ATLA Monograph Series
edited by Dr. Kenneth E. Rowe

1. Ronald L. Grimes. *The Divine Imagination: William Blake's Major Prophetic Visions.* 1972.
2. George D. Kelsey. *Social Ethics Among Southern Baptists, 1917–1969.* 1973.
3. Hilda Adam Kring. *The Harmonists: A Folk-Cultural Approach.* 1973.
4. J. Steven O'Malley. *Pilgrimage of Faith: The Legacy of the Otterbeins.* 1973.
5. Charles Edwin Jones. *Perfectionist Persuasion: The Holiness Movement and American Methodism. 1867–1936.* 1974.
6. Donald E. Byrne, Jr. *No Foot of Land: Folklore of American Methodist Itinerants.* 1975.
7. Milton C. Sernett. *Black Religion and American Evangelicalism: White Protestants, Plantation Missions, and the Flowering of Negro Christianity, 1787–1865.* 1975.
8. Eva Fleischner. *Judaism in German Christian Theology Since 1945: Christianity and Israel Considered in Terms of Mission.* 1975.
9. Walter James Lowe. *Mystery & The Unconscious: A Study in the Thought of Paul Ricoeur.* 1977.
10. Norris Magnuson. *Salvation in the Slums: Evangelical Social Work, 1865–1920.* 1977.
11. William Sherman Minor. *Creativity in Henry Nelson Wieman.* 1977.
12. Thomas Virgil Peterson. *Ham and Japheth: The Mythic World of Whites in the Antebellum South.* 1978.
13. Randall K. Burkett. *Garveyism as a Religious Movement: The Institutionalization of a Black Civil Religion.* 1978.
14. Roger G. Betsworth. *The Radical Movement of the 1960's.* 1980.
15. Alice Cowan Cochran. *Miners, Merchants, and Missionaries: The Roles of Missionaries and Pioneer Churches in the Colorado Gold Rush and Its Aftermath, 1858–1870.* 1980.
16. Irene Lawrence. *Linguistics and Theology: The Significance of Noam Chomsky for Theological Construction.* 1980.
17. Richard E. Williams. *Called and Chosen: The Story of Mother Rebecca Jackson and the Philadelphia Shakers.* 1981.
18. Arthur C. Repp, Sr. *Luther's Catechism Comes to America: Theological Effects on the Issues of the Small Catechism Prepared In or For America Prior to 1850.* 1982.
19. Lewis V. Baldwin. *"Invisible" Strands in African Methodism.* 1983.
20. David W. Gill. *The Word of God in the Ethics of Jacques Ellul.* 1984.
21. Robert Booth Fowler. *Religion and Politics in America.* 1985.
22. Page Putnam Miller. *A Claim to New Roles.* 1985.
23. C. Howard Smith. *Scandinavian Hymnody from the Reformation to the Present.* 1987.
24. Bernard T. Adeney. *Just War, Political Realism, and Faith.* 1988.
25. Paul Wesley Chilcote. *John Wesley and the Women Preachers of Early Methodism.* 1991.
26. Samuel J. Rogal. *A General Introduction of Hymnody and Congregational Song.* 1991.
27. Howard A. Barnes. *Horace Bushnell and the Virtuous Republic.* 1991.
28. Sondra A. O'Neale. *Jupiter Hammon and the Biblical Beginnings of African-American Literature.* 1993.
29. Kathleen P. Deignan. *Christ Spirit: The Eschatology of Shaker Christianity.* 1992.
30. D. Elwood Dunn. *A History of the Episcopal Church in Liberia, 1821–1980.* 1992.
31. Terrance L. Tiessen. *Irenaeus on the Salvation of the Unevangelized.* 1993.
32. James E. McGoldrick. *Baptist Successionism: A Crucial Question in Baptist History.* 1994.

33. Murray A. Rubinstein. *The Origins of the Anglo-American Missionary Enterprise in China, 1807–1840.* 1995.
34. Thomas M. Tanner. *What Ministers Know: A Qualitative Study of Pastors as Information Professionals.* 1994.
35. Jack A. Johnson-Hill. *I-Sight: The World of Rastafari: An Interpretive Sociological Account of Rastafarian Ethics.* 1995.
36. Richard James Severson. *Time, Death, and Eternity: Reflecting on Augustine's* Confessions *in Light of Heidegger's* Being and Time. 1995.
37. Robert F. Scholz. *Press toward the Mark: History of the United Lutheran Synod of New York and New England, 1830–1930.* 1995.

PRESS TOWARD THE MARK

History of the United Lutheran Synod of New York and New England 1830–1930

by

ROBERT F. SCHOLZ

ATLA Monograph Series, No. 37

The American Theological
Library Association
and
The Scarecrow Press, Inc.
Metuchen, N.J., & London
1995

A project of the Lutheran Archives, Metropolitan New York Synod of the Evangelical Lutheran Church in America.

Harry J. Kreider, *History of the United Lutheran Synod of New York and New England. Volume I: 1786-1860.* Philadelphia: Muhlenberg Press, 1954.

Robert F. Scholz, *Press toward the Mark: History of the United Lutheran Synod of New York and New England, 1830-1930.* Metuchen, NJ, & London: Scarecrow Press, 1995.

British Library Cataloguing-in-Publication Data available

Library of Congress Cataloging-in-Publication Data

Scholz, Robert F.

Press toward the mark : history of the United Lutheran Synod of New York and New England, 1830-1930 / by Robert F. Scholz.

p. cm. — (ATLA monograph series ; no. 37)

Includes bibliographical references and index.

ISBN 0-8108-3026-4 (alk. paper)

1. United Lutheran Synod of New York and New England—History. 2. Lutheran Church—New York (State)—History. 3. Lutheran Church—New Jersey—History. 4. Lutheran Church—New England—History. I. Title. II. Series.

BX8061.N78S36 1995

284.1'74—dc20 95-11378

Manufactured in the United States of America

Printed on acid-free paper

DEDICATION

to

Helen M. Knubel

and

C. Francis Scholz

And I believe one holy, catholic, and apostolic church.

From the Latin text of the Nicene Creed
Chapter 1, "The Three Chief Symbols"
Augsburg Confession

We must begin by knowing ourselves and being true to that knowledge. Let us not with our rich coffers play the part of beggars and ask favors where we have every ability to impart them. No church can maintain its self-respect or inspire respect in others which is afraid or ashamed of its own history and which rears a dubious fabric on the ignorance of its ministry and of its members. Whatever flickerings of success may play around it, it will yet sink to rise no more, and, worse than this, no honest man will lament its fall, for however such a moral dishonesty may be smoothed over, every reflecting man sees that such a church is an organized lie with a ministry, congregations, churches and societies united to sustain a lie.

Charles Porterfield Krauth
from "The Relation of our Confessions to the Reformation," 1849

CONTENTS

ILLUSTRATIONS

FIGURES

GRAPHS

MAPS

TABLES

LISTING OF ABBREVIATIONS AND DATA SOURCES

ABBREVIATIONS

BC *The Book of Concord. The Confessions of the Evangelical Lutheran Church.* Theodore G. Tappert, trans. & ed. Philadelphia: Fortress Press, 1959.

CA The Augsburg Confession, in *The Book of Concord. The Confessions of the Evangelical Lutheran Church.* Theodore G. Tappert, trans. & ed. Philadelphia: Fortress Press, 1959.

FC The Formula of Concord, in *The Book of Concord. The Confessions of the Evangelical Lutheran Church.* Theodore G. Tappert, trans. & ed. Philadelphia: Fortress Press, 1959.

LCR *Lutheran Church Review*

LQ *Lutheran Quarterly*

LQ(NS) *Lutheran Quarterly* New Series

LW *Luther's Works. American Edition.* Pelikan, Jaroslav, and Helmut T. Lehman, eds. Philadelphia and St. Louis: Fortress Press and Concordia Publishing House, 1955-.

MCAL Microfilm Corpus of American Lutheranism, Robert C. Wiederaenders, Editor.

RG Record Group, Archives of the Metropolitan New York Synod, ELCA, Wagner College.

SC Special Collection, Archives of the Metropolitan New York Synod, ELCA, Wagner College.

DATA SOURCES

Press toward the Mark includes a number of tables and graphs containing statistical data on population and church membership. Unless otherwise acknowledged by table or graph, following are the sources with numbers in parentheses as they appear in the tables:

(1) Population statistics for New York City are taken from Ira Rosenwaike, *Population History of New York City* (Syracuse: Syracuse University Press, 1972).

(2) New York and New Jersey county statistics are taken from the several censuses of the United States Bureau of the Census.

(3) New York State and national statistics are taken from the U. S. Bureau of the Census, Historical Statistics of the United States, (Washington D. C.: 1960), Section A ("Population"), 1-16.

(4) Denominational statistics are also taken in part from Historical Statistics of the United States, Section H. ("Social Statistics: Religious Affiliation"), 226-229, and from Edwin Scott Gaustad, *Historical Atlas of Religion in America*, revised ed. (New York: Harper & Row, 1976).

(5) Synodical membership statistics are taken for the years noted from the Minutes of the New York Ministerium, the Hartwick Synod, the New Jersey Synod, the New York Synod, the Synod of New York and New Jersey, the Synod of New York, the New York and New England Synod, and the Journals of the Franckean Synod; New York area Missouri Synod statistics are taken from the Parochial Reports for 1880, 1890, 1900, 1910, and 1920 of the Eastern and Atlantic Districts of the Lutheran Church-Missouri Synod provided by the Concordia Historical Institute, St. Louis, Missouri.

(6) Range of U. S. Church statistics, and national Lutheran figures extrapolated from Gaustad, *Historical Atlas*, 111, Fig. 93; and National Lutheran Council, *The Lutheran World Almanac* for 1921, 572-3, and *The Lutheran World Almanac 1931-1933*, 381.

Individual table column sources are indicated by numbers in parentheses corresponding to these six sources.

ACKNOWLEDGMENTS

In keeping with the origins of the New York Ministerium's history, *Press toward the Mark* is written as a church history for a community of faith. Its shape and argument have emerged out of this scholar's conviction that the dynamics of both denominationalism and the "confessing church" profoundly shaped the development of a United Lutheran Synod in the northeastern United States. Understanding this is crucial to the self-understanding of the community of faith out of which this work arises, and to those outside of that community who would understand its origins and development. It is the story of an evolving religious community which developed a united confessional identity within the context of denominational pluralism. This kind of secular, cultural influence is something which people of faith find difficult to understand, let alone appreciate. For that community of faith—especially its community of church historians and theologians—it is hoped that *Press toward the Mark* might contribute a chapter in American Lutheran church history. We need to remember Karlfried Froehlich's observation that church history is both an independent historical discipline, and an auxiliary theological discipline which assists theological self-understanding in religious communities too often given to pious romanticism, sectarian self-justification, the reinforcement of communal prejudice, and the mythicizing of history.[1]

As an exploration of how pluralism and denominationalism affected one regional religious body, *Press toward the Mark* is also intended as a contribution to the field of American religious history. This study has emerged out of a close and extensive reading of nearly four hundred minute books of New York area synods, and of the General Synod and the General Council. Congregational histories, as primary sources, have also been consulted where congregational life seemed relevant to synodical developments. Themes and emphases which have emerged in this study thus reflect the public religious life and issues of New York area Lutheranism as they were recorded at the synodical level of its corporate existence. A series of illustrations—lithographs, maps, tables, and graphs—depict the growth of the separate synods involved in this study, and delineate their eventual mergers. An important conclusion reached in the writing of Volume II is that growing religious communities with a mission do not merge; communities past their mission peak do merge, often in the hope that new size and augmented resources will make growth possible once again.

Press toward the Mark deliberately raises questions regarding the

---

[1] Karlfried Froehlich, "Church History and the Bible," *Lutheran Quarterly* (new series) 5.2 (1991): 131.

sometimes disproportionate emphasis placed upon religious pluralism in a political culture committed to the First Amendment disestablishment of religion. What other forces, of a countervailing nature, shaped the drive toward religious unity which among northeast Lutherans took the form of pressing "toward the mark" of one church body. Is the "confessional church" (*Bekenntniskirche*) radically defined, and promoted with evangelical fervor where the confession was both the rule of faith and life, and the unifying center of fellowship, not possibly one such force? Recently historians of American religion have begun to answer this question more positively and in detail.[2] Are such forces, and their results, perhaps ignored by a modern scholarship enamored of religious pluralism? And are they not overlooked at the peril of a comprehensive description of the role religion plays in American life? Religion considered anthropologically may well focus on human diversity originating in a human need to be religious in specific times and places. It can also be argued that the unity of deity, especially in a religious culture shaped by monotheism, has also profoundly shaped the course of American religion, though that force is eclipsed by a religious pluralism which on the face of it seems more reflective of American democratic values.[3] Yet even as the list of American religious denominations grows, a countervailing religious force can be seen at work in American religion, including the Lutheran bodies in this study, especially in the ecumenical convergence in our day which is bringing closer together a significant majority of Christians in churches committed to the ancient ecumenical creeds.

No historian is an island. A debt of gratitude is owed to many for their interest, suggestions, and support during the preparation of *Press toward the Mark*, beginning with a dedicated group of archivists and historians within the Lutheran Church. Drs. David Gaise and Helen Knubel, Metropolitan New York Synod archivists, have been helpful with their enthusiasm, support and suggestions as have David Wartluft, Librarian at the Lutheran Seminary in Philadelphia, and John Peterson, archivist for the Region 7 Lutheran Archives housed there. August Suelflow and Marvin Huggins of the Concordia Historical Institute have shown an interest in this history, and provided materials for the sections on the Lutheran Church Missouri Synod. Also gratefully acknowledged are members of the Lutheran Historical Conference

2 Mark A. Noll, *A History of Christianity in the United States and Canada* (Grand Rapids, Michigan: William B. Eerdmans Publishing Company, 1992), 160 ff.

3 On this see Wolfhart Pannenburg, *Systematic Theology* (Grand Rapids, Michigan: William B. Eerdmans Publishing Company, 1991) I: 136-151, esp. 142.

(LHC), an association of librarians, archivists, and historians dedicated to Lutheran history, which provided an opportunity to clarify my thinking on the role of Pietism in American Lutheranism at its 1990 Gettysburg Conference on "Lutheranism and Pietism."

Press toward the Mark is written both for scholars and the interested lay person. Special thanks are due two members of LHC who read the first draft of this study—Dr. Christa R. Klein and The Reverend Richard W. Dishno, formerly on the faculty of the Lutheran School of Theology at Chicago. At a crucial stage of the book's development they provided helpful encouragement, useful comments, and specific suggestions for further exploration. Drs. David Gaise and Charles E. Deitz, and the Rev. Paul Britton, all members of the Metropolitan New York Synod's Archives Advisory Committee, also read the manuscript at my request for general content and readability. Committee member Walter Jensen provided many helpful suggestions in the preparation of the manuscript for publication. In a study such as *Press toward the Mark* the balance between breadth and depth warrants special consideration. Questions may be raised for which there are no ready answers, or which would require a greater depth of inquiry than is possible here. Some areas have been explored more fully than others in seeking to guarantee the adequacy of this study. Where further investigation would benefit our understanding of Lutheranism in New York it has been so noted in the Notes. Perhaps this may benefit other scholars who, like Klein and Dishno, understand the collegial nature of the historian's enterprise. Finally, the Reverend William Gentz, editorial consultant to religious authors, was especially helpful at that point where a first-draft manuscript had to be transformed into a publishable book.

My circle of supportive and helpful colleagues also includes John Auh, Librarian of the Horrmann Library at Wagner College, and his staff, who have extended every courtesy possible to the Synod Archives, to the archivist, David Gaise, and to myself, in support of our work. Also Hofstra University History Department colleagues Natalie Naylor and Jack Moore, and Dr. Barbara M. Kelley, curator of Hofstra's Long Island Studies Institute, have provided support and suggestions especially in the area of New York History. My colleague in ministry at St. Davids, the Reverend Joanne Bond, has managed to coexist with grace and good humor though this historian is not the tidy traditionalist she had expected to work with at St. Davids. Parishioners Grover Cordts and Silvia Happ gladly aided with translations from the German as did another colleague, the Reverend Paul Schmiege, Our Redeemer Lutheran Church, Seaford, Long Island. The members of St. Davids, a large and busy parish, have graciously tolerated a working synod historian as their pastor with much patience, and they take justifiable pride of accomplishment in this volume. Parishioners Marge Collelo and Joan Grutzmacher, together with St. Davids's pastor already mentioned, the Reverend Charles E. Deitz, provided important documentation for this study with their monumental *New York Ministerium Legacy* (New York City: 1986) published under the editorship of Charles Deitz. Joan Grutzmacher has also been indispensible as editorial assistant in the preparation of the manuscript for publication. Collectively their concern for the history of their own and other religious communities represents the kind of commitment to nearby history which is essential if local religious history is to take its place alongside other subdisciplines in a growing field.

Finally, some special people need recognition and thanks. My wife Dorothy and my children Anna and Charles, lived daily with someone who could be found (too often) at the computer, "working on the history," when his energy and attention might be needed elsewhere. Two special people are also recognized in the dedication—the late Dr. Helen M. Knubel, for her extraordinary archival work over many decades on behalf of Lutheran history nationally and in the northeast, and who had hoped mightily that this history would be completed; and my father C. Francis Scholz, who taught me to love history as much as he did.

SERIES EDITOR'S FOREWORD

Since 1972 the American Theological Library Association has undertaken responsibility for a modest monograph series in the field of religious studies. Our aim in this series is to publish two studies of quality each year. Titles are selected from studies in a wide range of religious and theological disciplines. We are pleased to publish *Press toward the Mark* by Robert F. Scholz.

The author studied at the University of Minnesota, where he received a BS in American Studies, and a Ph.D. in history and political science. Subsequently he studied at the Lutheran Theological Seminary at Philadelphia where he earned his Master of Divinity degree. He has published in the field of American religious studies, most recently concentrating on the history of Lutheranism in North America. He is a member of the American Society of Church History, the American Historical Association, and the Lutheran Historical Conference (LHC). He currently serves on the LHC's board of directors, and as the historian of the Metropolitan New York Synod of the Evangelical Lutheran Church in America.

Drew University Library
Madison, NJ 07940
USA

KENNETH E. ROWE
Series Editor

FOREWORD

An archaic sermon illustration had the village infidel at the head of the bucket brigade. He was the most arduous of the villagers who were pouring water on the burning church; he outbucketed the most earnest believers themselves. He was asked why he who usually ignored or scorned the church was first to climb the hill and show interest when it was burning. His answer: "Because this is the first time the church has ever been exciting."

I can picture that some potential readers who, being told that *Press toward the Mark* is the story of church mergers and efforts to merge, would expect to find it dull. Maybe when they hear that it is also about conflict and schism they might find it exciting. But I would argue that taken together the merging and de-merging make up a single tantalizing plot that will hold the interest of any serious person who gives these pages a chance. Grab your figurative bucket and come up the hill for the experience of reading this book.

Press toward the Mark is a case study. No, strike that. It is a case *story*. Recently I read a remark by a medical humanist who was a bit tired of case studies. He was glad to hear some of them called "case stories." Why? Case studies make specimens out of patients. Case stories allow for us to get inside the world of the patients. The physician who deals with a single patient needs the case story in order to know what to prescribe and do to help a sufferer. But physicians read about other cases to make sense of those that come before them.

So it is with this study, which focuses on Lutherans. Most Americans are not of their company, though eight million are, and we take their interest for granted. But Mormons and Moravians, United Methodists and Unitarian Universalists all are "cases" and they have "stories" that can inform each other. No two patients are alike, nor are two diseases, nor two stories of disease. But by overhearing or looking in on case stories, people with imagination find analogies. They hold up a mirror to their own past, their own people.

Dr. Scholz chose to make his case a set of people who were trying to make sense through the mazeways of American life. They were an immigrant people, as are all 260 million of us, including the Native Americans. They were uprooted, capable of being lost in the thicket of earlier America, prone to wandering on its not well charted paths. They formed groups and named them, in response to the call of God and the creeds that were in them. Some of these have names that sound eccentric to us: "Hartwick Synod" and "Steimle Synod," for example. The names we use to describe our denominations in the phone book's Yellow Pages, between "Chiropractors" and "Cigars," where "Churches and Synagogues" get located, are much more bland or, in village atheist terms, less "exciting."

The Hartwickians and Steimleites and all the rest did live exciting lives, and when there was danger of dullness, they found something about which to have controversy of sorts that was meaningful to them if not always immediately to us. What sense would they make of our conflicts today? I don't know, but I know they would use them as a mirror to be held up as they looked to see who they were, what they believed, what they hoped for, toward what mark they would press.

These are not then "old, unhappy, far-off things, and battles long ago" that we can easily dismiss out of mind. Scholz as an historian wants to read something of their mind and ours. Jacob Burkhardt, the great nineteenth-century historian of culture, once said that history was the story of what one age found remarkable in another. Our current age finds religious people trying to find themselves in the midst of the pluralism, the multiculturalisms that include so many lures in the American milieu. Our times find Christians seeking to see their churches grow and get defined, to make sure their conflicts are meaningful. They can learn by reading of people who have been through the maze, along the path.

If a case story that informs us all is from the world of sports, we are entertained or we learn even if we are not going to be figure skaters and quarterbacks. We read biographies of opera stars or business women even if we are not going to become either. With author Scholz, we have to take the subjects where we find them. They belong to a different time, not our own. The past, someone says, is a foreign country; they do things differently there. He has to work with the people who left records and who got or put their names in them. So his case story has much about clergymen, that is clergy+men. The laity play supporting roles and women, often implied on these pages, were given few chances to have their names put forward. But they are there.

Just as historians of politics spend more time with the candidates than with the generally anonymous voters, yet by treating the candidates and their rhetoric and action they can infer much about the public, so historians of the churches write more about the special moments—conventions, committee sessions, and the like—than about the quotidian existence, the ordinary daily life, of people who had other things to do in addition to preaching or hearing sermons or starting new churches or going to conventions.

Dr. Scholz is not one to shun elements of the case story wherever he finds them. If this means going through the dusty sources to denominational conventions, he will do so, until he can help us find our way through them. If it means dealing with consistories and ministerial minutes, he blows the dust off the archives and shows us the treasures under the dust. In a time when many get turned off by "organized religion," he is patient about following the disorganized pioneers around, until we learn why organizing was so important to them.

There are some today who show interest chiefly in the "spirituality" of the isolated, lonely, entrepreneurial person who in the spirit of St. Francis (Sinatra) says "I'll do it my way." Forget about them, as most of us soon will. When two or three band together in order to make sense of things, to celebrate, or to make fighting meaningful in the name of God, they stand more chance of making history and making it interesting; of becoming not case studies but case stories.

Press toward the Mark is about pioneers, pathmakers, trailblazers of the spirit; serious people with sometimes grand visions and sometimes petty ones, people who wanted to play their part ministering to mainly German-speaking people who were making their way in an English-speaker's environment. But you do not have to be of a German heritage to identify with their plot. All languages in unfamiliar settings are bewildering and offputting. They also wanted to minister to people who they thought were threatened; sheep without shepherds, they were vulnerable to false shepherds, some of them representing their own faith. They wanted to build up the faith of the believing and half-believing, Christian and semi-Christian, Lutheran and maybe-Lutheran who were so much like most of us with our puzzlements today.

They wanted to be faithful to God in Christ, to scriptures and creeds. They wanted to and did put together agencies that could generate mission, stage theological inquiries, build schools and colleges, found benevolent institutions, just as most of us would and must today. The dictionary says that to "invent" means to "find" and "to make something new," so they were inventors on the church scene. In their particular case study some wanted to put creeds first ("confessionalists") and some concentrated on prayer and devotion ("pietists"), and together they left traces that still mark church bodies. Some compromised where they had to and others turned their backs in rejection when others of their faith did not meet their standards. Case stories are not pretty on every page. Just exciting, as the village atheist at the fire scene could have told you.

Some of the leaders in this story tried to borrow from their rivals, with mixed results. In their tradition, revivalism had played little part. But on the American scene, revival fires burned. Some got singed, some inflamed, some enlightened; their varied experiences are part of Scholz's case story. Professor Scholz pauses to explain to us, more than some might wish at times but always informatively, why words like "denomination" and "sect" are important. Most of the time he moves the plot along, catching the unsuspecting of us—unsuspecting that we will get carried away—in cases and stories that still help define people of faith and learning and energy today.

The University of Chicago — MARTIN E. MARTY

INTRODUCTION
"Press toward the Mark"

On June 5, 1929, representatives of four hundred and two Lutheran congregations from New York, New Jersey, Connecticut, Massachusetts, and Pennsylvania gathered in St. Johns Lutheran Church, Albany, New York, to form a new Lutheran church body—the United Lutheran Synod of New York. This is the story of their merger.

It was a time of optimism, at least in June of 1929, a fitting end to the Roaring Twenties. While the wealthy frolicked on the Gold Coast of Long Island's north shore, in imitation of the Great Gatsby at East Egg, more sober-minded folk, including many Lutherans, moved into new towns and suburbs along the south shore, bringing with them hopes for a better life and plans to build new churches. They built there as they built elsewhere in new suburban areas throughout the Northeastern United States (including the environs of Albany and other upstate cities) for it was a time of prosperity—a good time to build.

Guggenheim money finished the Museum of Modern Art in 1929. The Rockefellers were building an entertainment and communications center—Rockefeller Center—scheduled for completion in 1931. The Empire State Building was still a large hole in the ground, but it too would be finished by the time Rockefeller Center was completed. The United Lutheran Synod began as a religious edifice of comparable dimensions—a very large synod covering seven states in the northeast, but identified primarily as a new and stronger church body situated in the dynamic Empire State. The Reverend Samuel Trexler would speak at the opening of the United Synod's second convention of "the new vision of the stronger Synod," a vision of a "stronger and more living Church" which emerged from the merger. The newly united and strengthened synod stood (in his view) "at the threshold of a new life for the Church on this territory which holds so many of the forces which dominate this nation as well as the world." Like Paul, writing to the Philippians (Trexler observed) the United Synod had not yet attained this most excellent goal of a common mind: "but I press toward the mark for the prize of the high calling of God in Christ Jesus."[1]

Building such a synod would prove difficult. The good times were about to end, not on October 28—"Black Friday"—when the stock market plummeted, but slowly and painfully as prosperity ebbed away among working class people, leaving an ever deepening depression. The new United Lutheran Synod, with its many mission churches, entered this modern era heavily in debt, and the approaching Depression would greatly influence its future.

But it is not with the development of the United Lutheran Synod that we are concerned, but with its origins in a period rich with promise for a more prosperous Lutheran future when the most mature among New York Lutheran leaders, like those among the Philippians whom Paul exhorted to "press toward the mark," struggled also to "be of the same mind." With them the struggle for single mindedness meant embracing the same confessional outlook, a necessary precondition among Lutherans for a truly "united" synod. This volume in the history of the New York Ministerium and its successor bodies, is (therefore) a study in confessional convergence.

The watchword that fifth day of June, 1929, was "united." It was a time for coming together throughout Christendom. Most of Scotland's Presbyterian churches had united in 1929 to form the Church of Scotland; Lutherans worldwide were already meeting for a second time in a World Conference at Copenhagen. It was eleven years since three major American Lutheran bodies—the General Synod, the General Council, and the General Synod of the South—had met in New York City to form the United Lutheran Church in America (ULCA).[2] And now, in upstate New York three ULCA synods—the New York Ministerium, the synod of New York, and the synod of New York and New England—which themselves already represented the merger of six previous Lutheran synods in the region, were at last coming together for a historic reunion. (See figure 1.)

For some it had been a brief separation. The 1929 merger was a reunion of two synods—the New York Ministerium and the synod of New York and New England—both members of the General Council which had only split apart in 1903 over the problem of mission work among a new generation of suburban, English-speaking Lutherans whom the Ministerium, in its German-language exclusivity, was reluctant to recognize and to serve. Joining them was the synod of New York. Its involvement made the merger also a reunion of two main streams of Lutheranism in American life which had diverged in mid 19th century—the older, more liberal, Americanized and Protestant form of Lutheranism in the General Synod tradition; and the newer and more confessional outlook of the General Council, expressing the confessionalism of conservative American Lutherans and recent German immigrants. For all it represented the union of Lutheran bodies whose histories had brought to this historic moment of change.

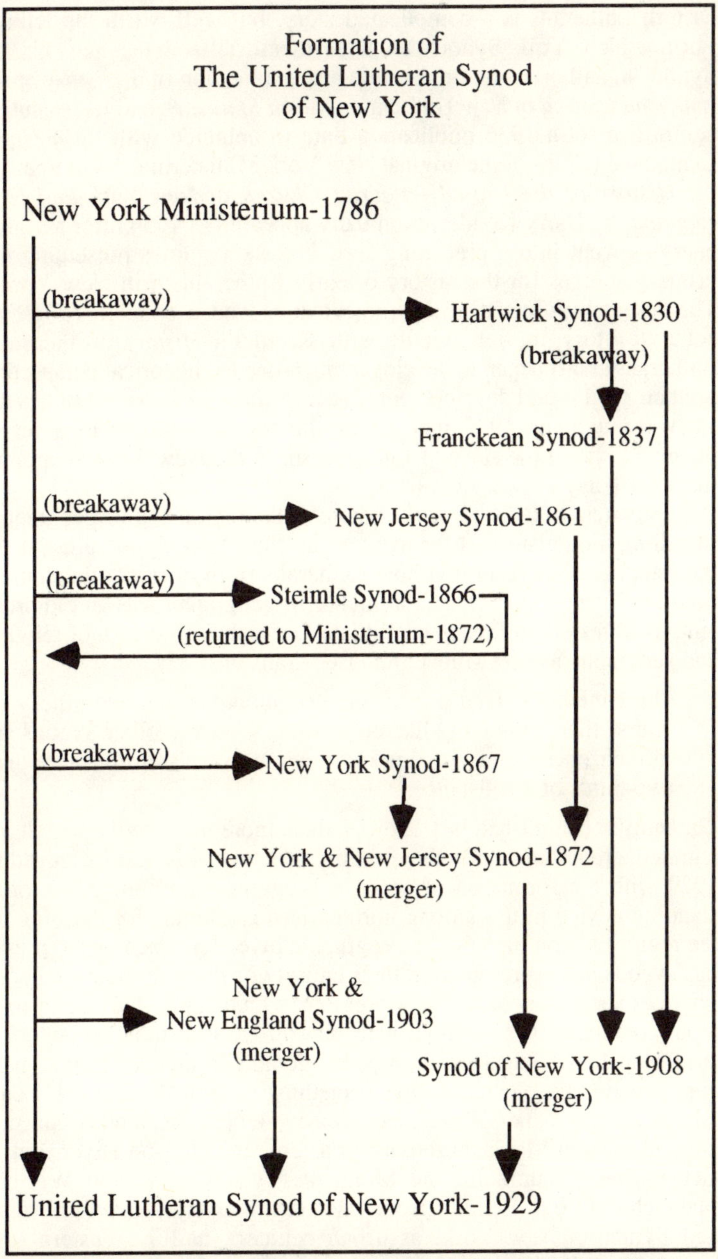

figure 1 Formation of the United Lutheran Synod of New York

The development of these schisms and their healings among north eastern Lutherans is a complicated story, but well worth the telling. Former New York Synod delegates memorialized the new United Synod "to authorize the preparation and publication of a *History of the Lutheran Church of New York and adjacent States...*"; and its executive committee set a 1936 publication date to coincide with the Sesqui-Centennial (1936) of the original New York Ministerium.[3] Volume I of the *History of the United Lutheran Church of New York and New England*, by Harry Kreider, eventually appeared in 1954 after research energies went into a preceding series of six volumes presenting the primary sources for the history of early Lutheranism in New York.[4] The research volumes in the project displayed a concern to tell an accurate story in rich detail; with Kreider's *History* northeastern Lutherans at last began to develop a much-needed historical perspective on their origins and development. *Press toward the Mark* continues the story through the 1929 merger, as the second volume in a series planned to bring the story of Lutheranism in the New York area up to the present day.

Important to the story is the nature of the region and its geography. In calling for a history of the merger, the New York Synod understood the importance of recording how Lutherans from different theological traditions came together. The influence of geography was an old problem, as Ministerium President William D. Strobel observed, of religion and geography among Ministerium Lutherans in 1852:

> Our churches extend over a space of about six hundred miles—of course there is nothing like compactness—while other Synods are in their operations, crossing our track at every step for more than two-thirds of the distance.[5]

The unity accomplished in 1929 was, then, more than theological. It integrated a religious region the diversity of which was acknowledged in 1929 with the formation of seven subregional conferences (a long-standing device in use among northeastern Lutherans for dividing up the region) to comprehend its geographic diversity. Each of the previous synods had represented in their entirety or through their own conferences specific geographic subregions which supported strong religious communities, sometimes with very different theological outlooks. (See Map 12.1.) Together, these subregional conferences formed new conferences whose names tell us something of their diversity: 1. Long Island, 2. New York (City), 3. New Jersey, 4. New England (Connecticut and Eastern Massachusetts), 5. Eastern (the Hudson River, Lakes George and Champlain, the Mohawk River Valley, and Western Massachusetts), 6. Central (from Canada to Pennsylvania with Rome and Syracuse, New York, as urban centers), and 7. Western (the Rochester-Buffalo axis).[6] Perhaps it was that geography and theology had closer than usual connections among New York Lutherans, for a history of division and merger among New York Lutherans requires a closer look at the geographic influences on developing Lutheranism in the New York region. What will be found in the subregions of New York is a geographic shaping of religious pluralism among New York Lutherans, one of the most significant characteristics of American religious life.

Having pointed to the influence of geography, it is essential to understand that the history of Lutheranism in the region (as, indeed, throughout the Lutheran world) was first and last the history of a Christian denomination seeking its own confessional identity in a time of rapid change and increasing pluralism. Even as the Lutheran Church was being "denominationalized" a strong counter-movement to transcend denominationalism in the name of catholicity within "the one holy, catholic, and apostolic church" was also at work in the formation and development of General Council Lutheranism. This drive for catholicity was (and is) easily misunderstood to be more catholic and ecumenical than indeed it was. Philip Schaff, the American church historian, saw it as an imported "European Lutheranism" that not only isolated itself from the Reformed mainstream of American Christianity but looked only backwards to the Reformation in seeking out the final form which evangelical catholicity should take.[7] From the time of the Civil War Lutherans in the northeast faced a denominational dilemma when it came to catholicity—whether to choose between a minimal confessional distinctiveness in the name of generic Protestantism (a weak denominational identity), or to insist upon a confessional distinctiveness in the name of a somewhat sectarian catholicity (strong denominational identity).

One way to look at this developing Lutheranism is in terms of a distinct Protestant denomination increasingly claimed by a confessional movement seeking concord on doctrinal questions as normed by Holy Scripture. Fidelity to the Lutheran confessions in the *Book of Concord* denominated the New York area churches as "Lutheran." In resolving intraLutheran conflicts during the sixteenth century, Lutheran leaders developed certain confessional ground rules in a "Formula of Concord," rules which provide an intrinsic historical perspective from which to view the history of Lutheran confessionalism in the New York area. What were these "rules"? In the first place the "Formula" acknowledged that "the prophetic and apostolic writings of the Old and New Testaments are the only rule and norm according to which all doctrines" must be "appraised and judged." The "Formula" also acknowledged the centrality of the ancient symbols "which were accepted as the unanimous, catholic Christian faith—namely the Apostles', Nicene, and Athanasian Creeds." If these ancient symbols defined orthodoxy overagainst ancient heresy, it was the Augsburg Confession—"the symbol of our time"—together with Philip Melanchthon's "Apology" for the

Augsburg Confession, and Luther's Smalcald Articles, which formed "the unanimous consensus and exposition of our Christian faith" at the time of the German Reformation. In addition to these statements of Lutheran belief, Luther's two Catechisms—"the layman's Bible"—were thought to contain "everything which Holy Scripture discusses at greater length and which a Christian must know for his salvation." The Augsburg Confession, the Smalcald Articles, Melanchthon's "Apology," and the two Catechisms, collected and bound between the covers of one *Book of Concord* together with the "Formula of Concord," formed a confessional canon. As the "Formula" itself defined the function of the canon, "all doctrines" pertaining to Lutheran matters "should conform to the standards" of these confessional norms.[8]

In interpreting the history which follows, the present volume explores how indifference or faithfulness to this canon shaped the story of New York Lutherans working out their confessional identity in a changing world. Some New York Lutherans (in the General Synod tradition) would give primacy to a faith in which scripture was the "only rule and norm," finding in the Word a vital Christian piety which shaped belief and practice. Others (in the General Council tradition) would find in subscription to the Augsburg Confession an additional element considered essential to being Lutheran. Still others (strict confessionalists within the New York Ministerium and the Missouri Synod) would go so far as to include one or all of the other symbols of the *Book of Concord* in their definition of an adequate Lutheran identity. But because a confessional identity required conformity to agreed upon confessional norms, Lutherans who would unite synodically would have to agree on a confessional formula that all could accept. It was the successful process of evolving agreement among northeastern Lutherans by 1929 which brought this history of confessional merger to its conclusion. Like leaders in churches admonished by St. Paul himself, they pressed toward "the prize of the heavenly call of God in Christ Jesus." Still unfulfilled in 1929, Paul's admonition was doubtless also President Samuel Trexler's: "Let those of us then who are mature be of the same mind; and if you think differently about anything, this too God will reveal to you. Only let us hold fast to what we have attained."[9] Aiming for the mark meant adhering to confessional choices that were made in dealing with northeast Lutheranism's denominational dilemma—and aiming once again in the light of continuing change.

Because each body of Lutherans who took part in the 1929 merger of the United Synod settled within the greater New York area at a different time and place, various expressions of Lutheranism took root in the different soils of the region's complex culture. We begin the story of the United Synod, therefore, with a closer look at that interaction of geography, culture, and theology which created such diversity, exploring the development of various synodical expressions of confessional Lutheranism within the watershed of the Hudson River system.

NOTES

1 United Lutheran Synod of New York, *Minutes of Second Annual Convention* (1930), 37. Philippians 3: 14.

2 See Abdel Ross Wentz, *A Basic History of Lutheranism in America* (Philadelphia: Muhlenberg Press, 1955), 279ff.

3 United Lutheran Synod of New York, *Minutes of the First Annual Convention* (1929), 101, 117.

4 The six volumes, in order of publication are:
Harry J. Kreider, *Lutheranism in Colonial New York.* New York: The United Lutheran Synod of New York and New England, 1942.
The Lutheran Church in New York. 1649-1772. Records in the Lutheran Church Archives at Amsterdam, Holland, trans. Arnold J. F. van Laer. New York: The New York Public Library, 1946.
Harry J. Kreider, *The Beginnings of Lutheranism in New York.* New York: The United Lutheran Synod of New York and New England, 1949.
Harry J. Kreider, *History of the United Lutheran Synod of New York and New England, Volume I, 1786-1860.* Philadelphia: Muhlenberg Press, 1954.
Protocol of the Lutheran Church in New York City, 1702-1750. trans. Simon Hart. New York: The United Lutheran Synod of New York and New England, 1958.
Lutheran Church in New York and New Jersey, 1722-1760. Lutheran Records in the Ministerial Archives of the Staatsarchiv, Hamburg, Germany, trans. Simon Hart and Harry J. Kreider. New York: The United Lutheran Synod of New York and New England, 1962.

5 New York Ministerium, *Minutes* (1852), 33.

6 ULSNY, *Minutes* (1929), 94.

7 Klaus Penzel, "Philip Schaff's Mercersburg program of 'Evangelical Catholicism,'" *Lutheran Forum* 26.2 (1992): 38.

8 BC, "Formula of Concord," "Epitome," 464-5.

9 Philippians 3: 14-15 (NRSV).

1

DENOMINATIONAL ORIGINS

The Development of Five Lutheran Parishes and the Beginnings of Denominationalism in the New York Area, 1649–1840

The United Lutheran Synod and its predecessor bodies represented an extensive array of theological, social, and historical influences spread across the entire watershed of the Hudson River region. Geographic diversity reflected theological and organizational differences among Lutherans. Together they represented what C. M. Jacobs (leading theologian of the newly established United Lutheran Church in America) described as "environmental" influence—the combined influence of doctrine, ethnic origins, "social and cultural inheritance," and geographic distribution which differentiated one Lutheran body from another.[1] More recently we have learned to understand such developments in the language of cultural geography.[2] Of the forces leading to this extensive diversity among Lutherans, we look first at the geographic nature of the greater New York area; then examine the theological forms of Lutheranism—orthodox and pietistic—which Lutheran immigrants brought to the region; outline the five subregional expressions of Lutheranism that developed out of immigration and the influence of orthodoxy or pietism; and (finally) explore the resulting denominational developments among northeast Lutherans.

THE NATURE OF A REGION

How did the New York environment create a Lutheranism peculiar to the region? Consider, for example, the conferences formed by the United Synod of New York, in 1929. They were etched like the sign of Zorro across the face of the region, east from Buffalo to Albany, south from Albany to the greater metropolitan New York/New Jersey area on either side of New York harbor, and east along both shores of Long Island and of Long Island Sound. (See Map 1.1.) Though Lutheran churches could be found in city, town, village, and countryside throughout the region, Lutherans were more urbanized than many other religious groups. What William Strobel, Ministerium president, complained about was a dispersal of Ministerium congregations along a growing industrial and urban belt stretching east from Lake Erie and Buffalo along the Erie Canal and Mohawk River to Albany, down the Hudson River Valley to metropolitan New York and New Jersey, then east along Long Island Sound incorporating southern New England and Long Island into a single demographic entity.[3]

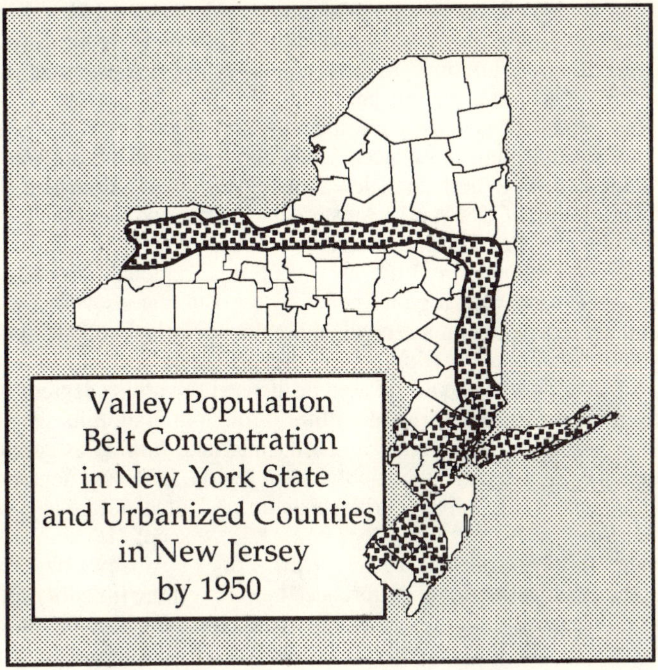

Map 1.1 New York/New Jersey Urbanization[4]

Conference names like "New York," "New Jersey," and "New England" reflected state or regional origins; clearly these were geographic areas which crossed state lines. (See Map 12.1.) How, then, could the regional name "New York" be used by the uniting churches to identify themselves synodically? State and regional identities and loyalties surely must have been set aside, or at least temporarily ignored, that June in 1929 at Albany! The twentieth century has forgotten that previously regions were defined as much by rivers and other bodies of water as by political boundaries or governmental charters. Geographers call this "hydrographic definition."[5] To someone sailing down Long Island Sound, through New York Harbor, up or down the Hudson River, or "from Albany to Buffalo" along the Erie Canal, the region lay on either side of the waterway, and could easily be reached by water travel up this watercourse and its tributaries. What lay to either side of these navigable bodies of water within the greater Hudson River watershed included most of New York as well as areas of northeastern New Jersey (colonial East Jersey), southern Connecticut, western Massachusetts, and portions of upper and lower Canada.

Hydrographic definition was what the earliest Lutheran settlers in the region experienced. They brought this experience with them to the New World where they understood their new territory by analogy to the Old. The Hudson River was the American "Rhine," a vital New World waterway ending in a New Amsterdam—"a broad avenue through highlands to a rich interior." Like its namesake, New Amsterdam (later New York) was a trading city in a commercial region, serving a rich, complex estuary of islands, bays, alcoves, and radial rivers, a counterpart to the canal- and river-laced lands about the Scheldt and Zuider Zee in the Dutch Netherlands. New Amsterdam quickly became a New World miniature of Old World Amsterdam in form and function.[6]

Manhattan Island, at the center of this hydrographic basin, served as the region's island core. From its inception as regional port of entry, New York City was the region's nerve center. But regions can have peripheral centers also with a second, subregional culture which is potentially antagonist to the predominant center. "Upstate" Albany and environs, a frontier and agricultural area influenced to various degrees by a different New England regional culture through migration in the early nineteenth century, functioned in good hinterland fashion as counterpoise to the "Downstate" metropolitan subregion. Differing degrees of influence meant that Albany, with its enduring Dutch culture and river connections to New York City, was less susceptible to Yankee influence than central and western New York or Albany's own rural environs. Such subregional differences help to tell the full story as far as the Lutheran Church in New York is concerned. Each subregion was further subdivided into geographic areas served by clusters of Lutheran congregations which formed local "parishes" along segments of rivers, tributaries, canals, and around lake ports. As different from one another as their Lutheran inhabitants, these various parishes would interact with one another in ways that contributed to the development of a distinctive New York Lutheranism noted, like the New York region, for a formally tolerant pluralism in which different religious and ethnic groups kept both their distance and their prejudices.[7]

Beyond this distinctiveness New York was also unique in its regional geographic significance to the northeast. Together with Philadelphia, Metropolitan New York formed part of a nation-building geographic corridor shaping the American nation in ways other geographic regions could not.[8] In politics and government, religion and commerce, the northeast provided cultural leadership to a growing nation. The existence of this corridor meant that New York Lutheranism was to have a special influence on American Lutheranism growing in part out of the interaction between Hudson River and Delaware Valley regional cultures. Within its own borders New York Lutheranism could be distinguished from that of the Delaware Valley: whereas the Delaware Valley culture of this bipolar region embraced a *mediating* Lutheranism—an moderate, integrated expression of Orthodoxy and Pietism originating with Henry Melchior Muhlenberg of Pennsylvania—the Lutheranism of the Hudson River basin was characterized by a *tension between* these two forms of Lutheranism. Given the significance of the extremes of Pietism and Orthodoxy in the New York area, let us look more closely at the nature of Lutheran Orthodoxy and its supposed nemesis, Lutheran Pietism.

EARLY LUTHERAN THEOLOGY—ORTHODOXY AND PIETISM

Luther's recovery of the doctrine of "Justification by Grace through Faith" is the essential point of departure in Lutheran faith and practice. God is God, and humankind cannot by its own reason or strength either approach God or fulfill His Law through human righteousness. The original nature of sin is just radical enough to prevent human beings from using natural ability to do any good work which might contribute to righteousness or sanctification. No Christian, therefore, can stand before God justified in His sight by human merit, "reason or strength." Instead persons stand before God simultaneously justified and sinners—*simul justus et peccator*—in this Reformation perspective. That perspective, first developed by Luther, was amplified in Article IV of the Unaltered Augsburg Confession (1530):

> It is also taught among us that we cannot obtain forgiveness of sin and righteousness before God by our own merits, works or satisfactions, but that we receive forgiveness of sin and become righteous before God by grace, for Christ's sake, through faith.[9]

Within a century this Lutheran understanding of justification developed into an "orthodox" Lutheran theology sharply differentiating the Lutheran Church from both Roman "Catholicism" (which some Lutherans were still seeking to reform) and the Reformed Church (with which other Lutherans were still interested in uniting). Lutheran Orthodoxy's point of departure on such disputed points as Christ's "real presence" in the Eucharist, and the predestination of saints and reprobates to their respective fates, was developed in the "Formula of

Concord" where sharp lines drawn between Lutheran and Reformed traditions were incorporated into the 1580 *Book of Concord.*[10]

This systematic development of Lutheran doctrine began with Philip Melanchthon, Luther's young colleague at Wittenberg University. Beginning with Holy Scripture, Melanchthon laid out a series of doctrinal loci to form a biblical theology for the instruction of his students which emphasized the "modern" topics of "Law," "Gospel," "Grace," and "Justification."[11] Several generations of Lutheran theologians including some of his students—most notably Martin Chemnitz and Nicholas Selnecker, as well as their distinguished successors Leonard Hutter, John Gerhard, and Abraham Calovius—built upon this foundation an elaborate orthodox system of Reformation theology which served the Lutheran Church for centuries in educating its pastors. Pastors (for example) trained in the Pennsylvania Ministerium of Henry Melchior Muhlenberg prior to the American Revolution were prepared for ordination using Leonard Hutter's *Compendium Theologiae.*[12] By the end of the Civil War this orthodox theology was reintroduced to New York Lutheranism in compendium form by means of Heinrich Schmid's *The Doctrinal Theology of the Evangelical Lutheran Church.*[13]

Melanchthon's approach was meant to open up scripture to systematic analysis and deeper understanding. As a method for explicating biblical theology, it reflected the spirit of the "Formula of Concord" in which scripture was "the only rule and norm according to which all doctrines and teachers alike must be appraised and judged."[14] But with the reintroduction of Aristotelian logic into German education, this developing Orthodoxy became highly "scholastic." The needs of faith were subordinated to the doctrinal interests of logic and rationality. A preoccupation with dogmatic definitions over-intellectualized faith, confusing faith with belief in the life of the Lutheran church. Though in the *Book of Concord* scripture was the ultimate source of authority in doctrinal matters, too often holy writ simply became a proof-text for orthodox doctrine.[15] With an overemphasis on this objective side of religion, theological aridity, and formalism in worship also developed. The Biblical kerygma was lost to such an extent that parishioners could be subject to the likes of a 1605 sermon reported by historian Gerald Cragg preached on the text "The very hairs of your head are all numbered." The sermon's parts referred to the origin, style, form and natural position of hair, its correct care, reminiscences, reminders and warnings derived from the hair, and how to wear it in good Christian fashion.[16]

Looking back, Lutherans would hold conflicting opinions about Orthodoxy's worth. None though would deny its important influence in Lutheran history, including its role in the New York story. Lutheran Orthodoxy is too easily caricaturized and insufficiently understood. As an expression of the Teaching Office in the church, its strength and genius were not in the pulpit or congregation, but in the university and the consistory (governing body) of the church. Developed at a time when Lutheran Pietism was on the ascendancy, it had a confessing and norming function which resisted heterodoxy while seeking to educate those called to the Office of the Ministry. Those who could penetrate its objectivism could find a vital faith in search of understanding. Two of its most able exponents contributed enduring expressions of Lutheran faith—Paul Gerhard, through his hymns, including "O Sacred Head Now Wounded," expressed a deep and abiding faith life; Johann Arndt, a powerful and popular preacher, developed a practical theology and vital system of Christian piety based on Orthodox loci.

Both Gerhard and Arndt expressed that personal, subjective, and experiential side of faith which critics of Orthodoxy found missing in its rationalistic emphasis on belief. Arndt, in particular, gave expression to a deep-seated Christian mysticism in his *True Christianity*, a popular pietist treatise which drew upon the same *German Theology* which Luther (like Arndt) had once commended to German Christians. Like Luther, Arndt also drew guidance and inspiration from the German mystic Johannes Tauler (who was erroneously thought to have written the *German Theology*).[17] Tauler, like Arndt, Gerhard, and Luther, had also drawn inspiration from the mysticism of Bernard of Clairvaux and, ultimately, from St. Augustine himself.[18] Together these Lutheran theologians shared with Tauler and Bernard an ancient biblical faith, inherited from the Patristic age and transmitted to the western church through the medium of contemplative monasticism, which emphasized an experiential (mystical) theology and the soul's search through love for the Good. The spirituality of the Western Church and its piety were fundamentally shaped by this monastic theology, though its influence is often unrecognized.[19] Pietism centered on a devotion to Christ through the experience of justification by grace through faith.[20] Here was the very heart of the mystical tradition, traceable to St. Bernard, for whom Christ's saving grace was also all important—not the soul soaring to divine heights which Bernard emphasized, but pardoned sinners lifted up by forgiveness. Though developed in numerous writings, Bernard said it most simply in the hymnic poetry which survived in Gerhardt's "O Sacred Head, Now Wounded":

> What language shall I borrow to thank thee, dearest friend,
> For this thy dying sorrow, Thy pity without end ?
> Oh, make me thine forever, And should I fainting be,
> Lord, let me never, never Outlive my love to thee.[21]

Arndt's emphasis on "true repentance" stressed a genuine, inward attitude of selfless contrition as the essence of true Christianity. True repentance was, we may remember, also the starting point of the Reformation which Luther articulated in his 95 Theses. Written in a popular, devotional style, True *Christianity* was second only to Luther's

Small Catechism in popularity among Lutheran emigrants to the New World. Both volumes profoundly shaped popular Lutheranism among both clergy and laity in the northeast for several centuries.[22] This concern also led to the development of a more practical Christianity, and a new emphasis on pastoral theology, which focused on the experience of repentance and holiness as essential to Christian faith.[23]

The chief exponent of this new Pietism was Philipp Jacob Spener (1635-1705).[24] Spener published a program for the reform in his *Pia Desideria*, arguing that reform was necessary because of the overemphasis on an arid orthodoxy in the Lutheran Church, and because much of German life and culture, including its moral and spiritual life, had been devastated by the Thirty Years' War.[25] He called for the establishment of *collegia pietatis* (small devotional gatherings of Christian laity to study scripture under the guidance of a pastor); re-emphasize of the Reformation doctrine of the priesthood of all believers; the use of practical sermons to strengthen faith; and a clerical education which emphasized personal piety and spiritual edification as found in the *German Theology*, the writings of Johannes Tauler, Thomas à Kempis *The Imitation of Christ*, and *True Christianity*.[26]

In August Hermann Francke (1663-1727) Spener found an extraordinarily able ally and disciple.[27] Francke was a faculty member at Halle University, and founder of the highly influential Halle Orphan School in which so many European and American Lutheran pastors received at least some of their schooling as teachers and assistants. At Halle, the University faculties embraced a pietistic form of Lutheranism emphasizing the experience of sin and grace, a return to the Reformation emphasis on scripture and biblical studies, and an understanding of Scripture "deepened" in small Bible study groups.[28] This "new form" of Pietism (as the German historian Kurt Aland styled it)[29] was noted for its ethical activism, its charitable and educational work among orphans, and its extensive mission endeavors in Asia and America.[30] Most distinctive was Francke's insistence on a conversion experience as the sign of true repentance, his relative indifference to the Sacraments and intransigence towards Orthodoxy, and his emphasis on "sanctification" leading to an ethical activism in a church dominated by orthodox quietism.[31] Both organizational orthodoxy and mission-minded Pietism had a significant impact on the development of the Lutheran church in New York.

REGION, SUBREGIONS, AND PARISHES —1649-1735

The initial form of the Lutheran church in New York was already regional. It consisted of one elongated parish, stretching the length of the Hudson River, from New York Harbor to its confluence with the

Mohawk River in the Albany area, with two foci at its port of entry (metropolitan New York) and its peripheral center (Albany). Over a period of fifty years five distinct, subregional "parishes" or clusters of congregations developed on this landscape.[32] (See Map 1.2.) They were frequently served, in their earliest years, by one pastor traveling a circuit. In later years these clusters reflected not only the distinctive influences of diverse clergymen with different theologies, but the doctrinal diversity of the laity themselves. Thus did doctrine and geography interact in shaping subregional expressions of Lutheranism in the New York Area almost from the outset.

THE ALBANY CLUSTER

The earliest congregations in Albany and New Amsterdam were composed primarily of Dutch Lutherans with an admixture of other nationalities, and were served by pastors educated in Lutheran Orthodoxy. The earliest Lutheran parish in New York, the Albany cluster, developed in the region's peripheral center in Albany and (eventually) Loonenburg (now Athens). The Lutheran church in the area dates from at least 1649 when Dutch Lutherans, identifying themselves as "adherents . . . of the Unaltered Augsburg Confession," petitioned for a Dutch-speaking pastor from the Amsterdam Lutheran Consistory.[33] The congregation formed from among these Lutherans—Ebenezer (eventually the First) Lutheran Church of Albany—dates its origins to 1644, though 1649 probably identifies more accurately the time when an intentionally Lutheran community was actually organized. This organization was accomplished against great odds, overcoming (in the earliest years) the opposition of New Amsterdam's Calvinist leaders; doctrinal antagonisms with Calvinism in the *Book of Concord* no doubt reinforced the confessional adamancy of this struggling congregation.[34] The Albany congregation was revived three times in the seventeenth century, and again in the eighteenth century by Pastor Justus Falckner who labored diligently on behalf of the scattered clusters of Lutherans trying to maintain themselves along the Hudson River. Their desperate condition turned Falckner to a life of pastoral itinerancy in caring for such groups in Pennsylvania and New York. He learned the Dutch language, preaching to polyglot communities composed of High Germans, Swedes, Danes, Norwegians, Poles, Lithuanians, and Transylvanians (among others). Given the difficulties of maintaining a confessional identity in Calvinist America, Falckner published (in 1708) a Lutheran compendium of anti-Calvinist doctrine, thereby extending the life of early Lutheran Orthodoxy.[35] He was succeeded by William Berkenmeyer, an orthodox Lutheran pastor from Hamburg (by way of Amsterdam), and an old world hierarch. Slowly, under the influence of Falckner and Berkenmeyer, a cluster of congregations formed around this Albany-Loonenburg axis in Albany and Rensselaer counties.

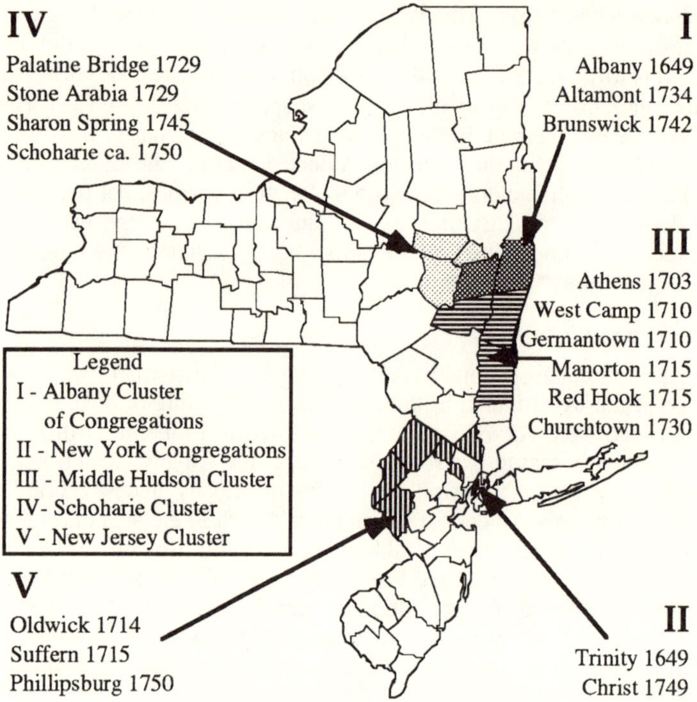

Map 1.2 New York Classis to 1750

THE NEW YORK CITY PARISH

Almost as old as First Lutheran was the Lutheran Church in Manhattan, which actually dated to about 1664, though Manhattan residents were to be found among the 1649 petitioners which eventuated in Albany's First Lutheran. Working together with Albany Lutherans as a single parish, and sharing a common destiny, the New York church was repeatedly revived and reorganized until more firmly established in the eighteenth century by Justus Falckner, his brother Daniel, and William Berkenmeyer. In the case of Falckner and Berkenmeyer, Albany shared clergy, ministries, and a common theological orientation with New York City. But whereas the Albany parish developed into a cluster of like-minded congregations, divisions occurred within the New York City parish. By the mid-eighteenth century, the parish had split into Trinity (fig. 1.1) and Christ (fig. 1.2) Churches over language differences. While both Albany and New York parishes were originally composed of different nationalities—five in Albany, seven in New York—the New York parish more clearly reflected the polyglot character of the more complex lower Hudson Valley area.

figure 1.1 Dutch Trinity Church, Broadway and Rector Street

This urban New York area was a subregion of stunning diversity, an urban environment composed of "ethnoreligious villages" that were internally homogeneous and often quite hostile to one another, to strangers and to change.[36] By the mid-eighteenth century the original Lutheran parish in Manhattan had divided into Dutch- and German-language congregations; thereafter, the swinging pendulum of language change lent momentum to periodic divisions and reunions among metropolitan New York Lutherans for nearly two centuries. Because of its leadership role, these changes in urban New York influenced the Lutheran Church throughout the region.

The changes caused by language segmentation in the New York parish were an important dynamic in the development of Lutheranism in the region. So, too, was its function as port of entry to the region. The parish's close connection with Henry Melchior Muhlenberg, and the Pennsylvania Ministerium is a case in point. Being trilingual—Muhlenberg spoke German, Dutch, and English—he served the New York City parish at a time of language and ethnic tension, and had thereafter, together with a son (Frederick Augustus Conrad), and a son-in-law (Johann Christopher Kunze), a significant influence on the New York church in both organization and theology. In this case New York became the port of entry for a mediating theology that was confessional in outlook and experiential in piety. Though part of growing religious pluralism that characterized the religious climate in New York City this mediating theology would become the source of a reviving confessionalism.

figure 1.2 German Christ Church ("The Old Swamp Church"), Frankfort Street

THE CENTRAL HUDSON CLUSTER

Congregations in the central Hudson River valley were first formed by colonies of Palatine Germans brought to New York in the early 1700s by the English Crown to produce naval stores. The Palatines were part of a major migration of Germans from the Palatine and Wurtemburg caused by political upheaval in the area of the Rhine Valley and south-west Germany. These immigrants introduced a different element into New York Lutheranism. The Rhenish Palatinate and Wurtemburg were especially fertile soil for the growth of a Lutheran Pietism rooted in the tradition of Rhenish mysticism. The German Theology and the "Devotio Moderna" of the Brethren of the Common Life originated in the region, as well as two forms of Wurtemburg Pietism, one radical, the other thoroughly integrated into the parish life of the region.[37] The area of emigration was devastated by the Thirty Years' War (1618-1648), and further ravaged by war between France and Austria over Spanish succession to the throne of the Holy Roman Empire.[38] An uprooted population fled, including many Lutherans with Pietist leanings, migrating to the American colonies. There they were joined in "mixed" communities by like-minded Reformed Church adherents. In all about twenty-five thousand Germans emigrated by the time of the American Revolution, ten thousand of which were at least nominally Lutheran.[39] At a popular level it was reported that their religious outlook was not grounded in the idea of divine Law but in the gospel idea of God's love, a traditional faith which was fertile soil for Pietism.[40]

In 1708 a group of these Palatine immigrants moved into the valleys of the Mohawk River and its tributary, Schoharie Creek. The remnant, which remained at Eastcamp and Westcamp, helped form congregations of German-speaking Christians in the middle Hudson Valley between the Catskills and Berkshires. Their worshipping communities often began as union churches of German-speaking Protestants, consisting of both Reformed and Lutherans, which lasted until sufficient immigration of Lutherans and Reformed permitted division into separate, self-sustaining congregations. The congregations in the Central Hudson cluster were served briefly in the mid-eighteenth century by the rather individualistic Johann Christoph Hartwick, and later by the leading American exponent of German rationalistic theology, Frederick Quitman.[41] The middle Hudson congregations had an affinity for the German language and culture, and a conservative religious orientation that became both mildly rational and openly ecumenical, a sign of Pietism and the common bond which adversity formed between Reformed and Lutheran émigrés. Slow growth and acculturation made them steady reflectors of the religious *status quo* in the regional church.

THE SCHOHARIE CLUSTER

Congregations were formed in the area by Palatine Germans who either moved up the Mohawk River and into the area from the central Hudson region after 1720, or who came directly into the Mohawk Valley from Germany. From there, Lutheran influence spread into the Schoharie Creek area. Two churches were established at Palatine Bridge (fig. 1.3) and Stone Arabia, initially including both Lutheran and Reformed Christians. Served for a time by Berkenmeyer, and then for an extended period by his son-in-law, Peter Nicholas Sommers, the area was distinctive throughout the history of Lutherans in the region.

Some of this difference originated with German Palatine resistance to English colonists and officials who would deny them secure land titles. Another factor was the religious differentiation between Palatine Pietism and the Lutheran Orthodoxy of Albany. A third was the continuing rural nature of the area, by contrast to the growing importance of Albany as an inland city. Finally, the essential feature of German social life during this period—particularism—must be acknowledged. With religion playing an unusually large role in social and political life, and with the Germans' "excessive preoccupation with local, even parochial concerns," the particularistic differentiation of this religious subregion, as of all subregions, had roots in these parishioners" ethnic origins.[42]

figure 1.3
Evangelical Lutheran Stone Church of Palatine, Erected, 1770

German particularism (especially strong among immigrant groups to America), reinforced by religion, would continue to influence northeastern Lutheranism throughout the period under consideration.[43] The resulting religious differentiation amounted to a distinctive geographic area dominated by an ethically activist form of Lutheran Pietism.[44] It was a dissident area of Lutheranism, affected by the waves of revivalism which swept upstate New York in the 1830s, which did missionary work in the rural and village regions of upstate New York.

THE NEW JERSEY CLUSTERS

Shortly after the settlement of the Central Hudson parish, German immigrants moved up the Raritan River valley forming several congregations, the oldest of which— Zion at Oldwick—dates from 1714. Quite likely the new immigrants were mostly members of the great migration of Palatinate Germans who migrated to the British colonies after 1710.[45] An important mission congregation and a significant "mother church" in mission and leadership, the Oldwick congregation was served by both Falckners, Henry Melchior Muhlenberg, and several Muhlenberg sons. A second area emerged in New Jersey along the upper Ramapo River in the Ramapo, New York/Mahwah, New Jersey area. Originally served by Justus Falckner, the congregation was also served by the Muhlenbergs and the Pennsylvania Ministerium. Here was a core group of Lutherans which developed into a number of congregations, eventually extending its mission interests into the Saddle River area in the late eighteenth century.

Though Palatine and presumably Pietist in outlook, like their fellow refugees along the central Hudson, Lutheran churches in the area had a stronger and more exclusive Lutheran identity, due to numbers and organization; their Lutheranism was also confessional in outlook.[46] They were receptive to the Lutheranism of the Pennsylvania Ministerium which had elements both confessional and pietistic. However, over time the Lutheran churches in the New Jersey area developed in a more decidedly pietistic direction. A similar differentiation among Dutch Calvinists. Like German Orthodoxy, a form of Dutch Calvinist Orthodoxy had developed along the Albany/Manhattan axis, while the Pietism of the German pietist and revivalist Theodore Frelinghuysen, who served Dutch Reformed congregations in the area, found an alternative outlet on the New York frontier of eastern New Jersey, especially in the Raritan Valley. Evangelical Presbyterians, led by Gilbert and William Tennent added a significant English-speaking expression of Pietism in the same area, while the Great Awakening's successes there provided another measure of the area's evangelical and pietistic predilections.[47] Because of their geographic location, Raritan area Lutheran churches were at the center of the two-region corridor. They had significant links with the Lutheran Church in Pennsylvania but were inclined to go their own way, seeking connections alternately with the Pennsylvania or New York Ministeria and attempting to form their own organization.

Regional and Bi-Regional Synodical Organizations—1735-1786

With growth these five clusters of congregations began developing a synodical expression of Lutheranism in the New York area by the middle of the eighteenth century. New York Lutherans joined Anglicans, the Reformed, Presbyterians, Baptists, and Quakers in the northeast, becoming part of a process of church building well under way by the 1750s. Throughout British American colonies, but especially in the middle colonies of New York, New Jersey, and Pennsylvania where no established church prevailed, Old World churches finally became established on a New World basis of voluntarism after a century of modest beginnings. With increased numbers of professional clergy, and as ecclesiastical structures stabilized, the church became a basic institution of provincial life, with increased influence among people, and expanded power in public life.[48]

This process of institution building was especially prevalent among German Lutherans and Reformed, including the Lutherans of New York. The need for pastoral leadership, for synodical guidance, for adjudication from outside the congregation, for cooperative arrangements in educational and mission activities, all led to the emergence of a synodical organization in New York by 1735. In Europe a system of state-organized territorial churches evolved a system of church government which became the initial instrumentalities of organization in colonial New York as well. The elements in this system included:

- the CONSISTORY (having administrative and judicatory functions; also ordination and the certification of clergy)
- the SYNODICAL ASSEMBLY (borrowed from Calvinism, gatherings of church leaders, lay and clerical, for mutual guidance and deliberation; not well developed in most German territories until the nineteenth century)
- the MINISTERIUM (gatherings of clergy for fellowship, consultations, and certain kinds of ecclesiastical business requiring theological reflection; also licensing, examining, and ordaining candidates for the ministry—the primary embodiment of the Office of Ministry among Lutherans in America)
- the SUPERINTENDENT (a church administrator responsible for the everyday administration of the consistory)

THE NEW YORK CLASSIS—1735

New York area Lutherans at first developed their own organizations using European institutions for support and guidance and as models for their new world counterparts. The earliest congregations in Albany and New York relied on the Amsterdam Lutheran Consistory for support, guidance, and pastoral supply. In the eighteenth century, with the appearance of William Berkenmeyer, a member of the orthodox Lutheran Hamburg Consistory who was called to serve in New York by the Amsterdam Consistory, ecclesiastical government among the churches took its next step. Berkenmeyer began to serve as a "superintendent," among other things gathering area congregations into a "Classical Assembly" in 1735. Dutch Calvinists used the term "classis" for certain, sub-synodical organizations, and its use in New York no doubt reflected the Amsterdam Consistory's influence. The classis consisted of pastors and congregations, meeting in consultation for advice and consent.[49] Berkenmeyer organized a "General Church Order" and in a brief time the assembled congregational leadership worked out a number of understandings, settlements, and congregational "submissions," effectively creating synodical government among eighteen scattered Lutheran congregations throughout the New York region. (See Map 1.2.)[50]

Assembly in synods was a practice widely used also in the New England region from the earliest settlement of Puritan congregations.[51] It mattered little whether the congregations were Congregational or Presbyterian. Both kinds needed the direction and guidance which deliberative synods and the corporate office of the ministry could provide. With no European ecclesiastical machinery in the American colonies, colonial churches quickly learned to organize into representative church bodies to manage their common affairs. Berkenmeyer's efforts can be seen as a first attempt to impose church discipline and doctrinal norms on a grouping of Lutheran congregations having diverse origins and more or less strong pietistic inclinations, something Lutheran Orthodoxy considered its special task in both Germany and America. Under Berkenmeyer's "General Church Order" congregations and pastors subscribed "to our Symbolical Books," and pastors were forbidden "even the use of any new phrases which would contradict the same."[52]

THE PENNSYLVANIA MINISTERIUM—1748

Shortly after New York's first experiment in Lutheran Church government, Henry Melchior Muhlenberg began the task of organizing Philadelphia-area congregations into a similar organization. These "United Congregations" (a group which had called Muhlenberg to America), together with their pastors, joined to form what was eventually to become the Pennsylvania Ministerium. Given Muhlenberg's key position as pastor of this original congregational union, he served off and on during his lifetime as Ministerium president and superintendent. Though begun in 1748 as an organization of congregations, this "Ministerium" met most frequently throughout the colonial period in what was often referred to as a "college of preachers." The clergy assembled to examine and ordain ministerial candidates and conduct other business of the churches including the development of church liturgies, hymnbooks, and catechisms. While the priesthood of all believers was clearly evidenced in the formation of congregations, and calling pastors, in the earliest period it was the "Ministerium" (the Office of the Ministry expressed in collegial form) which decisively influenced the development of American Lutheranism.[53]

The Pennsylvania Ministerium was but one expression among many of a new associational denominational authority developed more fully in the Delaware Valley region than elsewhere.[54] By the 1750s the

Ministerium had extended its influence and good offices into the New Jersey cluster and New York City parish, where Muhlenberg, who was especially adept at adjudicating congregational disputes, brought order and the prospects of regular, ordained leadership to the region's parishes. He was especially helpful in the City, a polyglot community, for the patriarch of the Lutheran Church could both converse and preach in Dutch, English, and German. Since 1730, New York had seen an influx of German-speaking Lutherans who preferred worshipping in their native tongue rather than English or Dutch.

This Pennsylvania influence helped introduce the irenic Lutheranism of Muhlenberg and the Pennsylvania Ministerium, which Muhlenberg actively promoted as an alternative Lutheranism to the Orthodoxy of Berkenmeyer and the New York Classis. Muhlenberg practiced a mediating theology which traveled a middle way between the extreme forms of Orthodoxy and Pietism.[55] His theological stance was decidedly confessional in distinguishing between Lutheran faith and practice on the one hand, and the Pietism of Moravians or other Protestants who considered themselves Lutheran. Orthodox Lutheran pastors in New York and Pennsylvania considered Muhlenberg and his colleagues to be out and out pietists because they emphasized "sanctification" as well as justification in their pastoral work.[56] Lutheran congregations, on the other hand, generally appreciated both their clear-cut Lutheran confessional identity and practical Pietism. By the 1750s most New York congregations had transferred allegiance from a (now largely defunct) New York Classis to the Pennsylvania Ministerium. With Muhlenberg's triumph in the area, the New York church began also to reflect a mediating Lutheranism which was both confessional and reformist in outlook. Its theology emphasized the experience of forgiveness and renewal, and the changed, sanctified life which comes of putting off the "old Adam." As developed by Muhlenberg, this piety drew upon Luther's experiential emphases, as well as the theological outlook of Arndt and Spener, focusing in particular on the lifelong struggle of justified faith simultaneously in the grip of human sinfulness.[57]

THE LUTHERAN MINISTERIUM IN NORTH AMERICA —1781

Ironically, by 1750 all but the Schoharie cluster had joined forces with the Pennsylvania Ministerium. The holdout was an area of Lutheranism with strong pietist inclinations but served by Berkenmeyer's son-in-law. While this area remained separate, other and more orthodox-leaning areas willingly joined an expanding Ministerium. Clearly this was a triumph for the moderate, mission-minded Lutheranism of a Ministerium which sought to build a larger church on a basis at once confessional and pietistic. Something of the "nation-building" influence of the Hudson and Delaware Valley Regions can be seen in this evolution of the

Pennsylvania Ministerium and its theological emphases. At first restricted to Southeastern Pennsylvania, the Pennsylvania Ministerium spread to adjacent areas and colonies, including (besides New Jersey and New York), Delaware, Maryland, Virginia, and North Carolina, by the end of the colonial period.

For a brief time, at least, the New York region of the Hudson Valley emerged as an institutional part of a nation-building, "national corridor," an important center of economic, social, political, and also religious change.[58] This national Lutheran body included congregations from Canada to South Carolina along the eastern seaboard and as far west as the Appalachian frontier. Accordingly, the Pennsylvania Ministerium's new 1781 constitution created "An Evangelical Lutheran Ministerium in North America."[59] Formed at a time when European colonial church life had to be organized on a new, American basis, the Evangelical Lutheran Ministerium of North America was one of many newly organized or reorganized denominations to be found throughout the new American states. All were ecclesiastical structures forming a legal foundation for the free exercise of religion in a nation then beginning to replace its colonial religious establishments.

The North American Ministerium anticipated by more than a century the formation of the United Lutheran Church. Yet its formation was premature. Church structures and growth were still primarily regional, rather than national, in nature. The formation of new states, and the need for legal incorporation led to the development of state, and regional expressions of Lutheranism instead.[60] Accordingly the 1781 Constitution was revised in 1792 to create a Lutheran Ministerium for the larger Delaware Valley—"The German Evangelical Lutheran Ministerium in Pennsylvania and Adjacent States."[61] At this time a Ministerium was developed for the New York region of the Hudson Valley watershed.

THE BEGINNING OF A REGIONAL MINISTERIUM 1786-1816

Lutheran congregations in New York state had already begun developing their own organization with the establishment of "The Evangelical Lutheran Ministerium of New York" in 1786, modeled on the North American Ministerium.[62] The move was initiated by the group's prime organizer and first president, Johann Christoph Kunze (fig. 1.4), Henry Melchior Muhlenberg's son-in-law. Kunze was called to the New York parish of German-speaking Lutherans which had been reunited under the continuing influence of the Pennsylvania Ministerium. Originating in the region's port of entry (New York City), the new Ministerium began organizing the core Lutheran groupings in the area, namely the Albany, Schoharie, and Central Hudson clusters of Lutheran congregations.

figure 1.4 Johann Christoph Kunze

THE NEW YORK MINISTERIUM—1786

The Ministerium's initial meeting took place in 1786 and it was understood that a synodical meeting would be called "whenever a sufficient number of preachers and congregations should desire it." The desire did not materialize until six years later when the Ministerium held its second meeting. It met more regularly thereafter. The 1786 synod indicated one of its purposes was the examination of a preacher's "orthodoxy," a term then undergoing redefinition. "Orthodoxy" was nowhere spelled out in the New York constitution, but the Pennsylvania Constitution of 1781 indicated orthodoxy to consist of the "plain teachings of the Holy Scripture and our Symbolical Books." Composed while

Muhlenberg was still alive and active, the constitution still maintained a working definition of that mediational theology that was both pietistic and confessional.

By 1792, shortly after Muhlenberg's death, things had changed. In that year the New York Ministerium adopted the new (1792) constitution of its Pennsylvania counterpart with minor modifications. Orthodoxy was still a concern of the New York and Pennsylvania clergy, but it was now limited to a proper understanding of "the Word of God in its purity according to the law and the gospel." The objectives of both Lutheran Orthodoxy and Pietism were still in evidence however. Candidates in preparation for ministry were expected to acquire "a systematic knowledge of Christian doctrines and ethics" and "above all things a practical knowledge of experimental religion."[63]

The resulting Lutheran Church in New York was now united linguistically, geographically, and theologically from New York to Albany. Reflecting these new circumstances, the church changed its name in 1794 to "The German Evangelical Lutheran Ministerium in the State of New York and Adjacent Parts."[64]

There were no "adjacent parts" however, at least not that were ready to affiliate with the new organization. New Jersey Lutherans seem to have led an independent existence for several decades during this period of transition. The Raritan cluster was last referred to by the Pennsylvania Ministerium in its *Minutes* in 1790, and then in circumstances suggesting it was an outside group being invited to attend Ministerium sessions.[65] What was by now known as "New Germantown" waited until the ordination of Pastor Ernest Hazelius in 1809 to reestablish formal ties with a Lutheran synod. This time it chose the New York church, when Hazelius's Lutheran congregation in that area requested Ministerium membership through their new pastor.[66] With time other "adjacent areas" including upper Canada (across the Niagara and St. Lawrence Rivers, at either end of Lake Ontario), lower Canada (across the state's northern border and in the area around Montreal), western Massachusetts, western and southern Connecticut, and extreme northeastern Pennsylvania would join the New York Ministerium. All of the congregations were in a region whose commerce and cultural life flowed into the hydrographic basin of New York and the Hudson River watershed.

The initial group of New York Ministerium congregations developed slowly, confused as to its own long-term identity. Ironically, the new *American* church in New York was more self-consciously *German* than the old Pennsylvania Ministerium of Muhlenberg, or Berkenmeyer's bilingual Classical Assembly. In 1800 the New York Ministerium went on record as discouraging German-speaking congregations from becoming bilingual, and English-speaking congregations from thinking of themselves as "Lutheran" at all. Membership was to be denied the latter group. With the exception of one English-speaking New York congregation already in existence, which was admitted with the provision that its admission not invalidate the German-language rule, English-speaking Lutherans were encouraged to join the Episcopal Church! The Ministerium's intentions were unambiguous on this point:

> That in consideration of the connection that exists between the Anglican Episcopal and Lutheran Churches and the similarity of doctrine and the close resemblance of the church organization of the Ministerium (the latter) will never sanction a newly founded Lutheran congregation that uses English only in a place where members may participate in the service of the Anglican Episcopal Church.[67]

Such thinking fostered an "ethno-religious village" mentality and served as a survival mechanism in the polyglot culture of the lower Hudson Valley.[68] Language, ethnicity and religion conspired to create a tiny church with a limited vision of its future in the new and strange world of Revolutionary America. Strobel's words—"There is nothing like compactness"—take on a certain irony in the context of late eighteenth-century New York Lutheranism. Only as its German Lutherans would dare to venture out upon the terrain of their region, would a larger vision of Lutheranism arise. And that would require crossing psychological barriers more foreboding than New York harbor. But the journey was about to begin.

1807-1816—A TIME OF CHANGE

For Lutherans in the New York region, 1807 was a year of transition, marking the beginnings of its denominational era.[69] Pastors and representatives of area congregations met that year in the first of a series of annual meetings. Meetings of increased frequency were required by the growing pace of ecclesiastical business. The transition came with the surprising swiftness of death. It began, so the Ministerium's "Minute Book" noted, with a "solemn gloom [which] overspread this Synod upon account of the decease of the Revrd. John Christoph Kunze," DD, Pastor of the United Lutheran Church of New York, president of the Ministerium, and theological professor at tiny Hartwick's Institute (later Academy). Kunze had "happily presided [over] their religious councils in a course of twenty-two years, a father in Christ to many that are now Teachers in ours and other Churches."[70] However distraught Kunze's colleagues might have been, they composed themselves sufficiently to immediately change the Ministerium's official language from German to English, and to lift the ban on the one English congregation which could not receive new members from German-speaking congregations. They also elected an architect of change, the Rev. Frederick H. Quitman (1795-1832) to preside over the Ministerium, and to instruct its candidates as the new "Professor of Divinity" in Hartwick's Institute. Quitman, a graduate of Halle University, represented the new emphasis in the Lutheran Church on philosophy and reason which had replaced Orthodox Lutheran theology, especially at Halle. There, as at other Universities, the German *Aufklarung* (the Enlightenment) dominated intellectual life by the late eighteenth century, resulting in a new generation of "enlightened" clergymen for whom faith and doctrine were less important than the moral and pedagogical role of religion.[71] Perennially controversial, Quitman's "rationalist" approach to theology angered more orthodox colleagues in his own time, and made him a favorite scapegoat for later Lutheran confessionalists.

Kunze, like father-in-law Muhlenberg, knew the Gospel must be preached in German and English if the Lutheran Church was to survive in America. But he was incapable of doing so himself. On the one occasion when he tried, delivering the good news of universal redemption ("God is not willing that any should perish"), a group of boys who overheard the sermon put it about that "God is not a villain."[72] The language change of 1807 was not from one language to another, however, but involved the more subtle redefinition of primary and secondary languages in a bilingual community needing to educate its young in the language of the host culture.[73]

Crucial decisions followed year by year:

- At its 1808 synod gathering the Ministerium proposed developing a new constitution, and "a new Catechism in the Engl.[ish] language adapted to the wants of the rising generation."[74]
- 1809 saw a proposal for a "new Hymnbook & Liturgy in the English language."
- The proposed English Catechism was published in 1814.
- A year later (1815) the Ministerium agreed to the purchase and use of "the Hymnbook & Liturgy in the Engl. language" then being printed in Philadelphia.
- Also introduced by the Ministerium, probably for the first time among American Lutherans, was an "unguarded" invitation to the Lord's Supper which knew no confessional limits.[75]
- In December of 1815 the new Hartwick Seminary was opened in frontier Oneonta County (fig. 1.5).
- 1816 saw the new Ministerium constitution appear.
- Two years later (1818) a home mission fund would be established.

By themselves these and other decisions added up to change. Taken together they represented a transition to a new kind of corporate religious life in America—denominationalism—with its emphasis on growth and expansion.

figure 1.5 Hartwick Seminary, Opened December, 1815

1816—AN AMERICAN DENOMINATION EMERGES

A decade after Kunze's death, it was apparent that a Lutheran denomination was emerging in New York. Although the term "denomination" was used at the time by Lutherans as well as by other Christian groups, it does not derive from the church's confessional tradition. In the Augsburg Confession, the Church is understood confessionally as "one holy Christian church," an "assembly" of saints in which the Gospel "is taught purely and the sacraments are administered rightly." "Church" was used in a double sense—for the church catholic, and for what Luther described as "a Christian congregation or assembly."[76]

To "denominate" a Christian body is to give it a name and identity which distinguishes it from other church bodies. A "Denomination"—a religious organization of like-minded congregations—was therefore an institution with a distinctive "something" which *denominated* that group as Lutheran or Reformed or Presbyterian by comparison with other groups (denominations) differently denominated. Contrary to the Lutheran confessional emphasis upon orthodox catholicity—the one holy catholic and apostolic faith to be found always and everywhere—denominationalism distinguished church bodies in terms of their sectarian particularities and doctrinal peculiarities.

The American church historian, Sydney Mead, has characterized the denomination in this way.[77] Its primary feature is the *voluntary principle* of organization. A necessary corollary of religious freedom guaranteed in the Bill of Rights, a voluntary association is based upon freedom of assembly and the free and uncoerced consent of its members. A second feature is a *sectarian tendency* to justify a denomination's peculiar beliefs by appeal to scripture. A third is the denomination's *mission outlook*—a mixture of evangelical zeal inherited from Pietism, a commitment to works of outreach and charity, and a desire to win converts and increase membership. *Revivalism*—the use of rural camp meetings and the urban protracted meeting to effect religious conversion—was a fourth hallmark of the emerging denomination, and a primary means of evangelization. Still another feature was a tendency to *flee from reason and religious rationalism*, favoring, instead, an emphasis upon revelation and experience as the bases of Christian faith.

Taken together, the characteristics of denominationalism represent a pattern of attitudes and behaviors among American Christians which successfully restructured Protestant Christianity between the American Revolution and the end of the War of 1812.[78] Colonial religious establishments and immigrant outposts of European Christendom were transformed into voluntary organizations with an increased capacity for membership adherence, outreach, and growth. In an era which witnessed the emergence of free-market economies in the United States and in Europe, it has been argued that denominationalism in North America took on some of the qualities of a competitive religious economy. Mead has noted the "competitive relationship" of religious "voluntary associations," noting that competitors whether "selling" religion or another item seldom stress the virtues of the competition. More recently Roger Finke and Rodney Stark have seen successful marketplace competition as a major reason for growing church membership.[79]

Estimates of church membership on the eve of the Revolution vary widely from as low as 6.6 percent to a recent calculation of 17 percent of the total population; it is generally agreed that a reasonable ballpark figure is between 10 percent and 20 percent. Yet whatever the percentage of actual membership, Church attendance was high in colonial America, and when attenders are added to communicant "members" (in the ratio of three or four attenders for every one communicant member) adult adherence to the major denominations by the early nineteenth century could well have been as high as 62.5 percent of the population. Probably hardcore adherents of various emerging denominations doubled between 1776 and 1812, increasing from 1 member for every 15 Americans (6.6 percent of the population), to about 1 in 8 (12.5 percent), a dramatic change which in itself indicated the increasing importance of church membership per se. What these figures do indicate is the growing involvement through membership in religious denominations that but a generation before had been expressions of state churches and established religion.[80] Lutheranism too was transformed—from an immigrant church dependent upon Europe for its identity and existence, to an American denomination capable of self-sustaining growth. Almost all of the above features—voluntary association, a sectarian tendency, revivalism, a mission outlook, and the flight from rationalism to emotions and experience—were accepted by Lutherans in the process of Americanization, and can be found shaping New York Lutheranism.

The new Ministerium Constitution proposed in 1808 and completed by 1816 exhibits this process of transformation. Its American orientation and identity was displayed in a new seal consisting of two fields—on the right a double eagle hovering over a vine, "in commemoration of Germany and the Evangelical church planted in that country"; and on the left, an eagle flying from east to west and hovering over the vine, "intimating that the Evangelical church in America is a branch transplanted from Europe." On the top was a crown, sun, and twelve stars, with the moon below, the emblem of the Church described in Revelation 12:1.[81] A year later the New York legislature was to be approached to ensure that the "Luth[eran] Church in this State" would be incorporated upon the same basis as, and enjoying equally privileges with "the Episcopal English & Dutch Reformed Churches."[82] To seek competitive parity rather than noncompetitive compatibility with the Episcopal church was symbolic of how far New York Lutheranism had come as a separate denomination since agreeing that all of its English-speaking members should become Episcopalian.

As significant, the denominational language of voluntarism and the spirit of liberty and democracy permeated the revised constitution. The old constitution suggested the evolution of a Ministerium out of a "Consistory" in keeping with European thinking and practice.[83] The new organization was to be a united body of representatives and ministers forming an "association." Elections and business went on much as before, for this new constitution reflected two decades of democratic practice dating back at least to the New York Ministerium Constitution of 1792. New, however, was the idea that a congregation was an associating body for "mutual counsel and assistance" entering into "common measures for the promoting of knowledge and religion." Henceforth congregations were to "have rights which ought to be protected and secured to them" through the practice of representative government.[84] All ministers, meanwhile, were to be considered "perfectly equal as to rank, title, and privileges, having no power, the one over the other," except for the limited power of officers designed to maintain order in the association. As for the Ministerium proper, that body of clergy which met apart to examine, license, ordain, and admit ministers to the organization, its deliberations were to be conducted by "the first principle of Protestantism, the right of free inquiry" with no infringement and no attempt "to erect the Ministerium into an inquisitorial tribunal."[85]

The Ministerium was meant to promote "the best methods of discharging ministerial functions," and "the spread of truth and piety." In addition, weighty "articles of faith" or "cases of conscience . . . may receive a friendly discussion" it was argued, the latter in the spirit of "the first principle."[86] As the Frenchman Tocqueville found when visiting America later, here everyone had an opinion to which he or she felt entitled. The first principle of Protestantism was a form of etiquette meant to allow religious discussions in a democratic society. In all denominational bodies, including the Ministerium, such ettiquette would shape theological discussion. Developed as a means, this principle would quickly become an end in itself, and a fundamental principle of theology in an emerging American Lutheran denomination.

PLAN ENTWURF AND THE GENERAL SYNOD OF 1820

The logic of denominational differentiation and associationalism meant the growth of more general synodical structures as well. In 1818 the New York body formed a standing committee of correspondence with the Pennsylvania Ministerium on the "state of the sister churches."[87] Within a year the two groups advanced a "Proposed Plan for a Central Union of the Evangelical Lutheran Church in the United States of North America" (or "Plan Entwurf"). The Plan emerged from the 1818 session of the Pennsylvania Synod, that "venerable Ministerium" which had assumed the responsibility "to prepare a plan for a closer union . . . and to see to it that this union . . . be brought about, if possible." If adopted the plan would consolidate the national corridor of New York and Pennsylvania Lutheranism uniting it with a band of southern congregations organized in the Synod of North Carolina.[88]

The plan was to form a "General Synod" with powers 1) to establish new synods; 2) to introduce new worship services and "improve the present Liturgy"; and 3) to serve as a court of arbitration for disputes of doctrine or discipline in constituent synods. Scrupulously honoring the first principle of Protestantism, the General Synod was to have "no power to make any change in the doctrines hitherto received among us."[89] The organization which emerged from the General Synod's organizational meeting had a primary commitment to Christian unity. Organized to deal with the growing pluralism and diversity within American Lutheranism, the General Synod was committed by "all their powers" to prevent schism and to be "incessantly regardful" of the rise and progress of "unity of sentiment among Christians." Its goal was nothing less than to "heal the wounds and schisms already existing in the Church of Christ and to promote general concord and unity."[90] To this end the General Synod was to examine the proceedings of its constituent synods "that they may obtain some knowledge of the existing state and condition of the Church."[91] As for the books, writings, catechisms, and liturgies published in various parts of the church, these were to be examined by the General Synod to provide "advice, counsel, or opinion" to its constituent synods. No synod was to introduce such items into its congregations without such a review. When the General Synod deemed "it proper or necessary" the general body itself could propose catechisms, liturgies or other written material "for general or special, common or public use" however it was specifically not allowed "to possess, or arrogate unto itself the power of prescribing among us uniform ceremonies of religion for every part of the Church." Nor could it introduce alterations in what was considered the fundamentals of faith underwriting the General Synod—"the Gospel of Jesus Christ."[92] The General Synod was to serve in an advisory manner, but not as a "Tribunal of Appeal." It was not to be a body which established confessional norms, but one which arbitrated different theological opinions "according to their best insight of right, equity, brotherly love, and truth."[93]

Growth however, not regulation, was the General Synod's *raison d'être*. Fulfilling the great commission was considered a "sacred duty" and it was the district synod's responsibility to adopt all measures necessary to extend the kingdom through mission work.[94] The General Synod was therefore expected to regulate Lutheran growth by encouraging the formation of new synods where twenty-five or more ministers within a given area applied to the General Synod, thereby assuring the creation of new regulatory bodies. By 1829 a model constitution was available for new groups seeking membership in the general body. District synods were expected to examine ordinands and administer the following ordination vows:

- "Do you believe the Scriptures of the Old and New Testament to be the word of God, and the only infallible rule of faith and practice?"
- "Do you believe that the fundamental doctrines of the word of God, are taught in a manner substantially correct, in the doctrinal articles of the Augsburg Confession ?" [95]

Confessional norms, which were applied at the level of the district synod, also applied in the General Synod's seminaries. The oath of office given to professors at the new seminary at Gettysburg stated "I believe the Augsburg Confession and the catechisms of Luther to be a summary and just exhibition of the fundamental doctrines of the Word of God." [96]

THE MINISTERIUM REJECTS THE NEW GENERAL SYNOD

The New York Ministerium rejected the plan for a General Synod as "at variance with the spirit of the constitution of the Ministerium of New York" and with its understanding of the first principle of Protestantism, favoring its own approach to greater Lutheran unity, namely the mutual exchange of voting delegates from other synods.[97] Freedom of expression not confessional unity was uppermost in its mind. As President Quitman's three sermons on the "Jubilee of the Reformation" (October 31, 1817) made abundantly clear, commemorating the Reformation meant celebrating a Christian freedom which liberated one from subscription to the Reformation's theological norms![98] Its diminished confessional identity and aversion to synodical solidarity, as expressions of its Protestant principle, were one sign of the democratic transformation through which American Lutheranism was then passing.

While the name "Lutheran" remained in the Ministerium constitution, the term "evangelical" was operative. Gone were all references to the symbolic books (they had disappeared in 1792), or to a knowledge of law and gospel. It was a pious, courteous, and above all learned ministry which was desired. Even the "practical knowledge of experimental religion"—code words for Pietism—had been dispensed with. The Ministerium's ordinands now were to be well acquainted with the language and doctrine of scripture, and "the evidences of Christianity" (i.e., its rational basis of existence); and to be able to read the New Testament in the original Greek. They were to be proficient in Latin, Hebrew, and German; competent in church history, natural and moral philosophy; and able to compose and deliver a sermon. Indeed, any minister "ordained by a Bishop, Convention, Presbytery, Association, or Council" (i.e., any Episcopal, Methodist, Presbyterian, Baptist, or Congregationalist clergyman) if a person of piety, character, and literacy, could be received into the association of clergy without examination or ordination![99]

DENOMINATIONAL GROWTH AND SYNODICAL DIVISION

After 1820 however, a new set of realities overtook the Ministerium. By 1823 the Ministerium had grown to include twenty-three congregations some of which were vacant and in desperate need of pastoral leadership. Originally formed by three congregations in 1786, the New York Ministerium increased to four by 1792, but included only thirteen in 1800, a number that remained fairly constant until the third decade of the nineteenth century. The largest single group of congregations came from the Albany area, and included the Albany and Schoharie clusters of congregations. The Central Hudson region was represented by one or two congregations, New Jersey and New York by one or two each. Now, however, other areas were beginning to grow and seek Ministerium involvement.

The years between the War of 1812 and mid-century were decades of unprecedented growth in America including New York. Natural population growth, swelled by a new wave of European immigration, peopled the farms and villages, the towns and (increasingly) the cities of the new American nation. Americans moved west, pushing the frontier past the Mississippi. Everywhere they settled new churches were established. And wherever villages developed into towns, and towns into cities, old congregations grew and subdivided the better to accommodate a growing population. Where new congregations were established throughout frontier America, old synods grew, developing new conferences of pastors in frontier areas which eventually separated from older synods to form new synods. The Pennsylvania Synod spun off The Ohio Synod in 1817, Maryland-Virginia in 1820, and the Western Pennsylvania Synod in 1823. Ohio itself subdivided into eastern and western districts in 1831. New synods also formed. In 1820 the Tennessee Synod was organized over differences in confessional loyalties. 1835 saw the organization of the Henkelite Indiana Synod with congregations in Indiana and Missouri, while other congregations in Illinois, Indiana, Kentucky, and Middle Tennessee formed the "Evangelical Lutheran Synod of the West" in the same year.[100]

Yet while ranks of new states formed north and south of the Mason-Dixon Line, eastern states like New York continued to grow. During the 1820s the New York frontier, from Albany to Buffalo, developed into a region of farms, villages, and towns spreading along the Mohawk River and then the Erie Canal—an extension of the Hudson and Mohawk rivers westward across the state "from Albany to Buffalo"— forming the beginnings of what would become New York's urban belt. (See Map 1.1.) It was only a matter of time before the New York Ministerium reached a similar point of self-division to better serve the new west region along the Erie Canal. New Jersey evolved a distinctive group of congregations within the Ministerium as did a growing population of Lutherans around Albany and to the west. Significantly, both areas were mission conscious and concerned to deliver the faith through English versions of Luther's catechism. In response to Erie Canal growth a missionary fund was established, followed by the formation of a Home Mission Committee of the Ministerium in 1823, and a separate Home Missionary Society in 1828. Mission trips undertaken by Ministerium appointed clergy in 1819 and 1823 eventuated in the appointment of a full-time mission pastor by 1823, John P. Goertner.[101]

THE GENERAL SYNOD STRUGGLE IN NEW YORK

The General Synod was organized at just that point in American Lutheran history when congregational growth and synodical subdivision made its existence both desirable and necessary. Its self-assigned right and power to establish new synods was meant to prevent disorderly growth that "might in the end be the means of bringing about unnecessary and injurious divisions and departures" from the Great Commission. [102] Thus the General Synod's provision in its constitution allowing local groups of clergy (twenty-five ministers living in close proximity in a fixed district) to form new synods.[103]

Now given subregional realities of New York Lutheranism, such a right to organize, or the potential for an organization that could grant such a right, could become an important element in shaping New York church growth. The Hudson axis of the New York Ministerium, from Albany to New York City, was the oldest and most established part of the Ministerium. Moreover, the Ministerium in these parts was (for the most part) religiously conservative and tied theologically through President Quitman to German rationalism. The New Jersey and Schoharie clusters, to the contrary, long influenced by the Pietism of their Palatine immigrant founders, had developed ties with the Pennsylvania tradition of Muhlenberg theology with its emphasis on a confessional identity, piety, and mission. Synodical officials in these circumstances were not regional leaders as much as they were subregional politicians. While Quitman led a kind of rationalist, status-quo party, Ernest Hazelius of New Jersey, now president of Hartwick Seminary, represented a more confessional, pietistic and mission-minded alternative. So, too, did Pastor Frederick Shaeffer of New York City's breakaway, English-speaking St. Matthews Lutheran Church, who had an interest in Ministerium mission work in northern New Jersey. Pastor George Lintner of Schoharie County shared a similar outlook and an interest in mission activity west of Albany.

It was Shaeffer and Lintner who provided the leadership which formed a standing committee on missions in 1823. Together with Hazelius, Henry N. Pohlman, pastor in New Germantown, New Jersey, and Hartwick Professor George B. Miller, Lintner helped form the synodical Missionary Society in 1828 "to propagate the gospel among the destitute, to organize new churches, and to assist feeble congregations in supporting the gospel ministry." And it was Lintner who annually raised the question of membership in the General Synod with the New York Ministerium after 1821. He was aided by Hazelius after the latter became president of the Ministerium in 1829. Both wanted a General Synod which could be helpful to the preachers west of Albany who had formed a separate conference in 1826 without Ministerium approval.[104] The needs of the church in the west were great, but the Ministerium seemed unable or unwilling to respond. When it refused again in 1830 to consider General Synod membership, the Western Conference withdrew and formed a separate synod, naming itself after a colonial pastor and his namesake Seminary, both of which had the mission interests of the Lutheran Church at heart.

The new Hartwick Synod joined the General Synod in 1831. The Ministerium followed in 1836, concluding that membership would "give an increase of character and respectability to our church," and produce "greater harmony and concern of action in our benevolent enterprises, and thus will increase our means of usefulness in the wide field now occupied by the destitute of our common household of faith." Besides membership was thought advisable "for our own security against undue encroachments."[105] Since the Hartwick separation, territorial disputes had complicated relations between synods in the

New York area. The General Synod was now considered a desirable bridle on unrestrained competitiveness. The overriding reason for joining the General Synod, however was mission. The Ministerium was growing concerned about the influx of German immigrants into New York by the 1830s. "There is no calculating the number" its mission committee reported "who have settled down in the State of New York. They are to be met with in every city, town and village; and the tide which has for several years been flowing to the west, instead of being stayed, seems to be rolling on with increased force."[106]

PROTESTANT REVIVALISM AMONG LUTHERANS

Meanwhile Yankee immigrants flowed into New York's primary geographic subregion, skipping over the Hudson Valley and the subregional culture of Albany Yorkers (with its continuing Dutch influence) moved west along a rapidly expanding frontier, leaving behind them a settled agricultural belt and industrial economy, a well-developed canal system, and a line of growing cities from Albany to Buffalo. As the region's economy, social structure, and political life matured, an intense interest in religion developed, creating the circumstances for a wave of religious revivals during the 1820s—themselves part of a Second Great Awakening of Protestantism in America which had begun in the previous decade. The revival's eventual demise left a region and culture known all too accurately as the "Burned Over District."[107] Though the revival's most intense phase seems to have occurred in western New York, from Oneida County and Rome (at the head of the Mohawk River) west after 1824, it is clear from Lutheran developments further to the east that New York Lutheranism in at least two of its five upstate clusters was remolded in its heat.

The progress and development of upstate revivalism followed the classic pattern. It began with denominational interest in mission and evangelism among Presbyterians, Methodists, and Baptists. The resulting local revivals spread like fire through the work of itinerant preachers moving like so many of Samson's foxes from town to town. By 1825 these revivals had appeared throughout the region, partly due to a Jefferson County lawyer-turned-evangelist who would become its most prominent leader. Charles Finney, converted at Adams, New York, in 1821, brought revivalism to the growing towns and cities along the Erie Canal through the "protracted meeting," a series of lengthy, nightly religious gatherings of several weeks duration, designed to awaken the spiritual life of community members.[108]

The protracted meeting was one of several "New Measures" in a developing technology of Protestant revivalism, which also included intensified preaching of sometimes theatrical proportions; small-group prayer meetings which invoked divine power to convert persons; and the use of exhortation and prayer which focused on specific individuals (i.e., sinners), sins (such as drunkenness), and reforms (like temperance).[109] Lutheran revivals used all of these methods including an "invitation" to come forward and receive an "interest" in the prayers of the congregation. Though criticized by conservative confessionalists, to aggressive evangelists the New Measures were the very "lever of Archimedes" destined to lift the Lutheran Church out of its apathy.[110] These included S. S. Schmucker who had endorsed "special conferences for the purpose of holding stated protracted meetings" among the institutions of General Synod Lutheranism; also New York Ministerium President Ernest Hazelius who reported in 1829 on a "gradual increase of the numbers of professors of religion" because of New Measures.[111]

Moral reform also became an important objective of the revival culture, including the causes of temperance and the abolition of slavery. In its most extreme form, revivalism included experiments in achieving "perfect sanctification." There was an urgency about the entire movement, for the revivals fostered eschatological hopes in a rapidly approaching millennium, for which the larger society must be prepared.

By the mid-1830s, what contemporaries referred to as religious "ultraism" was rampant in upstate New York.[112] Ultraism in its turn spawned heterodoxy and schism as denominations and mission societies divided into old and new light factions, and orthodox and revivalistic camps. But all was not radical ferment. For the revival movement itself was by and large a sober affair of urban professional and business people. Finney's greatest success was in Rochester! Nor were the consequences entirely negative. Church growth developed through missionary societies, and Sunday school unions promoted new educational activity in congregations.[113]

Most importantly, upstate New York revivals during this Second Great Awakening built a solid religious foundation for the family. A study of several Utica congregations suggests that while revivalism brought new male converts into American churches, increasing the number of males in these congregations, female converts were the agents of family religious development and congregational growth. The first family member to enter a church was twice as likely to be female as male. The men were "led into the churches by pious wives, mothers and sisters." Many husbands and brothers joined the church later, and on their own but a majority affiliated when a female relative was converted. Successive revivals brought the grown children of these parents—especially of the mothers—into growing congregations. They represent the echo effect of previous harvests of souls.[114] Converted women, seeking Baptism for children and drawing men after them into the congregation, were essential to religious development in upstate New York along the corridor of commerce and industry created by the Erie Canal.[115] This will become abundantly evident in the histories of the Hartwick, Franckean, and New York and New Jersey Synods.

REVIVALISTIC LUTHERANISM AND THE FRANCKEAN SYNOD—1837

By the 1830s upstate revivalism had reached the Hartwick Synod. Talking shop among themselves, the Hartwick pastors discussed the usual topics—baptism and confirmation, but also the New Measures of upstate revivalism—"Prayer Meetings and the manner of conducting them, and the means most proper to be used to promote revivals." Three years later the synod recommended employing the protracted meeting throughout its jurisdiction.[116] Finally in 1837 a small group of revivalist pastors concerned about mission work in rural, upstate New York, broke away to form the Franckean Synod, named after the German Lutheran pietist leader, August Hermann Francke (1663-1727).

The movement developed among rural Lutherans surrounding Albany (but outside of Albany County) in Rensselear County to the east, toward the New England origins of revivalism, and to the west in Herkimer, Schoharie and Montgomery counties, on either side of the Mohawk River. Revivalism itself was not limited to the Burned Over District. A significant revival had occurred in and around Albany itself among Presbyterians in the 1820s. It was the effects of this and other revival work, including Finney's visits to Troy, an urban center in the midst of Hartwick (and breakaway Franckean) congregations, which set the stage for Lutheran revivals. Significantly, both synods, but especially the Franckean breakaway, developed new Lutheran congregations to the west and northwest using revivalistic techniques within the Burned Over District itself.[117]

Again it was a synodical conference breakaway, Hartwick's Western Conference in this case, and again it was "for the purpose of organizing another Synod in the Lutheran Church."[118] But unlike the Hartwick Synod, the new group was susceptible to ultraism, quite probably because of the Halle Pietism and moral activism which had permeated this corner of New York Lutheranism, but a result as well of Franckean penetration into the heart of Burned Over upstate New York.[119] This area of intense religious and moral fervor was part of a larger area influenced by moral reform. Albany, which lay in between two groups of Franckean congregations, had a strong Temperance Society whose *Temperance Recorder* was the Temperance movement's national organ, and was the capital of a state many of whose politicians took an early lead in advocating the abolition of slavery.[120] The religious revival's progress in the new Synod can be measured by the extent to which a receptive piety allowed ultraism to shape its Lutheranism. The new synod's constitution provided that no delegate "shall be a slaveholder, nor engaged directly or indirectly in the manufacture and traffic of intoxicating liquors," rendering it thereby one of a number of comeouter breakaways to occur among Protestant denominations over the issue of slavery, and an early advocate of temperance.

Even clergy were excluded who would "not sign the pledge" of total abstinence or who were slaveholders or advocated "the system of slavery as it exists in these United States."[121] According to the Franckean Synod's "Declaration of Faith" sanctification through the Holy Spirit, which begins with repentance, produces saving faith, sanctifies the soul and perfects human holiness, was considered of equal importance to justification. Only those Christians giving credible evidence of having been born again through a radical change of heart, and who live "according to the precepts and requirements of the Gospel," could be admitted as church members.[122] Its "chief object" the group proclaimed at its second meeting, "is to promote the Redeemer's kingdom by cultivating deep-toned piety . . . and by expansive benevolence."[123]

Ultraism, and a certain looseness of tradition and pedigree, carried this expression of Lutheran Pietism beyond the pale. Though the synod's theology and agenda were classic expressions of Halle Pietism, synod leaders had by now turned to the thought and work of a widening circle of Christians leaders, including English Puritans, American Calvinists, and Methodist pietists. The synod's self-professed intellectual pedigree included "a Luther, a Francke, a Wesley, a Baxter, a Whitefield, an Edwards," betraying the mixed influence of Luther, Lutheran Pietism, upstate Methodist revivalism, English Puritanism, Great Awakening Revivalism and New England Edwardianism.[124] Even in a day of latitudinarian Lutheranism, the Franckeans transgressed recognizable Lutheran limits. In Franckean Synod congregations infants were baptized, but only "professed Christians" could be members. Its leading theologian was inclined to reserve Baptism still further for adult converts only, a hint that Franckean thinking was seeking to differentiate itself from confessional Lutheranism in an area influenced by regular and Freewill Baptists. Significantly Baptists were also the leading northern anti-slavery denomination though even its contingent of Freewill Baptists were not so militant on the subject as the Franckean Synod, perhaps another sign of denominational competitiveness. Though Franckeans believed that persons were "not justified on account of any merits or works of their own," they also insisted that keeping the moral law was mandated for all who would call themselves Christian. War and peace became vital issues, it being the duty of members "as disciples of Jesus Christ" to "secure the immediate, universal and permanent abolition of war."[125]

Franckean Synod leaders considered themselves religious radicals but were they still Lutheran?[126] To the charge that the synod had "renounced" the *Augsburg Confession* he asked: "Where in all our proceedings is there one word found about or against the Augsburg Confession? . . . We have waged no war against that instrument. We have left it where it is and just as it is."[127] The confessional tradition was neither affirmed nor rejected, used nor discarded, and insofar as articles of the *Augsburg Confession* agreed with scripture, "so far it agrees with our declaration." Put to a confessional test, however—"whether we believe all that is contained in the *Augsburg Confession*"—"we do frankly and candidly declare, that we do not. Do the great body of Lutheran ministers and people in the United States" he asked rhetorically? It was as "Protestants," Lawyer argued, that the Franckeans judged the *Augsburg Confession,*[128] and as radical democrats (quoting Hartwick Seminary professor George Miller):

> Let us regard the Augsburg Confession as a venerable legacy; the first effectual stand against spiritual tyranny! but let us not convert our boon into a band, by making it a shackle for our consciences. Let us rather imbibe its spirit and follow up the glorious path which it has opened for us.[129]

For the Franckeans it was the American experiment in religious freedom which determined their attitude toward the Confession and the democratization of American Christianity which (as historian Nathan O. Hatch has rightly observed of numerous comeouter groups in antebellum America) denigrated religious orthodoxies, individualized religious conscience, and subverted the authority of an established, educated clergy in the name of bringing an evangelical faith to the people.[130]

CONCLUSION: THE DENOMINATIONAL NATURE OF NEW YORK LUTHERANISM

Alas the Franckeans were Lutherans in their eyes only. The new synod's 1837 application to join the General Synod was rejected at the general body's 1839 convention. Eschewing religious extremes was the order of the day in a group seeking to build a General Synod church composed of congenial and cooperative synods. And so the Franckean Synod was rejected for "introducing practices which we consider contrary to the Word of God, thereby causing disturbances and divisions."[131] Franckean piety was a potent religious force with a program of moral reform which led to the most significant nineteenth-century Lutheran confrontation with racism.[132] For this offense (and not for its lax confessionalism) it was excluded from the General Synod, though it managed to help move five synods in the direction of abolition between 1837 and 1859.[133]

The Franckean Synod had developed into a classic case of the sect-type. Intensely preoccupied with the essential elements of the gospel, living independently of others, deliberately existing outside of the ecclesiastical mainstream, and accusing others of falling away from true Christianity, the Franckean synod introduced elements of religious revival and innovation associated with the sect. In this context a sect is a religious group that rejects the social environment in which it exists, living in a high degree of tension with it. Separatism, withdrawal, and defiance are the hallmarks of this tension, together with exclusiveness, emphasis on conversion, a spirit of regeneration, and an attitude of ethical austerity.[134] But to view the sect (and this synod) as compared with the church type which accommodates itself to the prevailing culture, as a religious phenomenon *external* to the denomination (even though it was formally excluded from the General Synod), is to oversimplify the nature of American denominationalism. Within denominations, especially in the eighteenth and nineteenth centuries, sub-networks of discontented individuals developed creative, sectarian schisms in the name of innovation and renewal. This was a countervailing process of revival and innovation, a self-limiting denominational adjustment to secularization. Franckean Pietism was thus a historical expression of sectarian renewal which emerged within American Lutheranism in reaction to accommodationists in the General Synod, and to extreme rationalists tendencies within the New York Ministerium.[135]

By 1840, then, with the formation of the Hartwick and the Franckean Synods, the New York area Lutheran Church assumed a new and more complex denominational form reflecting the long-term realities of geography, theology, and regional organization stretching back into the seventeenth century. The denominational reorganization of synodical life had initially created a mission-driven, two-district synodical system operating under the aegis of the General Synod, with a third, sectarian expression existing beyond the Lutheran pale but still shaping its religious culture. The system stretched from New York Harbor and the lower Hudson River region through the upper Hudson region and the Albany area, and on into the Mohawk River-Erie Canal basin. To some extent each synod within the system functioned as a subregional organization of the Lutheran Church in New York with roots in the earliest clustering of colonial Lutheran congregations. Where they inhabited the same region, the three synods members were differentiated into urban, town, and rural congregations, each with its own theological configuration.

What they shared in common was a "denominational" outlook. In search of converts, American religious bodies grew apace, forming new synods and subdividing old ones. They had learned to be competitive in outreach and sectarian in approach. Revivalism, which was intended to fill the mourning bench and pack the pews, found expression in its most extreme form within the Franckean Synod. Franckean pietism, however, was only one source of religious renewal in the territory and within American Lutheranism. Likewise rejected for membership in 1839 by the General Synod was the strictly confessional Tennessee Synod whose outlook was expressive of a new interest in the confessing church. It is to this confessional renewal movement that we must now turn to understand the further diversity introduced onto the territory of mid-nineteenth century New York Lutheranism by a new breed of Lutheran.

NOTES

1 C. E. Jacobs, "Review of H. Richard Niebuhr's *The Social Sources of Denominationalism*," *LCQ* 4 (1931): 100.

2 For a detailed discussion of geography and regional culture see David Hackett Fischer, *Albion's Seed. Four British Folkways in America, America. A Cultural History* (New York: Oxford University Press, 1989), 1: esp. "Conclusion," 783 ff.

3 See David M. Ellis, James A. Frost, Harold C. Syrett, and Harry J. Carman, *A History of New York State* (Ithaca, New York: Cornell University Press, 1967), 471. By 1950, 85+% of the state's population would reside within this twenty-five-mile-wide belt, including the vast majority of northeastern Lutherans in New York, New Jersey, and New England.

4 Map adapted from Ibid., 462 & 471; and John E. Bebout and Ronald J. Grele, *Where Cities Meet: The Urbanization of New Jersey* (New York: Van Nostrand, 1964), 82-3.

5 D. W. Meinig, *Atlantic America, 1492-1800, Colonial American Geography as Matrix of Culture. The Shaping of America. A Geographical Perspective on 500 Years of History* (New Haven: Yale University Press, 1986), 1: 249-51.

6 Ibid., 119.

7 On the Dutch origins of this regional outlook see Fischer, *Albion's Seed.* I: 816-817. On New England expansion and its influence see Lois Kimball Mathews Rosenberry, *The Expansion of New England. The Spread of New England Settlement and Institutions to the Mississippi River 1620-1865* (New York: Russell & Russell Inc, 1962), Ch.VI, 139-170, and interleaf maps 154-5, 158-9, 168-9.

8 Ibid., 403.

9 Augsburg Confession, BC, 30.

10 See Formula of Concord, "VII. The Holy Supper," and "XI. Eternal Foreknowledge and Divine Election," BC, 568ff, and 616ff.

11 *Melanchthon and Bucer,* Wilhelm Pauck, ed. (Philadelphia: Westminster Press, 1969), 7; "Loci Communes Theologici," 21, 20 n. See also "Loci Theologici, "*The New Schaaf-Herzog Encyclopedia of Religious Knowledge*, 76.

12 Ibid., 404.

13 Heinrich Schmid, *The Doctrinal Theology of the Evangelical Lutheran Church*, eds. Charles A. and Henry E. Jacobs Hay (Philadelphia: Lutheran Publication Society, 1889). For a detailed study of Lutheran Orthodoxy see Robert. D. Preuss, *The Theology of Post-Reformation Lutheranism. A Study of Theological Prolegomena* (St. Louis: Concordia Publishing House, 1970).

14 FC, "Epitome," BC, 464.

15 Arthur Carl Piepkorn, *Profiles in Belief. The Religious Bodies of the United*

States and Canada. Volume 2: Protestant Denominations (New York: Harper and Row, 1978), 25.

16 Gerald R. Cragg, *The Church and the Age of Reason 1648-1789* (Harmondsworth, England: Penguin Books Ltd., 1970), 100.

17 On Pietism and its origins see Dale W. Brown, *Understanding Pietism* (Grand Rapids: Wm. B. Eerdmans), 17ff. On the origins of Lutheran Pietism see Kurt Aland, *A History of Christianity* (Philadelphia: Fortress Press, 1986) 2: 234ff. For a discussion of this relationship to a mystical emphasis on religious "experience" and knowledge, as it affected American Lutheranism, see Robert F. Scholz, "Henry Melchior Muhlenberg's Relation to the Ongoing Pietist Tradition," a paper delivered to the Lutheran Historical Conference, Gettysburg Lutheran Seminary, Gettysburg, Pennsylvania, Nov. 1, 1990 (published in The Lutheran Historical Conference's "Essays and Reports"), 14, 1990.

18 Piepkorn, *Profiles in Belief,* 2:25.

19 See Jean Leclercq, *The Love of Learning and the Desire for God. A Study of Monastic Culture* (New York: Fordham University Press, 1961), 236, 262.

20 Henry E. Horn, "Steps toward a Modern Piety," *Word & World* VIII (winter, 1988): 19.

21 "Bernard of Clairvaux," in *The New Schaaf-Herzog Encyclopedia of Religious Knowledge* (Grand Rapids, 1977), 2:64-5.

22 The volume in an abridged edition is readily accessible as Johann Arndt *True Christianity. The Classics of Western Spirituality,* ed. Peter Erb (New York: Paulist Press, 1979.)

23 Aland, *A History of Christianity,* 2: 239.

24 For a biography of Spener see K. James Stein, *Philipp Jakob Spener: Pietist Patriarch* (Chicago: Covenant Press, 1986). A representative anthology of pietist writings can be found in *Pietists. Selected Writings, Classics in Western Spirituality,* ed. Peter C. Erb (New York: Paulist Press, 1983). Superficially Spener's Pietism resembled new theological directions in the Reformed Church, with its emphasis on moral earnestness and biblicism. Such a view makes too little of the high confessional walls erected between Reformed and Lutheran communities in Germany, however, and ignores Pietism's debt to Luther and his writings. Aland, *History of Christianity,* 2: 236, 341.

25 Arndt, *True Christianity,* "Preface," xiii. For a description of the social impact of Pietism see Eda Sagarra, *A Social History of Germany. 1648-1914* (New York: Holmes & Meier Publishers, 1977), 107 ff.

26 "Pietism," in *New Schaaf-Herzog Encyclopedia of Religious Knowledge,* 9: 54.

27 On Francke see K. James Stein, *Philipp Jakob Spener: Pietist Patriarch* (Chicago: Covenant Press, 1986).

28 "Franke" in *New Schaff-Herzog Encyclopedia of Religious Knowledge*, IV, 367 ff. Aland, *History of Christianity,* 2: 261-3.

29 Stoeffler considers Halle Pietism to be part of a major Pietistic movement which he describes as Spener-Halle Pietism. Aland notes that besides, the "four varieties of German Lutheran Pietism" (referring to Spener, Francke, Zinzendorf and Wurttemberg). (Aland, Ibid., 248, 257).

30 On "ethical activism" see Paul P. Kuenning, *The Rise and Fall of American Lutheran Pietism. The Rejection of an Activist Heritage* (Macon, Georgia:

Mercer University Press, 1989), esp. 7-31.

31 Kuenning, *Rise and Fall*, "The Theology of Ethical Activism," 17 ff.

32 Charles H. Glatfelter in *Pastors and People: German Lutheran and Reformed Churches in the Pennsylvania Field, 1717-1793* (Breinigsville, Pennsylvania: The Pennsylvania German Society, 1980), 215-221, suggests a similar arrangement of parish clusters among both Reformed and Lutheran congregations. See pp. 206-214 for a similar treatment of New Jersey congregations.

33 *The Lutheran Church in New York. 1649-1722. Records in the Lutheran Church Archives at Amsterdam, Holland,* trans. Arnold J. F. van Laer (New York: The New York Public Library, 1946), 5.

34 Harry J. Kreider, *The Beginnings of Lutheranism in New York* (New York, 1949), 16-19.

35 "Falckner, Justus" in *Lutheran Cyclopedia* (St. Louis, 1975), 290. Lucy Forney Bittinger, *The Germans in Colonial Times* (New York, 1901), 53, 55. William B. Sprague, *Annals of the American Lutheran Pulpit* (New York, 1869), 14 n. Also see Delberr W. Clark, *The World of Justus Falckner* (Philadelphia: Muhlenberg Press, 1946); and Julius Friedrich Sachse, *Justus Falckner, Mystic, and Scholar* (Philadelphia: New Era Printing, 1903).

36 Meinig, *Atlantic America*, 225.

37 See *Devotio Moderna. Basic Writings, The Classics of Western Spirituality*, ed. John Van Engen (New York: Paulist Press, 1988).

38 Bittenger, *Germans in Colonial Times,* 12ff.

39 Thomas Jefferson Wertenbaker, *The Founding of American Civilization. The Middle Colonies* (New York, 1938), 263-269. On the migration see Albert Bernhardt Faust, *The German Element in the United States* (New York, 1969), I, Chapter IV, "The First Exodus—The Palatine Immigration to New York."; Ibid., 285; Theodore G. Tappert, "The Church's Infancy. 1650-1790," *The Lutherans in North America* (Philadelphia, 1975), 37, Table 1. For a more extensive treatment of the Palatine background see Kuenning, *Rise and Fall,* 42ff.; also Robert Kuhn Mc Gregor, "Cultural Adaptation in Colonial New York. The Palatine Germans of the Mohawk Valley," *NY History* 69.1 (January 1988): 5-33.

40 Heinrich H. Maurer, "Studies in the Sociology of Religion and American Sectionalism. The Pennsylvania German," *American Journal of Sociology,* XXX (1925), 412-414.

41 Sprague, *Annals,* 30.

42 See Sagarra, *A Social History of Germany,* 13.

43 See for example Stanley Nadel, *Little Germany. Ethnicity, Religion, and Class in New York City, 1845-80* (Urbana: University of Illinois Press, 1990), 155ff.

44 The story of the Palatine struggles in colonial New York is documented in Faust, *The German Element*, 74-105. On Sommers see Sprague, *Annals*, 13-16. On the pietistic orientation of this area see Kuenning, *Rise and Fall,* 42 ff; also Paul P. Kuenning, "New York Lutheran Abolitionists: Seeking a Solution to a Historical Enigma," *Church History,* 58.1 (1989): 52-65. A similar kind of differentiation occurred between English Anglicanism and Dutch Calvinism, with the latter becoming either orthodox or pietist in outlook. See Randall Balmer, *A Perfect Babel of Confusion. Dutch Religion*

and English Culture in the Middle Colonies, Religion in America Series, ed. Harry S. Stout (New York: Oxford University Press, 1989), 109. Balmer identifies a cluster of pietist religious attitudes and orientations that makes them, by contrast to the dominant English culture, peripheral, informal, conversion oriented, and inclined to withdraw from the larger world and culture. See also Richard W. Pointer, *Protestant Pluralism and the New York Experience* (Bloomington: Indiana University Press, 1988).

45 Bittenger, *Germans in Colonial Times*, 53-4.

46 Faust, *The German Element*, 152.

47 Balmer, *A Perfect Babel*, ix, 103 ff, 119ff.

48 Patricia U. Bonomi, *Under the Cope of Heaven. Religion, Society, and Politics in Colonial America* (New York: Oxford University Press, 1986), 8, 10, 81-82.

49 "The Constitution of the First Lutheran Synod in America" is to be found in the *Concordia Historical Institute Quarterly* 9 (1936): esp. 5-8.

50 These developments are treated in detail in Harry Julius Kreider, *Lutheranism in Colonial New York* (New York, 1942), 100-119. Examples of agreements reached can be found in *Protocol of the Lutheran Church in New York City, 1702-1750,* trans., Simon Hart and Harry J. Kreider (New York: United Lutheran Synod of New York and New England), 245; and *Lutheran Church in New York and New Jersey. 1722-1760* (New York: The United Lutheran Synod of New York and New England, 1962), 103ff. See also Kreider, *History of the United Lutheran Synod,* 10ff.

51 See Robert F. Scholz, "'The Reverend Elders' Faith, Fellowship, and Politics in the Ministerial Community of Massachusetts Bay, 1630-1710" (Ph. D. diss., University of Minnesota, 1966). The viewpoint shaping this section was first developed in graduate seminars at the University of Minnesota and benefited from ongoing discussions with and the explorations of fellow seminar member Jon Butler. On Butler's approach and emphasis see note 56.

52 Harry Julius Kreider, *Lutheranism in Colonial New York* (New York, 1942), 100, 103-119, describes these developments. See also "The Constitution of the First Lutheran Synod in America," *Concordia Historical Institute Quarterly*, 9 (1936): esp. 5-8.

53 General Council, *Documentary History of the Evangelical Lutheran Ministerium of Pennsylvania and Adjacent States* (Philadelphia: General Council Board of Publication, 1898), 3 ff.

54 See Jon Butler, "Power, Authority, and the Origins of American Denominational Order. The English Churches in the Delaware Valley 1680-1730," 68.2 (February, 1978); also his *Awash in a Sea of Faith. Christianizing the American People* (Cambridge: Harvard University Press, 1990), 118ff.

55 See Robert F. Scholz, "Was Muhlenberg a Pietist?," in *Concordia Historical Institute Quarterly,* 52 (summer, 1979): 50 ff.

56 See Robert F. Scholz, "The Confessional Stance of Henry Melchior Muhlenberg and the Early Pennsylvania Ministerium," *Lutheran Quarterly,* I.4 (winter 1987): 439-456.

57 See Robert F. Scholz, "Henry Melchior Muhlenberg's Relation to the Ongoing Pietist Tradition," a paper delivered to the Lutheran Historical Conference, Gettysburg Lutheran Seminary, Gettysburg, Pennsylvania,

Nov. 1, 1990 (to be published in The Lutheran Historical Conference's "Essays and Reports," 14, 1990.

58 See Meinig, *Atlantic America,* 438 ff.

59 *Documentary History*, p. 165.

60 Meinig, *Atlantic America*, 400.

61 *Documentary History*, 248.

62 *Minutes of the Evangelical Lutheran Ministerium of New York,* trans. Theodore E. Palleske (New York: typescript of original in possession of the Synod Archives, Wagner College), 2 ff.

63 New York Ministerium, *Minutes* (1786-1818), 2, 7ff; General Council, *Documentary History,* 173, 25, 1-2, 254.

64 Typescript "Minutes," 19.

65 *Documentary History,* 234.

66 *Minutes*, Palleske trans., 19.

67 Ibid., 53.

68 Meinig, *Atlantic America*, 225.

69 An excellent survey of the transition period American Lutherans can be found in H. George Anderson's Chapter 6: "The Crisis Years, 1800-1817," in *The Lutherans in North America,* ed. E. Clifford Nelson (Philadelphia: Fortress Press, 1975), 95-111.

70 Typescript "Minutes," 46.

71 Sagarra, *Social History of Germany,* 204 ff.

72 Sprague, *Annals,* 58.

73 Typescript "Minutes," 45-7.

74 Ibid., 50.

75 The term is that of Charles Porterfield Krauth who made the observation in his "The Relations of the Lutheran Church to the Denominations Around Us," reprinted in *Lutheran Confessional Theology in America 1840-1880,* ed. Theodore G. Tappert (New York: Oxford University Press, 1972), 115.

76 CA, BC, 32; "The Large Catechism," BC, 417.

77 Sidney E. Mead, *The Lively Experiment* (New York: Harper & Row, 1976), 103 ff.

78 On denominationalism see also two essays by Timothy L. Smith, "Congregation, State, and Denomination: The Forming of the American Religious Structure," and "Religious Denominations as Ethnic Communities," in *Denominationalism* (Nashville: Abingdon, 1977), Russell E. Richey, ed., 47 ff, and 185 ff); and Winthrop S. Hudson, "Denominationalism as a Basis for Ecumenicity" in Ibid., 21 ff.

79 Sidney E. Mead, "The Fact of Pluralism and the Persistence of Sectarianism," in *The Religion of the Republic*, ed. Elwyn A., Smith (Philadelphia: Fortress Press, 1971), 256. See Roger Finke and Rodney Stark, *The Churching of America, 1776-1990. Winners and Losers in Our Religious Economy* (New Brunswick: Rutgers University Press, 1992), esp. 16 ff. Finke and Stark provide a provacative interpretation of church growth among American denominations that warrants serious though not uncritical consideration. A number of conclusions reached in this study of Lutheran churches in New York , though derived independently of the methodology and conclusions provided in *The Church of America*, are not dissimilar.

80 Winthrop S. Hudson, *Religion in America* (New York: Charles Scribner's Sons, 1981), 4th ed., 129. Patricia U. Bonomi, *Under the Cope of Heaven.*

Religion, Society, and Politics in Colonial America (New York: Oxford University Press, 1986), 88-9. See also Patricia and Peter Eisenstadt Bonomi, "Church Adherence in the Eighteenth-Century British American Colonies," *Wm. & Mary Qtr.* 3rd Ser., 39 (1982): 245-286; see especially 252, 273-4. Finke, *Churching of America*, 24

81 "The Constitution of the Evangelical Lutheran Ministerium of the State of New-York and Adjacent States and Countries," in the *Minutes of the Evangelical Lutheran Ministerium of New York. 1786-1818,* "Appendix," Synod Archives, Wagner College. See also *The Constitution of the Evangelical Lutheran Ministerium of the State of New-York, and Adjacent States and Countries* (New York, 1836), 2nd. edition, 23.

82 Typescript Minutes, Part II. "Minutes of the Evangelical Lutheran Ministerium of the State of New York and Adjacent States and Countries for the years 1807 to 1818 inclusive," transcribed by Harry Julius Kreider, 60, 67.

83 Title page of typescript "Minutes of the Evangelical Lutheran Ministerium of New York," translated by Theodore E. Palleske ("Protokol Des Evangelisch Lutherischen Consistoriums Im Staat Von New York. North America"). On voluntarism in American life and religion see James Luther Adams, "The Voluntary Principle in the Forming of American Religion," *The Religion of the Republic*, ed. Elwyn A. Smith (Philadelphia: Fortress Press, 1971), 217-246; also Elwyn A. Smith, "The Voluntary Establishment of Religion," Ibid., 154-182.

84 *The Constitution of the Evangelical Lutheran Ministerium of the State of New-York, and Adjacent States and Countries* (New York, 1836), 2nd. edition, 3, 17.

85 *The Constitution of the Evangelical Lutheran Ministerium of the State of New-York,* 7-8, 21-2.

86 John Nicum, *Geschichte des Evangelisch-Lutherischen Ministeriums von Staate New York und angrenzenden Staaten und Landern* (Reading: 1888), 22.

87 Typescript "Minutes," 70.

88 "A Proposed Plan (Plan Entwurf) for a Central Union (zu einer central-verbindung) of the Evangelical Lutheran Church in the United States of North America, Baltimore, 1819," in *Documentary History of the Evangelical Lutheran Ministerium of Pennsylvania and Adjacent States* (Philadelphia, 1898), 541 ff.

89 Ibid., 541-44; Kreider, *History of the United Lutheran Synod,* 64.

90 General Synod, *Minutes* (1820), 10.

91 Ibid., 6.

92 Ibid., 7-8.

93 Ibid., 8-9.

94 Ibid. (1829), 36.

95 Ibid., 39.

96 Henry Eyster Jacobs, *A History of the Evangelical Lutheran Church in the United States,* IV, *American Church History,* Second ed. (New York: Charles Scribner's Sons, 1899), 367.

97 N. Y. Ministerium, *Proceedings of the Evangelical Lutheran Synod of the State of New York . . . 1819,* 10-11.

98 Typescript "Minutes," 67.

99 1816 Constitution in typescript "Minutes," 13, 11.

100 See H. George Anderson, Chapter 7: "Synodical Growth and the General Synod, 1817-1840," in *Lutherans in North America*, 112-127; also Abdel Ross Wentz, *A Basic History of Lutheranism in America* (Philadelphia, 1955), 68-72.

101 The Rev. John Molther, pastor of the Schoharie-Cobleskill parish, undertook the first of the Ministerium's missionary journeys in 1819 into the new west. A typescript copy of the record of his trip is in the synod archives, Wagner College (NY Ministerium, "Missionary Journey," 1819).

102 *Documentary History*, 541.

103 Ibid., 542-3.

104 Harry J. Kreider, *History of the United Lutheran Synod of New York and New England. Volume I: 1786-1860* (Philadelphia: Muhlenberg Press, 1954), 76. See Lintner's remarks in *Minutes of the First Session of the Hartwick Synod and Ministerium of the Evangelical Lutheran Church in the State of New York* (1831), 22-23.

105 NY Ministerium, *Minutes* (1836), 14.

106 Ibid., 29.

107 See Whitney R. Cross, *The Burned-over District. The Social and Intellectual History of Enthusiastic Religion in Western New York, 1800-1850* (New York: Harper & Row, 1965).

108 Hudson, *Religion in America*, 141 ff.

109 See Cross, *Burned-over District*, Ch. 10.

110 F. Seilhamer, "The New Measure Movement among Lutherans," *Lutheran Quarterly* 12 (May 1960): 123-31.

111Wentz, *Pioneer in Christian Unity*, 98. NY Ministerium, *Minutes* (1829), 15.

112 See Cross, *Burned-over District*, 173.

113 Hudson, *Religion in America*, 144ff.

114 Mary P. Ryan, "A Women's Awakening. Evangelical religion and the Families of Utica, New York, 1800-1840," *Women in American Religion*, ed. Janet Wilson James (Philadelphia: University of Pennsylvania Press, 1980), 90-101, 91, 99-101. See also Barbara Leslie Epstein, *The Politics of Domesticity. Women, Evangelism and Temperance in Nineteenth-Century America*, (Middletown, Connecticut: Wesleyan University Press, 1981), esp. Ch. 2, "Religious Conversions in the Nineteenth Century: Men's and Women's Diverging Experiences," 45 ff.

115 See Charles Sellers, *The Market Revolution. Jacksonian America, 1815-1846* (New York City, New York: Oxford University Press, 1991), 225 ff.

116 Hartwick Synod, *Minute Extracts* (1834), 18; Kreider, *History of the United Lutheran Synod*, 86ff.

117 Douglas C. Stange, *Radicalism for Humanity: A Study of Lutheran Abolition* (St. Louis: Oliver Slave, 1970), notes this Franckean entree into the Burned-over District as "several fingerlings of territory served by the synod," 2. For possible New England influence see Lois Kimball Mathews Rosenberry, *The Expansion of New England. The Spread of New England Settlement and Institutions to the Mississippi River 1620-1865* (New York: Russell & Russell Inc, 1962), Ch. VI. Nelson R. Burr, *A Critical Bibliography of Religion in America. Religion in American Life*, ed. James War and A. Leland Jamison Smith. (Princeton: Princeton University Press,

1961) IV, Parts 1-5: 157. Cross, *Burned-over District*, 154, 163, 3. Compare especially Ibid., Map XXII, "Churches showing antislavery feelings," 228; and Map 6, "Congregations of the Franckean Synod 1837-1908," Appendix.

118 Franckean Synod, *Proceedings of a Convention of Ministers and Delegates From Evangelical Lutheran Churches, in the State of New-York* (Albany, 1837), 3.

119 Kuenning, *Rise and Fall*, 82-3.

120 Charles Sellers, *The Market Revolution. Jacksonian America, 1815-1846* (New York City, New York: Oxford University Press, 1991), 125, 127-9, 164.

121 Kuenning, *Rise and Fall*, 8, 9. John R. McKivigan, *The War against Proslavery Religion. Abolitionism and the Northern Churches, 1830-1865* (Ithaca: Cornell University Press, 1984), 93, 105, identifies this break with the Hartwick Synod as a new phenomenon in the abolitionist movement, the emergence of the "comeouter sect" which separated from a parent denomination over the issue of slavery. The others besides the Franckean Synod were the Wesleyan Methodist Connection, the American Baptist Free Mission Society, the Free Presbyterian Church, and the Indiana Yearly Meeting of Anti-Slavery Friends.

122 Ibid., 11, 12.

123 Franckean Synod, *Journal of the First Annual Session of the Franckean Synod of the Evangelic Lutheran Church* (Albany, 1838), 6-7.

124 Ibid., 21.

125 See John D Lawyer, *A Scripture Guide to the Mode of Baptism: Being a Discourse Delivered by Request of the Evangelic Lutheran Church at Argusville, N. Y., May 12, 1844* (Albany: E. H. Pease, 1844), 3-10. Forrest G. Wood, *The Arrogance of Faith. Christianity and Race in America from the Colonial Era to the Twentieth Century* (New York: Alfred A. Knopf, 1990), 318-328. Franckean Synod, *Journal* (Albany, 1838), 17-18.

126 Stange, *Radicalism for Humanity*, 27.

127 *Journal of the Special Meeting of the Franckean Synod* (Albany, 1837), 28-29.

128 Ibid., 28-9, 30.

129 Ibid., 32.

130 Nathan O. Hatch, *The Democratization of American Christianity* (New Haven: Yale University Press, 1989), 4-5, 64; see esp. Ch. 2.

131 Kreider, *History of the United Lutheran Synod*, 101.

132 See Stange, *Radicalism for Humanity:* also his "The 125th Anniversary of Fraternal Appeal," *Concordia Historical Institute Quarterly* 40 (1967): 354-59. On American Lutheranism and slavery see Abdel Ross Wentz, *A Basic History of Lutheranism in America* (Philadelphia: Muhlenberg Press, 1955), 162-172; also Forrest G. Wood, *The Arrogance of Faith. Christianity and Race in America from the Colonial Era to the Twentieth Century* (New York: Alfred A. Knopf, 1990), 346-353.

133 See Timothy L. Smith, *Revivalism and Social Reform* (Nashville, Abingdon, 1957). Kuenning, *Rise and Fall*, 116-133, 198-207. The five synods—all small and new—were East Ohio, Wittenberg, Allegheny, Northern Indiana, and Pittsburgh, identified in Abdel Ross Wentz, *Basic History*, 164-5.

134 See Ernst Troeltsch, *The Social Teaching of the Christian Church* (London: Allen & Unwin, 1931), I, 331-37. A significant development of the sect/church typologies is to be found in Rodney Stark, and William Sims Bainbridge, *The Future of Religion. Secularization, Revival, and Cult Formation* (Berkeley, California: University of California Press, 1985). See especially 21-26, Ch. 5 (99 ff). Stark and Bainbridge consider social tension a better indicator of sect membership than conversion since sects like the Amish are socialized from birth; conversion is rare or nonexistent.

135 Ibid., 101, 131, 2, 23 ff., 51, 65ff. What Stark and Bainbridge observe of an immigrant Roman Catholic Church regarding its relatively sectarian outlook can be said of immigrant Lutheranism as well.

2

CONFESSIONAL AWAKENING

The Development and Influence of Confessionalism in the New York Synods, 1830-1860

The Lutheran Church in the early nineteenth century could not have survived by itself as a competitive, sect-like denomination with a high confessional profile, cut off (as the Tennessee Synod was cut off) from the American Protestant mainstream. It survived, as did American Christianity, through revival of a Protestant religiosity which Lutherans shared with other denominations. Only with a secured existence, accommodated to new American circumstances, would Lutherans have the strength to begin differentiating themselves confessionally in ways that strengthened rather than weakened their identity. When they could finally say with Charles Porterfield Krauth, "I am First a Lutheran, Then an American," they had begun to gain a critical detachment from American values and institutions, permitting them to forge a confessional identity as Lutherans in America.

The newness of the experiment in religious freedom and a preoccupation with anything which could impinge upon personal religious liberties limited confessionally differentiated denominational growth in the long run however. For though a revival of Protestantism could recover the religious ground lost to a secularizing culture, it was doctrine which played the all important role in maintaining denominational particularity, a lesson in denominationalism that American Lutherans had not yet learned. Theologian George Lindbeck has put the matter in this way:

> The privatism and subjectivism that accompanies the neglect of communal doctrines leads to a weakening of the social groups (*Gemeinschaften*) that are the chief bulwarks against chaos and against totalitarian efforts to master chaos. One can argue, in other words, as did some of the more agnostic founders of the American

> republic, that an open society needs doctrinally committed religious communities to inculcate the moral and creedal absolutes that are necessary in order to maintain openness.[1]

The need to establish confessional "absolutes" as something American Lutherans soon would discover with the confessional struggles developing in the General Synod. These efforts would give rise among New York Lutherans first to a confessional movement, and then to the formation among eastern Lutherans of a general Lutheran body—the General Council—which became a strong confessional alternative to the General Synod. As key institutions in the formation and development of a national Lutheran denomination, the New York synods—most especially the Ministerium and the Franckean Synod—would play distinctive roles.

Revivalism, Mission, and Church Extension

The core of the Lutheran confessions is scripture's testimony to the saving work of God through faith in the gracious justification of the sinner in Jesus Christ—the Good News. This identifiable confessional core survived within the New York Ministerium where it was articulated, for example, by the president of Hartwick Seminary and Ministerium President Ernest Hazelius. Consider his 1829 synodical sermon on I Corinthians 4:12—"It is required in stewards that a man be found faithful"—a challenge to the rationalism of his predecessor which summarized Biblical theology in the language of old Tuebingen "orthodoxy." A truly faithful minister he began, is instructed by Jesus Christ to deliver the Gospel—the "evangelion" which is Christ, his teachings, and his coming into the world, to save sinners. This work is part of an act of reconciliation in which we are justified freely "by his grace." "Whoever therefore will be a faithful minister and ambassador of Jesus Christ," he informed the assembled clergy, "must set forth repentance towards God, and faith in our Lord Jesus Christ."[2] For Hazelius's colleague, George Lintner, president of the Hartwick Synod, the Augsburg Confession protected this core evangelium:

> In this day of bold and reckless encroachment on the landmarks of Gospel truth, we cannot too faithfully adhere to those scriptural standards which the Reformers instituted for the defence and preservation of the true faith. If we give up these standards, we relinquish one of the safeguards of the purity of the Church,—we open a door for all manner of abuse in the faith and order of God's house,—we give up the principle of a uniform and uncompromising devotedness to what we conceive to be the truth.[3]

Accordingly the Hartwick Synod published a correct translation of the Augsburg Confession in 1837, insisting as their justification for the reprint that "our prosperity and usefulness as a Church depend" on its doctrines.

No developed confessional theology lay at the center of such a concern nor any understanding of a confessional church, though the preconditions for both existed. Yet the Augsburg Confession was beginning to function among at least some New York Lutherans as originally intended—to guarantee sound Biblical theology and doctrine. It also demarcated rather clearly the differences between Lutheran and Roman Catholic positions on many issues in dispute between Protestants and Roman Catholics at a time when early nineteenth-century "orthodox" Lutheranism was viewed as a genuine expression of Protestant fundamentals with which other Protestant denominations could agree. Its important purpose was to establish the boundaries of true faith—the limits of genuine Protestantism—at a time when Protestant anxieties about Roman Catholicism had reached epidemic proportions.[4] There was, then, a growing sense within New York Lutheranism that sound doctrine and the sacraments were contributing factors to a mission church, though revivalism and its practices were still recognized as the Archimedes lever of renewal and growth.

"THE PROGRESS OF OUR CHURCH"—1819-1850

But how did this form of church growth fare among American Lutherans who were reestablishing their European religious heritage on a denominational basis? Was it successful among Lutherans? More importantly, was it Lutheran? If not was something lacking? These questions, posed by New York Ministerium President William D. Strobel in 1850, were framed to assess the "Progress of Our Church" in a period of extensive denominational growth. The questions were inevitable, given the three-way division existing within the New York Lutheran Church. Within the new synods, as within the parent body, where and how the church was growing had become a matter of compelling interest. The questions are also important to us, for they yield information about, as well as insights into, the nature of Lutheranism in New York at mid-century.

What stimulated Strobel's musings was a table of data (see Table 2.1) prepared for the 1850 Ministerium indicating the number of clergy, communicants, baptisms, confirmations, and monies collected for the preceding year. He noted that the reception of new members which was 10 percent of total membership in 1819, had dropped to 5 1/4 percent by 1849. Infant baptisms, 43 percent of membership in 1819, had dropped to 23 percent by 1849. He wondered whether Baptism (and Confirmation) were not being neglected in the churches, especially (it was implied) in the more revivalistic synods. "Have we lost our faith in its validity, or what is the true cause of the facts exhibited above?"[5]

Strobel asked the key question regarding Lutheran synodical

growth in the nineteenth century. Interested in Ministerium statistics, he might have wondered about the rates of baptism in the Hartwick (8.9 percent of communicant membership) and Franckean (3.8 percent) Synods as compared with the Ministerium (20.9 percent) in 1849. Compared with the flourishing, revivalistic synods, his own Ministerium showed a far greater potential for growth. Indeed, the importance of infant Baptism to congregational (and thus synodical) growth would become more apparent as the century progressed.[6] (See Chapters 9-12.) Strobel might have considered a second factor—per capita giving for local and mission development—that is the funds needed to help form new congregations. Here the proportions were reversed, with the Franckean Synod providing the most support ($ 0.15 per communicant member), and the Ministerium the least funding ($ 0.08); once again the Hartwick Synod was in the middle ($ 0.11).

Table 2.1[7]
Ministerium Congregations Statistics for 1849

Synods	Clergy	Baptisms	Confir-mations	Commun-icants	Collec-tions
New York	28	1529	386	7332	$ 565
Hartwick	23	291	206	3235	$ 367
Francean	18	74	70	1941	$ 282

Also of interest was the new statistical orientation itself, since it tells us something about New York Lutheranism at mid-century. Strobel's retrospective was based on a quarter-century's accumulated statistics. In 1825 the Ministerium had begun publishing relevant data in a simple "Tabular Expose." The term reflected the French influence on the fledgling science of statistics. By 1850 Americans had a growing awareness of the statistically identifiable dynamics of church growth and population change in a growing nation. At about the same time tables of data were being charted by Scottish mathematicians, most notably William Playfair, in the form of line graphs similar to those presented in this chapter and throughout this study. Though line graphs did not come into widespread use until the early twentieth century, the statistical tables upon which they were based were widely used a century before. By the nineteenth century, as one historian of American demographics has put it, Americans knew "that statistical methods helped illuminate the pattern of meaning of their collective vital events and population movements."[8] Thus Strobel's musings!

MOTIVATION FOR GROWTH—1825-1850

It was the hope of mission "progress" which motivated the Franckean Synod's breakaway in 1837. The Synod's rationale for separation from the Hartwick Synod was the freedom "to license pious intelligent men, sound in the faith, although they may" not be "classically educated, or have pursued a regular theological course." They wanted committed pastors to serve destitute congregations, and to form new ones along New York's expanding frontier. The Hartwick Synod had been formed for similar reasons. Their purpose in separating was "to awaken and convert sinners and to edify believers, by close and practical preaching of the Gospel." The principle difference between the two synods was that the Franckeans would admit only born-again Lutherans into their new churches. Two of the three synods of Lutherans in New York had every hope that revivalism would lead to a growing Lutheran church.[9]

The mission impulse in synod formations needs to be examined closely among American Lutherans. It is too easy to suppose that synods were formed to organize the churches in specific geographic areas, or among different ethnic groups, or to promote confessional differences. Synod formation, in other words, was motivated by something besides geography, confessional theology, or ethnic identity. Saxon immigrants in Missouri, for example, formed the strict confessional Missouri Synod. Swedes in upstate New York, in northeastern Pennsylvania, and in New England developed an eastern branch of the Augustana Synod with a history that parallels rather than intersects the history of German Lutherans in New York. Language, ethnicity, geography, and confessional differences, would also influence synodical developments among English- and German-speaking Lutherans in New York between 1837 and 1867. Yet, these were sufficient reasons for developing new Lutheran synods in New York without adding a key denominational factor—mission.

The Great Commission was an imperative that could not be ignored among Lutherans in New York. A part of the reason, no doubt, was Luther's use of the mission commandment in defining the sacramental nature of Baptism in the Small Catechism. Baptism was not "merely water" but water used "according to God's command and connected with God's Word."

> What is this Word of God ?
> Answer: As recorded in Matthew 28:19, our Lord Christ said, "Go therefore and make disciples of all nations, baptizing them in the name of the Father and of the Son and of the Holy Spirit."[10]

No wonder that by 1850 a Lutheran pastor like Ministerium President Strobel would come to consider Baptism as essential to the mission progress of the church in America. Such an attitude was widespread among American Christians, and Lutherans were no exception: as political institutions are supposed to govern, and economic institutions to generate wealth, churches were intended to grow and multiply by spreading the Gospel and baptizing new members. This was especially true of the American denomination whose mission outlook could be traced to pietist influence, including Lutheran Pietism.

THE NATURE OF NEW YORK SYNODICAL GROWTH

Given the mission imperative and its consequences, how did the Lutheran church in New York progress? The beginnings were modest. In 1786, the year of its organization, only four of twenty-five New York area congregations joined to form the New York Ministerium. By 1800, thirteen of twenty-seven congregations had joined the new denominational organization, three more churches having been formed in the meantime. Two decades later (1820), the number of Lutheran congregations in the area had grown to thirty or more, twenty-three of which now belonged to the Ministerium. Ten years later (1830) at the time of the Hartwick division, and with the formation of at least another fourteen congregations, the Ministerium and the Hartwick Synods contained between them fifty-five congregations. By then, however, synodical growth was no longer simply the outcome of incorporating existing congregations into an expanding synod but was the result of three distinct processes. Older, independent congregations had now joined one or another of the two synods. Also some older congregations had subdivided with growth and maturity, each half joining a separate synodical organization. Finally, the growth of new congregations in frontier areas with growing populations had also begun. It was the latter which stimulated the Hartwick division.

ORGANIZATION FOR MISSION

This subdivision of mission territory was followed by organization for mission in each synod. The Hartwick Synod set up a home Missionary and Education Committee in 1833 to procure funds for the support of missionaries and the education of theology students as ministers for a growing synod. Three missionary trips grew out of this initial enthusiasm.[11] Pastor John Selmser of the Richmondville church traveled north and west along Lake Ontario to Rochester, then south and east, over a course of five hundred miles, organizing new congregations and assessing possible mission fields. Philip Wieting, pastor at Sharon, also in Schoharie County, traveled to congregations and settlements in the north and Canada, covering a circuit of four hundred miles. Licentiate Martin Stover of Dansville returned to the area between the Erie Canal and Lake Ontario in Monroe and Orleans Counties, following the westward course of the canal and the population spreading along this new route to the west.

In 1836 Selmser was called as missionary for a year, and again traveled to the six-county region of canal-stimulated growth, extending his work in Orleans and Niagara counties all the way to the southern border of Lake Ontario. This time he took with him Hartwick Seminary student Reuben Dederick to do the German preaching. Everywhere there was a need to serve both English- and German-speaking Lutherans, a situation complicated by the prejudice against English in

German-speaking communities, especially in Niagara County. The Hartwick Synod contemplated an English-speaking mission in Rochester, where the German Lutheran church belonged to the Ministerium. Eventually it would attempt an English-speaking mission in Buffalo, reflecting a preference for a language (and perhaps mission methodology) that would limit its mission outreach among German immigrant Lutherans. Yet the Hartwick Synod did establish a successful German-language mission in Boston by 1855 which, in its ability to elicit local support among its adherents, proved more effective than the Buffalo mission.[12]

The resulting mission effort within the Hartwick Synod resulted in a healthy period of synodical growth (as can be seen in Graph 2.1). For all but a few years—from 1845 to about 1850—the synod grew more rapidly than the population pool in the New York counties where most of its congregations were located and from which it drew its members. As can be seen from the growth of the German population in the New York City area—a rough indicator of German immigrant population in the state—the fortunes of the Hartwick Synod were not closely related to patterns of German immigration after 1850. Rather, revivalism among susceptible populations contributed both to the growth of established congregations, and formed the basis for new missions as well. The Synod's traveling missionary divided his time therefore, laboring for the harvest wherever the revival of religion was occurring. This emphasis on revivalism led to at least one cycle of growth and decline. After fifteen years of revivalism, the Hartwick Synod underwent a time of retrenchment between 1845 and 1850, a "sad decline of vital godliness" and a time of "spiritual dearth." Its president attributed the problem to "a hasty admission of members into the church." Many were admitted "when their feelings alone were too much excited, without having their minds sufficiently enlightened with divine truths." Others had a head religion with no support from the heart.[13] No doubt it was this slowdown which contributed to President Strobel's reassessment of mission growth in the New York church. As we shall see, it was a dynamic that would continue to trouble the Hartwick Synod despite its renewed growth in the 1850s.

Ministerium mission work on the other hand, moved steadily in the direction of providing German-language preaching and worship to communities of German-speaking immigrants. It established a Missionary and Education Board in 1836, also for the purpose of funding home missionaries, aiding destitute congregations, and educating theological students for a growing church. Its concern was of two kinds—for its young members, forced by high land prices in settled areas to move onto a growing frontier; and for the immigrants from Germany, of which the city of New York alone contained an estimated 20,000 in 1836.

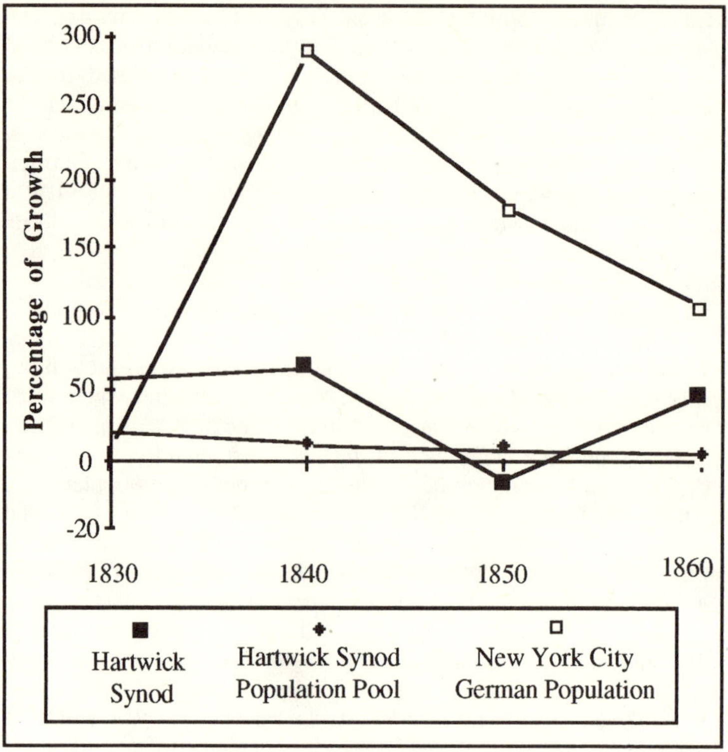

Graph 2.1 Hartwick Synod Growth

The previous year the Ministerium had made a momentous decision: "We want clergymen, particularly native-born clergymen, who can preach German and English, and who can go forth possessing not only the spirit of the gospel, but also that of our American institutions . . ." To this group of second-generation, bilingual clergy was added a small but growing number of German-born and German-speaking candidates for ministry like Carl F. E. Stohlmann, who would eventually help carry the synod in a more conservative, confessional direction.[14]

The results of mission activities within the New York Ministerium can be seen in Graph 2.2. It, too, was a dynamic church but with growth rates slightly less than the population pool from which it drew new members. Since the makeup of that population was affected by heavy German immigration, immigrant population dynamics were more evident in Ministerium growth than among the upstate Hartwick congregations. Thus by 1855 and with a growing ability to minister to foreign-language Lutherans, the Ministerium for the second time in its history showed greater rates of growth within its congregations than the surrounding population. Soon it would outstrip its offspring in growth and size.

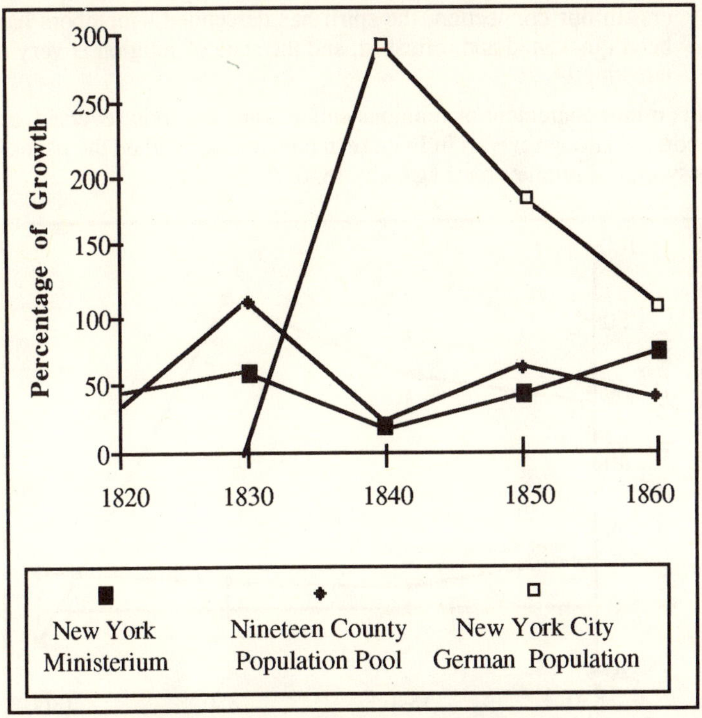

Graph 2.2 New York Ministerium Growth

The Franckean Synod's experience of growth presents another, and somewhat contrasting case for consideration as Graph 2.3 indicates. From its inception the Franckean Synod sustained higher growth rates over a longer period of time than its parent, the Hartwick Synod, and without experiencing the spiritual dearth which that body did during the later 1840s. Adult baptism was its most important source of membership. The Synod's close attention to the "state of religion" in its midst with a yearly report to the synod, meant that the quality of adult faith and life was uppermost in its mind. Like its namesake, August Hermann Francke, the synod held to a special expectation of dramatic conversion to a life of vital piety for its members.

While mission outreach was important, spiritual attractiveness seemed the key to the Franckean Synod's growth. In the same year (1845) that the Hartwick Synod's President Thomas Lape analyzed the general consequences of too-quick membership accessions, his Franckean counterpart Nicholas Van Alstine noted:

> That notwithstanding some of our churches have had reason to mourn over the low state of religion among them; and that they have not been so signally blessed as in former years, still upon others, in our connection, the spirit has descended—members have been quickened and refreshed, and the state of religion is very interesting.[15]

This minor abatement of religious enthusiasm was soon reversed, and reports of strong revivals in Franckean congregations filled the pages of its synodical minutes once again by 1850.[16]

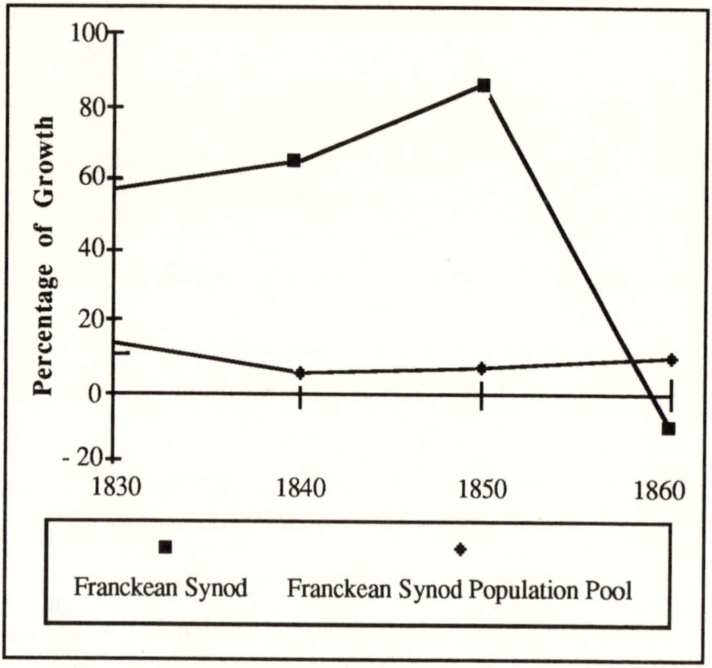

Graph 2.3 Franckean Synod Growth

By contrast to Hartwick Synod practice, a stricter standard of membership (higher standards of behavior and financial support) served both to attract and to retain new members in the Franckean Synod. This impression is borne out by the Synod's revised Constitution, published in 1847. Regarding "Admission to Membership":

> there is a necessity of a radical change of heart, and that no one should be admitted to the membership and privileges of the Church, but such as give a credible evidence of being born again, and are living according to the precepts and requirements of the gospel. [17]

Yet even strictness could not dampen the cycles of revivalism, being perhaps but a delaying mechanism. By 1855, and even in the midst of strong revivals in some congregations, there was "much sorrow of heart" expressed regarding the "sad and unfavorable condition of others." "There is reason to fear [the Synod's President reported] that pure religion is declining among us." One must look closely to find the reason, but it is possible to detect a shift away from former emphases. The issues of peace (pacifism), temperance, and slavery—moral questions of the highest order, which the synod addressed with strenuous concern, and which were indicative of "living according to the precepts and requirements of the gospel"—were still very much present. By 1860 however, the reports on the state of religion noted modest revivalistic success, while a less shrill tone informed social concerns (with the exception of slavery). Although also long blessed with Sunday schools in some of its congregations, new to the synod (1854) was a sabbath school system similar to that which Hartwick employed, an indication of a shift to more extensive educational measures then being introduced in the face of declining revivalism.[18]

Between 1837 and 1850 it had become a classic case of the sect-type. Intensely preoccupied with the essential elements of the Gospel, living independently of others, deliberately existing outside of the ecclesiastical mainstream, and accusing others of falling away from true Christianity, the Franckean Synod's growth was like the bright, burning arc of the comet—brilliant but brief. The Franckean Synod is perhaps best described by 1860 as a tired sect—consumed (perhaps) by its social issues, certainly exhausted by the fever pitch of religious intensity and the militancy of a persecuted Lutheran minority. Though tired, it was not exhausted however. Instead it showed every sign by 1860 of evolving into something more like a mainstream expression of American Lutheranism, having begun the transition from sect to a more church-like structure. Does this mean that the Franckeans were at first reaping the fruits of a "truer" Christianity, as they claimed after their formation in 1837? Again, did their growth slow down as they lost their uniqueness among New York synods? Can numbers validate such sectarian theological claims? It can be said that the two revivalistic upstate synods were more effective at incorporating and holding members than the downstate Ministerium in the first half of the nineteenth century. It can also be said that of the two, the stricter synod (Franckean) enjoyed a higher rate of growth. Revivalism was a potent force for recruitment in the middle nineteenth century, creating unusual growth in churches with strict membership. Yet that is not a full answer to the question. For as we shall see, the neglect of infant Baptism in upstate New York would significantly reduce the growth potential of both the Hartwick and Franckean Synods after the Civil War including, of all things, the fortunes of revivalism itself.

CHURCH EXTENSION—COMPARING THREE SYNODS

When comparisons are made between the Ministerium, and the Hartwick and the Franckean Synods, the differences between two different types of church growth—*autogenous* and *allogenous*—became very clear.[19]

Autogenous (self-generated) growth occurs from the "recruitment" of the children of members, and is related to congregational demographics. Allogenous (outside) growth, on the other hand, involves the recruitment of outsiders and their children. The latter form of growth occurs when the pool of potential converts increases through (for example) revivals or immigration. Real church growth can only result from the incorporation of children of members *and* of adult nonmembers, thereby outstripping population growth in the larger community. Revivalism can lead directly to allogenous growth as it did in the two upstate New York Synods. But it also contributes to the cyclical pattern noted above in the case of the Hartwick and Franckean Synods. More important than revivalism over the long term—especially as percentages of growth decrease—is the recruitment of young members directly through baptism and indirectly through Sunday schools.[20]

Understanding the two forms of growth help explain membership dynamics in the three New York synods. It is clear, for example, that the Franckean Synod underwent a period of allogenous growth from its inception until just prior to the Civil War; the Hartwick Synod, which grew more slowly, also underwent allogenous growth during most of its prewar period, with the exception of the downside of the revivalistic cycle in the latter 1840s; the New York Ministerium, in contrast, enjoyed no such growth until the late 1850s when it began incorporating more German immigrants into its churches. The experiences of revivalism, including the slowdown of growth just before the Civil War, and the beginning of a shift to a greater emphasis on Sunday schools, indicate a growing recruitment problem in the two revivalistic synods. Likewise the slow growth in the Ministerium and the slowdown in the Hartwick Synod prompted the musings of President Strobel about Baptism and confirmation and the need to re-emphasize both sacraments for the sake of church extension.

THE LUTHERAN CHURCH AND IMMIGRATION

But were even these periods of exceptional growth real allogenous growth? None of the synods were growing at rates equal to or greater than the primary pool of potential adherents—the German immigrant population. The only synod for which this was a real problem, however, was the New York Ministerium. It was the only synod with a growing percentage of German-speaking pastors and members. It (alone) would become exclusively German-speaking during the nineteenth century, seeking (as it did) to serve the Lutheran immigrants coming to

American shores from the "Fatherland." By 1860, as Graph 2.2 indicates, though its growth now outpaced that of the larger population, it had not yet caught up with the German immigrant population. In fact it would lag behind throughout the nineteenth century, growing at its own pace and by its own logic, sometimes when immigration itself was declining. Delayed marriage and child rearing among immigrant males who preceded wives and sweethearts to America doubtless accounts for part of the lag. Marriage, families, and baptisms, and the church growth which resulted, occurred sometime after the arrival of immigrants and at its own delayed and slower pace, producing a church whose strength did not mature until the 1880s and 1890s.[21]

The gap between the two—the growth of the immigrant population and their own congregations—was an ever-present challenge to Lutheran leaders. A comparison between membership in German-speaking Lutheran congregations and the larger German immigrant community in New York City, especially that third of the population which General Synod officials identified at this time as nominally Lutheran, indicated something of the gap. With the increased number of German immigrants in the New York City population by 1840, the size of the city's Lutheran congregations decreased in proportion to the number of potential adherents living in the city. In 1850 just under 1 in 6 members of the immigrant population (18.5 percent) was a member of a German-speaking Lutheran congregation (belonging either to the New York Ministerium or to the somewhat smaller Atlantic District of the Lutheran Church, Missouri Synod), as Table 2.2 indicates. By the eve of the Civil War just over 1 in 10 (11.8 percent) in the larger community were Lutheran church members.

Table 2.2
Communicants as Percentage of Lutheran Immigrants

Year	NY Ministerium (5)	Missouri Synod (5)	Total
1830	43.2		43.2
1840	19.4		19.4
1850	13.9	4.6	18.5
1860	8.5	3.3	11.8

In 1830, by comparison, the ratio of members to potential adherents was almost 1 in 2 (43.2 percent). This percentage of membership probably reflected a long-standing level of religious commitment and attendance in German and German-American Lutheran congregations going back to the colonial period. Then (1790–1800), after a period of heavy immigration in the late colonial period, the ratio of congregants to immigrants ranged anywhere from 1 in 2 (50 percent) to 1 in 3 (33 percent) though with some estimates as low as 30 percent. The higher number (50 percent) is probably more accurate, being similar to other estimates (59 percent).[22] By 1860, as we have seen, that rate had dropped from 1 in 2 or 3, to 1 in 7.

Why the changed level from 1830? In America agricultural life was more rural and isolated, making church organization and participation more difficult than in Germany. Certainly this was one reason for the low percentage of congregants. Another was the apparent nonaffiliation of half the Lutheran immigrant population with any American congregation, a phenomenon which first appeared in colonial America. Half gave up the faith of their fathers by choice! They either left religion behind in departing Europe or found it too difficult to incorporate in their new American lives. Clearly some immigrants preferred the lax faith and private judgment allowed Americans but which so vexed revivalists, who complained incessantly of this widespread problem among the unchurched. Important for other immigrants was the growing power of secular life in nineteenth-century European thought and culture which was brought to American shores. This occurred especially in the form of political ideologies among the working class, providing a political substitute for religious belief and practice. For still others the humanism of philosophy and education became effective substitutes and (sometimes) aggressively promoted options to the "superstitions" of organized religion. Whatever the reasons, the result was a relative paucity of religious adherents in America, a situation especially prevalent (as we shall see) in New York City.[23]

THE PROBLEM IDENTIFIED

It was this growing problem which prompted President Strobel to share the results of Table 2.1 with the New York Ministerium in 1850. Acknowledging the "external" (or cultural) factors, especially physical and economic growth in the Empire State, as instrumental to church expansion, he went on to identify "internal" factors contributing to the problem. It was the internal factors—not the organization of new congregations, but their ability to draw in new members—which puzzled and troubled him. In a pessimistic mood, he saw the implications of his 1849 table of statistics well enough—it was a halving of membership accessions between 1819 and 1849 which caused the decline in Ministerium growth rates as well as the declining ratio of members to potential adherents. What proved especially troubling was the Ministerium's seeming inability to include new members from among the immigrant population at rates commensurate with German population growth—"those coming from the fatherland"—"an almost boundless field for church extension" according to Strobel.[24] In this he was correct. Relative to the general population, Lutheran churches in the Ministerium were growing more rapidly; relative to the German immigrant population, they were growing more slowly. Paradoxically, German immigration was causing the Lutheran church to grow everywhere and in every way except in relation to the German immigrant community from which its drew new members!

Strobel addressed the Ministerium in 1852 regarding these internal congregational factors. Preaching for membership growth (i.e., conversion) had for a time "seemed a mighty lever, and great accessions followed from it," but not lately. Also "in former years catechization was universal and all the youth being brought under its direct influence" had swelled congregational membership. But to this rite, as with the Sacrament of Baptism, there had been growing indifference.[25] The result was that preaching was out of fashion while catechetics and confirmation were forgotten. Little had been done for "church extension" because of a lack of preachers (itself a result of the slowdown) and would not improve until other changes of attitude occurred. In a repentant mood, Strobel suggested that he, himself, might reflect a wrong orientation, since in his own ministry he was guilty of having labored to improve the "tone of religious feeling" rather than for an effective increase of church membership.

A CONFESSIONAL ALTERNATIVE

Strobel's analysis suggests a Ministerium at the crossroads in 1850, its leadership troubled by slowing growth and a sense of confessional apostasy. It was neither aggressively revivalist nor conscientiously confessional. Rather, it was somewhere in between—like the lukewarm church at Laodicea—existing in an apathetic no-man's land, its membership rolls filled with inactive members, and plagued by low and declining rates of membership relative to the population it most wished to attract, yet unable to mount an effective home mission effort on behalf of the new German immigrants. Decisive choice and action were necessary, but nothing was immediately forthcoming, save half-measures.

Perplexed by past results, American Lutherans like Strobel were beginning to rethink their mission strategies and to think, once again, in terms of traditional, confessional emphases and practices. The dynamics of change had made them ripe for a new confessional movement just then reaching maturity in Europe and America. What they did not yet know—what Strobel but half understood—was that the confessional understanding of the church would lead to both renewed vitality and growth among Lutherans in America. That understanding was in crucial ways anti-denominational in its assessment of the American scene, and post-denominational in its aspirations to catholicity. Eventually it would provide the foundations for a united Lutheranism among eastern Lutherans first in the United Lutheran Church, then in the United Lutheran Synod of New York. For the present, however, it would interact with the New York landscape creating another powerful expression of Lutheranism and contributing to further synodical differentiation and religious pluralism among Lutherans in the northeast.

BEYOND CONFESSIONAL MINIMALISM

As late as 1840 American Lutherans were not able to make doctrinal distinctions essential to establishing an institutional denominational identity. In the previous year the General Synod rejected the Franckean Synod's application for membership on seemingly confessional grounds. In that year confessionally minded Lutherans had managed to draw a line identifying a minimal Lutheranism beyond which Protestant bodies could not go in their religious practices and still be considered Lutheran. But to identify these distinctions as confessional would be to give credit where credit is not due. The Franckean Synod was censored in that year by the general body for "introducing practices which we consider contrary to the Word of God, thereby causing disturbances and divisions in our churches." It was deemed a "sacred duty" to publicly disavow such practices and to exhort all "Evangelical Lutheran churches in the United States, to beware of the efforts of these men to cause divisions and offences contrary to the spirit of the Gospel."[26]

A DENOMINATIONAL DEFINITION OF LUTHERANISM

The Franckean Synod's differences concerned just what it was that Lutherans practiced as a denomination. To "denominate" something is to describe, categorize, or otherwise distinguish it from other like objects, in this case the practices of other church bodies in American life. It is therefore a term of classification which is more apt to establish limits at the periphery than core doctrines. Though contrasting the practices of Synod critics with his own, Franckean president, John Lawyer, spoke of "the practice of many Christian denominations" when he sought to classify his form of Franckean Lutheranism as still being part of a larger denomination. An extract by Lawyer from *Buck's Theological Dictionary* on the "Evangelical Lutheran Church in the United States" suggested that among Lutherans, for example, conversion was not considered "indispensable" for partaking of Holy Communion, though "a sense of sin was." If any pastor should think proper to pursue a stricter course, although it would be an anomaly, "it could be done" the extract continued. The anomalous Franckeans, Lawyer noted "require a credible evidence of a change of heart." [27]

Such was the nature of Lutheranism in America—a form of Protestant Christianity, suffused with a "sense of sin," where conversion was emphasized but not considered essential to membership. New York Lutherans represented one denomination divided into three synods, two of which were affiliated with the General Synod. The Franckean Synod was not a member, though it considered itself a part of the Lutheran denomination by virtue of its faith and practice. Others did not consider them Lutheran! But then, just what it was to be Lutheran in America was a question whose answers were becoming more, not less varied with time. General Synod Lutheranism could provide no definitive answer to the Lutheran puzzle even though it drew a line at the practices of the Franckean Synod in 1839. Other Lutheran synods—indeed the two largest American synods, the Ministerium of Pennsylvania, and the Joint Synod of Ohio—remained aloof from the General Synod, frustrating the drive to establish a comprehensive denomination in a land of religious freedom. This distancing was even then making room for a more confessional Lutheranism being brought to America from Europe by a new wave of immigrants.

DEVELOPING CONFESSIONALISM IN EUROPE AND AMERICA

Most General Synod Lutherans failed to recognize that a fundamental shift of perspective was taking place in Christian circles on both sides of the Atlantic which made the confessionalism of German immigrants more appealing than the mild confessional outlook of American Lutheranism. And so they resisted the birth of a newer confessional perspective more suited to changing times. What were these changes? They were many, varied and not always tending to the same end.

First the reviving fortunes of confessionalism derive from a growth of denominational consciousness, not only among Lutherans, but throughout American Protestantism. It was becoming more important to know what it meant to be a Lutheran as compared with a Methodist for example. Such differences hastened a decline in ecumenical cooperation after 1830, as various American bodies formed their own denominational organizations for the development of faith, life, and mission in the United States and abroad. Revivalism, which historically had minimized doctrine, theology, and denominational organization, while encouraging cooperative, ecumenical ventures, had come under a cloud of suspicion thereby weakening the ecumenical force of American Protestantism. American Lutherans underwent a "deep-going disenchantment with the prevailing revivalistic modes of American church life . . ."[28] They also experienced loss over the changes revivalism had wrought. With the controversy surrounding the stagnation of the late 1840s, another way to speak of change was by invoking the memory of a lost Lutheranism (Baptism, catechetics, and Confirmation) in a time of waning revivalism. It was this sense of having lost something important which underlay the revival of confessional Lutheranism then taking place both in Germany and America.

Theirs was the disappointment of a love affair gone sour, for Lutherans had been unusually sympathetic to revivalistic measures, given their confessional background. They were singled out for criticism in the most influential attack upon revivalism to be mounted by the new confessionalism in American—John W. Nevin's 1843 "Anxious Bench," a conservative German Reformed attack on revivalism in general and especially the work of upstate New York's Charles G. Finney in particular. "The spirit of the Anxious Bench" Nevin argued "is at war with the spirit of the Catechism. . . . The Bench is against the Catechism, and the Catechism is against the Bench." To this way of thinking, high-pressure revivalism was considered "unfavorable to deep, thorough and intelligent piety . . . absolutely fatal to the true idea of devotion . . ." and "injurious to the worship of God."[29]

Nevin's outlook reflected the *second influence* as well: after 1825 Germany came to have the greatest influence on American theology, whether directly through German-language publications, or indirectly through the mediating thought of English and Scottish Romantics like Samuel Taylor Coleridge and Thomas Carlyle. This was the result of a fundamental shift in intellectual perspective after 1815 away from Enlightenment liberalism and toward a Conservative and Romantic outlook. Once again tradition was appreciated for the enduring values and established institutions which it bequeathed to a modern age. God and history were now the only legitimate sources of such things in a world where reason and skepticism had begun demythologizing Christianity. Quite suddenly all that the Enlightenment had devalued was being revalued by those with a historical consciousness able to think the thoughts of the past in a way vital to the present. A decline in church attendance and of interest in things religious resulting from the *Aufklarung* was offset by a religious "Awakening" among many segments of German Christianity, especially the nobility, who were then developing renewed interest in religious matters.[30]

THE CONFESSIONAL REVIVAL IN GERMANY FROM 1817

In 1817, on the 400th Anniversary of Luther's 95 Theses, Prussia's King Frederick William proclaimed a Union of Lutheran and Reformed Churches, a *fait accompli* made possible by years of moderating religious influence traceable to the Enlightenment and to Halle Pietism. The threatened loss of inherited teachings and practices caused a tremendous reaction among some Lutherans affected by this decree. Claus Harms (1778-1855) a Lutheran pastor at Kiel, republished Luther's 95 Theses in 1817 together with 95 of his own. Paraphrasing Luther's attack on the Roman Catholic sacrament of penance, he wrote:

> When our Lord and Master Jesus Christ says, "Repent," he wills that men should be conformed to his teaching; he does not conform his teaching to men, as is now done in accordance with the altered spirit of the times.[31]

The threatened loss of Lutheran tradition precipitated a sudden transvaluation of the discredited sixteenth-century confessional symbols and the ecumenical creeds of the early church. By comparison with the questionable results of rationalism, Lutheran tradition represented "Old Belief" in a Romantic age looking to the past for what was both good and true.[32]

For another decade the outlook of Harms and a few other pioneers was that of a prophetic minority. [In New York, as we have already seen, 1817 was the occasion for celebrating the very opposite—the autonomy of Enlightenment reason as freedom from the claims of Lutheran confessionalism.] Thereafter, however, the lost strands of Lutheran Pietism and Orthodoxy were recovered and rewoven into a tradition-oriented neo-Lutheranism which emphasized both intellect and experience. One result was a resurgent confessional dogmatics and a recovery of the church's historic liturgy.

Here was no mere repristination of the past, however. What emerged was a "newly minted" idea of the "confessional church" (*Bekenntniskirche*) radically defined, and promoted with evangelical fervor. A demand for a "church theology" proved intolerant of opposing views which were considered "unchurchly." A church was considered no older than its confession, since the confession was both the rule of faith and life, and the unifying center of fellowship; with no confessional agreement, there could be no Christian fellowship. The confession could sustain the church and give life to the community only in completeness "without alteration or exception." It was also symptomatic of a broader comprehension of the objective forms of church life, including confession, pastoral office, sacraments, liturgy, and the Bible.[33]

A peculiarity of this religious revival was that persons *first* discovered an experienced need for faith in Christ, forgiveness of sins, and justification through grace, *before* developing an active, confessional awareness of faith. As Gottfried Thomasius, a leader of the Lutheran revival in Bavaria put it, "we were Lutherans even before we knew it." In searching for an understanding of this experience, they rediscovered the explanative power of the Lutheran confessions, so "we became Lutherans voluntarily, from the inside." Here, perhaps, was a particular expression of the more general Romantic imagination which led to a yearning for faith and the reaffirmation of the supernatural.[34]

Such statements point to a new source of religious renewal at work in Europe and America. In a complex religious world, with traditional beliefs and practices buffeted by the cross winds of rationalism and unionism, and where religious pluralism (especially in America) further undermined the historic churches, the perennial religious experience of sinfulness and the need for grace refocused on creeds, confessions, the historical liturgy, and the sacraments as the objective realities of faith. As the resurgent confessional dogmatics would have it, the passion of personal faith in search of God (*fides qua creditur*) found focus once again in the historic faith (*fides quae creditur*) of the church. The subjective and the objective were thus deemed compatible rather than contradictory, and now formed a psychological basis for the remarriage of Pietism and Orthodoxy.

For one lay theologian, Soren Kierkegaard, the crisis of faith existing behind the neo-Lutheran revival was described as a "sickness unto death," an existential anxiety created through human estrangement from God for which the only solace was a "leap of faith." Of little influence in his own generation, Kierkegaard's theology, which would eventually lend substance and depth to religious awakening through existential awareness, was a major expression of this refocusing. For this solitary poet and essayist Denmark was merely an expression of "Christendom"—a highly religious, but pseudo-Christian community bewitched by numbers. Christendom was a mere "adding up units which are not Christian, getting the result by means of the notion that the big number does it. For true Christianity this is the most dangerous of all illusions . . ." Kierkegaard's confrontation reminds us that Lutheranism's ecclesiastical conservatism, could and did lead to an alliance between "throne and altar" in Europe and to the political conservatism which dominated European politics after 1815. The result was state-controlled churches in which (as Kurt Aland recently put it) the "Christian substance was more and more lost . . . until at the end of the age there was nothing but a facade left. This facade was beautiful and impressive to see, but behind that facade secularization had taken on frightening proportions."[35]

The neo-Lutheran revival in Silesia (southeast Prussia), where an independent Breslau Synod was formed by self-styled "Old Lutherans" in 1841, was one of the rare exceptions to this repristinated conservatism which fed the confessional revival.[36] Freedom there permitted a more open kind of repristinating neo-Lutheranism. Likewise in Bavaria the theologian Wilhelm Loehe encouraged the development of a more open form of orthodox theology so long as nothing essential to traditional orthodoxy was contradicted. A more progressive viewpoint developed in the Bavarian Erlangen University which avoided a literalist interpretation of either scripture or the confessions, seeking the best of the past understood in conjunction with contemporary knowledge.

For these moderate confessionalists, Christianity was seen not as doctrine but as a relationship to God experienced through regeneration, a relationship at once experiential and subjective but also mediated objectively through the church and the sacraments. In this Erlangen school subjective Pietism and objective Orthodoxy could come together in a new synthesis which emphasized both the structures of the church and the religious experience of its members, thereby reversing a process begun several centuries before. The Erlangen approach found permanent expression in Heinrich Schmid's *Dogmatik* first published in 1843. As the conservative confessional movement gained strength in the United States, Schmid's *Dogmatik* would be translated for use as the primary textbook in a revival of confessional Lutheran theology among Eastern Lutherans. His *Dogmatik* was based on the *Book of Concord* and the tradition of loci theologies dating to Philip Melanchthon which eventually gave rise to Lutheran orthodoxy itself.[37]

Unlike the repristination of Lutheran orthodoxy within the old-Lutheranism introduced by the Missouri Synod, Schmid's approach began (as his American editors observed) by the reader "knowing the positions held by the leading Dogmaticians" of the tradition, "even though he [the reader] may often regard them open to criticism." The difference was that "Definitions in Theology are always to be interpreted historically." Schmid accomplished this by developing a Biblical theology whose "loci" reconstructed a historical Lutheran theology. His pages included the classic loci of the catholic faith while still being faithful to the salvific themes important to Luther and Melanchthon including Grace, Faith, Justification, Regeneration, Good Works, Efficacy of the Divine Word, Law and Gospel, the two Sacraments, and the Three Estates in the Church.[38]

THREE FORMS OF LUTHERANISM IN AMERICA

The appearance in America, after 1840, of these two positions—repristinated, and historical/critical orthodoxy—helped create three major groups of Lutherans in the United States. The three groups and their differences were accurately described near mid-century (1857) in William Julius Mann's *Lutheranism in America.*[39]

GERMAN CONFESSIONALISM AND IMMIGRANT SYNODS

On the right, according to Mann, were the newer synods of immigrant Germans, most notably Missouri and Buffalo, which considered the Lutheran church "Lutheran by virtue of its peculiar Lutheran confession and not without it." They clung to the confessions believing them to be in accord with Scriptures, and showed a similar devotion to old Lutheran traditions in theology, worship, and piety. Conscious of other forms of Lutheranism in America, they staked out their position employing a contentious politics of exclusivity. They drew their inspiration and guidance from "Old Lutheranism" in Germany and from the repristinating neo-Lutheranism of Wilhelm Loehe, whose influence was especially great in the conservative but somewhat more flexible neo-Lutheranism of the Iowa Synod, erstwhile partner of Missouri, but also one of its most troublesome critics.

These two synods, organized among new German immigrants to America, were composed of old Lutherans fleeing persecution, victims of enforced religious union who established congregations in the middle west and in western New York around Buffalo during the 1830s and 1840s. One group of congregations in western New York formed the Buffalo Synod in 1845, just when the Hartwick Synod and the New York Ministerium were developing an English-language mission in that port city. Meanwhile the Evangelical Lutheran Synod of Missouri was organized in Chicago two years later. With them emerged a host of new, conservative German-speaking church leaders—most notably J. A. A. Grabau of the Buffalo Synod, and Carl F. W. Walther of Missouri. Iowa owed its origins and guidance to the prominent German confessionalist, Wilhelm Loehe; in America the Iowa Synod was led by Sigmund (1833-1900) and Gottfried (1836-1889) Fritschel. Other, similar bodies followed shortly—the Wisconsin Synod (1850) which was originally centrist, and the Iowa Synod (1854) which Mann classifies the Iowa Synod with the conservative right. Another centrist synod to emerge over time as a conservative, confessionally oriented body was the Joint Synod of Ohio. First established in 1812 as a conference of the Pennsylvania Ministerium, Ohio was organized as a separate synod in 1818 and reorganized as the Joint Synod of Ohio in 1831, with eastern and western districts; a separate English district was organized in 1836. German immigration led to a growing, German-speaking group within the synod, and greater confessional interest. The result was a body with opposing forces and theological factions—one sought greater confessional strictness, the other adjustment to American culture. Under the leadership of William F. Lehmann and (especially) Matthias Loy this bilingual synod (and its Evangelical Lutheran Seminary at Capital University, Columbus, Ohio, founded in 1830) managed to develop a coherent, moderate confessionalism, not equally acceptable to all members of the synod.[40]

A NEW AMERICAN CONFESSIONALISM

In the center of this emerging Lutheran continuum (Mann noted) were English- and German-speaking Lutherans in the East (including Mann and the Pennsylvania Ministerium), as well as Swedish and Norwegian immigrants in the Middle West, who eschewed the confessional laxity of the left and the rigidities of the right. Their worship and piety avoided both undisciplined revivalism and inflexible traditionalism.[41] This group also embraced a moderate German confessionalism, and the historical approach to scripture and doctrine of the Erlangen School.

C. P. KRAUTH—"FIRST A LUTHERAN, THEN AN AMERICAN"

If Samuel Simon Schmucker was the most significant leader of the left, and if C. F. W. Walther of Missouri was the pre-eminent spokesman of exclusive, neo-Lutheranism of the right, the moderate center, was largely the province of Charles Porterfield Krauth (1823-1883), an American Lutheran leader of the stature of Walther, Schmucker, and Muhlenberg. Krauth (fig. 2.1) was educated at Gettysburg College, where his father, Charles Philip Krauth, was president, and then at Gettysburg Seminary. The mild confessionalism established at Gettysburg Lutheran Seminary by Schmucker, took on stricter and fuller form under the influence of the elder Krauth whose own mild confessionalism became more conservative with extensive reading in the newer currents in German theology. [42]

figure 2.1
Charles Porterfield Krauth

What is typical of the immigrant experience once summarized by the social historian Marcus Lee Hansen (himself a Lutheran reflecting upon Scandinavian immigration) is that the grandsons and granddaughters of immigrants seek to remember what the sons and daughters hoped to forget. Charles Philip Krauth was the son of immigrant German Lutheran parents. Initially his was the second generation immigrant's infatuation with American Lutheranism at a time when both the Pennsylvania and the New York Ministeria had shed their German language and come to look upon themselves as an American denomination. But what he might have hoped to forget his son Charles Porterfield Krauth ended up by remembering. In his own lifetime the elder Krauth began the difficult task of recovering his religious roots and developing a more centrist, conservative confessionalism. "Some call me a rigid Symbolist" he observed late in his career, "others an extreme New Measure man. I am neither. If I say so again I draw upon me the extremists of both sides. I acknowledge no standard of Lutheranism but the Augsburg Confession." In 1850 the elder Krauth relinquished the college presidency to devote full time to seminary teaching and to editing the *Evangelical Review*, making it the journal of eastern Lutheran confessionalism. He promoted Heinrich Schmid's *Dogmatik of the Lutheran Church* in the pages of the *Review* as an antidote to the prevalent theological ignorance among American Lutheran clergy. Sometimes (he observed) they displayed "a decided Calvinistic influence, sometimes an extreme Arminian, sometimes a Pelagian" viewpoint. True Lutheran theology on the other hand the elder Krauth argued, while informed by the Augsburg Confession, its Apology, the Smalcald Articles, Luther's Catechisms, and the Formulas of Concord, arose in a church which because of its catholicity and antiquity, was part of a wider Christian church. This kind of Lutheran confessional outlook was a "catholic" outlook which he took pains to distinguish from Roman Catholicism.[43]

It was this stance which the elder Krauth bequeathed to his son—third generation to the core—who would argue most eloquently for a recovery of Lutheranism's confessional past, becoming the most important American-born spokesman for this old/new form of Lutheranism in America. The younger Krauth graduated from Gettysburg Seminary in 1841, was ordained a year later, and as parish duties allowed he began collecting a library which eventually reached 15,000 volumes—the kind "out of which other books are made"—reading extensively in German theology especially early orthodox Lutheran dogmatics and the confessions.[44]

At twenty-six Krauth published a seminal essay in the first volume of his father's *Evangelical Review* (1849)—"The Relation of our confessions to the Reformation" (republished in slightly modified form in 1871 as the highly important *The Conservative Reformation and Its Theology.*)[45] Already an accomplished essayist whose aphorisms demolished the conventional wisdom of his fellow Lutheran clergy, Krauth challenging their basic assumptions about American Lutheranism, clearing ground for a new perspective rooted in a deeply felt conservatism and the historian's regard for the truth of texts and sources.

Krauth addressed an audience whose cherished historical perspective on things religious was that of Enlightened liberalism, a progressive view which assigned the Reformation to the dark ages. For them the spirit of the Reformation led to freedom of conscience from the thralldom of a dead past and its religious doctrines. They assumed, moreover, that outmoded confessional doctrines would be rejected by the reformers themselves were they to reappear in this modern and enlightened age. It was more important to share an ecumenical outlook with others, and to embrace a common-denominator theology which was biblically based, than to remain faithful to the theological anachronisms found in the *Book of Concord*. The result of this historical consciousness was a level of confessionalism consisting of a vague allegiance to the "symbols" of the church, a knowledge of Luther's *Small Catechism*; and little else beyond an understanding of the historic importance of the doctrine of justification.

It is clear from the essay's organization and direction, that Krauth sought to challenge this conventional wisdom:

> "While it [the Reformation] established broadly and deeply the right of private judgment, it did not make that abuse of it which has since been so common."[46]

Regarding the superficial historicism of his colleagues:

> By a careful study of the symbolical writings of our church, commencing with the Augsburg confession and its Apology, a more thorough understanding of the history, difficulties, true genius, and triumphs of the Reformation will be attained than by reading everything that can be got or that has ever been written about that memorable movement. It is, indeed, too much the fashion now to read about things to the neglect of the great original sources themselves."[47]

Again, concerning the supposed familiarity of his contemporaries with the intentions of resurrected reformers:

> "Every objection which is now urged was then brought to bear upon the truth. Controversy has added nothing to its stores; they know perfectly those superficial, miscalled reasons which make men now so confident in saying that had the Reformers only lived in our time they would have abandoned much to which they held."[48]

Not satisfied to challenge these assumptions, Krauth continued by exploring the meaning of authentic religious existence in America. He challenged the immigrant's over-identification with American institutions and its idolatrous distortion of the country's place in human history. Are the confessions "after all of any value to the American Lutheran preacher?" One question was answered with another: "Must Lutheranism be shorn of its glory to adapt it to our times or our land? No! Our land is great and wide and glorious and destined, we trust, under the sunlight of her free institutions long to endure, but our faith is wider and greater and is eternal." "The world owes more to the Reformation than to America," he continued. "America owes more to it than to herself. My country is my mother, but my church is her mother, the source under God of all that is great and good in it. Through my church Christianity, peace with God, redemption in Christ, immortality have been given to me, and therefore I am first a Lutheran and then an American."[49]

Krauth continued by reflecting on the need for Lutheran self-reliance after a period of too-close identification with evangelical Protestantism. The historian Sydney Ahlstrom in described the origins of this indigenous confessionalism as arising from a "deep-going" disenchantment with the prevailing revivalistic Christianity; it appeared with a "spontaneity akin to the rise of Transcendentalism." Like the religious outlook of Ralph Waldo Emerson, which gave original voice to the words "know-thyself" and "to thine own self be true," there was more than a superficial measure of self-reliant truth in the seminal essay of Krauth. Thus Krauth critiqued religious existence in a world of sectarian denominationalism "which threatens the welfare of pure Christianity on our shores more than all other causes combined." How would it be possible, he asked, to "lift ourselves out of the sphere of that pitiful little sectarianism which is crawling over us and biting us continually? We must begin by knowing ourselves and being true to that knowledge. Let us not with our rich coffers play the part of beggars and ask favors where we have every ability to impart them . . ." "No church," he continued, "can maintain its self-respect or inspire respect in others which is afraid or ashamed of its own history and which rears a dubious fabric on the ignorance of its ministry and of its members. Whatever flickerings of success may play around it, it will yet sink to rise no more, and, worse than this, no honest man will lament its fall, for however such a moral dishonesty may be smoothed over, every reflecting man sees that such a church is an organized lie with a ministry, congregations, churches, and societies united to sustain a lie."[50] He lamented "the pressure of surrounding denominations" which produced past apostasy, and Lutheranism's inability to survive acculturation with its integrity intact. He hoped for a renewed confessionalism in his church:

> that, after all the changes of national existence and of language, all pressure from the churches and the people around us, our holy faith shall come forth in all its purity and power eventually to perform, in the great drama in our western realm, a part as important as that which it bore in its original glory in the history of the world.[51]

With Krauth, then, a new and self-transcending form of confessional Lutheranism was emerging among native Lutherans who desired to live a more authentic faith, by transcending the cultural pressures of denominationalism because many were tired (in Krauth's words) of "living a lie," an "organized lie" meant to "sustain a lie."

GENERAL SYNOD CONFESSIONAL CHANGES—1829-1860

Desire for a more authentic faith shaped such confessional developments as these within the Pennsylvania Ministerium (and to a lesser extent within the New York Ministerium), though the General Synod itself was decidedly to the left of the Krauth's centrist position. *On the left,* according to Mann, were American Lutherans represented by the mild confessionalism of Schmucker and the General Synod. Zwinglian in theology Mann argued (rather than Calvinist), they were Calvinist in piety, if Calvinism could be represented by the practices of revivalism and the neglect of catechization. The position was represented by about twenty American Lutheran synods (including the Hartwick Synod and the New York Ministerium) originating in early nineteenth-century America. At the time of the General Synod's formation (1820) there had been a growing curiosity about, if not actually, a renewed interest in the Augsburg Confession. The Confession itself was viewed more as an expression of Protestant thought and a bulwark against encroaching Roman Catholicism than as a source of theology. As we have seen, the oath of office given professors at the General Synod's new Gettysburg Seminary stated "I believe the Augsburg Confession and the catechisms of Luther to be a summary and just exhibition of the fundamental doctrines of the Word of God."[52] The General Synod's model district synod constitution of 1829, the only other place where the General Synod took anything like a confessional stance, spelled out what was asked of Lutheran ordinands:

> Do you believe the Scriptures of the Old and New Testament to be the word of God, and the only infallible rule of faith and practice? Do you believe that the fundamental doctrines of the word of God, are taught in a manner substantially correct, in the doctrinal articles of the Augsburg Confession?[53]

"Substantially correct" was a position the General Synod would espouse for a number of years. The partisans of American Lutheranism, led by Gettysburg's Schmucker, tried spelling out what was substantially correct in a "Definite Platform" proposed to the General Synod for adoption in 1855 while the forces of American Lutheranism and old Lutheranism were still evenly balanced. To streamline Lutheran confessional theology the Platform presented an "American Recension of the Augsburg Confession," abbreviating or modifying twenty-one articles of the unaltered Augsburg Confession, together with a list of errors in the *Book of Concord* including the ceremonies of the mass, exorcism, private confession and absolution, the doctrines of baptismal regeneration and the personal union of the two natures in Christ, the outward form of baptism, the sin-forgiving power of the Lord's Supper, and the real presence of Christ in the Eucharist.[54]

THE CONFESSIONAL CENTER EMERGES

By 1860, however, a growing conservative Lutheranism had begun to assert itself more powerfully in the General Synod. The turning point came in 1853 when the centrist and more confessional Pennsylvania Ministerium rejoined a General Synod it had helped form in 1819 but subsequently left for confessional reasons. Under the guidance of young leaders like Krauth, the Pennsylvania Ministerium had recently returned to the pre-1792 confessional position of its predecessor body, the Lutheran Ministerium in North America, by acknowledging "the collective body of symbolical books as the historico-confessional writings of the Evangelical Lutheran Church" with preeminence given to the Unaltered Augsburg Confession and the Small Catechism. Now the Pennsylvania Ministerium led the fight to defeat the *Definite Platform.* After vigorous debate in some synods (other synods ignored the Platform entirely) the "Definite Platform's" rejection was assured when only three small General Synod bodies ratified the document. None was from the New York area where a growing confessionalism could be seen at work in the Ministerium and Hartwick Synod.[55]Like the Pennsylvania Ministerium, by 1855 the New York Ministerium was returning to its own pre-1792 confessional origins. Its confessionalism arose from two sources. One, as expressed by Krauth, was the yearning among American-born, English-speaking Lutherans for a confessional system that reappropriated a heritage lost in becoming acculturated to American Protestantism. The other was the conservative confessionalism arriving in the baggage of immigrants known (as immigrants in general were known) for their conservatism.[56]

MINISTERIUM GERMAN-SPEAKING CONFESSIONALISM

New York entered the 1830s with one struggling English Lutheran Church body—St. James—and with another conducting services in both languages. This situation changed in 1838 when St. Matthews called Carl F. E. Stohlmann who had come to America in 1836 to serve German Lutherans in Albany. He was the first of a steady stream of German-born pastors who emigrated to New York with the support and encouragement of the Ministerium. It included two future leaders among strict confessionalists in the Ministerium who served as Stohlmann's assistants at St. Matthews, F. W. Steimle (1855) and Christian Hennicke (1861-1865). By 1840 St. Matthews served a growing German-speaking constituency drawn from Manhattan, Brooklyn, Hoboken, Jersey City, and Staten Island. In the next decades the congregation helped form St. Marks, Manhattan; St. Pauls, Brooklyn; St. Matthews, Hoboken; and St. Johns, Newark, while also giving financial assistance to fifteen German-speaking congregations.[57]

The Ministerium provided its own sources of mission development. Besides Steimle the Ministerium brought in John Muehlhaeuser in 1838 to serve a growing German population in Rochester (he soon left for Wisconsin, where he eventually formed the Wisconsin Synod), and George J. Kempe in 1838, who was assigned to those Germans gathering for worship in Syracuse who formed "Die deutsche evangelish-lutherische St. Johannis-Kirche (fig. 2.2)." They were but the first of a large group of clergy who emigrated in the 1840s and 1850s from such schools as Halle, Rentz, Bremen, Dresden, Saxe, Meiningen, Basle, and Berlin. With this growing group of pastors, the first clear signs of a confessional resurgence were seen at the synodical level with increased use of German, making bilingual publications necessary to communicate with all Ministerium members.[58]

figure 2.2
St. Johannis-kirche Syracuse, NY, Founded December 18, 1838

The same synod which created conferences to supervise the needs of cluster congregations, also began developing regulations to govern new congregations seeking admission. Of greatest importance, the model constitution for new congregations required adherence to the Augsburg Confession and Luther's Small Catechism. By 1852 recognition of the unaltered Augsburg Confession became mandatory for all congregations seeking admission to the New York Ministerium, while pastors after that date were required to teach "the true doctrine of our church, according to Luther's Catechism." Meanwhile, it was expected that new members of these congregations would be baptized, commune and contribute regularly, live in conformity with the Gospel and "uphold and cherish our Lutheran Church with its doctrine and practice before any other denomination or society whatever."[59] Inclusive denominationalism was rapidly disappearing in the changing Ministerium. Strangers seeking membership on a confessional basis were immediately accepted, as was a pastor applying for his German Lutheran congregation outside of Buffalo, as "a minister of our confession."[60]

The 1850s marked a transition for the Ministerium as its German population rapidly increased. Nearly a million German immigrants emigrated to the United States between 1850 and 1860. Many entered through Castle Garden in New York City before embarking up the Hudson River system to the Erie Canal and Lake Erie—the preferred route to the American frontier. Rochester's pastor J. G. Kempe, reporting religious awakenings and renewal from that city, noted: "The German Population of the Lutheran denomination in this city is increasing so fast, that our newly built and much enlarged church, is filled nearly every sabbath with attentive hearers."[61] What took place in Rochester and Buffalo also occurred in the region surrounding New York Harbor. From Buffalo to New York City substantial brick and stone churches were built in growing urban areas attesting to the existence of substantial communities of German Lutherans in their midst. (See fig. 2.3.)

figure 2.3
Erste deutsche evangelish-lutherische Zions-Kirche
Rochester, N. Y.—Founded 1839

CONFESSIONALISM WITHIN THE HARTWICK SYNOD

Confessional positions varied from synod to synod within New York. The Hartwick Synod, situated in an area of upstate New York where there was no great influx of German confessionalists to influence it, also began rejecting the confessional position of American Lutheranism in the 1850s, but its doctrinal position would have given little comfort to the old Lutheranism of some immigrant groups. Hartwick took a stand against the "Definite Platform" because the Lutheran Church in the United States "has for some time been agitated by a controversy in reference to the authority of the Augsburg Confession as a standard of faith for our synods and churches." Accordingly they reaffirmed the "doctrinal basis" of the General Synod, "receiving the Scriptures of the Old and New Testament as the only infallible rule of faith and practice" and at the same time endorsing the sentiment "that the fundamental doctrines of the word of God, are taught in a manner substantially correct, in the doctrinal articles of the Augsburg Confession."[62]

Characteristically, the Hartwick Synod also went on to embrace the criticism of the Augsburg Confession which American Lutheranism had made in the *Definite Platform*. In so doing the synod claimed the right to "enumerate" the doctrines which were fundamental to Lutheranism, listing "The articles concerning God," "The Trinity," "The divinity of Christ," "The Son of God and his mediatorial work," "Repentance," "Justification by faith," "Obedience as an evidence of our faith," "The resurrection of the body," and "A future judgment, and a state of rewards and punishments in a future life." As for the articles "which are susceptible of different constructions," the synod (without "stopping" to argue whether they teach objectionable views when properly interpreted) enumerated those objectionable views:

> this Synod, resting on the word of God, as the *sole* authority in matters of faith, on its infallible warrant rejects the doctrine of baptismal regeneration—rejects the Romish doctrine of the real presence or transubstantiation, and with it the doctrine of consubstantiation; rejects the mass, and all ceremonies distinctive of the mass; denies any power in the sacraments as *opus operatum*, or that the benefits resulting from the sacraments can be received without faith; rejects auricular confession and priestly absolution; hold that there is no priesthood on earth except that of all believers, and that God only can forgive sins; and maintains the sacred obligation of the Lord's day, as of divine appointment, to be sacredly regarded by all Christians.[63]

A part of this position reflected the pietist critique of Lutheran orthodoxy developed in Germany several centuries before, and brought to the American colonies by Henry Melchoir Muhlenberg. Meanwhile, the Hartwick Synod's position on confession, absolution, and the real presence reflected the American recensionists. In the meantime a Protestant twist had been added further modifying the Hartwick Synod's position:

> That whilst this Synod, gives this public expression to its doctrinal basis, it will ever be regardful of the views and feelings of our brethren who may differ from us, and will cheerfully extend to them the same freedom of opinion in all matters of faith, which we claim for ourselves. [64]

For the Hartwick Synod the paradigms of denominationalism still prevailed.

CONCLUSION: "I AM FIRST A LUTHERAN, THEN AN AMERICAN"

Hartwick had in mind its sister New York synods—the New York Ministerium with its growing confessionalism, and the Franckean Synod, which steadfastly refused any kind of confessional subscription. The three together represented a range of confessional interests and practices as great as anywhere in the church. Hartwick's stand on behalf of tolerance and freedom of opinion was meant to prevent confessional differences from causing deep divisions within the New York Church. While they could not yet say with Charles Porterfield Krauth, "I am First a Lutheran, Then an American," they had gained some critical detachment from English-American values and institutions, permitting them to begin developing a confessional identity as Lutherans in America. What the Hartwick Synod could not anticipate, nor prevent, was the way in which New York confessional differences were about to cause a deeper division in the national church and General Synod. While the Franckean Synod adamantly maintained its anti-confessional stance, the New York Ministerium was moving quickly toward a new confessionalism that would make it among the most conservative Lutheran bodies in the United States. Driven by diverging confessional concerns, Lutheranism in New York was about to make an important contribution to the restructuring of the national church as part of a new Lutheran middle way.

NOTES

1 George Lindbeck, *The Nature of Doctrine* (New York: Westminster, 1984) 77-78; see also Mark Horst, "The Problem with Theological Pluralism," *Christian Century* 103 (Nov. 5, 1986): 971-974.

2 NY Ministerium, *Minutes* (1829), 26.

3 "Preface" quoted in Harry J. Kreider, *History of the United Lutheran Synod of New York and New England* (Philadelphia: Muhlenberg Press, 1954), 86.

4 Abdel Ross Wentz, *Pioneer in Christian Unity: Samuel Simon Schmucker* (Philadelphia: Fortress Press, 1967), 250 ff.

5 New York Ministerium, *Minutes* (1850), 55, 30-32.

6 See "Dynamics of Baptism" in Chapter 11; also "Confessional Basis of the General Synod, 1829-1868" in Chapter 12.

7 Ibid., 55, 30-32.

8 Nigel Holmes, *Designer's Guide to Creating Charts and Diagrams* (New York: Watson-Guptill, 1984), 13-21. James H. Cassedy, *Demography in Early America. Beginnings of the Statistical Mind, 1600-1800,* (Cambridge: Harvard University Press, 1969), 309.

9 Synod, *Journal* (1837), 25ff. Kreider, *History* 71, 86.

10 See "The Sacrament of Holy Baptism" in the Small Catechism, BC, 348 ff.

11 Hartwick Synod, *Minutes (*1833), 13. For a more detailed description of mission activity among the three synods see Kreider, *History,* Chapter 8, "Mission," 189 ff.

12 Hartwick Synod, *Minutes* (1845), 12; (1848), 16; (1849), 13-14; (1855), 17 ff. In a note to this author Richard Dishno reports evidence of an independent German-speaking church in Boston founded in 1839 which apparently joined the Hartwick synod during the mid 1840's. See George Adams, *The Boston Directory for 1848-1849* (Boston: James Smith & Charles, 1848).

13 Ibid. (1843), 22, 33, 39; (1845), 21.

14 Kreider, *History*, 191 ff, 193. New York Ministerium, *Minutes* (1835), 22.

15 Franckean Synod, *Journal* (1845), 21.

16 Ibid. (1850), 18.

17 Ibid. (1847), 34.

18 Kreider, *History*, 169-70. Frankean Synod, *Journal* (1855), 22, 6, 15, 11, 10; (1860), 20-22.

19 Robert Currie, Alan Gilbert, and Lee Horsley, *Church and Churchgoers. Patterns of Church Growth in the British Isles Since 1700* (Oxford: Clarendon Press, 1977), 79 ff.

20 Ibid., 39; 51 ff; 86 ff.

21 Stanley Nadel, *Little Germany. Ethnicity, Religion, and Class in New York City, 1845-80* (Urbana: University of Illinois Press, 1990), 26, notes this lag in marriage and families with the immigration, first, of German males.

22 The first estimate is made from information provided in Theodore Tappert, "The Church's Infancy. 1650-1790," *The Lutherans in North America,* ed. E. Clifford Nelson (Philadelphia: Fortress Press, 1976), 36-7, 57; the second estimate is based on the number of nominal Lutherans indicated above and the report of Lutheran congregants for 1800 provided in Edwin Scott Gaustad, *Historical Atlas of Religion in America,* Revised ed. (New York: Harper & Row, 1976), fig. 40, p. 52. Conclusions similar to these for the colonial period are to be found in Jon Butler, "A Spiritual Tower of Babal: Shifting Structure and Functions of Religious Diversity in Colonial Pennsylvania, 1680-1760," 1983, 19. Patricia and Peter Eisenstadt Bonomi, "Church Adherence in the Eighteenth-Century British American Colonies," *Wm. & Mary Qtr.* 3rd Ser., 39 (1982): Table 3, 274.

23 Thomas Jefferson Wertenbaker, *The Founding of American Civilization. The Middle Colonies* (New York: 1938), 271-72. For a possible interpretation see Peter F. Williams, *Popular Religion in America. Symbolic*

Change and the Modernization Process in Historical Perspective (Englewood Cliffs, New Jersey: Prentice-Hall, 1980), 58 ff; see also Jon Butler, "A Spiritual Tower of Babal," 22ff. There is little evidence to substantiate such a hypothesis among nominal Lutherans in the northeast.

24 NY Ministerium, *Minutes* (1850), 33.

25 Ibid. (1852), 32.

26 General Synod, *Minutes* (1839), 17.

27 Franckean Synod, *Proceedings of a Convention of Ministers and Delegates from Evangelical Lutheran Churches, in the State of New-York* (Albany, 1837), 21. Charles Buck, *A Theological Dictionary, New American (corrected) Edition revised by the Rev. George Bush* (Philadelphia: Thomas Cowperthwait, 1838), 471. Franckean Synod, *Journal of the Special Meeting of the Franckean Synod* (Albany, 1837), 39.

28 On the changing religious scene in America, especially as it pertained to Lutherans, see Abdel Ross Wentz, *Pioneer in Christian Unity: Samuel Simon Schmucker* (Philadelphia: Fortress Press, 1967), 170-78. Sydney E. Ahlstrom, "Theology in America," in *The Shaping of American Religion*, eds. James War Smith and A. Leland Jamison (Princeton: Princeton University Press, 1961), 275.

29 Ibid., 272. John Nevin, *The Anxious Bench* (Chambersburg, 1843), p. 56; quoted in Ahlstrom, "Theology in America," p. 268.

30 Kurt Aland, *A History of Christianity*, 2 vols. (Philadelphia: Fortress Press, 1986) II: 291-2, 338ff. See also Klaus Epstein, *The Genesis of German Conservatism* (Princeton: Princeton University Press, 1966); and Hans Georg Artur Viktor Schenk, *The Mind of the European Romantics. An Essay in Cultural History* (London: Constable and Co. Ltd, 1966).

31 Theodore G. Tappert, *History of the Lutheran Theological Seminary at Philadelphia, 1864-1964* (Philadelphia: Lutheran Theological Seminary, 1964), 7.

32 Ibid. See also Walter H. Conser, Jr., *Church and Confession: Conservative Theologians in Germany, England, and America 1815-1866* (Macon, Ga.: Mercer University Press, 1984), 55-98 for Neo-Lutheran confessional developments in Germany.

33 Claude Welch, in *Protestant Theology in the Nineteenth Century*, 2 vols. (New Haven: 1972), I:196-7, summarizes the new confessional viewpoint with great clarity.

34 Tappert, *Lutheran Confessional Theology*, 9. Schenk, *The Mind of the European Romantics*, 49ff, 81, 88ff.

35 Soren Kierkegaard, *Attack Upon "Christendom,"* in Hugh T. Kerr, ed., *Readings in Christian Thought* (Nashville: Abingdon, 1966), 283-4. Aland, *A History of Christianity*, II: 339, 338.

36 Ibid., 335-6.

37 See Arthur Karl Piepkorn, *Profiles in Belief*, II, 28ff; also Tappert, *Lutheran Confessional Theology*, 12-15. Samuel Macauley Jackson, ed., *The New Schaaf-Herzog Encyclopedia of Religious Knowledge* (Grand Rapids: Baker Book House, 1977), X, 250. For the English translation see Heinrich Schmid, *The Doctrinal Theology of Evangelical Lutheran Church, verified from the original sources*, trans. Charles A. Hay and Henry E. Jacobs (Philadelphia: Lutheran Publication Society, 1875).

38 Schmid, *Doctrinal Theology*, 3-11.

39 William Julius Mann, *Lutheranism in America: An Essay on the Present Condition of the Lutheran Church in the United States* (Philadelphia: 1857). Mann's work was written to counter S. S. Schmucker, *The American Lutheran Church , Historically, Doctrinally, and Practically Delineated, in Several Occasional Discourses* (Springfield: D. Harbaugh, 1851). It was also the basis for Philip Schaaf's classification of American Lutheranism in his *America: A Sketch of the Political, Social, and Religious Character of the United States of North America* (New York: 1855). Mann's position is summed up in Tappert, *Lutheran Confessional Theology*, 26-27.

40 Nelson, *The Lutherans in North America*, 183-4. Ibid., 168, 174, 179.

41 Tappert, *Lutheran Confessional Theology*, 27.

42 Ahlstrom, "Theology in America," 235; Wentz, *Pioneer in Christian Unity*, 190-91, 205-6, 223-24; on Krauth's position, when he bequeathed to his son, Charles Porterfield Krauth, see Tappert, *Lutheran Confessional Theology*, 30; Tappert's "Introduction" provides a good analysis of the origins of American Lutheran confessionalism on both sides of Atlantic. See also Walter H. Conser, Jr., *Church and Confession: Conservative Theologians in Germany, England, and America 1815-1866* (Macon, Ga.: Mercer University Press, 1984).

43 Marcus Les Hansen, "The Problem of the Third Generation Immigrant," Augustana Historical Society *Publications* [Rock Island, Illinois] 8:1 (1938), 12. Walter H. Conser, Jr., *Church and Confession*, 263-268. Though Conser emphasizes the importance of Charles Philip Krauth in Lutheran confessional developments to the neglect of the son, Charles Porterfield Krauth, he gives due credit to a neglected figure in the history of eastern Lutheran developments.

44 *Dictionary of American Biography*, VIII, 502-3.

45 "Relation" in Tappert, *Lutheran Confessional Theology*, 44

46 Ibid., 43.

47 Tappert, *Lutheran Confessional Theology*, 44.

48 Ibid., 46.

49 Ibid., 47.

50 Ahlstrom, "Theology in America," 275. Ibid., 48.

51 Ibid., 49.

52 Henry Eyster Jacobs, *A History of the Evangelical Lutheran Church in the United States, American Church History*, Second ed. (New York: Charles Scribner's Sons, 1899), 367.

53 General Synod, *Minutes* (1829), 39.

54 Went, *Pioneer in Christian Unity*, 212-213.

55 Abdel Ross Wentz, *A Basic History of Lutheranism in America* (Philadelphia: Muhlenberg Press, 1955), 142. Abdel Ross Wentz, *Pioneer in Christian Unity*, 216-223.

56 Marcus Lee Hansen, *The Immigrant in American History* (New York: Harper & Row, 1964), 82.

57 See Harry J. Kreider, *History*, 193 ff. H. Brueckner, *Seventy-Fifth Anniversary of St. Matthew's Evangelical Lutheran Church, Eighth and Hudson Sts.* (Hoboken, N. J., 1933), 18-21; Carl T. Uehling, *St. John's Evangelical Lutheran Church, Newark, New Jersey, Founded October 10, 1833. The One Hundred and Twenty-fifth Anniversary* (Privately published, 1958), 4-5; Hugo W. Hoffmann, *The History of St. Paul's Evangelical*

Lutheran Church, Brooklyn, N. Y., from 1853-1903 (Mt. Vernon: Wartburg Printing House, 1903), 18-21; Karl Kretzmann, *The Oldest Lutheran Church in America. A Brief Chronicle of Events in the History of the Evangelical Lutheran Church of Saint Matthew in the City of New York, 1664-1914* (New York City: privately published, 1914), 36, 41.

58 *Minutes* (1851), 16.

59 Ibid., 19; (1852), 38.

60 Ibid. (1853), 11.

61 Ibid., 12.

62 Hartwick Synod, *Minutes* (1856), 30.

63 Ibid., 31.

64 Ibid.

3

A HOUSE DIVIDES

Divisions within the New York Area Church, 1861-1867

Trying to be tolerant of others, the Hartwick Synod sought to adjust to the rapid confessional changes which were creating growing pains among New York Lutherans in an effort to prevent division. In the end the stress would be too great and like the nation, engaged in a great civil war, Lutheranism too would become a house divided. The two divisions were not unrelated. Eastern Lutheranism of the Muhlenberg tradition would separate into two general bodies—a General Synod and a General Council—because of attempts among New York Lutheran synods, in time of civil war, to move closer to one another by arranging the admission of the Franckean Synod into the General Synod. In the meantime, however, the old "environmental" elaborations of Lutheranism on the territory, and their theologies, now aggravated by a language split, led to still further divisions among New York area Lutherans.

DIVISION BEGINS: THE NEW JERSEY SYNOD FORMS

In 1861 New Jersey's growing church resorted to the (by now) time-honored practice of subdivision, first as a separate New York Ministerium conference of New Jersey pastors in 1855, and then as a separate synod within the General Synod. (See Map 7.1.) Reporting on the reasons for forming the New Jersey Synod in its founding convention, its president noted in his report:

> For a length of time some of us have felt that it was desirable and important that we should have a synodical organization in our State, as a common bond of unity, and centre of operation for the benefit of all concerned in the prosperity of our particular communion. [1]

Again mission was important, with mission fields developing in New Jersey's Salem and Cumberland counties, where it was hoped "something effectual will be done to supply our destitute people there with the ministration of the Gospel."[2]

The New Jersey withdrawal was harmonious enough, at least on the surface. Its constitution, which reflected changing confessional directions within the General Synod, went beyond the mild confessionalism of the general body itself. In declaring its "Doctrinal basis" the New Jersey Synod moved in the direction of Old Lutheranism:

> we receive with the Evangelical Lutheran Church of our fathers the Word of God, as contained in the Canonical Scriptures of the Old and New Testament as the only infallible rule of faith and practice; and the Augsburg Confession, with Luther's Smaller Catechism, as a correct exhibition of the fundamental doctrines of the Divine Word, and the faith of our Church founded on that Word.[3]

Yet given its peculiar subregional character, with an evangelical and confessional interest like that of the Hartwick Synod, time would demonstrate New Jersey's proclivity for the moderate confessionalism of General Synod Lutheranism. A few years by themselves would also uncover other reasons for their separation from the parent body across New York Harbor, which itself was undergoing a rapid change in language and confessional theology. Eventually its president would confess to a more complex set of motives including the growing German character of the Ministerium and the fact that it conducted its business in German—"a language which a considerable portion of" New Jersey members "did not understand"—also necessitated the division.[4] As a result Lutheranism in New Jersey would be divided into an English-speaking General Synod form and a German-speaking form which developed in urban New Jersey along the western shore of New York Harbor under the influence of the Ministerium and its German congregations in Manhattan.

German Immigration Changes the New York Area

In all things, including its own peculiar development as a subregion, the greater New York City area, led by New York City proper, reflected the greater pressures of European immigration. City population more than doubled between 1850 and 1880, from 500,000 to 1,200,000.[5] In this period New York's German population increased from 20,000 to 151,000 (between 1840 and 1870), as Table 3.1 indicates. Between 1850 and 1860 alone the German population doubled as did the pool of German Lutherans (estimated at one third total German immigration). By 1880 only Berlin and Vienna had larger German populations, making New York's *Kleindeutschland* ("Little Germany") the third capital of the German-speaking world. Whereas the older (pre 1860) immigration had come mainly from the German Rhineland territories (with its pietist bias), two-thirds now came from all over northern and eastern Germany. Largely artisans, shopkeepers and skilled workers, these workingclass Germans and their families were compressed into the lower east side of Manhattan, from the Bowery to the East River, between East Fourteenth Street on the north and Division Street on the south. Endogamy—marriage within the group—was strong among German immigrants, the preference for marriage with a *Landsmann* of the same religion contributing to an exceptionally strong ethno-religious particularism expressed in highly exclusive neighborhood blocks. German immigrants were more self-segregating than the Irish, with second generation German-Americans being even more exclusive than their immigrant parents. Endogamy, a preference for the nuclear family, and high birth rates (inherited from Germany) meant relatively large German families. Between 1860 and 1880 family size grew as the number of children per family increased from 2.66 to 3.16. By 1880, 46.6 percent of the *Kleindeutschland* population was under the age of 21. While repeated waves of immigration added new members to the community, rapidly growing families were Little Germany's major source of growth in times of slackened immigration.[6]

Table 3.1
German Lutherans in New York City 1840-1880

Year	NYC Germans (1)	Grmn Luths	Percent Grwth	Congre-gations (5)	Percent Grwth	Communi-cants (5)	Percent Grwth
1840	19693	6564	29.3	41	78.3	4654	143.9
1850	56141	18714	185.1	33	19.5	6672	43.4
1860	118292	39431	110.7	55	66.7	11688	75.2
1870	151216	50405	27.8	58	5.5	12936	10.7

Here was growth with more than its share of pain. Fourteenth Street divided English-speaking uptown New York from a downtown dominated by Germans and Irish. Fifty percent of the metropolitan population was crowded into the old city, a vital, teeming area of tenements plagued by congestion, poverty, disease, and environmental deterioration. By 1876 half of New York lived in tenements, yet 65 percent of adult deaths occurred there, as well as 90 percent of all infant mortality. Uptown mortality rates were 20.44 per thousand. There fewer children died, while adults lived longer. Below Fourteenth Street the rate was 37.72! The difference was as stark as the late twentieth-century distinction between first and third world countries.[7] The religious needs of *Kleindeutschland's* growing families with many children—both living and dying—was an elemental fact that fundamentally reshaped Lutheranism in the northeast.

As immigration grew, the number of congregations in the

Ministerium increased from 33 to 55 between 1850 and 1860, a growth of 66.7 percent; communicant membership increased 75 percent. While these increases represented healthy growth for the Lutheran Ministerium in both New York City and State, the growth rate in the church was only three quarters that of the population, causing a sense of urgency for the church. However it was figured, the percentage of Lutherans in the community was small—somewhere between 6 percent and 12 percent.[8] Table 3.1 suggests that Lutherans in the New York Ministerium made up 8.5 percent of the *Kleindeutschland* population. Corrected for upstate Lutherans, and adding in the small but growing Lutheran congregations of the Missouri Synod a figure of under 12 percent is realistic. [9] However the percentage is figured, the small number of Lutherans distinguishes German New York from other immigrant communities in America as relatively secular in orientation, organization and outlook.[10]

The urban experience among American Christians already displayed a diversity which would increasingly characterize the urban church between 1860 and 1920. Urbanization produced at least four distinct responses among Christian groups: 1) A desire to maintain homogeneous congregations along ethnic and class lines led some Protestant congregations to relocate in the face of undesirable changes in their neighborhoods. Between 1870 and 1890, for example, as 200,000 immigrants were moving into lower Manhattan, seventeen Protestant churches moved out of the area demonstrating one kind of response to immigration and changing neighborhoods. 2) Many other congregations stayed in place, making few if any conscious adjustments to urban life, or developing any urban mission strategies to remain where they were. 3) A third kind of response occurred among a few old, established congregations which became denominational "cathedrals" drawing upon a scattered but mobile membership and sometimes becoming "institutional churches" with special programs and facilities for the surrounding community. 4) Finally, many congregations were simply "transplantations" of rural and village life (whether native or immigrant), seeking to replicate traditional community life within an urban neighborhood.[11]

In New York City the *Kirchendeutschen* (Church Germans) were neither so large nor so well organized as the *Vereindeutschen* (Association Germans). This may have been due to the peripheral nature of the church. Few German Christian churches—Roman Catholic, Reformed or Lutheran—were located in the Manhattan ghetto. They demonstrated a decided preference for building outside of *Kleindeutschland* in lower Manhattan, moving uptown (well above Fourteenth Street) or to Brooklyn, in the latter two cases following newly well-to-do middle-class Germans out of the ghetto, rather than remaining to serve the new immigrant working class which stayed behind. Many Lutherans seemed susceptible to this kind of move though their churches displayed all of the various responses to urbanization already noted. The three congregations most closely associated with the development of bi-lingual Lutheranism in New York City indicate two specific responses.[12]

St. Matthews became a "cathedral" church which attracted German-speaking Lutherans not only from Manhattan, but from Brooklyn, Staten Island, and New Jersey. It started life in 1822 on Walker Street, east of Broadway, but moved in 1866 to Broome and Elizabeth Streets—inside Little Germany (in the Fourteenth Ward) just outside of the increasingly German Tenth ward. In this case, the cathedral church was also a "Mother" church spinning off congregations in Little Germany, Brooklyn, Newark, and Hoboken. Its nearest offspring, St. Marks, situated on Sixth Street, was the only Lutheran congregation that was inside of the German ghetto (fig. 3.1).

figure 3.1
Die deutsche evangelisch-lutherische St. Markus-kirche

From its vantage point on the near periphery however, St. Matthews developed a successful ministry to the German community. The community used its facilities to develop its various religious and secular associations, while over time a day-school developed into a full-blown German-language academy.[13]

St. James displayed characteristics of types 1 and 2. It moved several times because of changing neighborhoods, but in the process, and because of its English mission, developed an institutional church program. At its inception in 1827, the congregation moved into the recently vacated Irish Presbyterian Church on Orange Street, between Hester and Grand, in the heavily commercial and industrialized 10th Ward. The undesirable neighborhood led to a rapid loss of membership, and a move first to a temporary home with St. Matthews and then to a second home (in 1844) a block away on Mulberry between Broome and Grand. The Orange Street experience repeated itself however, the rapid change in the lower city not having been foreseen. Though beginning to attract people of means, the congregation still struggled to survive and so decided in 1856 to search for still another site "in a more central and respectable locality." It moved once again to Fifteenth Street near Third Avenue, one block above Little Germany. There it not only continued its English mission to the German community, but helped develop a Swedish congregation, Gustavus Adolphus; in subsequent years it ministered to a variety of other ethnic groups.

Along the way it also developed other congregations, most notably George U. Wenner's Christ Church.[14] Christ Church was a cathedral church in the sense that it, too, developed an urban strategy that proved successful throughout the sixty-six year ministry of Wenner. St. James's support proved crucial to a ministry already underway. While attending Union Theological Seminary from 1866 to 1868 Wenner came into contact with leaders of a Presbyterian Sunday School on Fourteenth Street in the Peterfield section (the "Gas House District") of Little Germany who were then seeking a seminary student to look after the children's attendance, visit their parents and conduct a Sunday evening worship service. Wenner took up the ministry with the help of another student accomplished in German who was to preach. Upon graduation both the Presbyterians and the Episcopal Bishop offered to ordain Wenner to continue the ministry. But at that point Wenner, who was a Pennsylvanian long urged by his mother to enter the Lutheran ministry, approached the newly formed New York Synod of the General Synod. St. James's pastor, A. C. Wedekind proposed Wenner for ordination and the Presbyterian Sunday School soon had a Lutheran pastor. In October of 1868, sixty-five parents organized the Evangelical Lutheran Church of Christ and moved into an English Protestant congregation on Fifth Street. At this point St. James and the General Synod's Board of Home Missions provided crucial financial support. In 1873 the growing congregation moved into a Baptist Church on Sixth Street, and into an Episcopal Church in Stanton Street three years later. Finally, in 1882 the congregation purchased the Episcopal Chapel of St. Georges as its permanent home on Nineteenth Street.[15]

Wenner's particular strategy for survival in Little Germany, which he began to develop under the Presbyterians, was educational. Providing worship services in English and German for the adults whom he evangelized assidously in person and through his German language parish paper *Der Sonntagsgast* ("The Sunday Visitor"), Wenner taught religion in English-speaking classes to the children of German immigrants, depending on the children of recent immigrants to "replenish our classes in religion" decade after decade. He maintained Christ Church into the twentieth century well after migration from Little Germany had caused the demise or removal of most other Lutheran congregations. Of the 10,000 families to whom he ministered in his first sixty years of ministry, there were probably not a dozen descendants in his Sunday School. All had moved. Wenner provided (in recorded ministerial acts) Baptism (7,949), Christian education and catechization (2,140) to three generations of German immigrant families, with many catechumens among the members of an organization of the "Catechumens of Christ Church" residing throughout the metropolitan area. Always adept at making new mission opportunities, Wenner built on his Sunday school experience to persuade the public schools to allow the religious education of students in "off hours," thereby beginning what became the Week Day Religious Education movement in America. Unlike St. Matthews and its preoccupation with maintaining a German-language culture and religion, Wenner's strategy was bi-cultural. Having been raised in an English-speaking family, Wenner learned German after college and seminary to undertake his German language ministry. Besides *Der Sonntagsgast* he wrote a German language column "Germanicus" in the *Lutheran Observer* and otherwise staunchly promoted a bilingual German-American culture in which the German language was preserved alongside English for the sake of both religion and literature. He thus maintained Christ Church in Little Germany while recognizing that in the long term his kind of urban mission strategy was contributing to the growth of a much larger, English-speaking Lutheran Church within the metropolitan New York area.[16] Ever solicitous for the social and material welfare of the immigrant community he served, Wenner could write of "The Great Migration" which caused his own congregation's decline:

> It is not necessary for me to speak of the social and material progress wrought by these changes. They have given New York a chance to breathe. They have given little children a chance to grow. They have supplied the keys for homes to tens of thousands who formerly scarcely knew what it was to have a home.[17]

A contemporary described Wenner as "a veritable Americanization process" by which generation after generation of Germans "came to the East Side, there to be instructed, catechized, and confirmed . . . only to move out into suburban districts as their worldly means permitted them, there to become the very pillars of new Lutheran missions." In later life Wenner developed "a mental obsession" with the process he developed repeatedly recounting before audiences how his people filled the churches in Brooklyn, Jersey City, Westchester, and Long Island.[18]

St. Johns Lutheran Church on Christopher Street to the West of Little Germany was formed in 1855 as a split-off from St. Marks (on 6th Street) led by St. Marks pastor A. H. M. Held. For several decades, and after a difficult start because of the financial crisis of 1857, St. Johns prospered as a cathedral church, drawing large German-speaking crowds from both Greenport, L. I., and Hoboken, New Jersey. However the church was plagued by poor financial management and with the movement of German-Lutherans from Little Germany uptown and to Brooklyn, and with the formation of congregations there and in Hoboken, St. Johns went into a period of decline. It emerged a decade later as an important English-speaking congregation in the rapidly changing urban scene of lower Manhattan.[19] Its history suggests that St. Johns, like St. James, found a changing neighborhood a difficulty as well, but stayed put, developing its own strategies for urban survival. Besides these congregations, key pastors also remained. St. James's pastor A. C. Wedekind resided within *Kleindeutschland's* "best" residential ward (the seventeenth) in the northwest sector of the ghetto, as did George U. Wenner. The Seventeenth Ward was the least industrialized and most spacious part of Little Germany, and included first-class brick and stone houses set back from crowded streets; it also contained the fewest "new immigrants" from Prussia and elsewhere in northern and eastern Germany, and the largest number of older immigrants from the Rhineland.

However most German Churches and their leaders isolated themselves socially as well as physically. They intentionally developed parallel *verein*, organizing a religious subculture in a hostile urban milieu. This beleaguered survivalism profoundly shaped immigrant Lutheranism in greater New York. By far the most common experience of urbanization among immigrant Lutherans was the first response to urbanization—"transplantation" of former lives, values, attitudes, and experiences to a new urban setting under the most favorable circumstances obtainable. While few German Lutheran congregations physically moved uptown or to the suburbs, their parishioners did. The result was a few aging congregations in the vicinity of Little Germany with a mushrooming cluster of communities and new congregations outside the ghetto in Yorkville, Queens, and Brooklyn. To some extent the migration was a sign of upward mobility—up and out of the ghetto. Just as significant was the desire to escape exploitation and harassment by established Americans. A desire to maintain their ethnic-religious identity and the opportunities offered by German-American employers (like Steinway in Long Island City) hastened the exodus. As Manhattan's German population dwindled, Brooklyn's German-speaking population increased between 1860 and 1890, leading to the development of strong German-speaking communities in Yorkville, Williamsburgh, Brooklyn Heights, and East New York.[20] A second ring of communities, this time bi-lingual or English-speaking, but still Lutheran, would subsequently develop in eastern Queens and western Nassau Counties in newly developing suburban areas.

The pattern of extreme isolation in *Kleindeutschland* did not hold everywhere in the Ministerium. In Buffalo, with the second largest urban concentration of Germans and German-speaking Lutherans, the more familiar and common type of transplanted immigrant community and church emerged. This difference would persist into the twentieth century, primarily in terms of church life and sociability.[21] A multitude of voluntary associations (*verein*) appeared in organizing Buffalo's German community on the east end of the city—among them singing societies, physical culture organizations, mutual aid societies, political factions, and churches. These secular, religious, and political associations were not voluntary societies "with narrow, specialized purposes, but corporate moral communities that exacted obligations for good conduct, fellowship, and participation" from their members, each being guided "by their own codes and aspirations."[22] Buffalo's German-speaking churches—Lutheran, Reformed, Evangelical, and Roman Catholic—with their welfare, recreational, and spiritual *verein*, Sunday schools, day schools and orphanages, seminaries and cemeteries, were not peripheral but (in fact) central to the re-creation of a face-to-face German ethnic community.

Still, a strong sense of particularity caused differentiation within the community. Lutheran German-Americans of colonial extraction, plus early nineteenth-century immigrants from Rhineland Germany and France (Alsace and Lorraine), created the first Lutheran congregation in Buffalo, St. Johns (fig. 3.2); by 1860 services in this New York Ministerium congregation were already being conducted in English. Old Lutherans from Prussia formed their own congregations—Holy Trinity (1839) and St. Andrews (1858)—which were affiliated with the Buffalo Synod of Pastor Johannes A. A. Grabau. First Trinity (1839) which formed out of a splinter group of Silesians and Pomeranians following a doctrinal conflict, became a member of the Missouri Synod, as did St. Pauls (1843) and St. Andrews (1858). Eventually German St. Pauls sustained a withdrawal of Reformed members to form St. Stephens United Evangelical Church (1853), leaving behind the nucleus of St. Pauls Lutheran Church.

figure 3.2
Deutsche evangelical-lutherisch St. Johannis-Kirche,
Buffalo, formed February 10, 1833

Unlike St. Pauls and St. Andrews, other Lutheran congregations preferred not to join the Ministerium, nor the Buffalo or Missouri Synods, exercising their American prerogative for an independent congregationalism of a type which was prevalent in all sectors of the German religious community. This Lutheran congregationalism had its parallel among Buffalo Catholics who displayed a decided preference for both local and ethnic autonomy within the Roman Catholic Church, partly because of the Alsatian experience of lay control guaranteed under French law. Grabau's high view of the ministry which developed after his arrival in America was in some measure an antidote to this attitude in Buffalo Synod congregations.[23] Lutheran congregationalism—also expressive, perhaps, of the *verein*-intense nature of German life—would also have a profound influence on both the Missouri Synod and the New York Ministerium.

Despite the mediating influence of these social institutions, immigrant ghetto stress produced social problems and spiritual crises. What occurred in lower Manhattan was simply repeated elsewhere in America (like Buffalo) though in less desperate terms. The General Synod took the measure of the problem in 1864:

> Many of these, spiritually, are in great destitution, and the duty, which the Lutheran Church owes to those of the same household of faith coming from the fatherland, should inspire her members with greater zeal, and with increased efforts to minister to their spiritual necessities.[24]

In New York City these spiritual problems began at the docks and Castle Garden, port of entry for German immigrants. By 1862 the New York and Pennsylvania Ministeria were negotiating to establish a missionary at Castle Garden, an effort supported in particular by the New York City Conference of the Ministerium. Part of the reason for the mission was the feared loss of potential members to other denominations. A concerned General Synod reported two years later that the Methodist Church had 636 traveling ministers in the German immigrant field alone. One of those missionaries had formed the Deutsche Methodisten Kirche on Second Street in Manhattan's Little Germany; two other Methodist missions for German immigrants were organized at Buffalo in 1846 and 1852 (as were two Baptist missions in 1848 and 1859). To offset this advantage, a special edition of the Small Catechism was published with an appendix "exhibiting in the form of questions and answers, the peculiarities of the doctrines of our church, in contrast of other denominations." Its purpose was "to facilitate catechetical instruction, and to counteract all proselyting efforts being put forth by these denominations."[25]

What it meant to be Lutheran in a strange land was not readily apparent to the immigrant. American and European church practices were different. In the states the added dimension of congregational democracy gave rise to a thousand issues, great and small, requiring democratic resolution. Where German particularity had not created distinct congregations it created distinct problems, with conflict and acrimony part of the changing scene. President Henry Pohlman reported in 1861:

> Many of our congregations, as you are aware, are composed of immigrants from various parts of Germany, and have been accustomed to different modes of religious training. It is not therefore surprising that there should be a want of homogeneousness which

> frequently leads to a conscientious difference of opinion and action, producing divisions often fatal to the peace and unity of the church. Several cases of this kind have occurred during the past year. It is not necessary that I should specify them, or give details of the advice I have given to the contending parties under the varying circumstances presented for my consideration. Suffice it to say, that the investigation and settlement of these cases have involved no small amount of labor, and given occasion to the exercise of not a little of the "grace of patience."[26]

The crush of numbers posed its own problems. A Ministerium committee was formed to communicate with churches in Germany regarding those who transferred membership to American congregations. A German secretary was appointed to help expedite the publication of German minutes, and to increase the Ministerium's ability to communicate with its own. Universities throughout Germany were searched for divinity students to finish their education in American seminaries; mission societies were to be appealed to for mission pastors. A German professor was proposed for Hartwick Seminary in 1863 and German universities were again contacted for a suitable candidate. In the meantime the metropolitan New York Conference presented four candidates for the ministry all of whom were from Erlangen University, one of the important centers of confessional Lutheranism in Germany.[27]

After 1860 it become more and more evident with each year that the Ministerium was undergoing radical changes in focus and outlook with the growth of its immigrant population. The demand for change was everywhere—even for more German-speaking pastors to provide spiritual care and attention "to the sick and wounded German soldiers" being brought into New York hospitals from the Civil War battlefields in the South. Though in fact no different than the other needs forcing change upon a struggling Ministerium, this last request represented forces that would cause its rapid transformation, since no American institution could remain untouched by the destabilizing forces unleashed by the American Civil War, and certainly not when accompanied by the changes which immigrant confessionalism was bringing to the New York Church.

THE NATIONAL HOUSE AND CHURCH DIVIDE—1861

Those wounded troops in need of Lutheran pastors had fought valiantly, according to President Henry Pohlman in his 1861 report:

> I glory in the fact that the descendants of Luther's countrymen have borne no mean part in the battle for the Union, the Constitution and the laws. Missouri, if saved at all to the Union, will be saved by her German population; and an eye witness of the rout at Bull's Run

> records the honorable fact "that while he conversed with, or heard the voices of three or four hundred of the flying troops, scattered all along the road, on the night of that disastrous battle, *he did not once hear the German accent*."[28]

If true, Pohlman's remarks identify one of the few bright spots in the first Battle of Manassas (Bull Run). Fort Sumter fell to Confederate hands in April of 1861, and the first pitched battle of massed armies along Bull's small stream at Manassas, in Virginia, the following July proved conclusive for neither side. Close to victory, Federal troops retreated in a rout. The victorious Rebels, as disorganized after victory as before, but now lacking supplies and transportation, could not pursue the advantage. The American Civil War was to prove long, disruptive, and costly to the American nation and its churches.

For Lutherans the unraveling had begun with the fall of Sumter. The General Synod began to experience divisions that had long vexed other Protestant denominations. Within two years Southern Lutherans would "secede" from the northern synods, eventually forming the General Synod of the Evangelical Lutheran Church in the Confederate States in America. The New York Synods had been quick to support the Union after Fort Sumter, the Ministerium urging that "no concession or compromise should be made" until the rebellion of southern states was crushed. Even the pacifist Franckean Synod, long opposed to both slavery and warfare, lent its support to "a war for the maintenance of the American Constitution and the Union," making it clear that this support of a national "act of self defence" was not at variance with its longstanding opposition to offensive wars which it still considered "iniquitous and full of evil."[29] In the face of such opposition, southern Lutheran synods withdrew from the General Synod, beginning with the Virginia Synod in October, 1861. After another summer of devastation in the Old Dominion with pitched battles at Shiloh, Bull Run (a second time), and Antietam, the General Synod (in 1862) went on record condemning the rebellion as "wicked in its inception, unjustifiable in its cause, unnatural in its character, inhuman in its prosecution, oppressive in its aims, and destructive in its results to the highest interests of morality and religion."[30]

By now the profound nature of the conflict had been impressed upon the human mind. What followed were numerous blows to be struck at sedition, slavery, and racism, beginning with President Lincoln's Emancipation Proclamation issued on January 1, 1863. Another summer of numbing warfare followed—Chancellorsville, Gettysburg, Vicksburg, and Chattanooga—with appalling losses. That year America's naive idealism bled to death on a dozen battlefields. This loss of manpower could only be replaced by a military draft. New Yorkers rioted, causing further disorder and bloodshed. Lutherans in the South, now separated by grief as well as conflict, finally came to the point of forming another General Synod in the Confederacy by the summer of 1863.

FRANCKEAN MEMBERSHIP DIVIDES THE GENERAL SYNOD

Whether the accumulated changes caused by German immigration in the New York Ministerium after 1860 would cause a major reorientation, or a division by language into several synods was anyone's guess. What could not be anticipated was how the War and the realignments it caused among Lutherans would bring the New York situation to a head. A group within the Ministerium were concerned about the Franckean Synod's reapplication for General Synod membership in 1862. After years of separation, but following a decade of renewed fraternalism during which the General Synod rescinded its 1839 censure, the Franckeans reapplied for admission. When its own stand against the South, on grounds of rebellion rather than slavery, was taken up by the General Synod itself in 1862, the Franckean Synod thought that "a very marked change had taken place" in the larger body, and decided it was time to explore whether a union was in "the best interests of the cause of Christ."[31]

Sentiment among the other Synods for union with the Franckean Synod was mixed. Hartwick was incensed by the General Synod's recent repeal of the 1839 censure, and by the Franckeans' insulting comment in the midst of the religious revivals of the 1850s, namely that Hartwick was at last moving in the right direction because it seemed "more anxious to cultivate a spirit of prayer, and to stir up revivals of true religion . . ." The Ministerium, meanwhile, established fraternal ties with the Franckeans and began exchanging delegates in 1861, in part because they had offered generous help in raising $10,000 for Hartwick Seminary. Warm, fraternal greetings were exchanged thereafter as when the Ministerium delegate to the 1864 Franckean synod "expressed his pleasure in the privilege of meeting Synod, and a desire for a more fraternal union."[32]

Encouraged, the Franckean Synod applied for membership and its application was taken up for consideration in the 1864 meeting of the General Synod. It was proposed that the outcast Synod should be allowed to join "so soon as they shall give formal expression to their adoption of the Augsburg Confession, as received by the General Synod." The Franckean visitors in attendance indicated they believed that in adopting the General Synod's model constitution for district synods, with its confessional subscription for ordinands, they were "adopting the doctrinal position of the General Synod . . . 'That the fundamental truths of the word of God are taught in a manner substantially correct in the Augsburg Confession.'" Reconsidering its previous recommendation, the General Synod now proposed that the Franckean Synod be admitted "with the understanding that said Synod, at its next meeting, declare, in an official manner, its adoption of the doctrinal articles of the Augsburg Confession, as a substantially correct exhibition of the fundamental doctrines of the Word of God." The majority of the General Synod delegates agreed, including five members of the New York Ministerium, six of seven Hartwick representatives, and two of three New Jersey Synod members. But to the entire Pennsylvania delegation, and to another five members of the New York Ministerium, including its president, Henry Pohlman, this expressed degree of confessional loyalty was insufficient.[33]

The stricter confessionalists in the General Synod were plainly unhappy with the move to admit the anticonfessional Franckeans. Plans by Franckean visitors to attend the General Synod of 1864, in anticipation of their acceptance into General Synod membership, had brought a warning from Charles Porterfield Krauth of the Pennsylvania Ministerium:

> Let there be pure love for each other and just forbearance where there are conscientious differences, but let there be also a deep love for the truth and fraternal plainness of speech. Men cannot build together unless they are agreed as to what shall be built.[34]

When the Pennsylvania Ministerium rejoined the General Synod in 1853, after an absence of twenty years, it did so with the proviso that if the General Synod violated its own constitution and required of the Ministerium any condition of membership or continuance conflicting with "the old and long established faith of the Evangelical Lutheran Church," its delegates would be required to protest against such action and withdraw from synodical sessions. This they did after the vote to accept the Franckean Synod into membership. In a protest before its withdrawal, signed by its ten delegates plus numerous others, the Pennsylvanians charged the General Synod with violating its own constitution by admitting a synod which did not hold to the "fundamental doctrines of the Bible, as taught by our Church" which by universal consent are "expressed in the Augsburg Confession." The Franckean Synod's entire history demonstrated "no relation nor connection whatever with the Augsburg Confession" they asserted, and therefore it is not "a regularly constituted Lutheran Synod."[35]

Originally it was the plan to admit the Franckeans, who had never formally adopted the Augsburg Confession, by way of a compromise statement that it should "give formal expression to their acceptance of the Augsburg Confession" by adopting "the doctrinal articles of the Augsburg Confession as a *substantially* correct exhibition of the fundamental doctrines of the Word of God [emphasis added]." This was to be done at the next session of their synod in 1864, a move the Franckean Synod was now ready to undertake.[36] But near the end of the General Synod's 1864 meeting constitutional changes, some of them confessional, were approved and passed on to the district synods for consideration, including the newly admitted Franckean Synod. Displeased with Franckean confessionalism, it was Henry Pohlman who had proposed a change in the Constitution which revised the confessional basis of the General Synod. The change now identified "the Word of God as contained in the Canonical Scriptures of the Old and New Testaments, as the only infallible rule of faith and practice; and the Augsburg Confession as a correct exhibition of the fundamental doctrines of the Divine Word, and of the faith of our Church founded upon that word." Pohlman's formula would become the confessional basis in the new General Synod Constitution of 1868.[37] Thus as they gathered in 1864 the Franckean Synod was faced with an additional requirement:

> All regularly constituted Lutheran Synods, not now in connection with the General Synod, receiving and holding with the Evangelical Lutheran Church of our fathers the Word of God, as contained in the Canonical Scriptures of the Old and New Testament, as the only infallible rule of faith and practice; and the Augsburg Confession, as a correct exhibition of the fundamental doctrines of the Divine Word, and of the faith of our church founded upon the Word, may, at any time, become associated with the General Synod, by complying with the requisitions of this Constitution.[38]

The Franckean Synod was now faced with outright doctrinal subscription. The New Jersey Synod had done so upon formation in 1861 before this requirement was in place, anticipating the new, more confessional language of the General Synod. Now there was to be complete adherence to the entire Confession as a "correct exhibition" of fundamental doctrines (no qualifying "substantial" was to be allowed). President Marcus W. Empie suggested noncompliance in keeping with the Synod's traditional "gospel basis, according to the true meaning and intent of Lutheranism." He was concerned lest other Protestant denominations become isolated from the Franckean Synod by the "symbolists" who were "putting up partition walls in the house of Lutherans." Having made his point, however, the synod went on to comply with the stricter doctrinal standard and was admitted to the General Synod in 1865.[39]

FORMATION OF AN ENGLISH SYNOD—1865-1867

The split vote within the Ministerium's General Synod delegation over the Franckean admission indicated divided confessional loyalties within the New York body. A substantial portion of the membership were in sympathy with the Franckean position. Where the opposition group stood became evident enough in the Ministerium's 1865 synodical meeting. Submerged differences quickly surfaced when the New York City Conference, newly augmented by its Erlangen-trained pastors, made proposals challenging the English-speaking leadership.

Desperate for German-speaking pastors, they opposed Ministerium restrictions on the ability of licensed candidates to administer the sacraments. To assure an adequate supply of clergy, the Conference insisted it was in "the best interests of the German Lutheran Church" to support the newly formed Philadelphia Seminary rather than the Hartwick Seminary which was then being supported by all three New York synodical bodies. No doubt the Erlangen pastors found attractive the announcement that the Philadelphia Seminary was to be "unreservedly and unalterably based on all the Confessions of the Evangelical Lutheran Church." These same pastors insisted, as well, on an improved version of the German liturgy, which in its present form went back to Kunze and Muhlenberg. Finally they proposed that "in consideration of the equality of rights existing between the German and English languages, some member of Synod who is master of both languages be appointed Vice President."[40] The request was a slap at Pohlman whose bilingual capacities and genuine interest in his younger German colleagues and their churches were managing to keep the bilingual synod intact.

As this last proposal moved toward discussion on the synod floor, "notice was given" that a portion of the English members of Synod would subsequently ask permission to hold a convention, to consider the propriety of withdrawing "from this Ministerium and forming an entirely English Synod." Application for permission was subsequently made at the synod's 8th session, for a "purely English Synod, the reasons for which are too numerous to be mentioned." It was also resolved that the English pastors should withdraw to join the New Jersey Synod, but action was held over until the synod assembly of 1866.[41]

How could such a proposal have appeared so quickly on the Ministerium floor? Fifteen years had dramatically changed the Ministerium's makeup. At least twenty-four German-speaking congregations had been added to its thirty-three largely English-speaking congregations in that time. Another twenty or so German-speaking congregations which were formed on the territory in the same time period remained independent or joined the Missouri Synod. Where there was growth within the Ministerium territory, it was almost entirely German. In the meantime, as we have seen, seven English-speaking or bilingual churches had withdrawn to form the New Jersey Synod. Most growth within English-speaking congregations within New York had occurred recently in the Hartwick and Franckean Synods, then both undergoing another of their periodic revivals. (See Maps 8.1 and 8.2.)

As issues of language and theology combined to expose the considerable differences existing within the Ministerium, the English-speaking majority in the Ministerium came to feel like the vulnerable minority it was fast becoming, and it decided to withdraw. In justifying its position Henry Pohlman (as it was reported)

> alluded to the formation successively of the Hartwick, the Franckean and New Jersey Synods, taking with them from the Ministerium a large number of English members; and how, in consequence, the German brethren in the Ministerium had gradually acquired so large a preponderance in numbers.[42]

President Pohlman insisted the problem was a matter of language—the isolation of a former (English) majority—rather than confessional. That was not quite accurate. The New York Ministerium might have survived as a bilingual Lutheran synod, like the Pennsylvania Ministerium, or the Joint Synod of Ohio, but the confessional differences emerging in the General Synod caused by the 1864 Franckean vote deepened the division between the German and English groups in New York beyond the point of bridging. Pohlman simply could not fathom, let alone acknowledge the depth of these confessional differences. He saw the occasion of the Franckeans' admission to the General Synod as simply another occasion to sow seeds of distrust by troublemakers—"extraordinary efforts . . . to excite the passions and prejudices of our German brethren against the General Synod."[43]

However, the theological differences were real enough. The General Synod had made progress in a confessional direction with its 1864 constitutional amendment requiring district synod subscription to the Augsburg Confession as "a correct exhibition" of fundamental doctrine. But in the context of a changing confessional language, it was a somewhat neutral and detached attitude at best. Portions of the confessions were still suspect or objectionable to General Synod Lutherans, including many in the New York area. At the same meeting in which it had tightened up its confessional language, the General Synod also passed on to district synods for review and implementation a statement regarding the "alleged errors" in the Augsburg Confession. These "errors," which were agitating many churches in the General Synod as supposedly "grave and dangerous," had first been raised in Schmucker's "American Recension of the Augsburg Confession." An abbreviated version of the Recension's list of errors had been published by the Hartwick Synod in 1856. Now an almost identical statement was passed down to all of the synods by the General Synod in 1864, the difference being that the Hartwick statement added a preamble and conclusion which affirmed the essential soundness of the Augsburg Confession, something the Hartwick Synod failed to do.[44]

The two statements indicate that General Synod Lutherans held a bewildering variety of theological attitudes which, for example, confused "transubstantiation," "consubstantiation," and the "real presence," and failed to accept such matters as confession and absolution though both were expressly mentioned in the Small Catechism. Especially upsetting was its continued ambivalence towards a confessional understanding of the sacraments. When at its 1866 convention in Fort Wayne the General Synod reaffirmed the constitutionality of its reception of the Franckean Synod, the Pennsylvania Synod withdrew and began plans to development a more confessionally conservative seminary (already established in 1864 at Philadelphia) and general church body (the General Council). This time the New York Ministerium's six votes were cast in opposition to the General Synod stance, whereas Hartwick's six votes, New Jersey's two, and the Franckean Synod's six votes, were all cast in support.[45] Clearly within a one or two year period a conservative, confessional majority had emerged within the New York Ministerium!

The majority, led by Secretary G. W. Schmucker and German Secretary Reinhold Adelberg of the Ministerium, felt the underlying issue was that most General Synod delegates disliked the doctrinal position of the Pennsylvania Ministerium though it "is that of the Confessions of our Church" and therefore affects "the very faith of the Church itself." They argued, therefore, that because the General Synod violated its own constitution, and had a "tendency . . . to counteract the growth of pure and true Lutheranism in this country," the New York Ministerium should also withdraw from the General Synod to help form a new Council "on the basis of the Unaltered Augsburg Confession" and should therefore appoint delegates for that purpose. The minority report, meanwhile, made Pohlman's point all over again, namely that with its revised Constitution the General Synod "now stands on Doctrinal points and the Augsburg Confession on the same basis as our own Ministerium."[46] Given so momentous a proposal, the majority report was held over for the next meeting of synod (1867), and the congregations consulted. Meanwhile, "no action" was taken on the 1865 request of a minority to form an English Synod.

THE STEIMLE SYNOD FORMS—1866

While English-speaking Lutherans awaited the outcome of these important events, a small and highly orthodox, neo-Lutheran clique of German-speaking Lutherans could wait no longer. In March of 1866 three pastors of the Ministerium met together at Zion German Church in Brooklyn with a non-ordained professor of archaeology, Gustav Seyffarth, Ph.D., of Immanuel German Church in Yorkville, and a ministerial candidate, Louis F. T. Halfmann, to organize a new synod. Their leader was Zion's pastor, Frederick William Tobias Steimle; the other clergy were the brothers Johann F. Christian Heinnecke of St. Peters German Church, Manhattan, and George Henry Heinnecke of St. Pauls German Church, Brooklyn.[47]

Steimle was born in Wurttemberg, in Germany, and was trained at the Missionary Institute in Basle, Switzerland. He was ordained at Lorrach, in Baden, in 1851, and a year later arrived in New York where he was received into the Ministerium by its examining committee "with great pleasure." Steimle quickly became the protégé of the conservative German pastor Carl Stohlmann of St. Matthews, Manhattan, and part of the group of signers commending the *Lutherische Herald* to "inform our people respecting the confessions of our Church."[48] He served his first pastorate at Ellenville, New York, but was called within a half year as Stohlmann's assistant. Next he was called to St. Pauls German Church, Williamsburgh in 1855, but left within three months when a failed agreement by the congregation to ratify a new and more conservative constitution led him to resign. He was then called to Zion where he served until his death in 1880. His Zion charge adopted a new and confessionally advanced form of constitution with a very conservative Lutheran confessional basis:

> The congregation accepts all the canonical books of the Old and New Testaments as the true Word of God, and also all the confessional writings of the Evangelical Lutheran Church as contained in the Book of Concord of 1580 because they truly set forth and harmonize with the teachings of the Holy Scripture.[49]

From that point Steimle seems to have been on a collision course with the Ministerium, his strict confessionalism and high sense of conscience preventing him from serving congregations which compromised his high confessional standards.

By the time the Ministerium met in 1866, the three pastors had already withdrawn, forming "Die Deutsche Evangelishe Lutherische Synode vom Staate N. Y. und adren Staaten" because of the Ministerium's doctrinal laxness. The Ministerium's insistence that Halfmann, a ministerial candidate supported by the three pastors, continue his theological studies at a seminary for one year instead of proceeding to ordination as the four wished, provoked the move to form a new synod.

Whether there were doctrinal issues involved in the recommendation is not known. Subsequently the new synod justified its separation, insisting that its members had for years felt the need to establish a "pure, German Synod in the eastern states, especially in the state of New York, built on a true and full confessional basis." They wanted to "help the Lutheran Church rise again to propagate the pure doctrine of the divine Word, and to further the eternal salvation of souls, with this motto: 'One confession, one church, one school!' "For this "grievous sin of schism" they were roundly condemned by the Ministerium, and stricken from the rolls in censure. They received an equally severe censure from St. Matthews Lutheran Church and Dr. Carl Stohlmann. Both Steimle and Johann F. Christian Hennicke had served St. Matthews as Stohlmann's assistants. More galling perhaps, Hennicke had started St. Peters Lutheran Church with a gift of $2000 from St. Matthews which he took with him into the Steimle Synod. In anger, the mother church insisted that the sum be returned.[50]

Like the constitution of Zion Lutheran, the new Synod's constitution was equally conservative, and its confessional basis was to be adhered to "Mit Herz und Mund" (with heart and mouth) by every ordained member. The Constitution's introductory "Sendschreiben" (Open Letter), in challenging present day apostasy from the foundational beliefs of the Fathers, affirmed the *Book of Concord* as the church's fundamental confession "mit welchen die lutherischne kirche darim steht und fallt." Every member was required to "separate himself from all churches and synods, as well as from all tract, mission, and other societies which do not accept the confessional basis mentioned in Article 2" of the constitution. It was Steimle's task, as president, to "have oversight of the doctrine, practice, and various administrative functions of the officers, pastors, and teachers belonging to the Synod." Even in its purpose, the synod was considered primarily from a doctrinal point of view. Its "principal purpose" according to the constitution was "to strengthen the Church in faith and confession through God's Word," therefore "only such subjects are to be discussed . . .which relate to these important matters."[51]

The doctrinal discussions were meant to take place in the annual meetings of the synod, but New York City area pastors also joined them for weekly discussions. The agenda indicates a preoccupation with restoring a purity that it was believed would renew the church. Typically, in a three-day meeting of the synod in October of 1866, the following theses were debated:[52]

I. Theses on Luther
    A. What did Luther accomplish?
    B. Why is Luther's *work* (?) God's *work*?
    C. What follows from this?
II. Decline of the Lutheran Church.
    A. What is the decline?
    B. Reasons for the decline?
III.[Concerning Rationalism, Unionism, and Methodism]
    A. What are the rationalistic manifestations of a synod?
    B. Unionism.
    C. Methodism.
    [D.] How can this be corrected?
IV. Characteristics of True Lutheran synods.
V. Have we a true Lutheran synod?

More practical questions were also discussed. They suggest why it was that creating doctrinally pure churches among German immigrants in New York environment was no easy task.[53]

1. How must a good Lutheran preacher be equipped in order to perform his office honestly in this evil day?
2. How must a good Lutheran church member be equipped in his church, domestic, and civil life?
3. How is the Lutheran service of the congregation to be ordered,

and how is it that the week day and evening services are not better attended?
4. Why is so little done for missions in our congregations?
5. Why do so many congregations tire of their preachers so soon and why do so many preachers apply so often for other places?
6. Why do dissensions and parties arise in the congregations so easily.
7. Why do so many people have the official acts of the Church performed not in the church but rather in the home?
8. Why do so many German Lutheran parents send their children to other Sunday Schools?

Of course the last answer to be expected to such questions was that strictness and purity placed too heavy a burden on the synod's pastors, was a source of dissension in the congregations, and set up a standard of membership which immigrants could not meet. Another such discussion suggests the leadership yearned for a mythical member known as the "Upright Lutheran," as in the thesis debated: "How shall an upright Lutheran conduct himself in church, domestic, and civic relations ?" "Upright Lutheran" to the Steimle men meant a "*sincere* Lutheran who wishes to be faithful to the Confessions in word and deed."[54]

FORMATION OF THE GENERAL COUNCIL—1867

While the Steimle Synod was moving off in a sectarian confessional direction, the more churchly elements in the Ministerium were becoming involved in the efforts to establish a new general synod upon a stronger confessional basis. Pohlman, Schmucker and Adelberg were to attend a special meeting at Reading, Pennsylvania, December 12-14, 1866, to lay plans for the General Council. There the group was addressed by Charles Porterfield Krauth. His fundamental concern as expressed to the delegates was that "the acceptance of doctrines and the avowal of them without equivocation or mental reservation make, mark, and identify that Church which alone in the true, original, historical, and honest sense is the Evangelical Lutheran Church."[55] He was asking for a level of spiritual and intellectual integrity not unlike the Steimle call for confessional subscription "Mit Herz und Mund."

With division in the air, the atmosphere was tense at the Ministerium meeting in 1867. The Ministerium had subdivided once since it's last meeting, and was in danger of doing so again. The delegates met in Reinhold Adelberg's Second German Evangelical Lutheran Church in Albany—a congregation formed by a fraternal division within Pohlman's own recently renamed "First Lutheran"—where the body was addressed by President Pohlman himself. It was clear to all that his long, distinguished, and influential Ministerium career was now in great jeopardy.

Born in 1800 of German parents, raised in Albany's Ebenezer

Lutheran Church, Hartwick's first graduate, ordained by Henry Frederick Quitman together with George Miller, Pohlman had served parishes at Saddle River, Ramapo, and in Hunterdon County, New Jersey before being called back to Ebenezer, Albany, to succeed his pastor F. G. Mayer. Pohlman was active in both the Ministerium, where he presided for twenty-one years, and in the General Synod whose presidency he held three times. Those closest to him recognized that this accomplished leader was also noticeably ambitious. Most simply recognized Pohlman as a natural leader known for his wit, repartee, wisdom, common sense, and good judgment, qualities which he displayed from the beginning of his synodical career. Colleague P. A. Strobel observed that as a "presiding officer of a deliberative body he had few equals. Prompt, decided, familiar with parliamentary rulings, he was always clear and courteous." A. C. Wedekind said of Pohlman whom he observed presiding over the 1845 session of the General Synod that "his commanding presence—his magnificent voice—his perfect familiarity with parliamentary law—his quick and accurate decisions of all questions submitted to his ruling" made him especially attractive to young pastors like himself. Indeed, Pohlman was known for his aid to both young and new pastors and congregations, finding them positions and helping congregations in difficulty. At the beginning of German immigration only one Ministerium congregation was German-speaking; by the middle 1860s two-thirds were, and many had been helped along the way by the supportive Pohlman. Doing so as one admirer observed of Pohlman "required great tact and mutual forbearance to secure the harmonious action of these elements."[56]

Now his tact and forbearance had reached their limits. His ambition as a leading General Synod advocate was being thwarted. It would probably be his last meeting, or so Pohlman announced rather dramatically at the outset of the Ministerium gathering, for he was approaching the end of his career, and was tired of the many disputes and divisions occurring in the Ministerium, a situation which could only worsen with the impending proposal for division held over from last year. He had served in the office of president for the preceding twenty-one years, a period of unprecedented growth in the Ministerium, he observed. In that time sixty-one candidates had been licensed to preach; forty-four were ordained to the Lutheran ministry; and sixty-two were installed in congregations. Moreover, the cornerstones of thirty churches had been laid, and forty-four church buildings had been erected for worship. This "desirable growth and efficiency" Pohlman attributed to the "union of the English and German element in our ecclesiastical councils." "But if I read 'the sign of the times' aright" he continued, "this happy union is now greatly imperiled," and it depends "upon the action which shall be taken at our present Synod whether we shall continue to press onward in the good old way." He was referring to the present, stated synodical understanding of the Augsburg Confession "as a correct exhibition of the fundamental doctrines of the Divine Word, and of the faith of our church founded upon that word."[57]

As in the previous year, the president's report was tabled and the preceding year's resolution for Ministerium withdrawal from the General Synod was debated. The congregations reported twenty-six to twelve (26 to 12) in favor of withdrawal. Five congregations took no action. Immediately a vote was taken to dissolve "the connection of this Ministerium with the General Synod." It passed fifty to twenty-eight (50 to 28). Next Pastors Schmucker and Adelberg, noting that President Pohlman differed with them about the nature of the Reading meeting and the New York Ministerium's responsibilities, delivered a majority report which resolved that the Ministerium adopt the General Council's proposed constitution and elect delegates to a constituting convention.

Before a vote could be taken, a synod minority, in support of the General Synod, reissued its two-year-old request to withdraw to form a new Synod. English-speaking, General Synod supporters, were fraternally dismissed and withdrew to Pohlman's historic First Lutheran Church, the first Lutheran church in the New York area, and site of the Ministerium's organization eighty-one years before. There they formed yet another synod of New York area Lutherans, the Evangelical Lutheran Synod of New York. Doing things decently and in order, a fraternal delegate from the new synod appeared two sessions later and was given seat and voice by the still sitting Ministerium. At the same time President Pohlman asked to withdraw as well, citing the growth of the German contingent in the Ministerium and the periodic hiving off of English-speaking Lutherans into the Hartwick, Franckean, and New Jersey s. It was his sad conviction that with the Ministerium's withdrawal from the General Synod he could no longer remain in connection. His ordination mate, Hartwick Seminary's venerable president and professor, George Miller, asked for dismission on similar grounds, adding "he could not conscientiously consent to put a yoke on his neck" by remaining in a General Council organization. When appeals to remain failed, dismissals were granted both leaders with resolutions of thanks and gratitude "as Fathers of this Ministerium" that "we will continue to honor and love." Pohlman, in particular, was thanked for his twenty-one years service as a president who "presided over our sessions with great ability, and to the perfect satisfaction of all the members, who by his impartiality and affectionate regard for the opinions and feelings of all has contributed immeasurably to the peace and harmony which have marked our meetings." His vacant chair was filled by Adelberg with the unanimous consent of the remaining delegates. Having dismissed congregations wishing to join the new synod, the Ministerium finally adopted the proposals to form and join a General Council.[58]

OLD MINISTERIUM AND NEW

The division was complete, the house divided, the union of English and Germans dissolved. Where there had been one Ministerium, there were now two synodical organizations. Which was the true Ministerium carrying on the traditions of New York Lutheranism? According to the withdrawing delegates, the new New York Synod was "in reality, the old New York Ministerium under another name." Now it remained for the congregations in the state to decide whether or not they would join the New York Synod "in perpetuating the *real* New York Ministerium."[59]

From the minority's point of view, the differences concerned not so much doctrine as doctrinal subscription and the onerous implications which enforced subscription had always had for American Lutherans, especially for those in the New York Ministerium. At issue was not only the correct posture in relation to the Augsburg Confession, but also the deeply felt sense of freedom of conscience which American Lutheranism associated with the Reformation. In the new Synod's "Historical Statement" on the separation which it addressed to New York Lutheran congregations, this position was made abundantly clear. Blame for the division was laid at the feet of a few English-speaking confessionalists who used "our German brethren"

> to lord it over the consciences of their American brethren, and over the heritage of God in our Church which they shared with them in this land; and forgetful of the past, and reckless of the future, have sought to deprive them of their church lineage and birthright, equal with their own, and of the very freedom which Luther achieved in the Reformation, and with which Christ has made his people free.[60]

Henceforth, two different understandings of the Reformation would find expression among New York Lutherans. There was the position of the old New York Ministerium/new New York Synod, held in common with the General Synod, which

> receives and holds, with the Evangelical Lutheran Church of our fathers, the word of God contained in the canonical Scripture of the Old and New Testaments, as the only rule of faith and practice, and the Augsburg Confession as a correct exhibit of the fundamental doctrines of the Divine Word, and of the faith of our Church founded upon that Word.[61]

The other, the confessional position of the New York Ministerium remnant and new General Council, embraced not only the Augsburg Confession "but all the Symbolical Books, including the Apology to the Confession, the Smalcald Articles, the two Catechisms of Luther, and the Form[sic] of Concord." Moreover these confessions (to quote the General Council)

> must be accepted in every statement of doctrine in their own true, original and only sense. Those who set them forth and subscribe them, must not only agree to use the same words, but must use and understand those words in one and the same sense.[62]

Not since the Synodical Assembly dominated by the orthodoxy of founder William Berkenmeyer had such a rigorous subscription been imposed upon New York Lutherans. For more than a century the freer religious outlook of American Lutheranism had prevailed. Here, in the New York Synod's own words, was an attempt "to introduce into our Church" a "rigorous confessional system which our fathers were unwilling to endure, and which is unsuited to the age in which we live, to the genius of American institutions, and to the Protestant character of our Church."[63]

For English-speaking Lutherans of American descent the rigorous confessionalism of German-speaking immigrants was nothing but

> a retrograde movement towards the darkness of a darker age, assuming, in direct conflict with the spirit and principles upon which our Church was founded in the Reformation, that all Christian doctrine received its perfect expression in the Form of Concord, nearly three hundred years ago.[64]

Perhaps the American contempt for the immigrant newcomer colored English-speaking Lutherans' regard for immigrant confessionalism. Their theological differences with the newcomers were too easily dismissed, however. These were not simply "extraordinary measures" brought into Ministerium councils "by our German brethren." While Germans took only one side in the dispute, English-speaking Lutherans were to be found on both sides. Some remained with a Ministerium—still a bilingual body—which published its 1867 deliberations on the schism in both English and German! What the New York Synod could not admit may well have been closer to the truth, namely that the General Council's theological position had an appealing explanative power which many Lutherans, English-speaking as well as German-speaking, found compelling because it was more authentic to their understanding of the Christian faith. With Charles Porterfield Krauth they were willing to confess that "I am First a Lutheran, Then an American."

NOTES

1 *Minutes of the Convention . . . which resulted in the formation of the Evangelical Lutheran Synod of N. Jersey* (Easton, Pa., 1861), 6.

2 Ibid., 7.

3 New Jersey Synod , *Minutes* (1861), 2.

4 Ibid. (1861), 2; (1867), 6-7.

5 Albert Fein,"Centennial Years, 1850 to 1880," in Milton Klein, *New York:*

The Centennial Years 1676-1976 (Port Washington, NY: Kennikat Press, 1976), 75-95.

6 Stanley Nadel, *Little Germany. Ethnicity, Religion, and Class in New York City, 1845-80* (Urbana: University of Illinois Press, 1990), 1, 20-22, 29-32, 43-44, 51. Laurence Admiral Glasco, "Ethnicity and Social Structure: Irish, Germans and Native-Born of Buffalo, N.Y., 1850-1860," (Ph. D. diss., State University of New York at Buffalo, 1973), 166-69, provides statistics on relative birthrates among immigrants and native born Americans.

7 Klein, *New York: The Centennial Years,* 75-95.

8 The New Yorker Staats-Zeitung estimated in 1860 that fewer than one in five (20 percent) Kleindeutschlanders were regular church attenders. One-third of that number (the Lutheran percentage of the total German population) would be 6.6 percent. Other figures indicate even less religious involvement. A recent history of Little Germany indicates an active Protestant population of 7.5 percent, with Lutherans constituting just over 6 percent of the total population. Plans to establish a German Protestant newspaper led to estimates of 8000 potential subscribers in a population of 85,000 (9.4 percent). Using the same ratio just reported this would be an average of 7.5 % Lutherans. Nadel, *Little Germany,* 91, 95.

9 See Chapter 2, Table 2:2.

10 Ibid., 91-103.

11 Jacob H. Dorn, "Religion and the City," *The Urban Experience. Themes in American History*, ed. Raymond A. and James F. Richardson Mohl (Belmont, California: Wadsworth Publishing Company, 1973), 152-55.

12 See Chapter 1 for a discussion of these developments. The following analysis is based, in part, on that summary.

13 Karl Kretzmann, *The Oldest Lutheran Church in America. A Brief Chronicle of Events in the History of the Evangelical Lutheran Church of Saint Matthew in the City of New York, 1664-1914* (New York City: privately published, 1914), 30-38; Nadel, *Little Germany*, 30-31.

14 A. C. Wedekind, *Jubilee of the English Lutheran Church of St. James in New York City* (New York: Robers & Sherwood, 1877), 24-35; *Seventy-fifth Anniversary 1865-1940. The Church of Gustavus Adolphus, New York City, N.Y.* (New York: 1940), 21-26.

15 *Encyclopedia of the Lutheran Church,* III (Minneapolis: Augsburg Publish House, 1965), 2469. George U. Wenner, *Sixty Years in One Pulpit* (New York: The Petersfield Press, 1928), in Unpaginated. MNYS, SP 1.

16 Ibid. Frederick H. Knubel, Remarks "Read at memorial service at Concordia, December 17, 1934." MNYS, SP 1, "George U. Wenner." George U. Wenner, *The Lutherans of New York* (New York: The Petersfield Press, 1918), 86-88.

17 Wenner, *Sixty Years in One Pulpit,* Unpaginated.

18 Frederick H. Knubel, Remarks, "Read at memorial service at Concordia, December 17, 1934." MNYS, SP 1, "George U. Wenner."

19 John J. Young, *This History of St. John's Evangelical Lutheran Church 79-83 Christopher St., New York City from 1855-1905* (New York: 1905), 9-39.

20 Nadel, *Little Germany*, 91-103, 29-36, 161; also Table 2, p. 38, and Appendix B, Tables 1-3; Map 2, 30-31. Clergy addresses can be found in the annual Minutes of the New York Ministerium. James Sigurd Lapham,

"The German-Americans of New York City 1860-1890" (Ph. D. diss., St. John's University, 1977), 23-5. Hugo W. Hoffmann, *The History of St. Paul's Evangelical Lutheran Church, Brooklyn, N.Y., from 1853-1903* (Mt. Vernon: Wartburg Printing House, 1903), 21, 34, 52-3, 63.

21 See Samuel Trexler, *Crusaders of the Twentieth Century. A Lutheran Story in the Empire State* (New York: The Macmillan Company, 1927), 62-67. "I never failed to be impressed with the contrast between the church life of Buffalo and that of New York City. Buffalo was essentially a city of homes. This in turn created the atmosphere which was most favorable to a strong church life . . . . My pastorate in Redeemer Church was enriched by my relations throughout the city. I experienced a contrast here as over against the life in the metropolis. In Buffalo one has increased opportunities for friendships, and one meets friends at every turn" (64, 67).

22 David A. Gerber, *The Making of an American Pluralism. Buffalo, New York, 1825-60* (Chicago: University of Illinois Press, 1989), 167. Ibid., 190, 194.

23 Ibid., 194-5.

24 New York Ministerium, *Minutes* (1864), 42.

25 Ibid. (1862) ,43; (1865), 31. New York Ministerium, *Minutes* (1864), 42. Nadel, *Little Germany,* 31. Gerber, *Making of an American Pluralism*, 195. New York Ministerium, *Minutes* (1862), 50.

26 Ibid. (1861), 59.

27 Ibid. (1862), 36, 43; (1865), 31; (1863), 37; (1864), 11.

28 Ibid. (1861), 65.

29 Ibid. (1861), 42; Franckean Synod, *Journal* (1861), 19-20.

30 Virginia Synod, *Minutes* (1861), 10. General Synod, *Minutes* (1862), 30.

31 Franckean Synod, *Journal* (1857), 7, 24, 30-31; (1862), 7-8.

32 Hartwick Synod, *Minutes* (1857), 26; Franckean Synod, Journal (1856), 24-5; New York Ministerium, *Minutes* (1861), 34, 49; Franckean Synod, *Journal* (1864), 9.

33 Ibid. (1864), 12, 17, 18.

34 Krauth's warning appeared in the *Lutheran and Missionary* of May 5, 1864; the quotation is to be found in General Council, *Documentary History of the Evangelical Lutheran Ministerium of Pennsylvania and Adjacent States* (Philadelphia: General Council Board of Publication, 1898), 71-72.

35 Ibid., 67. General Synod, *Minutes* (1864), 23-24.

36 Ibid. (1864), 18.

37 General Synod, *Minutes* (1864), 40. James W. Richard, "The Confessional History of the General Synod," *The Lutheran Quarterly* XXV (Oct., 1895): 471; *Memorial of the Rev. Henry N. Pohlman, D. D.* (Albany: J. Munsell, 1875), 36.

38 General Synod, *Minutes* (1864), 39; Franckean Synod, *Journal* (1864), 20-21.

39 Ibid. (1865), 8-9; (1866), 27. General Synod, *Minutes* (1866), 4-5, 17.

40 *Minutes* (1865), 30-31. Theodore G. Tappert, *History of the Lutheran Theological Seminary at Philadelphia, 1864-1964* (Philadelphia: Lutheran Theological Seminary, 1964), 30.

41 Ibid. (1865), 33.

42 New York Synod, *Minutes* (1867), 10.

43 "Historical Statement," in New York Synod *Minutes* (1867), 4.

44 General Synod, *Minutes* (1864), 40.

45 See Pennsylvania Ministerium, *Minutes* (1866), appendix 9-18; *Documentary History,* 105-117.

46 Ibid. (1866), 35-6, 37.

47 German New York Synod, *Minutes,* 1:1.

48 Ibid. (1851), 27-8, 34.

49 E. C. J. Kraeling, *Unser Zion, Die Geschichte der Zion's Gemeinde,* trans. T. G. Tappert (Brooklyn, NY), 18.

50 *Lutheran Cyclopedia* (1899), 445; (1954), 972. Steimle Protocol; *Minutes* (1865), 10, 24, 48-9; (1866) 39, 60, 51. Edward F. Moldenke, *Geschichte der St. Petri Gemeinde* (New York, 1887), 140.

51 German New York Synod, "Protokoll Der Deutschen Evangelisch-Lutherischen Synode Vom Staate New-York und Andern Staaten," transcribed by Ruth Krulish, (Metro Synod Archives,Wagner College, Staten Island, New York, 1956), p. 1. Article 3, Section 2; Article 5, section 1. Steimle Protocol, Tappert trans.

52 Steimle Synod, *Minutes* (1866), 43-8, 51-60.

53 Ibid. (1869), 2:41.

54 Ibid.

55 Krauth quoted in E. Clifford Nelson, ed. *The Lutherans in North America* (Philadelphia, 1975), 234.

56 *Memorial of the Rev. Henry N. Pohlman,* 7-43, 22, 45, 35, 15.

57 New York Ministerium, *Minutes* (1867), 7-17, 9.

58 Ibid., 25, 27; (1867), 10, 29, 28-31.

59 New York Synod, *Minutes* (1867), 16.

60 Ibid., 5.

61 Ibid., 15.

62 Ibid., 5.

63 Ibid., 15.

64 Ibid.

4
CONCORDIA
Forming the General Council, 1867-1876

Even as the New York Ministerium broke apart in 1867, bringing disorder to itself and to the General Synod, a unified Pennsylvania Ministerium withdrew, forming a new general Lutheran body. The opportunity was significant. For the first time conservative Lutheran confessionalism had the opportunity to create a confessional church *de novo*. With division imminent in the General Synod over Franckean Synod membership, those Lutherans rejecting Franckean pietism as genuinely Lutheran could redefine their denomination in language reserved for this historic moment by the Book of Concord!

"THE MAINTENANCE OF UNITY IN THE TRUE FAITH OF THE GOSPEL"

They hoped to assure "the maintenance of unity in the true faith of the Gospel," with a new council for Lutheran unity which would (it was hoped) transcend denominational distinctiveness. Instead, they fostered a major confessional division unwittingly generated by four points of denominational controversy over altar and pulpit fellowship. Within the New York Ministerium the (so-called) language of "unity" and "true faith" encouraged a radical confessionalism which was anything but unifying. Nevertheless, this new confessional approach to the Christian faith as an expression of the one, holy, catholic, and apostolic church, was established for the first time among Lutheran congregations in the northeast. Eventually it would reshape northeast Lutheranism into a more confessionally unified expression of Christianity.

A GENERAL COUNCIL PLANNED—READING, PA., 1866

By August 10, 1866, five pastors from the Pennsylvania Ministerium had completed a Fraternal Address to Lutherans interested in creating a new body. The group included Charles Porterfield Krauth, theology professor at the new Philadelphia Seminary, and Pastor G. F. Krotel (the committee's chair) who would shortly move to Holy Trinity Lutheran Church, in New York City. Krauth was the most important spokesman of the new confessionalism. Long an advocate of a stronger confessional position within the General Synod, he had until recently put the best construction on that body's confessional outlook, even defining S. S. Schmucker against charges of unsound doctrine. By 1865, however, he recanted his former moderation in favor of a belief in the necessary agreement over confessional fundamentals.[1]

The manifesto—for such it was—began with an indictment of General Synod Lutheranism. It called for a new "general organization, first and supremely for the maintenance of unity in the true faith of the Gospel and in the uncorrupted Sacraments, as the Word of God teaches and our Church confesses them." The General Synod no longer represented such an entity, embracing (as it did) less than "half the membership of the Lutheran Church," while excluding precisely those synods "which are most thoroughly consistent with the faith of the Church." Its member synods, to the contrary, were "in undisguised or covert warfare with the Confession of our Church." Needed, then, was an organization dedicated to the "pure Gospel and its Sacraments, the preservation and extension of which can alone give to Synods a true value." Considering American Lutheranism's infatuation with Christian liberty and freedom of religion to the neglect of their confessional origins, what the church now needed was "an organization in which Christian liberty shall wisely work under the law of love and in the grace and beauty of Divine order, in which shall be unmistakably acknowledged the common faith once delivered to the saints." Beyond these extraordinary reasons for forming a new synod, other needs demanded a General Council—home and foreign missions; Christian education in congregations, colleges and seminaries; social welfare institutions; and, religious publications.[2]

Of the five New York area synods—the Ministerium, and the Franckean, German New York (Steimle), Hartwick, and New Jersey Synods (the New York Synod had not yet officially been formed)—only the Ministerium received a copy of this invitation. The Steimle group existed beyond the pale while the other three, given their General Synod orientation, were not approached to help reform Lutheranism in America. The New York Ministerium thus joined a select group of twelve other synods at Reading, Pennsylvania, on December 11, 1866, for the General Council's organizational meeting. Besides the New York and the Pennsylvania Ministeria, the group included the English Synod of Ohio, the Pittsburgh Synod, the Minnesota Synod, the Joint Synod of Ohio, the English District Synod of Ohio, the Synod of Wisconsin, the Michigan Synod, the German Iowa Synod, the Norwegian

Synod, the Missouri Synod, and also the Evangelical Lutheran Synod of Canada.[3]

"FUNDAMENTAL PRINCIPLES OF FAITH"

Charles Porterfield Krauth presented nine "Fundamental Principles of Faith and Church Polity" for the delegates' consideration upon gathering. Now that delegates had been appointed to consider superseding the General Synod with a new organization, the "Preamble" to the Fundamentals suggested other reasons for forming a General Council beyond the failures of the General Synod. The danger was great that "the genuinely Lutheran elements" in the American Church "may become gradually alienated" and lost in "a vast and ever-widening territory," with a "ceaseless tide of immigration," "the diversity of surrounding usages and of religious life," and "various nationalities and tongues." All of these forces—immigration, religious pluralism, and ethnic diversity—would prevail over confessional Lutheranism given the crying need for pastors and the church's "imperfect provision" for such urgent wants. The sad result would be "that our Church, which alone in the history of Protestantism has maintained a genuine catholicity and unity, should drift into the sectarianism and separatism which characterize and curse our land." A plurality of centrifugal forces in America would thus destroy the confessional center of the Lutheran faith, namely its catholic unity. Comprehending diversity in a spirit of toleration was the General Synod's strategy for survival. A theologically coherent unity seemed a better strategy to the General Council.

THE NINE THESES

The nine theses which followed, were composed by Krauth for the occasion. They were intended to provide a sure foundation for faith and doctrine in an American denominational setting. From beginning to end the fundamental principles reflected the confessional heritage of Lutheranism, understood in the context of an American denomination. The first principle, for example, insisted that there must be and abide through all time one holy Christian Church, which is the assembly of all believers, among whom the gospel is purely preached, and the Holy Sacraments are administered, as the Gospel demands.[4]

This *raison d'être* for a General Council of confessional synods closely paraphrased Article VII of the unaltered Augsburg Confession: "Our churches also teach that one holy church is to continue forever. The church is the assembly of saints in which the Gospel is taught purely and the sacraments are administered rightly."[5]

As Thesis 3 expressed the nature of the "one holy church," it existed in two ways. First as a "generic Unity of the Christian Church in the general Creeds." This position was first articulated among Lutherans in Article I of the unaltered Augsburg Confession and subsequently affirmed in the Book of Concord (1580), which published "Three Chief Symbols" of catholic Christianity—"The Apostles' Creed," "The Nicene Creed," and "The Athanasian Creed"—as the prime confessional expression of generic unity.[6]

As for the General Council's *raison d'être* Christian unity was also understood as "the specific Unity of pure parts of the Christian Church in their specific Creeds." Thus the creation of a confessionally pure Lutheran body, organized on the unified basis of its own confessional tradition, was to be viewed not as a narrow-minded Protestant denomination, or as a schismatic Lutheran body, but as a specific testimony to the catholic unity of the Christian Church. Henceforth catholicity and denominationalism were to be at odds in General Council Lutheranism. Thesis 5 defined this Unity of the Evangelical Lutheran Church, as a portion of the holy Christian Church, depended upon her abiding in one and the same faith, in confessing which she obtained her distinctive being and name, her political recognition, and her history. Theses 7 and 8, meanwhile, spelled out the content of that "one and the same faith": sincerely held and truthfully confessed "doctrines of the Unaltered Augsburg confession"[7] acknowledged as being "in conformity with the pure truth of which God's word is the only rule."[8] Thesis 9 incorporated the rest of the confessional canon from the Book of Concord into the Council's confessional viewpoint "inasmuch as they set forth none other than its system of doctrine, and articles of faith, are of necessity pure and scriptural."[9]

"Specific unity" (then) was based on doctrinal adherence to the "unaltered Augsburg Confession" with its emphasis upon "justification" as the essence of Lutheran doctrine. It specifically affirmed what the General Synod tradition had always been in danger of denying—the full and distinctive theology of Article IV of the unaltered Augsburg Confession.[10] The General Council position differed from that of the Steimle Synod, which adhered to "the canonical books of the Old and New Testament" and "all the confessional writings of the Evangelical Lutheran Church as contained in the Book of Concord." It would also differ from the (soon to be formed) Synodical Conference, a conservative body organized in opposition to the confessionalism of the General Council. For the Steimle Synod and the Synodical Conference, sixteenth-century normative solutions to post-Reformation theological controversies were still considered genuinely Lutheran.

KEY ARTICLES OF THE AUGSBURG CONFESSION

A closer look at this and other key articles of the Augsburg Confession will make the nature of General Council Lutheranism somewhat clearer. The first three Articles of the Confession identified the ecumenical and catholic faith professed by those reformers who stood before Emperor Charles V at the Diet of Augsburg in 1530. No mere bow to tradition for the sake of appearances, this starting point of Lutheran confessionalism reemphasized the catholic substance of the Christian faith in the western (Latin-speaking) Church. The God confessed in Article I was the triune God of the Nicene Creed. The emphasis upon original sin in Article II placed the Lutheran confessional stance on sin and salvation squarely within the classical theological tradition first articulated in the western Church by St. Augustine. Article III, on the Son of God, both confessed faith in the Christ of the Apostle's and Nicene Creeds, and the Formula of Chalcedon, and reaffirmed the medieval understanding of God's plan for salvation. Christ's death was considered an atoning sacrifice for a sin both original and actual, at once a propitiation of God's wrath and a reconciliation of the Father with his children. This theological perspective, though thoroughly orthodox, could be a sticking point for sectarian Lutherans, as it was (for example) with the Steimle Synod in its reunion negotiations with the New York Ministerium. For while the Ministerium professed it to be no Lutheran peculiarity, but the substance of the catholic faith, the Steimle men would deny its catholic character in the desire to be peculiarly Lutheran.[11]

Article Four (in the German) of the Augsburg Confession spelled out what Krauth and the General Council identified as the "specific Unity" of a truly confessional Lutheran church:

> It is also taught among us that we cannot obtain forgiveness of sin and righteousness before God by our own merits, works, or satisfactions, but that we receive forgiveness of sin and become righteous before God by grace, for Christ's sake, through faith, when we believe that Christ suffered for us and that for his sake our sin is forgiven and righteousness and eternal life are given to us. For God will regard and reckon this faith as righteousness, as Paul says in Romans 3:21-26 and 4:5.[12]

Three other articles of the unaltered Augsburg Confession—Article V on "The Office of the Ministry"; Article VII on "The Church"; and Article XIV on "Order in the Church"—were also crucial to the developing confessionalism of the new General Council. Article V insisted that "To obtain such faith God instituted the office of the ministry, that is, provided the Gospel and the sacraments." Article VII, meanwhile, identified the exact nature of that "true unity" which the General Council's "Fundamental Principles" elevated to first importance: "it is enough to agree concerning the teaching of the Gospel and the administration of the sacraments."[13] Article VII would be critical to the General Council's understanding of that specific unity it was trying to achieve. In identifying what in the Gospel and the sacraments made unity possible, it was the one place the Book of Concord spelled out the conditions for unity. However, such unity would be achieved only with struggle in a new American Lutheran body where a number of its constituent synods had close pulpit and altar ties with other denominations.

GENERAL COUNCIL POLITY

After the nine theses were approved by the assembled delegates at Reading, deliberations continued on a polity for the new General Council. The proposed organization of the General Council was designed to avoid the centralizing authority which the General Synod presumably had exercised in ways prejudicial to conservative confessionalism. The constitutional foundations for a different kind of American Lutheran church avoided the risk of triumphalism by disavowing all right to absolute religious authority. "All power in the Church belongs primarily, properly and exclusively to our Lord Jesus Christ" began the first of eleven theses on "ecclesiastical Power and Church Polity." Ecclesiastical power is a "derivative" power and "pertains to her as the servant of Jesus Christ." It followed, for those assembled at Reading, that the church "has no power to bind the conscience, except as she truly teaches what her Lord teaches, and faithfully commands what He has charged her to command."[14] This ecclesiastical power "Christ commits derivatively and ministerially to his Church on earth, [which] are the Congregations" composed of both pastors and people. Congregations are to be represented in Synods organized by means of a "mutual congregational compact" called a Constitution.

What then is the authority of the synod in such a representative system? "The judgments of Synods are the judgments of the Church," the General Council insisted, using language to be found in the Book of Concord's "Treatise on the Power and Primacy of the Pope." The judgments of the Council were also binding "so far as the terms of mutual agreement make them binding." But if the final decision of such a body seemed to a synod "in conflict with faith, involving violation of the rights of conscience" it was the synod's duty to take such action to prevent compromise with error including withdrawal from the Council itself.[15]

It was assumed however, that in all but the most unusual circumstances, the decisions of synods and councils would and should prevail because of "a higher moral probability of their being true and rightful." What lay behind this assertion was the Conciliarism which Philip Melanchthon expressed in the "Treatise on the Power and Primacy of the Pope." The "Treatise" asserted (among other things) that it was the task of civil magistrates to restrain the pope so "that the church is not deprived of the power of making judgments and decisions according to the Word of God." What the General Council believed it saw in Melanchthon's "Treatise" was a "free, Scriptural General Council or Synod," and a synodical model of ecclesiastical governance such as they were then developing at Reading.[16] The rationale was decidedly different from the Enlightenment free-association model of church government to be found in the General Synod and its district synods.

Once the General Council model was approved, the delegates

wrote a formal constitution placing at its head the Fundamental Principles, and agreeing among themselves that when ten synods ratified the new document, the General Council was to formally come into existence. Some last minute business of a very important kind completed the meeting. Committees were appointed to edit English and German Hymnals. Subsequently it was determined that these new volumes should also contain Luther's Small Catechism and the Augsburg Confession.[17] With their plans concluded, the delegates returned home, having accomplished much, expectantly awaiting the Council's ratification by enough synods to give it life and begin its work.

FIRST CONVENTION AT FORT WAYNE, INDIANA—1867

With the "Fundamental Principles" accepted by ten synods, the General Council was ready to hold its first convention. In fact, eleven synods ratified the founding document, assembling in general council for the first time on November 20, 1867, at Holy Trinity Lutheran Church, Fort Wayne, Indiana. The choice was symbolic. Holy Trinity was the scene of the Pennsylvania Ministerium's humiliation the year before when the General Synod, meeting there to consider the Franckean Synod's admission to its ranks, left Ministerium delegates standing in the wings while it debated their credentials. Though more than the requisite ten synods ratified the new constitution, two synods which attended the Reading meeting the year before were conspicuously missing. The Missouri and Norwegian Synods decided not to proceed further with the plan of organization. The Joint Synod of Ohio, meanwhile, though attending, refused to enter into voting membership.[18]

Despite these withdrawals, the newly organized General Council was an impressive body. Between General Synod synods which had withdrawn to form the new General Council, and the other uniting synods from the midwest, the new body consisted of eleven synods, 538 pastors, 1030 congregations, and 133,300 communicant members.[19] What is more the new body at its founding was larger than the General Synod from which it had withdrawn. The latter body's numbers in 1866, before division, and afterwards (1868) are instructive—synods, 21 (21); pastors, 674 (590); congregations, 1055 (970); communicants, 101,450 (86,200).[20] At the synodical level the General Synod suffered little because synodical splits left it with as many district bodies as previously. But while the number of synods remained the same, the number of congregations dropped by 9 percent. At the congregational level, the losses were over 10 percent—13 percent for pastors and 15 percent for communicant members. A greater percentage of members than congregations leaving suggests that the losses to the right were taking place among the larger, urban congregations within the church.

When statistics for both bodies are taken together, however, it is clear that a larger portion of American Lutherans were organized into significant denominational bodies after 1866 than before. While the General Synod lost 15,250 members, the new General Council gained 133,300—a 16 percent increase in size over the old General Synod. More importantly, this rapid reorganization and the addition of other synods attracted to the new General Council, created major liberal and conservative bodies of Lutherans in the United States, with a decided majority of pastors and congregations forming a conservative counterpart to General Synod Lutheranism.

FOUR-POINTS CONTROVERSY

The new Council was not conservative enough for some groups which pushed for an even more conservative definition of Lutheran practice in Council churches. The Joint Synod of Ohio's reluctance to enter into full membership soon found expression in four points of controversy which it raised in the new body. After several days of cordial discussions at the Council's first conference, the Ohio Synod presented a paper in which it insisted that "unLutheran doctrine and practice . . . despite the reception of the Confession or 'Doctrinal basis,' nevertheless is [to be] found to exist in some synods" of the General Council. To uncover the problem the Joint Synod delegates asked specifically "What relation will this venerable body in future sustain to chiliasm?" It also inquired what the Council's position was on "Mixed Communion," "The exchanging of pulpits with Sectarians," and on membership in "Secret, or unchurchly Societies?" "Especially, would we earnestly desire a decided answer with regard to the last item," the Ohio Synod's delegates insisted "inasmuch as the Joint Synod, for years already, in view of certain relations in one of its District Synods, has had its difficulties in consequence of four pastors belonging to Secret Societies, and would not, therefore, again burthen its conscience." The challenge represented a significant constitutional crisis on both theological and ecclesiastical grounds. Almost immediately after the formation of the General Council in which its decisions should have prevailed because of "a higher moral probability of their being true and rightful," a sympathetic synod involved in the founding had concluded that the new Council condoned religious practices "in conflict with faith, involving violation of the rights of conscience." Either they would be resolved to prevent compromise with error, or they would serve as a legitimate reason for withdrawal.[21]

Among other things the Joint Synod was troubled by the growing prominence of the pre-millennial theology of Dr. Joseph A. Seiss (1823-1904), a leading figure in the Pennsylvania Ministerium and an author of the Fraternal Address. Seiss taught and wrote that Christ would return before the millennium (therefore being "pre-millennial" in his theology) to usher in a thousand-year reign of peace before the final judgment. He had attended Gettysburg College before studying theology privately and entering the Lutheran ministry. He was known as a student of liturgics and hymnody, wrote widely on these subjects in various periodicals, and is credited with some one hundred publications including a notable sermon collection for the church year. It was these writings which made Seiss's literary reputation rather than his views on the second coming. In fact, his chiliastic views, though amply expressed during the later 1860s, were not published for another ten years when they were put forward in his *The Last Times and the Great Consummation* (Philadelphia, 1878).[22]

Though chiliasim as such argues from Revelation 20:4-5, that Christ will return to earth to establish a thousand-year reign of peace before the final judgment, the weight of scripture is against this heterdox position. No pre-millennial material is to be found in the synoptic Gospels which announces the Kingdom of God as "at hand" rather than lying in some indefinite future, and where the final judgment is preceded by a thousand-year reign or utopian triumph of peace and goodwill.[23] Nevertheless, belief in a pre-millennial age was rather widespread by the patristic age and continued thereafter as a dissenting viewpoint within the church. Augustine, returning to Biblical understandings, finally established the orthodox position on the matter in Latin Christendom—that the Church was the kingdom of God upon earth—and from there it passed into the medieval Church.

But so, too, did chiliasim in the thinking of the Spiritual Franciscans and Joachim of Fiore. Pre-millennial thought also recurred during the Reformation as did other heterodox positions, and the doctrine was therefore condemned in Article XVII of the Augsburg Confession:

> Rejected . . . are certain Jewish opinions which are even now making an appearance and which teach that, before the resurrection of the dead, saints and godly men will possess a worldly kingdom and annihilate all the godless. [24]

Thus chiliasm and its proponents were highly unorthodox in the eyes of the General Council's conservative membership. No matter that chiliasm was, in popular American theology, the only alternative to the postmillenialism of a liberal Protestant establishment convinced that its task was to prepare for Christ's return by bringing in a thousand-year reign of faith and peace through revivalism and social reform.[25]

Seiss's literary reputation in religious circles made him a good choice to chair the Board of the General Council's new Philadelphia Seminary, a position he held for four decades from 1865 until his death. Yet it was surely an embarrassing inconsistency to have an author of the Fraternal Address and Philadelphia Seminary director embrace so unorthodox and unconfessional a position. Besides, it made him a vulnerable player in the game of confessional politics. Perhaps reference to Seiss in the Missouri Synod's *Lehre und Wehre* as "the thorough-going

Chiliast Pastor Seiss, president of the Board of Directors of the new Seminary at Philadelphia," had alerted the Ohio members to his current beliefs.[26] In any case, he was highly suspect, reason enough (therefore) for the questions raised by the Joint Synod of Ohio. The Council, however, joined ranks behind its leader, putting the burden of proof on the delegates:

> So soon as official evidence shall be presented to this body, in the manner prescribed by the Constitution, that unLutheran doctrines or practices are authorized by the action of any of its Synods, or by their refusal to act, it will weigh that evidence, and, if it finds they exist, use all its constitutional power to convince the minds of men in regard to them, and as speedily as possible to remove them.[27]

The offended delegates from Ohio removed themselves from the Convention, however, feeling the above resolution evaded the points raised. The leadership's strategy worked for the time being. With the Joint Synod's withdrawal, there seemed little reason to pursue the remaining three points, and so only the first of the Four Points raised by the Joint Synod was addressed by the General Council.[28]

The German Iowa Synod picked up where their fellow conservatives from the Midwest had left off, presenting a paper the following day which sought clarification on the second and third points. Midwestern Lutherans were completely baffled by union churches. Accordingly the synod asked the General Council to "expressly acknowledge what is according to the understanding of the delegates . . . virtually acknowledged" in the Fundamental Principles,

> That according to the Confession of the Evangelical Lutheran Church there must be, and is, condemned all church fellowship with such as are not Lutheran; for example, ministers serving congregations such as are mixed and not purely Lutheran, receiving such congregations and their pastors into Synodical connection, the admittance of those of a different faith to the privilege of communion, the permission of those not Lutheran to occupy our pulpits, etc.[29]

The Iowa Germans were concerned about practices in union churches throughout the east where Reformed and Lutheran Congregations worshipped in the same sanctuaries and sometimes also maintained a union Sunday school. These were facilities which served old, Protestant German communities bound together through intermarriage for generations by culture and language. They were especially prevalent in the Pennsylvania Ministerium, although union churches were also to be found elsewhere, including the New York Ministerium, and in the Hartwick and Franckean Synods where there were a significant number of union Sunday schools.[30]

Whether these practices were unconfessional was a matter of dispute, as well as of viewpoint. Everything depended upon which confessional stance was to be taken—the official position of the General Council, with its emphasis upon the unaltered Augsburg Confession; or that of the Synodical Conference which embraced the entire Book of Concord. There was nothing in the Augsburg Confession which applied to the German Iowa Synod's concern. It was only in the Book of Concord that a strict confessionalist could find that condemnation of Zwinglian attitudes towards the Eucharist upon which the historic condemnation of the Reformed church by Lutherans had taken place, a condemnation which often extended to the prohibition of intercommunion where union churches existed. It was probably because such arrangements did not fall within the confessional strictures of the General Council position that the Council treated the Iowa Synod's questions in the same way that those of the Joint Synod of Ohio had been dealt with before—when the evidence of unionism was presented, the Council would officially take it up.[31]

This response, of course, did not satisfy the Iowa delegates. Like their Ohio counterparts, they never accepted voting responsibilities in the General Council. However, unlike them, they continued to attend Council conventions for twenty years, having adopted the "Fundamental Principles" and therefore having the privilege of voice without vote. Their leaders, the brothers Sigmund and Gotfried Fritschel, kept urging the strictest interpretation of the Council's confessional position, functioning as a loyal opposition which never found it necessary to provide contributions to the Council's general fund.[32]

The behavior of both groups of delegates reflected a general restiveness among Midwestern Lutherans with the eastern synods in the Council. Unlike the newcomers to American denominationalism, eastern Lutherans already had a long history of cooperative involvement and interdenominational fellowship which made them a significant expression of American Protestantism. Regional differences of a largely historical nature separated the two groups. More importantly such differences reflected two differing confessional attitudes developing within the General Council itself.

THE PITTSBURGH DECLARATION

These differences became clear as the General Council set about officially answering the Four Points at its second convention held at Pittsburgh in 1868. Two full days were devoted to a discussion of the points before the matter was turned over to a special committee consisting of a pastor from each of the eleven synods attending. Minnesota was missing; Iowa was in attendance but without vote so it had no seat on the special committee. Given the emergence of two parties in the Council, majority and minority reports should not have been surprising.

In what became known as the 1868 Pittsburgh Declaration, the Council answered its critics on the four points—chiliasm, mixed communion, shared pulpits, and secret societies. Regarding chiliasm: "This council holds firmly the doctrine of our Lord's coming." It "has neither had, nor would consent to have, fellowship with any Synod which tolerates the 'Jewish opinions' or 'chiliastic opinions' condemned in the XVII Article of the Augsburg Confession."[33] Since it was an official, rather than a synod which had taken up the "heresy," the Council managed to avoid dealing with the first point beyond a pious reaffirmation of the Augsburg Confession.

Its approach to secret societies sought without condemning "mere secrecy in association" to "beseech all good men" to consider whether their benefits outweighed the great mischief often done by them, and whether the same goals might be reached by other means. However,

> any and all societies for moral and religious ends which do not rest on the supreme authority of God's Holy Word . . . which do not recognize our Lord Jesus Christ as the true God and the only Mediator between God and man—which teach doctrines or have usages or forms of worship condemned in God's Word and in the Confessions of His Church—which assume to themselves what God has given to his Church and its Ministers—which require undefined obligations to be assumed by oath, are unChristian, and we solemnly warn our members and ministers against all fellowship with, or connivance at associations which have this character.[34]

Pulpit fellowship and intercommunion, however, were not treated so strictly. The western synods did not like the long-standing practice of exchanging pulpits which occurred in eastern Lutheran churches as well as at General Council convention time. Eleven of the pastors present had, in fact, preached in nonLutheran Pittsburgh pulpits while the Council was in session. The "Exchange of Pulpits" was thus treated as a matter of principle, not of prohibition, with the insistence "that no man shall be admitted to our pulpits, whether of the Lutheran name or of any other" where there is reason to doubt he will preach "the pure truth of God's Word as taught in the Confessions of our Church." Lutherans may preach in other pulpits wherever there is an opening, providing such fellowship does not imply error or schism.

As for communion, the Majority report distinguished between "a discriminating as over against an indiscriminate Communion." English-language Lutherans had introduced a "general invitation" to communion into their liturgies, beginning with the New York Ministerium in 1814. While the pastor's right and duty to examine persons for scriptural fitness who apply for communion was upheld, the majority cautioned against the errors of persons who in their "simplicity" might not measure up to examination standards but "who do not speak reproachfully of the truth of the Divine Word." To this statement the Council would add the counsel found in Article IV of Melanchthon's "Apology of the Augsburg Confession": namely, "there are many weak ones who have built upon the foundation perishing stubble . . . and yet . . . are still Christians, and their faults may be forgiven them or even be emended."

CONTINUED DISSENT AND SYNODICAL REALIGNMENT

Such was the viewpoint of the committee majority drafting the Pittsburgh Declaration. The minority on the committee were not so forgiving. Originally intending to issue their own report, they withdrew it because many "truths are confessed" by the Majority. Yet they felt constrained to make their faith and confession clear with three points of dissent:

> In regard to point I, we reject each and every form of chiliasm as contrary to the Scriptures and the Confessions.
> In regard to point II, we declare that we consider secret societies, such as the Free Masons, Odd Fellows, etc., as anti-Christian and soul endangering associations, and earnestly warn against them.
> In regard to points III and IV, respecting Mixed Communion and Interchange of Pulpits, we designate such fellowship with those not Lutheran as a unionistic practice, dangerous for our Lutheran Church, and which we most decidedly reject.[35]

These condemnations were voiced by delegates from three synods—the Wisconsin and Michigan Synods, and the New York Ministerium—two of which (New York and Michigan) would continue to play the role of radical confessionalists in the General Council. Being unhappy with the General Council's majority report, Wisconsin withdrew from the Council the next year (1869) in continued opposition to the Pittsburgh Declaration. The Michigan Synod would keep up its opposition for another twenty-six years, before finally withdrawing in 1894. The New York Ministerium, represented by its president, Albany pastor Reinhold Adelberg, remained in the Council for the time being, though its leader did not. Within another year Adelberg accepted a call to Watertown, Wisconsin, where he subsequently helped organize the Synodical Conference, became a leader in the Wisconsin Synod, a professor of its Northwestern College, and (eventually) an instructor in its Wauwatosa Seminary.[36]

Despite this majority triumph the Four Points would not remain answered to the satisfaction of radical confessionalists. Some real dialogue was in order. The Minnesota Synod raised questions about the Four Points in 1870 by attacking the Pittsburgh Declaration. The Council majority for its part, seemingly ready after continued dissent to take such objections more seriously and seek real answers to these questions, conscientiously desired "by the Divine blessing to contribute to the establishment of a pure faith, and good order throughout the Church." As a start the question about secret societies was sent down to the district synods to solicit their advice and opinions. By then, however, the Minnesota Synod had withdrawn. Those synods which reported back simply indicated their own actions against secret-society membership. There the matter rested until the original points and answers were referred once again to the synods in 1879.[37]

Restiveness over the Four Points was but a sign of a confessional realignment taking place at the conservative end of the American Lutheran spectrum. Of the seven midwestern synods which originally affirmed the "Fundamental Principles," three withdrew—the Joint Synod of Ohio in 1867, the Wisconsin Synod in 1868, and the Minnesota Synod in 1871. Meanwhile, several other western bodies united with the General Council—the Texas Synod joined in 1868, remaining a member for twenty-six years before becoming a part of the Iowa Synod; the Illinois Synod joined in 1867 only to withdraw along with the Minnesota Synod in 1871. Minnesota and Illinois then joined ranks with the other departing Synods—the Joint Synod of Ohio and the Norwegian and Wisconsin Synods—and together with the Missouri Synod formed the more conservative Synodical Conference in 1872, a group which the Michigan Synod eventually joined also. The same year, however, a fateful union occurred when the Swedish Augustana Synod joined the fledgling Council adding its strong, moderate confessional voice to that of other moderates in the General Council.[38]

What lay behind the restiveness and reshuffling was the repristinating conservatism of immigrant Lutherans with no history or experience involving the complicated relationships between eastern Lutherans and other Protestant groups. What might have been desirable confessionally in a *de novo* situation, like the Missouri Synod encountered as a new immigrant group, was considerably more difficult in the complex religious culture of established American Protestantism. For that reason, immigrant Lutheran conservatism formed a strict, radically confessional party not only outside of the General Council but inside as well—a party which included most midwestern Lutherans plus the more German elements in the New York Ministerium—working in opposition to moderate Council leadership originating in the Pennsylvania Ministerium. If the radicals insisted upon conformity and discipline, accusing the moderates of inconsistency, the moderates resented such accusations and the persistent agitation for discipline, insisting instead upon a general process of education in lieu of discipline.[39]

AKRON DECLARATION AND GALESBURG RULE

With this process in mind, the Minnesota questions about the Pittsburgh Declaration were taken up again by the General Council held in 1872 at

Akron, Ohio. President Krauth sought to summarize the policy of pulpit and altar fellowship for the meeting, doing so in what eventually became the standard and popular expression of the Council's position, known as the Akron Declaration:

> 1. THE RULE is: Lutheran pulpits are for Lutheran ministers only. Lutheran altars are for Lutheran communicants only.
> 2. The Exceptions to the rule belong to the sphere of privilege, not of right.
> 3. The Determination of the exceptions is to be made in consonance with these principles, by the conscientious judgment of pastors, as the cases arise.[40]

Three years later, at the General Council held in Galesburg, Illinois (in 1875), the Akron Declaration came up for discussion because it included exceptions to the rule about pulpits. This time the issue was raised by Pastor Justus Ruperti of St. Matthews Church, New York City, a delegate from a New York Ministerium just then experiencing a conservative shift in its own confessional outlook. In response, citing the progress on Lutheran practice in this area and the testimony of associated Lutheran bodies, especially the clear testimony on the subject just adopted by the Augustana Synod at its 1875 convention, the General Council this time established its rule in very simple language, without exceptions, insisting "the rule, which accords with the word of God and with the confessions of our Church, is: 'Lutheran pulpits for Lutheran ministers only—Lutheran altars for Lutheran communicants only.' "[41] Presumably this Galesburg Rule would end the controversy.

With the nature of pulpit fellowship supposedly defined, the Council turned to the subject of altar fellowship. It drew upon a recent statement on the subject by the Augustana Synod. The Swedish synod insisted that the Lord's Supper is a means of grace which can be of full benefit to none other than believers, who also believe what God's word teaches concerning the Lord's Supper. . . . Fellowship in the Supper with those who have and hold a doctrine differing from our Confession, especially relative to the Lord's Supper, is in a greater or less degree a denial of our own faith and confession . . . No others, therefore ought to be allowed to partake of the Lord's Supper within the Church, than those who belong to the Church or have the same faith and confession with our Church.[42] This position the Council affirmed as its own, thereby concluding the business of the Four Points.

At this point in the controversy, however, words no longer clarified positions, but simply confused them with more statements, opinions, interpretations and misunderstandings. When the Galesburg Rule on altar fellowship reached the "nonLutheran" religious press, and then the public newspapers, a moderate stance was portrayed as a narrow-minded position, and the moderate Council as a highly prejudiced body. Meanwhile, the radical confessionalists in the Council tried to make certain that the exceptions to altar and pulpit fellowship made in the Akron Declaration (which had not been repeated as part of the Galesburg Rule) were not to be considered a conditional part of the Galesburg Rule itself. Since they were not repeated, the strict confessionalists insisted that the accompanying preamble to the Galesburg Rule—that it "accords with the Word of God and with the confessions of our Church"—applied only to the rule and not the exceptions, rendering the exceptions null and void.[43]

President Krauth insisted, however, that the exceptions would remain intact as "the declaration of the General Council." Krauth had begun his professional life in support of pulpit and altar fellowship but had changed his mind out of the logic of confessionalism. The conversion was not easy for him since "I carry both sides within my own heart." Even then he stressed that the Galesburg Rule was educational rather than legalistic in intent within a fellowship of congregations accustomed to receiving only advice from general church bodies.[44] To test the sense of the Council delegates each synod delegation present at Galesburg was asked how they understood the adoption of the Galesburg Rule. Most accepted President Krauth's interpretation, but a few, including the New York Ministerium, insisted on the narrower (without exceptions) interpretation.

MODERATE CONFESSIONALISM VS. MINISTERIUM ORTHODOXY

That insistence reflected significant theological changes which had taken place in the New York Ministerium during the course of Council debates transforming it into a radical confessionalist synod on the right end of the General Council's theological spectrum. The loss of its more liberal, English-speaking wing and the development of a radically confessional and largely German-speaking wing which insisted upon the letter of the law regarding altar and pulpit fellowship differed considerably from a conservative confessionalism which sought to conserve the spirit of the confessions in an environment of Christian freedom. It is the source of this change which occurred with the reconstruction of the New York Ministerium after 1867 that we will now examine.

NOTES

1 David A. Gustafson, *Lutherans in Crisis* (Minneapolis: Fortress Press, 1993), 148-55.

2 *Proceedings of the Convention held by representatives from various Evangelical Lutheran Synods in the United States and Canada accepting the Unaltered Augsburg Confession* (Pittsburgh, 1867), 3-5.

3 General Council, *Minutes* (1866), 3-5, 19ff. See "General Council" in *Lutheran Cyclopedia*, Edwin L. Lueker, ed. (St. Louis, 1975), 325-6. The

entire proceedings covered below are to be found in General Council, *Minutes* (1866), 19.

4 The theses are to be found in General Council, *Minutes* (1866), 19ff. The first thesis states in full: 1. There must be and abide through all time, one holy Christian Church, which is the assembly of all believers, among whom the Gospel is purely preached, and the Holy Sacraments are administered, as the Gospel demands.

5 CA, BC, 32.

6 Thesis 3. The Unity of the Church is witnessed to, and made manifest in, the solemn, public and official confessions which are set forth, to wit: The generic Unity of the Christian Church in the general Creeds, and the specific Unity of pure parts of the Christian Church in their specific Creeds.

7 The only Churches, therefore, of any land, which are properly in the Unity of that Communion, and by consequence entitled to its name, Evangelical Lutheran, are those which sincerely hold and truthfully confess the doctrines of the Unaltered Augsburg confession.

8 Thesis 8. We accept and acknowledge the doctrines of the Unaltered Augsburg confession in its original sense, as throughout in conformity with the pure truth of which God's word is the only rule. We accept its statements of truth as in perfect accordance wit the Canonical Scriptures.

9 Thesis 9. In thus formally accepting and acknowledging the Unaltered Augsburg confession, we declare our conviction, that the other confessions of the Evangelical Lutheran Church, inasmuch as they set forth none other than its system of doctrine, and articles of faith, are of necessity pure and scriptural. Pre-eminent among such accordant, pure and scriptural statements of doctrine, by their intrinsic excellence, by the great and necessary ends for which they were prepared, by their historical position, and by the general judgment of the Church, are these: the Apology of the Augsburg confession, the Smalcald Articles, the Catechisms of Luther and the Formula of Concord all of which are, with the Unaltered Augsburg confession, in the perfect harmony of one and the same scriptural faith.

10 Thesis 6. The Unaltered Augsburg confession is by pre-eminence the confession of that faith. The acceptance of its doctrines and the avowal of them without equivocation or mental reservation, make, mark and identify that Church which alone is the true, original, historical, and honest sense of the term as the Evangelical Lutheran Church.

11 CA, Articles 1-3, BC, 27-30. See Jaroslav Pelikan, *The Christian Tradition A History of the Development of Doctrine. Volume 1: The Emergence of the Catholic Tradition* (100-600) (Chicago, 1971), esp. Ch's 4, 6 & 7; and Volume 2: The Growth of Medieval Theology (600-1300) (Chicago, 1978), Ch. 3, "The Plan of Salvation."

12 CA, BC, 30.

13 CA, BC, 31. Ibid., 32.

14 General Council, *Proceedings* (1866), 12.

15 Ibid., p. 13.

16 "Treatise on the Power and Primacy of the Pope. Compiled by the Theologians Assembled in Smalcald in the Year 1537," BC, 319, 329-30. General Council, *Proceedings of the Convention . . . at Reading,* Pa, 13.

17 General Council, *Minutes* (1867), 27.

18 *Lutheran Cyclopedia*, 325.

19 General Council, *Minutes* (1867), 14.

20 Ibid., (1867), 14; (1866), 58; (1868), 68.

21 H. E. Jacobs, *History of the Evangelical Lutheran Church in the United States* (Philadelphia, 1899), 471-483.

22 *Lutheran Cyclopedia,* 710. *The Encyclopedia of the Lutheran Church,* Julius Bodensieck, ed. (Minneapolis: Augsburg Publishing House, 1965), 2152.

23 See "Millennium" in *New Schaaf-Herzog Encyclopedia of Religious Knowledge*, VII, 374ff. Seiss's form of Chiliasm was one of three kinds to gain prominence in mid-nineteenth-century America. The others, far more popular, included pre-millenialism of the Seventh-day Adventists, and the widely popular Christian pre-millenariamism of leading American evangelists.

24 CA, XVII, BC, 39.

25 See Timothy L. Smith, *Revivalism and Social Reform* (New York: Harper & Row, 1965), 227-9.

26 Theodore G. Tappert, *History of the Lutheran Theological Seminary at Philadelphia. 1864-1964* (Philadelphia, 1964), 34. *Lehre und Wehre,* April 1866, 121.

27 General Council, *Minutes* (1867), 17.

28 Ibid. (1868), 29.

29 Ibid. (1867), 17-18.

30 Harry J. Kreider, *History of the United Lutheran Synod of New York and New England* (Philadelphia: Muhlenberg Press, 1954), 170.

31 General Council, *Minutes* (1867), 17.

32 Jacobs, *History of the Evangelical Lutheran Church*, 476, 481. General Council, *Minutes* (1868-1888), "Treasurers Reports."

33 Ibid. (1868), 37; *Lutheran Cyclopedia,* "Four Points," 306-7.

34 Ibid. (1868), 22.

35 Ibid.

36 Ibid. (1869), 33. "Reinhold Adelberg," Lutheran Cyclopedia, 4.

37 General Council, *Minutes* (1869), 19-20; (1870), 27, 34-6. Ibid. (1870), 42; (1871), 26; (1879), 32.

38 *Lutheran Cyclopedia*, "General Council," 324; "Synodical Conference," 748.

39 Jacobs, *History of the Evangelical Lutheran Church,* 481. Neve, *Brief History of Lutheran Church in America,* 223.

40 General Council, *Minutes* (1872), 47.

41 Ibid. (1875), 17.

42 Ibid. (1875), 38, quoting Augustana Synod Minutes (1875).

43 Jacobs, *History of the Evangelical Lutheran Church*, 482. General Council, *Minutes* (1876), 6-7, 25-31.

44 Donald L. Huber, "The Controversy over Pulpit and Altar Fellowship in the General Council of Evangelical Lutheran Church, 1866-1889," (Ph. D. diss. Duke University, 1971), 277. Huber quotes Krauth in H. E. Jacobs, "Pathways," p. 151.

5
"THE STANDPOINT OF OUR FATHERS"
Portrait of a Changing Ministerium, 1868-1876

The New York Ministerium which gathered in 1868, was a Synod undergoing change. This was apparent enough from the events of 1867. A small core of radical German confessionalists had already withdrawn to form the German Evangelical Lutheran (Steimle) Synod of New York. Though small, its commitment to confessional change was of immense importance to the history of New York area Lutheranism. Subsequently a second group, this time English-speaking pastors and congregations sympathetic to General Synod Lutheranism also pulled out of the New York Ministerium to form the New York Synod because the Ministerium was shifting its institutional and confessional loyalties from the General Synod to the new General Council. The remnant of the Ministerium which met in 1868 would have to identify its own place on the spectrum of New York Lutheranism somewhere between the confessional poles represented by these two bodies. They chose to do so by returning (they thought) to the pre-1792 confessional "Standpoint of our Fathers." What they created however in a restructured Ministerium was a new ethnoreligious Lutheran community defined confessionally in old Lutheran terms.

NEW SYNOD OR OLD? ESTABLISHING AN IDENTITY

The German- and English-speaking pastors and congregations remaining within the Ministerium gathered for their 1868 convention at Zion's German Lutheran Church in Rochester, New York, then under the care of A. Uebelacker, the synod's German secretary. The assembled group consisted of forty-six (46) pastors and representatives of fifty (50) congregations, down in numbers from the sixty-eight (68) pastors and fifty-five (55) congregations which had met at Albany in

1867. (See Maps 11.1 and 11.2.) The New York Synod, meanwhile, assembled as a new Lutheran body composed of sixteen pastors and ten congregations at St. Pauls Church, Red Hook, New York.[1]

The emergence of the new and/or changed synods gave a sharper regional focus to New York Lutheranism. Whereas there had once been five distinct subregions of New York Lutheranism, there were now six. Let us look at them a bit more closely. The Hartwick (1830), Franckean (1837) and New Jersey (1860) Synods represented those geographic areas of New York Lutheranism—the old Schoharie and New Jersey clusters, composed of congregations with a decidedly pietist orientation—which developed a consistently American Lutheran outlook. The New York Synod, meanwhile, represented central Hudson Lutheranism with its mixture of rationalism, unionism, and steady acculturation to American ways. It was as though with the Red Hook assembly, the New York Synod withdrew to its home territory to regroup its forces.

To be sure, there were churches in Albany and New York—parts of the old Albany-New York parish which formed the ancient backbone of New York Lutheranism. Yet it was really the Ministerium which drew its strength from the greater number of congregations loyal to it in these urban areas of an expanding, German-speaking Lutheranism. The rest of the Ministerium's strength was to be found in upstate New York to the west of Albany, especially in the large towns and cities like Buffalo, Rome, Utica, Syracuse, and Rochester. It was largely an urban body situated in the urbanized parts of the New York population belt.

The Ministerium's 1868 gathering proved one of the most significant in its history. Since an old standing resolution required the discussion of substantive issues at the outset of each annual gathering, the Ministerium's opening session was spent debating the Four Points raised at the recent meeting of the General Council—"viz, Secret Societies, Chiliasm, Close Communion, and Exchange of Pulpits." A resolution was passed on to the business session of the Ministerium concerning secret societies—"that no member of a Secret Society can be or become a member of this Ministerium." But the session ran out of time before Close Communion could be adequately discussed and so that topic was simply "laid on the table."[2]

At its second session President Reinhold Adelberg delivered his report observing that "we have assembled . . . under circumstances which render it both needful and desirable to take a brief retrospective view of the History of our Body." He began by reference to a historic founding document—the 1807 "Protocol" 0s formation, which Adelberg noted with obvious delight was "kept" in German. The Ministerium's founding was based on the Constitution of the Evangelical Lutheran Ministerium of Pennsylvania, he reported. Its "Fathers held to the Symbolical Books of our Church." What is more, the 1807 reception into the Ministerium of Pastor J. F. Earnst of

Hudson, New York, had depended upon his acceptance of "the divine word of the Old and New Testaments and the doctrine of the Symbolical Books." If "History is what one age finds worthy of note in another" as their contemporary, Jacob Burkhardt believed, then it can be said that the Ministerium began recovering a usable confessional history on this occasion.[3]

Chapter 1 has already indicated 1807 to be a year of transition for the Ministerium, a time when a rapidly fading confessional theology was giving way to rationalism and Protestant denominationalism.[4] Without knowing it, Adelberg was manufacturing an orthodox confessional pedigree out of the founders' attenuated understanding of Lutheran confessional theology. In the same spirit of unintended irony he went on to assert:

> The charges of our opponents [in the New York Synod] therefore, who assert, that by adopting the "Fundamental Principles" of the General Council, we have introduced something new in the history of our Ministerium, fall entirely to the ground. On the other hand we may rejoice that we have returned as a body, to the standpoint of our Fathers; that we stand with them on the complete and pure Confessions of our beloved Church and that we are one in faith with all true Lutherans. If we now build upon this good foundation of our Church, and to a firm adherence to the Confessions and correct practice and a holy zeal for the kingdom of God, the blessing of the Lord cannot fail to rest upon our work.[5]

In this Adelberg was mistaken. The New York Ministerium was reversing direction, not turning back the clock!

The rest of Adelberg's report dealt with the mundane details of the year gone by. It, too, indicated something of the old-new Synod's direction. Twelve congregations were dismissed to the New York Synod as per the agreement reached the previous year. Also several more pastors were dismissed to the New York, Pittsburgh, West Pennsylvania, and Pennsylvania Synods. Not all departed in a spirit of fraternal fellowship. Pastor J. Von Brandt left charging the Ministerium "with conformity to the world and lawlessness," assertions he repeated in the *Lutheran Zeitschrift*. Adelberg refused his request for an honorable dismissal to the Missouri Synod, though he would be more at home there. Meanwhile Pastor C. Schimmel left the Ministerium because it "chooses to be Lutheran in such a way as neither Luther, nor the demands of the times would justify, and which encourages union." For Schimmel the stricter confessionalism of the Ministerium meant no chance of "union" with the Roman Catholic Church which he subsequently went off to join before entering the United States Army.[6]

This initial loss of pastors and congregations was nearly made up by new congregations and pastors entering the Ministerium in 1868.

Nine pastors and nine congregations (the numbers were coincidental) applied for membership. More would follow year by year. In one case the losses and gains were especially noteworthy. With the withdrawal of pastors and delegates to form the New York Synod, St. James's congregation in New York City underwent a division between General Synod and General Council factions, with the strict confessionalists leaving to form Holy Trinity. The remnant at St. James, formed as an English-speaking breakaway in 1827 from the United Congregation of New York City, reaffirmed its English-language General Synod confessional heritage by withdrawing to join the New York Synod.

Interestingly enough Holy Trinity affirmed the same commitments within the General Council. At the point of the General Synod division "a few enterprising men" at St. James took steps "to organize another English Lutheran congregation, on the west side of the city, in which shall be taught the doctrines of our Church, in accordance with the principles of the General Council. . . ." They proceeded to call Pastor G. F. Krotel from Philadelphia. "As the German Lutheran churches of this city, connected with the New-York Ministerium, were now deprived of the only English Lutheran church in this city," Krotel later observed, "the establishment of another English Lutheran Church, in connection with the New-York Ministerium, and, thereby, with the General Council, appeared to be highly desirable and was warmly urged by earnest Lutherans in New-York and elsewhere." Krotel had received a unanimous call from St. James three years before since it was deemed desirable to call someone familiar with the German language "as the growth of the English Lutheran Church must largely depend upon the anglicized German element." Now the appeal to Krotel by former St. James members said rather bluntly: "It is very evident that if the Lutheran Church is ever to make her mark in this city it must be done now." If Krotel did not accept the call, they insisted, "many of our best people will be lost to the faith entirely." Appeals from members of the Lutheran clergy in New York City amplified the reasons for his accepting the call.[7] As one anonymous pastor pointed out to Krotel, by contrast to the prominence of the Lutheran Church in Philadelphia,

> Here she is, so far as the public regard is concerned, scarcely known, and utterly without influence. What you are wanted to do in New-York is not only to build up a single English Lutheran Church, but Lutheranism itself, for in this city Lutheranism has always been in the background, always at a disadvantage. . . . It is evident that the work not only should be undertaken now, but that the work *must* be done by somebody, if our English Church is to have a future in this city. . . . I do not see why the Mother Church of the Reformation should not succeed, as well as *sects* less favored in their doctrine and ritual. . . . I have no doubt that, as you

are personally so highly acceptable to our German brethren here, they will do all in their power to assist.[8]

Quickly organized by an influential group of English-speaking Lutherans who could and did put their money where their mouths were, Holy Trinity was one of the first applicants received from among a large group of Lutheran congregations (many German Lutheran) which applied to the Ministerium within a few days of its first 1868 session. Krotel, meanwhile, was the first clerical applicant for membership in the Ministerium. This addition to the clerical roster was especially significant. Krotel was a leader in both the Pennsylvania Ministerium and the General Council, having been one of the five Pennsylvania pastors issuing the call to organize the Council at Reading, Pennsylvania. He would continue to provide leadership for a conservative confessionalism even when it brought him into conflict with a changing New York Ministerium. Given his stature, it is not surprising that before the 1868 Ministerium had ended, Krotel was elected to its two standing committees—the examining committee, and the executive committee. Within a year, he would be the Ministerium's new president![9]

Despite these shifts in loyalty and leadership the Ministerium's confessional pedigree was still open to question. The troublesome departure of the New York Synod clergy continued to vex the Ministerium. Adelberg noted in his report that he was "grieved to say that the synod of New York . . . with whom we had hoped to stand in friendly relations, have pursued a course which must destroy this hope and greatly jeopardize our friendly relations." The problem lay with the New York Synod's publication of its "Historical Statement" in which the new Synod claimed to be the old Ministerium, while labeling the old Ministerium a new and unheard of confessional entity. In this claim the New York Synod were substantially correct, having withdrawn to preserve the mild confessionalism existing in 1807. However, a vulnerable Ministerium could not accept this reading of their common history.[10]

A Committee was appointed to examine relations between the two bodies and to make a report before synod adjourned. They noted that while, after the new Synod's formation, fraternal delegates were appointed by both synods to be exchanged this year, the recent Red Hook meeting of the New York Synod had complicated the relationship by approving the "Historical Statement." Its judgmental character was appalling the committee thought as was the imputation of motives to the Ministerium which would be considered "dishonorable in men of the world, not to say, very sinful in Christians, and Christian Ministers." Such vilification aside, the Ministerium committee objected to the New York Synod blaming the division "upon the Germans," and for insisting that all the "Fathers and oldest Members" of the pre-1867 Ministerium had united with the New York Synod. Most galling was the assertion that "the new Synod is the true New York Ministerium under another name, and that therefore our Synod has no just right to the name it bears." The committee quickly added that it "can be shown" from President Adelberg's brief history of the Ministerium's formation that "we now stand in entire harmony with the doctrinal standpoint of the men who established the Ministerium more than eighty years ago."[11]

The Committee urged the Ministerium to forward their report to the New York Synod "to so consider and act upon its contents" that the Ministerium might, "in conformity with just and necessary self respect," hold fraternal correspondence with their New York Synod brethren. The recommendation was accepted with two resolutions. The first said, in blunter language, what the Committee only suggested: "*Resolved* that we will not exchange Delegates with the Synod of New York until it explains the charges that have been made against them, and sent to them." The second resolution uncovered another part of the problem:

> Resolved that the officers of the synod are authorized to take all necessary measures to bring into the possession of Synod the monies that have been paid or subscribed, for a German Professorship.[12]

What troubled a majority of members was Adelberg's announcement that monies collected for a German professorship by "the Agent of Hartwick Seminary" had not been turned over to the Ministerium.[13]

NEW DIRECTIONS—A GERMAN PROFESSORSHIP

Plans had been afoot for some time to establish a German professorship at Hartwick Seminary because of the growing numbers of German congregations in the Ministerium. With the General Synod/General Council division, however, it would seem that monies already collected were being held by someone to assure that they were contributed to a seminary friendly to the General Synod. Whatever hands held the monies kept them from being diverted to the German professorship at the new Philadelphia Seminary. President Adelberg mentioned the entire matter because the Philadelphia Board of Directors had asked the New York Ministerium's cooperation in establishing such a professorship.[14] The proposed professorship was one of several significant projects in the Ministerium which marked out new directions for an old synod. Over the next decade the Ministerium would shift its educational resources from the Hartwick Seminary to the new Philadelphia Seminary, becoming an active junior partner with the Pennsylvania Ministerium.

NEW MISSION EFFORTS

Also new was the mission and social welfare work among German immigrants begun under the supervision of the Ministerium's Executive

Committee on Missions and Education. At the 1868 meeting of the Ministerium, the Committee resolved "to appoint Prof. Mohldenke [sic] of Prussia as traveling Missionary of the Ministerium" with the task of nurturing German-language congregations among new immigrants. Edward Frederick Moldehnke had recently returned to America from a pastorate in his native Germany. He first came to the United States in 1861 to serve the Wisconsin Synod as a traveling missionary and stayed to teach in that body's Watertown Seminary before returning to Germany in 1866. The appointment was timely, for the mission task was immense! "It is necessary, highly necessary, that greater efforts be made for the gathering of the forsaken and scattered members of our Church" the Committee asserted, for otherwise "they will wander away to other denominations and sects, or fall into unbelief and thus be entirely lost to the Lutheran Church." A sense of crisis pervaded the committee. Quoting Revelation 3.2—"Be watchful and strengthen the things that remain, that are ready to die"—the Committee characterized the forces of apostasy and atheism which threatened the German immigrant population as very real forces that were already curtailing growth among urban immigrant congregations.[15]

The problem was viewed not as apostasy but as a lack of funds. Sounding a note of financial exigency which would haunt the new Synod for decades, the Committee pointed to clergy and congregations without a financially aggressive mission effort. "Many congregations might be established in the bounds of our Ministerium with assistance according to their necessities, but the difficulty is ever the same. Your Committee is ready and willing to persecute with zeal the work of the Lord and his Church, but they are hindered on every side by the want of funds" for buildings and pastors. Unfortunately "Great work is accomplished, and numerous congregations are established among our German brethren in the faith, by the industry of other denominations who . . . show themselves unfriendly to the Lutheran Church and Doctrine:

> Wach auf, du Geist der esten Zeugen! Yes! Spirit of the Lord, breathe upon thy Church and arouse our hearts anew, and render us more willing to work for thy Kingdom while it is day.[16]

A second New York City project was the Lutheran Emigrant Mission, a joint effort of the New York and Pennsylvania Ministeria begun in 1862. It too employed a missionary, Pastor Robert Neumann, formerly a General Synod missionary in China, who had been called to serve the German Lutheran immigrant population passing through the United States port of entry at Castle Garden near the southern tip of Manhattan Island. An ambitious Committee was supporting plans for a third mission project—"Emigrant's House"—also near Castle Garden, a dormitory facility with "an office and Chapel" under development by Pastor Wilhelm Heinrich Berkemeier, a former German immigrant himself. This project was also to be a joint effort of the New York and Pennsylvania Ministeria. Going forward simultaneously with the Lutheran Emigrant Mission and Emigrant House created friction between Neumann and Berkemeier however. To coordinate matters better, the Ministerium abolished its committee on Emigrant House, turning its responsibilities over to the Executive Committee on Mission and Education and augmenting that Committee's membership by the appointment of G. F. Krotel.[17]

NEW LEADERSHIP

When the Ministerium assembled again in 1869, Pastor R. Hill of the English-speaking Lutheran congregation in Rochester and English secretary was serving as president, *ad interim*. Reinhold Adelberg had accepted a call to a Lutheran congregation in Watertown, Wisconsin, and had joined the Wisconsin Synod. Meanwhile the last year's host pastor, A. Uebelacker, German secretary, had also departed the territory, having been dismissed by his congregation for a "guilt" which made him "unworthy of the sacred office of the ministry." The particular sin was never reported, thereby establishing an enormity of unworthiness that made his departure inevitable.[18] Elections for president and a new German secretary were held at the first business session. Krotel was elected the new president for three years and E. Hoffmann, an Albany pastor, the German secretary. Together with an emerging group of new leaders, Krotel and Hoffmann would lead the Ministerium for a decade in directions more suited to its changing constituency.

THE PROBLEM OF BENEVOLENCE

The Ministerium established most of the new directions in its 1868 meeting. The impediments which kept the Ministerium from its goals were also evident by then. One of the most serious was synod finances. The Ministerium congregations remaining after the division could not (or would not) provide sufficient funding for the basic needs of an expanding synod. President Krotel called attention to this problem in his 1870 report. If the church "would prosecute the work of Missions and Education," then it was "absolutely necessary" for the congregations to contribute more liberally than at the rates reported in the 1870s Treasurer's "Annual Report." Contributions were being received at the rate of $0.23 per communicant, a very low figure compared to the $1.81 per member contributed through congregations in the newly organized New York Synod. The New York Synod's level of financial support translated into a "very active" involvement "on the field of Missions, Foreign as well as Home, in the latter especially, also among the Germans." Lower per capita giving in the Ministerium meant that mission support in the Ministerium was also low at the congregational level. The Ministerium's level of congregational giving for missions—by far the largest single synodical expenditure—amounted to $51.18 per congregation. But this was monies received from only twenty-one of fifty-eight congregations for an average of $141.36 and that was further skewed by the generosity—$300—of Krotel's Holy Trinity.[19]

Krotel had several reasons for raising the issue, including the poor support of other congregations which gave less than his newly formed congregation. Another reason had to do with his experience in the Pennsylvania Ministerium, for he called upon the synod to adopt a system of "Systematic Benevolence" as had "the Mother Synod," noting with assurance that in Pennsylvania such practices had "gratifying results." Following his lead the Ministerium adopted its own plan of Systematic Benevolence by which congregations were to "consider it a duty to place at the disposal of Synod a yearly contribution of at least fifty cents for every communing member." Lest this quota system be taken for what it was, the Committee hastened to add that according to the Word of God, no motive should be relied upon except free Christian love alone. For financially hardpressed German immigrants already accustomed to robbing *Petri* without necessarily paying *Paulus*, such assurances doubtless confirmed their belief that if one cannot give freely and generously, one should not give at all. By 1871 per communicant giving for synod work, as reported by the treasurer, dropped from $0.23 to $0.22! Therefore in 1872 the synod added another wrinkle to "Systematic Benevolence" motivated by pure love—a list of "Minimum contributions" quotas assigned to each congregation. Again the response was no better. Fortunately however Ministerium congregational membership was steadily increasing and so, too, was the dollar amount of contributions. In 1872 $4208 of a projected $5990 was raised, allowing the "Committee on Parochial Reports" to claim success regarding "the Minimum set down for the Congregations last year." Five years later, in 1877, the per communicant giving was still at $0.22! And there it hovered for the next decade, slowly drifting towards $0.21 without actually dropping another whole penny.[20]

This long-range picture presents a curious state of affairs. Missionary efforts, however effective they might otherwise have been, produced very few new congregations. There were fifty-eight (58) congregations in 1870 when President Krotel called for "systematic benevolence" to support home missions. And there were sixty-four (64) in 1877, five years after the merger with the Steimle Synod had brought at least ten new congregations into the synod. There had been accessions and mission starts besides the numbers received from the German Synod, but there had also been losses to other synods, most notably the Missouri Synod. President Krotel noted in his 1876 address that "many" might reach the conclusion the Ministerium "has already passed its meridian." What he failed to realize was that the Ministerium was growing not in numbers of congregations but in congregational size, something that was not happening in his English-language congregation because of the failure of Anglicized Lutherans to "cross-over" to English Lutheranism.[21] They remained with the German-speaking congregations where ethnic and cultural loyalty assured healthy congregational growth. In the same period of time that the number of congregations remained more or less constant, communicant membership increased almost 100 percent, from 12,936 to 24,733. Growth was taking place in the congregations—they were growing in size and in their capacity to sustain synod financial needs without increased per capita giving. Whatever per capita increases in giving occurred in congregations went into congregational activities.

HOME MISSIONS AND IMMIGRATION

What mission efforts the Ministerium managed to sustain at a synodical level were nonetheless significant. Such efforts had begun in the early 1860s through the Emigrant Mission, administered jointly with the Pennsylvania Ministerium. Coordination problems plagued the joint enterprise, including the New York Ministerium's unpaid indebtedness to the Emigrant Mission treasury as late as 1870. Another part of the problem concerned unresolvable conflicts between the joint representatives and the Missionary, Pastor Robert Neumann. For these and other reasons, the Emigrant Mission was put under the direct care and supervision of the General Council, relieving the Ministerium of its responsibility for the Mission. Yet New York Lutherans remained involved through their General Council support of Missions on their home territory at Castle Garden.[22]

Whatever the nature of the dispute, Pastor Neumann could report in 1869 on the important work which the Emigrant Mission was accomplishing. Worship was held Sundays for immigrants "lying over"; the Lord's Supper was administered to forty-five (45) communicants; eighteen (18) couples were married; thirteen (13) children were baptized, and two (2) buried. The mission also dealt with New York's nineteenth-century version of homelessness and poverty. Sixteen hundred and twenty (1620) cases of hunger were "appeased" and suffering "alleviated," while lodging was provided to homeless immigrants in sixty-six (66) cases. "Fifteen sick persons, whom I found in the evening without a place to remain all night, were provided for in like manner." "Men, women and children were supplied with boots, shoes, shirts, coats, dresses, caps, etc." in eighty-five (85) cases. "Thankfulness" and "praise" were words Pastor Neumann used often when summarizing his work: "more than ever, in hundreds of cases, has every request been granted, when I have bought to the notice of the authorities in Castle Garden, the sick, the hungry, the homeless and the discouraged. These miserable beings, according to the circumstances, were supplied with medicine, supports, shelter for the night, or sent to the hospital."[23]

Besides these efforts (Neumann's report continues), 468 persons "were received and sent forward" for strangers—presumably a service searching out immigrants which sent them on to their final destination with family or friends. $1,049.29 was loaned to seventy-five (75) persons so they could reach friends; of that $973.01 had been returned. Besides direct loans, money was exchanged for immigrants at Castle Garden and "in Wall-street" to the sum of $35,353.39. Also an immigrant post office, 1,967 letters were received for immigrants by the Emigrant Mission, and 1,134 sent on their behalf.[24]

However good the results, the Ministerium considered such efforts insufficient to the pressing needs of the immigrants. Neumann's problem centered on a rivalry between the Emigrant Mission and plans for an immigrant center to incorporate the Mission itself. These more inclusive plans were realized in 1873 with the founding of Emigrant House, with an office and chapel, near Castle Garden. A property was purchased in that year at "no. 16 State Street, opposite Battery Park, and . . . near Castle Garden (the place of landing)" for immigrants. The new Emigrant House (fig. 5.1) was to be opened in October and was looked upon as a "precious gift of God" since it would "remove the deplorable need of emigrants which existed until now and to carry on the Emigrant Mission effectually." A Ministerium visitor's committee reported two years later that they could whole-heartedly "join in the praise which so frequently is uttered regarding this house." Certain ethnic virtues were much in evidence, such as the "order and cleanliness dominating everywhere" as well as the "punctual care" of the business books and correspondence.

Missionary Berkemeier was praised for his work, including his "impressive admonitions" given youthful immigrants. A subsequent evaluation by a sympathetic historian drew the same general conclusions, adding details for emphasis. During thirty-seven years of operation, Emigrant House entertained 359,846 guests; of these 282,014 contributed to their own support; 67,832 were too poor to do so, and received shelter and food free of charge. Also, 26,450 free meals were distributed to unemployed immigrants in the City of New York. The institution had also written 140,351 letters, and issued over 500,000 pamphlets. Of 360,000 immigrants who were touched by the church, "hundreds have entered its fold," a point not lost on a Ministerium struggling to compete with other denominations for immigrant loyalty.[25]

Emigrant House did not see the worst cases however. They were sent to Ward's Island, the city immigrant station where "all emigrants who are sick and without means, friends, or a definite destination, are sent . . . until they can find other means of support, or until the time allowed them by law has expired" when they returned to Europe sick and destitute.

figure 5.1
Das deutsche Emigrantenhaus

By 1871, the New York City Commissioners of Emigration had determined that the largest percentage of the indigent Protestants on the island "belonged to the Lutheran Church, or were in some way connected with it," so the Ministerium was requested to provide a Chaplain for them. The Ministerium elected G. A. Schmidt, formerly pastor of St. Marks Church in Brooklyn, to serve in the post. Immediately taking up his duties he preached in German and English on Sundays, devoting "his whole time to the immigrants." Though his salary was paid by the Commissioners, some aid was also provided by the Ministerium's "Missionary Society of the City of New York," making it thereby a part of the synod's missionary efforts.[26]

This Missionary Society of the City of New York provided the other major focus of mission work in the Ministerium. It was formed November 1,1869 as "a Society, whose object is to prosecute the Mission work in the city of New York and vicinity." Until then the Executive Committee of synod had administered the mission work of the Ministerium. Besides being involved in the plight of arriving immigrants through Emigrant House and the Ward Island Chaplaincy, the synod needed a shepherd to gather immigrants into new congregations once they had arrived at their destination in the New York Area. As noted already, the 1868 Ministerium had called the Rev. Dr. Edward Moldehnke to do just that as its traveling missionary, a service he had performed previously for the Wisconsin Synod. Upon arriving in New York, Moldehnke chose instead to accept a call to St. Peters Church in Manhattan, joining the New York German (Steimle) Synod instead of the New York Ministerium. No substitute was found for Moldehnke, though the Ministerium's 1870 minutes reported a great need for someone to gather in the "scattered members of our beloved Church" living along the Erie Rail Road in New York, as well as in Massachusetts, Connecticut, and New Jersey. Instead of replacing Moldehnke the Missionary Committee was formed to oversee several on-site missionary pastors, all of whom were called to specific mission congregations. In addition the Committee administered synod funds disbursed in support of several congregations and divinity students.[27]

The new Missionary Society, actually a separate auxiliary of the Ministerium, was composed of twenty-five clergy and twenty congregations of the Ministerium. Though not representing the interests, resources or efforts of the entire synod, the Committee achieved impressive results by the time its first report was issued to synod in 1871. From the sites chosen and developed, it is clear that the Missionary Society rather than the Ministerium was responsible for the fateful policy which established new congregations away from *Kleindeutschland.* Mission congregations or Sunday schools (often a first mission step) were begun in Yonkers; Newark Bay; East Morrisana; at Wakefield, near Mount Vernon; and in New York City, at Thirty-fourth Street and 8th Avenue, and at Eighty-third Street, near Ninth Avenue. Three established congregations were also supported with funds, as was the Chapel on Ward's Island, which the Society also supplied with hymnals and a communion service.[28]

The Committee's work continued apace, which is to say it managed to do a fraction of what it could have done with sufficient funding. This should not be surprising. Poverty did, as poverty does, work in a vicious circle. The preponderance of Lutherans on Wards Island, and the great want seen in the Emigrant Mission, suggest a substantial number of impoverished Lutheran immigrants who would not be able to support either their own congregations or their synod as handsomely as did the

English Lutherans. Poor members supported poor congregations which supported a poor synod whose financial efforts on behalf of immigrants drew down funds for the support of new congregations! Poverty and underfunding were to persist as long as the flood tide of German immigration ran into New York Harbor. The same Ministerium (1876) which heard President Krotel wonder if the Ministerium had reached or passed its zenith also heard from its Executive Committee (which Krotel chaired) "regrets, that the means which it had to carry on the work of the Lord, were so insufficient."[29] As a result poor congregations established in upwardly mobile parts of the metropolitan area slowly prospered with the fluctuating (if rising) fortunes of the surrounding community and its upwardly mobile immigrant members.

THE PANIC OF 1873

The nation's economic depression had much to do with this financial state of affairs. The financial crisis had begun very close to home—on Wall Street—with the failure of Jay Cooke and Company, a leading investment banking firm heavily committed to postwar railroad construction. A prestigious firm which had managed government finances during the Civil War, the Jay Cooke and Company failure caused panic selling which precipitated a stock market crash. This September "Panic of 1873" in turn led to a depression lasting a full four years. Within months 5,000 businesses had gone bankrupt, and a half million workers were jobless—12 percent of the work force. Meanwhile the Federal government sought to alleviate the situation with an anti-inflationary policy detrimental to debtors and the poor.[30]

Depressed conditions remained through 1877, giving way thereafter to prosperity which lasted until the crash of 1893 and another round of depression and poverty. At the century's end, one in eight (1 in 8) Americans remained in poverty with the unskilled earning an average of $286 per year; by comparison skilled manufacturing workers earned $435, the average annual wage for railway employees was $560, business clerical workers average earnings were $848, postal employees made $878, while clergy income averaged $794. Wages remained fixed or declined slightly in the latter decades of the nineteenth century. However, real wages and purchasing power increased during this same period because the cost of living decreased with the growing standard of living industrialization brought.[31] This prosperity was part of a long-term economic growth in the United States which saw per capita living standards double every 47 years.

Financial hardship, then, was mostly short-term, being related to boom and bust cycles of economic growth which were part of a strong but immature economy. While real per capita growth in industrial output and personal income increased on average 1.5 percent per year during this period, the fluctuations because of the business cycles could be as much as plus or minus 10 percent.[32] The fluctuation was greater than minus 10 percent in the 1870s, a condition not repeated until the 1930s, which suggests how severe the Panic of 1873 and the resulting depression were to the working poor in the large immigrant population served by New York Ministerium congregations.

ORPHAN HOMES AND AID SOCIETIES

It was the new immigrant and the working poor—those who started at the bottom and lived in temporary poverty until a rising standard of living, family income, and upward mobility moved them beyond poverty level—who suffered most in America's economic circumstances. This suffering most often took the form of psychic pain and stress, poor health, alcoholism, illness, and premature death. Growing city populations, augmented by immigration, meant maximum demand on available housing, high real estate prices, and overcrowding in unhealthy tenements. Overcrowding, in turn, led to life-threatening epidemics—smallpox, cholera, measles, typhus, scarlet fever, diphtheria.[33]

These related problems were especially acute in urban areas like New York City which felt the greatest pressure from European (including German) immigration. City population more than doubled between 1850 and 1880, from 500,000 to 1,200,000. Fourteenth Street divided English-speaking uptown from a downtown dominated by Germans and Irish. Fifty percent of the population was crowded into an area of tenements, congestion, poverty, and environmental deterioration. By 1876 half of New York lived in the tenements, yet 65 percent of adult deaths occurred there as well as 90 percent of all infant fatalities. Uptown mortality rates were 20.44 per thousand. There fewer children died, while adults lived longer. Below Fourteenth Street the rate was 37.72! The differences were as stark as the contrast between first and third worlds and it would not improve until cities became healthier places to live with improved public health, something that did not occur until the turn of the century.[34] The daily reminders of endemic disease were marked by adult illness, many funerals, and orphaned children. No wonder the Ministerium started two orphan homes at Buffalo and Sulphur Springs (fig. 5.2) and jointly supported a third (started by William Alfred Passavant) at Mt. Vernon (fig. 5.3). Nor should synod commentators on parochial statistics have wondered that most congregations buried many beside their own members. In one case thirty-three (33) times as many non-members as members![35]

The Wartburg Orphan's Home at Mt. Vernon was one of several established by Passavant, American Lutheranism's most articulate spokesman for "inner missions" and its most successful organizer of inner mission social institutions. This Pittsburgh pastor, who had built up a sensitive, aggressive, expanding pastoral ministry in that city during the 1850s, was driven by a pietist's devotion "to the cause of mercy among the poor and suffering" to expand his inner mission empire to hospitals, orphans homes, schools, and deaconess communities. Once chided for "laying down" the ministry of Word and sacrament, Passavant replied that he refused to separate spiritual and secular concerns." "The gospel must be lived as well as told, or men disregard it as an idle dream."[36]

figure 5.2
Evangelical Lutheran St. Johns Orphan Home
(for Boys) Sulphur Springs, N. Y.

Passavant's vision was comprehensive:

> These are missions within the church, such as Scriptural revivals of religion; the instruction of the children of the church, comprehending Sunday-schools, infant schools, catechetical classes, Bible classes, etc.; the education of our people, comprehending Church schools, academies, colleges, theological seminaries and education societies; the relief of the temporal need of the members, including the Institution of Protestant Deaconesses, together with the various funds, societies, and institutions for the indigent, the aged and infirm, for disabled ministers, for the widows and orphans of the clergymen, etc.; the improvement of church architecture, of congregational singing, of the liturgical service, of the better observance of the order and worship of God's house.[37]

Passavant realized early on that hospital work and orphan work were related since the death of parents sometimes left hospital personnel with the difficult task of providing for the children who remained. His Orphan's Home in Pittsburgh (1852) soon developed into an Orphans' Farm School for Boys at Zelienople, Pennsylvania (an Orphans' Home for Girls at Rochester, Pennsylvania established in 1868 merged with the boys' Farm School at Zelienople in 1895).

figure 5.3
Wartburg Orphans' Farm School
Mount Vernon, New York

The Mt. Vernon home (fig. 5.3) followed in 1866 under the direction of Pastor G. C. Holls. By then the principles established as an experiment at the Farm School had proven sound. Above all the orphanage was to be a well-regulated Christian family. Children of all denominations were received at the home. Only "entire orphans" were accepted, since children with one parent experienced a conflict of authority between home family and parent. Legally indentured to the home, children were to remain there until coming of age. They were to be carefully instructed in "religion" based on Holy Scripture and Luther's Small Catechism. Early impressed with "the duty and the dignity of labor," the children were also taught a trade. Eventually half-orphans were admitted, and the institutional setting modified by the introduction of a cottage system, but Passavant's working principles remained operative into the twentieth century. While Mt. Vernon was an independent institution, Passavant pursued there as elsewhere a strong effort to enlist the support of the whole church, especially Lutheran organizations. It was in this spirit of cooperative inner missions that the Ministerium supported the work of Mt. Vernon, led by its president, New York pastor G. F. Krotel.[38]

Another kind of inner mission organization arose out of a need to support a family in the midst of illness or economic depression. Thus the appearance of "Aid Societies for the Sick," one of the most important kinds of *verein* to be organized within the German-speaking Lutheran congregations of *Kleinedeutschland* and as forerunners of benevolent insurance and savings-and-loan institutions in the United States. The Synod first took notice of these self-help organizations in 1871, when five were reported in Ministerium congregations, and urged their introduction into all congregations as "beneficial." Two years later, all four synodical conferences were urging adoption of aid societies "for the sick and poor within our congregations, according to principles of true Christian love and mercy . . . as a pressing need." The need was indeed great. By 1873—at the beginning of the Panic—the five (5) societies had multiplied threefold to fifteen (15), and would grow to a total of seventeen (17) by its end in 1877.[39] The Biblical concern for widows and orphans found a very immediate focus in daily life on New York streets and in its tenements. As expressed by a special synodical committee formed to examine the problem in 1874:

> As the royal law of holy love should have the dominion in every Christian congregation, and the first Christian congregation gives us the exalted example of a comprehensive and effective care for the needy, so it is and remains the unremitting duty of every Christian congregation, faithfully to care for their needy, especially their sick, poor, widows and orphans.[40]

However, this "holy duty" was frequently not "practiced aright" or at all, with the result that Lutherans were turning to others for support. Accordingly the synod proposed "a regulated system and definite rules" but not an organization apart from the congregation.

The synodical committee on aid societies thought aid should be administered by congregation officials and be well funded by whatever means, like setting aside 10 percent of congregational revenues, or collecting a minimum fee from all members, while those who could afford more might show their liberality with free-will offerings. Levels of support should be determined ahead of time and a strict distinction made between support in cases of death, sickness, and poverty.

Necessity was forcing the synod to think big. The preferred method for handling death, illness, and poverty, was to include all of these need-related crises as part of an overall "systematic beneficence" by which a great sum could be raised "for the different objects of God's kingdom."[41] Whether or not such aid societies, and the social needs of the congregations, were drawing funds away from support of the Mission Society during a time of economic depression, it was clear that the combined social ministry and mission needs of the Ministerium and its congregations ran well beyond its fund-raising capacities. If congregational resources were used in anything like the proportions suggested by the synod, money spent in the congregation meant less would be spent for mission and relief work at the synodical level.

A PAROCHIAL EDUCATION SYSTEM

The auxiliary Mission Society was but one of two organized expressions of mission in the synod. The other was the Committee on Missions and Education which was also concerned with the educational development of the Ministerium and its congregations. Mission work—organizing congregations, providing pastors, employing missionaries for further congregational organization and outreach to immigrants—had an educational dimension which made the yoking of mission and education in one Committee a natural combination for the New York Ministerium.

That body had long needed a seminary for new pastors, and by 1868 (as already noted) the Ministerium was actively negotiating with the new Philadelphia Seminary to established an endowed German professorship to facilitate the education of pastors for the home synod. But this provision only helped provide theological education for the Ministerium's seminary students. What of those who had not yet reached this stage in their education? The Ministerium early on realized that there were no facilities to prepare students for the seminary. A need for a proseminary was only part of the total problem. In the 1869 meeting of the Ministerium the Second and Third Conferences noted that there were no facilities to educate "Parochial School Teachers" as well as "no preparatory School for Theological Students." In response to this challenge the synod appointed two committees to plan for the creation of academies—one in the eastern part of the synod, and one in the west—to educate young Lutherans beyond the parochial school level in preparation for seminary. It was proposed, meanwhile, that training parochial school teachers would occur in schools attached to Ministerium Orphan Houses at Mount Vernon and Buffalo. By 1870 the Ministerium was ready to establish "an Anglo-German School-Teachers' Seminary in the East" at the Wartburg Orphan House at Mount Vernon, partly because it meant supporting a project already under way among Lutheran congregations in the east. Because this was a project of interest to Lutherans beyond the synod, the Ministerium asked the General Council to see it through.[42]

In 1871, meanwhile, the synod committee appointed the previous year to explore establishing an academy in the western part of the state reported favorably on such a proposal. This was to be a "literary and classical institution" capable of giving "our youth" a "liberal education, who would otherwise have neither the desire nor ability, and probably lead many into the ministry who without such an institution would never think of entering it." Its eastern counterpart reported favorably on already-existing St. Matthews Academy in Manhattan, a parochial school of St. Matthews Lutheran Church, which offered to receive pre-theology students tuition free. Finally, a 1871 special report to the synod on efforts to find seminary graduates in Germany concluded that few would be available in the future and that "it is of the highest importance to establish institutions of our own."[43]

Yet other educational plans went forward along lines developed in the New York Conference of the Ministerium. After thoroughly discussing "the question of establishing a Lutheran Sunday School Union" a meeting of pastors, church officers, and Sunday school teachers was called to meet at St. Matthews Church in March of 1870. Fourteen Sunday schools and 300 teachers were represented, a large group which was "unanimous" in its enthusiasm for such a union. A committee was appointed and a constitution drafted for a union which fully expected "to exert a beneficial influence upon our Sunday Schools and congregations." A year later President Krotel noted that "we have no higher institution of learning, such as a College." He proposed involvement with the new Muhlenberg College where "our students would enjoy the advantages of a proper training in the spirit of our Church." A special committee on the subject of education pulled most of these strands together in an 1871 report which set a new educational agenda for the synod. Whereas the lack of ministers would force the synod to "abandon some fields to other communions, or to leave them entirely neglected," as well as to watch synod congregations organized by them separate to join other Lutheran bodies which could supply pastors, three resolutions were passed to deal with the problem: 1) Congregations were admonished to work hard for the "elevation and improvement of the existing Parochial Schools"; 2) The synod was called upon to establish two academies in the eastern and western parts of the state "which shall ensure to young men a solid education in the spirit of our church, both in the German and English languages, as a preparation for College and Theological Seminary"; and, 3) the synod was urged to go forward with plans to establish a "Professorship in the Theological Seminary at Philadelphia."[44]

What emerged with these proposals amounted to a system of religious education consisting of five parts: 1) *Sunday church schools,* with schools and teachers organized into a comprehensive Union for planning and development; 2) *Parochial day schools* established for the total education of children in the community, including their religious instruction; 3) *Academies* in the eastern and western portions of the state to provide a liberal education for students of the parochial schools and others who wished or needed such an education, especially those with plans to pursue a call to the Lutheran ministry; 4) Two *teachers seminaries* to educate some of these Lutheran students for work as teachers in the Ministerium's parochial schools, undertaken in cooperation with the General Council; 5) the beginning of cooperative efforts in *support of a college* (Muhlenberg) of higher education; and, 6) cooperation with other General Council synods, most notably the Pennsylvania Ministerium, in the development of a *confessionally conservative seminary* at Philadelphia.

Such educational enthusiasm reflected an abiding Lutheran interest in general education with a Christian focus. Martin Luther advocated universal education in Germany for the sake of both laity and clergy—so that each individual might be able to read scripture and faithfully discharge his duties to God and man; also to prepare suitable persons for the ministry. "Where the Holy Scriptures does not rule" he observed, "I certainly advise no one to send his child." Though Biblically centered he envisioned a general education which embraced languages, history, math, science, physical training, music, and practical instruction for various callings. In the United States with its separation of church and state individual Lutheran congregations especially in New York, Pennsylvania, Delaware, New Jersey, Maryland, the Carolinas, Virginia, and Georgia began the practice of establishing this European state curriculum in Lutheran schools (342 schools were established by as early as 1820). Though the growth in public education eventually reduced the need for this parochial education, among the German congregations in the New York Ministerium the strong tradition of parochial education reasserted itself by 1870 specifically as an alternative to public education. One reason for their strength was the language of instruction—German. While secular German immigrants and their offspring prized the mother tongue to preserve culture and values (given up far less easily by Germans than by other ethnic groups); among church people it was often observed that "Language saves faith."[45]

The Ministerium's 1871 parochial reports indicated that religious schools existed in only a third of the parishes—approximately twenty (20) schools. The American Sunday School was more popular, and considered by some to be sufficient to a child's religious education, an attitude that we have seen vexed the Steimle Synod. But the Ministerium Committee on parochial education was

> thoroughly persuaded that the Sunday School can never take the place of the Parochial School, and that a congregation can only have a true life and vigor when the youth are trained up in the bosom of the Church, but this cannot be done as long as they are sent to [public] schools that do not teach religion.[46]

To promote the interests of parochial education a list of "school questions" was prepared for inclusion in the Ministerium's standardized parochial report form. The Committee also recommended synodical visitation to realize "the object we strive for." With such a push, the number of parochial schools increased, though slowly—from twenty

(20) in 1871, to twenty-four (24) in 1872, to thirty-one (31) in 1873. The big jump between 1872 and 1873, a reporting committee warned, resulted from the merger with the Steimle Synod. All did not survive, however, for the 1877 report of the synod indicated only twenty-eight (28) schools in existence. Some congregations gave reasons for having no school, others "mention substitutes, e.g.: Saturday Schools, Bible Classes, etc." The reporting committee considered this state of affairs a sign of "important progress." Whether 50 percent compliance seemed an optimistic or a pessimistic sign, statistics for the year ending 1877 suggest a significant parochial system at work: there were thirty (30) schools (not 28, as reported by the committee), fifty-three (53) teachers (nine of whom were pastors), and 2,431 pupils. What is more, it was a system which the synod sought to integrate into its leadership structure with the formal involvement of parochial school teachers in synodical deliberations.[47]

The plans for teachers, seminaries to educate parochial school teachers did not go as smoothly. In 1875, the synod was still trying to collect $15,000 to establish a seminary at the Wartburg Home. The financial crisis of 1872 had slowed the rate of collections. So, too, had a lack of enthusiasm for the project in the synod at large. Only a part of the synod was enthusiastic—presumably the 50 percent which conducted the parochial schools. But there was enthusiasm and support from outside of the Ministerium in other eastern synods. Therefore an 1874 decision establishing synodical jurisdiction over the proposed Wartburg Seminary was reversed in 1875; it was concluded that "a more limited association is more beneficial for the founding" of the seminary. Thereafter the Wartburg Seminary evolved into an auxiliary Lutheran institution with which the synod was in sympathy but which was only supported by churches and synods active in parochial education.[48]

The high stakes involved in parochial education and teacher-training can be understood by noting the reason given for such support. (Also, perhaps, the reason for resisting public education.) Great educational ferment was at work among German Americans, and not always of a kind to benefit the church. The lack of a "German-English Teacher's Seminary" was noted by those in support of the Wartburg endeavor. Two other teachers institutions had been established—one by the German-American Teachers Union of New York, the other by an Association of "influential Germans in this city." The teachers union openly declared its intent to "extirpate every root of Christian faith from the heart of the youth," while the Association's more neutral plans called for the introduction of German pedagogical methods to reform the American school system. Both efforts were looked upon, however, as having "anti-Christian purposes void of religion." The Wartburg Seminary supporters noted that the German immigrant population contained "thousands of . . . professed unbelievers" and even those nomi-nally religious had "imbibed infidel principles in Europe." The low-rate of church affiliation in *Kleindeutschland* and the high rate of secular associations were proof of the problem the church faced. Given this state of affairs (and point of view), there could be no neutral ground in the field of education. Educational options were stark in the immigrant community: it was either religious or antireligious. Only by the former (the supporters insisted) could the command be fulfilled to "Feed my lambs!" And that could not be done, the Ministerium believed, without daily instruction in the Word of God, without parochial schools, and "without able and true confessional teachers."[49]

Religion was not the only consideration, however. The Ministerium's plan of Lutheran Christian education would also carry forward the liberal educational tradition which had developed in Medieval Europe. Here the Ministerium had the best and worst of results. The Academy associated with St. Matthews Church, traceable to a school established by New York City Lutherans in 1752 or 1753, proved from the outset to be an ideal academic institution for the synod's purposes. It was well run and academically sound. The synod's 1875 visitors to St. Matthews Academy reported on a school ably managed under the "untiring zeal of the director, Mr. Bohm, with 267 scholars, forty-three (43) more than 1874, and eighty-two (82) more than 1873. The "higher classes are especially well filled" with Greek and Latin students, while two "young ladies" were "preparing to be teachers." However the western seminary never developed at all! The Academy of the West was established at Newark, in Wayne County, and was to be wholly owned and supported by the synod. A class was organized for the 1874 academic year. It gathered for a second year at the beginning of 1875, though with nine fewer scholars due to differences with its director, the Rev. Mr. Giese. A protracted dispute proved too much for the new and very small institution and its doors were closed in 1876 with the synod forced into the time-consuming task of trying to sell the property. As a result the synod was urged to direct its limited financial means to the exclusive support of St. Matthews where four of the six members of the advanced class were financial "beneficiaries of the N. Y. Ministerium." By 1877 four students had completed "the prescribed course of study" and "will now attend the Seminary at Philadelphia (figure 5.4)."[50]

MINISTERIUM SUPPORT FOR THE PHILADELPHIA SEMINARY

The new seminary was the capstone of the Ministerium's parochial education system. Invited to participate in its direction and financial support while Reinhold Adelberg was still president, the Ministerium moved to establish a German professorship at the new institution. The monies already collected by the Ministerium, before the withdrawal of General Synod Lutherans, and intended for such a post at Hartwick

Seminary, were left in the hands of the Seminary's collector, but the uncollected portion of the subscription was "called in" and reallocated. In 1871 President Krotel, one of the original Philadelphia Seminary faculty until his call to New York, suggested soon after becoming Ministerium president that the "proper time had come" to establish a similar position at Philadelphia since "Our people possess the means." The Synod agreed, and by 1872 it was reported that the president and Seminary Board of Directors were negotiating the terms of support and involvement.[51]

figure 5.4
Lutheran Theological Seminary, Philadelphia, Pa

To stimulate interest, Krotel also reported that a member of his own congregation, Mrs. Anna Burkhalter, "had resolved to found an English Professorship" at Philadelphia with financial support in the sum of $30,000. Widow of Charles Burkhalter, a wealthy leader in the successful effort to form Holy Trinity and to call Krotel, it was of special consequence to her that "our Ministerium might be animated by it as soon as possible to accomplish the founding of a German Professorship." When a single woman "lays such an offering upon the altar, should it be impossible for an entire Synod to do the same?" So challenged, the synod went on to propose the professorship, accepting the Seminary's terms of support and governance, and began raising an annual subscription of $2000 for its support from among the Ministerium clergy. It also nominated Philadelphia pastor, August Spaeth, to the post (with prime responsibility in the New Testament), while Mrs. Burkhalter nominated Charles W. Schaeffer, DD., Pennsylvania Ministerium president, as the new English professor "ordinarius."[52] Schaeffer and Spaeth joined three colleagues to form the new faculty—W. J. Mann, C. P. Krauth, and Charles F. Schaeffer.

The Burkhalter legacy made possible Schaeffer's full-time devotion to the seminary where he taught Church History, New Testament, and Practical Theology in the English language. It also strengthened the fortunes of conservative confessionalism in the Philadelphia Seminary. Spaeth's uncle and the faculty chair, C. F. Schaeffer, now taught the Lutheran confessions from the perspective of old Lutheran orthodoxy while Krauth, a more sophisticated theologian with responsibilities for teaching Dogmatics and church polity, promoted the conservative revival of Confessional theology among American Lutherans. His colleague, W. J. Mann, a German with developed interests in American history, besides teaching Symbolics (the confessions), Ethics, German Homiletics, biblical exegesis, and Hebrew, collaborated with the eminent church historian Philip Schaff, of Mercersburg Theological Seminary, in editing *Der deutsche Kirchenfreund*, a cultured monthly journal commenting on American religious life. His *Plea for the Augsburg Confession* (1856) and his history *Lutheranism in America* (1857) placed the emerging General Council confessional trajectory at the moderate center of American Lutheranism, to the right of the General Synod which (Mann believed) sacrificed its Lutheran heritage and made gospel into law, but to the left of the Missouri and Buffalo Synods which repristinated its confessional "heritage uncharitably and pharisaically."[53] However, changes were about to take place in the New York Ministerium which seriously challenged this moderate conservatism.

MERGER WITH THE STEIMLE SYNOD

Mann, the Seminary historian, might have added the Steimle Synod to the new synods on the Right except that it had not yet been formed. The synod remained a separate organization for only three years, suggesting how changeable Lutheran confessionalism was in the New York area. The Ministerium was in transition during the late 1860s and early 1870s with its slowly developing plans for a parochial educational system. Not until after the Steimle Synod reunited with the Ministerium did the larger body finish this evolution into a conservative Lutheran synod and because of the return of the Steimle radicals.

It was the General Council's 1867 statement of Fundamental Principles, accepting all the Lutheran confessions, which first stimulated merger talks between the Ministerium and its radical breakaways. In 1869 the Ministerium's New York Conference proposed reunion and Steimle officials concurred. Since the Ministerium had "adopted the full confessional basis of the Lutheran Church," there were now no obstacles "which could stand in the way of a brotherly union." Yet obstacles emerged, which required several years of intensive negotiations before merger would actually occur.[54]

The Steimle Synod balked at joining a group which had not yet incorporated its new confessional position into its constitution (then being revised) and said so in statements published in the press. What lay behind its concern was the still significant if narrowing gap between the two groups' confessional positions. In 1866 the German Evangelical Lutheran Synod of New York, in considering the apostasy from the confessional foundations of the fathers, had committed itself in an "Sendschreiben" (open letter) to the fundamental profession of faith as found in the 1580 Book of Concord, by which it believed the Lutheran church to stand or fall.[55] The Ministerium, on the other hand, until the adoption of its 1870 constitution, had merely committed its clergy, upon ordination

> To receive . . . the Word of God . . . as the only infallible rule of faith and practice; and the Augsburg Confession, as a correct exhibition of the fundamental doctrines of the Divine Word, and of the faith of our church founded upon that word.[56]

The revised constitution (1870), committing the Ministerium to acceptance of the unaltered Augsburg Confession as in agreement with the Word, and a correct demonstration of it, closed this gap somewhat by now including Melanchthon's "Apology, Luther's Catechism, the Smalcald Articles, and the Formula of Concord as true developments of doctrine." [57]

President Krotel strongly objected to the Steimle Synod's going public over these differences. It gave a wrong impression of the Ministerium's confessional basis he believed. Personally he had no idea how the Ministerium would respond to such an uncharitable statement.[58] At this point personal differences and procedural problems dominated merger talks. The Ministerium's New York Conference insisted the Steimle pastors admit that the treatment of Pastor Halfmann and not confessional differences was the real ground of the original separation. This, they insisted, was not sufficient reason for separation. The Steimle Synod, meanwhile, debated the idea of merger for two days, deciding to remain a separate synod until plans formed to create a Lutheran synod for New York City and vicinity. However, Steimle pastor Dr. Edward Moldehnke, who had originally been called to the New York area as a Ministerium mission pastor, pushed for renewed discussions. These occurred as a series colloquia with the New York Conference on the articles of the Augsburg Confession. Renewed contact and growing trust led Conference members to invite German Synod members to attend the 1871 meeting of the Ministerium. By then the Steimle pastors had reached the point of negotiating particulars. They presented several points for discussion involving the merger: no individuals (presumably Halfmann) were to be excluded from the merger;

the Ministerium should absorb the German Synod's church newspaper (the *Kirkenblatt*); and its city mission program. To these the Ministerium agreed, adding that members received from the German Synod should be "bound by our Synodical constitution." Predictably the Steimle pastors objected, given the still significant differences in confessional viewpoint. One more round of discussions ensued on the adequacy of the Ministerium's new Constitution before the smaller synod agreed in its 1872 synodical gathering to a merger of the two groups.[59]

At the merger, all but F. W. T. Steimle joined the Ministerium, the German Synod's president having been opposed to merger from the outset. His opposition seems to have been more cultural than confessional since he was (himself) a staunch confessionalist. Steimle remained without synodical affiliation until his death in 1880, though in 1872 (the year of the merger) he did organize the German Pastoral Conference of New York and Brooklyn. Perhaps it was Steimle who was holding out for a New York City area Lutheran Synod. Certainly he did not propose a Protestant German-speaking conference, for as the theses which he proposed for debate in the 1871 synod clearly indicate, there could never be any church union with Roman Catholics, Greek Orthodox, or other Protestant churches. All must give up their errors, for the "faith of the Lutheran Church is securely founded on the Word of God of the Old and New Testaments. It is therefore the right faith." "German" was probably the operative term for his conference. A colleague characterized Steimle as "German, with life and soul German." German-speaking homes and schools which spoke often "about Dr. Martin Luther" were his formula for keeping the faith of the fathers in a new land. For him, the old was better, especially the imperial Germany then emerging under Kaiser Wilhelm I and his Iron Chancellor, Otto Von Bismarck. "Germany is the leading power of the world" he believed, and in the world "there are no people like the German people," who are "the most sincere and upright and have taken to themselves most completely to the word of God."[60]

ETHNICITY AND RELIGION

Such sentiments might easily be misunderstood as racial chauvinism, nothing more. Instead they point to a persistent relationship between ethnicity and religion which profoundly shaped life and culture in Europe as well as America.[61] Ethnicity itself is not an anachronism, nor is the long-perceived relationship between ethnicity and religion to be considered an anachronism which disappears among immigrant groups with assimilation into a new land and culture. Indeed, ethnic religious bodies, like the Steimle German Synod, or the reorganized Ministerium, functioned as progressive agencies of acculturation and opportunity, meeting new challenges in a changing environment to enhance the fortunes of the communities which they served, in this case the German immigrants in the more urban centers of the greater New York area. The Ministerium's rapid restructuring to include German-speaking congregations, mutual aid societies, parochial schools, and social service agencies all point to a preoccupation with building an immigrant community.

Religious institutions—Protestant congregations, Roman Catholic parishes, Jewish synagogues—were especially important to this process. Though in competition with other cultural definers (such as education societies with an atheistic bent), it was the institutions of religion which were the enduring, mediating sources of meaning and value in the new immigrant communities. A variety of historians, anthropologists, sociologists, theologians, and biblical scholars have recently come to emphasize the unique role religion plays in shaping ethnic communities. While language and ethno-genetic factors are themselves important, it is belief and ritual which provide the overarching umbrella of meaning, legitimacy, and identity that make community possible in a world of distinct communities.

Thus the experience of immigration required theological reflection and interpretation. The individual's uprooting from old world ties, and transplantation to a new world community of compatriots, involved experiences requiring the ministration of the church—the moral confusion and conflicts involving the decision to emigrate, guilt over parents and family left behind, loneliness in a new land, a search for community and friendship, spiritual neediness in sickness, in want, and in death. The religious dimension was especially prominent in two regards. One was the ethical dimension—a heightened regard for correct behavior in a strange land which demanded bewildering choices—what the historian of immigration, Marcus Lee Hansen, styled "immigrant Puritanism." The other was a redefinition of ethnic boundaries in religious terms, and in the case at hand, more restrictive confessional ones.

Neither language nor ethnic origin made new communities of immigrants in the United States; it was the immigrant's willingness to become a member of such and such a community, most often by joining the church or synagogue at its psychic and spiritual center. Yet the community was wider still, including those who were not officially church members. It is little wonder, therefore, that in congregations of the restructured Ministerium the privilege and comforts of Baptism and Christian burial were extended far beyond the confines of membership into the tenements of the German community in Manhattan.[62] Yet this occurred even as these same communities were establishing strict confessional boundaries between themselves and the larger urban world. The ethnoreligious pattern developed within the Steimle Synod, then, was not an amusing anachronism among confused and homesick Germans. Managing the crucial transition, they brought their ethnoreligious stance into the New York Ministerium with them at a time when it was being restructured to suit the needs of an immigrant Lutheran community. The resulting political upheaval within the Ministerium contributed to a decided theological shift to the right within the General Council. Historically speaking, "The Standpoint of Our Fathers," which really shaped the changing Ministerium, was not that of the late eighteenth-century Kunze generation of colonial "Fathers" but one associated with German language, religion, and culture. It is to the interaction of this changed Ministerium and the General Council in the latter half of the 1870s that we now turn.

NOTES

1 New York Ministerium, *Minutes* (1867), 5-6; (1868), 6-10. New York Synod, *Minutes* (1867), 2-3.
2 Ibid. (1868), 4-5.
3 Burkhardt is quoted in Carl E. Schorske, *Fin-De-Siecle Vienna. Politics and Culture* (New York: Vintage Books, 1981), xxv.
4 See above, Chapter 1.
5 *Minutes* (1868), 13.
6 Ibid., 17.
7 G. F. Krotel, *A Discourse Delivered on the Tenth Anniversary of the Evangelical Lutheran Church of the Holy Trinity, of New York City* (New York City: privately printed, 1878) SC 1: 4-5.
8 Ibid., 8.
9 *Minutes* (1868), 11, 23, 3.
10 Ibid., 27.
11 Ibid., 61ff.
12 Ibid., 63.
13 Ibid., 28.
14 Ibid.
15 *Lutheran Cyclopedia* (1975), 52. New York Ministerium, *Minutes* (1868), 57. See Ch. 4.
16 Ibid., 58.
17 *Lutheran Cyclopedia* (1975), 85, 405. New York Ministerium, *Minutes* (1868), 61.
18 Ibid. (1869), 23, 38.
19 New York Ministerium, *Minutes* (1870), 35-6. Ibid., 11; (1874), 52. The figures are to be found in Ibid., 6-8, 10-11, 41-2.
20 Ibid., (1870), 36, 49, 58, 29, 68-70; (1872), 41, 67; (1877), 17, 67-8; (1874), 60.
21 Ibid. (1876), 15. Krotel, *Discourse* (New York City: privately printed, 1878) SC 1: 15-17.
22 *Minutes* (1869), 19, 48; (1870), 15-17.
23 Ibid., 49.
24 Ibid., 48-9.
25 The difficulties dragged on to the point of charges being aired in the 1874 meeting of the Ministerium. See Ibid. (1875), 61; (1873), 60; (1875), 81. Charles R. Keiter, "Immigration in the Nineteenth Century in Its Relation to

the Lutheran Church in the United States," *Lutheran Church Review* 31 (1912): 275.

26 *Minutes* (1871), 22-23.

27 Ibid. (1869), 29; (1870), 28, 51-2; (1868), 56.

28 Ibid. (1870), 28; (1868), 56; (1871), 48-9.

29 Ibid. (1876), 59.

30 Richard N. Current, et. al., *American History. A Survey. Volume II: Since 1865* (New York: Alfred A. Knopf, 1987), 455. Joseph R. Conlin, *The American Past. Part Two. A Survey of American History Since 1865* (New York: Harcourt Brace Jovanovich, 1987), 474, 503.

31 Conlin, *American Past,* 503.

32 Robert L. Heilbronner and Lester C. Thurow, *Economics Explained* (Englewood Cliffs: Prentice-Hall, 1982), 47-8.

33 Conlin, *American Past,* 530-31.

34 Milton Klein, *New York: The Centennial Years 1676-1976* (Port Washington, NY: Kennikat Press, 1976), Albert Fein, "Centennial Years, 1850 to 1880," 75-95.

35 New York Ministerium, *Minutes* (1873), 51; (1874), 59.

36 Robert H. Fischer, "William Alfred Passavant and the Church's Ministry of Mercy," (paper delivered to The Passavant Society of the Wartburg Home, Mt. Vernon, N. Y.; copyright 1992 by The Wartburg Home of the Evangelical Lutheran Church in America), 4. Quotation to be found in George H. Gerberding, *Life and Letters of W. A. Passavant* (Greenvile, Pa.: Young Lutheran Co., 1906), 195-6. To be published in 1993 as a monograph, by The Passavant Society of the Wartburg Home, Mt. Vernon, N. Y.

37 Passavant quoted in August Sueflow and E. Clifford Nelson, "Following the Frontier," *The Lutherans in North America,* ed. E. Clifford Nelson (Philadelphia: Fortress Press, 1975). The original is to be found in Gerberding, *Life and Letters of W. A. Passavant,* 281, 283-4.

38 Fischer, "William Alfred Passavant and the Church's Ministry of Mercy," 14-16.

39 *Minutes* (1871), 10-12, 56; (1871), 51, 78; (1877), 66-8.

40 Ibid. (1874), 57.

41 Ibid., 57-8.

42 Ibid. (1869), 42-3; (1870), 48, 59.

43 Ibid., 42-3; (1870), 34-5, 56, 39; (1871), 46, 67.

44 Ibid. (1870), 28-9; (1871), 67.

45 Luther quoted in "Christian Education: Day Schools," *The Encyclopedia of the Lutheran Church,* ed. Julius Bodensieck (Minneapolis: Augsburg Publishing House), 420. For a detailed summary analysis of "Christian Education" see *Lutheran Cyclopedia* (1975), 163ff. Walter H. Beck, *Lutheran Elementary Schools in the United States* (St. Louis: Concordia Publishing House, 1965), notes that in this period the Pennsylvania and New York Ministeria together had 62 parochial schools, with the latter having a much greater percentage relative to its total number of congregations. Heinz Kloss, "German-American Language Maintenance Efforts," *Language Loyalty in the United States*, ed. Joshua A. Fishman (New York: Humanities Press, 1968), 206-252.

46 New York Ministerium, *Minutes* (1871), 55.

47 Ibid., 77; (1873), 78; (1877), 62, 73, 31.

48 Ibid. (1875), 72-3, 79.

49 Ibid., 72-3. See "Report of the Committee on the German Population in North America," in General Synod, *Minutes* (1864), 43-44.

50 *Lutheran Cyclopedia* (1975), 164. Because St. Matthew eventually joined the Lutheran Church, Missouri Synod, St. Matthew's Academy is honored as the oldest school in that church body. New York Ministerium, *Minutes* (1875), 29; (1874), 25; (1875), 38-9; (1876), 26-7; (1876), 26-7; (1877), 20-21.

51 Ibid. (1869), 36; (1871), 30; (1872), 28-31.

52 Ibid. (1872), 30. G. F. Krotel, *Discourse* (New York City: privately printed, 1878) SC 1: 7, 11. New York Ministerium, *Minutes* (1872), 57, 61, 63, 70, 76; (1873), 26. The minutes incorrectly identify him as F. W. Schaeffer.

53 Theodore G. Tappert, *History of the Lutheran Theological Seminary at Philadelphia. 1864-1964* (Philadelphia, 1964), 50, 71, 44-49.

54 German New York Synod, *Minutes* (1869), 2: 8, 10-11, 22. New York Ministerium, *Minutes* (1869), 41-2.

55 German New York Synod, *Minutes* (1866), "Sendschreiben," 1.

56 New York Ministerium, *Constitution* (1856).

57 New York Ministerium, *Constitution* (1870), p. 4. (Both the 1856 and 1870 constitutions are to be found in the Ministerium Archives, Wagner College.)

58 New York Ministerium, *Minutes* (1870), 21, 66, 68-70.

59 Steimle Synod, *Minutes* (1870), 2:34, 39, 42-3. Ministerium, *Minutes* (1870), 66-73. Steimle Synod, *Minutes* (1871) 2:65-7: 72-3; 76-8, 82, 98; (1872) 2:126-7, 134-5, 141-2. New York Ministerium, *Minutes* (1871), 31, 41; (1872), 24-28, 57-9.

60 *Lutheran Cyclopedia* (1975), 734-5. Steimele Synod, *Minutes* (1871), 2:92. Kraeling, *Unser Zion,* 45-6. *Kirchenblatt,* April, 1871.

61 For a detailed treatment of the subject see Timothy L. Smith, "Religion and Ethnicity in America," *AHR* LXXXII (1978): 1155-1185; also Timothy L. Smith, "Religious Denominations as Ethnic Communities: A Regional Case Study," *Denominationalism,* ed. Russell E. Richy (Nashville: Abingdon, 1977), 185-206.

62 Timothy L. Smith, "Religion and Ethnicity in America," *AHR* LXXXII (1978): 1160-61. Smith notes, in particular, the work of the Biblical scholar William F. Albright and his students; also Jurgen Moltmann's *Theology of Hope.* An important account of this process can be found Norman Gottwald's, *Tribes of Yahweh* (Maryknoll: Orbis Books, 1979).

6
CONGREGATIONALISM
The Changing New York Ministerium and the General Council, 1872-1882

"PASSED ITS MERIDIAN?"

In his Annual Report for the year 1876, President G. F. Krotel made a fateful observation about the destiny of the New York Ministerium. Viewing it primarily as a clerical body—a gathering of ordained colleagues—he observed that while the Ministerium had recovered from the crisis of the late 1860s, it was not as strong as it had been in previous years. Thinking primarily of pastors, and of the recent decrease in their numbers, he observed:

> Although we have sustained such losses, by the death and withdrawal of some of the brethren, that many a one might come to the conclusion; that the New York Ministerium has not only reached, but has already passed its meridian, and is now suffering with infirmities of old age; we will not therefore, be discouraged.[1]

If counting pastors was all that mattered, he was correct. Yet his assessment of the Ministerium's probable future was wide of the mark. He was out of touch with important trends in the Ministerium and its congregations, trends which were changing the face of New York Lutheranism.

True, the Ministerium's clerical leadership had decreased in size while the number of congregations remained static. But the congregations themselves were increasing in membership at a very healthy rate. As the following graph 6.1 indicates, the Ministerium had entered a phase of *allogenous* growth by the middle 1870s, incorporating new members from outside existing families and their baptized offspring![2]

The Ministerium was growing faster than the 19-county population where it enjoyed its greatest numerical strength. It was growing faster than the German community from which it drew its members. More interesting still, its density (the percentage of Lutherans in the

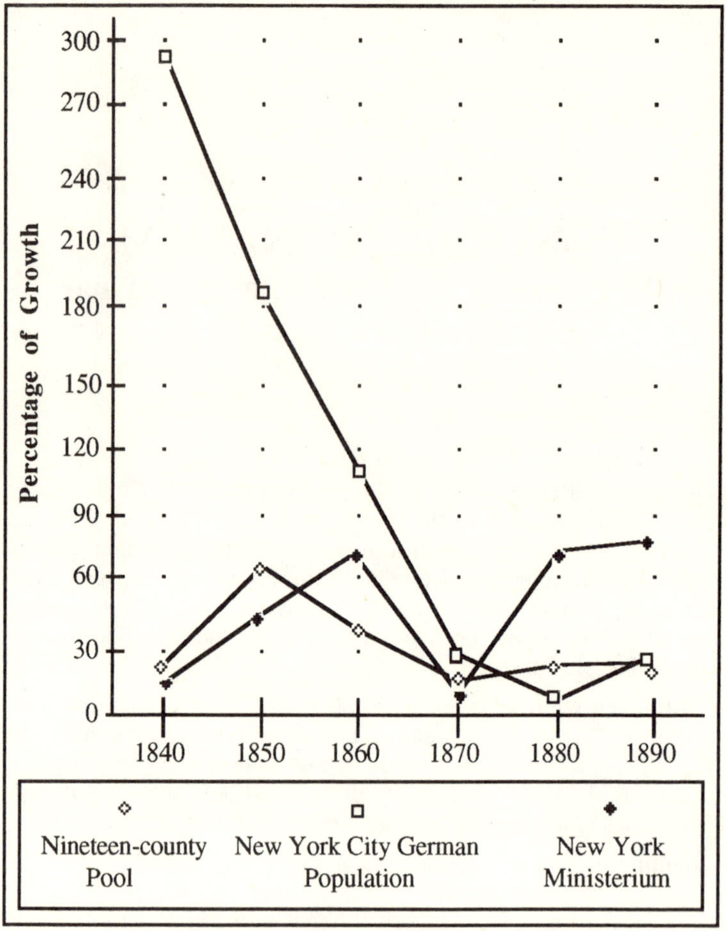

Graph 6.1 New York Ministerium Growth

population) was increasing while the density of the German community (the percentage of Germans in the total population) was decreasing! By a number of measurements the New York Ministerium could be considered a fast-growing mission field. As indicated in Chapter 4, recent growth in the German community was due to delayed marriage among German immigrants, which meant an expanding community of young families in the 1870s and 1880s. Responding to this situation (as seen in Chapter 6), a changing Ministerium restructured its congregational life, developing a ministry reaching out into the community through the Sacrament of Baptism with followup through an expanding system of parochial education.

Much of this growth was in the larger cities in New York State, especially New York City, Rochester, and Buffalo, the last a home mission field the New York Ministerium shared with the Buffalo and Missouri Synods. Some idea of their success can be had by comparing the size of the German foreign-born population with that of the German-language congregations in New York City. Table 6.1 provides a comparison of adult Lutheran communicants and the German Lutheran population in this largest urban area.

Table 6.1
Lutheran Communicants
as Percentage of Lutheran Immigrants in New York City

Year	NY Ministerium (5)	Missouri Synod (5)	Total
1850	3.9	4.6	18.5
1860	0.9	3.3	14.2
1870	10.3	8.4	18.7
1880	17.2	10.9	28.1
1890	13.3	9.4	22.7

Like snapshots of change taken at ten-year intervals, the above percentages indicate the relative size of the German Lutheran church in New York and the larger German-speaking population of nominal Lutherans between 1850 and 1890. In 1850, for example, the German-speaking Lutheran churches were recruiting just 1 in 6 members of the larger community, a ratio that dropped to 1 in 7 by 1860. With a substantial increase in the size of the larger community between 1860 and 1870, that ratio had nevertheless decreased to about 1 in 5. By 1880 with a growing system of congregations and parochial schools in New York City, the ratio of converts to community members was slightly less than 1 in 3. A decade later the ratio had declined once again, to just over 1 in 5.

What was different about this kind of growth was its congregational basis. The history of the Ministerium until now had been a story of a church being planted congregation by congregation. Growth had meant an increasing number of congregations, and a growing roster of clergy. Both trends continued in the Ministerium, but at a slower rate. What was different was the growth in *congregational* membership, resources and influence. With such growth, questions arose. What was a congregation, and how did it relate to a synodical body, especially given the growth of large congregations which immigration had stimulated? Where did the authority of the church reside and how should a synodical jurisdiction be organized? These were questions which came to the fore after 1872 as a newly reunited New York Ministerium worked towards its own understanding of what a confessionally sound Lutheran Ministerium should look like in a world of growing congregationalism among immigrant Lutheran bodies.

THE OFFICE OF MINISTRY

As if from nowhere, a resolution appeared in the 1873 Ministerium requesting the "Rev. Dr. E. Moldehnke, to prepare these[s] on the Doctrine of the Ministerial Office" and to publish them in the *Lutherische Herold* for discussion among the clergy in their conferences. The results were to be reported to the 1874 synod for further deliberation. President Krotel had requested no such theses in his Annual Report, nor were there any issues on the floor of synod that might have required such a resolution. The Ministerium, through the General Council, was preparing a model constitution for congregations. It would appear in 1880, yet the result gives no hint of the concerns behind the Moldehnke theses. The former Steimle congregations were then requesting admission to the Ministerium, and their constitutions were under scrutiny to assure conformity to Ministerium constitutional language, but no questions arose from this quarter.[3]

However the Steimle men had a history of interest in such questions and the request for one of their number to submit theses on the topic suggests where the request probably arose. American Lutheranism was then going through doctrinal conflicts over such issues. At one extreme stood the Buffalo Synod and its founder J. A. A. Grabau who held a doctrine of the ministry which considered ordination a divine institution. For Grabau good church order consisted of congregational obedience to pastors in all matters not contrary to the Word of God. For a time the Steimle Synod had considered uniting with the Buffalo Synod, and though the subject was dropped because of differences over the doctrine of the church and pastoral office, a subsequent discussion of theses on the subject indicated growing agreement with the Buffalo position among the Steimle pastors. No doubt Dr. Moldehnke had played a part in such discussions, and the divine right theories which Moldehnke introduced in his own theses suggest a proximity of the Steimle pastors to the Buffalo position (which, by the way, was just then moving *away* from the extremism of Grabau).[4]

Moldehnke submitted eight new theses to the synod for discussion and possible adoption in 1874:

> 1. The Ministerial Office is instituted and ordered by Christ himself, and is therefore no human institution.
> 2. The Ministerial Office is well to be distinguished from the Universal Priesthood of all believers.
> 3. As the Spiritual Priesthood, so the Ministerial Office also has it rights and duties, *jure divino*.
> 4. These rights and duties of the Ministerial Office—jure divino, consist in the public administration of the means of grace, i.e., in feeding, supervising, and governing by means of the Word of God and the Sacraments.

5. The keys are given by Christ (immediate), without means to the Church.
6. Every baptized person has a certain common ability and in peculiar cases, for instance, of need, the authority to make use of the power of the keys.
7. A Christian obtains the right or authority of officially executing the power of the keys, by vocation, only when he has a call to do so.
8. The public administration of the means of grace is according to God's order, conferred upon the ministers regularly called, so that a minister officiates at the same time in the name of Christ and the Church.[5]

The first four theses were unanimously adopted by the Ministerium after discussion, while the fifth was prefaced by a curious statement—"(Verbally from the Articles of *Schmalkald,* therefore not voted upon)."[6] Presumably because the thesis was not derived from the Augsburg Confession itself but from elsewhere within the *Book of Concord*, it carried only unofficial weight under the recently adopted Constitution of the Ministerium.

A quick reading between the lines suggests a Ministerium at pains to reaffirm the confessionally defined Office of Ministry, but in unconfessional language of divine rights and duties, somewhat reminiscent of the Buffalo Synod, and without the qualifications of Thesis 5. These rights and duties were presumed separate from and equal to those of the laity, and in no way inferior to, or derived from them. As the last three theses suggest, a clear-cut distinction needed to be made between lay administration of the sacraments in extraordinary circumstances, and the clergy's right to the ordinary exercise of the power of the keys and to administer the sacraments as conferred by call and ordination.

Ministerium theses notwithstanding, the issues raised by such distinctions were not so easily resolved. Applying sixteenth-century confessional statements to nineteenth-century circumstances meant facing different political realities. On the one hand, the Augsburg Confession described the office of ministry as instituted by God to provide gospel and sacraments for the sinner's justification. In the northeast among Lutherans, this office was ordered collegially as a Ministerium with authority to oversee the proper exercise of the office in congregations. After the Revolutionary War, congregational delegates sitting in synodical assembly came to share responsibility for the office as for other matters handled through collective deliberations. On the other hand, the Augsburg Confession also stated (in opposition to Papal authority) that the power of the keys—not only loosing and binding, but also the proclamation of law and gospel, and the absolution following confession—was given to the whole church (as Moldehnke insisted in thesis four).[7] In Lutheran practice, congregations exercising this right given to the priesthood of all believers, called suitable candidates for ordination into the office of ministry. Theirs was a right to call, but not to create, administer or control. In so doing, they exercised their right without infringement upon the ministerial office. Yet misunderstandings could arise where either sets of rights were advanced at the expense of the other.

ST. MATTHEWS PROPOSES CONSTITUTIONAL CHANGE

St. Matthews Evangelical Lutheran Church in New York City sought to advance the congregation's rights in July of 1874 when it submitted a revised congregational constitution to President Krotel for synodical approval. Revision had become necessary after the synod's reorganization to bring St. Matthews' constitution into harmony with the Ministerium model constitution for congregations first adopted in 1870. The process took St. Matthews four years and included a paragraph by paragraph reading in successive congregational meetings with the membership frequently exercising its right of amendment. A hint of congregationalism was to be found in a new Paragraph 9: "The Meeting of the Congregation is the final authority in the direction of all Congregational affairs, the execution of which it transfers to the Church Council." Perhaps this declaration of independence was meant to protect another peculiarity of the new document: its confessional standard and definition of membership. Whereas the model constitution for congregations which was emerging in the General Council would confess (besides scripture) the normative character of the unaltered Augsburg Confession and the Small Catechism, St. Matthews subscribed to the entire *Book of Concord.* And whereas the General Council defined voting membership as open to male communicate members over twenty-one who contributed to the congregation's support, St. Matthews added pew-renting, worship attendance, and reception of Holy Communion (at least yearly) to the requirements, *as well as* confessional subscription to the *Book of Concord* and the demonstration of "a Christian way of life." The finished document was forwarded to synod in 1874, but was returned almost immediately by President Krotel for further revision. Reexamined again paragraph by paragraph, the revised constitution was resubmitted, this time with a covering letter by St. Matthews pastor, the Rev. Dr. Justus Ruperti.[8]

At issue, as Ruperti indicated in his covering letter, was the relationship of the congregation to the synod. The new constitution represented an "adequate expression of the state of things which has long practically existed . . . or has long since been recognized as necessary." Its "sincere loyalty and firm attachment" to the synod Dr. Ruperti observed, was "always done . . . under the presumption, that the congregation is, and is to remain exclusively mistress in her own house; and that the Synod is not a commander, but a venerable adviser." Therefore St.

Matthews's new constitution would only be acceptable if the synod's constitution was also revised as it applied to congregations. Such constitutional revisions were submitted by St. Matthews to the synod president shortly thereafter as "new propositions" for amending the present (1870) constitution. "They refer mainly," Pastor Ruperti indicated, "to a proper determination of the relation of the congregation to the Synod."[9]

Considering the congregation's position and their amendments, what prompted the Moldehnke theses on Ministry is obvious. How was that office expressed in Ministerium polity? The "Ministerium" was originally a body of ordained Lutheran clergy responsible to examine, license and ordain candidates for the ministry. Lay delegates were included in ministerium gatherings in the New York Ministerium from its inception in 1786. As a synod assembly of pastors and delegates representing congregations, the Ministerium entered the nineteenth century serving the expanded purposes of representative church government while the ongoing work of the ministerium proper was conducted at the end of synod in a special session limited to the clergy under the rubric "Ministerial Business." By 1852 bylaws stated that the congregational pastor was to "hold his holy office, so long as he teaches and lives as an Evangelical Lutheran minister should do; but if to the contrary, which God forbid, his case shall be brought by the elders of his church before the Ministerium." This trend toward centralized and hierarchical synodical authority, which was carried a step further in the 1870 Constitution, also reflected the thinking of the General Council in its model constitution for congregations. It was the synod's appellate authority which St. Matthews Church challenged under the principle of the priesthood of all believers. "The point in question is especially the placing aright of the relation between congregation and synod." According to practices at St. Matthews "the congregational meeting is the highest court in all congregational affairs." St. Matthews interpreted the Smalcald statement that the power of the keys was given to the whole Church, to mean that "the congregation, assembled around the Word of God, is the possessor and bearer of all churchly power." The congregation must judge "the doctrine of its pastors, and remove false doctrine, but must not permit true teachers to be taken from her by any exterior power." "No other corporation can therefore form the highest court in congregational affairs[;] the congregation itself governs in its own house . . ."[10]

The logic of St. Matthews congregationalism and its new proposals would have transformed a synod into a confederation of congregations represented by pastors and delegates. Such a confederation would have little influence on the congregation. Whereas the Ministerium could designate the liturgy and hymn-books for congregational use, St. Matthews proposed synod would only recommend. Whereas the Ministerium would only receive congregations with compatible constitutions,

St. Matthews revised synodical constitution would make the compatibility a matter of confession rather than polity. According to the Constitution of 1870, once admitted, congregations could only withdraw with synod approval. In the congregational model, congregations were free to come and go after consultation. A whole series of other changes, dealing with clergy problems and clerical responsibilities, would have emerged from this shift of authority. Certain initiatives once residing in the Ministerium now would lie with pastor and congregation. Congregations were free to prepare candidates for ordination. Pastors in congregations were to be free to change the boundaries of existing parishes, form new ones, or divide old ones, powers which resided with the Ministerium and were normally exercised by the conference.[11]

Why the changes, and what did they represent? For one thing a basic shift in the confessional center of gravity had occurred within the Ministerium. Prior to its reorganization of 1867, the New York Ministerium was an aggregation of congregations and pastors with a variety of confessional viewpoints, when there was any serious interest in confessional theology at all. Candidates for ministry came from a variety of backgrounds and some were plainly subconfessional in their theological acumen. A strong synod with increasing confessional standards and synodical authority made good jurisdictional sense. After 1867, and with reorganization, emphasis was placed on developing confessionally strong congregations, served by orthodox pastors trained in German-speaking seminaries, whose laity were educated in parochial schools and who could function as theologically informed members of church councils. St. Matthews's proposals would have shifted the locus of doctrinal influence to the congregation.

Parallel to this emphasis on congregational orthodoxy was an emphasis on congregationalism itself—a political move to strengthen congregations at the expense of synod. Clearly St. Matthews' proposals were designed to foster the kind of congregationally planned growth which (as we have seen) was significant to the mission life of the German-speaking church in the New York area. Such growth required congregations which were open beyond the limits of strict membership to the religious needs of the larger community (St. Matthews strict membership standards notwithstanding). An intensive congregational effort and extensive congregational resources were needed to deal with immigrant population growth and its social and spiritual problems. Congregational Aid Societies, as well as women's aid groups, both strong local organizations, contributed significantly to congregational growth and to the support of home and foreign missions. A strong and centralized Ministerium might dampen or rechannel this initiative.

Synod officials found problems with this kind of congregationalism. New congregations "springing" from older ones without synodical supervision were often deplored by synodical officials where "one grows at the expense of another." Synod officials and synodical committees admired the more orderly "English churches" (the New York Synod), whose "firm organization of congregations" "is yet greatly wanting with us." They deplored the unwillingness of many congregations to categorize "members entitled to vote" or "entitled to communion." They also had the same difficulty with congregations where the number of funerals conducted was way out of proportion to the number of burials of church members. And they deplored the disproportionate number of communicants to those "entitled to communion" for the same reason.[12]

In a word, synod parochial reports suggest a synod leadership which felt there should be organizational conformity and subordination in the face of congregations with considerable independence of attitude and judgment. It was a clearcut case of the difference between *Gemeinschaft* and *Gesellschaft*, between an ethnoreligious community and a denominational association. A significant number of the immigrant parishes with aid societies and parochial schools seem to have fallen into this category. A clear-cut pattern of independence and confessional orthodoxy went hand in hand among such Ministerium churches. St. Matthews was one of them, and its proposals spoke their mind. The support of five pastors and congregations (including St. Matthews) assured that the 1875 proposals would receive a hearing on the floor of the Ministerium, which they did two years later. A thorough discussion of the doctrinal questions involved took place in two separate sessions of the 1877 meeting of synod. When it was resolved that the president appoint a member of synod "to prepare theses *upon the relation of the Congregation to Synod*," St. Matthews's delegate, Director Bohm of St. Matthews's Academy, delivered a declaration which stated, in effect, that St. Matthews intended neither to withdraw from the synod "except under pressure of necessity" nor recede from its position of independence. It sought to buy time to persuade the Ministerium of the rightness of its position.[13]

But time did not heal a growing division. For congregationalism and the right of congregations to be masters in their own houses was meant to protect a developing orthodoxy more radical than the confessionalism to be found either in the New York Ministerium or the General Council. The situation worsened under Ruperti's successor Pastor Johann Heinrich Sieker. He had been president of the Minnesota Synod before called to New York, and as a strict confessionalist was instrumental in persuading the Minnesota body to withdraw from the General Council in 1872 and join the Synodical Conference. Sieker never joined the Ministerium though his congregation was bound to encourage him to do so by a Ministerium requirement written into their constitution. Perhaps their insistence that pastors be tried and disciplined by the congregation rather than the synod was meant to protect a shepherd who had introduced confessional subscription and private confession to St. Matthews. So radical a departure attracted intense criticism in the Synod's *Herold,* which labeled St. Matthews's members firebrands and "Missourians." But such criticism also encouraged "a good number of Pastors and congregations" to support the principle: "The Congregation gathered for the Word of God is the bearer and possessor of all ecclesiastical authority." At first St. Matthews formed an emerging "Protest Party." But finally its Church Council recommended leaving the Ministerium in April of 1880 because of the "Doctrine of Congregational Autonomy." Sieker, who had maintained his affiliation with the Minnesota Synod and the Synodical Conference, joined the Eastern District of the Missouri Synod in 1881 followed by St. Matthews congregation in 1885 for by then St. Matthews's position on the congregation was identical to that of the Missouri Synod. Among the reasons for organizing "Die Deutsche Evangelisch Lutherische Synode von Missouri, Ohio und andern Staaten," was the "protection and maintenance of the rights and duties of pastors and congregations." The decision was made "with very good participation" by the voting membership and with only one dissenting vote who was branded as "wrong, as it easily can happen to a man." The move was justified because "One always knows where the Missouri Synod stands—in doctrine and practice it leads an open and truthful life." Besides, by joining, the congregation would come to peace since "according to her history and her knowledge she cannot belong to another church body and continually be disturbed, standing alone."[14]

REVISED CONSTITUTIONS, 1878 TO 1894

St. Matthews's confrontation was part of a larger conflict within the Lutheran Church in America. The Buffalo and Missouri Synods, representing opposing models for the development of polity among Lutherans in America, engaged in bitter strife over these issues, brought unrest and confusion into other church bodies as well. The Moldehnke theses and St. Matthews's proposals, in staking out these extremes within the New York Ministerium, brought the heat of controversy to the Hudson Valley. The withdrawal of this historic congregation was doubly tragic for the Ministerium because it was apparently so unnecessary. St. Matthews's objections eventually carried the day within the Ministerium which subsequently undertook a thorough reconsideration of the relationship between synod and congregation. The result was a series of constitutions published between 1878 and 1894 in which the Ministerium redefined that relationship.

Three years after the original St. Matthews's proposals were brought to the synod floor, the first draft of a new constitution (1878) was completed. In Chapter One, immediately following a revised confessional stance, the new document clearly indicated that the synod had "nur eine berathende Autoritat" (only an advisory authority), though the congregation was expected to consult the synod in important difficulties and honor its advice. Revised in 1883, and again in 1887, the final form which the definition of this relationship took appeared in the 1894 Constitution. By then the language of authority had been changed to indicate that the "final decision of its own affairs shall at all times rest with the congregation." All such decisions were to be "based upon the Word of God as the absolute rule, and upon the Confessions of the Church," but after consultation with the synod in "all important cases." The synod's role, "on the other hand," was to "guard the purity of doctrine and the maintenance of discipline both among pastors and congregations" also "according to the Word of God and the Confessions of the Church." But its authority to do so was far more limited. From 1878 on the synod was no longer authorized to suspend a minister from his pastoral duties, nor from the office itself. Degrees of disenfranchisement as a synod member were all that remained of the synod's disciplinary power. As a general principle, the power to compel pastors and congregations was replaced throughout the document by the right to exclude a pastor or congregation from a synodical union of confessionally like-minded congregations and pastors.[15]

A MORE CONSERVATIVE CONFESSIONAL STANCE

The St. Matthews's proposals were but one reason for revising the 1870 constitution. The proposals were part of a more conservative view of confessional subscription which required adherence to the entire *Book of Concord*. If the clergy and laity supporting St. Matthews's proposals had an affinity for the Missouri Synod and its conservative, confessional congregationalism, former Steimle pastors also showed a similar preference for this more extensive form of subscription. They were joined by a young group of new pastors, many of whom were educated at the Philadelphia seminary. This new majority in the New York Ministerium displayed an increasingly historical awareness of the Lutheran confessional tradition. Four centuries after the Formula of Concord reunited Lutheran Germany in a confessional concord which embraced the *Book of Concord*, it became the official confessional position of the New York Ministerium. The symbolism was more than coincidental.

The 1870s marked a time of resurgent confessionalism in important segments of American Lutheranism, especially in the Synodical Conference and the General Council. In 1872 Philadelphia Seminary's Charles Porterfield Krauth had published his *The Conservative Reformation and Its Theology* providing one very cogent expression of this new outlook. The year 1875 saw the publication of an English translation of Heinrich Schmid's *Doctrinal Theology of the Evangelical Lutheran Church* by younger Lutheran theologians about to become influential seminary professors at Philadelphia (General Council) and Gettysburg (General Synod) Seminaries. Krauth's work has already been discussed in the context of the 1850s when it first appeared as an essay. Schmid's volume, a comprehensive Biblical theology in the tradition of Philip Melanchthon and his orthodox successors, drew upon the confessional canon in the *Book of Concord*. The resulting theological system included the themes of grace, justification, law, and gospel, four (count them!) uses of the law, conversion, and good works. It was Schmid's volume, together with Leonard Hutter's *Compendium* (1610), which informed the orthodox confessional outlook of Krauth's colleague, Dogmatics professor Charles F. Schaeffer, whose primary responsibility was the dogmatic and confessional education of the new pastors entering the Ministerium.[16]

Therefore it is not at all surprising to find this more conservative viewpoint appearing in the New York Ministerium draft constitution of 1878 and its final revision in 1894. In draft form the confessional article read:

> This body accepts all the canonical books of the Old and New Testaments as the revealed Word of God and the only rule of faith; also the confessions of the Evangelical Lutheran Church, as contained in the Book of Concord of 1580 as the correct presentation of the Christian Faith, to wit:
> The three oecumenical creeds;
> The unaltered Augsburg Confession of 1530;
> The Apology;
> The Smalcald Articles;
> The Large and the Small Catechisms of Luther;
> The Formula of Concord

The 1894 confessional position was identical to the above with the added proviso: "All questions concerning the faith of the Church, and the administration of the sacraments shall be decided in accordance with this rule of faith."[17]

NY ORTHODOXY CHALLENGES GC CONFESSIONAL STANDARDS

Such a stance represented a significant shift from the confessional position of the General Council, with its primary emphasis on the Augsburg Confession. A new willingness to address questions of faith and practice from the more detailed perspective of the whole *Book of Concord* meant a strictness about matters contained therein that other General Council synods did not share. In particular the Lutheran position on the sacraments and predestination, maintained over against the Reformed tradition could easily explain why the New York Ministerium took the lead among synods in the Council in demanding strict altar and pulpit fellowship among Council pastors and congregations. While St. Matthews's proposals stirred up the New York Ministerium over one set of confessional issues, the General Council's Galesburg Rule did so in another way. A report in 1876 on the General Council's new Galesburg Rule—"Lutheran pulpits for Lutheran ministers only—Lutheran altars for Lutheran communicants only"—prompted the Ministerium's First Conference to insist that the Ministerium declare its wholehearted assent. The Ministerium's General Council delegates, who reported on the matter, had made no such recommendation however.[18]

In framing its resolution of commendation, The First Conference included the Galesburg Rule but not the clause on exceptions to the rule. These were exceptions that Ministerium delegates to the General Council did oppose at the time, and would continue to oppose. Therefore a substitute motion was placed on the floor of synod by Council supporters which simply said "That we give our assent to the Galesburg action, in the sense in which the same was set forth by the president of the General Council, and accepted by the General Council itself." When this substitute motion came to the floor for debate and approval it was defeated by a vote of 46 to 23. Voting in the majority were pastors from the First Conference including two stalwarts of the old Steimle Synod, Pastors Moldehnke and Halfmann, and also the pastors and congregations (including St. Matthews Church) which had supported the St. Matthews's proposals for constitutional change. They were joined by a solid phalanx of newer clergy who had been called to the ministry since the Ministerium's reorganization in 1867, including a number of younger pastors trained at Philadelphia Lutheran Seminary.[19] Added up, this support for the Galesburg Rule (without exceptions) can be seen to have arisen among growing German-language, confessionally minded urban congregations serving segmented immigrant communities where exclusive associations differentiated subcommunities of faith. Rapprochement between Reformed and Lutheran Germans was the last thing one would expect to find on their agenda. As important, purity of fellowship in pulpit and altar likewise maintained loyalty to German-speaking Lutheranism, distinguishing it from its competitors for the loyalties of German immigrants—Methodists, Presbyterians, Baptists—as well as from its confessionally impure English-speaking counterpart. Crossing over was everywhere discouraged.

President Krotel voted with the minority, and when the motion failed, he abruptly resigned the presidency, the second presidential victim of confessionalism in less than a decade! The Ministerium "unanimously resolved" that he reconsider, but "after he had declared that he felt himself in conscience bound to resign his office" Krotel's resignation was accepted and a member of the majority, Rev. C. F. W. Hoppe, was elected president, *pro tempore*. The original First Conference proposal was then passed 66 to 2, with an addition stipulating "that the Synod calls upon its pastors to labor with all wisdom and faithfulness, to the end that this rule may more and more make itself felt in practice." By then Krotel had absented himself from the Ministerium and was no longer present to vote even among the "nays." [20]

His absence and the nature of the voting, indicate that a seismic shift in confessional attitude had occurred in the New York Ministerium. Perhaps Krotel felt he could no longer provide leadership in both the New York Ministerium and in the General Council, given their diverging viewpoints. He had been among the Council's founders and leaders, and an architect of its confessional middle way which opposed the Galesburg Rule understood as existing without the moderate Akron Declaration on the nature of exceptions. This was a position he would continue to take against Old Lutheranism after Krauth's death (in 1883) together with the controversial millenialist J. A. Seiss, making Krotel an important leader in a moderate conservatism which eventually carried the day in the General Council. The position taken by the New York Ministerium (on the other hand) placed it in conflict with a majority in the Council and its leadership, as well as with the Pennsylvania Ministerium. Since it was now abundantly clear that the New York Ministerium was no longer any place for the more moderate, bi-lingual confessionalism of G. F. Krotel and Holy Trinity Lutheran Church in Manhattan, Krotel and the congregation withdrew from the New York Ministerium in 1877 to unite with the Pennsylvania Ministerium. The move was made, according to Krotel, "because I am assured that I can labor with greater success and peace as a member of the Pennsylvania Synod; at the same time I wish God's blessing upon every good work of the N. Y. Ministerium." Ironically, this congregation which was formed by conservative members withdrawing from St. James Lutheran Church at the time of the New York Ministerium split, was now leaving the Ministerium as St. James had done before it.[21]

Without Krotel's restraining hand, the New York Ministerium presented its actions to the General Council at its next (1877) sitting. Further, it proposed that the General Council go on record indicating that exceptions to the Galesburg Rule "shall neither be claimed nor considered a special privilege," and that district synods work to bring their practices into line with the rule as the New York Ministerium was then doing. The New York motion was tabled, but out of the exchange came the resolution which led President Krauth to develop his 105 Theses on the nature of the Church. It was the theses, and the Council's willingness to discuss the Galesburg Rule, which prevented the New York Ministerium's withdrawal from the General Council. They were still ready to launch out on their own however, should the Council's debate over the exceptions to the Galesburg Rule not be resolved to their satisfaction.

KRAUTH'S 105 THESES OF 1877

From the beginning it was clear that for Krauth there was a moderate interpretation of the "rule" which escaped the strict confessionalists. The word "rule" was "not used in the sense of 'prescriptive regulation,' but in the sense of 'general principle,' a principle of intrinsic validity and right." The distinction between 'prescriptive regulation' and 'general principle,' and again between a rule meant not "legislatively" but "morally," drew an important distinction between the voluntarism of the General Council and the disciplinarian orientation of its more conservative opponents. It is not at all farfetched to find here an echo of the debate in the New York Ministerium between those General Synod proponents who withdrew to form the New York Synod and the remainder who reshaped the Ministerium itself. The sense of freedom from coercion, the need to appeal to conscience, the matter of a moral solution based on conscience and judgment, the preference for voluntary assent over enforced compliance—all suggest that the majority in the General Council, long accustomed to voluntary action in a free society, were recasting American Lutheranism in a moderate Confessional mold. This was a moderate confessionalism, at once more faithful to the confessional tradition than the General Synod, yet more in keeping with the American spirit than German immigrant confessionalists.

On the other hand the rule was also a careful way of spelling out for an interested public the warrants by which a confessional communion responsibly derives rules of governance for establishing its norms and standards. It is a question of how, in a democratic polity, rules of the game are derived an issue almost as important as the rules themselves.[22] Accordingly theses five through eight spelled out in greater detail the meaning of Lutheran "pulpits" and "communicants," and how exceptions to the rule were to be made. Number nine continued by reaffirming that exceptions were a matter of privilege not right, while number ten noted that exceptions are circumstances which "arise" rather than simply exist as a normal state of affairs. Where exceptions are made, it must be done in "*consonance with the principles*," and not in any way which implies that the Rule is not in accord with Word and Confession, or is simply a "human rule" or "rule of order," or is made out of regard to any claim of right that a nonLutheran might make to pulpit or altar. Most importantly, for whom the General Council thought exceptions might be made was spelled out in thesis twelve. No official statements defining exceptions were made either at Akron or Galesburg. At Akron it seemed clear that "the occasional admission to our pulpits and altars of such ministers and people of 'the Evangelical denominations' as 'preach and hold the pure truth of God's Word as taught in the Confessions of our Church' " was what came "within the sphere of exceptions."

By the time the issue was aired again at Galesburg, the debate made it clear that a majority "had reached the conviction that the exceptions are *not of this class*." The "interdenominational" invitations to altar and pulpit, whether regular or occasional, were regarded not as legitimate exceptions, "but as pre-eminently the cases which need to be guarded against by the Declaration." The more it discussed the matter, the further the General Council moved toward the conservative end of the confessional spectrum on the Galesburg Rule. The strict confessionalists like those of the New York Ministerium were "right" after all in their relentless push for clarity on the issues involved! Clearly the Galesburg Rule and its discussion surfaced rather widely held assumptions of a broad ecumenical nature among churches in the General Council regarding what was considered legitimate altar and pulpit fellowship, assumptions more in keeping with General Synod Lutheranism. But opened up to further reflection and exposed to the light of scripture and the Confessions, those practices were seen as suspect "exceptions" against which a Rule should apply.

On the other hand, the Council's moderate stance required avoiding the excess of exclusiveness in relation to other Christian bodies or Lutheran groups. Accordingly it argued that we "admit our own preachers to our pulpits, because after their voluntary subjection to as thorough a test as the limitations of human knowledge render possible," while other preachers "have offered themselves to no such test, and we have no right to form an official judgment in regard to them, or to act without it as if we had it." Likewise, no Lutheran pastor was to be admitted to a General Council pulpit simply "on the knowledge of their being members of the Church invisible." In avoiding excess, thesis fifty-one attempted to deal with the troublesome problem of Lutherans separating from one another over confessional issues as had occurred during the formative period of the General Council and the Synodical Conference. "When a Church holds and confesses the very truth of God in all its parts" the thesis began, "*no man has a right to leave it*, because of any human defects which may exist in its actual state." Rather, "he must labor and pray to correct them; must apply the Church's own principles to remove her own evils, must reform within the Church." To remain means one is pledged to a church's "officially confessed faith." For, if "a Church has the pure Word and Sacraments it has the essential means of correcting its actual practical defects; and the forming of a new denomination, simply as an easier mode of securing any human ends, however important, is schismatic."

THE FINAL CONFLICT AND RESULT

Alas a "new denomination"—the Synodical Conference—had already been formed. Hopefully, such theses and the admonition to "labor and pray" for confessional change, would prevent the more conservative elements within the General Council, like the New York Ministerium, from changing affiliations as well. The temptation was great to jump ship however, for (so far as the strict confessionalists were concerned) the abuses continued. Council leaders continued preaching from Protestant pulpits in host cities during annual conventions of the Council and at its district synods—clearly unwarranted violations of the Galesburg Rule in the eyes of the stricter members of the Council. In 1877 the New York Ministerium objected to this practice among Pennsylvania Ministerium members when it occurred at Reading, Pennsylvania in the previous year, while both the Ministerium and the Reformed Church Classis were meeting. The debate in the General Council was an emotional one, and was resolved against the New York Ministerium by a narrow vote of 29 to 23.[23]

Meanwhile, the Michigan Synod, which had endorsed the New York Ministerium attack, objected to the practice at Council gatherings when the annual Council was held on their territory, in Monroe, Michigan. The pastor loci, who usually helped arrange the guest preaching for attending Council dignitaries, introduced a resolution at the end of the 1884 Council censuring those who had stepped into other pulpits during the Council meeting. After all, "Lutheran pulpits for Lutheran preachers" seemed to apply in such matters.[24] On this occasion the Council members were extracted from the dilemma "by the leaders who control all the business" (so a not unfriendly General Synod critic reported)

> by moving that the resolution be laid upon the table, inasmuch as the "offenders" were not present to vindicate themselves, and it was not known in what manner these services were conducted, and above all, as the protest was not against the action of the General Council, but merely against individuals.[25]

The same practice occurred in Reading, Pennsylvania, in 1885, at which time the Council adopted a rule that at conventions of the Council preaching arrangements should be made for delegates by the president and the pastor loci.

Again the Michigan Synod objected, this time in 1886, asking if the practices of the Pennsylvania Ministerium in such matters were "in accordance with the principles adopted by the General Council with reference to Pulpit Fellowship?" This time the Council leadership referred the objecting synod back to its 1877 "decision" on the matter. The Michigan Synod responded by withdrawing in disgust! Only then did the Council leadership seem to take the question seriously. After a thorough review, it was decided that the 1885 rule was the correct one. This time the New York Ministerium asked if the Council's understanding of the Galesburg Rule was that adopted by the Ministerium—namely the rule without the exceptions. Again they were told "no."[26]

BI-POLAR CONFESSIONALISM IN THE NATIONAL CORRIDOR

There matters ended. In the Council itself, the Galesburg Rule and the Four Points were not taken up for debate again! The New York Ministerium maintained its strict interpretation of the Galesburg Rule, but also maintained its membership in the General Council as a synod on the right, refusing (as it were) to become schismatic and form yet another denomination, presumably because the General Council still had the pure Word and Sacraments.

Some would say the "nitpicking" had ceased. What seemed like "nitpicking" to outsiders, however, was (in fact) an effort by like-minded Christians to establish the kind of internal coherence and consistency at a congregational level which a confessional position demands of those who would try to be honest about the nature and meaning of their theology. What these differences obscured was the rather substantial confessional agreement and theological clarity which occurred with the General Council's formation and which continued to develop throughout the extensive debates which took place over the rules of the game.

Those rules were important for a special reason. As indicated at the beginning of this history, the Lutheran Church which existed along the nation-building New York-Philadelphia axis, in the Hudson and Delaware River basins, played a formative role in the affairs of the nation and its institutions. This was a nation-building corridor with considerable influence throughout the rest of the country. In Lutheran affairs, as in so many other matters, the metropolitan areas of Philadelphia and New York and the dynamic relationship between them were formative in shaping Lutheran doctrine. The influential career of G. F. Krotel and his shifting membership was an important case in point. The debate over the Galesburg Rule was not the first time that staunch New York orthodoxy and a mediating theology in Philadelphia interacted to shape the fortunes of the church on the eastern seaboard. Nor would it be the last.

There was, then, a bipolar quality about the conservative confessionalism of the General Council, thanks to these geographic dynamics. The same thing could be seen, however, in General Synod Lutheranism. Because of their geographic position, the Hartwick, Franckean, New Jersey, and New York Synods played a role in the General Synod similar to that played by the New York Ministerium in the General Council. It is to this English-speaking side of New York Lutheranism that we now turn, in our continuing exploration of the New York Ministerium's complex legacy. As with the Ministerium, the story begins with changes in the parent body, in this case a restructuring of the General Synod which occurred after formation of the General Council.

NOTES

1 New York Ministerium, *Minutes* (1876), 15.

2*Autogenous* (self-generated) growth occurs from the "recruitment" of the children of members, and is related to congregational demographics. *Allogenous* (outside) growth, on the other hand, involves the recruitment of outsider's and their children.

3 *Minutes* (1873), 75. See S. E. Ochsenford, *Documentary History of the General Council of the Evangelical Lutheran Church in North America* (Philadelphia, 1912), 192ff.

4 *Lutheran Cyclopedia* (1975), 117. Steimle Synod, *Minutes* (1868), 1: 180, 185, 191, 210-215, 224-5; (1869) 2:13; (1870) 2:35, 54; (1872) 2: 116-18, 120.

5 New York Ministerium, *Minutes* (1874), 47-8.

6 Ibid., 47-8. See "Article VII. The Keys," Smalcald Articles, BC, 311-12.

7 CA, BC, 30-31. "Smalcald Articles," 311; Martin Luther, "Treatise on the Power and Primacy of the Pope," BC, 324.

8 Ochensford, ed., *Documentary History*, 196-7. St. Matthews Lutheran Church, Transcript & Translation of manuscript "Protocol," 1868-1886, 1870: 177, 1874: 177, 317, 308-317, 44.

9 New York Ministerium, *Minutes* (1875), 19-20; (1874), 20, 47ff.

10 *Lutheran Cyclopedia* (1975), 542. See *Die Versassung des Evangelish Lutherischen Ministeriums des Staates New=York und angrenzenden Staaten und Lander* (New York, 1859). New York Ministerium, *Minutes* (1861), 68-74; (1852), 35-42. Article II, part 5, 1845 bylaws, Ibid. (1852), 36. *Constitution und Nebengestze des Evangelish=Lutherischen Ministeriums des Staates New-York und angrezender Staaten und Lander* (New York, 1870). Ochensford, ed., *Documentary History,* 139, 196ff. New York Ministerium, *Minutes* (1875), 47.

11 Ibid., 48-9, 50-55.

12 Ibid. (1874), 59; (1875), 50-51, 59, 29.

13 Ibid., 56 (the pastors and congregations besides Ruperti and St. Matthews were E. F. Giese, German Evangelical Lutheran Church, Newark; W. Hoppe, St. John's German Evangelical Lutheran Church, Rochester; A. E. Frey, St. Matthew's, Brooklyn; G. W. Drees, German Evangelical Lutheran Church; (1876), 65; (1877), 31, 40, 46. New York Ministerium *Minutes* (1877), 45-6.

14 Karl Kretzmann, *The Atlantic District of the Evangelical Lutheran Synod of Missouri, Ohio, and Other States and Its Antecedents* (Erie, Pa.: Erie Printing Company, 1931), 34; Edwin L. Lueker, ed., *Lutheran Cyclopedia* (St. Louis: Concordia Publishing House, 1975), 716. St. Matthew Lutheran Church, "Protocol," (1868-1886), 1876: 75-7, 123, 150. *Lutheran Cyclopedia,* 716, 489-90. "St. Matthew Lutheran Church, "Protocol," (1868-1886), 1877: 156-7, 158-9, 149; 1880: 18-19; 1881: 99; 1885: 306.

15 *Entwurf der Constitution und Uebengesetze des Evangelish=Lutherischen Ministeriums des Staates New-York und angrenzender Staaten und Lander* (New York: Lutherischen Verlags-Vereins New York, 1878), 4, 15; *Constitution und Uebengesetze des Evangelish=Lutherischen Ministeriums*

des Staates New-York und angrenzender Staaten und Lander (New=York, 1883), 4; *Constitution and By-Laws of the Evangelical Lutheran Ministerium of the State of New York and Adjacent States and Countries* (New York, 1894), 4-5, 14, 21-2, 23-4.

16 *Entwurf der Constitution*, 3. *Constitution of the Evangelical Lutheran Ministerium of the State of New York and adjacent States and Countries* (Mount Vernon, NY: Wartburg Orphans' Farm School Print, 1894), p. 3. Herbert J. A. Bouman, "Retrospect and Prospect: Some Unscientific Reflections on the Four Hundredth Anniversary of the Formula of Concord," in *The Sixteenth-Century Journal* VIII (Number 4, 1977): 96. Heinrich Schmid, *The Doctrinal Theology of Evangelical Lutheran Church, verified from the original sources,* trans. Charles A. Hay and Henry E. Jacobs (Philadelphia: Lutheran Publican Society, 1875). Theodore G. Tappert, *History of the Lutheran Theological Seminary at Philadelphia. 1864-1964* (Philadelphia: Lutheran Theological Seminary, 1964), 46, 71.

17 *Entwurf der Constitution*, 3; *Constitution and By-Laws,* 3.

18 New York Ministerium, *Minutes* (1876), 30, 54.

19 Ibid., 53, 56, 55-6. For the roster of clergy in 1876, listed in the order in which they entered the ministry, see pp. 4-6.

20 Ibid., 54-56.

21 Donald L. Huber, *The Controversy over Pulpit and Altar Fellowship in the General Council of Evangelical Lutheran Church, 1866-1889* (Duke University, 1971), 277. New York Ministerium, *Minutes* (1877), 11.

22 On the nature of theology and rules, see George Lindbeck, *The Nature of Doctrine. Religion and Theology in a Postliberal Age* (Philadelphia: Westminster Press, 1984), 16-18.

23 General Council, *Minutes* (1877), 6, 8, 22-24; (1879), 49.

24 John G. Morris, *Life Reminiscences of an Old Minister* (Philadelphia, 1896), 281-2; General Council, *Minutes* (1884), 105.

25 Ibid., 281-2.

26 General Council, *Minutes* (1885), 64; (1886), 70-71; (1888), 13, 45-6; 81-2.

7
UNION OF EFFORT
The Reorganized General Synod and Its Lower Hudson Basin Synods, 1860-1890

GENERAL SYNOD REORGANIZATION

We have seen how the General Council was organized in reaction to the American Lutheranism of the General Synod and have described the role played by the New York Ministerium in the General Council's organization and theological development. Now it is time to turn to the General Synod and its district synods—the Hartwick, Franckean, New Jersey, and New York Synods—examining developments within General Synod Lutheranism after the division of 1867. There, too, congregationalism and Protestant individualism (as well) hindered synodical development. But now free of conservative critics and confessional "distractions," the general body was able to work on "Concentration and union of effort" in rebuilding American Lutheranism. Because of the New York area's significance on the national scene, its synods would play a role roughly comparable in importance to that of the New York Ministerium within the General Council. Again, we begin with confessional matters.

GENERAL SYNOD CONFESSIONAL ATTITUDES

One way to describe the confessional stance of the General Synod was that it believed that it advocated neither too much nor too little by way of a Lutheran identity. The partial acceptance of the Augsburg Confession which the "Definite Platform" represented, would have left too little that was doctrinally Lutheran. To include more than the Augsburg Confession would have accepted too much that was binding. The General Synod sought a middle way of unity between what it perceived to be the extremes of American Lutheranism and Old Lutheranism, always with an eye to maintaining itself as an identifiably Lutheran Protestant denomination. Unlike the exponents of Old Lutheranism however, those of American Lutheranism never left the General Synod. The result was—in the 1860s at least—a strong liberal wing with no conservative counterweight, and (therefore) an immediate tilt to the left in the world of American Lutheranism.

This tilt became evident enough when, in preparing a new constitution, the General Synod sought to clarify its doctrinal position. The finished document was no different in the extent of its doctrinal conscription than previously when the Franckean Synod was forced to move beyond its nonconfessional stance in 1865. However, in 1868 the General Synod passed the following resolution which was taken almost verbatim from the Definite Platform's criticism of the "nondoctrinal" articles of the Augsburg Confession:

> this General Synod, resting on the Word of God as the sole authority in matters of Faith, on its infallible warrant rejects the Romish doctrine of the Real Presence or Transubstantiation, and with it the doctrine of Consubstantiation; rejects the Romish Mass, and all ceremonies distinctive of the Mass; denies any power to the Sacraments as an *opus operatum*, or that the blessings connected with Baptism and the Lord's Supper can be received without faith; rejects Auricular Confession and priestly Absolution; holds that there is no priesthood on earth but that of all believers, and that God only can forgive sins; and maintains the Divine obligation of the Christian Sabbath.[1]

Drawn from the *Definite Platform*, this statement had first appeared in the minutes of the Hartwick Synod as a partial critique of the Augsburg Confession; it had reappeared in 1864 (before the division into General Council and General Synod), this time with a preamble and conclusion meant to affirm the soundness of the historic Lutheran confession. By 1868, after the historic break of 1867, it was again used to qualify historic Lutheran confessionalism, this time to "prevent all misapprehension and misrepresentation as to the doctrinal position of the Lutheran Church as represented in the General Synod."[2] It was to have just the opposite effect, however!

Considering the neglect for the Sacrament of Baptism which we have seen in the Franckean and Hartwick Synods, and the relative neglect in the General Synod by comparison with the New York Ministerium and the General Council, it becomes clear that post-Civil War General Synod bodies continued to maintain a low confessional profile on sacramental grace in the Lutheran church, a position which put them at variance with the General Council. By contrast to the rapid changes in doctrine within that more conservative body, confessional developments in the General Synod would occur far more slowly as its own confessional perspective developed. It would occur, however, for the same reason that the New York Ministerium changed during the 1870s—from the slow accretion of new pastors joining its district synods as each year's cohort of divinity students were trained in a more confessional outlook at Gettysburg Seminary where (for example) Schmid's *Doctrinal Theology* was also in use. There, Schmucker's successor, James Allen Brown, though something of a conservative, established the seminary "on the basis of a broad, liberal but genuine Lutheranism, that knows to distinguish between slavery to the letter and freedom of the spirit."[3] Not to be outdone by the General Council, it was in other areas that General Synod Lutheranism would excel, most notably in more practical matters of organization, especially for home missions and the alleviation of human suffering. Here, too, fundamentally different perceptions of reality would mark General Synod and General Council understandings of church polity.

NEW CONSTITUTION AND FORMULA OF GOVERNMENT

At its first biennial meeting following the Pennsylvania Ministerium withdrawal, the General Synod undertook a major reorganization involving a rewritten constitution and a restatement of the "Formula of Government and Discipline" recommended for congregations. If the General Council's sense of polity was rooted in the Confessions, that of the General Synod was grounded in the Enlightenment, betraying (as it did) a lingering rationalism that had been prominent in the first half of the nineteenth century.

The Formula's argument was an interesting anachronism, originating as it did in that mixture of human reason and Biblical revelation used in both Halle University and the old Tuebingen School favored by S. S. Schmucker. Instead of beginning with a confessional understanding of the church, the General Synod proceeded from "an examination of the works of nature and the course of events" to find evidence for God's existence and the prominent truths of natural religion. Because this knowledge of God is insufficient, revelation "at sundry times and in divers manners, unto the fathers and in later days by his Divine Son Jesus Christ" has been delivered in the Old and New Testaments. This revelation binds every individual as an "infallible rule of faith and practice . . . to be governed by it." It is stated immediately, however, as if to put this uncharacteristic term "infallibility" in its proper perspective, that "liberty of conscience and the free exercise of private judgment in matters of religion" were insisted upon as "natural and inalienable rights of men" of which no government, civil or ecclesiastical, "can deprive us."

The associative capacities of natural man, going back in popular form to the political thought of John Locke, is based on a human need for good order. Therefore congregations are free to create government and discipline "as appear . . . most consistent with the spirit and precepts of the New Testament" and best calculated to serve the interests of the church of Christ. Finally, men "exercising the right of private judgment" agree that Christianity requires a "social connection." As experience proves they will differ "in some of their views of doctrine and discipline," and as too much difference is prejudicial to the purposes and ends of association, "reason dictates that those holding similar views of faith and practice should associate together." Once associated, it is their duty to require of church members and those inducted into the sacred office of the ministry, "such terms as they deem most accordant with the precepts and spirit of the Bible."[4]

The organizational outcomes of such a philosophy can be exaggerated, especially in terms of differences in polity between the General Synod and the General Council. After all, organizationally speaking, congregations are congregations, church councils are church councils, and synods are synods. Nor were the differences of a kind one might expect. Ironically it was General Council congregations in the New York Ministerium which limited the authority of synods to depose pastors and to reverse the decisions of church councils, whereas it was the associational philosophy of the General Synod which created that authority in the first place! But it would be a mistake to reduce the differences in outlook to inconsequentiality or dismiss them because of ironic consequences. The General Synod had a profoundly American view of human nature and political institutions based on the Enlightenment, which embraced the inalienable rights of human nature as a fundamental part of creation. Its real shortcoming was that it was not theologically informed by those Biblical and Reformation understandings of freedom which Luther had so profoundly expressed in 1520. Theirs was a natural-philosophy outlook which could go nowhere confessionally, being cut off from its own confessional roots by General Synod indifference to the Lutheran theological heritage. Had it been otherwise, American Lutheranism might have made a lasting contribution to Lutheran confessional theology in America in the area of a mature Christian freedom. As it was, the General Synod simply proved itself better able to organize and structure its form of denominationalism than the General Council.

REORGANIZATION OF 1868

Besides a new constitution and updated principles, important new projects were started as well. Planning for a new liturgy and a new hymnbook for General Synod congregations went forward; also the development of a more adequate edition of the Small Catechism; and the formation of a German language newspaper to reach the increasing numbers of German Lutheran immigrants coming to the United States. In the case of worship and doctrinal materials, the authority of the General Synod was appreciably increased while the right of synods to publish their own material was curtailed. A more detailed program of general benevolence for the church was also worked out, including:

1) plans for Home and Foreign Missions (planting churches and missions at home and abroad); 2) encouragement of Church Extension (financing mission church construction); 3) provisions for developing "a Church Literature"; and 4) plans for developing and maintaining charitable institutions.[5]

Reorganization affected parts of the enterprise differently.

1) The Foreign Missionary Society of the General Synod had already been in existence for some time, issuing its fourteenth report in 1868. Well established missions in India and Africa remained a part of the reorganized General Synod, but without the support of former synods like the Pennsylvania Ministerium.

2) The Home Mission Society, in existence already as an auxiliary organization of the General Synod, was continued in the reorganization. But upon motion of the Society, it was resolved in 1869, that in keeping with the new constitution, its interests be transferred to the General Synod. A new Home Mission Board was therefore created and the district synods were requested to transfer their home mission funds to this general body for redistribution and use as the overall mission needs of the General Synod dictated. For more permanent funding a system of apportioned benevolence was established by which each synod was assigned a fair share of the General Synod's total support for home missions. A Jubilee Offering was established in 1868 by the General Synod to commemorate the 350th anniversary of the Ninety-five Theses.

3) When insufficient benevolence contributions (during the Panic of 1873) became a problem by 1877, a report on "Limited benevolence" was published which surmised that those in the churches who contribute little or nothing either "love their money more than Christ" (a plausible enough assumption) or are ignorant of the importance of home missions. This latter problem was laid at the feet of the male clergy who did little about it; but its solution was discovered in creating Female Missionary Societies in the synods and congregations. The 1877 convention of the General Synod earnestly recommended the formation of "Female Missionary Societys [sic] in all the churches where it is practicable, in order that the influence and efforts of Christian women may be fully enlisted in the cause of Christ among us." In short order the General Synod was able to report "a wonderful development of the Church during the last decade in mission work." "A vigorous and aggressive spirit now characterizes the General Synod" it was reported by 1881 in that body's annual State of Religion report, partly as a result of the new women's organizations. The official organization to emerge out of the General Synod recommendation was the "Women's Home and Foreign Missionary Societies" which was to be formed in congregations and organized into synodical societies and a general (national) association. Such organized efforts were part of a movement of women's missionary societies organized in Protestant America

during the late 1860s and the 1870s. The Congregational Church was the first to form a denominational organization with its Woman's Board of Mission, organized in 1868. The Methodist, Presbyterian and Episcopal Churches followed in 1869, 1870 and 1871 respectively. The Baptists, African Methodists, Disciples of Christ, and the Reformed Church followed throughout the 1870s with the Woman's American Baptist Home Missionary Society being organized the same year (1877) as the Lutheran Women's Home and Foreign Missionary Society. These groups and their "remarkable efforts and achievements" can be traced, it was reported, to the American Christian woman's "deep sense of Christian responsibility for the unconverted in an age of millennial fervor."[6] The harvest was great and the male laborers needed help before the Messiah's expected return. The proposed partnership of men and women seems to have been entered upon cheerfully and with great expectation by the men, quite probably secure in the sharp religious division of labor which by the nineteenth-century thought of the woman as the Angel of the Home, responsible for her children's religious upbringing. Now she was being granted a more prominent role in the public affairs of the church.

4) The Church Extension Society of the General Synod was reorganized in this same period. It was a separate auxiliary until 1869, the year the Society petitioned the General Synod to create a Board which would assume its assets and responsibilities. The resulting Church Extension Board also earmarked funds from synods for its purposes—lending funds at interest to mission congregations for building or renovating houses of worship. Again to anticipate, efforts by New York area synods to establish new missions without adequate facilities would retard mission development, often to the point of jeopardizing a mission congregation's future. As the new Board reported in commenting on the importance of its work, what it so often heard from new congregations was that "We must have a House of Worship of our own if this Mission is expected to succeed"; or "we cannot possibly build up a congregation here while we are obliged to worship in rented, and inconveniently arranged, and most generally in very unaccessible halls."[7]

5) A somewhat different plan of reorganization occurred with the Lutheran Publication Society. First proposed by the Maryland Synod in 1852 or 1853, the Society was acknowledged as an auxiliary by the General Synod in 1855 and given membership on the Synod's Board of Publication in 1857. Thereafter this Board provided the Synod with an annual report on the work of the Society. As stated in its constitution, the society assumed "the doctrinal basis of the General Synod" and had as "its object the diffusion of religious knowledge, by means of translations and original productions, and thus to furnish and circulate a suitable literature for the Church." In 1868 the constitution of this independent organization was amended to strengthen its relationship

with the General Synod, but not at the expense of its independent editorial integrity. Also strengthened was the system of local agents and synodical involvement to enhance the Society's presence among local congregations. The Society produced a number of significant publications, among them a Sunday school hymn book, religious materials for the Sunday school, family worship materials, study outlines of the Old and New Testaments, biographies of Luther, a history of the Reformation, and a study of the Augsburg Confession. Twenty-five of forty publications were prepared for Sunday schools; and a separate Sunday School Department had been established for that purpose.[8]

The Society was in the right place at the right time, seeking to serve the church in the midst of a growing Sunday School movement. However it faced competition from the American Sunday School Union whose inexpensive publications were widely used and highly competitive. Also the Society's independent existence weakened a sense of ownership and identification on the part of synods and congregations. At the congregational level the struggle involved getting congregations to use Society publications. Though sometimes slightly more expensive, they should be used (it was argued) because Lutheran Publication Society curricula contained a Lutheran point of view. Even the Franckean Synod, least Lutheran of any district synod, began promoting Society publications in the face of cheap competition, although in some cases the Sunday School Union material was more congenial to its own theology. That the Franckean Synod was doing so suggests the impact which the Lutheran Publication Society was having in shaping Lutheran identity at the grass-roots level of the Church.[9]

A NATIONAL CHURCH SOLIDIFIES

The Franckean Synod's concern to promote Lutheran Church literature, suggests something of the organizational solidification that was occurring even among the most independent district synods of the General Synod. This solidification occurred by degrees. Trends and countertrends could be seen almost simultaneously. The 1873 State of Religion report listed as the first of "OUR WANTS"

> concentration and union of effort in all our various Church associations. Our Church is large, wealthy and influential. Nor are we, compared with other denominations, inactive in good works. Our plans of operations also, as carried forward by our different Boards, are admirable. We have capital Church machinery, but we lack concentration. We lack earnest and faithful cooperation in and through the modes adopted and recommended to the districts Synods and Churches by this General Synod. Everywhere there is still too much more congregationalism and individualism; and this is, today, one very great source of our comparative inefficiency.

> Because of this our power is weakened, the operations of our Boards are hindered and crippled, and we fail, as a Church, to accomplish our portion of work in the grand aggressive movements for the overthrow of the kingdom and power of Satan in the world. In union there is strength.[10]

Yet barely two years later, in the biennial report on religion's state, one of the signs of promise was listed as

> a better general apprehension of the true mission of the Church, and a more manifest desire and effort to accomplish that mission. No longer distracted and rent by exciting controversy, a conviction of fixedness of purpose obtains, and the talent and energy of the Church are being more generally put forth in the aggressive work of Zion. . . . There is a growing sense of obligation to the authority and demands of the Church; less of separatism and reckless independence, and more of harmony and concentration; less of confusion in method and purpose, and more of order and consistency.[11]

INTEGRATION AT THE DISTRICT SYNOD LEVEL

By the middle 1870s something approaching a monolithic national Lutheran church body appeared within the General Synod. There was a "growing sense of obligation to the authority of the General Synod" among district synods and a greater degree of cooperation and integration. Local circumstances were pushing district synods in this direction even as the General Synod provided a national structure with which to integrate. After all, it was a time of developing national institutions everywhere within American society—within government and business, as well as within the church.

THE NEW YORK SYNODS

Turning now to the four New York area district synods within the General Synod, we shall examine developments within each synod in this and the next chapter. Again, to anticipate, what we shall find is that some very diverse synods were becoming more like each other in organization and theology, under the aegis of the General Synod. Most importantly, we shall begin to find expressed a number of reasons for merger between New York Synods living and growing as district synods under the umbrella of the General Synod. Even as its New York synods moved in this direction after 1865, confessional issues raised by problems of growth, development, and acculturation, would also surface. Among them was the question of Baptism. Relative indifference to the sacrament of Baptism and what this meant for the future growth of the denomination, was to become a confessional leaven among American Lutherans in the New York area.

As an ecclesiastical organization the English-speaking half of New

York Lutheranism was alive and well. It survived the formation of the General Council and the division of the New York Ministerium with a sense of renewed vigor and purpose. Its ability to organize and to develop mission-funding was enviable compared to New York Ministerium mission capabilities. And yet this ability to function effectively in an increasingly urbanized, industrialized milieu also indicated a growing accommodation to materialism and to the changing status quo. Between 1860 and 1890 the General Synod remnant of the New York Ministerium grew, adjusting well to its environment. Yet by 1890 the material circumstances of its existence had brought it imperceptibly, and quite unexpectedly, to a spiritual and organizational crisis which it could no longer ignore.

THE NEW JERSEY SYNOD—1861

The breaking of fraternal ties and unraveling of a tradition had begun much earlier—in 1861 by some accounts. Six pastors and lay delegates from New Jersey churches gathered at German Valley, New Jersey, in February of that year to form a New Jersey Synod. To recapitulate, the reason given was that the time had arrived to establish an "efficient agency within the State, which shall more successfully look after the varied interests" of the church. Six years later, as the New York Synod was being formed, the president of the New Jersey Synod confessed to a more complex set of motives, indicating that it was originally the remoteness of the New York Ministerium meetings, the inability of small (i.e., New Jersey) congregations to host the synod, and the conducting of Ministerium business in German—"a language which a considerable portion of" New Jersey members "did not understand"—which necessitated the division.[12]

Basically the religious interests of the English-speaking church in New Jersey seemed best served by a state-based, English-language synodical organization. German-language confessionalism and its affinity with the General Council, like English-language loyalty to the General Synod, began to complicate the picture as the new synod developed its relations with other Lutheran bodies. The New Jersey Synod managed to maintain ties with both the New York Synod and the Ministerium after the 1867 split. Yet when both bodies sent fraternal delegates to the 1867 gathering of the New Jersey Synod, its president "returned in courteous manner the fraternal greetings" of the Ministerium but expressed "hearty approval of the course of the New York Synod, and assured the delegate of this Synod [New York] that our sympathies were with them in their new organization." President J. I. Burrell of New Jersey spoke for all in approving the New York Synod's withdrawal from a body which itself withdrew "from the great bond of union of our Church in this country," i.e., the General Synod.[13]

The New Jersey Synod, then, was a General Synod body when it was formed, and remained so throughout the General Council schism. This was so because the core congregations could trace their roots to the Lutheran pietism characteristic of this subregion of greater New York area Lutheranism. Originally consisting of two congregations in the New Germantown area served by Pohlman in 1830, the core increased to eight congregations by 1840. The inactivity of German-language St. Johns, Newark, and the reduction of three New Germantown congregations to one large congregation, reduced the number of active New Jersey congregations in the New York Ministerium to four by 1850. But that number had increased again to eight by 1860. It was this small group together with two eastern Pennsylvania congregations—in all ten congregations, seven pastors, and 1,395 communicant members—which formed the New Jersey Synod in 1861.[14]

Organized for mission, the new body's per capita mission support was only $0.28, and on that basis the synod sought to maintain a mission and missionary to two groups of German immigrants at Bridgeton and Salem. During the first eight months of its life the president reported that "little requiring my supervision had occurred," a level of inactivity which continued throughout the decade.[15] Since its initial *raison d'être* was that of an "efficient agency" intended to improve the condition of the church within the borders of New Jersey, the synod's brief life and history must be understood on the basis of this presumed efficiency.

AN EFFICIENT AGENCY?

The New Jersey Synod would use General Synod mission methods to bring prosperity to a small and somewhat out-of-the-way corner of the Lutheran church. This meant developing new congregations and reviving religious zeal in those already established. By now—1861—Lutheran church leaders were experienced nose-counters who understood the Kingdom's progress in terms of statistical growth. What is more, the strength of their faith and their mission effort had become linked to the good news of church growth. Or so one could easily conclude from the 1864 report of a synod committee on the "Minutes of the General Synod." The Committee complained, for example, that it was impossible to present any statement on the progress of the church in the United States "in the absence of . . . statistical tables." Their omission was to be regretted "as we are thus left without much information in reference to the progress of our Zion." A sense of such progress was important, moreover, because it "would have encouraged our faith, and strengthened our hearts in the prosecution of the work to which the Master has called us."[16]

For better or worse New Jersey Lutheran church leaders were

acutely aware of church growth and related it to the fortunes of church mission work. The President's report for 1866, for example, called "for us to double our diligence in the cause of Missions" because last year's statistical report indicated a "falling off of communicants."[17] This was indeed the case, as Table 7.1 indicates:

Table 7.1[18]
New Jersey Lutheran Communicants

Year	Communicants (5)*	Churches	Stations (5)
1861	1395	10	0
1862	1467	11	0
1863	1499	10	0
1864	1508	9	16
1865	1368	10	18
1866	1575	10	17
1867	1517	11	7
1868	1621	13	8
1869	1753	13	8
1870	1759	11	13
1871	1988	14	14

But New Jersey church growth was also part of a much larger, and more complicated picture.

The fluctuation in numbers during the early 1860s reflected the fortunes of revivalism. Parochial reports for the year 1865 had indicated few revivalist efforts (protracted meetings) with poor results (conversions and new members). Thus the decline in membership between 1864 and 1865. It was a season of spiritual dryness, having much to do with the physical and spiritual exhaustion resulting from four years of civil war. Parochial reports noted membership losses from death on the battlefield, and the hardships associated with church members being drafted. In one case members of a single congregation were called up to serve the Union together with their pastor. The years 1861-1863 on the other hand, had been times of religious awakening—again partially war-related. In one case, a revival had added fifty-four members to a church, half of them young men who had continued their spiritual renewal with an ongoing prayer meeting. These same young men soon went to war as volunteers with the 31st New Jersey Regiment and all returned "except two noble young men" (their pastor reported to synod) "who died in the hospital in Virginia, with their religious character" intact.[19] This cycle of revivalistic growth from 1861 to 1864, and the religious decline of 1864 and 1865, began anew in 1866 with the war's end. Revivals occurred once again with an increase in church membership throughout 1866, 1867, and 1868.

Table 7.1 suggests a second reason for church growth after the Civil War in New Jersey—the growth of new congregations to serve a growing population. The two German-language missions became self-sustaining as these and other new congregations were added to the total number belonging to the Synod. More important, the preaching stations (which the Synod began reporting on in 1864), established by pastors in territories adjacent to their own congregations, had great potential for developing still more congregations. The new congregations were formed in the midst of a crisis which gripped the Synod at mid-decade, leading the president to call for renewed mission efforts. His 1864 report had sounded a note of doom. The Synod had an excess of ministerial candidates with no work to do, and they were being exported when they might better be employed at home. A possible mission to German-speaking immigrants had just failed for lack of interest by the people themselves and a pastor who could help it along. Another in the German Valley at High Bridge failed in similar circumstances. A traveling missionary was needed who could preach in German and English. At a time of stagnant growth in New Jersey the much admired Hartwick Synod—"one of the most energetic Synods" in the General Synod—had added 200 members. And so the lament went.

The preaching stations seem to have been a self-generated remedy for this malaise. Two of them—at Ramsey and Belvidere—were the work of a group of synod pastors who had been unusually successful at revivalism in their own congregations. Theirs was part of an overall pattern of church growth in New Jersey, despite presidential reports to the contrary. Between efforts at revivalism and the development of new mission fields, the New Jersey Synod grew by a most respectable 42.5 percent between 1861 and 1871. Given such results, could the New Jersey Synod be considered an "efficient agency" in promoting the fortunes of Lutheranism in the State as the founders had hoped? Some overall conclusions can be drawn from Graph 7.1.

Under the old New York Ministerium the New Jersey congregations had grown from a small cluster to a significant handful with an *allogenous growth rate* (i.e., greater than that of the surrounding population).[20] That exceptional growth had declined however after 1850, continuing well below the general population. By 1860 New Jersey pastors were prepared to go it alone, as a distinct synodical entity, seeking to improve this lackluster performance for the sake of the Kingdom in New Jersey. In one sense they were successful—an increase of 46.5 percent over the decade was significant for a new organization. However, as Graph 7.1 also indicates, that rate of growth did not keep up with the overall population growth in New Jersey.

The problem was especially acute in the urbanized areas of New Jersey around New York harbor. In 1866, for example, the Synod Mission Committee noted 12,000 Germans in the growing city of Newark (population 80,000). Four German congregations were flourishing (none of them members of Synod), while the Baptists, Methodists, and

Presbyterians were all laboring among the Germans. The result was Presbyterian congregations composed almost solely of German Lutheran immigrants whose clergy were asking Lutheran synod pastors "Why do not you Lutherans do more for your people in this place?" There were also Germans in Hoboken, Hudson City, Jersey City, Camden, "and many other places" including "Boiling Spring," where a "pious Episcopalian" had established a Sunday school for German immigrant children. Some things had been accomplished, yet much remained to be done. It was this unfinished work, and the greater resources of other groups, which troubled New Jersey Lutherans.

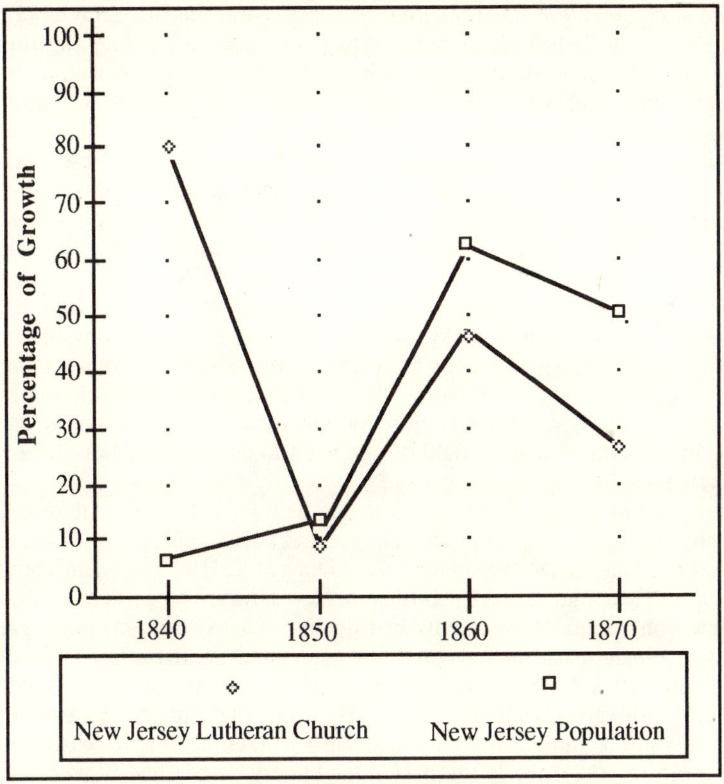

Graph 7.1 New Jersey Church and Population Growth

TO MERGE OR NOT TO MERGE?

At this point in the synod's development the question of merger was raised from outside the synod itself. In 1865 New Jersey's synod president E. DeYoe reported that in the present meeting of the New York Ministerium, which seemed to be contemplating "a separation between the English and German elements," it was anticipated that there would be a "union between the English brethren of that synod and the Synod of New Jersey." The matter was raised again by President DeYoe in 1867 as a point of information. He informed the synod that the recent division of the New York Ministerium with the creation of the New York Synod had removed the old reasons for forming the New Jersey Synod—the old Ministerium's size, distance and foreign character—so that a merger might now occur. Wisely, the New Jersey Synod decided to test the proposition, asking its congregations to instruct their delegates to the 1868 meeting of synod on the matter.[21]

The 1868 session of synod was opened by the usual president's address, in which President Matthias Sheeleigh, who was also secretary of the General Synod, delivered a strong case against "disbanding this synod." It was asserted that the merger of two small synods would "be an advantage to both." Yet dissolution would break up the New Jersey Synod with a part surely going to the East Pennsylvania Synod, and the other minute fragment providing no great advantage to the New York Synod. "How then" he asked, "could the death of this Synod sensibly contribute to the advantage of any other? " Looking at the matter from New Jersey's vantage point, being "torn to shreds and scattered to the winds" was not an act of faithful stewardship. The New Jersey Synod had been created "with the view of effectually developing this field for Christ." To expect a larger synod to devote more energy to New Jersey when it had a larger mission field than before, and thus provide more mission help, "would probably not soon be realized. The result would be a failed Synod and the creation of a half-century's hiatus before another such organization could devote itself to the needs of New Jersey Lutherans.[22]

Should not New Jersey Lutherans be admonished to "labor and pray together a little longer in patience and hope?" Sheeleigh asked. A new life was already apparent in the infant synod. How rarely until now was a new congregation established in New Jersey. The germ of several new congregations were now in evidence. The Synod was but eight years old and had already met and withstood great trials. Why not "stand still a little longer, that we may see the salvation of God?" Sheeleigh recognized that New Jersey was one part of the eastern Lutheran corridor whose geography had worked against it. What had the old regime done in the past? One hundred years had proven that New Jersey—"this fair and promising territory, lying between the largest cities of the land"—was little more than "a roaming ground for the spoiler so far as our beloved Church was concerned." If nothing was done in a hundred years, "*twice* nothing might be realized" in another century. Why not continue the little synod then, "that we may labor and pray and weep together for the church?" Accordingly he recommended that a union with the New York Synod be considered inexpedient "and that we unitedly seek grace from on high to make us and our churches more earnest and self-denying in organizing and sustaining new congregations amongst us."[23]

Sheeleigh made a splendid speech. What is more, he was right. More had been done for New Jersey Lutherans since 1861 than in the previous 100 years. But had enough been done? And could not more be done with a larger group? Sheeleigh made a good case for small synods, with subregional responsibilities, as the geography and ethnic landscape of the New York area became more complex and diversified. It was a case for local responsibility and governance made at a time when such "littleness" was still understood and valued. Yet it was also a time when Americans were beginning to discover the "economies of scale." Some things are better done with greater size and larger resources. And the question of the moment was whether a merged synod of New Jersey and New York might be able to do more in the struggle to increase the size of the church relative to a growing population.

The question was not to be answered for several years. By then Pastor Sheeleigh had taken another call outside of the Synod. As late as 1869 it was reported in the New York Synod that there was "an almost unanimous opinion" among New Jersey Lutheran leaders that they "have a very large field in which to work, and they feel assured that this work can be better accomplished" if their separate organization was maintained. Yet in that same year Pastor David Kline, president of the New Jersey Synod for 1870, proposed formation of a joint committee to work out terms of merger. By then it was assumed, at least by Kline, that a larger synod was a good idea. The New York, Hartwick, and Franckean Synods had recently met without New Jersey to consider educational matters of common interest. The snub had shaken and angered Kline, having been an indication (perhaps) that New Jersey's desire to go it alone was a disadvantage where size and cooperation counted.[24] Still the New Jersey Synod's conferences—local organizations of congregations and pastors—voted against merger in 1871.

THE NEW YORK SYNOD

The New York Synod with which the New Jersey Synod considered merging, was a body of similar size. It began life in 1867 with sixteen pastors, ten congregations, and 1,445 communicants, and included among its leaders President Henry Pohlman, presiding officer of both the new Synod and the General Synod. Its commitment to the General Synod was central to its existence. It had been formed, after all, by the withdrawal of pastors and congregational delegates from the Ministerium, because as Pohlman insisted "We are personally and conscientiously attached to the General Synod of the Evangelical Lutheran Church of the United States." Separating from the General Synod, as the Ministerium had done, "would sever our connection with all past associations and future hopes of our Church." It was a body whose past history had shown it to be "under God, and will continue to be, the most influential and efficient organization . . . for the cultivation of sound Christian doctrine and practice . . . of the Lutheran Church in this country." It was also, as Henry Pohlman noted at the time of the division, the English-speaking remnant of an increasingly German Ministerium which had experienced three previous withdrawals of English-speaking Lutherans—the Hartwick, Franckean, and New Jersey Synods.[25]

The New York Synod would continue the confessional tradition of the General Synod. That tradition, Pohlman argued, was *also* the doctrinal basis of the old New York Ministerium. Until the confessional changes brought about by the General Council, involving subscription to "not only the Augsburg Confession, but all the Symbolical Books," and that by acceptance "in every statement of doctrine in their own true, original and only sense," the old Ministerium had received and held

> with the Evangelical Lutheran Church of our fathers, the word of God contained in the canonical Scripture of the Old and New Testaments, as the only rule of faith and practice, and the Augsburg Confession as the correct exhibition of the fundamental doctrines of the Divine Word, and of the faith of our Church founded upon that Word.[26]

Now German elements wished to introduce "in this land a rigorous confessional system which our fathers were unwilling to endure, and which is unsuited to the age in which we live, to the genius of American institutions, and to the Protestant character of our Church." This was a "retrograde movement towards the darkness of a darker age," an effort to "enforce precise uniformity of belief on minor aspects of doctrine, on which there always have been, are now, and always will be differences of opinion" which the Word has not clearly revealed, and which neither the Augsburg Confession nor Luther's writings assumed to define.[27]

JUBILEE SPRINGBOARD FOR THE NEW SYNOD

The New York Synod appreciated its Reformation heritage, such caveats notwithstanding. The year 1867, Pohlman continued in his first report to synod, was the "*Seventh Semi-Centennial Jubilee Year* of the glorious Reformation." The most important work of the new Synod, aside from organizing itself, was laying ambitious plans to celebrate the Jubilee Year in suitable fashion. As with Israel's Jubilee this was to remind church members of "the numberless mercies bestowed upon them" by the Reformation—"the unspeakable blessings of a redeemed church, an open Bible, an untrammeled judgment in its interpretation and a purified Christianity." Above all it was to be a time for recollecting the revival of that cardinal doctrine "*of a standing or falling church*"—"JUSTIFICATION BY FAITH ALONE." In true pietist fashion, thanksgiving was to be married to active plans for attaining "a higher degree of spirituality" in the new synod.

How was this to be done? In several ways. On the first sabbath of each month in each congregation a sermon was to be preached on a cardinal doctrine of the Reformation. Also Jubilee Festivals were to be celebrated in each church under the personal supervision of President Pohlman. Finally, the Synod was to raise $18,000 for general benevolence, especially for home mission and Church extension, and for the endowment of Hartwick Seminary. All members of the congregations and Sunday schools were to be persuaded to contribute towards this goal, with efficient committees appointed in each congregation for monthly collections using a proper book to record amounts. A "large, handsome book," stamped *Jubilee Volume,* was also to be used in each congregation listing all contributors and their contributions, with a special section for *Memorial Contributions* to honor some cherished departed friend, or relative of the family. The volume was to be preserved as a reminder at the next Centennial "of our liberality, church love and interest in the spread of the doctrines of the Reformation."[28]

The opening session of the new Synod demonstrated several things (as our extensive quotations indicate). The first was loyalty to a Lutheran confessional heritage which preserved the core of Lutheran doctrine but in the context of American religious liberty. Reformation and Enlightenment co-existed in what for General Synod Lutherans was an easy truce. The heritage was celebrated, but as something safely past. A useful distinction can be made among Lutherans in America regarding their attitude towards the confessions. For General Synod Lutherans the confessions were an honored heritage, for General Council Lutherans they were a living tradition. Each drew a different value, meaning, and theological content, therefore, from the pages of the *Book of Concord.*

The second thing the opening of synod demonstrated was the systematic way in which General Synod Lutherans managed to raise funds for the work of the church. Neither revivalism in General Synod congregations, nor an extensive parochial school and college system in General Council congregations, could do anything to encourage growth and development of new congregations. Entering new mission fields required money—for missionaries, pastors, and places of worship. As we have seen, neither the New York Ministerium nor the New Jersey Synod had managed very well in this aspect of mission work, resulting in a loss to the church of new members. The New York Synod, on the other hand, demonstrated an organizational ability to solve these and other problems which vexed the Lutheran Church in the United States.

Within a year it was apparent what an honored heritage could do to motivate a church organization in the service of mission. The Jubilee offering itself exceeded $33,000 by the end of 1868; nearly $30,000 was earmarked for local mission work. Meanwhile, regular ongoing home missions were supported at a per capita rate of $0.32, considerably greater than rates in either the New York Ministerium or the New Jersey Synod. Succeeding years were as productive. The year 1869 saw further contributions to the Jubilee fund of $7,600. The per capita support for home missions dropped to $0.29, not because of any decline in the amount of giving, but because of a very healthy increase in communicant membership (new members gave less well at the outset). The increase for that year was not the result of new missions however, but represented the addition of four more congregations to the Synod. And 1870 saw further growth—Jubilee contributions in excess of $46,600 and, despite the addition of two more congregations, an increase in per capita giving to home missions to $0.92! Not only was per capita giving up. Communicant membership had jumped by 45 percent, an increase that could not be attributed to new congregations alone. And the pattern continued in 1871—nineteen congregations, $24,100 for the Jubilee fund, and a percapita support of home missions of $1.15.[29]

And all of this without a plan of systematic benevolence. The increases were noted by the committee on systematic benevolence which quickly added that such increases were "no more than our people can readily give under proper motives and methods." Insisting that a method should be available by which church members can "contribute regularly and frequently" to the extension of the Kingdom, the "Lord's Treasury," a system of regular contributions in special collection boxes, was proposed for introduction into the New York Synod. The system was promoted by the General Synod itself with the recommendation that it be introduced with a request that each church member contribute at least one dollar "for the benevolent operations of the church." The next year, 1872—the year of merger—$26,200 went into Jubilee coffers, while home mission contributions jumped to $1.42 per capita in the New York part of the joint synod.[30]

Increased monies meant expanded mission efforts. The 1868 report of the Missionary and Education Committee noted, for example, "an extended and promising field" of mission, but "our means are very limited." An appeal by New Jersey to support a new field in Patterson was taken under advisement and several other mission fields were continued. By 1870, however, and with the growth of benevolence monies, the mission work of the Synod was "considerably enlarged." A Swedish mission in Boston had been stabilized, and another started in Brooklyn under the licensed ministerial candidate P. J. Kallstrom.[31]

ANOTHER MERGER EMERGES

By 1870 strengthened mission resources were becoming apparent to all who were concerned with New York Synod mission efforts, presumably including those in the New Jersey Synod trying to decide about merger with their twin synod across the Hudson. Two years before, the New Jersey Synod was almost unanimously of the opinion to go it alone. At the same time the New York Synod resolved that it did "not deem it expedient to form a union with the New Jersey Synod at this present time." Much happened in the two year interval besides the improved fortunes of New York missions to change some minds.

The proposal to merge New York and New Jersey Synods was but one of several merger suggestions made in the uncertain days following the General Synod's reorganization. Just when New Jersey congregations were deciding to remain a synod to give attention to Lutheranism in New Jersey, New York's synods were focusing on religious needs in their state. In 1868 for the first time New York Lutherans thought about a joint urban ministry. The Franckean Synod proposed that itself, Hartwick, and New York cooperate in supporting a "domestic missionary at large" to supply destitute congregations and explore mission fields throughout the state, especially in "the most cultivated portions of the country."[32] As the nation moved into its period of urban growth, newly urbanized areas were becoming a new kind of mission field which the old, subregional synods could not manage by themselves. For the same reason, even as the New Jersey Synod was seeking to better serve its own constituency, it was also exploring joint mission efforts with New York to serve the newly urbanized areas of greater New York on the western (New Jersey) shores of New York Harbor.

Though the New York Synod declined the Franckean overture of 1868, a year later it established a committee to explore a merger of the three New York bodies after such a merger was proposed by the Rev. P. A. Strobel, the Hartwick delegate to the 1869 meeting of the New York Synod. By 1870 the Hartwick and New York Synods had agreed that a union of General Synod district synods in the New York area was "both desirable and feasible," and that both the Franckean and New Jersey Synods should be so notified. But at the same session, President Pohlman proposed the creation of a joint union committee with New Jersey, assuring the New York delegates that New Jersey and its president, David Kline, were so inclined.[33] A year later President Pohlman reported further progress on the two converging plans of merger.

Within three years of its founding, then, the New York Synod had emerged as a resourceful synodical organization capable of sustaining expanding mission fields, of promoting intersynodical cooperation in mission matters, and of leading the way to a potential merger of General Synod elements in greater New York. The result would have been a region-wide district of the General Synod equivalent to the General Council's New York Ministerium. However when the Hartwick Synod discovered in 1872 that the New York-New Jersey merger was a foregone conclusion, it withdrew from further merger talks insisting that "a union with the combined Synods does not coincide with the views of the brethren." The reason was not difficult to fathom. Hartwick was not ready for fraternal ties with the New Jersey Synod since they were locked in a dispute over whether or not Pastor G. W. Enders had been properly dismissed from the Hartwick Synod when he received a call in New Jersey. As if this were not enough, New Jersey Pastor Philip A. Strobel had taken a call in the Hartwick Synod in 1868 and upon his departure had pocketed as severance pay funds presumably earmarked for his incoming successor. Strobel had sued synod members in 1868, necessitating a special session of Synod.[34] Cool relations between the two bodies made a further merger impossible at this time.

THE SYNOD OF NEW YORK AND NEW JERSEY—1872

In New Jersey on the other hand, sentiment was shifting towards merger. While the synod conferences opposed merger, the joint committee formed to explore the idea favored union because of "the substantial benefits of united action in the work of the Synods of New York and New Jersey"—the New Jersey Synod would continue as a separate conference in the new, super synod. A joint session of the two synods would occur soon after adoption to quickly effect the merger. Despite conference opposition, the plan of merger was adopted at the 1871 meeting of the New Jersey Synod and the joint session was set up for the following year. Meeting first by themselves in brief session for the last time in 1872, nine New Jersey pastors and thirteen New Jersey congregations conducted their final business. Perhaps it was just as well. Once again they were informed that "Our fields of missionary ground . . . remain as ever unattended to ... not for want of interest, but that of means." In particular a new mission field was opening up at Phillipsburg ("and some others that might be named") which must sit fallow. It was hoped that measures would be adopted to meet these longstanding circumstances in the merged synod.[35]

Shortly thereafter the two Synods met in joint session as the first gathering of the Synod of New York and New Jersey. A new constitution was adopted after three sessions of discussion, and committee reports were given. A financial accounting was provided by both Synod treasurers and reports were made on systematic benevolence campaigns in both synods. Figured for our purposes in terms of per capita giving, New Jersey's thirteen congregations had contributed $0.17 to home missions while New York's nineteen congregations had given about ten times as much to the cause—$1.27. Shortly thereafter the Mission and Education Committee of the new synod reported on its work and recommended that the potential Phillipsburg, New Jersey mission field be surveyed "in the interests of our Home Missionary work."[36] For the moment at least the question "To Merge or Not to Merge" had been answered. The new merger's economy of scale, given New York's outstanding mission benevolence, seemed the wiser choice.

The new Synod formed in 1872 was the first of a two-step reunion process by which all New York area General Synod districts were reunited in 1908 as the Synod of New York. (See Maps 7.1 and 7.2.) In the meantime, General Synod Lutheranism along both sides of the Hudson from Albany to New York harbor underwent a significant reorganization and a slow but profound spiritual change. Over the next two decades the new combination of General Synod Lutherans along the Hudson showed steady if unspectacular growth. The Synod of New York and New Jersey began life as a synod of twenty-one (21) pastors, thirty-nine (39) congregations, twenty-seven (27) preaching stations, and 5,295 communicants. By 1890 it was a larger body of fifty-four (54) pastors, forty (40) congregations, ten (10) stations, and 7,684 communicant members.

At the 1872 merger a number of active clergy, in the prime of life served a host of congregations and preaching stations nearly twice as numerous as themselves. By 1890 the Synod consisted of an aging clergy, more numerous than the combined total of congregations and preaching stations, some of whom were in retirement. The field of endeavor had shrunk in that time. Between withdrawals to other synods (many from the New Jersey field) and additions of new congregations (twelve new congregations joined the synod between 1872 and 1890), the two decades showed a net increase of one congregation (though membership within the congregations increased significantly in that time). The number of preaching stations had decreased, however, by seventeen (17). In that time the size of the New Jersey portion of the Synod had shrunk—both from withdrawals and a lack of development. By 1890 there were only ten (10) New Jersey pastors (3 retired) and seven (7) New Jersey congregations left in the joint synod.[37]

What had begun in New Jersey as an enterprise of hope proved a mixture of light and darkness (a favorite image of New Jersey pastors seeking in parochial reports to capture the annual state of religion in their congregations)! The area's churches were not strong enough to develop on their own, yet were unsure of their future submerged in a larger body.

CHURCH EXTENSION IN THE NEW SYNOD

Such growth was at best autogenous—the self-generated results of baptism, revivalism, and conversion. Unlike the New York Ministerium, there was no increasing percentage of the population incorporated into the synod's congregations, and no rates of growth greater than the surrounding population. (See Graph 7.2.)

The Ministerium—the German-speaking and German-seeking part of New York Lutheranism—despite the pullout of English-speaking

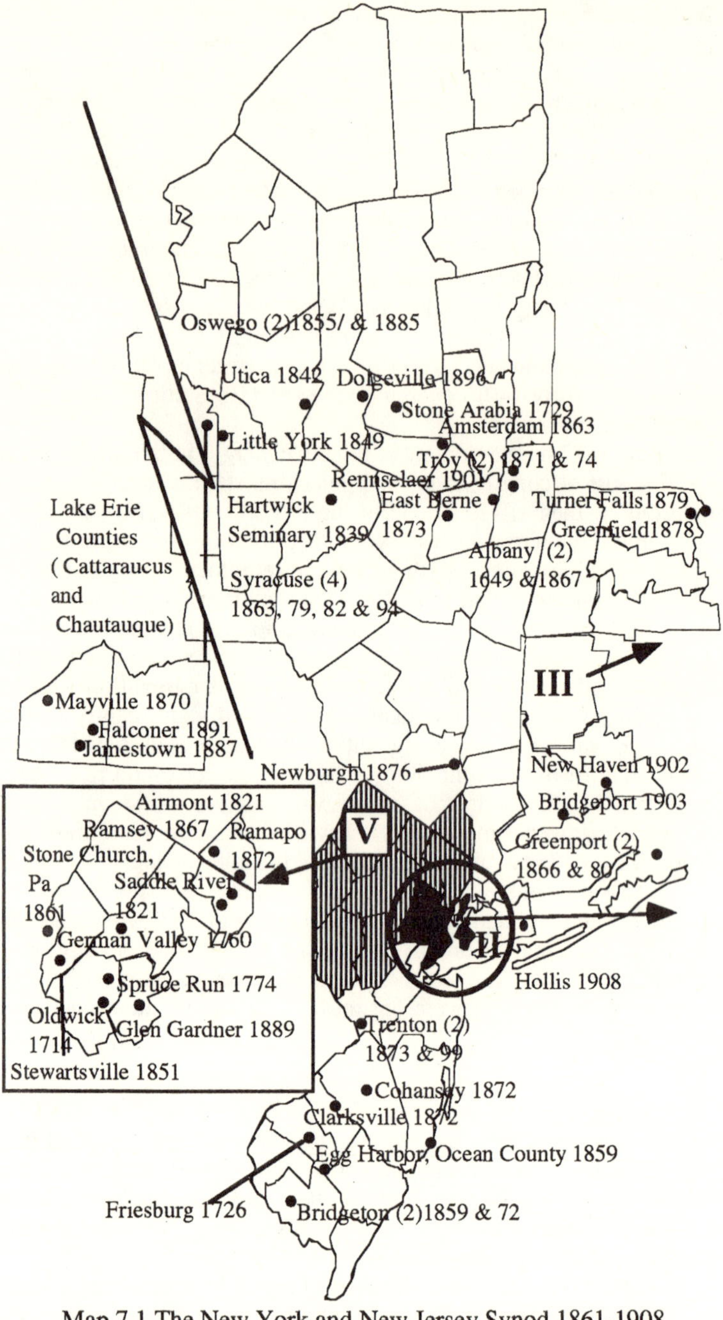

Map 7.1 The New York and New Jersey Synod 1861-1908

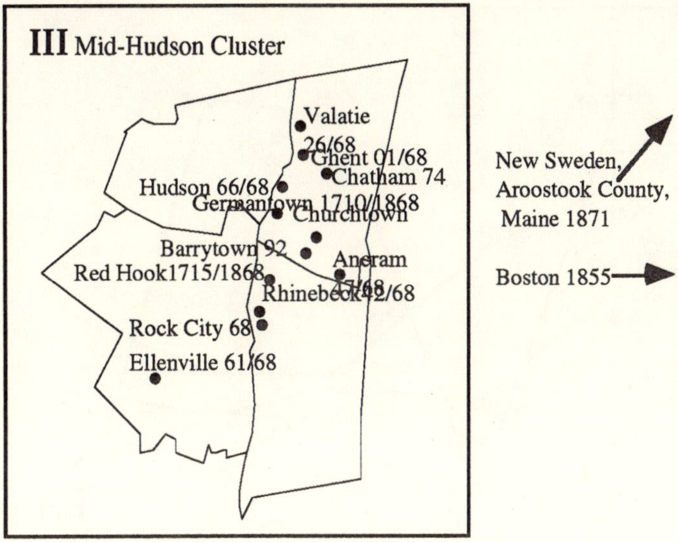

Map 7.1 New York and New Jersey Synod, 1861-1908

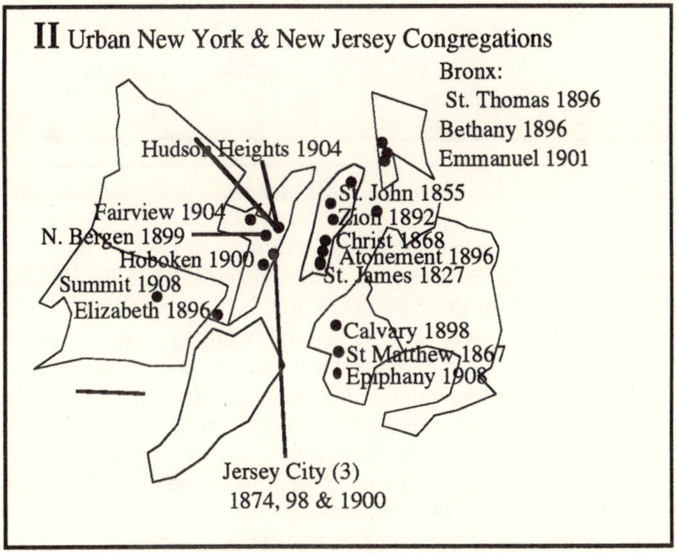

Map 7.2 Urban and Mid-Hudson Congregations

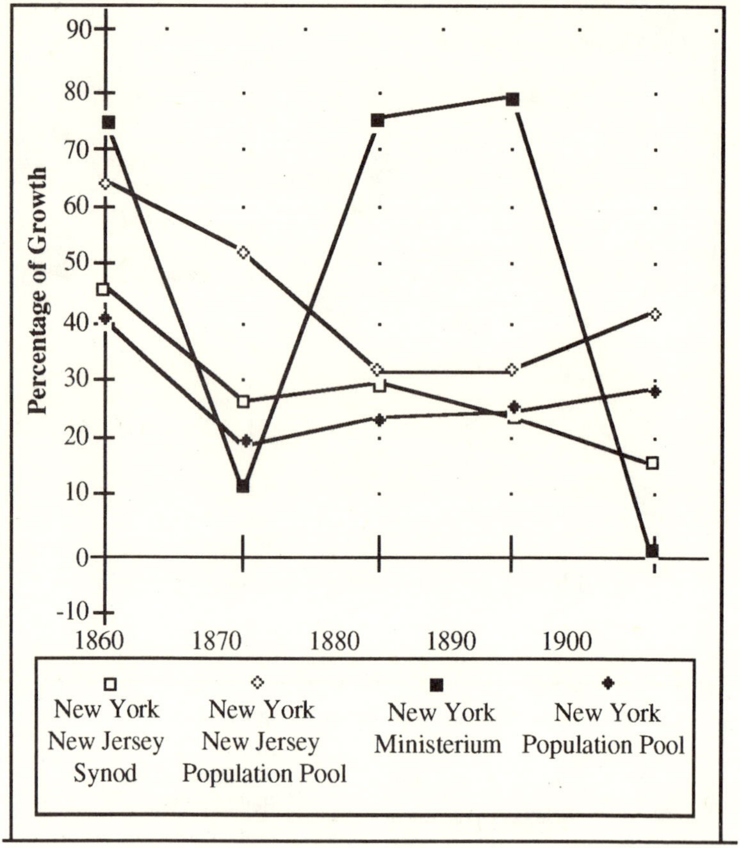

Graph 7.2 New York/New Jersey Church and Population Growth

New Jersey and New York elements, continued to grow at rates faster than the surrounding population until the middle 1890s. English-speaking Lutherans in the New York and New Jersey Synod, to the contrary, failed to grow at rates in keeping with population expansion in New York and New Jersey, as a comparison of growth rates between the synod and its *total* population pool indicate. However, if the synod's growth rate is compared with the New York population pool, it is apparent that the New York and New Jersey Synod was growing more rapidly until 1890. The synod was growing more rapidly in New York, but less rapidly (relative to population) in New Jersey, because of the very rapid urbanization occurring on the west shore of New York Harbor, partly the result of German immigration. All of which is to suggest that the English-speaking, General Synod portion of the Lutheran Church was not growing as rapidly in New York as the German-speaking, General Council part. Yet English-speaking New York Lutheranism still grew at a healthy rate. Why? There were two reasons. First, by a conscientious use of Baptism it incorporated an increasing portion of the children in its population pool into the church.[38] Secondly, because as the German immigrant population matured it was producing mission opportunities for English-speaking Lutheranism among a growing number of second-generation daughters and sons.

To describe the New York and New Jersey Synod as exclusively English-speaking, however, is inaccurate. The Synod was actually bilingual; it published its minutes in both languages, and sought mission opportunities among both language groups. President Pohlman, a second-generation, bilingual English-speaking pastor, had sought to maintain that language and cultural balance in the old New York Ministerium even as it was being overwhelmed by German-speaking Lutherans, and he (among others) carried over this objective into the new New York and New Jersey Synod. So strong was the commitment to a bilingual church without segregation of language groups that the Synod of New York and New Jersey complained to the General Synod when, in 1877, the General Synod proposed the separation of mission efforts into English and German departments. More precisely then, the New York and New Jersey Synod was bilingual, but English-"leaning," with a special sense of responsibility for English-speaking Lutherans and for a Lutheranism which was bilingual.[39]

ENGLISH-LANGUAGE MISSION STRATEGY

If the Synod had a mission strategy, it was in finding areas to establish English-speaking congregations where maturing immigrant populations were producing an anglicized second generation. If the German-speaking congregation was General Synod all the better, since there would be no questions of pulpit or altar fellowship to further impede crossover in a Lutheran population that was more resistant to acculturation than most other ethnic groups. In his 1878 report to synod, President A. C. Wedekind called attention

> to the many fields in our State for the establishment of English missions. . . . I hesitate not in saying that there are few fields anywhere more inviting or more promising than most of our large inland cities, where usually from two to three and even more, large German congregations exist, without any provision being made for the young whose education and associations are English, and who thus, alas! are generally lost to our church.[40]

Syracuse, for example, had two German-language churches, St. Stephens and St. Johns, both members of the Ministerium. A third, Zion, belonged to the New York and New Jersey Synod. In 1879 the Synod started an English-language congregation, First English, as a new mission field. Oswego had two Lutheran congregations in the early 1880s—an independent German-language church, Grace, and St. Pauls, which originally had belonged to the Ministerium. But it changed affiliation, joining the New York and New Jersey Synod as a German-speaking congregation in Oswego. Subsequently the Synod formed an English-language mission, St. Matthews, from an English-speaking group which broke away from St. Pauls. The transfer was arranged by the president of Synod because St. Pauls was thought to have "a special mission" among the Germans of Oswego which an English-language worship service "may only cripple." English-speaking St. Matthews, meanwhile, was seen as an equally important mission field which would not encroach on St. Pauls and which would in time "be a home for their children in the faith of their fathers, and so prevent them from being absorbed by the surrounding denominations."[41]

Another variation on the theme was to be found in the ministry of President Wedekind. He served for a number of years as pastor of St. James Lutheran Church in Manhattan (the struggling English-speaking break away from German-speaking St. Matthews) with the purpose of ministering to descendants of eighteenth-century immigrants who were rapidly being anglicized. St. James's (it will be remembered) had sustained a reverse-breakaway in the 1860s when Holy Trinity was formed, calling G. F. Krotel from Philadelphia; it joined the New York Ministerium in protest against St. James's decision to join the New York Synod. With his peculiar experience in serving English-speaking Lutherans, the bilingual Wedekind was called to St. Johns German Lutheran Church in the city (now Greenwich Village), a Ministerium congregation, "a large and flourishing congregation, which has been able to retain within its fold many of the younger members, who are now among the active workers in this interesting field." Wedekind accomplished this by adding "a service in the English language." Despite the congregation's Ministerium connection, Wedekind was able to maintain his Synodical affiliation resulting in the eventual shift of St. Johns congregational allegiance to the New York and New Jersey Synod![42]

St. Johns was one of at least eight among the forty (40) congregations in the New York and New Jersey Synod in 1890 which were identified as German-speaking. They constituted just less than a quarter of the Synod and represented a significant element in that body. What was observed above about the different growth rates for German- and English-speaking Synods held true for congregations within the New York and New Jersey Synod as well. Its German congregations were growing faster than their English counterparts, a fact troubling to the Synod. Without blaming the English-speaking pastors, the "low state of spirituality and efficiency" among English-speaking churches was nevertheless lamented. Synod officials, not yet understanding the demographic reasons for different growth rates (twice as great among immigrant Lutherans), blamed the differences on a growing "spirit of worldliness" and the "decline of family religion" among English-speaking Lutherans.[43] Obviously higher rates of membership growth in the German-speaking community resulted from ethnic-language churches serving as centers of ethnoreligious communities in immigrant America. Yet there was also an element of truth to the assertion about a growing decline of spirituality among English-speaking Lutherans.

TOWARD A MORE INCLUSIVE SYNOD

At the end of its printed minutes for 1890, the Synod provided statistics on world Lutheranism with an interpretative statement on the Lutheran Church in the United States and in the world. The New York and New Jersey Synod identified itself with "English Lutheranism" but also indicated that the Church in the United States was multilingual, containing communities using English, German, Swedish, Norwegian, Danish, Finnish, Icelandic, and French. The American Church was clearly part of a world-wide institution represented not only by these and other European languages, but by "every other civilized tongue" as well. "The Lutheran Church, though taking its origin in Germany, knows no fatherland or mother tongue. She is at home everywhere."[44] Something of this multilingual, multiethnic vision of a Lutheranism set free from fatherland and mother tongue was to be found in the Synod of New York and New Jersey itself, at least in embryo. Within two years of its formation a major mission thrust occurred into the Scandinavian communities. A Swedish Mission Church under the care of P. J. Kallstrom was receiving mission money. The Synod also established "a permanent foot-hold in the New England states" through support of Scandinavian immigrants congregations: the Scandinavian Evangelical Lutheran Church in Gloucester, Massachusetts; the First Norwegian Evangelical Lutheran Church in Boston; the Scandinavian Evangelical Lutheran Church of Lowell, Massachusetts; and a Swedish congregation in New Sweden, Maine.[45]

Eight different missions were being supported by 1874, thanks largely to the Jubilee mission fund established by the New York Synod in the early 1870s. "Ours is emphatically a missionary Synod" the mission board proclaimed. "*Eight Missions*, with an aggregate appropriation of *fifteen hundred dollars!*" One reason for this immigrant outreach, no doubt, was the Castle Garden Mission of Pastor Robert Neumann, begun under the Ministerium, but continued under New York and New Jersey Synod auspices when Neumann changed synod affiliation in 1875. The Synod considered the Castle Garden Mission's support "one of high Christian duty and mercy." Castle Garden Mission had managed to form colonies of immigrants sent to settle new lands in the west. One group, which moved from Russia and settled in Franklin County, Nebraska, forming a congregation there (St. Pauls German Lutheran Church of Wilhelmruhe), was at least temporarily affiliated with the distant Synod through the ordination of their spiritual leader, a pious schoolmaster, F. W. Scheibel.[46]

AN AFRICAN-AMERICAN LUTHERAN CHURCH IN GREENPORT

In such cases the Synod was willing to take risks, breaking its rules to qualify ordinands it might otherwise have rejected. Pastor Neumann's long acquaintance with Scheibel and a favorable report concerning his piety and general qualifications, made such flexibility easier. In another case the Synod moved into uncharted territory. After examination it admitted the Rev. Mr. Christie (a Baptist) to serve Trinity Church, Greenport, a "colored" congregation which had grown up beside St. Peters Lutheran Church, a German congregation in that Long Island village. Though Trinity was "anxious to procure the services of one of their own color," the president of Synod reported, they were willing to accept Mr. Christie.[47] This historic move was not accomplished without racial overtones. The Synod's Committee on Applications reported negatively to the Synod on the Greenport application:

> [W]e would respectfully submit, that whilst we believe that all men are created free and equal, and that our brethren of African descent are entitled to our prayers and our assistance in their efforts to extend the Redeemer's kingdom, yet we cannot see our way clear under existing circumstances to admit the said congregation as an integral part of Synod, because of the ecclesiastical difficulties that would in all probability follow . . .[48]

But the report was overturned by a substitute motion on the synod floor, and Trinity was welcomed into membership despite "ecclesiastical difficulties."

German St. Peters had been established as a German (Steimle) Synod mission to a farming community and fishing village in the vicinity of Greenport. Perhaps the German-speaking residents were farmers, and the African-Americans (as elsewhere in the New York area) a community which made at least a part of its living by fishing. An African-American Sunday School had existed in the area since 1855 when the church itself was known as Second Presbyterian Church (before its affiliation with the New York and New Jersey Synod). With the arrival of Pastor L. H. Schneider, who was ordained into the ministry in 1879 and sent by the Synod to Greenport probably to serve St. Peters, both Lutheran congregations benefited.[49] Trinity was reported to be a tiny congregation of eight (8) active members, with a Sunday school of eighteen (18) "scholars." The school's larger population suggests it may well have been the African-American Sunday school in existence since 1855. Trinity's parochial report to the Synod for 1881 indicated most of the scholars were temporarily away, suggesting (perhaps) a community whose younger adults were periodically at sea. Local newspaper reports, not so concerned with parochial report niceties, reported that the congregation numbered 150 "souls."

Schneider left in the spring of 1880 because of the "unfavorable influence of the climate" on his health, moving to Hartford, Connecticut to organize The Church of the Reformation for German immigrants there. With his departure Trinity Lutheran Church was listed on the Synod's rolls in 1880 and 1881 with the notation "supplied," yet its pulpit remained vacant. Its reason for remaining affiliated was simple: in the "Remarks Accompanying Parochial Reports" Trinity noted that "The congregation connects itself with Synod this year, to have some authority to which to turn in the many dangers which surround a congregation which is standing isolated, and, at that, is vacant." Its story, as told to the synod's delegates, is worth reading. "The Lord has blessed us in some measure since we joined the New York and New Jersey Synod" with periodic pulpit supply. "When there is preaching we have a fair congregation; our little church will seat about one hundred and forty comfortably, and we can get in one hundred and fifty. Yet "Our number of members has not increased on account of not having a pastor." With some preaching and a Sunday School in session each week that part of the church was growing. Besides the long-distance moral support of Schneider, the Spruce Run Sunday School had "sent to our school from seventy-five to eighty library books and papers," while St. Johns Lutheran Church on Christopher Street "has donated to the Trinity church, Greenport, the sum of $51.25, which was appropriated on the organ in our church." Thanking the Synod for its help, the report continued "We hope we shall have a man of God this year." [50]

Mr. Christie, the Baptist, may have served as Synod supply at Trinity, but he was never ordained. In 1882 the Rev. A. J. Tolbart, a recently resigned Deacon in the Methodist Church, was called to preach, but never sought ordination. Another supply pastor, Floyd Mills, was listed in the 1883 parochial report, but in 1884 Trinity's pulpit was again vacant, and by 1885 neither Trinity nor St. Peters (which remained vacant throughout its brief affiliation) was affiliated with the Synod of New York and New Jersey. Trinity disappeared from the rolls of the Lutheran Church. Its Lutheran phase did not outlast the support of its former pastor and benefactor, Pastor Schneider.[51] The last year in which their membership was reported, Trinity had grown to thirty-eight (38) members and St. Peters to seventy-two (72). Neither was in a position to be supported by the Synod. Both were too small to sustain a pastor, though together they might have done so, had each not had its decided ethnic preferences.

THE LIMITS OF INCLUSIVENESS

A part of the failure can be attributed to racial prejudice of a kind that appeared in the Applications Committee, a religious form of Jim Crow-ism then creating two separate and unequal societies in the South and encouraging segregation in the North. But this situation, like the story of African-American religion itself, is too complicated to simply dismiss as a case of racial prejudice.

African Americans had been associated with the Lutheran Church in New York since colonial times when New York Lutherans seemed less segregation-minded, though hardly less racist than their nineteenth-century counterparts. Dutch slavery introduced African-Americans to New Amsterdam and New York Lutheranism as it did somewhat later in its two Caribbean colonies of Surinam and Guyana. The New York Church included at least one black family in the seventeenth century. The Pieter Christiaan family, beginning with Christiaan himself, a slave and member of the Loonenberg (Athens) congregation, who was married twice by its pastors, were members of the Athens congregation for three generations at least beginning in 1716. His second wife was a Palatine German and his children by this marriage were designated "mulatto" in the record. Zion Lutheran, Oldwick, New Jersey, was established in 1714 in the home of Aree van Guinee, a freedman from Surinam (Dutch Guiana) whose prosperity probably also provided the land on which the church was built. There is no reason to believe these were isolated instances of African-American membership. Taken together, however, these two cases were part of a pattern in colonial America, North and South, in which Lutherans for the most part served those black Christians who came to them seeking services, but did not attempt any systematic mission to African-Americans. After the American Revolution and the nation's new emphasis on freedom, slavery hardened further into a repressive institution in the antebellum South; in the North separation of the races developed based on white hostility and black alienation, leading to the development of independent African-American churches and (eventually) denominations.[52]

An isolated but important exception was the case of St. Johns Lutheran Church in Charleston, South Carolina, served by the New York Lutheran pastor, John Bachman. From 1816 until the Civil War St. Johns developed a mission to South Carolina blacks, slave and free, which eventually created a separate African-American congregation within St. Johns that constituted 35 percent of its total membership by 1860. Among its parallel white and black organizations, St. Johns's black mission society helped send two African-Americans north—Jehu Jones and Daniel Payne—for mission work among African-Americans. Jones arrived in 1833 to be ordained by a group of New York Ministerium clergy who remained after an adjourned meeting of the Ministerium for the purpose of developing a mission in Africa.

Bachman and Ministerium leader P. A. Strobel arranged for Payne to come north in 1835 to receive an education at Gettysburg and though Payne had no intention of receiving Lutheran ordination, he was licensed by the Franckean Synod in 1837 and ordained two years later to serve a "colored" Lutheran mission in Troy. (In the 1880s the Franckean Synod also ordained two Liberian natives, David Davidson, and Joseph Steward, who were educated at the Muhlenberg Mission, to serve as General Synod missionaries in Liberia.)[53]

But Payne soon sought to be dismissed to the African Methodist Episcopal Church going on to become a distinguished AME Bishop and eventually the president of Wilberforce University in Ohio. Jones, meanwhile, moved to Philadelphia in 1834 and founded St. Pauls Colored Lutheran Church which he served until its demise in 1849. He returned to New York and the Ministerium seeking support to establish a black Lutheran congregation in New York City, but his free-lance attitudes and questionable financial dealings led to rejection by the New York synod. What the Ministerium's leadership could not see, at this point, was the important new mission potential which Jones's unorthodox ways would actualize. The process of forming separate black churches had begun with the Methodists in Philadelphia, but spread to New York in the antebellum North. More than any other American institution, the independent African-American church was the one place where blacks, expressing their sense of freedom, were in control of their own lives and could develop educational and political skills, a place (in other words) for self-expression, recognition and leadership. Payne and Jones expressed this outlook, associated as they were with St. Johns Lutheran Church in Charleston and its indigenous black Christian community. The experience of Trinity Lutheran Church, Greenport, and its relationship to the New York and New Jersey Synod must be seen in this changing context.[54]

At St. Johns, as at Trinity, Greenport, it was as much ethnic need (as racial prejudice) which shaped the histories of these two congregations. While many black and white Americans, including Lutherans, worshipped together in individual congregations up to the Civil War, integrated worship was not especially important to either group. The Civil War accelerated a movement towards African-American independence as formerly integrated congregations and denominations split into separate African-American and white organizations. Where there were significant numbers of congregations within a single denomination as (for example) among Baptists and Methodists, these formed congregational networks eventually leading to separate African-American Baptist and Methodist denominations. The African Methodist Episcopal Church which Payne served grew during his lifetime from 75,000 members in 1856 to 200,000 twenty years later. Included among the new African-American denominational bodies was the Alpha Synod of the Evangelical Lutheran Church of Freedman in America, formed in 1878 by African-American ordinands of the North Carolina Synod. By then black Baptists and Methodists had long practiced an indigenization of the Gospel within African-American culture. Lutherans, meanwhile, were just beginning to develop such indigenous institutions. In desperation, isolated and rejected by white Lutherans after the Civil War, the clergy of the Alpha Synod invited the Synodical Conference to assist in a new mission of indigenization to southern blacks.[55]

Isolated Northern congregations like Trinity, Greenport, on the other hand, had to make do with whatever denominational affiliation was available and so their Lutheranism (but not their Christianity) withered on the vine. What was true of German-Americans was true as well of African-Americans: the church formed the center of an identity-giving, ethnoreligious community. The existence of African-American congregations, with African-American leadership, was seen by them as essential to their freedom, independence and equality with whites. Little wonder Trinity preferred a pastor "of their own color" to a white ex-Baptist preacher. As for maintaining an African-American congregation, an organized religious life in the African-American community was a chief means of structuring its social life and an important way of providing social control and granting social status (at Trinity "our Superintendent, is a lady"). African-American congregations were also a primary agency of empowerment through education for work, freedom and dignity, a reason that the Sunday school was originally larger in size than the congregation. It was with a justifiable pride of status and achievement that Mrs. Nichols identified the school's superintendent as a "lady," and its secretary and librarian as "gentlemen."[56]

Given the importance of ethnicity the outcome was no surprise. An 1882 history of the area listed a "colored" Methodist society in Greenport, suggesting that Trinity now belonged to an African-American Methodist denomination under the guidance of the black Methodist deacon, the Rev. Tolbart. For similar reasons St. Peters had joined the German-speaking New York Ministerium in 1891. The complex but essentially positive relationship between ethnicity and religion first noted in the Steimle Synod can also be seen at work in both Trinity and St. Peters. Long-term affiliation in an integrated denomination was not a current reality for African-Americans (nor ethnic German-Americans). Even as Trinity was leaving its jurisdiction the New York and New Jersey Synod was urging support for an African-American Lutheran congregation, Our Redeemer in Washington, D. C. a key to resurgent black Lutheranism in the South.[57]

A CRISIS IN BENEVOLENCE

There was a limit to how many missions the Synod could support. Despite its promising start and large contributions on behalf of home missions in the early 1870s, by the end of the decade congregational support for mission work had slipped badly. Home mission support (for congregations) had dropped to $0.06 per capita; home extension contributions (to build new church buildings) to $0.03. President George Neff reported to Synod in 1880 that its support for foreign and home missions and church extension exhibited "a great falling off" in the past four years. His remarks were in response to an urgent appeal by the mission boards of the General Synod, which was then suffering a significant shortfall in mission support. Neff's personal observation on the matter was that "the churches will fail in this duty until the membership is educated and trained up to the standard of scriptural teaching; that giving is an important and indispensable feature of the Christian character, and that whosoever is wanting in this, comes as far short in the growth of the Christian life." A new effort at systematic benevolence—the "Envelope plan"—was introduced in 1881 whereby each individual or family voluntarily pledges a stated sum per week, "according as the Lord hath prospered, which amount is brought to the Lord's house as a thanksgiving and part of holy worship." The system produced some increased giving for home missions and local church extension—from $0.08 and $0.06 respectively per communicant member in 1880; to $0.12 and $0.11 in 1885. Despite this increase appropriations still fell short of contributions in the Synod. By 1890 per capita support was slipping once again—down to $0.11 and $0.10. Perhaps this was due to a drop off in membership, from 8,120 in 1886 to 7,684 in 1890. At the same time, however, the money congregations spent on themselves increased from $60,728 to $110,068 while congregational indebtedness jumped over $100,000 from $64,300 to $ 168,700 by 1890.[58]

THE PANIC OF 1873

What was happening? Why the preoccupation with funding at home? A new cycle of spending had begun on church buildings—new building, or renovation and expansion of old facilities—that had been impossible earlier because of a depression. As noted in Chapter 6 regarding finances in the New York Ministerium, the Panic of 1873 (a financial depression of five to seven years duration) had profoundly affected Lutheran churches in the area. Year after year pastors reported congregations struggling with crushing financial commitments from a previous round of spending for church development and expansion in the prosperous times after the Civil War.

The impact was felt by 1875 in most congregations of the Synod of New York and New Jersey. The church's "State of Religion" report for 1875 was thus summarized:

> The chief source of discouragement in many of our congregations, is the depressed condition of the financial and industrial interests of the country, which bears with great severity upon the laboring

> classes, especially in our cities, and affects more or less injuriously the spiritual and temporal progress of nearly all our churches.[59]

Pastor A. C. Wedekind described the malaise in his parochial report for 1878. "The causes of depression in business still exist as actively to-day as they have done the last five years, and I cannot say that our trials have brought us perceptibly nearer to God." The temptation in New York City is to "set one's affections on things below and not on things above. Worldly-mindedness is the sin that so easily besets our citizens." Pastor J. P. Kretching simply reported that "'Hard times! hard times!" is the cry daily, especially when the cause of missions and benevolence are presented. "But it is really so; we cannot shut our eyes to the stern fact." "The times *are* hard, and it is difficult to find fault with a man on account of the small sum he contributes for benevolence, when he scarcely earns a dollar a day, and has a wife and six, seven or more children depending upon him for daily bread. Such is really the case with a large number of my people." If Pastor Kretching's numbers are correct, then his congregation was composed of many unskilled day laborers, or semiskilled workers among whom unemployment stood at 12 percent or more. Businessmen and workingmen suffered a common fate. Pastor William Hull offered a somber post-mortem on his congregation: "The panic ruined nearly all the business men connected with the congregation, but now a number of our young men are becoming established in business with good prospects of success."[60]

This ray of hope appeared in 1881. By then hard times were passing. Congregational spending at home increased during the 1880s, (especially after 1885 as already noted) during a time of renewed hope and growing prosperity in industrial America. The early 1880s saw the retirement of the 1870s indebtedness which crippled the church's influence and paralyzed its mission efforts; the late 1880s saw a new round of indebtedness as prosperity tempted church councils to improve their aging physical facilities. With increased "material prosperity" it was reported to synod, churches were displaying "much enterprise . . . in the way of acquiring, enlarging, and caring for church property. In one instance there has been erected a large and attractive chapel. . . . In other instances there had been remodeling; in other repairing and beautifying the church or parsonage or both; and in others still, there has been the liquidation of interest-bearing indebtedness, which lifted heavy burdens from the hearts of devoted men and women."[61]

Severe as the panic was, it was part of an economic cycle with largely positive results. The 1880s, like the 1870s, were part of an epoch when per capita growth and personal income increased at a very significant 1.5 percent a year—15 percent in a decade, 100 percent in a half-century—and a doubling standard of living in less than a lifetime. It was the kind of financial improvement two generations in one family would notice as part of their improved standard of living: better housing (through a move uptown or to Brooklyn or Queens, or New Jersey), better food and health, increased consumer goods, more education and professional training, expanding business opportunities, conspicuous consumption among the very wealthy in this Gilded Age. There were material benefits for all, despite a cyclical economy which produced its moments of hope and despair. It also produced greater concern with material matters—a materialistic preoccupation according to church leaders. Perhaps this was the price to be paid in an age when life and values in America were shaped more and more by understanding economic prosperity (growth), and learning how to survive panicky economic downturns. Pastor Wedekind's 1878 assessment—a growing preoccupation with materialistic matters—was simply the beginning of a clerical lament which came to dominate synod reports on the state of religion throughout the 1880s.

SPIRITUAL CRISIS

President Neff alerted the Synod of New York and New Jersey to a form of the problem in his 1881 report. While the church in "this advanced age" should have the means "for bringing the people within the fold of the church, and in educating and developing to a higher degree that Christ-like character and life so essential to the true prosperity and working power of the church" pastors are perplexed and depressed that "the means of grace employed have not resulted in a greater development."[62]

The customary "Report of the Committee on the President's Report" replied with a devastating analysis of this "perplexing problem." The family had ceased to be "a nursery of the Church." Worldliness presides over it and parental influence has lost its force as evidenced by the decay of "family religion." Parents have forgotten covenantal responsibilities entered into at the Baptism of their children "*to teach them to observe all things whatsoever I have commanded you.*" And they fail to cooperate with pastors who would gather the young into catechetical classes. For this the Christian pulpit is to blame because of its "elevation of views and notions into primary positions which the gospel makes altogether secondary." Where Christ, and him crucified should be the central content of preaching, the new gospel offers no Christ and no sacrifice." "*Follow me*" now means enchanting bowers, feasts of joy, card-tables, and play-houses, dancing-saloons and masquerades, as showing "the cheerful side of religion," where to follow Jesus truly "means the giving up of the love of sin, the renouncing the vanities of the world, and the laying one's self upon God's altar as a living *sacrifice*, holy and acceptable to God."[63]

Throughout the 1880s, as the "State of Religion of 1883" indicated, the churches showed "progress in the financial and temporal condition" but a "similar degree of progress . . . is hardly manifest in the spirituality of our churches." Pastors were discouraged. Though attendance at worship, Sunday-school and the Lord's Table were good, "yet they have to lament a want of deep vital interest in spiritual things on the part of many." The 1886 Report, meanwhile, indicated that from all quarters "there comes the lamentation of the fearful increase of worldliness and a corresponding decrease of spiritual mindedness." Its diagnosis was as devastating as the diatribe on indifference in 1881. By now Christian life seemed to run close to the border between Christianity and the world where the disciples of Jesus can easily step over "into downright worldliness and an absolute forgetfulness of the purity of the Christian calling, or its essential separateness from the world." Moreover, "hands are quick and feet are swift in such work that has just religion enough in it, so as not to make it positively irreligious: while hands are sluggish and feet are leaden in the work and way of *entire consecration to Christ.*"[64]

The language and metaphors are revealing. The separation of Christ and culture, for the average Christian, had created a borderline situation with human existence on the boundary, a careful walking on the margins of Christian faith and life so as to avoid the crisis of agnosticism and irreligion. But there ignorance and misunderstanding "abound." God's order of salvation "is fearfully misunderstood," while many in the congregations "rest in means as an end": "They go to church, and to holy communion; they read the Bible and say their prayers, and are content therewith, as having met the full requirements of God their Saviour!"

> Meanwhile their desires remain as selfish, their conduct as unchanged, their conformity to the world as unbroken, their love of pleasure as intense, their worship of mammon as hearty, and their indifference to spirituality as open and undisguised, as can be found in the ranks of any class of worldlings.[65]

Further, there seems to be an intention to obliterate the boundary itself, and with it the boundary situation—"an effort to wipe out, as nearly as possible, the line that separates the Christian from the worldling." And hence "believers" have become "workers," accepting Christ "as their only and all-sufficient Saviour" is replaced by glib-tongued religion talk," and sacrifice has been replaced by the ten dollar bill prominently placed in the plate on collection day. "SELF, the real antichrist in the world, remains on the throne, his lordly sceptre undisturbed." For this and for the "spirit of regress" to be found in the churches, the spirit of the times was blamed. "Everywhere society has been convulsed from top to bottom as by a moral earthquake. The fearful conflict between labor and capital, by no means ended, has rolled like a mighty avalanche over the land." The one ray of light was that the Lutheran Church "has maintained her conservative character, taking sides with neither party in this period of industiral conflict, but fearlessly teaching their respective duties to both."[66]

THE END OF PIETISM

Clearly the English-speaking portion of the Lutheran Church was undergoing a fundamental spiritual crisis. Old-fashioned piety was being replaced by modern behavior, which embraced material concerns and refused to avoid life's more innocent pleasures. As a part of American Protestantism, English-speaking Lutherans were going through what historian Arthur M. Schlesinger identified as a "critical period" between 1875 and 1900. American churches were confronted by two fundamental challenges, one to their social systems with pressing problems of an urban industrial society, and the other to theology and doctrine by forms of modern thought, especially Darwinism, the higher biblical criticism, and the social gospel. In the process of adjusting, and out of a spirit of optimism, American Protestants came dangerously close to over-identification with industrial America, its values and its destiny, embracing a form of popular theology which could not distinguish adequately between Americanism and loyalty to the kingdom of God.[67] Lutherans were not as quickly influenced by these intellectual trends, as they were by the social changes.

The danger was that participation in economic growth, material prosperity, industrial might, and urbanization offered an enticing alternative to the traditional Christian faith and piety which for Lutherans had separated Christ from culture. Some Christians preferred to walk the border between Christ and culture to benefit from both. The growth of a marginal and minimalist Christianity was troubling as was the increased absence of many Lutheran church members from worship and their infrequent use of the sacraments. One sign was the decline of the family as a religious entity. Parents no longer active in the church made every effort to keep their children safely this side of the comfortable boundary between Christ and culture by having them baptized. So persistent was this trend toward religious minimalism that a joint faculty committee from Hartwick and Gettysburg Seminaries was convoked to determine just where the church should draw its own boundaries. Who was the proper subject of infant Baptism? Could children of non-professors or non-church members be baptized? The answer was that where parents do not "bring and keep" their children under the authority and education of the Church, and in the nurture and admonition of the Lord," Baptism should not be administered. Scripture and the "law of duty and responsibility" in the rite of Baptism itself dictate this position. To go beyond it is to treat the sacrament like an "*opus operatum*," an entirely objective work without regard for the intent of parents or sponsors.[68]

The Synod's concern for the Christian family was no isolated matter, but part of a complex of issues involving the Christian home in Victorian America. Domestic religion—"the divinized home" one historian has called it—was an important focus of American Christianity, with its emphasis on family worship, Bible reading, hymn singing, parlor altars, and the prominently displayed family Bible. At its center was the woman as wife and mother whose power and influence were considered essential to Christian faith and life. Women had become a vital influence in the church since the Civil War through mission societies and the Temperance movement. Their influence can be seen, as well, in the increased importance of infant (early) Baptism for their children and an emphasis on the more feminine aspects of Christian doctrine, an influence which has been described (somewhat exaggerated in the case of Lutheranism) as leading to "the feminization of American religion."[69]

Significantly, this increasing influence was part of a sharp gender division of labor in the American denomination, the woman being assigned to the home, the man to the public market place (outside of the home) to congregational governance, and to the public, ordained ministry in the church where his gender characteristics (competitive aggressiveness) prevailed. So sharp and absolute was the distinction that while men prevailed in the public sphere, women were considered supreme in the home. Writing in the 1874 issue of the *Lutheran Quarterly Review*, R. A. Fink observed that as mothers and heads of families, the woman's role in religious matters was comparable to that of the pastor. If her "delicacy of frame" unfits her for pastoral work, "she is wisely and kindly prepared for the duties of this relation, by a sympathy and tenderness of heart, which are characteristic of her sex." Fink made much of female tenderness, affection, and the power of feminine love. So equipped, the woman would provide religious instruction and prepare the child "for the service of God, for usefulness in the Church in this life, and for the joys and glories of heaven in the life to come." "It is not intended by the preceding remarks that the husband and the father has nothing to do in the education of children" Fink continued. "He has his own share of responsibility and his own duties to perform. It is assumed, however, that the mother's influence is greater than that of the father. The mother's influence is that of kindness and affection more than of authority, the father's is that of authority, more than of kindness."[70] The disturbing trend which the New York and New Jersey Synod found itself facing by the 1880s was precisely the failure of the American family to live up to this much-vaunted ideal of maternal love and paternal authority in the changing urban scene.

THE 1880S, A TIME OF TRANSITION

Given the enormity of the spiritual crisis which gripped the downstate, English-speaking portion of the New York area Lutheran church during the 1880s it is reasonable to ask after its outcome, to find out if and how it was resolved. For resolved it was after a fashion! As of 1889 the Synod of New York and New Jersey stopped reporting on the "State of Religion" in its congregations, having suspended publication, five years before, of the parochial reports on which the reported state of religion was based. Thereafter, it simply remained an unacknowledged problem in the Lutheran church!

A contemporary Lutheran historian, Pastor George U. Wenner, named Synod historian in 1871 by the New York Synod, made similar observations about the changing Lutheran church. Wenner worked patiently at the task for years, collecting the histories of individual congregations, devoting himself to a life of ministry in New York City during which he made the acquaintance of almost every Lutheran pastor in the metropolitan region. He knew the Lutheran church and its history better than anyone else in the metropolitan area. Out of this experience he wrote a book on the changing church in 1918—*The Lutherans of New York. 1648-1918*—which detailed its "Problems." In noting three problems that were especially troubling—membership, religious education, and lapsed Lutherans—Wenner pointed once again to the same perplexing syndrome first noted in the Synod of New York and New Jersey by the early 1880s.[71] It was a fundamental shortcoming of area Lutheranism which would not go away.

For such was the fundamental transformation being worked upon church and society by the forces of industrialization in the late nineteenth century. One phase in the life of the church was ending, another beginning. While the church might cease reporting on the state of religion within, it could not escape the powers of transformation from without. The revivalistic faith which converted church members from one lifestyle to another, by which they crossed the boundary from culture to Christ, found itself in a perilous boundary situation too close for comfort to the dividing line between traditional Christian morality and the ways of economic growth and prosperity. What is more, it was unable to define the boundary for lack of adequate doctrine.

Other boundaries needed redefining in this time of rapid change. The external boundaries between synods were geographically confusing and organizationally counterproductive. Because synodical jurisdictions overlapped geographic subregions, in 1887 the Hartwick Synod proposed forming new synods out of itself, the Franckean Synod, and the Synod of New York and New Jersey. An 1888 plan would have drawn the line for a southern synod at the Dutchess and Ulster county lines, creating a body incorporating downstate New York, New Jersey, and New England. A middle synod, beginning with Greene and Columbia counties along the Hudson and concluding along the Mohawk with Saratoga and Schoharie Counties, would center on Albany. The third would incorporate all remaining congregations in upstate

New York and Canada, an area roughly defined by Pennsylvania on the south, Lake Ontario on the north, and Lake Erie to the west. After considerable debate the motion was tabled by the Synod of New York and New Jersey. In 1889 a second and presumably more acceptable proposal from Hartwick was debated, this time a plan to create a single synod from a merger of the three to be divided into as many conferences "as would be found convenient and desirable." This too was tabled after considerable discussion, held over until the 1890 synod, and discussed again, when debate was cut off without decision "yea" or "nay."[72]

CONCLUSION: DRIFT WITHOUT MASTERY

By 1890, then, the New York and New Jersey Synod was in the midst of accelerating change. Such drift, without mastery, in an ever more rapidly changing world would soon require significant responses. For one thing, it could not much longer ignore a problem of merger and/or total reorganization which had been set aside at the time of its formation. Mission efforts on a coordinated scale with sufficient funding for success could no longer be effectively mounted by synods the size of New York's three General Synod bodies. For another, time was running out on the mildly confessional revivalism which had once been so essential an element in congregational and synodical growth and which continued until the 1880s to be important in the slow-growth, English-speaking congregations of Synod. Rural revivalism was no match for the material circumstances and spiritual condition of the urban dweller. The Synod could not long endure without being shored up by more adequate doctrinal underpinnings. The problem was most apparent in the areas of Baptism and church membership both of which needed theological clarification. Yet, drift it would, for another decade. While the Synod of New York and New Jersey could still afford to cut off debate on the merger question in 1890, the upstate synods could not. A series of proposals for union had emerged periodically from the Hartwick and Franckean Synods for three decades now, for they were in more straitened circumstances than their General Synod counterpart in downstate New York. It is to these two bodies that we now turn, in continuing to explore the history of General Synod bodies in the greater New York area after the Civil War.

NOTES

1 General Synod, *Minutes* (1871), 66; (1868), 63.

2 Ibid.

3 See Heinrich Schmid, *The Doctrinal Theology of the Evangelical Lutheran Church,* ed. Charles A. and Henry E. Jacobs Hay (Philadelphia: Lutheran

Publication Society, 1889). Brown quoted in A. Roger Gobbel, *On the Glorious Hill. A Short History in word and picture of the Lutheran Theological Seminary at Gettysburg* (Lancaster, Pennsylvania: Pridemark Press, 1976), 31.

4 General Synod, *Minutes* (1868), 63; (1869), 39-47.

5 Ibid., 11, 17, 15, 41.

6 Ibid. (1868), 64; (1869), 28; (1871), 82; (1873), 79; (1877), 30-31, 37-9; (1879), 98-9; (1878), 39; (1877), 39: (1881), 60-61, 88. Virginia Lieson Brereton, and Christa Ressmeyer Klein, "American Women in Ministry. A History of Protestant Beginning Points," *Women in American Religion*, ed. Janet Wilson James (Philadelphia: University of Pennsylvania Press, 1980) 174-175.

7 General Synod, *Minutes* (1869), 54, 87.

8 Ibid. (1868), 97-107, 117, 118; (1871), 104-111, 105-6.

9 Ibid. (1871) 107-8; 105. Franckean Synod, *Journal* (1884), 15.

10 General Synod, *Minutes* (1873), 48; (1875), 38.

11 Ibid.

12 New Jersey Synod, *Minutes* (1861), 2; (1867), 6-7.

13 Ibid. (1867), 14.

14 New York Ministerium, *Minutes* (1831), 19; (1840), 7; (1850), 9; New Jersey Synod, *Minutes* (1861), 14.

15 Ibid., 14, 17, 7.

16 Ibid. (1864), 18.

17 Ibid. (1866), 5.

18 See beginning note of "Select Bibliography" for listing of statistical sources.

19 Ibid. (1865), 12-15; (1864), 12-13; (1862), 4-5, 10-12; (1863), 10.

20 Ibid. (1866), 19-20. *Autogenous* (self-generated) growth occurs from the recruitment of the children of members, and is related to congregational demographics. *Allogenous* (outside) growth, on the other hand, involves the recruitment of outsider's and their children.

21 Ibid. (1865), 6; (1867), 7, 19.

22 Ibid. (1868), 8-10.

23 Ibid.

24 New York Synod, *Minutes* (1869), 19-20; (1870), 5-8.

25 New York Synod, *Historical Statement of the Evangelical Lutheran Synod of New York* (New York, 1867), 9; New York Synod, *Minutes* (1867), 4-5.

26 New York Synod, *Historical Statement,* 15.

27 Ibid.

28 New York Synod, Minutes (1867), 20-21.

29 Ibid. (1868), 24; (1869), 16; (1870), 11; (1871), 13.

30 Ibid. (1871), 18-20. Synod of New York and New Jersey, *Minutes* (1872), 33.

31 Ibid., 33-4.

32 New York Synod, *Minutes* (1868), 30.

33 Ibid., (1870), 17, 22, 9.

34 Synod of New York and New Jersey, *Minutes* (1872), 8. New Jersey Synod, *Minutes* (1871), 5 ff; (1867), 24.

35 Ibid., (1870), 8; (1871), 7-8, 18, 20; Synod of New York and New Jersey, *Minutes* (1872), 14.

36 Synod of New York and New Jersey, Minutes (1872), 16-33, 27, 28, 33.
37 See Ibid., 26a; (1890), 6-7, 44ff.
38 See Chapter 10, Table 10:3, "Baptism as a percentage of Communicant Membership in the Hartwick, Franckean, and the New York/New Jersey Synods, and the NY Ministerium."
39 Ibid. (1877), 25.
40 Ibid. (1878), 9.
41 Congregational Database. Synod of New York and New Jersey, *Minutes* (1879), 23; (1885), 14; (1886), 15.
42 Congregational Database. Synod of New York and New Jersey, *Minutes* (1879), 6.
43 Ibid. (1890), 44 ff; (1886), 15.
44 Ibid. (1890), 50.
45 Ibid. (1874), 74; (1880), 33.
46 Ibid. (1874); (1875), 19, 29; (1877), 7.
47 Ibid. (1881), 12, 42.
48 See Harry J. Kreider, "Negro Lutheran Work in New York," *Lutheran Church Quarterly* 20 (1947): 267. Kreider considers that the rejection "smacked of plain race prejudice."
49 Arthur C. Olsen, *Upon This Rock. St. Peters Evangelical Lutheran Church of Greenport, Long Island, N. Y.* (Greenport, L. I., N. Y.: 1959), 1-6; *History of Suffolk County, New York* (New York: 1882), 26; see also Carleton Mabee, *Black Education in New York State: From Colonial to Modern Times* (Syracuse: Syracuse University Press, 1979), 287-291. "St. Peter's," Greenport, Congregational Database. Synod of New York and New Jersey, *Minutes* (1879), 4, 27.
50 Ibid. (1880), 9, 44a; (1881), 44a.; (1881), 44; (1881), 12, 42.
51 Synod of New York and New Jersey, *Minutes* (1882), 10, 44a; (1883), 9, 48a; (1884) 56a.
52 *The Albany Protocol. Wilhelm Christoph Berkenmeyer's Chronicle of Lutheran Affairs in New York Colony, 1731-1750*, John P. Dern, ed., translated by Simon Hart and Sibrandina Geertruid Hart-Runeman; (Ann Arbor, Michigan: 1971), 545. Harry J. Kreider, "Negro Lutheran Work in New York," *LCQ* 20 (1947): 261; 263-5. Norman C. Wittwer, Jr., *The Faithful and the Bold. The Story of the First Service of the Zion Evangelical Lutheran Church Oldwick, New Jersey* (Redwood City, CA: Monocacy Book Company, 1984), 7-9. Jeff G. Johnson, *Black Christians. The Untold Lutheran Story* (St. Louis: Concordia Publishing House, 1991), 28-35, 67-104, 129.
53 Jeff G. Johnson, *Black Christians*, 113-125. Harry J. Kreider, "Negro Lutheran Work in New York," *LCQ* 20 (1947): 263-5.
54 Johnson, *Black Christians*, 123, 130-37; Kreider, "Negro Lutheran Work in New York," 261-4. John Hope Franklin, *From Slavery to Freedom. A History of Negro Americans*, 5th ed. (New York: Alfred A. Knopf, 1980), 110-113, 413-414. See also Winthrop K. Jordan, *White Over Black. American Attitudes Toward the Negro, 1550-1812* (Chapel Hill: University of North Carolina Press, 1968), 417 ff.
55 Michael L. Cobbler, "Useful Lives, Black Lutherans in Ministry Past and Present," *LCA Partners* (April/May 1984), 11. W. Kent Gilbert, *Commitment to Unity* (Philadelphia: Fortress Press, 1988), 18-19. See H.

Richard Niebuhr, *Social Sources of Denominationalism* (New York: World Publishing, 1963), especially Ch IX, "Denominationalism and the Color Line," 236 ff. W. Kent Gilbert, *Commitment to Unity* (Philadelphia: Fortress Press, 1988), 18-19. For a different view on the racial dynamics of denominationalism see Timothy L. Smith, "Religious Denominations as Ethnic Communities: A Regional Case Study," in *Denominationalism*, Russell E. Richey, ed. (Nashville: Abingdon Press, 1977), 183 ff. on the formation of the Alpha Synod see Johnson, *Black Christians*, 151-181, 231-238.

56 On these aspects of Black denominationalism see E. Franklin Frazier, "The Negro Church: A Nation Within a Nation," also in *Denominationalism*, 207 ff. Johnson, *Black Christians*, 158, notes the demise of the Greenport church due to lack of consistent leadership.

57 Arthur C. Olsen, *Upon This Rock*, 6; *History of Suffolk County*, 26. New York Ministerium, *Verhandlungen* (1891), 13. For a detailed treatment of the subject see Timothy L. Smith, "Religion and Ethnicity in America," *AHR* LXXXII (1978): 1155-1185; also Timothy L. Smith, "Religious Denominations as Ethnic Communities: A Regional Case Study," *Denominationalism*, Russell E. Richy, ed. (Nashville: Abingdon, 1977), 185-206. Synod of New York and New Jersey, *Minutes* (1885), 40.

58 Ibid. (1879), "Parochial Report"; (1880), 12-13; (1881), 37; (1885), 20. Parochial Tables, Ibid. (1880) & (1885); (1890), 48-9.

59 Ibid. (1875), 23.

60 Ibid. (1878), 33-35; (1881), 41-2.

61 Ibid. (1884), 47.

62 Ibid. (1881), 8.

63 Ibid. (1881), 31-3.

64 Ibid. (1883), 47; (1886), 51.

65 Ibid. (1886), 51.

66 Ibid., 51-2; (1886), 52.

67 Reginald W. Deitz, Eastern Lutheranism in American Society and American Christianity. 1870—1914. Darwinism—Biblical Criticism—The Social Gospel, University of Pennsylvania, 1958), 2-9. See Arthur M. Schlesinger, *The Rise of the City, 1878-1898* (New York: Macmillan, 1933), 68.

68 Synod of New York and New Jersey, *Minutes* (1888), 49-51.

69 Betty A. DeBerg, *Ungodly Women. Gender and the First Wave of American Fundamentalism* (Minneapolis: Augsburg Fortress Press, 1990), Ch. 3, 22, 22: n32. See especially Ann Douglas, *The Feminization of American Culture* (New York: Alfred A. Knopf, 1977), "Part One: The Sentimentalization of Status"; also Barbara Welter, "The Feminization of American Religion: 1800-1860," *Clio's Consciousness Raised. New Perspectives on the History of Women*, ed. Mary S. Hartman (New York: Octagon Books, 1976), 137-157.

70 DeBerg, *Ungodly Women*, Ch. 1, "Late Victorian Gender Roles." DeBerg provides a good introduction to an overlooked set of gender dynamics that shape American religion, including (especially) English-speaking Lutheranism from 1870 through 1930. On developing male attitudes see David G. Pugh, Sons *of Liberty. The Masculine Mind in Nineteenth-Century America, Contributions in American Studies*, ed. Robert H. Walker (Westport, Connecticut: Greenwood Press, 1983), Chapter 1, "The

Jacksonian Mystique." R. A. Fink, "Women in the Church," *LQR* IV (1874): 223-2273.

71 New York Synod, *Minutes* (1871), 26. George U. Wenner, *The Lutherans of New York. Their Story and Their Problems* (New York, 1918), esp. pp. 91-120.

72 Synod of New York and New Jersey, *Minutes* (1887), 14; (1888), 44; (1889), 14, 26-7; (1890), 25.

8

PARALLEL PROBLEMS

The Upstate Hartwick and Franckean Synods, 1860-1890

"THE DESIGN OF EVERY ECCLESIASTICAL ORGANIZATION"

The Hartwick Synod 's "State of Religion" Report for 1867 was unusually perceptive. Such reports were standard in the General Synod and its district bodies. Most assessed the bright and the not so bright spots in the life of the synod's congregations, and then summarized the results. This report differed. It included a trenchant definition of a synod. For one clear-sighted moment the Hartwick Synod willingly used that definition to assess its own life and progress. It could have been applied as well to any of the other Lutheran synods in the larger New York area. One reason, perhaps, was that the report's chief author was Phillip A. Strobel, until recently a pastor in New Jersey, secretary of the New Jersey Synod and a member of its Mission Society. Indeed Strobel's insights could have been applied with equal value to any ecclesiastical body influenced by American denominationalism and its view of the expanding church. We shall examine that definition as it helps explain developments in the Hartwick and Franckean Synods between 1860 and 1890. (See Map 8.1, The Hartwick Synod.)

THE HARTWICK SYNOD

"The design of every ecclesiastical organization," the Report began, "whether it be a Synod, a Classis, a Presbytery, or a Conference, is to promote the growth of the church, to develop its resources, and to increase its spirituality and usefulness." Statistically measurable growth, development, and progress—these were characteristic of a proper church body. Therefore "three points . . . naturally claim our attention. Its growth: 1, in numbers; 2, in liberality; and 3, in spirituality." When

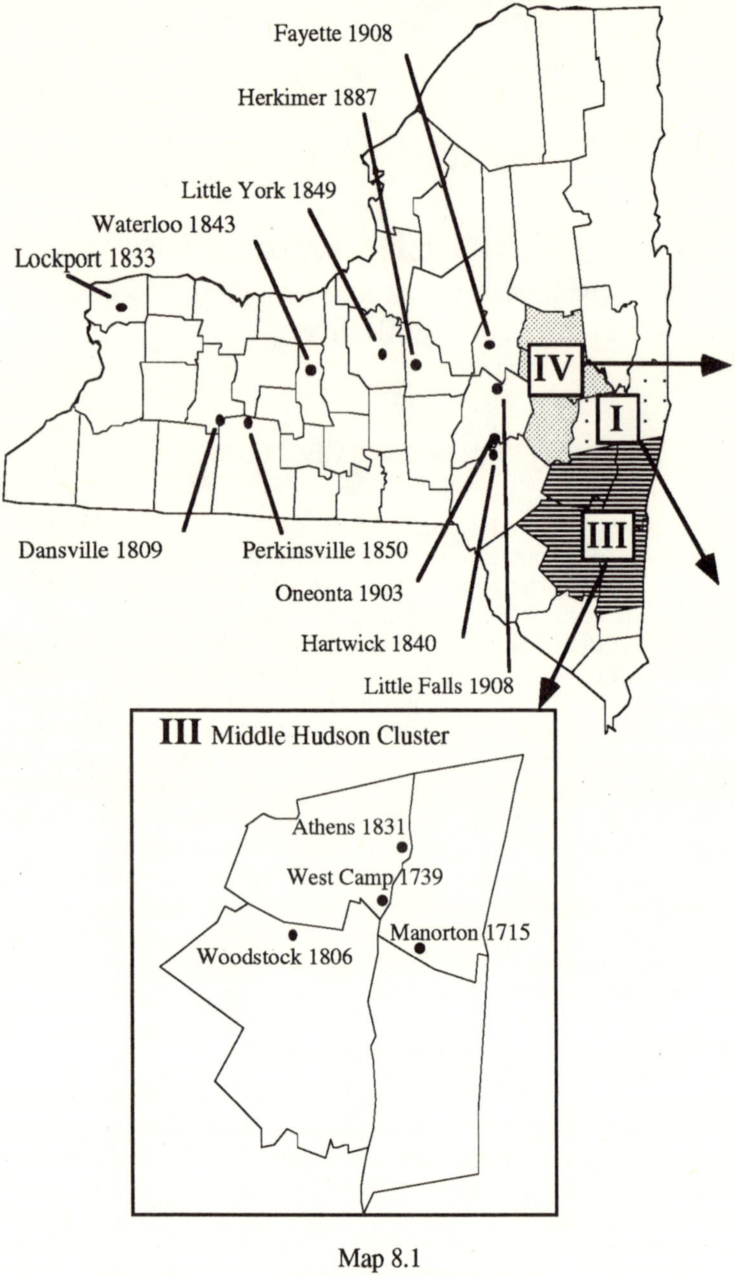

Map 8.1
The Hartwick Synod

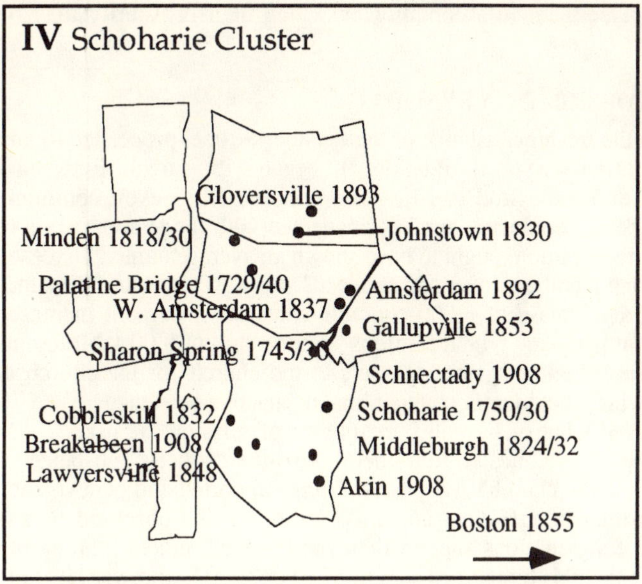

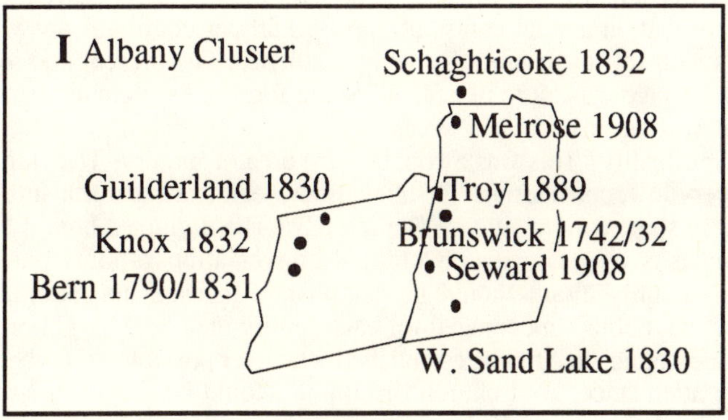

Map 8.1
The Hartwick Synod

(Strobel continued) "we meet in our capacity as a Synod, it becomes a question of deep interest, what during the past year, has been accomplished in carrying out the object of our organization?" Two questions were crucial in his view. "What has been done towards building up the true interests of the Redeemer's kingdom, and what measures is it best to adopt to promote the welfare of Zion?" "We meet" Strobel concluded "to very little purpose as a Synod, if our deliberations do not result in devising those measures which may correct any defects in our churches, and place them in a condition in which their prosperity may be secured."[1]

THE DESIGN OF A SYNOD

With the fresh perspective of the outsider Strobel proceeded to analyze the Hartwick Synod's situation. He began with growth. Between 1859 and 1865 the synod had lost one hundred fifty-seven communicant members. The thirty churches connected with the synod, if in a really healthy condition, ought to have shown an average annual increase of at least ten members "over and above all losses." This would have meant a 10-year increase of 3,000 communicants, a 75 percent increase (7.5 percent per year) with a resulting membership of 8,000. More must be accomplished "in gathering souls to the church" or the church is not "growing," but merely maintaining an "inactive existence."

And what of liberality in support of mission, he asked? Are the people being educated to a liberal devotion of their "substance" more freely to the church? Are pastors being supported and benevolence underwritten in sufficient amounts? In answer he observed that while some congregations support their pastors well, others "can hardly get above the old stereotyped sum of $500 or $600," a prewar level of support no longer reflective of the postwar "increase in the price of living." On the question of benevolence support for growth, Strobel went on to observe that an annual contribution of $0.50 per communicant would give synod sufficient funds for its benevolence. The present and inadequate average was more like $0.30. Some form of "systematic benevolence" was the answer.

Spirituality? This was Strobel's third area of inquiry. The standard was very low, considering "the alienations, jealousies and schisms" existing in some congregations. The remedy? The divinized home! More home visits by pastors with pointed conversations about "personal piety." Family altars should be established in each household, and "closet devotions" encouraged for each family member. Neighborhood prayer meetings need to be established wherever possible, with the pastor in attendance. And church discipline should be enforced—where Christian duties are shirked, censure or excommunication are in order.[2]

How perceptive was this particular report on the state of religion in the Hartwick Synod? Was it an accurate assessment of the situation? And were its suggested solutions the right ones? The answer to the first question is "very perceptive." Strobel (and his two committee members) provided an especially trenchant analysis of the Hartwick Synod and how it thought and worked. It had been a "progressive," mission-minded, growth-oriented synod from its inception and would continue so until its eventual merger some eighty years later. When its members met it was to assess the state of religion and to seek measures for its improvement. But Strobel's solutions were not necessarily the right ones to deal with the kind of synodical stagnation he was describing. Rather, it was the continuation of stagnation, and the slow and painful inquiry into the nature of a *Lutheran* synod which began to alter the measures Strobel prescribed.

COMPARISON WITH REALITY

As Graph 8.1 indicates, the 1867 report was accurate enough. The synod was in a state of virtual decline so far as congregational growth and communicant membership were concerned.

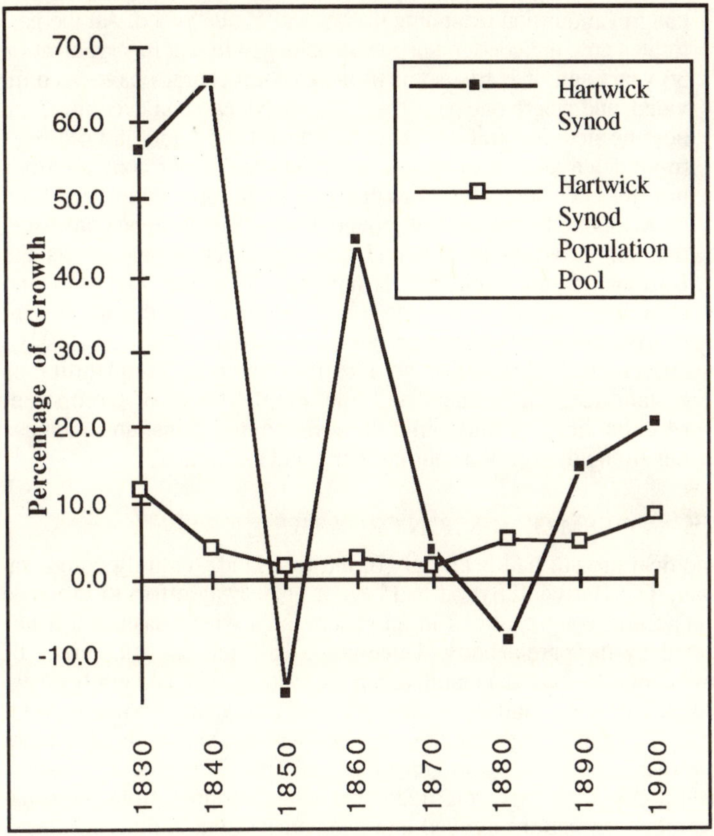

Graph 8.1 Hartwick Synod Growth

After a decade of growth during the 1850's greater than the surrounding population, Hartwick Synod growth began to decline in the middle 1860s, a trend which lasted until 1880 if not longer. Strobel's committee, then, was viewing an unfortunate trend in the making!

There were two ways in which the synod could develop the kind of numerical growth which it valued—through increased congregational growth (which at the time was marginal), and by increasing the number of congregations in the synod through new mission fields. It was the latter problem which was addressed by the synod's mission committee in an alarming report issued for 1866.

> It should be a question for very serious consideration whether as a Synod, we intend to abandon the work of Home Missions and church extension. It is a painful fact, that in the last fifteen years we have done comparatively nothing in the way of organizing new congregations and extending the borders of our Synod. All the pastorates now included in our Synod belonged to it at its organization 36 years ago. It is true some of the pastoral charges have been divided, and where one pastor was employed, two and even three are now needed. Several new churches have been built, and old ones re-modeled and renovated. But the number of our congregations has not been increased, and many of them have done very little more than to maintain their ground. It must therefore be confessed, that our progress as a Synod has been very slow. . . . Is the Hartwick Synod finished? Is our work in Home Missions and church extension completed? Are we content with our present limits, and do we never intend to attempt any aggressive movements? Are there no localities, where, by a Judicious expenditure of money and the employment of competent Missionaries, we may build up new congregations, and increase our strength, as well as our influence and usefulness?[3]

THE PROBLEM OF MISSION GROWTH

Synodical growth had been only of the first kind—entirely congregational. The Hartwick Synod had been a breakaway effort to organize Ministerium congregations in an upstate area where pastors felt neglected by the parent body. Three and a-half decades later many of those congregations had matured, but the mission field had not been extended. Nor were matters to change significantly. In 1866 there were twenty-nine (29) congregations affiliated with the synod, in 1888 there were twenty-seven (27) congregations and nine (9) preaching stations. Several congregations were added but others dropped from the rolls. Several congregations divided into two parishes, but in other instances congregations had merged. A few, like St. Marks Lutheran Church, Canahajoharie, were growing enough to renovate existing structures to accommodate larger numbers. (See fig. 8.1)

In the period from 1860 to 1890 two mission congregations were established—in Maryland, New York and Troy, New York, but only one (Maryland) survived. The Maryland, Otsego County mission was established principally through the efforts of a Hartwick theology student G. W. Enders in April, 1868. Enders occupied the territory after a similar mission by the Franckean Synod had failed.

figure 8.1
St. Marks Lutheran Church, Canahajoharie, New York
Rebuilt and Dedicated August, 1870

Though the Franckeans contested the move once the mission was a success, Enders entered upon the field with their knowledge and approval. A new church building was dedicated January 20, 1869, paid for in part with $800 in funds collected locally and from other congregations in the synod. At that point attendance improved steadily and the winter season saw a revival—"a very precious quickening of grace"—and "many were brought from darkness to marvelous light." In all fifty-one members joined the new church in 1869—ten through infant baptism, twenty-six through adult baptism, seven through Confirmation and eight by letter of transfer. Besides Sunday worship, a "sabbath evening prayer meeting" was introduced together with another weekly meeting. An active Sunday school was developed, its educational needs supplied in part with materials contributed by the West Sandlake congregation and a donor from Ohio. Besides his pastoral duties in the congregation, Enders preached in school houses in the district, an added effort which convinced him that the Maryland area was a "large and important field for missionary operations."[4]

The new mission struggled on into the hard times of the 1870s when congregations and the synod found money scarce because of the Panic of 1873; its condition was reported to the synod as "poor" by 1873 and "not in a very flourishing condition" in 1875. By then Pastor Enders had been gone for three years, and the church was either vacant or served sporadically by itinerant preachers. Without strong leadership, the congregation found its strength ebbing, and its numbers dwindled to twenty members. With a success to his credit, Enders had assumed pastoral status without examination or ordination. And he looked elsewhere for another call. When he asked for a letter of dismission to take a more lucrative call in New Jersey, the promised letter was refused and he was given, in its place, a letter recommending him for examination, a situation which further soured relations between the Hartwick and New Jersey Synods just prior to the 1872 merger talks with them and the New York Synod. Despite these setbacks, a new pastor provided new hope so that by 1878 the Maryland mission was reported prosperous and out of danger, with a resurgent membership of forty-two![5]

The mission in Troy, New York, was started within a community of 5,000 new German immigrants. The city was canvassed, and rooms rented in the local YMCA for church meetings. Success was apparent by May 1869 and a new congregation was started, this time with eighteen members. The synod had an abiding concern for the infant Lutheran church because of the great need among the Germans, "many of whom have become recreant to their church, but who, by faithful labor and devotion to their interest, may be brought back again to the fold." Within two years however, the mission was in trouble. A mission pastor could not be procured, while the founding pastors had to travel some distance to support this additional charge. Illness plagued one of them. The church itself was inaccessible to many in the community who lived some distance from its place of worship. Finally, a German Lutheran congregation was formed in the city by the New York Ministerium and a mission pastor was soon ordained and installed. This combination of circumstances proved impossible and by 1873 the Troy mission was abandoned and its property put up for sale. The synod contemplated attempting another new mission at Troy in the late 1870s but it never materialized. Kingston was surveyed in 1875 as a possible mission site. "The field is inviting" it was reported, " and an early effort is highly necessary if we wish to retain those who are willing to labor and sacrifice for the building up of our church." No early effort was forthcoming however. Nevertheless greater effort had been expended on this occasion than in 1867 when a plea by the president of synod to establish mission churches in the thriving villages along the new Albany and Susquehanna Railroad went entirely unheeded.[6]

Why so few mission explorations, and so little effort on their behalf? A lack of resources and motivation. Per capita giving for Home Missions involving synod contributions to General Synod mission efforts throughout the United States amounted to $0.10 in 1865, $0.11 in 1870, $0.13 in 1875 and $0.14 in 1880, a progression which just kept up with the growth of real income during the period. Comparatively, Hartwick support was about half that of the New York Ministerium during the same period, and perhaps a third of the Synod of New York and New Jersey. Despite the mission efforts resulting from European immigration, "*our own needy ones*" were being deliberately ignored (the synod reported) "with the un-Christian rebuff 'Am I my brother's keeper?'"

> What the church needed was a baptism of the Home Missionary spirit. The churches and synods, pulpits and pews have got to feel, and feel deeply, that this spirit is the spirit of the gospel; and that the work of Home Missions is the work and hope of the Lutheran church in this land of 40,000,000.[7]

This observation, which had been made in the General Synod by reference to the whole church, was repeated in the Hartwick Synod because it was especially applicable there.

A retrospective view of the problem by P. A. Strobel in the synod's *Memorial Volume* of 1881 attributed lack of mission effort to a lack of financial support and the synodical disorganization associated with General Synod district structures in upstate New York. "That we have failed to plant churches at many points which were opened to us, and that the development of our Synod has not been commensurate with our resources and our opportunities, candor compels us to admit." Missions were dropped at Buffalo, Troy, Waterloo, Saugerties "and other localities where churches might have been built, if more liberality and energy had been displayed." Granted the discouragements and embarrassments "connected with the divisions in our Synods, and the distractions in our congregations," yet "we might and should have made in these fifty years much greater progress in the multiplication of our churches and the increase of our membership."[8]

Like most Lutherans in America, members of Hartwick Synod's congregations had not yet come to realize the importance of mission efforts to the health of the church in the United States. The synod lacked understanding, therefore had low motivation, and consequently contributed inadequately to the task of transplanting a European state church to American denominational soil, a task which was primarily a mission effort.[9] Eventually this realization would dawn upon them. By 1885 per capita giving for Home Missions had increased to $0.19. What is more, a Church extension fund for local missions which had been started after 1870 began providing desperately needed mission money—$488.28 by 1885, or another $0.11 per capita.

IMPORTANCE OF WOMEN'S MISSIONARY SOCIETIES

What made the difference was the creation in the Hartwick Synod of a Woman's Home and Foreign Missionary Society by recommendation of the General Synod. Actually the Hartwick Synod was repeating an earlier, successful experience. The Lutheran Church in Dansville had formed a local Woman's Missionary Society in 1832, while the wives of Lutheran pastors from the Hartwick Synod, together with other women in the synod formed the first Woman's Synodical Missionary Society in the United States in 1839 at Cobleskill. Such organizations, while helping in local mission development, also represented a (by then) well-developed movement of religious advancement and moral reform undertaken by Christian women through voluntary associations. So the Hartwick Synod was no stranger to organized female effort when, in 1878, it urged synodical churches to form local women's missionary societies. Four years later (1882) seven congregational units with 228 met to form the synodical Society in its first annual meeting. The next year the number of units had increased to twelve. Local meetings, fund appeals, the distribution of mission materials, the development of a congregational contingent with this as its special enthusiasm—all helped the Hartwick Synod in its long struggle to break the encirclement of apathy which kept it from growing and from adequately supporting the mission growth of the larger church.

The Hartwick Society was perhaps the best of the societies organized within New York General Synod bodies, being ably lead for some years by Cobbleskill president, Ruth Hoag Larkin. She summed up a typical year's work and life for women of the synod with lines from an anonymous poet:

"—year hath been
The sum of all since time began,
The birth and death, the joy and pain
Of nature and of man."

Her group encouraged male pastors to "extend to us the right hand of Christian comradeship . . . to advance the Master's kingdom." Individual pastor's did so, helping develop within their congregations an important force for mission and family development. Larkin acknowledged the cost of "much labor and self-sacrifice" to the hundreds of women involved in keeping the mission message alive in the synod, but also "the blessings, the hours of peace and happiness that have been given to others, and in turn received into the hearts and homes of the faithful women in our Auxiliaries." Not one to depend on improved organization for better results, she led by encouraging that present methods "be more faithfully carried out."[10]

CONGREGATIONAL GROWTH

Despite these expanding efforts, however, it was not an increase in the number of congregations, but membership growth within congregations which reversed the declining fortunes of the Hartwick Synod in the late 1880s. Why did this occur? A growing congregation requires a healthy environment, one with an effective pastor and relative harmony in the congregation. In the middle 1860s, at a time of precipitous decline, there was an unusual high rate of itinerancy among the Hartwick clergy. A "well settled and permanent ministry" was deemed essential at this point in the synod's life, yet itinerancy was the rule. Some ministers, to be sure, had wanderlust. Yet the problem really rested with the congregations. It was assumed that no minister, no matter how well qualified, could serve effectively for more than three or four years. Many congregations employed a yearly call, subject to annual review at the congregational meeting, which reinforced the idea of impermanency. This practice, which surfaced complaints against the pastor both real and imagined, probably reduced the average call to several years' length. Inadequate salaries also encouraged itinerancy. A nominal salary of $500, set before the war, was now worth $200 because of deflated currency. The problem was so bad in 1864 that the lay delegates to the synod gathered for a special meeting to seek a remedy. The law of supply and demand seems to have reinforced the problem. Despite the low level of recruitment for the ministry in the Hartwick Synod, there were more clergy available than congregations to call them, while some congregations deliberately kept themselves vacant to make ends meet, further exacerbating the problem. Indications are that the situation improved in the late 1860s and early 1870s, at least in some congregations.[11] Thereafter, the complaints about clergy support were not so frequent. Small congregations like the Maryland mission went without a pastor from time to time for such reasons. Its experience of declining membership when its pulpit was vacant was a good indication of how important permanent clergy were to membership development.

REVIVALISM

In congregations where pastors were available and active, the conventional theological wisdom suggested adult conversion as the best way to membership growth. After all the Hartwick Synod, like its Franckean counterpart, had gone through a period of significant growth prior to the Civil War with such a revivalistic emphasis. It was simply a matter of trying harder. Hadn't P. A. Strobel called for such efforts in the 1867 report on religion?

From time to time, revivals of note occurred with the expected results. There was an 918 member increase between 1870 and 1871, an unusual growth rate of 27 percent. That year one pastor reported a "precious harvest of 119 souls" after a six-week series of revival meetings.

Winter revivals created less spectacular increases in other congregations as well—thirty-five of fifty-four persons converted at a revival meeting joined one Lutheran congregation; another congregation added thirty-four new members after a protracted revival among three cooperating Lutheran churches; a third included thirty new members as the result of a single-congregation revival.[12] A 13 percent increase in membership between 1875 and 1876, followed by another of 6 percent in 1876, led to this appreciative comment (by P. A. Strobel) in the synod's 1877 "Report on the State of Religion":

> From the parochial reports, it appears that a number of our congregations have been blessed with revivals, which have resulted in the conversion of very many amongst the impenitent, and the quickening of the spiritual life of the churches. As the result of these revivals, the membership of some of our churches has been largely increased, thereby adding to their strength and efficiency, as well as their financial ability. Even in some of the congregations in which there has been no special work of grace, there has been a gradual but steady growth, so that with a few exceptions, our churches during the past year have all been making progress.[13]

At such times the number of adult baptisms and confirmations increased in relation to infant baptisms. In 1871, for example, the number of infant baptisms in the synod was 160, while the number of adult baptisms was 114 and confirmations 249; the ratios of adult baptisms to infant baptisms was .7 and that of infant baptisms to confirmations was 1.6 respectively. By contrast, in 1873 (a year with no significant revivals) the ratios were .5 and .8. In 1876, the ratios were up again—1.6 and 2.9. Two years later (with no significant revivals to report) the ratios were down once more—.8 and 1.0. Clearly young adults were caught up in revivals and joined the church, contributing to a healthy membership increase. However, what happened in the synod before the Civil War in similar circumstances repeated itself on these two occasions. Between 1872 and 1873 membership dropped by 24 percent. The revival of 1875-76 did not recoup these losses with the result that Hartwick membership did not reach 1872 levels again until 1890. It came closest in the middle 1880s after an 8.5 percent membership increase between 1882 and 1883. Again, such an unusual increase was noted by the committee on the state of religion in the synod: "During this year fervent prayer and earnest preaching of the Word has borne fruit, and we can now report large gains, of whom many, we trust, will be gathered as precious grain for the *Master* in the skies."[14]

THE SIGNIFICANCE OF BAPTISM

Revivalism, then, to the extent that it influenced membership growth in the synod contributed very unevenly to the "progress" of the church.

Baptism was potentially a greater factor in the growth trends noted above. Extensive studies of church growth over long periods of time indicate that for a church to expand it "must increase its stock of young potential recruits . . ." It is not adult converts taken into a church in any given year which influence membership trends, but (rather) those formerly baptized members who join in their own right as adults. It is the number of children baptized "x" number of years before a particular membership increase, which is its chief determining factor. About fifteen years has been suggested as an appropriate "lag time" between baptism and its membership impact, though as we shall see it was more like a twelve or thirteen year lag in the history of the Hartwick Synod.[15]

The 1871 revival occurred thirteen years after a record number of baptisms in 1858 (282 baptisms). The revival of 1875-76 occurred thirteen years after another record baptism in 1862 (308). The more modest increase between 1883 and 1884 occurred thirteen years after another baptismal record for the period, this one a more modest 160 baptisms in 1871. The synod would enter the 1890s with another increase, this one associated with an 1877 baptism of 155. An examination of the high and low points of membership from decade to decade (as shown in Graph 8.1, above) makes the point clearly enough. An 1840 high occurred after a period of very high baptismal rates for the new Hartwick Synod (602 compared with 2,087 communicants, or 13 in 1831, the first year Hartwick statistics are available). The 1850 low echoed a drop to 7.7 for the year 1837. The 1860 high resulted from an increase to a more modest 11.9 in 1847. At its 1880 low the ratio reflected a low of 2.8 for the year 1867.

It would be impossible to determine the actual number of new members from the actual number of baptisms occurring thirteen years before. But the increase in baptisms indicates an increase in the population pool of thirteen-year olds, many of whom were then brought in through confirmation and (sometimes) revivalism. The fact that revivals tended to coincide with an increased pool of thirteen-year olds indicates that baptized and unbaptized members were being brought into the church by a combination of revivalistic and catechetical means. In the case of the Hartwick Synod revivalism had a greater role to play in membership acquisition than in several other New York synods. The reason for this was that a relatively small age group of the total membership in any given year (communicant and baptized) was being baptized in Hartwick congregations. Table 8.1, indicating rations of baptism to communicant membership for three New York synods, makes the point most clearly: while the numbers of confirmed members in years of revival harvest seem impressive, it is the number of adult baptisms, large by comparison with the other synods, which is more significant. For the low incidence of baptism meant a relatively low incidence of confirmation. It was, on the other hand, the high incidence of young, unbaptized adults that swelled the ranks of the converted and increased church membership.

Table 8.1
Ratio of Baptisms to Communicant Members

Year	Hartwick (5)	NY/NJ Synod (5)	NY Ministerium (5)
1863	6.7	(NJ) 6.7	28
1867	2.8	(NJ) 5.7	23
1870	2.8	(NJ) 6.9	25
		(NY) 13.5	
1873	2.8	11.9	21
1877	3.8	11.5	18
1880	1.8	12.9	18
1883	2.1	12.8	15
1887	2.3	14.1	15
1890	2.5	15.5	na
1900	3.2	11.4	12

By contrast, the New York Ministerium, especially while it was being organized congregation by congregation in the immigrant community, was very busy baptizing young children born into ghetto families with high birth rates. As the number of German-speaking congregations in the New York and New Jersey Synod increased, and as the baptismal rate settled down in the more mature Ministerium, the rates in the two synods converged until they were almost identical at the end of the 1880s. Clearly the German-speaking confessional churches placed a higher priority on baptism than did the English-speaking congregations. The English-speaking New Jersey Synod's rate was lower than the bilingual Ministerium in 1865, while the rate of the English-speaking New York Synod in 1870 was appreciably lower than that of the predominantly German-speaking Ministerium which it had left three years before. The Ministerium, meanwhile, without its English-speaking element, experienced a modest increase in its rate of baptism.

THE PROBLEM OF BAPTISM IN THE HARTWICK SYNOD

The fastest growing New York area synod, and the only one to show (allogenous) growth of new membership after the Civil War—the New York Ministerium—also had the highest rate of baptism in relation to its communicant membership. It was more successful than any, through baptism, in providing itself with a large potential for adult membership. Ironically, when Hartwick was itself displaying allogenous growth—from 1830 to the middle 1840s and again for a time from the middle 1850s into the middle 1860s—it too had a higher ratio of baptisms to communicant membership. Table 8.2 indicates the ratios.

Table 8.2
Hartwick Baptisms as Percentage of Membership (5)

Year	Baptisms	Membership	Percentage Baptism to Membership
1832	613	3537	17.3
1835	370	3988	9.3
1837	205	2647	7.7
1840	280	3555	7.8
1843	321	3669	8.7
1845	241	3187	7.6
1847	325	2723	11.9
1850	238	2943	8.1
1853	227	3178	7.1
1855	248	3144	7.9
1857	171	3328	5.1
1860	287	4255	6.7
1863	219	3230	6.7
1865	158	4253	3.7

By the 1860s the trend was apparent enough though not its consequences. Observed a Hartwick committee on its state of religion:

> The Committee regrets to state . . . that in some of our churches the baptism of infants seems to have fallen greatly into disuse, for which they can see no reason, but an utter carelessness and inattention to a positive and solemn Christian duty. Christians are bound by the most solemn covenant obligations to make an early consecration of their children to God in holy baptism; and yet there are thousands of children, whose parents are in the fold of the church, who are suffered to grow up aliens from the commonwealth of Israel, and strangers from the covenants of promise. . . . The Committee . . . hopes that the Synod will take some action.[16]

An 1866 report, while giving thanks for revivals which added many repentant sinners to the churches, noted another reason for the decline in spirituality—"neglect of the ordinances of religion and means of grace without which Christians cannot expect to grow in the divine life. . . ." The problem was dealt with again in 1874, a year after the synod experienced a 24 percent decrease in membership. On motion of Pastor P. Felts of Johnstown, it was resolved that the synod pastors preach on the subject of infant baptism once a year, and that they engage in home visitations, making "special efforts to convince Christian parents, who may seem inclined to withhold their children from the benefits of this sacred rite, of their culpable neglect." Another, and special synod committee on infant membership shed still more light on the problem in 1885 within the synod. Despite infant baptism (when it does occur), little is done beyond infancy for children in synod congregations.

Children's names are recorded "but here it ends." Though a great advantage is intended from this relationship, none is realized without the "actual use of the members." And how are these helpless ones to be helped? They must be instructed "doctrinally, experimentally, and practically." It is the pastor's duty "to enlighten in all the essential theories, the spiritual experiences and practical lessons of the Christian religion and life."[17]

The report recognized a closely allied problem—catechization. This too was much neglected in the church. No other method had ever been adopted in the church (so the report continued), "more efficient in bringing the young to Christ, and establishing them in the faith of the gospel." Negligent pastors must be urged on in this task as well, for poor membership increases require doubled diligence and prayer that God would bless the seed so sown. The next year (1875) the same point was made, this time urging a "return to the old paths" and "ancient and invaluable custom" of catechization. As late as 1884 it was noted that "Our good old system of catechetical instruction in the Lutheran church is not so generally and faithfully practiced by us as in some other Synods." Hartwick was out of step with a trend toward churchliness "in the best Lutheran sense" throughout the General Synod, failing to reflect the growing esteem and favor for the "practice of catechization" in the rest of the church.[18]

Such attitudes indicates a changing theological climate in the Hartwick Synod by the 1880s. Baptism was being re-examined, shortcomings in its administration studied, and the use of the catechism in confirmation encouraged. It was coming to be understood that baptism was the key to a growing church, and catechization a necessary kind of followup if this potential for growth was to be realized. What is more the synod had identified the heart of the problem—parental indifference—and sought a solution through home visitations that would persuade parents of the importance of baptism. As students of church growth elsewhere during this period observed, in order to grow "a church must increase its stock of young potential recruits by first increasing its stock of young adults members or adherents." The Hartwick Synod must persuade members and adherents to baptize and catechize if the young were to remain more than potential members.[19]

The results were not immediately apparent. The ratio of baptisms to communicant membership did not change significantly during the period, an indication that encouraging infant baptism in the particular subculture of rural and small-town New York was an uphill battle, given the indifference among parents, and the "second chance" opportunity which conversion presented for entrance into the church.Yet the struggle to introduce catechization seems to have produced good results. In 1887 the synod reported that "greater attention is being paid to the catechization of the young at the present time than in the past." A part of the victory lay in the realization through a growing confessional renewal that the "time-honored" institutions of the church could only be neglected at the synod's peril. By the 1880s the message of the synod's recent growth patterns was very clear—the "future of the church depends largely upon the training of the young."[20]

THE FRANCKEAN SYNOD

The Franckean Synod was drawing much the same conclusion, at the same time, from similar experiences, having experienced a history of change and development similar to that of the Hartwick Synod. The two histories developed in parallel, with only occasional points of contact. Even encouraging comments could be taken amiss. In 1865 the Franckeans observed of Hartwick that "We are glad to see in this body an advance in what we consider the right direction. They seem more anxious to cultivate a spirit of prayer and to stir up revivals of true religion among them than formerly." The Hartwick Synod responded rather defensively and "with the deepest regret" that the Franckean Synod had made "a most ungenerous and untruthful imputation on the past history of this Synod."[21]

That history had seen a division between the two bodies in 1837. Franckean concern for Hartwick laxness reflected an air of superiority toward their upstate sisters and brothers because of their own dependency upon revivals for church growth. The Franckeans' most recent remarks had been made in an encouraging spirit of fellowship and reconciliation at a time when Hartwick was becoming more like the Franckeans, or so it seemed. But Hartwick had taken them ill, perhaps because revivalism was at that moment working for the breakaway synod, whereas the Hartwick Synod was in a period of decline. This we have already seen from Graph 8.1. In this their histories were not identical. Graph 8.2 (page 250) indicates a somewhat different pattern for the Franckean Synod. (See Map 8.2 The Franckean Synod.)

After a decade or more of intensive growth during the 1850s the Franckean synod had slowed down in a time of consolidation. By the middle sixties however there was a resurgence of strength just as Hartwick was going into a period of membership stagnation. Graph 8.3 (see page 251) compares these two histories. After years of contrasting growth and development from their inception to the Civil War, postwar developments for the two synods were more alike. Both experienced a decline after 1860, and both a reversal of fortunes after 1890. Hartwick preceded the Franckeans by close to a decade in both directions. What were the similarities and the differences that account for these largely parallel histories? What delayed developments in the Franckean Synod of forces at work in the Hartwick Synod? And why did the Hartwick Synod reverse its fortunes more quickly?

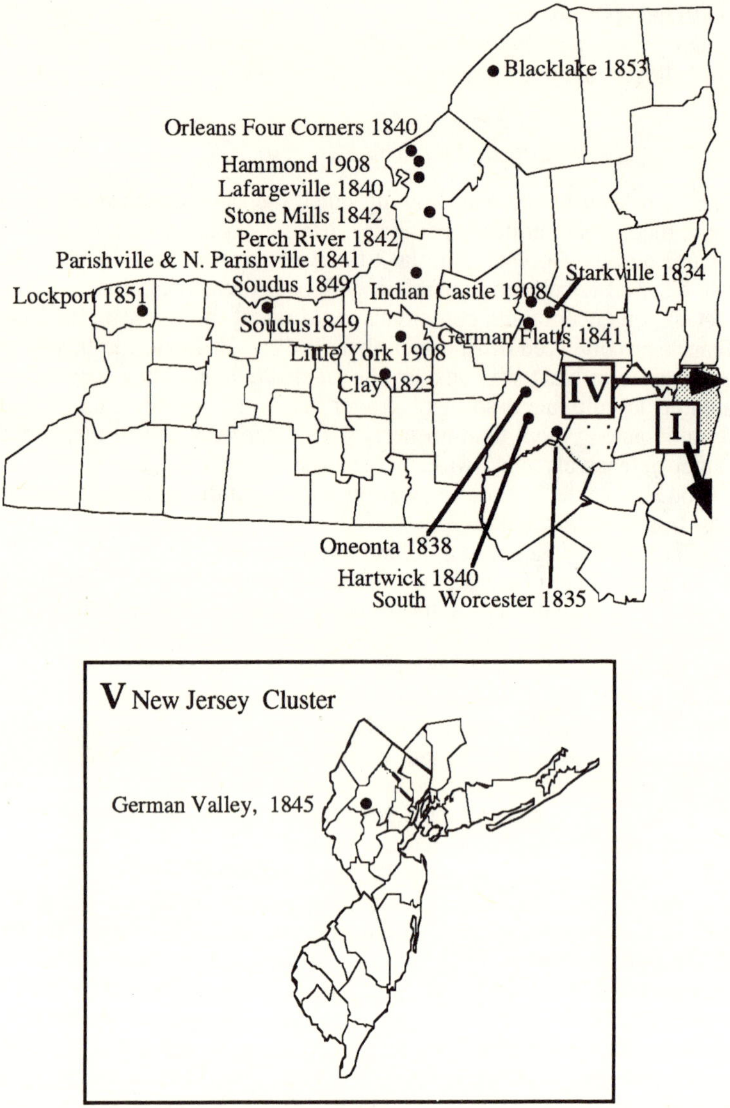

Map 8.2 The Franckean Synod

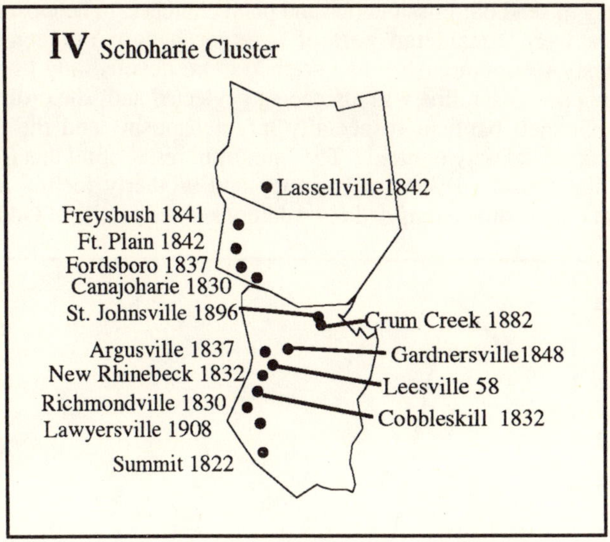

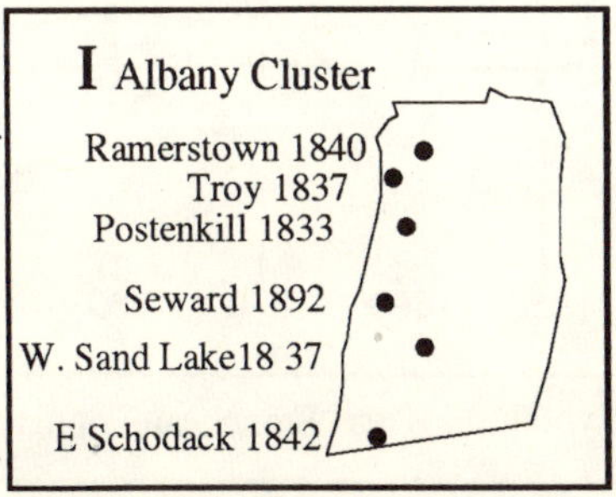

Map 8.2 The Franckean Synod

WAR BRINGS DECLINE

Just prior to the Civil War, the Franckeans went through their own spiritual doldrums. The synod's 1861 report on the state of religion indicated most churches to be in an "ineffective state." Membership had increased by a mere thirty-five additions, and there was "but little evidence of efficient effort as also of holy living." By 1862 the committee on the state of religion was reporting "some little progress in Christian activity" with formerly distracted congregations reunited, and some congregations receiving "refreshing showers of heavenly grace." The year 1863 was seen as a year with far fewer revivals than formerly, while 1864 continued the pattern. By 1865 the lack of church extension also came in for criticism, seeing that but "very little has been done by us as a Synod, of late years" whereas it was "characteristic of our body formerly to send out missionaries and plant churches." The most recent troubles were considered part of a larger pattern of declension. Previously the membership had seemed more devoted and liberal in their support. Discipline was also being neglected and "the ordinances of the Gospel, baptism (especially infant baptism) and the Lord's Supper are carelessly omitted." The "mournful result of all this is impiety in the church, a want of harmony and brotherly feeling among members, few conversions and few additions to the people of God."[22]

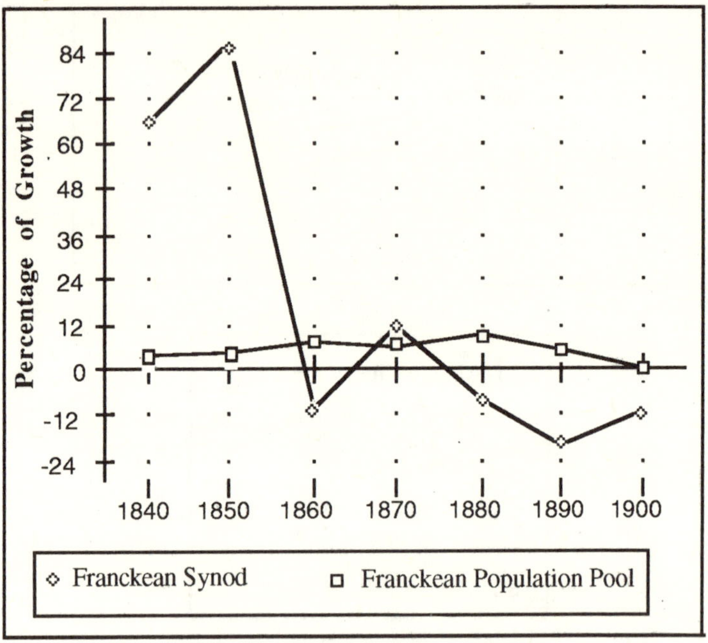

Graph 8.2 Franckean Synod Growth

For most of these matters the war was tó blame. Some in the churches "have been too much distracted by our national difficulties and political issues, hence fraternal feeling have become alienated and the love of God grown cold, the means of grace forsaken and the interests of Christ's cause forgotten." Many of the Franckean churches had been traumatized, politicized, and divided over the issues of the war, slavery and pacifism, much more so than other General Synod synods. From the outset the Synod had not compromised on the institution of American slavery, while other bodies avoided the issue as too divisive. It had gone on public record once again in 1860 advocating the overthrow of slavery, and vowing that their efforts "shall not cease until the end is gained, or we are laid in the silence of the grave."[23]

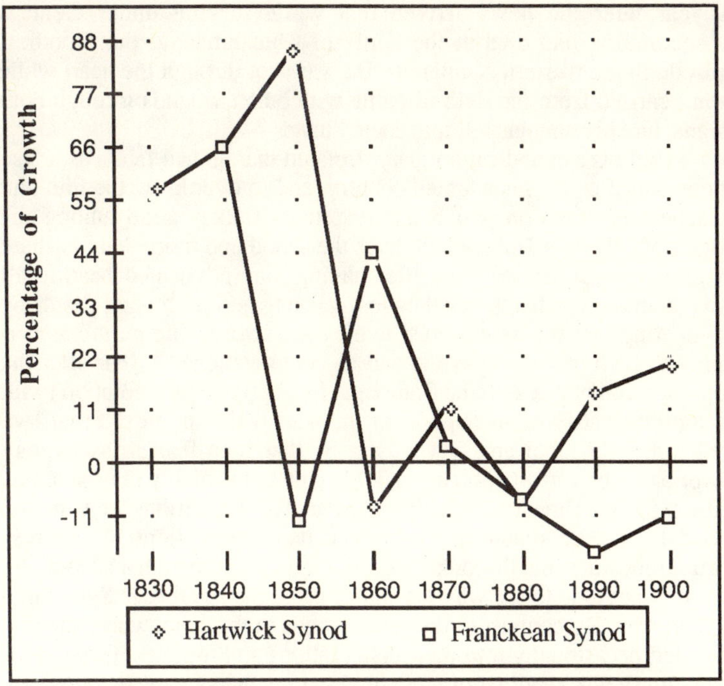

Graph 8.3 Hartwick and Franckean Synods Compared

These were incendiary words meant to heat up the moral issue of slavery at a desperate time of national compromise. Those unsympathetic to the cause thought such language could lead only to warfare, conflict and disunion. Neighbors of the Gardnerville congregation replied by firebombing that church's sanctuary. Nor did emancipation ease matters very much. As late as 1864 the congregation reported "We still have some alienations of feeling to us arising from the state of the country." While this particular dispute was with outsiders, other congregations were divided from within.[24]

The Franckean Synod also had made its opposition known to human warfare with testimonies bordering on pacifism. Now their advocacy of a defensive war in opposition to slavery made the synod's positions on war and slavery difficult to reconcile. Individual lives struggled with the contradictions. The synod was especially troubled by the fate of a young pastor, Justus Steinmitz, a recent German immigrant who had enlisted in the Union cause. He was prompted to do so "by love for my adopted country" he reported to the synod, and knowing the principles "which our Synod cherishes I hope so much more to be excused." Steinmitz saw the "hand of God" in the war. A proud nation was being humbled because God had heard "the cry of the oppressed."

A year later the news arrived that while serving under General Rosecranz he had died at the battle of Chicakmauga, the bloodiest episode in the western campaigns. He was shot through the heart while being carried from the field of battle with bullet wounds through both thighs, and his remains fell into enemy hands.[25]

Steinmitz's synodical obituary declared that he had fallen as a "patriotic sacrifice for his adopted country, and to overthrow the foul and treacherous rebellion which has reared its snakey head among the Altars of Liberty's Temple." Perhaps the synod had more than its share of guilt for advocating war, after having long advocated beating all swords into plowshares, for they lost a young and promising pastor by advocating that the nation must live by the sword. The guilt was certainly to be found in the synod and its congregations. A year after the conflagration had ceased the Franckean Synod passed a resolution (with preambles justifying its support of the war) which promised that "we will faithfully labor and fervently pray, that such fearful issues may never again be forced upon us, and that God in his mercy may save this nation for all time to come from the awful desolations of war and bloodshed." The synod also instructed its congregations to suppress their animosities and discords, praying for a time of national accord.[26]

It is possible to see why the war affected the Franckean Synod in a special way. By contrast to the other synods in the state, where the war intruded occasionally into their deliberations and minutes, the state of the country was reported on not only by a special synodical committee but frequently in the president's reports as well. For this Lutheran synod there were religious issues at stake in the civil conflict—moral issues of war and peace, slavery and freedom, rebellion against, and submission to lawful authority. The hand of God was seen to be actively involved in the affairs of the Christian republic, while the fortunes and outcome of a civil war had everything to do with their sense of Christian concern. Whereas other synods may have noted President Lincoln's death with regret, the Franckean Synod lamented the death of "the martyr President" with a long obituary and political statement.

> In many respects he was a remarkable man, and the people saw it more clearly and admiringly every year. To the wise he was wise; to the good and the pious, he was a good man, for their sympathy and religious interest were taught to cling to him at every altar of prayer; to the soldier he appeared as a true and tried friend, and his word and counsel were received and followed cordially into the battle-field, suffering death and the grave; and to the oppressed he was the Moses of God; in him they reposed confidence and cherished an esteem as for no other man. Such a man to fall by death, and that, too, by the hand of the assassin . . . is apparently an immeasurable calamity to our nation, and a calamity to the democracy of the world.[27]

The Franckean Synod was peculiarly responsive to this most profoundly religious of all American presidents. Above all they grieved. That Lincoln believed in a God who favored neither side did not diminish their deep regard and respect for the martyred president.

AN UNEVEN REVIVAL

For them the Almighty had intervened to save a nation. And now, the synod believed, "without a shadow of doubt" that God was "about to pour out his Spirit in copious effusion, and that every church that is waiting for and praying for this consolation of Israel will enjoy the most refreshing showers of divine grace." In this they were not mistaken. As in other synods, wartime spiritual depression gave way to growth and renewal with the advent of peace. There was little sign of revival or renewal from 1866 to 1868, but thereafter membership increases became significant. Membership jumped 21 percent between 1865 and 1870, continuing to climb another three years to an increase of 26 by 1873. Because of a temporary membership dropoff in 1867 the actual increase from that point to 1873 was 35 percent![28]

However it was still not the pre-war experience. "State of Religion" reports gave the synod and its congregations mixed reviews. Summarizing the parochial reports for 1871, the committee which drafted this annual barometer of spiritual health observed "that some of the churches in our connection have enjoyed the rich effusions of the Holy Spirit, while others are in a comparative state of coldness." There was simply "not the same degree of living piety . . . that used to prevail among us in the early history of the Synod."[29]

Whence the unevenness? Where was the strength and where the weakness? On the positive side, this post-war revival was also a period of mission growth. Though the Franckean Synod lost the Maryland mission to the Hartwick Synod, other missions were established at Avoca, Manheim, Bards (Beard's) Hollow (Schoharie County), all in New York, and in Williamsburg, Ontario. A mission field at Syracuse was explored, though nothing came of it. And a congregation from the Ministerium (Taghkanick) and the New York Synod (Churchtown) joined the synod.[30] In 1860 there were twenty-nine (29) congregations in the synod; after the new flurry of mission development and congregation-trading, there were thirty-three (33) by 1873. Throughout the period of growth, benevolence giving—always good by comparison with other synods—improved significantly. In 1862 support for synod missionary work amounted to \$0.42 per capita; in 1872 it was \$ 0.72; by 1882 it would increase (though more modestly) to \$0.77.

Strong congregations in the synod managed to support missions elsewhere as well as revivals at home. Weak congregations and vacant ones were a negative factor and a drain on synod resources. Preferring to take care of these problems at home, the synod refused in 1872 to transfer home mission funds in their entirety to the General Synod Home Mission Board. Without potential in such congregations, no amount of money withheld would help. Eventually, the synod advised that some weak or vacant congregations should disband, with members seeking spiritual fellowship in other, more active congregations in the area.

Other Franckean congregations were vacant by choice with the result that there were actually unemployed ministers in the synod. Synod communications on the matter indicate that some congregations were very fastidious about whom they would call, implying that competent if not charismatic pastors were refused calls because they did not quite measure up. As noted with the Hartwick Synod, pastoral vacancies contributed to congregational decline. Itinerancy and short pastorates, another drain on congregations, plagued the Franckean Synod as well. Historical statistics published in 1872 by the synod historian, Pastor H. L. Dox, indicate an average pastorate of 4.1 years, while thirty-seven (37) of the one hundred thirty-seven (137) recorded pastorates in the synod's history ran for less than two years.[31]

DECLINE OF FRANCKEAN PIETY

In Chapter 2, it was suggested that the Franckean Synod had become a "tired sect" by the beginning of the Civil War. The synod summarized its own condition in 1871 in this way: "we fear that in a great measure the church has assumed the garb of worldly conformity, and settled down, satisfied with the mere form of religion, in place of the experience and practice of vital godliness." Was the Franckean piety, with roots going back to Palatine Pietism, in a state of permanent decline with the onset of modern 'worldliness' (i.e., bourgeoisie values in the commercial and industrial economy of upstate New York along the Canal)? A similar state of affairs had been reported by both the Synod of New York and New Jersey and the Hartwick Synod. The question was partially answered by an 1874 report on religion in the church which pointed to an "alarming coldness" among many in the congregations. Members were no longer acquainted with one another. Friendship was on the wane and the differences between rich and poor were no longer overcome in Christian feelings of mutual regard. Discipline was lacking—those who lived by worldly standards and values were no longer disciplined. And the heart of Lutheran piety—self-examination, meditation, and corporate prayer in prayer meetings—was also on the decline.[32]

One indication of the change was with the use of the prayer meeting—always an important part of a revival and conversion-conscious religious movement. That year (1874) twenty-eight (28) prayer meetings appeared in the parochial reports. In 1870 during the recent revival, there had been thirty (30). In 1875 only twenty-two (22) were reported and the number declined thereafter—twenty (20) in 1881, thirteen (13) by 1885. By comparison, the pre-war years tell a different story. Coming into extensive use by 1845, the Franckean Synod reported forty-eight (48) prayer meetings in that year, fifty-two (52) in 1850, thirty-six (36) in 1855, and forty-eight (48) in 1860.

Clearly pre-war pietism and revivalism, though they survived the war, did not survive the growing materialism and secularity associated with the later 1870s and the 1880s. These were times of great change. "So rapid are the movements and transitions of the age" President Van Alstine reported in 1882, "that years of the past are now blended into one. . . . On every hand is hurry, breathless attention, increased activity, and all seem to be in excited expectation of momentous developments." The times made increased demands on the ministry "for the whole field of the world lies open and calls for work, to repel and suppress skepticism, and gather in the ripening harvest." Yet those who assessed the state of religion for the year, wondered how piety could improve "if the stream will never rise higher than the fountain"—that is higher than the standards set by the clergy.[33] This decline was significant in and of itself, but also because of the abnormally severe consequences it would have for Franckean church membership. Revivals there were, and one more burst of membership growth in the late 1860s and early 1870s. More than ever the synod depended on conversion to fill its pews.

THE DYNAMIC OF BAPTISM

Their situation was, once again, not unlike that of the Hartwick Synod already noted. Again, baptism was the key. The two pre-war high points in membership growth for the Franckean Synod were in 1843 and 1850. Another high point was reached in 1865. In all three cases they were preceded twelve to fifteen years before by unusually high numbers of baptisms. In fact, the initial growth of the new synod from 1837 to 1843 can be traced to very high baptismal rates in the Franckean Synod before the break. It was a time, as we have seen, when young women led the way into the church seeking baptism for their children and drawing their menfolk after them. The age of the members baptized twelve to thirteen years before the peak years of 1843, 1850 and 1865 were 17.3, 10.1 and 6.4 percent. (see Table 8.3.) The revival of the early 1870s, on the other hand was preceded by baptism rates around 3 percent. At the time of the revival, at another membership high-point in 1873, the rate of baptism was 4 percent.

In the early years then, despite the replacement of confirmation with a profession of faith as the rite of entrance into adult membership, it was the confirmation-age children of a baptizing church which fueled revivalism. By the 1870s, on the other hand, it was the more highly prized "Baptism of the Spirit," leading to adult baptisms and professions of faith, that were filling the pews, though at a more modest rate.

By then the church had all but ceased baptizing. So alarming had the situation become by 1870 that a resolution was offered in synod: "we deeply deprecate the apparent neglect of Infant Baptism, as indicated by the Parochial reports." It was considered a matter of "remissness" rather than a "change of sentiment" and therefore the "claims of this ordinance" were recommended as a subject for pastoral instruction.[34]

Table 8.3
Baptism as Percentage of Membership in NY Synods (5)

Year	Hartwick	Franckean	NY/NJ	Ministerium
1830				19.9
1832	17.5			
1835	9.3			31.8
1840	7.8	13.0		24.7
1845	7.6	6.4		21.4
1850	8.1	6.4		23.6
1855	7.9	5.0		26.1
1860	6.7	3.5		30.2
1865	3.7	1.8	(NJ) 7.8	29.0
1870	2.8	1.0	13.5	25.0
1875	3.0	2.1	11.9	18.0
1880	1.8	(1881)1.3	12.9	17.8
1885	2.7	0.5	14.8	15.0
1890	2.5	0.8	15.5	14.1
1895	3.0	1.0	13.6	13.8
1900	3.2	1.8	11.4	11.5
1908	2.7	1.9	9.0	

Doubtless parental attitudes had much to do with the low and declining rate of baptism. English-speaking Lutherans in upstate New York obviously did not have the same regard for baptism as did downstate Lutherans—either English- or German-speaking. The lower rates in the Hartwick and Franckean Synods attest to that subregional phenomenon. In particular the Franckeans had developed their religious attitudes in an area of western New York where Baptist influence had always been great. But the difference between the two synods is not simply explained on the basis of parental attitudes. The Franckean Synod's denial notwithstanding, a "change of attitude" toward Baptism did occur among the Franckeans with the growth of a synod dedicated to a membership of the converted. The Franckean Synod was a tired sect, but more sectarian in outlook than in its antebellum period!

DEVELOPMENT OF THE SUNDAY SCHOOL

Compared with the Hartwick Synod, which also began to lament the decline of baptisms in its congregations, the Franckean Synod's 1870 resolution was pretty much the end of the matter. Instead of continued concern it shifted attention to promoting the Sunday school movement within the synod as a way of preparing children for adult membership. An 1873 report emphasized, for example, that religious ignorance was destructive of human dignity, and that secular education alone was not "sufficient to meet the highest wants of the soul." The earlier this education is imparted the less likely the mind is to "be pre-occupied with evil." Everything points to the Sunday school as of high utility and importance, because "many extensive and powerful revivals of religion have originated in the Sabbath School."[35]

Somewhat more pointed sentiments were expressed throughout the 1880s—the Sunday school was "the nursery of the church" and it should be sustained by all church members in an aggressive war against Satan (1881); at a time of declining membership the Sunday school is "the most encouraging sign among us" (1882); year after year the Sunday school "becomes more and more the hope of the church" (1884). Again, there were two key institutions—the Sunday school and the prayer meeting—which together "constitute a thermometer" measuring the spiritual temperature of a congregation.[36]

And what did the thermometer indicate? As we have already seen, there was a significant decline in the number of prayer meetings in the church. (In 1884 there were only seventeen left). Conversely the number of Sunday schools was increasing. There were thirteen (13) in the 1840s, twenty-one (21) by 1860, twenty-six (26) in 1870, and fifty-six (56) in 1885. There was also an interesting parallel to be seen with adult Bible study. Arriving on the scene in the 1850s, there were fifteen (15) study groups by 1860. The number increased to twenty-six (26) by 1870, while in 1881 (1880 statistics are not available) there were thirty-eight (38). Four years later the number had jumped to sixty (60).

Ironically, while fifty years after the formation of the Franckean Synod a synodical report suggested that statistically the synod was dying, the increase in the number of Sunday schools and scholars indicated a healthy and growing educational religious movement in its midst. Along with it went, at long last, a reversal in the fortunes of baptism within the synod. While the change of direction was not dramatic, as Table 8.3 indicates, the per capita number of baptisms was on the rise between 1885 and 1900. With this reversal changes in adult membership occurred as well. Things had gotten so bad, that for years the synod had actually experienced an annual membership loss. What occurred was not a dramatic increase in adult or communicant membership, but simply a decrease in the rate at which the synod was loosing members. As Graph 8.3 indicates this occurred between 1890 and 1900 (at the appropriate lag in time) with decreasing (negative!) growth rates at a time when growth rates in the surrounding population were declining. It would take higher rates of baptism to again increase membership. But the synod was moving in the right direction at last!

FROM HOLINESS TO EARNESTNESS

The change in theological outlook which the Franckean Synod was undergoing can be seen in two reports on the "state of religion" delivered to the synod in 1888 and 1889. The 1888 report suggested subtle shifts in emphasis which highlighted the importance of education (over prayer) in shaping the heart, a somewhat radical shift for the likes of the Franckean Synod.

> Religion is reverence for and love to God, accompanied by holy obedience and charity. It is the outgrowth of faith in our Saviour crucified for us, with a renewed heart for the fountain. It is indispensable to accomplish successfully life's mission—to glorify God, to secure personal purity and peace, and to promote the general welfare. It is the special work of Christians to maintain and extend religion, by teaching and exemplifying gospel truth, and to bring our lost race under its saving and elevating influences. . . . It is very desirable that the "state of religion" in the Church, in the Synod, and generally, should be favorable and prosperous. . . . In proportion as religion increases, ignorance and sin will cease, and intelligence, right and virtue will prevail.[37]

The following year's report was written by Nicholas Van Alstine, senior minister of the synod (he was ordained in 1836), a leader who from the beginning of the synod moved it in a revivalistic direction. Often elected synod president, Van Alstine was given that honor one last time in 1887 for the fiftieth anniversary of the synod. By then he and one lay delegate were all that remained of the 1837 founders. A transition between generations was occurring. The change had been anticipated as long ago as 1875 when it was observed that before long the "younger brethren will be left to carry forward the work of the Synod."[38] Van Alstine's 1889 report was a last hurrah for the traditional theology of the older generation:

> In order to gauge the state, vitality and spirituality of religion as existing in our churches, it is quite essential to have a true conception of the Bible standard. A correct rule is necessary to measure the height, depth, or solidity of any object. A false measure will produce incorrect results. Therefore we need God's exact and infallible rule to determine the real state of religion among us.[39]

He continued, insisting that true religion "is evolved in a converted heart and life." It requires "a life of prayer and true devotion," an elevated piety requiring "consecration and holiness," a life of holiness and righteousness," and "full consecration and zealous works in the kingdom of Christ." Neither report found the synod in decline or advance, but in a *status quo* situation with some congregations showing greater vigor, others less. Both reports called for greater achievements, having some of the same ends in mind. However, the spiritual means was shifting—from the converted life of prayer, consecration, and holiness, to a life of faith, understanding, virtue, and earnestness which would improve rather than save persons. It was a new language—this shift from holiness to earnestness—for a new age of enterprise and reform. "In world enterprises, politics, business, and pleasure, people are in earnest; they talk, write, and in every way stir up interest by keeping their object before the people, inviting their attention and co-operation. . . . From this the church may take a lesson, and become in her generation and sphere, equally aggressive and successful. Then religion will flourish, and the gospel leaven will revolutionize our communities and the world."[40]

SLOW MOVEMENT TOWARD UNION

Compared with the New York Ministerium or the Synod of New York and New Jersey, the Hartwick and Franckean Synods experienced a downturn in their religious fortunes after the Civil War. It was characterized by a slowed rate of growth and periods of stagnation, a situation of which leaders in both synods were painfully aware. Neither was equal to the task of "church extension" in such circumstances. Instead they found themselves in competition with each other and with surrounding synods over mission fields and shifting congregational loyalties. While the conflict was occasionally dramatic, there were also overtures of cooperation and occasional plans of union proposed to improve the situation.

It was after a protracted conflict between the Franckean and Hartwick Synods over the Maryland mission field in 1868 that the Frankeans proposed a cooperative mission effort by the appointment of a domestic missionary jointly by themselves, Hartwick and the Synod of New York. This occurred just as the four synods began serious negotiations for a union of synods. As we have already seen, the results were a merger of New York and New Jersey, with the Hartwick Synod pulling out at the last minute, ostensibly because a union with New Jersey would create too large an entity to be manageable. Meanwhile plans were afoot to put the by now independent Hartwick Seminary on a more secure intersynodical footing, and to increase its offerings to make it "collegial" with the support of the four New York area members of the General Synod.[41]

In the same year—1875—the Franckean Synod proposed a joint conference of all three synods "to discuss all legitimate questions and draw a closer union in all our benevolent operations" (i.e., education and missions). The Synod of New York and New Jersey agreed to the exploration. At this point the General Synod became involved. At its 1877 meeting the parent body proposed a union of the Franckean and Hartwick Synods in the "Union Synod of New York" because they were both small but of a similar size, shared a common territory (sometimes with congregations in the same town "supporting two pastors where only one is needed"), and were already favorably "disposed to a union."[42]

The Hartwick Synod, in reporting on the resolution to its pastors and delegates, indicated that it would be a union like that of New York and New Jersey. The delegate to the Franckean Synod indicated widespread interest among synod members in the idea. Apparently congregations in both synods liked the idea of merger, especially if it meant supporting only one pastor in a town. By 1878 a plan had been proposed in a conference committee to create "The Hartwick and Franckean Evangelical Lutheran Synod of the State of New York." Since both synods were district synods of the General Synod, having adopted similar constitutions, they were therefore identical (by now, on paper at least) in doctrine and practice. Pastors from both synods would be entered on a common role. Congregations would be members of the new synod, and where "two churches are contiguous" merger and reincorporation was recommended.[43]

Both synods were to meet separately at their next conventions and ratify the proposal by a two-thirds vote. Then a joint meeting would be arranged to consummate the union. Though both synods met, only Hartwick managed the two-thirds vote necessary for union. It ratified the proposal 39-0. In the Franckean Synod, President Van Alstine, who had led the withdrawal from the Hartwick Synod in 1837, insisted that the proposal could only be brought to the floor by a three-quarters vote. Upon appeal his ruling was sustained 18 to 15. The Franckean Synod then resolved to table the proposal since "It is evident that the Synod is not prepared to act finally on the question of the union of Synods."[44]

Why were the Franckeans reluctant to do so? There appear to have been very few congregations where trouble with a potential merger would have caused a negative vote. Besides, the congregations were reported willing to consider a merger, especially those where resources were spread too thin. Quite probably it was the resistance of the chair, President Nicholas Van Alstine, and the questionable parliamentary procedures he used to keep the matter bottled up in the Franckean Synod, which kept the proposition from a vote and the two-thirds majority required for its passage. Eventually (1893) he would publish a brief historical review of the Franckean Synod in which he attributed its declining fortunes to a lack of home mission funds to reinvigorate weak congregations. The reason—"the organization of the Home Missionary Board of the General Synod, withdrawing all such funds from the district synods, and appropriating them in places, where, in their judgment, the most good would be effected." Not until then, at the end of his distinguished career, would Van Alstine finally insist: "Let all warfare be suppressed" in favor of "fraternal cooperation."[45]

But the Franckeans were not the only General Synod Lutherans in New York to oppose a merger. Ten years later (1888) a proposal to dissolve and reorganize the four General Synod district synods into three new synods was readily passed by the same body. This time one of its own, M. W. Empie, chaired the committee which developed the plan of reorganization. And this time another synod—the synod of New York and New Jersey—tabled a final set of proposals that would have made a four-way merger possible. On this occasion the Hartwick Synod accepted the inevitability of its own continued, independent existence, and dropped the subject from debate.[46]

CONCLUSION—PARALLELISM RATHER THAN CONVERGENCE

Resolutions for merger are moments of truth in the life of a church. With the number of proposals for cooperation and merger circulating among the three General Synod synods in the New York area, it was clear that the circumstances were ripe for a union of some sort. Three synods which had gone through periods of extensive growth reached points where their capacity for church growth—increasing the size of congregations, and mission outreach through church extension—had been reached or surpassed. Organizational frustration, confessional weakness, and congregational stagnation were enervating the future of General Synod Lutheranism in the greater New York area. The time was fast approaching when merger was inevitable and must therefore occur. But in the meantime New York General Synod districts continued the kind of parallel existence and development which characterized the history of the Hartwick and Franckean Synods in the latter half of the nineteenth century. Parallel developments within the three synods had not yet led to convergence at the district synod level. Such was the religious landscape that distinctive forms of Lutheranism remained in the Empire State well beyond the Civil War.

NOTES

1 Hartwick Synod, *Minutes* (1867), 14-15.

2 Ibid., 16-18.

3 Ibid. (1866), 58.

4 Ibid. (1868), 8; (1869), 32ff, 22.

5 Ibid. (1873), 25; (1875), 28; (1872), 13-14.

6 Ibid. (1869), 23; (1871), 18-19; (1873), 25; (1867), 47. Metropolitan New York Synod, *New York Ministerium Legacy* (New York City: 1986), UNYS-117.

7 Hartwick Synod, *Minutes* (1876), 28-9.

8 P. A. Strobel, *Memorial Volume to Commemorate the Semi-Centennial*

Anniversary of the Hartwick Lutheran Synod, of the State of New York (Philadelphia: Lutheran Publication Society, 1881), 70-71.
9 Hartwick Synod, *Minutes* (1876), 28-9.
10 Ibid. (1882), 6, 26; (1878), 19; *Proceedings of the Twentieth Annual Convention of the Woman's Home and Foreign Missionary Society of the Hartwick Synod,* in Hartwick Synod, *Minutes* (1901), 50-1.
11 Ibid. (1865), 37; (1864), 6, 41; (1866), 44; (1867), 48; (1868), 22.
12 Ibid. (1871), 43-46.
13 Ibid. (1877), 16.
14 Ibid. (1883), 14.
15 Robert Currie, et. al., *Churches and Churchgoers. Patterns of Church Growth in the British Isles since 1700* (Oxford: Clarendon Press, 1977), 51.
16 Hartwick Synod, *Minutes* (1864), 31.
17 Ibid. (1866), 43; (1874), 19; (1885), 24.
18 Ibid. (1874), 20; (1876), 14; (1884), 24; (1885), 10, 18, 24.
19 Currie, *Church and Churchgoers*, 51.
20 Hartwick Synod, *Minutes* (1887), 27.
21 Franckean Synod, *Journal* (1865), 30; Hartwick Synod, *Minutes* (1865), 24.
22 Franckean Synod, *Journal* (1861), 22; (1862), 19; (1863), 21; (1864), 5; (1865), 7.
23 Ibid. (1865), 22.
24 Ibid. (1861), 10; (1864), 15.
25 Ibid. (1863), 12; (1864), 6, 13. James M McPherson, *Battle Cry of Freedom. The Civil War Era, The Oxford History of the United States* (New York: Oxford University Press, 1988), 666ff.
26 Franckean Synod, *Journal* (1864), 13.
27 Ibid. (1865), 28.
28 Ibid., 23; (1867), 19; (1868), 27-8; (1871), 17-18
29 Ibid. (1871), 18.
30 Ibid. (1866), 19; (1868), 6, 20; (1870), 9; (1871), 14-16.
31 Ibid. (1872), 32; (1875), 6; (1871), 7; (1872), 10-12.
32 Ibid. (1872), 17; (1874), 18-19.
33 Ibid. (1882), 5, 17.
34 Ibid. (1870), 11.
35 Ibid. (1873), 18.
36 Ibid. (1881), 18; (1882) 17; (1884), 7, 14-15.
37 Ibid. (1888), 18.
38 Ibid. (1887), 6; (1875), 8.
39 Ibid. (1889), 12.
40 Ibid., 14-15; (1888), 19.
41 Ibid. (1868), 35. Hartwick Synod, *Minutes* (1872), 35; (1875), 41.
42 Franckean Synod, *Journal* (1875), 11. General Synod, *Minutes* (1877), 40-41.
43 Hartwick Synod, *Minutes* (1877), 9; (1878), 10; (1879), 19; (1878), 11.
44 Ibid., 10-11; (1879), 19.
45 Nicholas Van Alstine, *Historical Review of the Franckean Evangelical Lutheran Synod of New York* (Philadelphia: Lutheran Publication Society, 1893), 13, 19.
46 Franckean Synod, *Journal* (1888), 13-14; Hartwick Synod, *Minutes* (1888), 16.

9

CONFESSIONAL CONVERGENCE

The Common Service and the "Thirty Years' War," 1875-1905

The attempted union of the Hartwick, Franckean, and New York and New Jersey Synods indicated a growing closeness among Lutherans in the northeast. After years of parallel development since the Civil War, signs of convergence began to appear by the 1890s. Also New York synods associated with both the General Synod and with the General Council began to discover the developments in their histories which made them closer than they had thought. By then the three above-mentioned bodies had begun a final round of negotiations that would lead to a merged Synod of New York by 1908. In keeping with a new spirit of inter-Lutheran cooperation, this new Synod of New York would find itself almost immediately exploring cooperation in practical ministry with the newly created English-speaking Synod of New York and New England which broke away from the New York Ministerium in 1902. Even as these changes took place, the parent bodies—the General Synod and the General Council—were themselves also discovering that parallel efforts suggested practical union in certain matters like home missions and the exploration of other possible areas of convergence, including any possible changes of confessional climate and outlook that may have recently occurred.[1]

What they found was threefold. By the turn of the century a steady if unspectacular growth of a common confessional outlook had occurred among a centrist party of Lutherans in the General Council, the General Synod, and the United Synod of the South, a party which grew in strength and influence even as the forces of differentiation carried the day after the Civil War. This centrist group came more and more into its own after 1883, the four-hundredth anniversary of Luther's birth, which was commemorated in numerous pan-Lutheran celebrations held in November of that year. Celebration was followed by an extensive inter-Lutheran dialogue in many areas of Lutheran life. Of greatest significance, however, was a single liturgy—the Common Service—developed in 1888 for use among Lutheran congregations throughout the United States. Lutherans were discovering a common Lutheran service of worship though they could not yet worship together.

TOWARD A COMMON LUTHERAN LITURGY

A common liturgy had long been considered important to Lutheran unity in the three general bodies of Eastern Lutherans. While confessional agreement was important at a national level and among confessionally concerned church leaders, it was worship which shaped the identity of Lutherans in the pew. In no other way could the common faith of the church, expressed at the congregational level, be so influenced as by uniform rites and symbols of the Christian faith. This the old General Synod itself recognized, the development and deployment of worship materials being one of its basic reasons for existing. The search for a common liturgy had a long history.

THE LITURGIES OF 1832, 1837, 1847, AND 1856

The General Synod's approach to the development of a common liturgy was derivative at best. After an 1832 attempt by George Lintner, Hartwick Synod president, to construct a liturgy for the General Synod's supporting bodies (a liturgy which followed closely the New York Ministerium's Liturgy of 1814) the General Synod found itself supporting whatever liturgy seemed most acceptable to its synods and congregations. This approach encouraged change rather than continuity, magnifying whatever shortcomings or strengths existed in current liturgical practice. While a working committee continued developing the Hartwick liturgy, in 1837 the General Synod simply appended the English liturgy of the New York Ministerium to its own hymnbook, thereby establishing the first common liturgy per se. New York Lutheranism thus played a prominent role in early liturgical developments, by exerting what was considered (at best) a dubious influence. Most objectionable of all was the general invitation to "approach the table of the Lord" made in "the name of Christ our common and only Master . . . to all who own Him as their Saviour, and resolve to be His faithful subjects: ye are welcome to this feast of love."[2]

The years 1814 to 1837 certainly did mark the lowpoint of *Lutheran* liturgical development. By then the colonial liturgies, based on fifteenth- and sixteenth-century German liturgical practice, had been reduced to very simple forms of worship under the influence of American Protestantism. The traditional elements were all but eliminated, including all congregational responses, thereby depriving the worshipper in the pew of any active involvement in what had anciently been known as the "work of the people." This "free liturgy" (so called) enjoyed considerable popularity among American Lutherans. Liturgies (then) were primarily collections of public confessions, prayers, and (perhaps) scriptural selections commonly used in the churches, joined together with a series of occasional orders including Baptism and the Lord's Supper. The 1814 liturgy, while providing a table of readings commonly used in American Lutheran churches, discouraged the use of a lectionary because it neglected the "great facts, truths, and lessons, contained in Holy Writ, especially of those which are most interesting to Christians." While the Apostle's Creed was used at infant Baptism, alternative affirmations of faith were made available for use, and were the only forms used for Confirmation and Adult Baptism.[3]

THE TRADITIONAL LITURGICAL STANDARD

The traditional elements had been a normative part of Lutheran worship in areas under the influence of the Pennsylvania Ministerium from 1748 until after the close of the American Revolution. But what was traditional? Its particular agenda for worship, taken from the liturgy of the German Lutheran congregation in London (St. Marys) known as the London Agenda, and which could be traced back to the Lutheran church in Holland and the Antwerp Agenda of 1567, was itself a conflation of the London Agenda and those liturgies familiar to Muhlenberg and his colleagues. However each could be traced to Melanchthon and the theologians associated with the "Formula" and *Book of Concord*. [4]

The resulting Pennsylvania Agenda was more elaborate than the Protestant liturgy used by nineteenth-century Lutherans. A hymn invoking the Holy Spirit was followed by a confession of sins, an exhortation, the *Kyrie,* the *Gloria in Excelsis*, the Collect, Epistle of the Day, a hymn, the Gospel for the day, the Nicene Creed, a hymn, and the sermon. Next followed The General Prayer (of the Church) with intercessions, and the Lord's Prayer. Announcements, the peace, another hymn, the closing collect with responses, and the Aaronic benediction with Trinitarian invocation concluded the service. The collects and appointed readings were not a part of the Pennsylvania Agenda, but taken from the Marburg hymnal published in Germantown by Christopher Sauer.

A NEW CONFESSIONAL DIRECTION—THE LITURGY OF 1855

By the 1850s however, with the growth of conservative confessionalism in the United States, serious efforts were underway to return to the forms of the Pennsylvania Agenda and to recover the historic expression of Lutheran worship for the American Lutheran church which lay behind it. The repristination of traditional language and practice was not at issue here; the objective was to recover the worship language and faith of the "one holy, catholic and apostolic church" with its ancient and ecumenical creeds, the Lord's Prayer, and the liturgy of the sacraments. Becoming less Protestant and "free" was not the problem, but confessional faithfulness in a church "in which the Gospel is taught purely and the sacraments are administered rightly" (to quote the Augsburg Confession) certainly was.

This was no easy task. The eighteenth-century Pennsylvania Agenda was just that—a brief list of things to be done in worship—but without the details of the liturgy which a congregation could follow. Moreover, it relied for propers on the nonLutheran Marburg Hymnal. The Pennsylvania Agenda was like its predecessors, a listing of liturgical elements with more or less detailed direction for their conduct by the officiating clergy. Most of the agendas revealed the influence of Luther's *Deutsche Messe* (German Mass) of 1526 which the Reformer developed for the worship of laymen in towns and villages. Unlike the more elaborate *Formulae Missae* (of 1523) to be conducted in Latin, the German Mass which was to be conducted in the vernacular included German hymns (a major form of congregational participation) and a simplified celebration of Holy Communion that focused on an exhortation to communicants. Both the *Formulae Missae* and *Deutsche Messe* were stripped of the canon of the mass—the elaborate development of prayers and ritual actions which Luther had come to believe represented a form of works righteousness. In its place he proposed in both liturgies a simple consecration of the bread and wine by use of the *Verba* (Words of Institution) a rite which also included the Lord's Prayer, *Sanctus* and Post-Communion collect. (The Formulae Missae included, in addition, a Preface, Elevation of the elements, and the Peace).[5]

Both the *Formulae Missae* and the *Deutsche Messe*, like the various territorial church orders and agendas based upon them, were only outlines which left texts for the propers to be supplied by the ministers and choirmasters from the ancient office books of the church. They ordered with confessional clarity (rather than replaced) a rich liturgical tradition of prayers, readings, music, ceremony, and vestments. Tragically this religious culture was devastated in German territories most affected by the Thirty Years' War (1618-1648), especially with the destruction of the missals, breviaries, graduals, and other pre-Reformation books which shaped the liturgical outlines. Moreover, as Luther Reed has observed, the War prevented a new generation from being trained in the reformed "liturgical and musical tradition and understanding" of catholic worship. Pietism further undermined formal worship with its emphasis on individual experience and emotions and its neglect of many ancient liturgical forms. Religious rationalism, which followed with the Enlightenment, rejected both the form and content of traditional liturgical worship, all but eliminating it from the practice of worship in German life. Church leaders in Germany and America who would recover the historic liturgy of the church had, therefore, to reconstruct this detailed liturgical culture almost from scratch by adding flesh to the barebones agendas it began working with.[6]

In Germany Wilhelm Loehe, who established a seminary and missionary institute for training clergy for the American church, produced an *Agende fur christliche Gemeinden* in 1844 which institute graduates brought to the United States where it influenced midwestern Lutheran circles (including the Missouri Synod) and the liturgical studies of Charles Porterfield Krauth and Beale Melanchthon Schmucker. Under the leadership of the Ministerium of Pennsylvania and with the cooperation of the New York Ministerium, the Synod of Ohio and the General Synod, a German liturgy was prepared and published in 1855—the Liturgy of 1855—which reintroduced the traditional worship elements, including the Introit, generally in proper order (though the epistle followed the Gospel). A committee of the Ministerium including G. F. Krotel and Schmucker (son of S. S. Schmucker, a stricter confessionalist than his father, and a close student of Lutheran worship) prepared an English edition of the 1855 Liturgy in 1860 entitled *A Liturgy for the Use of the Evangelical Lutheran Church.* Introit and *Gloria Patri* preceded the Confession, which was followed by the Kyrie, Gloria in Excelsis, and the Collect for the Day. The Epistle, Gospel, Creed, Litany, or other General Prayer preceded a hymn and Sermon. The Lord's Prayer, a hymn, and a benediction followed. Throughout congregational responses were introduced or "reintroduced" as the worshipper was reminded in the Preface to the 1855 liturgy: "if we can restore this right to the congregations . . . we shall have essentially contributed towards promoting a well-ordered, living activity in the spirit of our fathers, who were very far from wishing to reduce the people to a condition of mute inaction."[7]

A NEW STANDARD OF WORSHIP—THE *CHURCH BOOK* OF 1868

With the division of eastern Lutheranism into General Council and General Synod by 1868, the General Council would develop a full liturgy with ministerial acts for its congregations. Now with the aid of Charles Porterfield Krauth, a new liturgy was planned—the General Council *Church Book*—which was modeled on the colonial Pennsylvania Agenda with modifications based upon a broader study of sixteenth-century Lutheran liturgies. The principle of historical precedence had been introduced—the oldest elements were to prevail over newer innovations, establishing thereby a basic model for Lutheran liturgy until the middle of the twentieth century. Confession and absolution were to be used, the Introit was to follow the Confession and the Kyrie. The Collects for Sundays were to be replaced by the "old Collects, arranged by festival days and seasons, with general and specific collects to be included for use in Sunday worship. Congregational chanting was encouraged—the Creed itself might even be sung—and congregational responses (also chanted) included the versicles before the Collects, and the "Hallelujah" before the Gospel.[8] Quickly finished, the Church Book was approved at the General Council's 1867 convention and printed for its second convention a year later.

For the first time then in American Lutheran circles the attempt was made to recover the full historic liturgy of the western Church as modified by the Lutheran reformation. The result was a standard of liturgical renewal which "returned the Lutheran Church to the ancient ways of the Church of the West of which Lutheranism had theologically and confessionally always been a part, even when it did not remember it." But using the colonial Pennsylvania Agenda meant more than simply a return to the immediate past or to a tradition committed to a single liturgy for all American Lutherans. Like the colonial Pennsylvania Agenda, the Church Book replaced particular liturgies, indigenous to separate areas of Lutheran Germany, with one, common liturgy. This practice, when based on the best liturgical scholarship and the principle of consensus of particular liturgies, deliberately transcended the provincialism of German church life in favor of a common liturgy for all Lutherans which was (in the words of Luther Reed) "thoroughly American in breadth of view and provision for practical use by the people."[9] The recovery of the traditional Lutheran liturgy was no exercise in nostalgia but a new and concerted effort, in an age of renewed confessionalism, to recover in detail the forms of worship rooted in the historic liturgy which could give modern expression to a confessionally reformed Christian faith. Though based on the traditional liturgies, it was also something new!

THE WASHINGTON LITURGY OF 1869

Throughout this period of new liturgical developments, the General Synod followed in the wake of the General Council and its most advanced district body, the Pennsylvania Ministerium. The General Synod committee charged with liturgical development originally published the English translation of the Pennsylvania Ministerium's pathbreaking Liturgy of 1855 in a pocket edition. With the 1868 restructuring, after the General Council withdrawal, another liturgy was proposed for General Synod congregations which was published in 1869. Taken from the English Liturgy (1860) of the Pennsylvania Ministerium, it had first been proposed to the General Synod in 1862 by Beale Schmucker, but had not been approved at the time. It introduced the *Gloria Patri* after the opening sentences, the *Kyrie* after Confession of Sin and Prayer, and the *Gloria in Excelsis* after the Apostles' Creed, but lacked the Collect and a General Prayer. Nevertheless, the Washington Liturgy represented "the first approximation to anything resembling a historical Order of Service " since the General Synod's organization.[10] However this "Washington Liturgy," named after the meetingplace of the historic 1868 General Synod Convention, also contained elements which represented a partial throwback to a more Protestant service, though important new elements of traditional worship had been introduced into General Synod congregations.

A CONFESSIONAL SHIFT—1875

While the General Council began its life with a satisfactory worship book for its English-speaking congregations—the *Church Book*—the General Synod spent the next decade fruitlessly seeking an alternative to the "Washington Liturgy." This phantom ideal was to include rites for special occasions, the "ordinances" (sacraments of Baptism and Holy Communion), and occasional services. A larger committee was appointed to accomplish the new task. The more important new forms of worship developed by the committee were to be printed in the General Synod periodical—the *Lutheran Observer*—for criticism before final revision. A provisional form of the new liturgy was presented to the General Synod in 1873, but its language proved unsatisfactory and it was never subjected to the kind of public review through its *Observer* as recommended by the General Synod. After further revision, a "cheap edition" was published in 1875 while a copy was sent to the church periodical for publication and criticism. The copy was mysteriously destroyed while in the editorial office, so that the document was not ready for publication until 1877. But in 1879 the results were found unsatisfactory once again and resubmitted to a further-enlarged committee. At every step of the way critical voices prevented a consensus. It might be assumed that this successful opposition to liturgical revision arose among those who resisted change in a more confessional direction. Perhaps so. But there was an equally adamant group who may have found the proposed revisions insufficiently confessional. Apparently such a group had existed since 1875 when it had proposed (unsuccessfully) the creation of a new Lutheran liturgy to replace the Washington Liturgy.[11]

PROPOSAL FOR A COMMON SERVICE—1879

Two centuries previously, Henry Melchior Muhlenberg had entertained the idea of a "Common Service" for Lutheran congregations in America. In 1870 the Rev. Dr. John Bachman, educated and ordained in the New York Ministerium, but for five decades a leader of southern Lutherans, revived the idea by urging it upon the General Synod of the South. The idea of a Common Service was rejected as "not likely to meet with a favorable response from other Lutheran Bodies," but a similar proposal to appoint a committee to cooperate in "preparing a

Service Book" for all three bodies emerged from the 1876 session of the General Synod South and was carried by its delegates to the General Synod and General Council in 1878. At this point the General Synod's beleaguered liturgical committee—stalled in the development of its own common service—was given a momentous directive: they were to correspond with the "Liturgical committee of the General Synod South, and to invite their cooperation in the publication of a Liturgy and a Hymn and Tune Book, with the view that both these general bodies may adopt these books of worship in their churches."[12]

The desire for a Hymn and Tune Book was another indication of powerful currents moving through General Synod and its congregations for the development of genuine Lutheran liturgical practices. A "Hymn and Tune Book" committee had been appointed two years before to explore two questions: 1) "Is there a general demand for such a book?"; and, 2) "Is it financially expedient, at the present time, to undertake to issue it?" What the committee inquiry uncovered was an English-speaking Lutheran church looking with "great anxiety" to the General Synod to provide what they would otherwise have to look for elsewhere. The assumption was that Lutherans were not "unlike" other denominations. Methodists, Presbyterians, Congregationalists, and Baptists not only had similar needs, but those needs could only be met with the publication of new hymnals.

What was "Lutheran" about this new denominational project was summarized in three ways by the committee. A distinguishing characteristic and chief glory of the Lutheran Church was that "she is eminently a singing Church." She had her nativity in a "land of song" among the most "music-loving people in the world" and was marching to victory "by the great hymns" of Luther and his successors. A second consideration was that the new generation of Lutherans would not receive this great inheritance without such a book, but would turn elsewhere for the music to animate Lutherans' joyful worship. Finally, it was an age of music-making "when music, secular and sacred, is more generally cultivated than ever before" and where music reading was taught in secular classrooms as well as in Sunday Schools. Texts alone would no longer do. There was a need for printed music in the church. Unless the General Synod realized this need, there would be a "comparative decline in the joyful service of song."[13]

The beginnings, then, of an inter-Lutheran quest for a fuller liturgy cannot be understood simply as the recovery of traditional texts and practices. It included a revival of both hymnic and liturgical music as well, for music was becoming an important element in a new style of Lutheran worship and piety then emerging in the rapidly changing world of American Lutheranism. The pursuit of a "common service" would logically culminate, therefore, in a Common Service Book with texts and music integrated into a new Lutheran system of worship.

The General Synod Committee on liturgical revival presented its report in 1881, providing the synod with another version of the much revised Washington liturgy and a comment that it was too late to do much by way of cooperation with the General Synod South in a "Common Service Book." A similar committee in the General Synod South communicated a like view to its constituency, having just prepared its own *Book of Worship*. Yet the committee had also found in both General Synods, and in the General Council a "desire for such a Book." While both general synods went forward with their own liturgical enterprises, a committee was nevertheless formed on the basis of this "desire" to include the General Council in a three-way exploration of how feasible a Common Service book might actually be. It was to be based, as the General Council had insisted in 1879, on the "common consent of the pure Lutheran liturgies of the sixteenth century, and when there is not an entire agreement among them the consent of the largest number of greatest weight." Two years later, in 1883, the General Synod agreed that "a common Service for all English-speaking Lutherans" could be developed on the "generic and well-defined basis of the Common consent of the pure Lutheran Liturgies of the 16th century."[14]

This assent opened up a new confessional direction for American Lutherans. The General Synod was just beginning a period of liturgical exploration and doctrinal self-education as it began to pursue the goal of a Common Service Book. Leading the way, fifty-five petitioners requested the 1883 session of the General Synod appoint a new liturgy committee "to prepare an order of service and liturgical forms more in harmony with the doctrine and usages of the Evangelical Lutheran Church than the Liturgy at present authorized by the General Synod." If the petition's appearance was startling so, too, was the General Synod's formal response. The delegates viewed the petition favorably as a "desire for a book more in harmony with historic Lutheran books of worship, and enunciating more clearly the doctrines of the church." It noted the recent action taken to join with the General Synod South and the General Council in preparing a common liturgy. But it also noted that within the General Synod there was no scholarly basis for an outline of such a book. Though no committee could therefore be appointed, the Synod resolved that the Publishing Committee keep on hand a limited supply of the present liturgy, that district synods be asked to develop an "intelligent sentiment" on the subject, and that ministers gifted with "a liturgic spirit . . . and a style of writing characterized by scholarly excellence" develop papers and projects to help inform ministers and people on this subject.[15]

THE COMMON SERVICE OF 1888

Unlike the General Synod, the General Council and General Synod South had seasoned liturgical scholars ready to pursue the creation of a common liturgy in Beale Melanchthon Schmucker and Edward Traill Horn, leaders who had been instrumental in communications on the subject between the two General Synods. In the General Synod of the north the invitation to students of liturgy would bring forward a new generation of liturgical leaders, the most able among them being the New York pastor, George U. Wenner, pastor of Christ Church in Manhattan and a member of the Synod of New York and New Jersey, who would chair the General Synod's liturgical committee from 1883 to 1915.[16]

A committee of six from the three general bodies met in Pastor Horn's study in Charleston, South Carolina during late April of 1884. Schmucker was chosen chair of the committee and Horn the secretary. They, together with Wenner, formed the subcommittee which created the first draft of a common service. There was substantial agreement on the form of the liturgy with the exception of differences about the placement of the Lord's Prayer and Words of Institution. A larger committee was gathered the following May which produced a finished liturgy for submission to the three church bodies. The direction of the liturgy's development went in favor of the General Council because General Synod representatives, though more interested in a "free Service," now willingly accepted the principles of historic Lutheran worship as the basis for a common liturgy.

The results presented no difficulties to the General Council since any changes from its 1870 liturgy had already been anticipated in a later German version. The General Synod, on the other hand, heard a detailed report and argument for historical liturgical forms by its representatives on the joint committee, and a plea that "after so many anxious years of waiting and effort the time has come, when, forgetting the prejudices of the past, we should make a determined and faithful effort to demonstrate to the world the substantial unity of the church." The report was unanimously adopted by the General Synod and the General Synod South, and the original subcommittee was reassembled to provide a finished draft taking into considerations the criticism which had been raised in the three bodies.[17]

Many of the General Synod's suggestions for liturgical diversity were incorporated in the final draft. Rejected, however, were pleas for alternate forms of the confession, the permissive use (in the rubrics) of other prayers than the Collect for the Day, the omission of the proper prefaces in the Communion rite, and the minor responses in the services of Matins and Vespers. None of these differences were very surprising given the General Synod's use of free and general prayer in its worship services and its lack of an elaborate liturgy with responsive forms. One difference remained—whether the Lord's Prayer should be incorporated before or after the Words of Institution in the rite of Holy Communion. Here the committee agreed to disagree and three slightly different services were published in three separate editions. Each appeared in separate hymnals with different occasional services. There were minor variations in text, rubrics, and the position of parts (most notably the Verba and Lord's Prayer), permitting variations of practice in the three general bodies.

With these exceptions, English-speaking Lutherans in the east and south had arrived at an important point of unity—one worship service recognizable to a majority of Lutherans in the United States. For General Synod Lutherans it represented a change from its old *Book of Worship*—a publication with only sixteen pages of liturgical material with a few historical liturgical elements arranged in an "unhistorical order," and with no provision for historical Introits, Collects, Epistles, and Gospels, or a rite of Holy Communion with a proper liturgical order. Despite such differences, as the "Preface" to the Common Service noted, the Liturgy of 1888 had received the approval of the three bodies "with a remarkable unanimity. There seems to be a strong desire for this bond of union," it was noted; "a general wish for the restoration of the pure Services of our Fathers; a hearty consent to the principles which ruled them in their revision of the old Services; a longing for unity in the services of worship between all believers; and a conviction that a historic Service furnishes the only basis of such agreement."[18]

CONFESSIONAL DIALOGUE

Joint efforts to develop a Common Liturgy had opened up other opportunities for cooperation between the three general bodies of eastern Lutherans, and for a theological dialogue about other confessional matters. Besides the Common Liturgy, this dialogue could be considered the second major force for eventual unity at work among Lutherans in the east and south.

THE FREE DIETS OF 1877 AND 1878

At the time it was wrestling with its liturgical future in the 1870s, the General Synod proposed (in 1873) through its president, Henry Pohlman, the exchange of fraternal delegates with the General Council. That body, increasingly concerned about altar and pulpit fellowship, rejected the offered hand of fellowship. Such an exchange would evade and ignore "the important points upon which we differ," implying a formal recognition of each other's confessional position when in reality "each body at heart condemns the position of the other." Instead, the General Council proposed the holding of a Colloquium "for comparison of views" regarding the Augsburg Confession. At the time the invitation was rejected by a majority of the General Synod delegates. Under the circumstances there was nothing to talk about. A minority, however, led by Gettysburg Seminary Professor Edmund Jacob Wolf and New York Pastor George U. Wenner, reluctantly called for such a conference in obedience "to the fundamental and historical principles of the General Synod." With no formal agreement for a Colloquium, members of the two church bodies met instead to hold two Free Diets at Philadelphia in 1877 and 1878 for discussion of questions on Lutheran faith and on Lutheran attitudes towards other denominations. Predictably, the meetings were marred by old animosities and suspicions.[19]

Organized by Henry Eyster Jacobs (1844-1932), a young historian and theologian educated at Gettysburg College and Seminary, who had recently returned to teach at the College, the First Diet opened with a paper by John G. Morris, of Baltimore, on "The Augsburg Confession and the Thirty-Nine Articles of the Anglican Church." The purpose of this historical background was to demonstrate that the "Augsburg Confession is the doctrinal *magna charta* of all Protestantdom." Like the great charter of liberties wrested from King John in 1215, which is the basis of free governments and free nations, the Confession has been the basis for all Formulas of Faith since written by Protestant churches.[20]

Charles Porterfield Krauth was the lighting rod of the first and most important gathering. He followed Morris with "The Relations of the Lutheran Church to the Denominations Around Us." Following up on his own written work of long duration, he carefully analyzed the American religious scene in terms of denominationalism. A denomination he defied as "a class or collection of individuals, called by the same name; a body of persons who have separated, or are separate from others, in virtue of their holding in common some special doctrine, or set of doctrines, or government, or usage, or discipline." The word is preferable to the term "sect" or "schism," he continued, as simply stating a fact without expressing judgment. But judge he did. The denomination had no right to exist, in his view, apart from the principle on which it vindicated its "right to exist." He distinguished therefore between those "primary forms of Protestantism" which separated from Rome, and those which continued the process of division and subdivision. The former were Protestants who remained steadfast to those principles and others who "desert the principles which gave them name." This "system of denominationalism," Krauth argued, was inaugurated by the writings and acts of Carlstadt and Zwingli. The Lutheran church, on the other hand, had established a relationship "*de jure*" (by right) with the denominations, claiming her right to exist because she was Biblical, confessional and historical. Scripture is her rule of faith and her confession the "whole truth of God," while her history "proves her divine origin and necessity."[21]

The Krauth essay was a well-reasoned piece of work, incisive in its presentation of Lutheran claims to uniqueness, and a brilliant interpretation of American denominationalism and the American Lutheran place within it. As the Reformer of Roman Catholicism the Lutheran Church was the primary Protestant body with legitimate scriptural, confessional, and historical bases for existence. Denominationalism, to the contrary, was a schismatic breakdown of this reformation unity. It was clear from the remarks which followed, that the paper and approach also managed to expose the differences in understanding between the General Council and General Synod views on Lutheranism and American denominationalism

F. W. Conrad, from the General Synod insisted that Luther maintained the supreme authority of Scriptures, and claimed the right of private judgment in interpreting them. He held a very different view on denomination. The liberty conferred by Christ on every believer to form religious opinions may be seen as their origin. "Various denominations have arisen, in the providence of God, in different ages and lands. They constitute the pure parts of the one holy catholic Church." J. A. Brown, S. S. Schmucker's successor at Gettysburg Seminary, paid close attention to Krauth's language. "The denominations around us" suggest that they are nothing more than simply denominations. The Lutheran Church to the contrary "has claims as a Church of Jesus Christ, which cannot be accorded to these denominations."

Setting up such a claim, for Brown, as for Conrad, ignored God's providential dealings with this church. It followed that the limitations on pulpit and altar fellowship that Krauth was promoting, were likewise objectionable. Other denominations are also "true Evangelical Churches." Therefore "who are we that we should undertake to legislate and prescribe the terms on which we will recognize" them? Krauth answered in rejoinder that "the Lutheran Church is not coordinated as one denomination with others. Her moral right to live turns upon the proof that she is a Church with the New Testament essentials—doctrine pure in every part, and right sacraments." Those who cut themselves off from her and erect "hostile denominations" reject her truth and in doing so "are heretics or errorists." It is "no fault of ours" that they have raised "sectarian banners." "We did not go out from them. They have gone away from us, or have followed those who abandoned us." Brown, he continued, claims for them the right to "forsake us," to "repudiate our distinctive faith," and yet to live by untested principles as children of the Reformation.

As Krauth observed elsewhere in the three-day dialogue, the "Augsburg Confession offers a point of union for divided Protestantism, but union will be effected" neither by changes in its meanings, nor by changing the sense in which it was first written.[22]

What the theologians could not achieve by their systematic inquiry, a historian and theologian began to accomplish by a careful survey of the kinds of convergencies noted in this study. Henry Eyster Jacob's paper on "The History and Progress of the Lutheran Church in the

United States" was valuable precisely because it demonstrated the convergence that had taken place among Lutherans in the last quarter century since the Civil War. The whole church had made "great progress" in "fuller acquaintance, higher appreciation and heartier acceptance of the theology of the Reformation." This was to be seen in the General Council, the General Synod, and the General Synod South as well as in synods and seminaries. "A leaven is working," he insisted, "slowly it may be, yet none the less surely" which encourages hope "that in the not very remote future we may be able to apply ourselves with greater harmony to the great work before us in this country." The greatest danger, meanwhile, lies in impatience that the progress is not rapid enough."[23]

THE PARAMETERS OF CONVERGENCE

The differing perceptions, entrenched positions, unresolved issues (like the General Synod's acceptance of the Franckean Synod which precipitated the General Synod-General Council division) and personal animosities (Brown vs. Krauth) expressed in the two Free Diets indicated that reconciliation and merger were still very much a thing of the future.

While the General Council was slow to promote inter-Lutheran unity, but quick to lead it in a confessional direction, the General Synod was slow in its own confessional development but quick to promote unity. It was, in a sense, animated by an doubly anachronistic ecumenical spirit—its panProtestant aspirations inherited from an earlier era were out of touch with the realities of a new era in which, as Martin Marty has recently observed, increased denominational differentiation (what Krauth was himself unwittingly promoting) was the only thing that could provide "religious identities and meaning in a corrosive climate" influencing America in the latter part of the nineteenth century. Yet its hopes for a Protestant union were idealistically premature. While preparing a Common Service with the General Council and the General Synod South, it was also negotiating potential mergers with both the Reformed Church in the U. S. and the Cumberland Presbyterian Church, and with the latter because the two bodies were "as one in doctrine"![24]

The Lutheran architect who could build a genuine church body in such circumstances had already appeared however. Henry Eyster Jacobs, who eventually inherited an ailing Krauth's mantle and teaching position at Mt. Airy, would be the theologian to preside over the convergence. He had the time and patience to await the slowly maturing confessionalism within the church and the acumen to urge it along at just the right moment. In the meantime, however, others in attendance agreed with Jacobs that cooperative effort was now possible. The first fruit of this new cooperation was the Common Service.

THE FREE CONFERENCES OF 1898, 1902, AND 1904

The Common Service created the circumstances for cooperation in other areas by the middle 1890s, most notably in the coordination of home mission efforts to avoid unnecessary overlap of mission fields. In this changing environment renewed efforts were made at further dialogue. A persistent United Synod of the South and its predecessors had been pushing for fraternal relations with the General Council since the middle 1870s, and it was out of these efforts that the General Council responded, first with an agreement to exchange delegates and then with a proposal for exchanging viewpoints in a General Conference. The resulting three free conferences of northeastern Lutheran leaders were organized in 1898, 1902, and 1904. Dissimilar to the two free Diets held in 1877 and 1878, the Conferences were not only composed of official representatives from the General Council, the General Synod, and the United Synod of the South, but were marked by a spirit of courteous dialogue. Of these, the gatherings held in 1898 and 1902 were most important, for they profitably explored the praxis and beliefs of American Lutherans. By the 1890s and with the experience of cooperation on the Common Service, the General Synod, the General Council, and the United Synod of the South had begun exchanging fraternal delegates once again. In 1895, at a General Council meeting at Easton, Pa., it was resolved in response to an invitation by the General Synod to hold a General Conference in an "unofficial way" to compare notes on the various doctrinal, liturgical, educational, and missionary interests "in which all are alike engaged."[25]

Jacobs, now of the Philadelphia Seminary, addressed the assembly ably setting the stage for the discussion to follow. He invoked the shared tradition of Henry Melchior Muhlenberg in briefly remembering the history of responsible confessionalism in America insisting that the assembled conferees were not there "for the purpose of projecting any plans for the ultimate unification of the Church" nor to debate past differences. Instead the group was there "to treat of the great principles we profess to hold in common, to descend beneath the surface to the foundations upon which they rest, and then again to rise to a proper conception of their manifold relations and far-reaching consequences." Present lines of church organization, adequate though they are for the efficient administration of church work, are inadequate as limits to "the interest which, as Christians and particularly as Lutheran Christians, we take in each other's life and progress." Jacobs was pointing to joint liturgical reform and a newly developed board of arbitration to adjudicate differences over mission development, to a fraternal exchange of delegates and a common support of deaconesses. Also at issue was the possibility of union itself. Inviting cooperation, the General Synod recognized the General Council as a Lutheran body. Accepting the invitation to a Conference, the General Council, however, indicated that it was bound by its Fundamental Principles regarding the General Synod's confessional basis, "properly interpreted, as not inconsistent with these principles." The time had come, then, to gather "in the fear of God to meet the issues that our calling demands; and to learn, by a comparison of judgments, where we are and whither Providence directs us."[26]

Though many issues were addressed in the first gathering, for our purposes the first two essays on "our Common Historical Antecedents" provide revealing glimpses into the mindset of convergence among northeastern Lutherans by 1900. The first was by Edmund Jacob Wolf, professor of Church History at Gettysburg Seminary, and author of a popular General Synod history whose *The Lutherans in America* (1889) was credited with shaping a common identity among American Lutherans. For Wolf, the General Synod was valued as a conserving force in the midst of a more liberal Protestant pluralism which acknowledged a need for (in Wolf's words) "a constant growth of Confessional and Churchly sentiment." From the General Council side, the second essayist Pastor John Nicum, president and professor of Wagner College (Rochester, New York) detailed the early orthodoxy of Muhlenberg Lutheranism and that of the early New York church, a subject familiar to him from having recently written a history of the New York Ministerium. For him the "almost universal" repudiation of S. S. Schmucker's "Definite Platform" and the American Recension of the Augsburg Confession "powerfully strengthened the cause of conservative Lutheranism in the East" with the happy result that with a fuller appreciation of the doctrines of the church "we understand each other better to-day than ever before." "Forming a closer union," he argued is possible therefore where Lutherans are faithful to their confessional heritage. Departure from the "faith of the fathers" has the opposite effect. Thus only "upon the basis of a healthy and evangelical confessionalism can a true union of the Lutheran Church be attained and maintained."[27]

Meanwhile Pastor Michael Wolf Hamma, president of the General Synod, spoke of the future and "The Problem of Co-Operation" among "the three synodical bodies." He provided details of the cooperative arrangements between the General Synod and the General Council in home and foreign missions, and bipartisan journalism, which Hamma clearly considered a "Providential movement, that . . . demands our most serious and thoughtful attention." He emphasized measures for the "practical unification of our glorious Church," noting in the language of the concords that these were to be considered a "sacred compact between the parties consenting thereto." The term "practically united" was used to distinguish the nature of this cooperative effort from "organically united" which was "not a distinct object of this movement." Despite this proviso, repeated often by many participants at the first conference, anticipations of a closer union were in the air. And a successful formula for merger was all but spelled out by Hamma, a practical formula which would be used time and again in the decades to follow: cooperation in practical matters led the way to a merger of doctrinal differences. United effort and common praxis created a solidarity of purpose which required abandoning old confessional formulations in favor of new ones which more adequately expressed the common faith of coworkers. Moreover, Hamma sensed a "historically orthodox majority" in all three bodies—a large majority to judge by the votes for cooperative efforts—is now in a position to lead American Lutherans in the "high and holy cause" of cooperation. Noting the convergence which can be permitted to occur "if Patience is permitted 'to have her perfect work'," influences were at work in the church "bearing all things towards a common center" before which all these old obstacles will become as the thin air and will some day ensphere and solidify the Lutheran Church now in fragments."[28]

Again in 1902 Hamma focused on theological matters as did the conference itself: "The mission of the Lutheran Church to the Twentieth Century is the theme of this discourse and the engaging consideration of the hour." What Lutherans might offer the twentieth century was "to contend with renewed earnestness for the absolute supremacy of the sacred Scriptures." Another offering was "to teach with renewed insistence the Permanence and Realism of the Fundamental Doctrines of Christianity as re-established in the Lutheran Reformation;" a third was "to preach a religion of Education and Intelligence as over against the superficial, the emotional, and the sentimental." Jacobs, meanwhile, offered a masterful statement bringing together the two sides in the most contentious dispute of the second conference—an exchange on Baptism between James W. Richards, Gettysburg Seminary Professor in responses to L. E. Busby's survey of "The Lutheran Doctrine of the Sacraments." Jacobs expressed regrets that more time could not be given the discussion since "We have reached a point where we can candidly express and treat of our differences with dispassionateness and respect for one another." Arguing that "the difference between us on this subject is not as great as may at first appear," he recalled the Wittenberg Concord "on Baptism" between Luther and Martin Bucer in 1536 when Luther had observed of faith that it is not lost in sleep and rebestowed upon waking. The conscious exercise of faith is not essential to its presence, Jacobs observed. And though it cannot be imagined that infants understand, nevertheless there are movements and inclinations "to believe Christ and love God" that are "in a measure like the movements of faith and love."[29]

By the turn of the century General Synod and General Council seriously engaged in exploring and developing a confessionally-based faith though sacramental questions—especially the efficacy of infant Baptism—still were the subject of intense discussion. The three

Conferences began a process of theological convergence which brought northeastern Lutherans closer to one another and to a time of merger. The process gave further exposure to Jacobs who emerged by their end as the theologian of convergence. But it was Hamma, perhaps, who best glimpsed the historic nature of what was taking place. A new process was at work in a religious denomination in a democratic culture in which common tasks developed common interests and a capacity for transcending older doctrinal formulations for the sake of new, more comprehensive and more adequate confessional statements of faith. This growing ability to become more inclusive with an enlarged perspective and with a more comprehensive and complex set of shared interests would within several decades be identified by the American philosopher, John Dewey, as at the heart of pragmatic thinking in a democratic society. This need in an age of religious pluralism to so act and think as to transcend particular and concrete (though limited and limiting) religious realities for the sake of something more adequately comprehensive Dewey would identify as at the very heart of life and education in a democratic society, a perspective that since has offered tantalizing possibilities for doing theology in a pluralistic context.[30] For such was the difference between the Free Diets and the Free Conferences that by the beginning of the twentieth century eastern Lutheran leaders had at last developed the skills necessary to the accomplishment of a major merger of different confessional outlooks and interests.

THE LAITY—A FORCE FOR UNITY

A third force for unity were the Lutheran laity who emerged as a significant organizing force within urban Lutheranism. This was evident with the Quadricentennial of Luther's birthday (1883), a significant turning point in the fortunes of a common Lutheran identity. Preparations for the celebration—which were held in various public halls in New York City—drew the attention of the local newspapers. Meetings in Steinway Hall and the Academy of Music brought Lutherans to public attention and gave to laity the opportunity of seeing in this public recognition and in the size of their gatherings, a Lutheran presence in New York hitherto undreamed of. Held in Manhattan, Lutherans newly moved to the suburbs—the as yet unincorporated boroughs of the Bronx, Richmond, Brooklyn and Queens—returned along elevated train lines and across the Brooklyn Bridge for the public events and learned something of church growth as well. The impact was especially great on the young, who growing up in suburban homes and inclined to leave a German-speaking church behind them, now "began to take an active interest in church questions and in church extension."[31] By 1883 then, the hoped-for crossover from German- to English-speaking Lutheranism, for which New York's Pastors Krotel and Wenner (themselves prominent in the growing work of convergence) had so long worked, was beginning to have its desired effect.

More puzzling than compelling were the apparent divisions among Lutherans which public exposure highlighted. Those sitting in the pews could not always understand their origins or the reasons for their continuance. The Quadricentennial led directly to the formation of the Martin Luther Society in New York in 1883, for an inter-Lutheran organizing body was required to prepare for the Quadricentennial itself. The Society's purpose was stated for area pastors in a circular letter:

> In view of the efforts made all around us to bring about a closer and more harmonious relation between the various Protestant denominations, the Martin Luther Society of the City of New York respectfully begs you to consider whether the time has not come to make an effort to bring about, if not a union, at least a better understanding and more fraternal intercourse between the Lutherans themselves. We all deplore the divisions that separate us; we believe that the reasons for these divisions are more imaginary than real, and we are persuaded that a free and frank interchange of opinions will materially help to remove whatever obstacles may be in the way.[32]

Like the Lutheran Social Union of Philadelphia, the Luther Society of New York represented an important new force for convergence among Lutherans in the northeast.[33] Differences, liturgical and confessional, with which church leaders had wrestled for generations, and which sometimes seemed insurmountable, now appeared "more imaginary than real" to an increasingly skeptical and impatient laity. This emerging viewpoint would prove decisive in future negotiations on unity. As we shall see, at crucial points lay organizations would intervene in stalled merger negotiations of the ULCA and the United Lutheran Synod of New York and New England, providing the necessary impetus to bring negotiations for merger to a necessary conclusion.

The year 1883 marked the development of the first such lay organizations. Others would follow, including the formation of The Luther League in New York City five years later. Its purpose was to rally and train young people in the various area-Lutheran synods for the support and service of the church. Beginning in the metropolitan area, the League slowly spread out among Lutheran churches in the state. The Synod of New York and New Jersey endorsed the organization in 1892, and in the following year encouraged its organization in all Synod congregations. The Hartwick Synod meanwhile created a standing committee on young peoples' societies and work in 1898. It is not clear whether the groups formed under its auspices were affiliated with the Luther League, but the results—increased loyalty and usefulness to the church—indicated a similar kind of organization. The Franckean Synod also heartily endorsed young peoples' societies, largely because of the church's failure to "utilize all her members" despite Sunday school missionary societies and young men's and women's Christian Associations. This most Protestant of the synods favored Christian Endeavor, an older Protestant organization developed in the 1880s, because of its proven ability to reach young people, but it was quick to add that such an organization "need not conflict with the Luther League."[34]

The extent to which such organizations united Lutherans in a common bond can easily be overestimated. Yet they indicate that Lutheran synodical bodies were not impervious to intersynodical organizations like the Luther Society, the Luther League, the Women's Home and Missionary Society, or to the Layman's Missionary Movement and the Lutheran Brotherhood when these two organizations appeared and became active in the area during the second decade of the twentieth century.

THE LIMITS OF CONVERGENCE

Despite major forces for unity at work among northeast Lutherans, there were limits to whatever Lutheran consensus was emerging. A sense of direction is important to understanding these limitations. The eventual merger of Lutheran bodies in the east resulted from all groups moving in a more confessional direction which simultaneously diminished intra-Lutheran differences while differentiating Lutherans from other Christian denominations. Convergence was limited to the extent that Lutheran bodies were moving in a non-confessional direction that would bring them closer, theologically, to other Protestant bodies, even as they gave up the distinctive expressions of their own theological heritage. While there were confessionally committed Lutherans in all three general bodies, it was therefore the longstanding agenda of the General Council which would prevail at merger—the establishment of a sound confessional foundation for a larger Lutheran body—not the somewhat indiscriminate compulsive unity of the General Synod towards Lutherans and other Protestants which would need to prevail.

It was the General Synod, therefore, which would have to grow in its Lutheran identity if merger was to occur. There were significant signs of change within that body. In 1895, the General Synod explicitly designated the unaltered Augsburg Confession as its doctrinal standard; six years later (1901) the General Synod dropped its troubling distinction between the fundamental and nonfundamental doctrines of that Confession. However, its leading theologians resisted the idea that subscription to the entire *Book of Concord* was essential to responsible Lutheranism. In particular they resisted subscribing to the fine distinctions of the "Formula of Concord," regarding them (incorrectly) as nothing more than efforts by one party of sixteenth-century Lutherans to destroy the influence of the other party, especially the theological perspective of Philip Melanchthon. In 1908 Henry E. Jacobs as the General Council's fraternal delegate to the General Synod would lay the conservative body's confessional misgivings before the more liberal group, indicating that a closer relationship between the two depended upon further confessional concessions.[35]

THE THIRTY YEARS' WAR IS OVER

The General Council was correct in its assessment of the General Synod. The reception of the Common Service—the most important indicator of a confessional outlook in either church body—within the General Synod and its synods in the greater New York area, indicate the very real limits to a common Lutheranism in its pews. Despite its acceptance of the Common Service of 1888, the General Synod's 1890 edition of its *Book of Worship* was published with both the "Washington Liturgy" of 1869 and the "Common Service" of 1888, arranged in chronological order. Preferred usage depended upon the worship leader's historical viewpoint—whether your religious identity looked to a Protestant past or a Lutheran future. Such an arrangement was reported upon favorably back home by the Franckean Synod delegate to the 1890 meeting of the General Synod; he also reported a good deal of debate over the Common Service, "some wise and some otherwise."[36] The New York and New Jersey delegate to the 1891 gathering of the general body reported continued controversy in the parent body over use of a common service. Its 1890 support for a common service and authorization of its use was reaffirmed in 1891:

> By this the Common Service retains the place unanimously given it at successive General Synods as the consensus of the various historical orders of the Lutheran Church, while congregations are left entirely free to use it as a whole or in part, or the old order, or none at all. Nevertheless the General Synod recommends the use of the Lutheran Service.[37]

It was further noted that such a position reflected the New York and New Jersey Synod's own stance against further agitation about the use of a Common Service, a fact attested to by the synod's united vote on behalf of the Common Service at the national meeting. The following year the same synod also went on record, affirming the historical character of the Common Service, and urging upon pastors the duty of using "all judicious and temperate means for its peaceable introduction." It also decided to use its regular and occasional services on synodical worship occasions.[38]

A decade later, in 1903, a delegate from the General Synod convention reported that the secondary divisions and accompanying prejudices that have existed in the General Synod are surely dying

> out, and that not by denominational indifference, but by the growth of a positive Lutheranism. The Common Service was used at all the services of the convention, and all parties gave indications of coming together in one Lutheran faith and in common Lutheran usage and practice.[39]

Nor could it "escape notice" that "the greater ratio of advance in the General Synod of late" was "synchronized with this growth in churchly usages and in appreciation of the historic worship and ritual of our Church." Whether one could actually make a case for church growth and the growth of a liturgical tradition going hand in hand, it was clear that an increasing historic awareness was no impediment to mission.[40]

Two years later (1905) another delegate reported that a colleague who had attended both the 1875 meeting of the General Synod, and the present gathering believed that the "Thirty Years' War" over liturgical renewal in the parent body was finally over. In 1875 the effort to substitute a Lutheran Liturgy for a Protestant one proposed by the liturgical committee had been unsuccessful. After thirty years of "Liturgical unrest," the General Synod at long last had "rendered the Common Service with a correctness and dignity which were edifying and impressive." As important, the thirty years had seen an advance "not only in the knowledge of our distinctive forms of worship, but also in the comprehension of those underlying principles and doctrines which differentiate us from other denominations and assigning to us a legitimate place in the work of 'the holy catholic church.'"[41]

THE PERSISTENCE OF LITURGICAL PLURALISM

While such optimism was justified at the national level, local practice left much to be desired. One of the principal architects of the Common Service, Pastor George U. Wenner, having been elected president of the Synod of New York and New Jersey for 1908, took the occasion to comment upon local usage. Noting the hope for the Common Service—that it would prove "to be not only a fitting mode of worship, but also a valuable bond of union among the separate branches of our Church"—he commented upon progress in the New York area since the synod's unequivocal affirmation of the Common Service in 1892. Much had been accomplished, especially at the national level. But congregational practice was "discouraging." German churches were using "the remnants of their inheritance from a score of German principalities, combined with selections from American Orders, that have long since been relegated to liturgical antiquaria." In addition pastors have added their own favorite practices "so that we have a veritable Joseph's coat of many colors—wonderful, at least, if not beautiful." Meanwhile, many English congregations continued using the Washington Liturgy adopted fifty years ago, while others use a combination of this liturgy and the

Common Service, a "hybrid production," also "wonderful to behold." In mistaken "Christian liberty" additions and alterations in the "form and substance" of the Service have been introduced, while rubrics are understood (as in the definition of one parochial school child) to be a "religious rule that can be stretched or twisted." The result is a most "uncommon Service" with sixty variations in sixty congregations.[42]

No such assessment can be made of the Hartwick and Franckean members of the General Synod, because no similar concern for the fate of the Common Service can be found in the minutes of either Synod. The Franckeans' favorable comment on the worship options provided by the General Synod in 1890 indicate their somewhat eclectic, Protestant outlook. It is probably safe to assume the multiple usages of the "uncommon Service" throughout New York-area General Synod congregations in the first decade of the twentieth century. Certainly the numerous reports on the State of Religion in the Hartwick and Franckean Synods do *not* indicate that the health or spiritual sickness of its congregations was in any way tied to the usage of the Common Service or accepted liturgical practice. Instead one must look to a time beyond the merger of 1908 in which one synod, dominated by the numerically larger Synod of New York and New Jersey, would move General Synod Lutheranism in New York onto a course of convergence with the synods and liturgical practices of the area's General Council congregations.

The multiplicity of liturgical practices which Wenner found (ironically of course) too "wonderful to behold" had it defenders as well as detractors however. A significant part of the Thirty Years' War over the Common Service involved an important theological skirmish between Wenner and Gettysburg Seminary theologian James W. Richards. Wenner argued that for corporate worship to be confessional it must subscribe to the liturgical forms and practices of the Common Service. Richard argued, to the contrary, that it was the doctrine to be found in various forms and orders, not the consensus of forms, that determined true Lutheran worship, a position which made considerable allowances for local conditions and customs so long as the doctrinal content of liturgical forms was pure. Accordingly Richards insisted upon "the law of liturgical adaptation" as cardinal to congregational worship. If Wenner argued for *uniformity* by usage of a common liturgy that transcended particular liturgies and the provincialism of religious life, Richards made a case for *diversity* and adaptation to local customs, language and circumstances. In doing so he lifted up a commitment to principles he believed to be enunciated by Luther—moderate conservatism, simplicity, an emphasis on the Word, and the principle of Christian freedom in ordering liturgical life.[43]

What elicited Wenner's scorn would have received Richards's approbation. Together they raised enduring issues and a creative tension regarding liturgical development and practice among American Lutherans that persist at the end of the twentieth century—the role and value of historical research, the relationship between doctrine and worship, and a contextualization of worship as liturgy that reflects contemporary and indigenous experience on the one hand, and a catholic and ecumenical sense of what worship is about on the other.[44] If convergence had its limits, it also had its irreducible divergencies.

NOTES

1 The United Synod of the South was formed in 1886 through a merger of the General Synod South, and the Holston and Tennessee Synods.

2 R. Morris Smith, "The General Synod." R. Morris Smith, ed., "Special Liturgical Section—Liturgical Developments within the Evangelical Lutheran Church in the United States," *LCR* XXXVI (1917): IV, 482 ff. See also Luther D. Reed, *The Lutheran Liturgy. A Study of the Common Liturgy of the Lutheran Church in America* (Philadelphia: Fortress Press, 1947), 175, 171. R. Morris Smith, "The Liturgical Development of the General Synod of the Evangelical Lutheran Church in the United States," *LQ* XLVII (1917): 493-496; Smith, "The General Synod," 483-485. J. A. Weyl, "Ministerium of New York," in Smith, ed., "Special Liturgical Section," 476.

3 New York Ministerium, *A Liturgy*, 1 ff, 36, 41-51. See also Harry J. Kreider, *History of the United Lutheran Synod of New York and New England. Volume I: 1786-1860* (Philadelphia: Muhlenberg Press, 1954), 172.

4 Reed, *Lutheran Liturgy*, 162-169; the Pennsylvania Agenda can be found in General Council, *Documentary History of the Evangelical Lutheran Ministerium of Pennsylvania and Adjacent States* (Philadelphia: General Council Board of Publication, 1898), 15-16.

5 Reed, *Lutheran Liturgy*, 92; 73, 77. See Bard Thompson, ed., *Liturgies of the Western Church* (New York: World Publishing, 1961), Ch. IV, "Martin Luther, Formula Missae and Deutsche Messe," 95-140.

6 Ibid., 92, 143-48.

7 Ibid., 153, 172-3; a copy of the liturgical outline can be found in Kreider, *History of the United Lutheran Synod*, 175. Smith, "The Pennsylvania Ministerium," 473.

8 General Council, *Documentary History*, 417-18. Reed, *Lutheran Liturgy*, 179-80. Philip H. and Carlos R. Messerli Pfatteicher, *Manual on the Liturgy —Lutheran Book of Worship* (Minneapolis: Augsburg Publishing House, 1979), 3.

9 Philip H. Pfatteicher, *Commentary on the Lutheran Book of Worship*, (Minneapolis: Augsburg Fortress, 1990), xv. Reed, *Lutheran Liturgy*, 194.

10 Ibid., 174-5; a copy is to be found in General Synod, *Minutes* (1869), 35-6. R. Morris Smith, The General Synod," R. Morris Smith, ed., "Special Liturgical Section—Liturgical Developments within the Evangelical Lutheran Church in the United States," *LCR* XXXVI (1917): 488.

11 General Synod, *Minutes* (1875), 27; (1877), 43; (1879), 9, 15, 35, 38-9.

Synod of New York and New Jersey, *Minutes* (1905), 29.

12 Luther D. Reed, "Historical Sketch of the Common Service," in R. Morris Smith ,ed., "Special Liturgical Section—Liturgical Developments Within the Evangelical Lutheran Church in the United States," *LCR* XXXVI (1917): 501-502. General Synod, *Minutes* (1871), 23, 34, 43; (1873), 40; (1875), 27; (1877), 43; (1879), 9, 15, 35, 38-9.

13 Ibid. (1879), 27.

14 Ibid. (1881), 15, 48, 51; (1883), 16-17, 32, 47. Reed, *Lutheran Liturgy,* 182.

15 General Synod, *Minutes* (1883), 32, 47.

16 [Knubel, Frederick H.] Remarks "Read at memorial service at Concordia, December 17, 1934." MNYS, SP 1, George U. Wenner. Documentary History Committee, "Obituary Entitled Wenner, George Unangst," *The Lutheran* (To be published November 17 & 22, 1934): MNYS, SP 1, George U. Wenner.

17 Ibid. (1885), 15-22.

18 Reed, *Lutheran Liturgy,* 187–90. Richard C. Wolf, ed., *Documents of Lutheran Unity in America* (Philadelphia: Fortress Press, 1966), 111.

19 General Synod, *Minutes* (1875), 29-32. Documents pertinent to the development of the Free Lutheran Diets of 1877 and 1878 can be found in Richard C. Wolf, *Documents,* 246-252. Wolf provides the copy of an 1874 affirmative response of the General Synod, but not of the 1875 rejection of the proposal for a Colloquium by that body. Eugene L Fevold, "Coming of Age, 1875-1900," *The Lutherans in North America,* ed. E. Clifford Nelson (Philadelphia: Fortress Press, 1975), 310, 373. See Henry Eyster Jacobs, ed., *First Free Lutheran Diet in America, 1877* (Philadelphia: J. F. Smith, 1878); *Second Free Lutheran Diet, 1878* (Philadelphia: Lutheran Publication Society, 1879).

20 Jacobs, *First Free Lutheran Diet,* 15.

21 Ibid., 27. C. P. Krauth, "The Relations of the Lutheran Church to the Denominations Around Us," Jacobs, *First Free Lutheran Diet,* 27-69.

22 Ibid., 70-75, 77, 79, 237.

23 H. E. Jacobs, "The History and Progress of the Lutheran Church in the United States," in Jacobs, Ibid., 130-31.

24 Martin E Marty, *The Irony of It All. 1893-1919, Modern American Religion* (Chicago: University of Chicago Press, 1986), 156. General Synod, *Minutes* (1881), 52, 50.

25 Wolf, *Documents,* 259-266. *The First General Conference of Lutherans in America Held in Philadelphia, December 27-29, 1898* (Philadelphia: 1899), 9; *The Second General Conference of Lutherans in America Held in Philadelphia, April 1-3, 1902* (Newberry, S. C.: Lutheran Publication Board, 1904).

26 Ibid. 30-34.

27 Abdel Ross Wentz, *A Basic History of Lutheranism in America* (Philadelphia: Muhlenberg Press, 1955), 280. See John Nicum, *Geschichte des Evangelisch-Lutherischen Ministeriums von Staate New York und angrenzenden Staaten und Landern* (Reading: 1888). *First General Conference,* 63-80.

28 Ibid., 297-299, 303-307.

29 *Second General Conference,* 5-16, 100-106, 114-119.

30 See Jerome Paul Soneson, *Pragmatism and Pluralism. John Dewey's*

Significance for Theology, Harvard Dissertations in Religion, ed. Bernadette J. & Francis Schussler Fiorenza Brooten. (Minneapolis: Fortress Press, 1993), 30, esp.. 87-91, and Chapter 6.

31 George U. Wenner, *The Lutherans of New York* (New York: The Petersfield Press, 1918), 49.

32 Ibid., 50.

33 Eugene L Fevold, "Coming of Age, 1875-1900," *The Lutherans in North America,* ed. E. Clifford Nelson (Philadelphia: Fortress Press, 1975), 373ff.

34 Wenner, *Lutherans of New York,* 51. Synod of New York and New Jersey, *Minutes* (1892), 26; (1893), 28. Hartwick Synod, *Minutes* (1897), 12; (1898), 13; (1902), 25-6. Franckean Synod, *Journal* (1891), 9; (1892), 13; (1896), 20.

35 Fred W. Meuser, "Facing the Twentieth Century. 1900-1930," *Lutherans in North America*, 374-5.

36 Synod of New York and New Jersey, *Minutes* (1881), 52, 50; Franckean Synod, *Journal* (1890), 15.

37 Synod of New York and New Jersey, *Minutes* (1891), 19.

38 Ibid. (1892), 20.

39 Ibid. (1903), 19.

40 Ibid., 19.

41 Ibid. (1905), 29.

42 Ibid. (1907), 17.

43 Michael B. Aune, "The Corporate and Confession Character of Worship: The Common Service Debate," *Word and World* VIII. Winter, No. 1 (1988): 32-41, see esp. 35.

44 Ibid., 38. Michael B. Aune of Pacific Lutheran Theological Seminary has helpfully identified the enduring questions and issues to be found in the Wenner/Richards debate.

10
A NECESSARY MERGER
Forming the Synod of New York, 1890-1910

The time-table of merger in New York—1901 to 1908—shows how closely restructuring paralleled the growth of modern American life and culture. The effects of urbanization, more and more apparent to Lutherans by the mid-1880s, became a powerful matrix of change by the beginning of the twentieth century. Merger seemed like a good idea in 1888; by 1908 it was essential. The need for closer organization and cooperation among synods whose antebellum scale of operations was inadequate to life in industrial America was painfully apparent after 1900. The new urban culture called for a more organized, cohesive, and self-conscious form if Lutheranism was to survive in America.

THE URBAN MATRIX

What New York Lutherans experienced between 1875 and 1905 was part of a major transition in American life, including religion. Historian Arthur Meier Schlesinger has described the period from 1875 to 1900 as "A Critical Period in American Religion." In an age of rapid urban growth and industrial development the Church was loosing its appeal; Protestantism (particularly) was in danger of dying with small town America.[1] The litany of complaints in the New York and New Jersey Synod during the 1880s (Chapter 9) showed some of the antireligious factors involved—indifferentism, materialism, worldliness, and the replacement of doctrine by secondary religious notions. It also hinted at a process of adjustment to new religious realities.

In assessing these changes, students of American religion usually focus on two indicators of change and crisis—the challenge to faith of evolution and the higher criticism in Biblical studies; and the effect of industrialization on Christian social ethics, especially as the church responded with the Social Gospel. A close study of eastern Lutheranism has determined that beyond its educated leadership, the theory of evolution and the higher criticism affected few Lutherans, while the Social Gospel was of little concern to Lutheran leaders or laity.[2]

What troubled Lutherans most during the period was a problem to other Christian denominations as well—the organizational challenge which urbanization presented. Henry Steele Commager has correctly noted that the "challenge which the new urban, industrial and corporate order presented to the church was less dramatic, but more immediate and complex, than that with which either Darwinism or the Higher Criticism confronted it"; historian Aaron Abell observed more specifically that the development of the city tested the structure of American religion "to the breaking-point." This was surely the case with the formation and early development of the Synod of New York, a process of merger among General Synod Lutherans in the greater New York area that began in the last decade of the nineteenth century and was finished by 1908. The merger and all that it called for occurred within an important decade for the American church (1895 to 1905), a decade which the social historian Timothy L. Smith describes as a time of "major adjustments of thought and practice to cope with new social conditions."[3] The growing city in America was an urban matrix which would remake the Lutheran Church in a modern image.

DEMOGRAPHIC CHANGES BETWEEN 1890 AND 1906

The 1890s to which Smith points was a major watershed in American history. Frederick Jackson Turner marked the passing of the American frontier in 1890. As important were the changes affecting the American city, then undergoing rapid urbanization. While small towns continued growing in size and number with rapid urbanization between 1890 and 1910, the major cities grew far more rapidly. Cities with 25,000 or more inhabitants nearly doubled, from 124 in 1890 to 228 in 1910; their population increased from 14 million to 28.5 million. In 1890, 22 percent of the national population resided in cities of 25,000 or more inhabitants; in 1910 the proportion was 31 percent. Conversely, in 1890, 61 percent of the population resided in villages with 1,000 inhabitants or less, a figure that decreased to 50 percent by 1910.[4] The urban population belt in the greater New York area was becoming more clearly defined as an emerging matrix of culture in the northeast—dominated by New York and New Jersey counties where populations had more than doubled between 1860 and 1910. (See Map 10.1.)[5]

What was important for the city was crucial for the church. Though extensive religious census statistics did not appear until 1906 (in the first specifically "religious" census conducted by the United States government), information from 1890 is helpful in understanding urbanization and denominational growth. In the period between 1890 and 1906, for example, the total population increased by 33.8 percent while churches grew at a rate of 59.9 percent. Church membership, as a percentage of the population, increased from 32.7 percent to 39.1 percent between 1890 and 1906. In cities 25,000 and larger the increase as percentage of population was from 38 percent in 1890 to 46.1 percent in 1906, an urban growth rate of 87.2 percent (compared with 59.9 percent for churches nationwide, and 33.8 percent for the population as a whole). With growing numbers of immigrants moving into American cities from central, eastern, and southern Europe, the Roman Catholic Church grew more rapidly both nationally and in the cities than did the religious institutions of Protestants or Jews. Yet American Protestantism increased by 44.8 percent nationwide between 1890 and 1906, and by 71.7 percent in the nation's growing cities, no small feat either.[6]

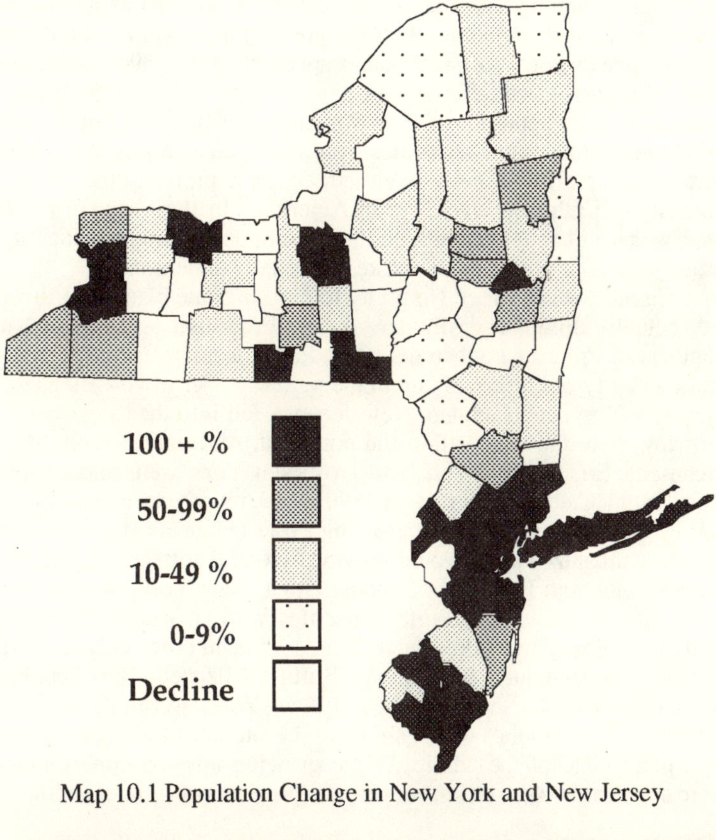

Map 10.1 Population Change in New York and New Jersey

Another feature of urban life was the increase of religious diversity resulting from mass immigration. For Protestant America this growing pluralism was something of a shock. Diversity was already great in a society marked for a century and a-half by religious pluralism. Already by 1890 the chances were high (about 4 in 5) that you could not pick two persons at random on a city street who would belong to the same Protestant denomination; by 1906 the chance of *not* being able to pick two Baptists or two Lutherans from a city population had increased to 84 percent. And with the growth of Roman Catholic and Jewish populations in the cities, the odds which were better than even that a stranger on the streets came from one of those unknown "religions" in 1890 had increased sixteen years later. There were simply more and different kinds of Protestants, besides increasing numbers of Roman Catholics and Jews in 1906 than in 1890, especially in growing midwestern and northeastern cities.

While ethnic differences and places of geographic origin increased this diversity among both Catholics and Jews, it was among an already diverse Protestant population that the greatest increases can be noted. Seventy-one distinct Protestant bodies appeared in the 1890 census; one hundred twenty-seven different bodies were identified in 1906. Of these sixteen were Lutheran in 1890, and twenty-four in 1906. Fourteen of these twenty-four Lutheran bodies were to be found within the greater New York area in the early twentieth century, probably the greatest diversity of Lutherans anywhere in America![7] In these circumstances the absolutes of religious faith and the certainties of religious identify, were easily relativized and therefore, potentially undermined.

Circumstances varied from city to city. In some places this diversity actually diminished slightly. A few Protestant cities gained in numbers of Protestant adherents while losing Roman Catholic inhabitants, a city-type which was rare in the northeast. Only two—Binghamton, New York, and Camden, New Jersey—fell into the category of a growing Protestant city within the northeast. And only Boston, Massachusetts, Erie, Pennsylvania, and Troy, New York, were among those cities with a Catholic majority in 1890 which recorded Catholic losses and Protestant gains. Of these growing Protestant areas, Troy and surrounding urbanized areas would provide favorable mission territory for the Hartwick and Franckean Synods. Utica, New York, on the other hand, fit the category of Protestant cities with an emerging Roman Catholic majority by 1906. Meanwhile, seventeen cities in New York and New England, including Albany, Buffalo, Elizabeth, Hoboken, Jersey City, Newark, New Haven, and New York, were city-types in which Roman Catholics were gaining and Protestants losing population as a percentage of the whole. While growing mission opportunities were apparent in these cities, so were the pressures of differentiation.[8]

DYNAMICS OF DIVERSITY, AND ITS LIMITS

That Protestant diversity increased during this period, and despite these changes, suggests a capacity for growth which occurred in conjunction with diversity. It has even been suggested that Protestantism flourished in such an environment, creating increasingly differentiated denominations to suit the religious marketplace. Diversity of religious groups and rivalry between them usually undermined the absolute nature of religion for urban inhabitants, something that does not occur as readily, if at all, in rural areas. Religious plausibility is usually decreased by religious pluralism. Why, then, such growth among Protestant groups when religious belief and practice tend to be reduced to matters of taste and fashion in urban environments? Because being "Protestant" was popular in urban America. It seems that even with diversification and competition, and even as denominational differences diminished in importance, Protestant bodies multiplied in number to serve a more diversified, urban self-consciously Protestant population. This was especially true where increases among Catholics and Jews in the population became a reason for tighter organization.[9]

Urban America, then, was beginning to move in these decades toward a tripartite religious division of Protestant-Catholic-Jew. Interestingly, even as a denomination differentiated itself to attract a certain segment of the population, it also engaged in interdenominational relations and organizations to more effectively reach out into the population. What was condemned by Populists and Progressives among business organizations as antitrust collusion to stabilize the marketplace, was in religious matters considered good "ecumenical" practice. Religious leaders engaged in building "cartels"; when addressing confessional differences, they had to "avoid drawing certain kinds of distinctions, and refrain from emphasizing distinctions where they may already exist." In this way certain denominational differences were minimized for the sake of common Protestant factors, as individual denominations came to be understood in the larger context of American Protestantism.[10]

None of this increased capacity for tolerance of differences, nor the ability to identify with the tripartite religious division of Protestant, Catholic, and Jew, should be taken as signs of a weakening of religious community in America. It was only the development of a more complex urban religious matrix and identity. That the religious landscape was populated by more and different Protestant, Roman Catholic, and Jewish groups in 1906 than in 1890, is evidence of continued strength in a growing variety of ethnoreligious communities. The urban matrix was less like a melting pot and more like a scene of kaleidoscopic diversity—always changing, but never disappearing. New colors and patterns were added by new immigrant groups and their religious organizations. It has often been assumed that conservative, tradition-oriented communities would disappear with assimilation in an urban environment. Instead such ethnoreligious communities actually flourished in abundance because whatever else they might be they were also forward-looking and progressive in meeting the challenge of immigration, urbanization, and modernization.[11]

This diversity was stubbornly persistent in twentieth-century America, encouraging a particularity which has survived the forces of urbanization. Religion reinforced ethnicity in neighborhood communities of Irish Catholics, German Lutherans, and Lithuanian Jews. It was the most important element in a mix of ethnicity, language, and religion which assured the survival of immigrant groups in urban America. Parochial education was a key factor in maintaining the ethos of ethnoreligious groups. Each group developed its own moral community with alternative visions of the American dream. Among Lutherans the parochial school systems in the Ministerium and the Missouri Synod helped maintain these separate communities. Like the growing importance of Baptism to be seen among Lutherans undergoing the urban transition, education was a mainstay of a community's strength. George U. Wenner recognized this when analyzing the problems of Lutherans in New York. Parochial education was vital to strong churches, and its absence directly related to weaknesses among communicant members, and to the high number of lapsed Lutherans. It was with real reason that he advocated parochial education in the General Synod sector of New York Lutheranism where it was weakest.[12]

THE URBAN MATRIX AND LUTHERAN UNITY IN THE NORTHEAST

After 1890, then, especially in the more highly urbanized and industrialized northeastern United States, religious diversity in an urban environment, though itself rooted in the identity of enduring ethnoreligious communities, introduced certain organizational dynamics which shaped the development of Protestant denominations. By the later 1890s this urban matrix was already having a profound effect on Lutherans in the northeast for they, too, were influenced by the new American search for adequate religious organizations. Even as Lutheran ethnoreligious communities maintained strong confessional identities such distinctive forms of Lutheranism became less important among some adherents of the General Council and General Synod, in the face of a growing pan-Lutheranism drawing members of these two bodies together into a party of convergence. Yet other General Synod types resisted this more generalized Lutheranism, identifying with a Protestantism becoming more important as the culture moved towards a major, tripartite religious division into what historian Will Herberg described as "Protestant, Catholic, and Jew."[13]

What was happening to Protestants on an *inter*denominational level was also happening to Lutherans on an *intra*denominational level. On the one hand, Lutheran diversity increased even as Lutherans were forced into closer proximity with fellow Lutherans, as with other Protestants, Roman Catholics, and Jews, in a close urban environment. There, forces of pluralism and syncretism which could relativize dogma, led Lutherans to question the confessional differences which separated them. At the same time however, the need to differentiate themselves, as a denomination, from other Protestant groups, especially with the growing threat of Roman Catholicism in most northeastern cities, encouraged cartel-like organizational behavior among Lutherans synods whose leaders were beginning to avoid drawing certain kinds of invidious distinctions between Lutherans and to refrain from emphasizing differences which weakened rather than strengthened this new cooperation. In sum, the urban matrix created circumstances of potential merger among Lutheran synods and a movement towards a pan-Lutheran religion—Lutheranism—a supradenominational possibility. The Free Diets of the 1870s and the Free Conferences at the turn of the century displayed all the behavior of church leaders slowly forging a Lutheran cartel. If, on the other hand, they were informed by Charles Porterfield Krauth's postdenominational vision of confessional union, they were led by Henry E. Jacobs who masterfully reduced invidious distinctions for the sake of a stronger confessional identity. The eventual result of these forces would be the creation of the United Lutheran Church and its largest district body, Synod of New York and New England.

The search for a differentiated Lutheran identity in such circumstances was nicely demonstrated by George Wenner who (as president of the New York and New Jersey Synod) reflected on just these puzzles and problems of Lutheran identity in a sermon preached at the synod's 1907 annual meeting. This was to be the last annual meeting before merger with the Hartwick and Franckean Synods created the new Synod of New York. It was appropriate to consider therefore, "The Church of the Augsburg Confession, her place in the Christian World, and her Mission to America in the Twentieth Century." The sermon's theme arose from a question often asked in a religiously diverse, urban environment, a question put by "Educated men of other faiths . . . when they learn that we are Lutherans"—"What is Lutheranism?"

What differentiates Lutherans from other Protestants ("if Lutherans are Protestants") or "from Roman Catholics, if there is a difference? " Lamenting such ignorance, Wenner insisted that a Lutheran clergyman "ought to be able to tell just what his system of religion is and means" and "be ready to state it with clearness to those whose minds are able to weigh critically his propositions." The problem for Lutherans, in the urban matrix, is that while an Episcopalian, Methodist, or Baptist could articulate her or his system in nine cases out of ten, Lutherans could not, the reason why members in the pew were "so ready to join other denominations."[14] Further differentiation was badly needed!

Wenner tried defining Lutheranism to comprehend Lutheran diversity, while explaining it to Protestants and Roman Catholics. While all Protestants shared the same Reformation origins, it was insufficient in differentiating Lutheranism to point to Martin Luther, for he stands "as a representative of universal Protestantism." Nor was it sufficient to note "that we have more members than all other Protestant churches combined." A Lutheran's Protestant pedigree as the elder son was not in question. A Lutheran identity was. One could not point to ecclesiastical unity—in the metropolitan New York area alone there were two-hundred congregations belonging to seventeen different synods. Nor was there a Common Service, if all possible congregational redactions is taken into account. The name itself was not "denominating"—"Congregations of the Augsburg Confession" is the designation in some places, and "Lutheran" in others; again, "Evangelical" is used in some places, and "Evangelical Lutheran in others." Doctrinal subscription was assumed by some as the "ultimate test of Lutheranism," but the churches of the General Synod did not hold this view. "We still hold with the confessors of Augsburg, 'For the true unity of the Church it is sufficient to agree concerning the doctrines of the Gospel'."[15]

Where Wenner emerged from this process of elimination was with "the catholicity of our Church" and an ongoing reformation that aimed "to bring back the Church to the common faith of Christendom." Rehearsing the history of the Reformation including Luther's own struggles, Wenner insisted that it was Christ's "person and work upon which the doctrine of our Church primarily rests." Pointing to the atoning work of Christ as confessed in Luther's explanation to the Second Article of the Apostles Creed, Wenner observed that it "was here that our Church pointed the way to a return to the simplicity of the Gospel by its Scriptural definition of justification." *Sola fide,* by faith alone, was the "keynote of the Reformation." After the doctrine of Christ's atoning work, justification by faith became the second and material foundation stone of Lutheranism. The third underlying principle relates to the means of grace. The word of God is regarded as the means of grace, and the Sacraments also "but because of the word." To summarize: "Lutheranism is that form of Protestant Christianity which makes Christ the only foundation, faith the only condition, and the word of God the only means of salvation."[16]

TOWARD MERGER, 1890-1908

Another dynamic dictating cartel-building among Lutherans was the relative rates of population change. Overall the urban church in the United States was growing more rapidly than the surrounding population, with Roman Catholicism increasing in numbers more rapidly than Protestantism. In New York State, however, where the largest urban population—the metropolitan New York area—was growing far more rapidly than the United States population, and the total state population itself was keeping pace with national growth, the Lutheran church was growing more slowly in country, village, town, and city (Table 10.1).

Table 10.1
Percentage growth among U. S. Churches and NY Lutherans

Year	U. S. Lutherans (6)	Ministerium (5)	Hartwick (5)	Franckean (5)	NY & NJ (5)
1890	68.2	79.2	14.7	-19.2	24.0
1900	43.8	23.2	0.4	-11.5	15.6
1910	32.3	0.4	merged 8.4	merged <-NY Synod	merged

Lutherans experienced atypical growth patterns compared with the national picture, patterns that gave less reason for optimism. Table 10.1 indicates the nature of the problem. New York area Lutheran churches were simply not growing at rates comparable to Protestant churches throughout the nation, nor were they as optimistic about maintaining their Lutheran "share" of the population.

Ministerium losses between 1890 and 1900 point to the wholesale removal of Lutherans to the English-speaking suburbs, to English-speaking congregations in Yonkers, Brooklyn, Queens, and elsewhere on Long Island, together with the very rapid growth in Manhattan of a Roman Catholic and Jewish population.[17] Even the losses experienced by the Franckean Synod were part of the overall pattern, because rapid urbanization and rural depopulation went hand in hand, simultaneously reshaping both the rural and urban segments of the Lutheran church. These rapid changes and a need for better organization in straightened circumstances added to pressures for merger. Let us look more closely at this situation synod by synod.

THE FRANCKEAN SYNOD INITIATES MERGER

In 1890 the Franckean Synod was a small, largely rural church body which had long depended upon revivalism in an unsuccessful effort to sustain its membership. Declining baptism rates adversely affected this method of bringing members into Franckean congregations, though increasing emphasis upon baptism, catechization, and Sunday schools maintained an adolescent population ripe for conversion, adult baptism, and full membership. While continuing to lose members into the 1890s, the Franckean Synod did so at a lesser rate, as Graph 8.2 has indicated.

Certainly a part of this modest reversal resulted from increased emphasis upon the Sacrament of Baptism, though catechetics continued to be a minor matter in Franckean parishes. As Table 10.2 indicates, per capita baptisms rates were up (if modestly) from their low point in the

1880s, more than doubling between 1890 and 1908. By the 1890s with increasing emphasis on Lutheran ways in the synod, this relative lack of emphasis on baptism was keenly felt. That it "deprives many of the young people of our churches of a solid foundation of Christian Lutheranism" was the lament in some parochial reports. At the synodical level, pastors were urged to "interest themselves in Lutheran and Christian doctrine by studying and imparting instructions from Luther's Catechism . . . so that our young people may have a sure and solid foundation upon which to build."[18]

Franckean pastors continued to report flourishing Sunday schools in their parishes, still considering them nurseries of the church. Sunday school membership had reached a high point of 1,998 pupils in 1885, dropping thereafter to 1,519 pupils by 1908. By then the synod had embraced the new young people's societies that appeared after 1890, promoting Christian Endeavor in particular, though also supporting the newly organized Luther League. The synod's "State of Religion" report for 1894 indicated what possibilities existed among such groups.

Table 10.2
Baptism as a Percentage of Communicant Membership (5)

Year	Hartwick	Franckean	NY/NJ	Ministerium
1875	3.0	2.1	11.9	18.0
1880	1.8	(1881) 1.3	12.9	17.8
1885	2.7	0.5	14.8	15.0
1890	2.5	0.8	15.5	14.1
1895	3.0	1.0	13.6	13.8
1900	3.2	1.8	11.4	11.5
1908	2.7	1.9	9.0	NA

Such successes doubtless led to the modest upturn in membership which the Franckean Synod experienced after 1890. Another factor—significant in past growth within the synod—was renewed mission work. The synod decided that it was time to employ a missionary. One reason was the continuing problem of weak and vacant churches which could not or would not support a full time pastor, let alone sustain a long-term pastorate. The synod was optimistic that such a missionary could "look up new fields in the bounds of our Synod." Having carefully perused the minutes of the Hartwick and New York and New Jersey Synods, the Franckeans were aware of new and extensive missionary activity in their sister synods. It also recognized what was in fact quite true—"Perhaps at no period in their history has the outlook been more favorable than at the present time" among Protestant churches.[19]

An 1896 synod committee reported for the first time in many years on hopeful prospects for "New Missions." Noting that the "Lutherans of New York have suffered much criticism in past years because of their unaggressiveness," the committee insisted that this criticism could hardly be directed against "the Synods of this State" of late. The Hartwick and the New York and New Jersey Synods, "have both been pressing forward in this direction," and "our own Synod is showing no less zeal in this good work than her sister Synods." The previous year a new congregation was organized in Indian Castle; at St. Johnsville a congregation was asking for admittance; new prospects existed, as well, at Lassellville, Little Falls, and Dolgeville. Other opportunities presented themselves as well. Urban growth had affected Troy, on the eastern bank of the Hudson River, in Rensselaer County. Among growing New York cities with over 25,000 inhabitants, Troy was the only Roman Catholic urban area where the Protestant population was increasing—from 27.3 percent in 1890 to 32.4 percent in 1906. Individual pastors from the synod's Eastern Conference had begun developing a Troy mission in 1897; by 1898 interested Protestants in Troy organized themselves as the First English Lutheran Church of Troy with rented facilities in the unused "Church of Christ" building. Meanwhile morning and evening services were conducted for the new congregation by Franckean pastors from the surrounding towns and villages. These reports of growth bear out the fact that immigration, population growth, and urbanization had an impact upon rural life or the village church. Even as people moved to the cities, rural villages benefited from population growth in the United States. In 1890 there were 7,838 villages in America with a population of less than 1000; in 1910 there were 9,113. Village life was certainly alive, if not well, in New York during the 1890s if mission opportunities in the Franckean Synod were any indication.[20]

Population drift from villages to towns provided a Protestant (and Lutheran) nucleus for new congregations in this population center on the east bank of the Hudson River. (Other mission opportunities were explored in 1901 at West Albany and Rensselaer indicate that limitations existed.) "No opening was found" in the state capital, but Rensselaer proved more favorable. It is probable that the Rensselaer opportunity proved more favorable because the town, like Troy, was a growing population center in Rensselaer County, a major stronghold of Franckean churches. As the upper Hudson valley's population grew, the synod attempted one more mission, proposing in 1908 to invite the Rev. Carl Zinssmeister, mission superintendent of the New York and New Jersey Synod, to "consider the advisability of starting a mission at Glens Falls" on the Hudson, in Warren County. This joint venture was possible because by then the two bodies, together with the Hartwick Synod, were completing negotiations for a three-way merger, a merger which occurred, in part, to enhance mission work among Lutheran synods in upstate New York.[21]

The Franckean Synod had initiated the new round of merger

discussions in 1900. President G. E. Harsh made the new proposal for merger in his annual report to the synod and it was approved by the committee on the president's report. Previous proposals for a three-way merger had occurred in 1878 and 1888. The former effort had been undermined by Franckean resistance, while the latter attempt was rejected by the New York and New Jersey Synod. Franckean opposition in 1878 had not been widespread however, being opposed at the time by Nicholas Van Alstine, senior pastor of the synod, and one of the Franckean Synod's founders who had withdrawn from the Hartwick Synod in 1837. But Van Alstine had retired in ill health in 1899. His death was announced by President Harsh a year later in his annual report; a few brief sentences of regrets, preceded his request for merger negotiations![22] After consultation with the Hartwick Synod, a joint merger committee met at the new First Lutheran Church of Troy in March 1902. Plans for union were presented and several proposed articles of incorporation were referred to legal counsel. Synod names were also proposed—"The Hartwick Synod," "The Hartwick and Franckean Synod," the "Joint Synod of New York," and the "United Synod of New York." The Hartwick delegates proposed that their own name be used to identify the merged body, while the Franckeans proposed "The Hartwick and Franckean Synod," a name approved by the Hartwick Synod in 1877 at the last merger talks. With neither delegation willing to accept the other's proposal, both groups reported back negatively to their respective bodies in 1902.

The Franckeans' report was mild considering the Hartwick delegation's tactics during the joint meeting. They had argued their case for a reunited Hartwick Synod by presenting a table of data (Table 10.3) which highlighted the relative strengths of the two synods:

Table 10.3
Relative Strengths of Hartwick and Franckean Synods

Category	Hartwick	Franckean
Ministers	36	24
Communicants	5733	2120
Value of Church Property	$427,800.00	$126,750.00
Local Expenses	$50,628.00	$15,415.00
Benevolence	$6,618.00	$3,009.00

The Hartwick name should be maintained, they insisted, because of both bodies' historic connection to the mother synod; because the stronger synod will need to assume the weaker synod's obligations; because both synods supported the Hartwick Seminary; and out of a desire to "honor and perpetuate a name that ought to be dear to all the Lutherans in the State." Their efforts came to naught because they foolishly joined the Franckean delegates though one shy of their full voting strength and were simply outvoted by a Franckean majority which rejected their insulting terms. When the Hartwick delegation reported back to its home body, its umbrage at having failed because of this "unfair" advantage led the Hartwick synod to vote an indefinite postponement of merger talks.[23]

THE RELUCTANT HARTWICK SYNOD

Hartwick's self-justification betrays a sense of superiority to its sister synod. It was larger in size and had experienced two decades of healthy growth after its own years of stagnation. That growth had begun during the 1880s, a decade earlier than among the Franckeans, eliminating the negative growth of the 1870s. A dramatic decrease in Baptisms during the 1860s had caused a membership decline in the following decades. But modest mission opportunities led to an increase in synod size (from twenty-seven to thirty-one congregations) and therefore of membership between 1880 and 1890. Four additional congregations were added in the 1890s. By then a modest increase in baptismal rates during the 1880s added to the membership increases of the 1890s (Table 10.3, above), though the synod continued to complain of insufficient catechization as a reason for slow membership growth.[24]

Why the difference between the two synods? More rapid population growth in the towns of New York State (compared with crossroad villages) where the Hartwick Synod had always done its best mission work began to present mission opportunities as early as 1891. In that year three new Hartwick missions were reported as receiving aid from the synod—St. James of Gloversville, the Church of the Redeemer of Lansingburgh, and St. Johns of Schaghticoke—joining the lone mission church of the previous decades at Maryland. St. James was organized in July of 1889 and quickly became all but self-supporting; The Church of the Redeemer, formed in 1890, was also soon flourishing. By 1892 the synod's Home Mission Committee could report what the Franckean Synod had already discovered. Many Hudson Valley urban areas were "growing faster in Lutheranism than in population" a situation similar to what was also happening in Rochester, Utica, and Syracuse. If this report was accurate, then such Lutheran growth in Utica and Syracuse might seem unusual since both cities (and possibly also Rochester) were cities in religious transition from Protestant to Roman Catholic majorities.[25]

The Hartwick Synod had never been successful with mission opportunities in such urban settings. Yet the synod reported that Hartwick Home Mission opportunities had never seemed "so prosperous and promising" in the synod's sixty-two year history. The First English Lutheran Church was then being organized in Schenectady by Pastors W. G. Thrall and T. J. Yost. St. Lukes of Amsterdam was organized in the same week of January 1892. Waterloo, outside of Buffalo, was also supporting a Lutheran congregation in a Union church building under the auspices of the Rev. Mr. J. C. Schindel. With such successes the Hartwick leadership spoke with pride of themselves as "the missionary Synod of New York." Besides present missions in place, prospects were good (it was reported) for mission starts in Troy, Cohoes, Niagara, Tonawanda, Buffalo, Fort Plain and Kingston. Especially promising were mission opportunities in east and west Buffalo, and Niagara Falls, where the synod resolved in 1893 to plant churches. But they never did. The decade proved disappointing from a mission perspective. The synod managed to maintain its support for new congregations already established, despite a financial depression gripping the country from 1893 through 1897, which "hung like a dark cloud over all the industries of our country." This was no small accomplishment for the new mission work was "mostly located in manufacturing towns" and "to an unusual degree, felt the effects of the hard times." In 1895, in the midst of the depression, another mission was anticipated in St. Johnsville, "a thriving village of 2,000," "and growing fast" because of German immigration and a "large piano-action factory" owned by a local Lutheran. Niagara Falls, Buffalo, Tonawanda (a Buffalo suburb), and Kingston were still looked upon as mission opportunities in 1895, but what had been observed in 1893 proved all too true. Limited resources and a shrinking small-town base provided very limited access to the larger urban areas of upstate New York. Even as the Hartwick Synod moved into small manufacturing towns to build new churches they were loosing ground because the general population was shifting from villages and small towns to small and middle sized cities in the upstate area.[26]

By 1901, then, when presented with an opportunity for merger with the Franckean Synod, the Hartwick Synod was mindful of its strengths more than and its weaknesses, but was also aware of rural Lutheranism's weaknesses in the Franckean Synod. Sensitive to its size, strength, accomplishments and prospects when compared with the smaller synod which had proposed the merger, it could not admit (indeed, may not have known) that its own mission base in small-town New York had reached growth capacity, and was in fact shrinking in numbers if not in wealth. Concerned about assuming the financial liabilities of the weaker synod, it was sensitive to assuming its name as well instead of trading on what the Hartwick Synod assumed to be its own stronger tradition. Without this prospect the Hartwick Synod was indifferent to merger and in 1902 once again postponed consideration of the proposal indefinitely.

The following year (1903) however, renewed mission activity in the Hartwick Synod again encouraged merger considerations. A new mission opportunity was available for a General Synod church at Oneonta which led to the English Lutheran Church of the Atonement in May of 1903. And in what was surely an early use of the word and instrument, Hartwick pastor N. E. Yeiser "telephoned" President J. H. Weaver with news of a second mission opportunity in Watervliet, a community of 18,000 on the west bank of the Hudson opposite Troy. Also a new mission was started at Cohoes, down river. This increased activity led to proposals to increase the size of and to restructure the Hartwick Synod's Home Mission Committee. It was to be divided into three working groups known as the Western, Southern, and Eastern divisions, with superintendents who would report to the committee of the whole, and to the synod. But just then a proposal arrived from the New York and New Jersey Synod for a total redistricting of the territory occupied by the three synods, an idea first proposed by the downstate synod's, Northern Conference, an organization whose jurisdiction overlapped that of the Franckean and Hartwick Synods. All three synods' conferences would be restructured into three multi-synodical conferences serving all General Synod congregations within a given geographic subregion. The heart of Hartwick and Franckean territory would be organized into a district covering Otsego and Schoharie counties on the south side of the Erie Canal and the Mohawk River; Herkimer, Fulton, and Montgomery counties would form a similar district on the north side. Schenectady, Albany, and Rensselaer counties would comprise a third district encompassing upper Hudson urban areas; while the growing cities of Syracuse and Buffalo would form the centers of two other districts. Organizationally more to its liking than the Franckean merger proposal, the Hartwick Synod adopted the New York and New Jersey proposal immediately, probably because it made good sense in light of its own imminent restructuring. The Franckeans were still nursing their differences with the Hartwick Synod, however, and did not become involved with the New York and New Jersey Synod proposal until 1904, by which time plans for reorganization had changed once again.[27]

NEW YORK AND NEW JERSEY SYNOD PROPOSES REDISTRICTING

The proposal for redistricting initiated by the Northern Conference independently of the New York and New Jersey Synod indicated that conference-sized jurisdictions were of growing importance in the synodical scheme of things. The Northern Conference did not go to the parent synod itself, but directly to the Hartwick and Franckean Synods, for there was no mention of such a proposal in the New York and New Jersey Synod at its Annual Meeting in October, 1903. When it did, it simply heard a report on negotiations between the Franckean and Hartwick Synods, resolving to await further developments. It was not until the 1904 meeting that the synod reported on a meeting of a Joint Committee on Redistricting of the Three synods, a committee whose work was already well underway.

The parent body was probably slow on the uptake because, for some time now, the fortunes of a rival Synod had been of more interest to it—the Evangelical Lutheran Synod of New York and New England—an English-speaking breakaway from the New York Ministerium formed in 1902, which it was believed had a great future and "should incite us to a friendly rivalry and to more ardent effort in speeding the forward movement of the Lutheran Church on this Eastern and New England territory." For the New York and New Jersey Synod interest in restructuring its own territory to incorporate the Franckean and Hartwick Synods was but part of a much larger regional concern for mission opportunities in the northeastern United States. Its state-wide territory was considerably greater than that of the two small up-state synods and also far more urban in character. The 1895 "Report of Committee on the State of Religion" indicates that its growing urban character was uppermost in its mind to the point of exaggeration. The Committee identified the synod as "One-half . . . located in villages or agricultural districts, the other half in manufacturing centres or in large cities." A count of congregations in cities of 25,000 or more reveal a tally which is closer to 33 percent.[28] However when compared with either the Hartwick or Franckean Synods, or with U. S. statistics on urban populations, the New York and New Jersey was decidedly more urban in character. What is more, this differential increased from 5 percent in 1890 to 24 percent by 1910. (See Table 10.4.)

Table 10.4
Urban Population in US and Synod Congregations

Year	US Population [29]	NY& NJ Synod (5)
1890	22	27
1895	24	33
1900	26	39
1908		55
1910	31	

Unlike the two smaller synods, with their limited ability to break into urban mission work, the more urban New York and New Jersey Synod enjoyed just that capability. Consider Buffalo, the litmus test in such things. While the town-based Hartwick Synod repeatedly cited unrealized opportunities for missions in Buffalo and its suburbs, the larger synod with its more urban base, was able to establish a second congregation in Buffalo by 1895. And Zion's, Buffalo, was one of five new mission congregations of the New York and New Jersey Synod in 1895. The others were to be found in Brooklyn, Herkimer, Oswego, and Erie. Like the Troy mission of the Franckean Synod, the Erie mission was in a city with a Roman Catholic majority which was experiencing Catholic losses and Protestant gains.[30]

Another new mission was formed in 1896—Bethany Lutheran Church of Bronx County—to meet a need for "an English Lutheran church north of the Harlem River." Bethany joined the synod in the same year, along with Zion German Evangelical Lutheran Church of Dolgeville, New York, a clear indication that the New York and New Jersey Synod continued the long-standing General Synod policy of seeking out places for English language Lutheran congregations in cities with second and third generation Lutherans as well as promoting new German-speaking congregations. Indeed, the General Synod itself received several German-speaking synods into its ranks during the 1890s, and supported its own German Theological Seminary in Chicago. The latter represented "an awakening to the vast importance of the German interests within our borders, as has not heretofore been seen in the General Synod." In the New York area, German-speaking congregations of the General Synod formed a separate German Conference within the New York and New Jersey Synod by 1896, the same year that the Synod printed 625 German copies of its annual minutes, along with 1,350 English language copies.[31]

The New York and New Jersey Synod was a more complex organization than its smaller, English-speaking counterparts, especially in the area of German-speaking mission. When Pastor Charles A. Dahlmann was called to the German Lutheran Church at Dolgeville, N. Y., his "very favorable testimonial from the Superintendent General of the Lutheran Church of the Duchy of Schwartzburg-Rudulstadt" was noted with approval. But while interested in the testimonials of confessional Lutherans, the synod's own Lutheranism was more irenic. The career of Pastor E. W. E. Hering, a member of the synod in 1871 and 1872, and (once again) from 1891 indicates something about this element in the General Synod. Emil W. E. Hering was born in Pomerania, Prussia, studied in Berlin and Halle, was ordained in Berlin in 1857, and for a time was assistant to the court preacher at Krummacher, at Potsdam. In 1871 he was called to the Lutheran Church in Stapleton, New York (Staten Island), and while there was a professor in the German Presbyterian Theological Seminary at Bloomfield, N. J. He returned to Germany in 1874, receiving a call to a congregation at Lagenfeld in Prussia. In 1883 he returned to the United States, accepting a call to the German Presbyterian congregation at Carlstad, N. J. Five years later (1888) he resigned and moved to Harlem, forming the Evangelical Church of the Augsburg Confession. While a pastor in Harlem he rejoined the New York and New Jersey Synod in 1891, but shortly thereafter moved to Chicago to fill the chair of Exegetical Theology and Church History at the General Synod's German Theological Seminary.[32] It is evident from his career that Hering was in fact an Evangelical pastor and theologian—a product of the union of Reformed and Lutheran churches in Prussia—and equally at home serving congregations in either the Reformed or Lutheran confessional traditions.

Both Hering and the General Synod were comfortable with this interdenominational "Evangelical" perspective. (In the far more confessionally orthodox New York Ministerium a pastor who "made application for admission to the Evangelical Synod of North America" was disciplined for "denying the Lutheran faith.") The Synod of New York and New Jersey clearly represented a breadth of German theology—Lutheran, Evangelical, and (perhaps) Reformed—that increased its appeal in some ways, but limited it in others. The availability of calls to German churches in the synod certainly was limited, with the result that pastors occasionally requested dismission to the New York Ministerium. Some congregations of German background also found the General Council tradition more to their liking, as with the German Evangelical Lutheran St. Pauls Church, in Torrington, Connecticut, which requested a transfer to the New York Ministerium in 1897. Most of the evidence suggests that relations between the two bodies was a one-way street with most of the business going to the Ministerium. The 1897 accords by which the General Council and General Synod coordinated their mission work, and which opened a dialogue on practical cooperation in the first of the Free Conferences, was rejected by the New York Ministerium "both as a matter of principle and because of its impracticability." This rejection rendered the accords "entirely inoperative" in the view of the New York and New Jersey Synod since the two synods occupied "corresponding territory." But eventually it broke through the New York Ministerium's theological aloofness by requesting a delegate exchange with the German-speaking body, a practice that had been suspended in the 1860s at the Ministerium's behest. Though the exchange itself did not occur, the president of the Ministerium expressed his hope that "relations of mutual comity and fraternal cooperation between the two bodies may ever continue and increase."[33] Relations between the two bodies were beginning to thaw by the turn of the century, thanks to the new spirit of dialogue and cooperation existing between the General Synod and the General Council.

The New York and New Jersey Synod viewed itself as a strong and dynamic Lutheran body with an important form of Lutheran mission to the metropolitan New York area. In a sermon preached before the synod at its twenty-fifth meeting at St. Johns Lutheran Church on Christopher Street in New York City, the preacher noted that since the division with the Ministerium the Synod of New York and New Jersey had made more rapid progress than either the Hartwick or Franckean Synods. Whereas the New York and New Jersey Synod had doubled its clerical and communicant members, increasing its congregations by 20 percent, Hartwick's increases had been far more modest while the Franckean Synod had actually shown a decrease in membership, and it was hoped that in the future "she may . . . cultivate well the territory which has providentially been committed to her keeping. May she continue to be pure in doctrine, vigorous and aggressive in action, and harmonious and affectionate in her membership."[34]

How accurate was this assessment? The new General Synod mission in Buffalo (Zion Evangelical Lutheran Church) which "now unfurls the banner of General Synod Lutheranism" was presented in the 1897 annual *Minutes* as having a churchly edifice in which the Common Service was used "with a pronouncedly distinctive Lutheranism." But three years later (1900), the synod's president, Junius B. Remensnyder, author of the widely acclaimed *Lutheran Manual* and a recognized confessional voice in the General synod, noted that many pastors in the New York and New Jersey synod were still under "an influence predominant in a past generation" when "non-Lutheran methods" were employed in most General synod churches. This problem was termed, however, but a "serious drawback" to a changing situation. Recently the territory of the synod, "after having long seemed a stationary field, has become the theatre of one of the most marked progressive movements of Lutheranism." This was true "of Greater New York, but all over its territory there are indications of renewed zeal, in renovating churches and going forward."[35]

"Progressive" in the New York and New Jersey synod meant a balance between growing confessionalism and the General synod tradition of religious freedom. As President Remensnyder put the matter in 1903, "our Lutheranism is of the conservative type as to liturgical forms and historic usages, yet we judge no brother whose heart is with us for any exercise of his evangelical freedom." In sum, this was a tolerant, "cosmopolitan" synod, attractive to young ministerial candidates, yet clear about what it considered its Lutheran identity. For this very reason the New York and New Jersey synod saw itself as well positioned, culturally as well as geographically, to respond to the mission challenge in the northeast. The General synod had recently noted the "inviting field for Home Missions in our larger cities," especially "Greater New York and Chicago." Scores of churches could be established in these circumstances and become self-supporting "within a few years." Significantly only two other synods had more missions receiving as much aid. The New York and New Jersey synod observed of itself that "our special territory has become one of the chosen missionary fields of the General synod. More progress, perhaps, had been made in this than in any other synod." So promising was the field, in fact, that the General synod gave "far larger aid to missions within our bounds than we sent to her treasury." The deficit was also responsible for the synod's phenomenal growth between 1899 and 1903—a 25 percent growth in size, with an increase of 2,000 new members in both newly organized and existing congregations.[36]

With these advantages of a progressive outlook and national support, New England was considered a special mission field. Approaching New England from its own theological perspective, the New York and New Jersey Synod believed Puritanism (i.e., native Protestantism) to be dying out, and that the populace was demanding "a more conservative Christianity and . . . looking to us and our type of theological teaching for spiritual guidance." Moreover the "large influx of foreign element of our Lutheran faith" especially in New England's cities, "are asking for Christian Lutheran Church privileges." On the basis of this mission potential the synod proposed in 1903 to appoint a full-time Missionary Superintendent with oversight of vacant congregations and new missions. The proposal was adopted and the advisory committees appointed. Eventually a Superintendent would be found from among the ranks of the committee itself—Pastor Carl Zinssmeister. Within a few years his would be a joint appointment with the Synod of New York and New England, as the two bodies began a cooperative mission on their common territory. It was also Zinssmeister to whom the Franckean Synod turned in 1908 for aid in developing a mission in the upper Hudson valley around Glens Falls. By then, a merger of the three New York bodies was all but completed.[37]

THE MOVE TOWARD MERGER—1903-1908

A few months into this far-reaching reorganization the Northern Conference proposed a further restructuring of upstate synods by realigning their respective conferences. The merger proposal which would carry the day was to be part of a regional restructuring of General Synod Lutheranism, not just a merger between two of its minor components. Friendly rivalry rather than cooperation with the Synod of New York and New England might be the order of the day, but competition gave way to cooperation among the state's General Synod bodies in the face of mission opportunities in the urban northeast. The Hartwick and Franckean Synods, while still capable of modest mission accomplishments, had neither the size nor the urban base for more effective mission results. The New York and New Jersey Synod, on the other hand, had the potential for effective urban growth. The differences are to be seen in Graph 10.1.

By the first decade of the twentieth century, the modest mission growth of the Hartwick and Franckean Synods was past while that of the New York and New Jersey Synod was really just beginning. Always more urban in character, the General Synod congregations in New York and New Jersey, whether in the old New York Ministerium (pre 1867) or the new English-speaking synod (post 1867), had displayed a more robust rate of growth. Now these trends and the circumstances which had created them were to be merged in a larger General Synod body (the Synod of New York).

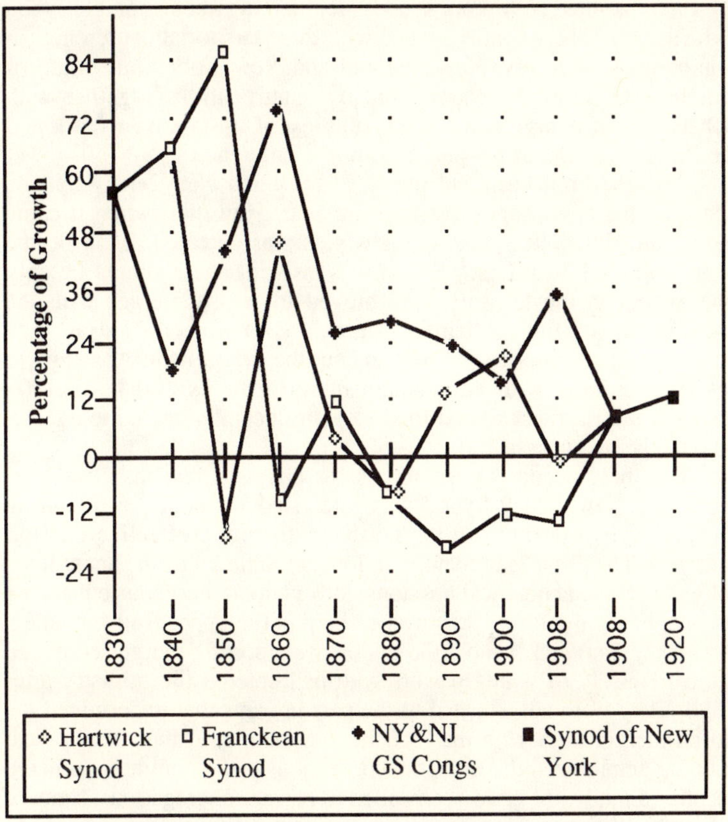

Graph 10.1 Growth Rates in New York Synod Bodies

Mission effectiveness was not the only reason for merger. The "Thirty Years' War'"over the Common Service was coming to an end and with it all General Synod divisions. Within the General Synod (as reported to the New York and New Jersey Synod), the "secondary divisions and accompanying prejudices that have existed . . . are surely dying out, and that not by denominational indifference, but by the growth of a positive Lutheranism."

Lutheran unity was advancing among the "General Lutheran bodies." Plans were afoot for a common annual meeting of the mission, education, church extension, publications, and Sunday School Boards of the General Synod, the General Council, and the United Synod of the South. And though perennially premature in its General Synod optimism, the remark of its president was nearly prophetic: "We have practically united all the English-speaking Lutheran organizations !"[38]

Cooperation, then, was moving towards more than restructuring. By 1905 the three New York synods were talking about a single synod to be named "The Atlantic Synod" with three territorial conferences—Southern (New Jersey, New England and New York State south of Dutchess County); Northern (Hudson congregations together with Schenectady County); and Central (the rest of upstate New York and the Province of Ontario)—plus a German Conference.

Both the Franckean and the New York and New Jersey Synods accepted the new proposal within the year. However, when it came before the Hartwick Synod, the new plan was defeated. By 1906 the New York and New Jersey Synod was insisting there should be only one synod on the territory, and moved toward a merger with the Franckeans in the "Atlantic Synod." A majority of Hartwick congregations supported the merger, but the synod itself was slow to resolve the issue with an adamant minority in its midst. By 1907 however the Hartwick Synod finally, and reluctantly agreed to a three-way merger to occur in 1908.[39]

The three synods joined forces for different reasons. The New York and New Jersey Synod was interested in totally restructuring General Synod territory in the northeast for more effective mission outreach. The Franckean Synod, no longer viable by itself, but still vitally concerned about local missions, looked upon merger as enhancing its own mission efforts. They wanted help in the upper Hudson valley. As for the Hartwick Synod, the majority supporting merger consisted almost entirely of young pastors who had entered the ministry after 1890. They were not attached to the past in ways that undermined the initial merger talks with the Franckean Synod. And their theological training emphasized the Lutheran confessions and a common Lutheran identity. Finally, they had been called to newer congregations, some of which had been mission congregations in the 1890s. President A. S. Hain, for example, voting with the majority, was pastor of the Troy Mission, the Church of the Redeemer. Also joining the majority was the oldest ordained member of the synod, I. J. Delo, who had served the Maryland, New York church, a congregation kept afloat for years when it was the only viable mission congregation in a stagnant synod.[40]

THE SYNOD OF NEW YORK—1908

Historic First Lutheran Church in Albany was the site of merger. The oldest Lutheran congregation in New York, First Lutheran was also the birthplace of the breakaway New York Synod in 1867. Now it witnessed another historic first—the healing of old divisions among New York Lutherans with a union of one hundred twenty-eight (128) congregations and one hundred thirty-two (132) pastors in the synod of New York. George U. Wenner of the New York and New Jersey

Synod, was elected the new Synod's president; Hartwick's W. M. Baum and J. G. Traver were elected vice president and treasurer, respectively; and the Franckean H. M. Oberholtzer became English secretary at the Synod's organizational meeting. The usual standing committees were organized—Executive, Examining, Education, Constitution, Apportionment, Hartwick Seminary, Home Mission and Church Extension, Temperance, State of the Church, and Memoirs. Perhaps most significantly for the future of the new Synod, a "Conference Committee, Synod of New York and New England" was also established to continue merger talks with the English-speaking General Council synod.

The old conferences were reorganized into Southern, Hudson, Hartwick, Western, and German Conferences. In the three oldest areas the congregations were evenly balanced—Hartwick (35), Hudson (33), Southern (33); the Western (13 congregations) and the German (12) Conferences were newer with fewer members. The Western and Southern Conferences were composed almost exclusively of former New York and New Jersey Synod congregations; the Hartwick Conference had a core of Hartwick Synod churches, retaining that synod's name as had been wished by a majority, but now at a conference level; while the Hudson Conference was made up of congregations formerly belonging to the New York and New Jersey Synod, and the Franckean Synod. With all of the congregations taken together, the new synod was 33 percent urban, and 66 percent rural—just slightly more urban than national averages. (See Table 10.1.) The conferences themselves varied widely however. The Southern Conference was 82 percent urban; the German Conference 33 percent and the Western Conference 31 percent; while the Hudson Conference was 91 percent rural, and the Hartwick Conference 100 percent rural.[41]

"PREGNANT WITH POSSIBILITIES"

The new synod's size dictated that crucial business would be conducted at the conference level. Mission work was restructured to facilitate supervision by committees at the conference level, an innovation begun in the New York and New Jersey Synod just before merger. Yet the first conference meetings continued to function largely as places of fellowship for considering learned theological papers. President Wenner indicated in his first annual report (1909) that the conferences "have not reached an adequate comprehension of their responsibility for the local interests of their respective territories. To the traditional view of the Conferences. . . . should now be added a thorough discussion of papers, and likewise a practical administration of local affairs, somewhat after the manner of Synodical work," though this would now require more frequent meetings.[42]

Atypically for a presidential report, Wenner's initial effort provided a trenchant analysis of its synodical circumstances that would be used by his successors as a blue print for change. In some way all of his observations addressed the size and growth of the church. A terse recommendation "that the first order of the day, for Thursday morning, be a doctrinal discussion on infant baptism, the paper to be read by Dr. Remensnyder" was meant to address a long-standing confessional problem in congregations of the former Hartwick and Franckean Synods. Another noted that the new synod might have been larger had its predecessor bodies not lost numerous congregations when "the power of a temporary or factitious majority" had taken a "congregation out of the Synod" over some disputed matter. The Synod of New York and New Jersey, for example, had lost forty-five churches in thirty-seven years by such withdrawals, he observed. Congregations should protect themselves with constitutional clauses "in which their connection with the Synod is defined and secured," a matter which the new Committee on Constitutions for Congregations should take under advisement.[43]

Wenner looked closely at religious life in the rural Hudson and Hartwick Conferences. Using topographical charts of the United States Geological Survey, he reported "suggestive glimpses of the scattered villages and hamlets located within a few miles of many of our congregations." "Some" are "relapsing into heathenism." Letters from two rural pastors noted hamlets with no churches near their congregations while "all over the hills here in almost every direction there are families with no church relations." There were similar circumstances in some twenty-five or thirty "cross-roads communities and out-of-the-way villages where the children and the young people are allowed to grow up godless, unbaptized, uninstructed, unconfirmed, and unsaved." They repeatedly asked that churches be organized in their communities. Wenner thought unchurched villagers might be served at worship stations in vacant school houses supplied from nearby towns by pastors or laymen motivated by their plight. Conference committees could organize these mission stations, leaving them with no excuse next year "for bringing no report or reporting that there is nothing of special importance for them to do."[44]

He next addressed marginal pastorates in smaller congregations of the synod. Twenty-one resignations had occurred in the last year he noted, 75 percent of them because of inadequate salaries. Of fifty randomly selected pastorates he surveyed, only twenty pastors indicated that they were adequately paid. In the new synod $200 (low by pre Civil War standards!) was considered a minimum salary, grossly inadequate compared to another denomination where the minimum was $1200. Though exceptionally high, this disparity revealed a basic problem in the synod. Consolidation of small congregations was one solution. A pastor could serve two to five congregations during the week, also providing monthly Sunday services in the right circumstances. Better this limited schedule than intermittent pastoral vacancies with congregations "slowly starving to death."[45]

Small size was another difficulty. Fifty-six congregations had fewer than one hundred communicants; all but thirty-two pastors in the synod served fewer than two hundred (200) communicants. Measured "by the ordinary standards of labor, which may be applied to men in good health, it is not enough of a job to keep a man busy." In parishes with less than one hundred fifty (150) families a pastor might well "enlarge his sphere of activity by establishing a station at some point in the adjoining territory. In view of the proximity of many of our churches to neglected neighborhoods, I deem this subject of sufficient importance to commend to the attention of the Conferences." Joint charges would improve under-productivity. Fourteen churches were presently so linked while circumstances "would warrant the establishment of many more such 'charges.'"[46]

As for "the age of our churches," Wenner noted that of twenty churches established in the last ten years, fifteen grew out of the "marvelous changes and growth of New York City." Only five congregations had been started in the other four conferences. A loss of four others meant a net gain of "one church in ten years." Considering "a steady growth of population in this part of the State," "such figures make one stop to think" and to question. "Are churches no longer needed as in former times?" "Can the Salvation Army, the Young Men's Christian Association or the itinerant evangelist supply all the spiritual direction that is needed?" "Does the net gain of one church in ten years adequately represent our response to the needs of the Empire State outside of New York City? "[47]

Urban mission was an obvious concern for a downstate clergyman like Wenner. It is surprising, therefore, that in his first report President Wenner sought a renewed vision for the rural church. What he attempted to motivate, by his close analysis, was mission activity in the neglected areas of the church where opportunity was not so evident. Admittedly this was the view of an New York City pastor, an urban clergyman with no rural parish experience. Harlem was not Harlemville. The productivity issue was raised unfairly perhaps, considering that it is far easier to visit a two hundred member congregation in a ten-square block area of New York City tenements than within a ten miles radius of an upstate village. Yet he tried at a time when the nation was beginning to hear alarming things about Christianity's decline at its rural point of origin in America.

In this, as in other matters, Wenner had "endeavored to magnify my office, believing that the first year of such a synod was pregnant with possibilities." He "endeavored to study the details of the entire field in all its various relations and to place upon record some of my observations with respect to its condition." At first the new synod responded, forming special committees to address fifteen issues raised in the president's first report. The "spiritual destitution" of New York's villages and hamlets was of such great concern that its special committee reported before the end of the synodical session. It asked that pastors and congregations "give careful oversight" to their immediate neighborhoods, organizing preaching stations, Sunday schools, and young people's societies wherever possible to revive Christianity in the rural countryside.[48]

ORGANIZATIONAL PROBLEMS

Size also proved to be a problem. While inadequate size hampered effective mission work previously, bigness was now proving an impediment. Wenner's mastery of detail was for the purpose of managing a complicated ecclesiastical organization. "Our Synod covers a large territory and in view of its history and development has a complicated constituency" he observed in his second Annual Report. "The work to be done, both extensively and intensively, is one of great delicacy and difficulty. Our organization is like a gigantic machine with many parts." Forty committees was one evidence of scale. Their reports, alone, would require a "parsimonious use of time." Another problem was the autonomous conferences with the potential for becoming five independent synods in their separate enthusiasms and projects. The Hartwick Conference had every opportunity to continue the former Hartwick Synod's emphases and interests without regard to the larger whole, while the large Southern Conference might easily become a semi-atonomous version of the old New York and New Jersey Synod. Urban imperatives had fostered Inner Mission "work" in this conference though it was undertaken without synodical approval. Though he himself was a member of New York's Inner Mission Society, apparently Wenner was concerned about the introduction of this independent, outside movement of social concern and its activities, because of its centrifugal influence at a time when synodical integration was necessary. The synodical president insisted upon the accountability of conference presidents in the same way that he was accountable.[49]

Wenner was most troubled by the synod's organization for mission. The Home Mission Committee functioned well, he reported with scarcely concealed irritation, but he had no official working knowledge of its activities. Private intelligence, and whatever could be gleaned from attending its meetings uninvited, gave him an inkling of their work. But he was informed of nothing except what was formally reported at synod. Ignorance prevented him from taking a more active role in mission development. This most activist of presidents would motivate the synod to swifter action in local missions fields. Going around the committee, he personally surveyed the territory through letters to each synod pastor asking them to identify "undeveloped fields within ten miles of his church." What he found through his greater determination were opportunities for a German mission in Utica, and English churches at Fulton in the Western Conference, Sidney in the Hartwick Conference, Cohoes and Watervliet in the Hudson Conference, plus "unlimited" opportunities in the Southern Conference.[50] Again, acting on his own authority, Wenner called attention to these five mission fields, expecting that the appropriate Home Missions Committees would act quickly.

His resoluteness also revealed, aside from the rural mission needs uncovered, that "in the upper part of the State, the territory is well churched," a matter that might otherwise have preoccupied the synod for years. Wenner continued urging aggressive local evangelism on rural pastors, but shifted his attention thereafter to urban missions—specifically to the work of the southern section of the Committee on Home Mission and Church Extension. Suburban growth caught his attention as the greater New York area invested "hundreds of millions" in constructing railroads, bridges and tunnels "for the distribution of our city population in the suburbs." Queens and Brooklyn were growing more quickly than the synod. While "we are planting one or even six new congregations, the city is growing so fast and so far, that a score of other places have to be neglected." "Under the present system of the synod we shall never catch up with the need" he complained, referring to the synod's rudimentary response. The mission superintendent was really a missionary temporarily in charge of two or three new congregations just starting up. Needed was an organized response that he could truly superintend.[51]

The synod must devise "comprehensive plans for the whole territory" which anticipated "probable needs" at least a decade in advance. He provided one model himself. Instead of the haphazard location of churches here and there, a "systematic chain of congregations, responsive and auxiliary to each other" must be created. The mission superintendent should administer a comprehensive plan, with lay organizations of men and of women for the promotion of local work. Instead of establishing congregations immediately, at great expense, new neighborhoods should have Sunday schools and preaching stations provided on a trial basis, in rented facilities, at a fraction of the cost. Unlike congregations, they could be easily abandoned if they did not become self-sufficient "within a reasonable time." It was necessary to adopt financial measures "commensurate with our ability" in mission, therefore it was imperative to repress "the inordinate desire of building expensive churches and mortgaging the future." Finally, with eighteen other Lutheran synods at work on the territory, cooperation rather than competition would also be necessary, for there "is work enough for us all to do."[52]

Wenner's proposals, and the operations of the synod committee supervising home missions, differed like night and day. Apparently oblivious to its president's ideas, the committee preferred a second mission superintendent for upstate churches. Zinssmeister's presence was needed locally as a temporary pastor, especially at St. Stephens, a new congregation in Hicksville on Long Island. When not so involved, the downstate Superintendent had an extensive schedule of travel, preaching, promotion and fundraising (as his synod report indicated). Instead of a comprehensive grasp of a region, the Committee's energy was absorbed by a few missions. At the moment, an Italian mission in West Hoboken seemed promising. Available funding was channeled into this single project. A pastor was engaged and paid for by committee funds, and a store-front church established. With a growing congregation, larger quarters were needed, especially considering the mission's seeming potential. Mission work was taking place among 16,000 Italians of whom 12,000 "have no belief," 3,200 are "indifferent" and 800 are diehard "Romanists." The plan was to "convert those who have no belief, to awaken the indifferent, to bring to Christ those who are Romanists." Besides the Hoboken and Hicksville charges, the committee had also conducted a "favorable canvass" of Brooklyn Hills and Brooklyn Manor.[53]

Preoccupied with leaves and trees, the Home Mission Committee was overwhelmed by the forest. To use their own metaphor, its members saw "many fields white unto the harvest" that would go unharvested without greater financial support. Where Wenner urged a more creative use of available funds, the committee lamented their lack of means. The Synod of New York, like its predecessor bodies, received more in General Synod mission funds than it contributed to the national church. Unless this already generous support increased (they argued) there would be no funds to build the chapels which every mission needed in two or three years if they were to survive as new churches. Many towns and cities had one hundred to two hundred families of unchurched Lutherans which could and should be organized. What was proposed was the creation by the Missionary Superintendent of an Emergency Fund to aid missions in their early struggles when they were especially vulnerable to collapse.[54]

Clearly, president and committee were working at cross purposes. Where Wenner urged a comprehensive plan with maximum coverage at minimum cost, using the available (though inadequate) supply of clergy, the committee proceeded piecemeal wherever a local community might be canvassed and a mission started up. Quite probably an ascerbic president and a detail-conscious committee had locked horns over such matters early on. Finishing up his two-year term, Wenner presented himself as the "watch dog of the Constitution" whose words and acts may have offended some. For this he asked forgiveness. But his brief tenure had been twenty-four months of unremitting effort to reorganize and refocus a new and enlarged synod which otherwise had little hope of meeting the challenge of urban life and growth in the New York area.[55]

Given the synod's very limited financial means, Wenner was more farsighted than its Mission Committee in facing the problem of urban mission work. In one sense it was an old story, synods having complained throughout the nineteenth century that they had insufficient funds to support necessary growth. It was one of President Wenner's specially appointed committees which spelled out the problem in detail. With eighty of one hundred fourteen pastors responding to its request for information about salaries, the special committee was able to determine that the average pastor received $896 in compensation—more in the city ($1,198), less in the country ($620)—with a total of $1,023 if perquisites were added. Their congregations divided almost evenly over the adequacy of such compensation—thirty-three thought pastor's salaries sufficient, while twenty-nine did not. On such incomes pastors supported an average family of three, but most could save nothing. Out of these salaries a minority (twenty-two) also had to rent housing, while most lived in parsonages.

The committee concluded that inadequate pastoral income caused "the paucity of ministers" to be found in the synod. "The unwritten law of capital and labor necessitates each profession or occupation to pay a salary that is adequate to meet its demands," it concluded. "When this is not done it must go begging for men, or fail to do the work." With other synodical bodies in the state reporting similar shortages, the committee's conclusions probably had some validity in the eighteen Lutheran synods in New York. Other denominations apparently had similar difficulties, for Synod of New York salaries were higher than the national average among 102 denominations and 164,229 congregations reported in the census—$100 higher in the city, and $47 in the country.[56]

No doubt low professional salaries contributed to the church's undersupply of clergy. Whether the congregations were doing all that they could—as the synod concluded *they were not*—is more difficult to determine. Other information gleaned from the clergy who were polled, indicated that eighteen of the synod's congregations gave all they could to support their pastors, while fifty-eight others did not. If pastors were underpaid, it is clear why mission apportionments were undersubscribed, and the synod had a lack of funds for new mission starts. Average giving was estimated at 2 percent throughout the church—higher in the city (2 1/2 percent) and lower in the country (1 1/4 percent). As revealing, the average country parson's salary ($620) was $205 less than the estimated average income of his parishioners. On the other hand, city pastors were paid nearly twice as much as their average parishioner earned—pastors averaged $1,198 in salary and benefits while their parishioners earned on average $638.[57]

Such figures suggest the crisis in rural religion was largely economic—many country congregations could not or would not provide adequate funds to support a full-time ministry. Whether this was because rural clergy were unproductive (as Wenner maintained), or whether rural clergy were ineffective because they were underfinanced, is impossible to say. It was a vicious circle, in either case, detrimental to religious needs in village and countryside.

The committee's data indicate something important about the Lutheran laity and their support of the church. At the century's end, one in eight Americans remained in poverty, with the unskilled earning an average of $286 per year—this by comparison with skilled manufacturing workers who earned $435, railway employees with an annual average wage of $560, business clerical workers earning $848, postal employees who made $878, and ministers with an income of $794.[58] The average urban Lutheran was more middle class than lower-middle class in origin, while the average pastor enjoyed a substantial middle-class income and status, though hardly the upscale existence associated with other well-educated professions. While the rural church, then, was hampered by a lack of economic resources, the majority of the urban church, on the other hand, had a middle-class economic base which took care of the pastor and the needs of the local congregation. However per capita giving levels of 2 1/2 percent seemed insufficient to finance the church's urban growth. That such giving levels have not been exceeded a century later (having slipped in fact), even as clergy compensation and status have declined, suggests that the urban, denominational form of the church has not been able to support itself as a voluntary association of church members financially based on discretionary income alone. This, perhaps, was the greatest consequence of the materialism which Lutheran leaders began to detect among church members by the 1890s.

URBAN MISSION GROWTH

With the conclusion of President Wenner's two-year term, leadership of the New York Synod passed into other hands. His immediate successor was Vice-President William Baum, a pastor of the former Hartwick Synod. Baum urged "careful examination" of Wenner's annual reports and his other communications with the synod, arguing that they "contain suggestions and recommendations" which are "capable of producing lasting practical results." Baum concluded his own two-year term of office still calling on the synod to give careful study to Wenner's two annual reports and to set his proposals "In active operation." Baum was convinced from his own observations and experience that a higher spirituality in the church would make its synodical efforts "more aggressive and efficient." The new synod lacked vision and commitment. The Committee which responded to President Baum's remarks was singularly unmoved, however, to make recommendations along the lines Wenner and Baum were suggesting.[59]

Instead, the synod responded piecemeal over the next decade to the issues being raised. Resolutions were passed in 1913 regarding "the shepherdless and weakened condition of many of our upstate country congregations," by once-again calling the attention of an overworked Missionary Superintendent to their plight. By 1917 it had become so pronounced and the synod's preoccupations with downstate missions so great that the synod finally decided to employ a second mission superintendent for rural upstate congregations. His first report, delivered in 1918 after a year on the job, detailed not only the deterioration itself but the "cold indifference [which] exists in reference to Rural Church work." Country churches have been seriously neglected because there is "so little remuneration for the work to be done." For ten years the synod had seen conditions worsen, but resolutions and committees had done nothing he noted with exasperation. Time was when churches were organized in every village; the time had come when they must be saved from extinction. Merger, then, had not helped the plight of the former Hartwick and Franckean congregations. The reason was the "paramount importance of Home Mission needs in the Metropolitan district of New York." The importance of downstate missions was not fully realized even by 1917, yet no "section of the United States can approach this field in vastness of possibilities," the Committee on Home Missions reported in that year. Moreover its problems took the entire time and energy of the synod's Mission superintendent, Carl Zinssmeister. The inadequate supply of clergy was a serious drain on his resources and upset his priorities.[60]

MISSION DEVELOPMENT ASSESSED

Clearly the New York Synod's bi-polar mission work and strategy produced inadequate results. Neglect and tardy reclamation efforts did little toward reducing the drag of the rural churches on the overall fortunes of the synod. Failure to develop more comprehensive plans, inadequate funding and a deficient supply of clergymen seriously retarded mission growth in the urban sector. *Yet* in terms of growth rates, mission efforts in the new synod had produced better results than the three former synods had done by themselves, and as a consequence (as seen in Graph 10.1) the synod increased its growth rate from 8.4 percent for the decade 1900-1910, to 12.6 percent for the years 1910-1920.

Even the increased growth, however, was well below national levels. Viewed conference by conference, there were surprises in the nature of that growth. As expected, the rural Hartwick Conference recorded a net loss of communicant members. The Western Conference, on the other hand, showed an increase of 20.9 percent, while the German Conference increased by 69.6 percent. Most surprising the Southern Conference, the largest potential mission field in the General Synod, despite an increase of eleven congregations through its mission efforts, registered only a 3.6 percent increase in communicant membership over the decade. This was far below both the overall growth rate of churches in the United States for the decade (26.2 percent), and that of its urban counterpart and friendly competitor, the Synod of New York and New England, which grew at a rate of 36.9 percent.[61]

Why this poor showing? The answer is to be found at the synodical level. By comparison with other church bodies, the New York Synod was not well organized to deal effectively with urbanization. According to historian Aaron Abell's assessment of the urban impact on American Protestantism, Protestantism in general made a "poor missionary showing" compared with Roman Catholicism, "from ignorance and lack of organization as well as from social indifference."[62] Lutherans fared less well than Roman Catholics because of their organizational deficiencies as noted by President Wenner, and their spiritual indifference as noted by President Baum.

An exception was in the area of social service or Inner Missions. Wenner's concern for uncoordinated Inner Mission activity indicates the extent of social ferment among urban Lutherans including (of course) Wenner. In 1906 Manhattan Lutherans, including Wenner, had formed the Lutheran Inner Mission Society in New York. Its leadership included English-speaking Lutherans in both the Ministerium and the Synod of New York and New Jersey, most notably Wenner and Holy Trinity's pastor, G. F. Krotel, but also Pastors Samuel Weiskotten, Frederick W. Knubel and Samuel Trexler. A Lutheran Hospital organized in Manhattan, formed in 1907 and led for years by President Wenner, provided extensive medical services for indigent Lutherans. Society efforts also included a young men's hospice; a summer camp—the Wilbur A. Herrlich Memorial Farm for poor children; missionaries who visited sick and troubled Lutherans at home, in hospitals, and prisons; and special homes for the disabled and for unmarried and deserted mothers. Cooperation with the Society for the Care of Indigent Germans resulted in "much needed work among the lonely and spiritually depressed inhabitants of Welfare Island."[63]

Though responding well with Inner Mission institutions and social service agencies, northeastern Lutherans did not undertake mission work in the cities on the same basis as other denominations. Most notable was the absence of city mission societies in which local churches in cooperation with denominational mission boards financed and built new parishes in growing cities. Income for such purposes in other Protestant denominations came from these two sources (local congregations and national boards), but also from trust funds and wealthy individual contributors. The result was that city societies among Baptists,

Methodists, Presbyterians, Episcopalians, and other main-line churches, provided between 35 percent and 50 percent of the funding needed for mission startups; in these denominations only an average of 14 percent came from denominational boards. With the New York Synod denominational funding amounted to 100 percent, because there was no additional support from other sources such as local congregations. In fact, synod congregations contributed less to the national church than their local missions received in help! The lack is all the more surprising since in Germany the same Inner Mission concern for social services also led new Lutheran synodical bodies to employ church building associations for that purpose. An important exception was in Rochester where the Rochester Lutheran Extension Society and its successor, the Rochester Mission Union of Lutheran Congregations, sought out new mission fields in the Rochester area in the early part of the century, building four congregations in this way before 1930. In Rochester's case, mission work led to social mission. An Inner Mission Society was formed in 1934, during the Great Depression.[64]

Why the unwillingness to master such development problems? President Baum had suggested a lack of "higher spirituality." This factor was highlighted by the synod itself in its 1916 report on the State of Religion. One-third of the members of the Hartwick, Hudson, and Southern Conferences were irregular in attendance at communion, while two out of three "are not informing themselves along Lutheran lines as they should" and are "unconcerned in this respect." What is more, there was a low percentage of male members (50 percent) active in the operations of the church, "one of the chief points of weakness in our denomination." Coupled with the paucity of men entering the ministry itself, this failure to attract men to the life and mission of the church was a serious problem. By contrast, in the more rapidly growing Western and German Conferences the "denominational spirit is very strong," and the Western conference reported "that the future is exceptionally bright and promising for all the Congregations."[65] Apparently denominational organization and differentiation—the two factors noted at the beginning of this chapter as having the greatest impact on the development of urban denominations—went hand in hand.

URBAN MISSION IN PERSPECTIVE

The New York Synod conferences with the lowest growth rates also displayed a relatively weak confessional identity while a more vital Lutheranism animated the more rapidly growing conferences. This can be explained in the Hartwick and Hudson conferences by the relatively weak Lutheran identity of the Hartwick and Franckean churches themselves. The secularizing effects of urbanization is probably the source of the problem in the Southern Conference. Congregations filled with ready workers but also with people indifferent to denominational matters, can be active at home but relatively indifferent to the mission work of extending the denomination in the growing urban scene. Given the size of urban New York and Buffalo, it is not difficult to imagine why a more committed Lutheran church developed rapidly in upstate urban areas, and more slowly in the downstate metropolitan area. The downstate church, in a more highly secular urban matrix, was more susceptible to the worldly complacency which the American church embraced between the turn of the century and the Great War. Upstate, in Albany, Rochester and Buffalo, congregations were more integrated into the life of developing urban areas.

What Lutherans experienced among themselves reflected a larger picture. A century of church growth and its problems hid both continuing growth problems and the power of secularization from all but the most discerning. "By every test but that of influence" wrote Henry Steele Commager "the church had never been stronger than it was at the opening of the twentieth century, and its strength increased rapidly . . .. Everyone was a Christian, and almost everyone joined some church, though few for reasons that would have earned them admission to Jonathan Edwards's Northampton congregation." The typical twentieth-century Protestant inherited his religion as he did his politics, "though rather more casually," and was quite unable to explain the differences between denominations. "He found himself a church member by accident and persisted in his affiliation by habit." Though such negative generalizations are too sweeping, Commager did note a troubling paradox. Though materially powerful and growing, the churches were filled with nominal Christians who were spiritually ineffective.[66]

Historian Winthrop S. Hudson has depicted the problem as the "church embracing the world." Declining church attendance and defunct family devotions were part of the new pattern of declension. Others beside Lutherans noted the signs of the times during the 1880s in the midst of prosperity and influence. The decline of the rural church was of special concern because village and town congregations had once been vigorous and well organized, the influential center of the church. Characteristically a 1908 White House commission voiced alarm at the plight of the rural church. They were being "diverted from the task of evangelism" by a preoccupation with Christianizing the culture, and therefore lost the "old vigorous advance" in church extension by a "withering evangelistic concern." The result was that old-line denominations slowed down in home mission efforts, and dissolved or merged more churches than they organized.[67] Such were conditions encouraging merger among New York General Synod bodies.

It was in such circumstances that eastern Lutherans began serious merger efforts, the first of which led to the formation of the New York Synod in 1908. Was merger interest fed by a crisis of opportunity and an awareness of decline, or by the illusion of strength and the hope of future growth? Perhaps by both, for American church leaders at the turn of the century were wrestling with contrary tendencies—urban growth and rural decline—as Graph 10.2 suggests.

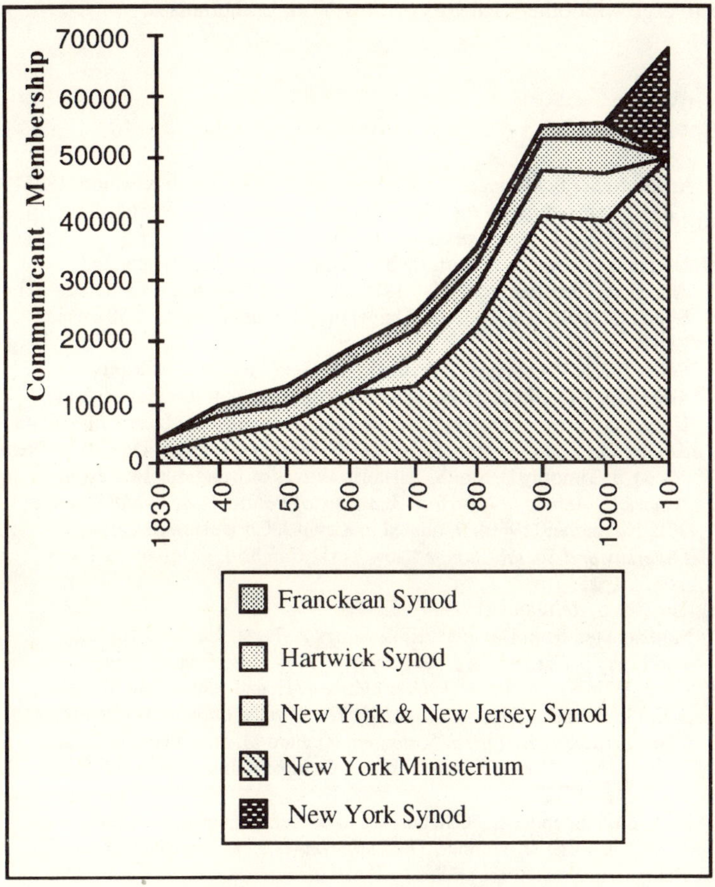

Graph 10.2 Formation of the New York Synod

The rural church in the form of the Hartwick and Franckean Synods provided few members to the Lutheran Church in New York between 1830 and 1910. The urban church was doing better, as the New York and New Jersey part of the bar graph indicates. Its growth between 1890 and 1900, and declining Ministerium membership in that decade, also indicate the relative fortunes of English- and German-speaking Lutherans at the end of the nineteenth century. Here was a problem which would challenge the Ministerium in the early twentieth-century. But as the Ministerium increases between 1870 and 1890 and again after 1900 also indicate, German-language mission was and would continue to be an important growth dynamic in the Ministerium. It is to this rather complicated situation that we now turn, to assess developments within a Ministerium that was beginning to converge with other elements of New York Lutheranism.

NOTES

1 Arthur Meier Schlesinger, "A Critical Period in American Religion, 1875-1900," *Proceedings of the Massachusetts Historical Society* 64, June (1932): 523-547; see especially 524-531.

2 Reginald W. Deitz, "Eastern Lutheranism in American Society and American Christianity. 1870—1914. Darwinism—Biblical Criticism—The Social Gospel," (Ph. D. Diss., University of Pennsylvania, 1958), esp. 280 ff.

3 Henry Steele Commager, *The American Mind. An Interpretation of American Thought and Character Since the 1880's* (New Haven: Yale University Press, 1950), 170. Aaron Ignatius Abell, *The Urban Impact on American Protestantism, 1865-1900* (Cambridge: Harvard University Press, 1943), 3; Timothy L. Smith, "Historic Waves of Religious Interest in America," *Annals of American Academy of Political and Social Science*, 332. November (1960): 9; quoted in Kevin J. Christiano, *Religious Diversity and Social Change* (New York: Cambridge University Press, 1987), 1, 15.

4 Christiano, *Religious Diversity*, 5.

5 Map adapted from David M. Ellis, James A. Frost, Harold C. Syrett, and Harry J. Carman, *A History of New York State* (Ithaca, New York: Cornell University Press, 1967), 462 & 471; and John E. and Ronald J. Grele Bebout, *Where Cities Meet. The Urbanization of New Jersey, The New Jersey Historical Series*, ed. Richard M. and Wheaton J. Lane Huber. (New York: D. Van Nostrand Company, Inc., 1964) 22: 82-3.

6 Ibid., 24ff; 19-21.

7 Ibid., 64; Appendix C. "Categorization of Religious Bodies, 1890, 1906"; 164 ff. "George U. Wenner, *The Lutherans of New York* (New York: The Petersfield Press, 1918), 73.

8 Christiano, *Religious Diversity*, Appendix E, "A Typology of Urban Religious Change, 1890-1906," 176ff; Appendix F, "Religious Diversity Scores for 122 Cities, 1890 and 1906."

9 Ibid., 129; 125; Chapters VII & IX; 155; 130-131.

10 Ibid.

11 Lawrence A. Cremin, *American Education. The Metropolitan Experience 1876-1980* (New York: Harper & Row, 1988), 116, 117-150. See Timothy L. Smith, "Religion and Ethnicity in America," *AHR* LXXXII (1978): 1155-1185, esp. 1156-67.

12 Wenner, *Lutherans of New York*, 91-120.

13 See Will Herberg, *Protestant-Catholic-Jew. An Essay in Religious Sociology*

(New York: Doubleday & Company, Inc., 1960), esp. 30ff; 33.
14 New York and New Jersey Synod, *Minutes* (1907), 76.
15 Ibid., 76-82.
16 Ibid., 84-7.
17 Wenner, *Lutherans of New York*, 57ff.
18 Franckean Synod, *Journal* (1891), 13; (1896), 10.
19 Ibid. (1891), 13; (1892), 17-18; (1891), 9; (1892), 13; (1896), 20; (1894), 15; (1891), 32; (1892), 14; (1896), 12-3.
20 Ibid. (1896), 12, 178, 175. Franckean Synod, *Journal* (1897), 9-11. Christiano, *Religious Diversity*, 5.
21 Franckean Synod, *Journal* (1901), 18; (1902), 27; (1908), 22.
22 Ibid. (1900), 7, 12. See Chapter 9.
23 Ibid. (1902), 24-6. Hartwick Synod, *Minutes* (1902), 18-20.
24 Ibid. (1890), 21.
25 Ibid., 177.
26 Ibid. (1891), 7, 19; (1892), 14ff; (1893), 9, 14, 18; (1895), 12-13; (1897), 18.
27 Ibid. (1903), 8-9, 11, 22-23; (1903), 12, 28; Franckean Synod, *Journal* (1904), 13.
28 Hartwick Synod, *Minutes* (1903), 25; (1904), 26, 27; (1895), 42; "Synodical Roll," 7-8; (1890), "Synodical Roll," 7-8; (1900), "Synodical Roll," 7-8; (1908), "Synodical Roll," 2-4; Christiano, *Religious Diversity*, "Appendix B."
29 Ibid., "Appendix B."
30 New York and New Jersey Synod, *Minutes* (1895), 13, 17-18.
31 Ibid. (1896), 12, 17; (1891), 21; (1896), 23.
32 Ibid. (1897), 10-11; (1896), 33-34.
33 Ibid. (1899), 19; (1897), 10-11; (1897), 22-23; (1898), 16; (1900), 13. New York Ministerium, *Minutes* (1897), 14.
34 Ibid. (1896), 62-63, 66-67.
35 Ibid. (1898), 9; (1900), 14. *Lutheran Cyclopedia* (1975), 671.
36 New York Ministerium, *Minutes* (1903), 11; (1901), 23; (1903), 10-11.
37 Ibid. (1901), 23; (1903), 10; (1902), 19-20; (1893), 19.
38 Ibid. (1903), 19.
39 New York and New Jersey Synod, *Minutes* (1905), 27-8; (1906), 13, 20-21; (1907), 47. Hartwick Synod, *Minutes* (1905), 33; (1906), 28; (1907), 21. Franckean Synod, *Journal* (1904), 13-14; (1906), 12-13.
40 Hartwick Synod, *Minutes* (1907), 22, 4.
41 Synod of New York, *Minutes* (1908), 8, 13-18, 20, 23-5; (1909), "Appendix A. Parochial Report," 104ff.
42 Ibid., 36.
43 Ibid., 45, 37.
44 Ibid., 41.
45 Ibid., 43-44.
46 Ibid., 47, 49.
47 Ibid., 45-6.
48 Ibid., 49, 91-2.
49 Ibid. (1910), 37, 35, 34, 37-8. On the Inner Mission movement see Kurt Aland, *A History of Christianity, 2 vols.* (Philadelphia: Fortress Press, 1986) II: 347; and Eugene L Fevold, "Coming of Age, 1875-1900," *The Lutherans*

in North America, ed. E. Clifford Nelson (Philadelphia: Fortress Press, 1975), 355-57.

50 Synod of New York , *Minutes* (1910), 29-30; 28.

51 Ibid., 38-39.

52 Ibid., 39-41.

53 Ibid., 53-56, 56-59.

54 Ibid., 52-59.

55 Ibid., 43.

56 Ibid., 65-7.

57 Ibid., 65.

58 Joseph R. Conlin, *The American Past. Part Two. A Survey of American History Since 1865* (New York: Harcourt Brace Jovanovich, 1987), 503.

59 Synod of New York , *Minutes* (1911), 32; (1912), 34, 54.

60 Ibid. (1913), 67; (1917), 36; (1918), 39-41; (1917), 37-42; (1920), 51-56.

61 Ibid. (1910), 96-109; (1920), 78-91.

62 Abell, *The Urban Impact*, 13-14.

63 I. Searles Runyon, *The Record of the First Twenty-Five Years 1906-1931. The Inner Mission Society of the Evangelical Lutheran Church in New York City* (New York: Privately published, 1931). Archives, Lutheran Social Services of New York. [Knubel,, Frederick H.] Memorial remarks "Read at memorial service at Concordia, December 17, 1934." MNYS, SP 1, George U. Wenner.

64 For a description of this social ministry response to urbanization see Abell, *Urban Impact*, 52-3; and Wilbur C. Hallenback, *Urban Organization of Protestantism* (New York: Harper and Brothers, 1934), 130-31, 90. Aland, *History of Christianity*, II: 344. Charles W. Kosbab, "The Rochester Lutheran Conference of the United Lutheran Synod of New York and New England and the United Lutheran Church in Americas 1809-1962" (Rochester, NY: Typescript by Charles W. Kosbab, 1962) New York Archives: 41-2.

65 Synod of New York , *Minutes* (1916), 43-44.

66 Commager, *American Mind*, 166.

67 Winthrop S. Hudson, *The Great Tradition of the American Churches* (New York: Harper & Brothers, 1953), 195ff, 203, 209.

11

CONVERGENCE AND COOPERATION

The New York Ministerium and the New York and New England Synod, 1890-1920

To examine the New York Ministerium for signs of convergence with other forms of Lutheranism might at first seem an exercise in futility. German immigration had transformed an English-speaking, General Synod Ministerium into a highly conservative expression of General Council confessionalism. Continued resurgence in German-language Lutheranism after 1900, even as English-speaking congregations emerged within the Ministerium, maintained its conservative direction. However in the quarter century after 1875 signs of convergence began to appear. Extremism bred reaction in a more moderate direction. Urbanization, too, began working its influence as in other Lutheran bodies. Acculturation likewise worked its (albeit belated) influence. Together these forces redirected the Ministerium towards a greater interest in other expressions of Lutheranism.

REALIGNMENT WITHIN THE NEW YORK MINISTERIUM

The Ministerium was transformed in the 1870s by a group of conservative, German-speaking confessionalists, including members of the re-merged Steimle Synod. They exerted a disproportionate influence pushing the Ministerium to the right within the General Council and agitating within the synod to safeguard the rights of congregations.

"DIE PROTESTPARTEI"

The Ministerium's historian, John Nicum, recounting the origins of this group in his 1888 history, described them as "Die Anhanger der missourischen Richtung" ("Adherents of Missourian tendencies").[1] Controversy over proposals for constitutional change introduced by St. Matthews, New York, the oldest congregation in the synod, dating (with First Church, Albany) to the seventeenth century, generated a supporting "Protestpartei." Thirteen pastors formed the nucleus of the party, though a majority within the Ministerium could apparently be counted on for key votes. They carried their case and viewpoint into the pages of the Ministerium's *Lutherischer Herold*, and when its pages were closed to them, they formed their own broadside, *Zeuge der Wahrheit* (*Witness to Truth*). Not content to keep the constitutional issue alive, they began raising other theological questions (most notably predestination) which were agitating German-speaking Lutherans especially within the Missouri Synod.[2]

The editors of *Zeuge der Wahrheit*—Louis Halfmann, William Busse, and August Emil Frey—were publicly censured for their efforts by Ministerium President J. H. Baden whereupon eight members of the party began a process of withdrawal which took them and four of their congregations into the Eastern District of the Missouri Synod. Halfmann, a Ministerium member serving a Missouri Synod congregation, Immanuel, New York, withdrew in 1880. Busse also left in 1880 together with his congregation, St. Lukes of New York, and though he joined the Missouri Synod, his congregation remained an independent affiliate. Frey withdrew in 1883 together with St. Marks, Brooklyn to join Missouri. Five other pastors left. Edmund Bohm withdrew to become professor and director of the new Eastern District proseminary which eventually became Concordia Institute. G. W. Drees, retired from St. Lukes and moved to the German community of Breslau (Lindenhurst, L. I.) to serve St. Johns; he joined the Missouri Synod in 1880, the year St. Johns withdrew from the Ministerium; it joined the Eastern District in 1885. J. P. Schoener left in 1883, perhaps with Frey, and took a Missouri Synod charge at St. Pauls, Port Richmond, on Staten Island, in 1885. Armand Bolquarts transferred directly to Missouri in 1883. Johann Mulhauser, the last to leave, withdrew in 1884, having walked out on the synod's disciplinary proceedings against Frey. In all eight clergy and five congregations left; of these, seven clergy and four congregations joined the Missouri Synod. Besides those which left with their pastors, two congregations withdrew separately. A new congregation at Yonkers, founded in 1870, withdrew during the height of the controversy to join the Missouri Synod in 1878. Most importantly, St. Matthews source of the controversy, and the oldest and most influential congregation in the Ministerium, withdrew in 1880, eventually joining the Eastern District of the Missouri Synod in 1886. When it left it took with it St. Matthews Academy, its extensive mission support, and an important chapter of the Ministerium's history and reputation.[3]

PREDESTINATION CONTROVERSY

It was Frey's departure in 1883 which finally involved the Ministerium in the predestination controversy. The controversy grew out of an 1877 meeting of the Western District of the Missouri Synod. Long accustomed to discussing doctrine as part of their synodical deliberations, like other confessional bodies including the Ministerium, the Western District dealt with the doctrine of election under the leadership of C. F. W. Walther. The doctrine, as found in the "Formula of Concord," was one of several discussed under the general rubric *soli deo gloria.* It was asserted in one thesis that the predestination of persons was seen to be the cause of salvation and the insurer that the elect would not lose their faith; yet election was not based on divine foreknowledge, i.e. God's foreseeing that it would occur. Faith was not the cause of election, yet damnation was not the result of predestination, but of the sinner's resistance to grace.[4]

Critics of Walther within the Missouri Synod and the Synodical Conference were concerned with what they felt was an overly deterministic, crypto-Calvinist emphasis in Walther's theses. If *soli deo gloria* was the orientation of Walther, his critics were concerned to uphold the sola *fide* emphasized in the Augustana doctrine of justification by faith. Eventually the dispute settled into a conflict between Walther and the Missouri Synod, and the Joint Synod of Ohio and its president, Columbus Seminary professor Matthias Loy. At issue for Loy was protecting the doctrine of the universality of God's grace and justification. He and the other Walther opponents were in turn accused of semi-Pelagianism (allowing free will a role in salvation) because in articulating the article of justification they insisted that where individuals were concerned, predestination takes place *intuitu fidei,* "in view of" faith. The New York Ministerium's "protest party" sought "to entangle the Ministerium in the Missourian predestination dispute" as part of its attempted criticism of Ministerium theology. Pastor A. E. Frey embraced the Missouri position, for which he was censured by the First (metropolitan New York) Conference of the Ministerium. The case was reviewed by the Ministerium and while Frey's own interpretation of the doctrine of election was put forward during the case's review, his reasons were never examined, and the Conference's accusation of "false teaching" was printed in the synod's protocol.[5]

It was at this point that Frey and Mulhauser withdrew from the synod, as much over the issue of unfair treatment as of presumed theological differences. Subsequently the Ministerium approached the Philadelphia faculty requesting an official opinion "Concerning the Dogma of Predestination." The Mt. Airy position reflected the progressive historicism of the Erlangen school found at Mt. Airy—a position which avoided a literalist interpretation of either scripture or the confessions, seeking the best of the past but understood in contemporary perspective. They wished to gain a proper conception "of the historical position of the Formula of Concord" in relation to early and later Lutheran theology. They also understood the inappropriateness of trying to solve new theological problems with old language, having developed a theological understanding of the anachronistic which was completely foreign to the repristinated theology of Missouri. Therefore the faculty assumed the "attitude of reserve" which they found in most of the *Book of Concord* regarding predestination. "It is a historical fact, that the early Lutheran Confessions . . . avoid any direct reference to the subject of predestination, and certainly do not teach an absolute predestination or determinism." With reference to the Augustana itself, "we know that silence on this particular doctrine was intentional." It is also a historical fact that Reformed declarations and confessions "openly declare an absolute predestinarianism and determinism" as the "very basis and starting point of their whole system." The "Formula of Concord" condemns outspoken Calvinism, on the one hand, and all "synergistic efforts," "but it also rejects those deterministic and ultra-predestinarian tendencies of early Lutheran theologians" which were uttered to counteract the Pelagianism of Rome. Diplomatically the faculty acknowledged the desire of those (Missourians) "to exalt the majesty of divine grace over against the prevailing Pelagianism and Synergism of modern times." But if "the attempt be made to interpret the Formula of Concord" in the extreme anti-Pelagian language of the early [orthodox] theologians, "we are constrained by the evidence before us to consider this a misconception of the historical position of the Formula of Concord, and an actual receding from its sounder and safer standpoint" to a position the Formula itself had sought to "overcome."[6]

CHANGING CONFESSIONAL LANGUAGE

The Mt. Airy faculty acknowledged in the extreme conservative anxiety to exalt God's majesty in reaction to the pelagianism and synergism of "modern times" the stress of modernity which could significantly warp confessional theology. The result was a sectarian mentality—the utter certitude of truth and right—which ultra-predestinarian tendencies simply reinforced as they had among Calvinists in the seventeenth century. It was this sectarian spirit in the "protestpartei" which the Ministerium condemned in its censure. The party's defeat and departure reduced the hard-core of extreme confessionalists within the Ministerium just as a steady stream of Mt. Airy graduates entered the synod through ordination, and with them the mediating theology of Mt. Airy and the more moderate confessionalism of the General Council. The change would not occur overnight, but over a generation of leadership with pastors moving into positions of leadership after 1885 who had no experience of the tumultuous 1870s. As late as 1894 the confessional article in the Ministerium Constitution stated:

> This body accepts all the canonical books of the Old and New Testaments as the revealed Word of God and the only rule of faith; also the confessions of the Evangelical Lutheran Church, as contained in the Book of Concord of 1580 as the correct presentation of the Christian Faith, to wit:
> The three oecumenical creeds;
> The unaltered Augsburg Confession of 1530;
> The Apology;
> The Smalcald Articles;
> The Large and the Small Catechisms of Luther;
> The Formula of Concord

However by 1900, a revision of the Constitution's confessional paragraph now indicated that the above-mentioned parts of the *Book of Concord* were no longer considered "the correct presentation" but simply "a true exposition of the Christian Belief." This shift in code words suggests a moderating confessional trend in a decade of changes.[7]

MODERATING ROLE WITHIN THE GENERAL COUNCIL

Another indication of change was the Ministerium's position within the General Council. Unlike the Michigan Synod which withdrew over the Council's interpretation of the Galesburg Rule—"Lutheran pulpits for Lutheran ministers only—Lutheran altars for Lutheran communicants only"—the Ministerium decided in the middle 1880s to remain in the Council, though continuing to interpret that rule "without exceptions." The Ministerium delegations of 1876 and 1877 which had pushed in the General Council for a strict interpretation of the Galesburg Rule, contained a majority of Ministerium pastors and lay delegates favoring no exceptions to the rule. These delegations included two leaders of "Die Protestpartei"—A. E. Frey and Louis Halfmann—as well as Halfmann's conservative colleague from Steimle synod days, E. T. Moldehnke. The previous three delegations (1873, 1874, and 1875), which had been active as well on behalf of a strict confessionalism, had contained other members of the group, including G. W. Drees and Justus Ruperti, pastor of St. Matthews. While General Council representation in the middle 1870s had been unbalanced in favor of "Die Protestpartei" and its supporters, with the party's demise after 1879 other pastors were chosen to represent the Ministerium in more balanced delegations. These included a mixture of moderate supporters of strict construction, continued opponents, and one or two neutrals. The key meetings of 1885 and 1886 (when the Michigan Synod withdrew) contained both opponents and supporters of strict construction, but no longer any members of "Die Protestpartei." After 1886 delegation personnel changed almost entirely with the slow turnover of generations then taking place. It was this shift in representation—the elimination of extremists in the

Ministerium, the return to more balanced delegations, and the generational turnover in the delegations—which kept the Ministerium from withdrawing and (perhaps) joining the Synodical Conference. As a result the Ministerium quietly laid the Galesburg Rule and its interpretation to rest by 1890.[8]

FORMATION OF WAGNER COLLEGE

The departure of St. Matthews with its Academy in 1880 left the Ministerium with no proseminary to educate ministerial candidates in preparation for Mt. Airy Seminary. By 1883 the situation had become critical. In August the Rochester Lutheran pastors appealed in writing to the Ministerium, asking where they were going to get their German clergymen. By October a Lutheran Proseminary had been organized. German Lutheran pastors were needed not only for missions in the west but for German congregations in the east. These congregations, too, needed pastors capable of providing understandable and edifying preaching, governance by God's Word, Luther's teachings in his German idioms, and German conversational ability. A large bequest by Rochester businessman and Proseminary Vice-President John George Wagner in memory of his deceased son who had hoped to become a Lutheran pastor soon led to the proseminary being renamed "Wagner Memorial Lutheran College." (See fig. 11.1.)

figure 11.1
Wagner College, Rochester, New York

The new College flourished for a time though it was no more than 10 percent the size of the much larger St. Matthews Academy. With the renaming administrative leadership was restructured and expanded to include two pastors and two lay members from each conference district. The Visitation Committee for 1887 reported twenty-six students in residence the previous year and a faculty of seven. Four languages were taught—German, English, Greek, and Latin—together with spelling, arithmetic, and religion. The last subject included "teachings of the Church and the book containing the creeds of the Lutheran, reformed, and Catholic Churches." At the closing ceremonies recitations were given in German and English, indicating a bilingual educational environment. Though not providing the classical liberal education found at St. Matthews, Wagner accomplished much in four years. But students were needed and more support from the congregations was required, a situation which did improve somewhat over the next few years. However, by 1900, with a declining need for German-speaking pastors, a proposal was made to broaden the curriculum and move the College to New York City. The following year a financial agent (fund raiser) was employed to develop support for the move throughout the synod. Eventually (1916) Wagner College would be moved to Staten Island with synod backing ($100,000 was to be raised). Through the efforts of Pastor Frederick Sutter of Trinity Lutheran Church of Stapleton, Staten Island, the college was relocated to the former Cunard family estate on Grimes Hill overlooking New York Harbor.[9]

REALIGNMENT AMONG CONSERVATIVE LUTHERANS IN NEW YORK

The fortunes of Wagner College reflect other changes taking place in the Ministerium. Unknown to Ministerium leadership, German immigration had peaked in 1882. Its decline over the next several decades, with emigration shifting to central and southern Europe, would change the Ministerium's makeup. It now found itself in competition with a strict form of confessional Lutheranism (the Missouri Synod) which was then showing considerable growth just when the pool of potential adherents was shrinking. While German-speaking pastors would still be needed, it was the English-speaking portion of the church which would grow more rapidly. The task at hand was to serve a multiple constituency—a declining first generation of German-speaking Lutherans, and their anglicized offspring. Though this phenomenon was apparent everywhere, it was especially apparent among subgroups of English-speaking Lutherans in German-speaking congregations in the cities of upstate New York. Even as it grew to cover the entire northeast, the New York Ministerium was becoming a complicated network of congregations. (See Maps 11.1, 11.2, and 11.3.)

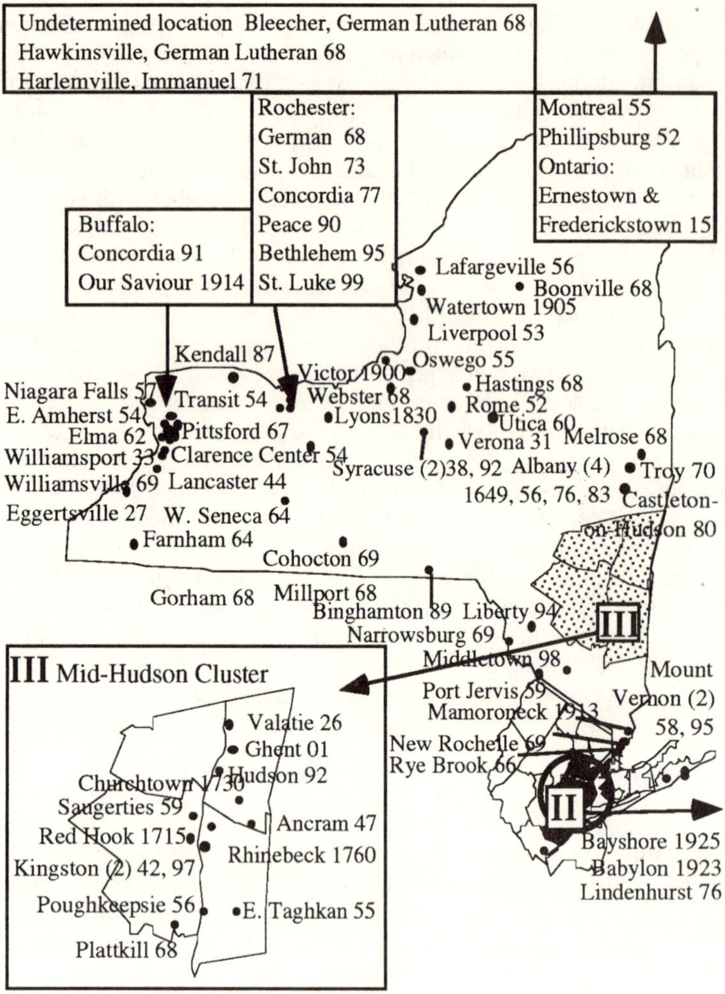

Note: two-digit dates are nineteenth-century

Map 11.1
Congregations of the New York Ministerium
1786-1929

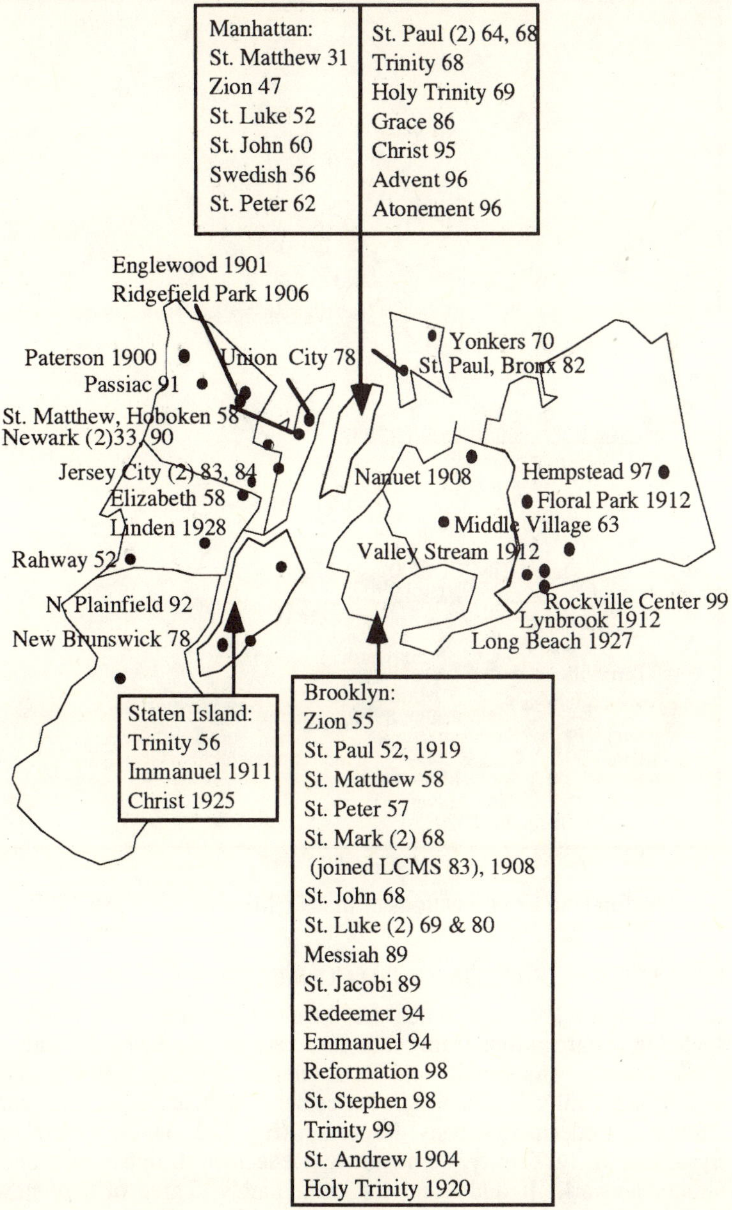

Map 11.2

Urban New York & New Jersey Congregations

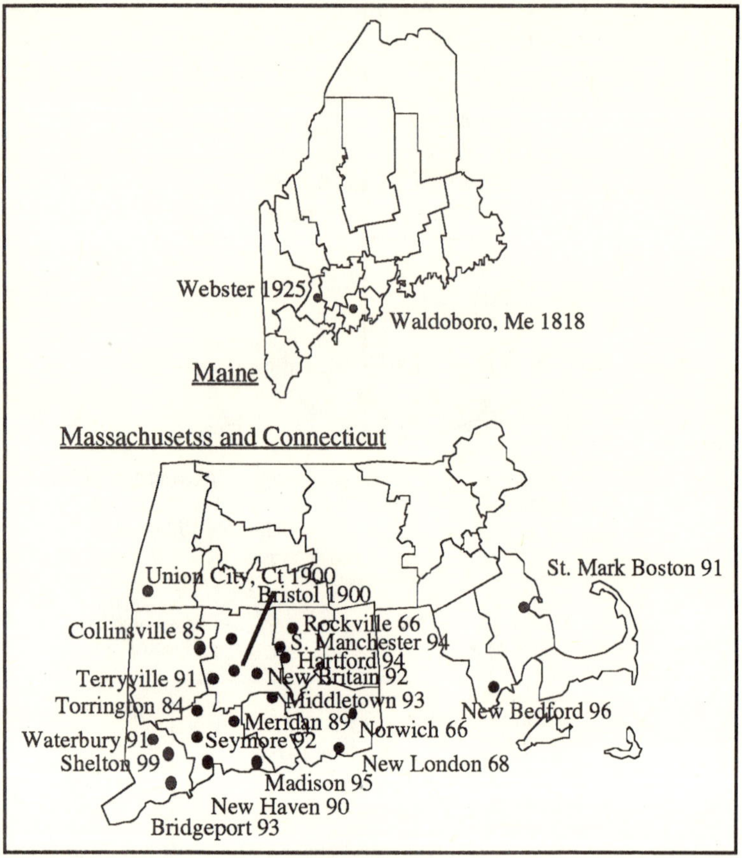

Map 11.3

New England Congregations of the NY Ministerium, 1786-1929

FORMATION OF THE ENGLISH CONFERENCE

In 1896 an English Conference was created by taking fifteen English-speaking congregations from other conferences for the new venture—Holy Trinity, Atonement, and Redeemer in Buffalo; Reformation, Grace, and Trinity, in Rochester; Redeemer, Christ, and Holy Trinity in Brooklyn; Redeemer, Albany; Redeemer (fig. 11.2), Utica; Redeemer, Syracuse; Holy Trinity, Jamestown; Redeemer, Binghamton; and, Grace, Newark. It added others immediately. Three of five new churches received into the Ministerium in 1895 were English-speaking, including Atonement, Buffalo; Redeemer and Christ, Brooklyn; and fully half of the new mission fields reported in 1896 were English-speaking.[10]

figure 11.2
Evangelical Lutheran Church of the Redeemer, Utica, NY

As the preponderance of the name "Church of the Redeemer" might suggest, the English Conference emerged out of an informal network of English-speaking Ministerium churches in upstate New York. Some shared common founders; all shared the common experience of seeking English-language worship in German-speaking cities. In Brooklyn the work of the Conference created difficulties almost as soon as it was formed. Bitter and apparently well-founded complaints reached the synod president that "English brethren have not shown the proper spirit of love and consideration" in founding English missions. In 1898 the New York Conference complained with specifics: the English Conference had failed to observe the synodical rules laid down at its founding. According to those stipulations, congregations were not to change conferences without synodical permission. And no mission was to be established by the English Conference without the consent of the Ministerium president and the local conference president within whose bounds a new congregation was to be formed. To make the rule stick, the two presidents were to be formed into a committee to "decide for or against" organizing a specific mission after consultation with neighborhood pastors.[11] By the next year (1899) the problem had increased, this time in an area where English-language Lutheranism was being aggressively promoted.

The Rochester Conference protested the formation of St. Pauls English Lutheran Church in Rochester on the grounds that the new procedures had not been followed. Whether or not the English Conference had acted unilaterally, it petitioned the Ministerium for equal status so that it could be master of its own affairs. Matters did not improve by 1900. An English-speaking west Albany parish was established over against protests of the German-language pastor in the vicinity, and only with the intervention of the Ministerium president. Again, in Brooklyn conflict arose over English efforts to organize in German neighborhoods. This time following procedures, members of the English Conference petitioned to start three congregations in Eastern Boulevard, South Brooklyn, and Greenpoint. Objections were made to all three. A subsequent request by Pastors Weiskotten, Steimle, and Knabenschuh, for a mission in Carroll Park suffered the same fate. The New York Conference president withheld his consent because the local pastor protested. Again a canvass was suggested, to which the English pastors replied that the only way to test the area was "to begin regular church services, when it would soon become evident, whether or not the necessity existed." The Ministerium president was again appealed to, but church services were also started, presenting him with a "fait accompli." The English Conference president declared (of course) that he had no official knowledge of work begun in the field. Matters went somewhat better in Borough Park, where Pastors Weiskotten, Steimle, and Knabenschuh proposed yet another mission. This time the New York Conference president made no objection because there was no German-speaking congregation with which to compete. But he insisted, "as a matter of principle and of doctrine" that a call to do mission work must be proven, and therefore a canvass was needed.[12]

Clearly German-language pastors and congregations were reluctant to allow English-speaking missions. While not standing in the way of such work, their outright veto power and insistence that the burden of proof must be met before a mission could be organized was in direct conflict with the desire of English-speaking pastors to start a mission to prove a need. Seeing this, the Ministerium president framed a series of questions for synodical deliberation in 1900. His conviction, based on several years' experience, was that synodical resolutions and opinions "will not banish all friction and unpleasantness between the representatives of differing interests in the Synod." There was, in other words, a fundamental conflict of interest at work within the Ministerium regarding "the English question" to the disadvantage of English missions![13]

Yet English mission work continued to grow. The Ministerium president summed up the situation well. One English-speaking church had existed in 1879; only three existed a decade later. By 1895, with the creation of the English Conference their numbers had reached fifteen (15); by 1900 the group had grown to twenty-five (25). There had been "rapid strides in missionary activity, but not without creating opposition and calling forth various protests against the founding of new missions." By 1902 the English question had become the all-consuming question in the Ministerium. Within the English Conference the opposition was carefully analyzed. While it was not thought that the German-speaking churches were opposed to mission efforts, undue prominence given to congregational interests were "shutting out the larger interests of the Kingdom." Meanwhile if the insistence that no mission could be established without canvass and call, although these were not to be the responsibility of the English Conference "because we are not a Synod, then there is but one course for us to pursue." Under the circumstances, where there was no mechanism for growth, separation seemed inevitable.[14]

In light of these circumstances English Conference president, W.F. Bacher recommended that the conference become an English Synod to be connected with the General Council. Thirty-one votes were cast in unanimous support of the move. The only nonvoting member, Ministerium President George Haas, counseled waiting and making a request for orderly withdrawal at the 1902 meeting of the Ministerium. Instead, twenty-four (24) pastors requested that Haas grant them an honorable dismission, and when he demurred, ten congregations withdrew outright. Subsequently, however, all requests and withdrawals were rescinded to be replaced by a petition of the English Conference for permission to withdraw from the Ministerium and to form an English Synod. This was granted at the 1902 meeting of the Ministerium, but an apology was demanded "for the irregularity of their course in withdrawing from the Synod." What followed was a very Lutheran ritual act of reconciliation and separation to purge the blame and guilt which had developed in the relationship between the two groups. The Conference expressed "deep regrets" on behalf of its members while recognizing "the magnanimity" with which the Ministerium had acted in the entire manner and "begged for forgiveness." A memorial from the offending group followed, expressing "deep appreciation" for permission to withdraw. The offended Ministerium majority, in a continued spirit of "magnanimity" noted with "great satisfaction" the minority's "moderation and kindliness" and the "peaceable and orderly manner" in which the final separation occurred. Magnanimous self-justification followed. Believing that "she thoroughly understand the peculiar conditions and necessities of her territory, the Ministerium indeed recognizes her devinely [sic] appointed mission to lie principally along German lines."

But having "watched the wonderful growth and development of the English work in her midst" the Ministerium "considers the interests of the kingdom of God paramount to the claims of nationality and language." Therefore "the interests of our Church at large should continue to be the bond of union" between Mother-Synod and her offspring.[15]

THE MISSOURI SYNOD AND THE NEW YORK MINISTERIUM

It was not until the resolution of the English question that the New York Ministerium realized how exclusively German were its interests within "the kingdom of God." The kingdom was a metaphor for a Lutheran ecology in the New York area composed of eighteen synodical bodies each seeking its own niche in an increasingly complex urban environment. Throughout the 1890s the New York Ministerium sought its place in this new landscape, but not without some frustration. Just as it decided for its German interests it found itself in intense competition for German Lutheran loyalties in the New York area with the Missouri Synod because of that body's rapid growth and aggressive congregationalism. As can be seen from Graph 11.1 the slowdown in the Ministerium growth rate occurred as that of the Eastern District (and then the Atlantic District) was increasing.

The Eastern District of the Missouri Synod was formed at St. Louis in 1854, at the eighth convention of the national body. It originally comprised all territory east of the Ohio state line (i.e., the northeast from the western Pennsylvania border), including parts of Canada. Eventually the Atlantic District was separated out in 1906 to form a separate body east of a line which ran through the center of New York State. At first the Missouri Synod was but a "little cloud, like the hand of a man, in the west," as the *Lutheran Observer* put it. C. F. W. Walther, using *Der Lutheraner*, drew together a network of sympathetic pastors before the Missouri Synod itself was formed. The network included Theodore J. Brohm, a Saxon immigrant who had studied theology at Leipzig and had migrated to America as secretary of Martin Stephan, original leader of the Saxon migration to Missouri. Brohm was called east in 1842 from Missouri by the new Buffalo Synod of J. A. A. Grabau and recommended to Trinity Lutheran of New York City as its pastor in 1843. Trinity itself had formed in 1839 from among the Prussian immigrants who remained in the city (rather than moving on to Buffalo) under the spiritual leadership of a tailor, Karl B. Schultheisz. A founder of the Missouri Synod and for years the vice-president "for the East," Brohm was leader of a group of Old Lutheran confessionalists who were determined, aggressive, competitive and moved by a sense of inevitable victory.[16]

The years from 1843 to 1880 were a seedtime for the Missouri Synod in the New York area. Besides Brohm's Trinity Church in Manhattan, there were Old Lutheran congregations at Port Richmond

(Staten Island) and Strattonport (College Point), Williamsburgh, as well as in Buffalo, and Boston, Massachusetts. During the 1850s, 1860s, and 1870s a total of forty-seven (47) Missouri Synod congregations were developed on the territory of the New York Ministerium including congregations in Yorkville, Hicksville, Harlem, Morrisania (Bronx), Locust Grove (L. I.), Narrowsburg, Rondout (Kingston), New Rochelle, Hudson, Hillsdale, Troy, Albany, Paterson, New Jersey, and Providence, Rhode Island. A Missouri Synod pastor, meanwhile, had been called to serve as chaplain and director of the Wartburg Orphan's Home and Farm.[17]

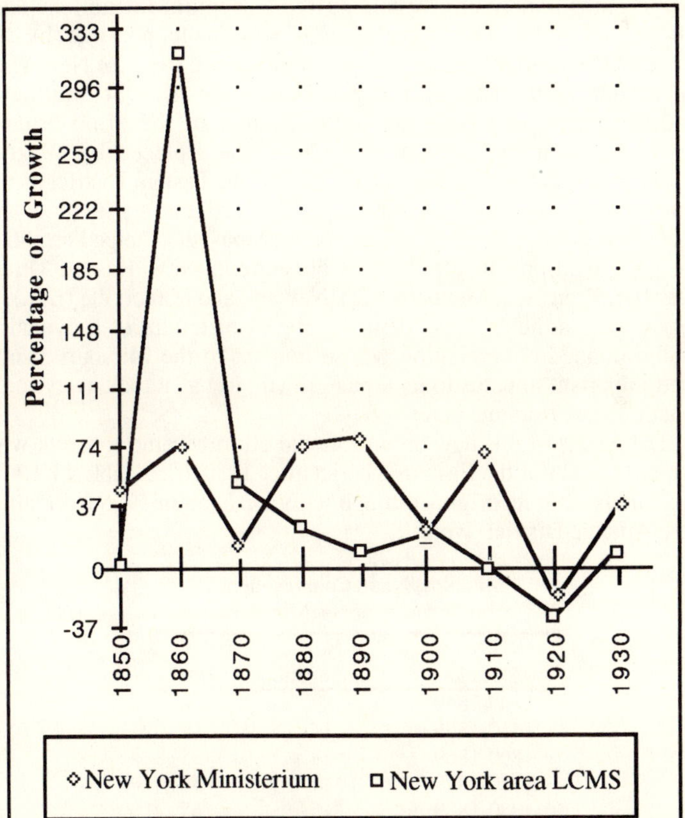

Graph 11.1
New York Ministerium and Missouri Synod

The next quarter century witnessed extensive growth at a time when the New York Ministerium's size had begun to stabilize. A Home

Mission Board was organized for the district in 1888 to assist the traveling missionary who had been on the territory since the 1870s, and a Church Extension Fund was established to assist mission congregations. The Eastern District was an important exception to the rule about the lack of city mission societies among eastern Lutherans. The District established the New York City Mission, and city mission organizations as well for Brooklyn, Schenectady, and New Jersey. These were cooperative mission groups (it will be remembered) which significantly augmented the financial support of regional and national Lutheran bodies in the work of home mission. A proseminary was also established for pastoral candidates in 1881 first as a *Progymnasium*, then as a *Mittelgymnasium*, finally becoming the Concordia Institution (later College) in 1893. This development was made possible by St. Matthews (Manhattan) recent transfer of allegiance from the New York Ministerium to the Missouri Synod Eastern District. St. Matthews Academy which had been an important part of the Ministerium's parochial educational system and had to be replaced by Wagner Proseminary and College was turned over to the Eastern District as the foundation for its own "Progymnasium." St. Matthews's affiliation, and its subsequent large donations to home missions, also helped establish new congregations in Danbury, Connecticut, New Haven, Utica, Rochester, Bronx (2), Manhattan (2), Newark, and Manorville (L. I.).[18] Clearly St. Matthews's loss deprived the Ministerium of a dynamic, mission-minded congregation whose transfer to the Missouri Synod added important impetus to its urban growth, just as it took away some of that impetus from the parent body.

The results of this new organizational effort became apparent with the rapid growth of the Eastern District after 1880. (See Table 11.1.) Its acquisitions from its origins through reorganization in 1906 (formation of the Atlantic District) were:

Table 11.1
Missouri Synod Congregations (5)
on Territory of NY Ministerium

Decade	New Congregations	Total
1840-1849	3	3
1850-1859	12	15
1860-1869	18	33
1870-1879	17	50
1880-1889	15	65
1890-1899	35	100
1900-1909	32	132
1910-1919	29	161

As noted above, a small but highly significant part of this growth came at the direct expense of the Ministerium with the loss of four congregations and seven pastors to the Eastern District in the early 1880s. The larger impact, however, was in terms of each organization's relative ability to attract congregational members and pastors from among the hundred or so independent, German-speaking Lutheran congregations organized between the Civil War and 1910. In eighty-nine known cases of independent congregations eventually joining a Lutheran synodical body in the area, fifty-nine joined the Missouri Synod while only one or two joined the New York Ministerium. By the 1890s both bodies reported a number of these affiliated but independent congregations. The Eastern District had been reporting its independent affiliates since 1855. The Ministerium did not need to make the distinction until 1897. The year before, it reported one hundred forty-eight (148) congregations, while in 1897 it finally distinguished between one hundred twenty-three (123) member congregations, and thirty-six (36) affiliates.[19] Competition was intense for new congregations, especially in urban areas where urban growth encouraged differentiation. (See Chapter 12.)

This was evident at Newark, where an independent congregation served by Ministerium pastors expressed a desire to reaffiliate with the Ministerium in 1899, and for its efforts was prominently mentioned in the president's Report. Rochester was more vulnerable with its large concentration of Zion Lutheran mission churches, its eight Ministerium congregations, and the existence of a growing Missouri Synod presence. In 1900 Rochester's "North German Evangelical Luth[eran] Concordia Congregation," one of Zion's mission offspring, withdrew from the Ministerium to the great dismay of Rochester Lutherans.

Fearing a chain reaction among the conservative string of Zion-formed Concordia congregations, the *Herold* reported that the loss of this "strong and thoroughly Lutheran German Church" would be the first among several in Rochester. Nearby Bethlehem Congregation of Penfield followed Concordia in 1901 under the guidance of its Missouri Synod pastor. Competition with "Missouri" was especially keen in the Rochester Conference where the Missouri Synod was seen "endeavoring to invade our territory in Brockport and Honeoye." The situation was so tense that the Rochester Conference asked the Ministerium president to lodge a complaint with the Missouri authorities over these "unChristian and dishonorable practices of Missourian Pastors."[20]

Yet the competition continued. Despite the Ministerium's reorganized constitution, it was also undergoing confessional changes in a more moderate direction as rapprochement occurred with the General Synod and its congregations. The loss of its "protest party" to the Missouri Synod removed a confessionally conservative element from the Ministerium. Though unwilling to resume fellowship, exchange fraternal delegates or coordinate mission efforts with the New York and New Jersey Synod, the Ministerium had established a more cordial relationship with its alienated sibling by 1900. Taken together these changes represent a restructuring of German-speaking confessionalism in the New York area with a growing Missouri Synod Eastern District, replacing the New York Ministerium on the right end of the spectrum, as the Ministerium drifted toward the center. There the Ministerium would begin to interface with the English-speaking church through its growing English Conference.

THE CHALLENGE OF URBANIZATION

Even as these events were taking place, the Ministerium found itself challenged by its urban setting. As already noted with English-speaking Lutherans in the General Synod tradition, the challenge of urbanization was taxing the New York Synod to the utmost. How did the Ministerium fare in comparison? As a synod of German immigrants, the Ministerium was more urban in character than its divorced sibling. In 1895, 47 percent of its congregations were to be found in urban areas, compared with 33 percent for the New York and New Jersey Synod. By 1900 that figure had grown to 48 percent, whereas the New York and New Jersey Synod increased by five percentage points to 39 percent. By 1908, even after merger with the more rural Franckean and Hartwick Synods, the New York Synod was still only 33 percent urban. Table 11.2 indicates this comparative urbanization by the sub-regional conferences in each synod:

Table 11.2[21]
Urban Congregations in NY Ministerium and NY Synod

NY Min. Conferences (1900)	Percent Urban Congregations	NY Synod Conferences (1908)	Percent Urban Congregations
Rochester	37	Western	31
Albany	25	Hudson	9
New York	51	Southern	82
English	84	German	33
Ministerium	48	Synod	33

Compared with the New York Synod, the German-speaking Ministerium had larger urban concentrations upstate in Rochester, Buffalo, and (especially) Albany; whereas the Ministerium had a sizable small town and rural concentration of German-speaking congregations in the Hudson valley and around the New York metropolitan area, the more rural New York Synod had a larger concentration of its German-speaking congregations outside of urban New York areas. Within the Ministerium the English-speaking church was heavily urban, as the children of German immigrants sought out English-speaking congregations. A comparison of Ministerium Conferences before and after the

English Conference's formation, as shown in Table 11.3, indicates something of these changes:

Table 11.3[22]
Urban Congregations in NY Ministerium, 1895 & 1900

Name	1895	Name	1900
Conference 1	58	New York	51
Conference 2	27	Albany	25
Conference 3	40	Rochester	37
		English	84

The restructuring, then, created a significant division in the Ministerium between a growing urban English-speaking conference and the remainder which was more rural and exclusively German-speaking.

Considering the role of urbanization in denominational identity, it was the strongly confessional, German-speaking part of the church which was least susceptible to ecumenical change in such circumstances, a situation which would ensure the continuance of conservative confessionalism in the German-speaking part of the Ministerium. Urbanization also had an effect on giving patterns with urban areas supporting the church better than rural areas. Though more urban than the New York Synod, the Ministerium was also poorer because of its immigrant status. By 1900, for example, the New York Ministerium percapita contributions for *congregations* and for benevolence were *$7.36* and $0.57; for the New York Synod, *$11.72* and $1.34. The English-speaking synod also had a better record of meeting its proportioned benevolence—71 percent of the benevolence costs apportioned to the synod and congregations by the General Synod; the Ministerium's congregations, on the other hand, contributed only 56 percent of their apportioned benevolence. Within the Ministerium the age met by conferences indicated that the more rural Albany Conference supported benevolence least well (46.5 percent), while the small but growing English Conference had the best record (67.7 percent).[23]

The portrait of the Ministerium emerging from these figures depicts a German-speaking synod with an ever more highly urbanized, and rapidly growing English conference in its midst. Though more urbanized than the New York and New Jersey Synod, the Ministerium was also poorer, and less able to support synodical growth at a time when it was important to urban church development. As a church of immigrants, the Ministerium had long been supported by new Americans who began near the bottom rung on the economic ladder where annual income (and giving) were below the middle-class levels of the English-speaking Lutheran Church. Also, European immigrants coming from state-supported churches were not used to the voluntary support of American denominations. Time, upward mobility, and socialization to denominational ways were required to approach giving patterns in the New York Synod and the English Conference.

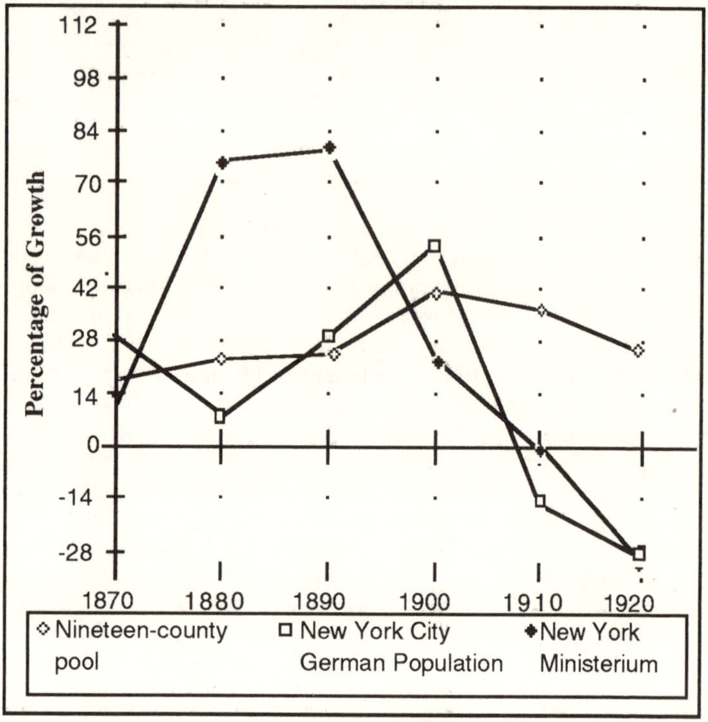

Graph 11.2
New York Ministerium and Population Growth Rates

With all the circumstances considered, it was not an optimistic picture for urban growth. If the New York Synod and its predecessor bodies had difficulties because of their levels of giving, the Ministerium had more. The result was that even as its population pool, including an urban German-speaking population, continued to grow between 1890 and 1900 the Ministerium experienced a decided slowdown in its growth rate (Graph 11.2).

The New York Ministerium's growth-rate was beginning to slow down just as the English-speaking church were beginning to grow once again. This was especially true of the New York and New Jersey Synod and its successor New York Synod. The decade of the 1890s and the process of urbanization, together with a decline in German immigration and the growth of a second generation of English-speaking Lutherans, combined to cause a dramatic reversal in the fortunes of General

Council and General Synod Lutheranism in the New York area. The reversal can be seem in Graph 11.3.

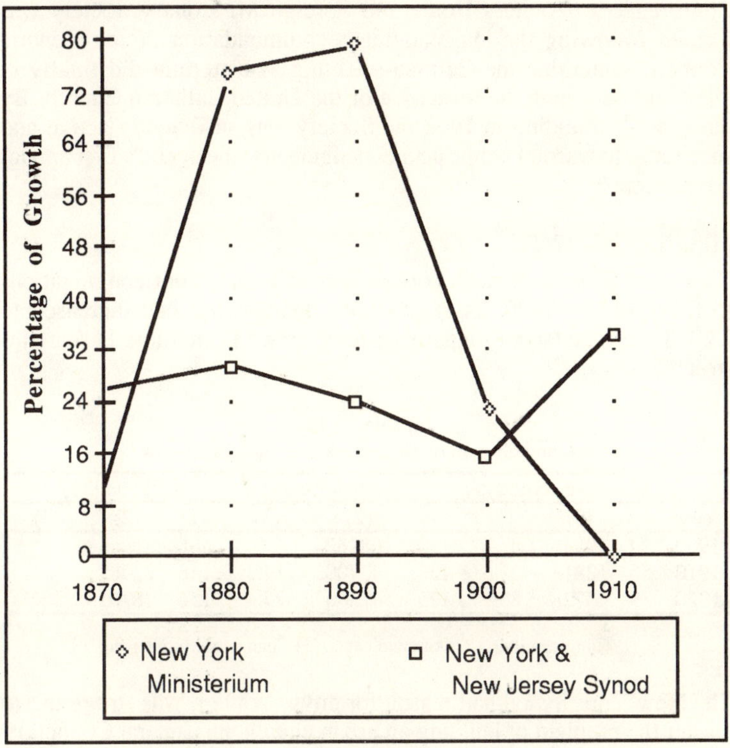

Graph 11.3
New York Ministerium & New York/New Jersey Synod

The decline began in 1890 and continued into the twentieth century. Changes after 1900 reflect the loss of the English Conference (of course) and the growth of English-speaking General Council Lutheranism which it lost with the formation of the New York and New England Synod.

THE NEW YORK AND NEW ENGLAND SYNOD

As the New York Synod looked on with competitive envy, after its organization in 1908, the Synod of New York and New England displayed a growth worth noting. (See Map 11.4 English Congregations of NY & NE Synods.) At its organization in 1902 the former English Conference of fifteen congregations had increased to thirty-four, with a communing membership of 10,536. By 1910 the new Synod of New York and New England had grown to fifty-four congregations with 12,813 communicants. Sometime during its existence as the English Conference a Women's Home and Foreign Missionary Society was formed following the longstanding recommendation of the General Council, something the German-speaking Ministerium did finally in 1919 and only with the formation of the United Lutheran Church. By the synod's founding in 1902 the Society was sufficiently active and successful to warrant public acknowledgment at the synod's first annual convention.[24]

MISSION GROWTH

Though the Synod of New York increased by only four congregations to fifty-nine by 1920, its communing membership had increased to 23,728 a decade later. Comparisons to be drawn from Table 11.4 are instructive:

Table 11.4
Size and Growth of New York GC and GS Bodies

	NY & NE Synod (5)			Ministerium (5)			NYSynod (5)		
Year	(1)	(2)	(3)	(1)	(2)	(3)	(1)	(2)	(3)
1900	34	10536		120	108067		not yet formed		
1910	55	12813	21.6	123	92700	-14.2	146	22069	
1920	59	23728	85.1	125	67300	-27.4	156	18761	-15.0

(1) Congregations, (2) Communicants, (3) Change of Membership

The New York Synod had reason for envy. While it was struggling to master the problem of building an urban church, its General Council rival was reaping a harvest. During a decade in which the New York Synod lost 15 of its membership, communicant membership in the New York and New England Synod increased by 85 percent. Of course the New York Synod had a rural and small town membership which significantly influenced its growth rate, while the New York and New England Synod was highly urbanized, and reaping the benefits of urban population growth. It also benefited from its upstate urban base, in which churches flourished by comparison with metropolitan New York.

Comparisons with the New York Ministerium produces the same conclusions. Again the New York and New England Synod had the advantage of an urban population base, plus the opportunity to serve a growing urban constituency among English-speaking Lutherans. Had the two bodies remained one, the growth of the English-speaking congregations within the Ministerium would have helped offset the precipitous decline of German-speaking membership. The Ministerium would have declined -11.0 and -13.7 for the two decades under consideration. Those losses might have been further reduced if cooperation rather than conflict between the English- and German-speaking conferences had eased the transition between the German and English Lutheranism for the offspring of immigrants. But the Ministerium's "devinely [sic] appointed mission" made that impossible. The New York Synod, and especially the New York and New England Synod, were establishing English-speaking congregations at a rapid pace often in cooperation with one another, but inevitably in conflict with the New York Ministerium. (See Maps 11.4 & 11.5, pages 350-51.) The growth was greatest along the urban belt of small and large cities, from Buffalo to New York City, resulting in more affluent congregations. Per capita contributions (Table 11.5) provide another clue to the success of the New York and New England Synod.

Table 11.5
Percapita Contributions in General Council and General Synod Bodies

Year	NY & NE Synod		Ministerium		New York Synod	
BASE	$30.91	**$0.56**	$7.36	**$0.57**	$11.72	**$1.34**
1920	$10.35	**$3.84**	$5.94	**$2.10**	$17.79	**$2.88**

Baseline for NYM = 1900, NY/E = 1903, NYS = 1908
Benevolence in boldface type

Benevolence giving for the New York and New England Synod as a just-separated part of the New York Ministerium was nearly identical to that of the larger body, though as a group of new congregations with newly developed church property, it was spending three times as much on itself. As noted above, the New York Synod contributed considerably more to benevolence including mission development. While all three bodies improved in support of missions, the New York and New England Synod made the greatest strides as a mission church. In the space of seventeen years an organization of highly indebted, new, English-speaking congregations had significantly reduced spending on themselves while steadily increasing their support for new mission starts. The New York Synod, to the contrary, had not supported missions as generously, while increasing spending at home, a stance reflective of its relatively weak mission identity noted in Chapter 12.

How did the New York and New England Synod achieve this turnaround? Its enviable record involved outside help. By 1909, with the aid of the General Council's Unification Plan, support for all local mission efforts were to be transferred to the Council's Home Mission Board in return for national funding which would be in excess of what the synod could raise by itself. Such help made it possible for the synod to call two field missionaries for greater New York and New Jersey while developing plans for a third to be called for western New York. It also meant the immediate establishment of four new missions—three on Long Island and one in New Jersey. The synod's representative on the national Board reported that the New York mission field was "recognized as the greatest Home Mission field of the Lutheran Church in America and being so regarded it receives the attention which its importance deserves. The amount expended upon its development since we last met exceeded by a considerable sum what was sent to the Board." In response, the synod urged a four-part fund-raising program upon its congregations which included special mission offerings, meeting (and if possible exceeding) the apportioned benevolence commitment set by the General Council, and by an appeal for congregations to increase their benevolence giving by one-third.[25]

With this aid the mission field grew. By 1913 fourteen new missions were organized—five in Brooklyn, one each in the Bronx, College Point, Corona, Yonkers, East Orange (NJ), Elmira, Dunkirk

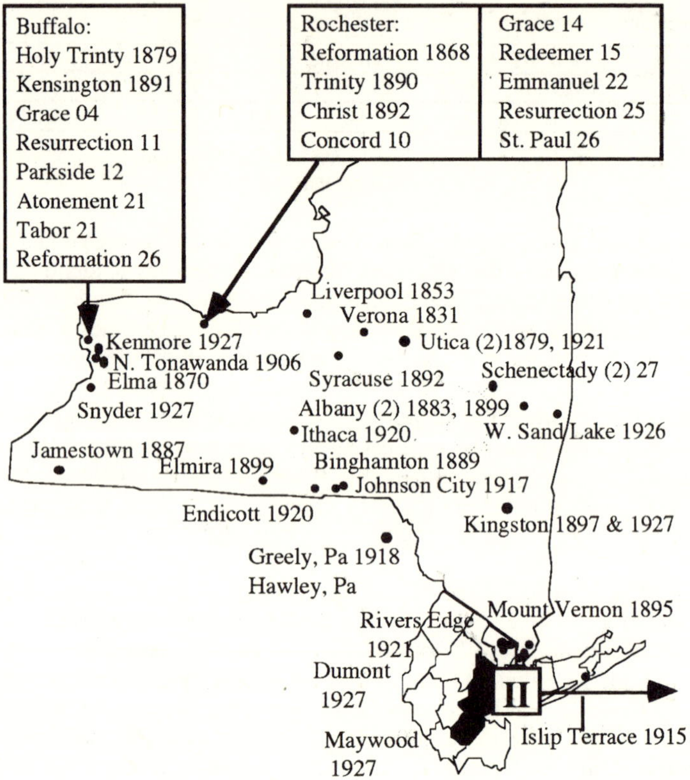

Map 11.4 English Congregations of the NY & NE Synods

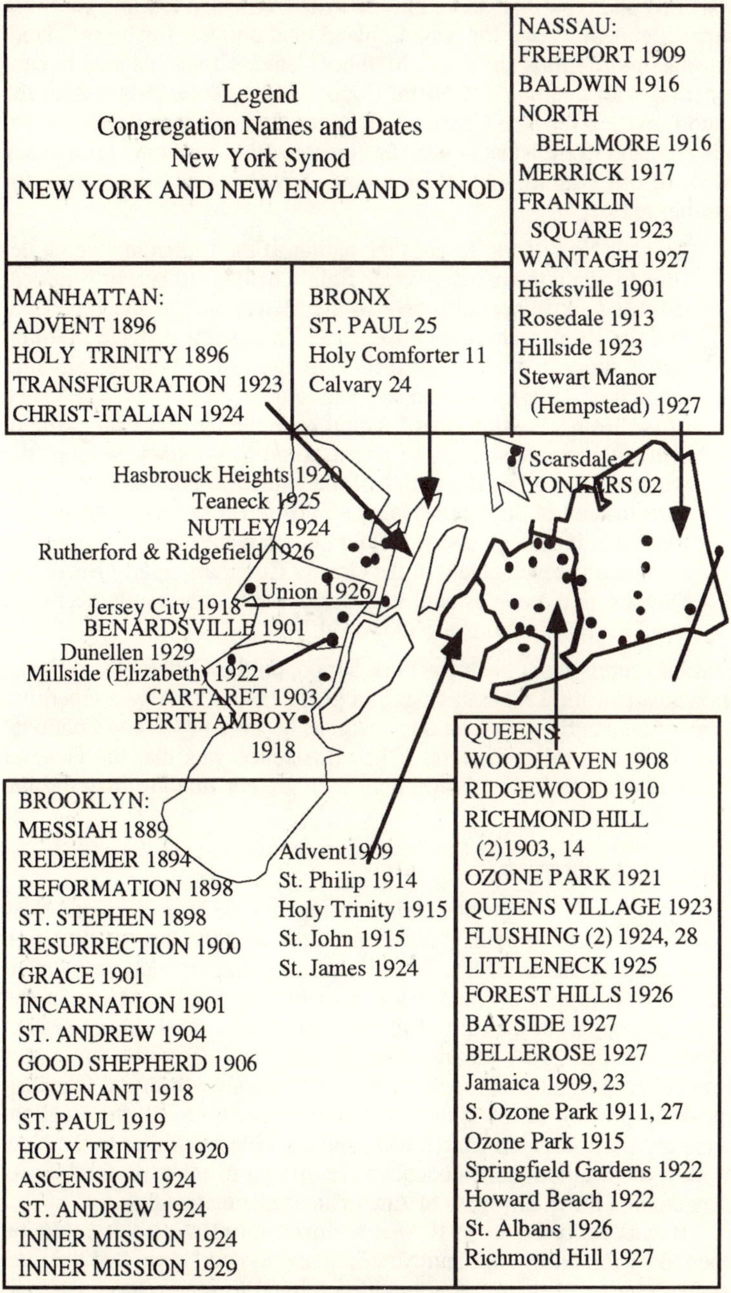

MAP 11.5 Urban Engl. Congregations of NY, and NY, & NE Synods

Hartford and New Britain (CT). The synod was also looking for more superintendents—one for New England, and another for Long Island. To raise more funds an "Every Member Canvass" was planned in conjunction with a national, General Council effort.[26] Leaders within the synod insisted that the Greater New York area—especially Brooklyn, Queens, and Long Island—was the "greatest field for home missionary work of our church." Apart from size, New York was important for another reason:

> As goes New York, so goes the nation. If the Lutheran Church desires to attain the prestige which rightly belongs to her, in America, it must seek to secure it here in the Metropolis, as the Episcopal and the Roman churches have done. This is not partisan opinion, but is supported by actual facts. The eyes of the entire Lutheran Church of America, should be focused upon New York. The office of the Home Mission Board should be in the Greater City, without doubt the greatest and the ripest home missionary field in the world. It should be the policy of the church to pour in money and men instead of attempting to make this territory self-sustaining at this time. If enough energy of our church were expended upon the missionary development of the Greater City, particularly Brooklyn, Queens, and Long Island, it is our opinion, the results accruing, would surpass anything in the world."[27]

Similar reports from the New York Synod, on the General Synod side, indicates that the Lutheran church in greater New York was emerging as a national entity—first among unequals because of the city's national prominence in other matters. A key difference was that the General Council supported the mission field with greater funding than did the General Synod.

CAMPUS MINISTRY

Money was only one problem which hampered the New York and New England Synod's growth. Another problem was the lack of qualified candidates for the ministry. The Ministerium had no such problem. It had an oversupply of candidates, part of a general problem in the General Council at the turn of the century. A parochial school system which included proseminaries (like Wagner College) and seminaries was generating an oversupply at a time when growth in the German-speaking portion of the church had slowed down.[28] But the English-speaking portion of the church had supply problems similar to the New York Synod. Good male students were turning to other professions as they entered the mainstream of American academic institutions.

It was reported in 1910 that a dozen more missions could be opened by the New York and New England Synod "if we had the men to take charge of them." A committee formed to secure more pastoral candidates reported on the problem at length the next year. Too many pastors have been called into other work in a growing church bureaucracy of church boards, aggravating the undersupply. Poor salaries and congregations with a "weak, short-sighted" policy of false economy have turned pastors into persons known to many only "as a solicitor of funds, a manager of sociables, or an advance agent for the Church fair." Part of the problem involved the church not attracting the "*right* men." A new breed was needed. "We want no man in the ministry who could not enter anything else."[29]

Such comments, reflecting shortages of pastoral candidates among English-speaking Lutherans, also indicates changing gender attitudes within the Lutheran ministry. Gender consciousness among American males had, by the end of the nineteenth century, placed a heavy emphasis on gender traits, making it more problematic for men and women to understand one another. A sharp division of labor between men and women in the church had left men in charge of public ministry within an increasingly feminized church. By the early twentieth century there was, as historian Leonard I. Sweet has noticed, a fear of effeminacy and an exaggerated emphasis upon masculinity in the American church.[30]

While the role of women in the church had expanded to the enormous benefit of religious life, men had become increasingly marginal to Protestant Christianity during the same period, except for the ministry which came to be jealously guarded as a male sphere. Lutherans, like other denomination bodies, discussed the desirability of ordaining women, a growing need and possibility given the lack of pastoral candidates. A remarkable three-way debate on the topic in the *Lutheran Quarterly* during 1903 and 1904 suggests the dynamics involved. J. L. Neve, professor of church history and symbolics at the General Synod's Western Theological Seminary (Atchison, Kansas), exegeting I Corinthians and I Timothy to deal with the matter for the attentive readers of the *Quarterly*, concluded (predictably) that women should not break in on the "ground rule of creation" by ordination and public preaching. Contributor Margaret R. Seebach, MA, dismissed Neve's argument as a modern extension of apostolic practice which she considered "degenerate" in a modern setting. Women might be equal to the call, but would lose their "moral influence by such indifference to home and children" if they worked outside the home. And if one could conceive of an unmarried woman with the time and the training for such a call Seebach continued, one doubted the feminine mind could persuade male worshippers. "Can a woman's preaching win and hold men in the Church?. . . [W]hen we consider that the great lack of the Church in all ages has been such a virile and logical interpretation of truth as will appeal to *men*, and hold their allegiance, this question assumes large proportions. The Church *has* the women—has always had them; she needs the men!"[31] Another contributor, Mary Dever, replied to both Neve and Seebach with a critique of Margaret Seebach's argument:

> The deep, the fundamental mistake is her assumption that we may choose to hear or not to hear those whom God has graciously prepared to speak to us of him, and of his love. Whether men or women, it is of his grace that they tell us, and it is of this that we long to hear. Whoever comes as the bearer of "good news from a far country," let him speak! It is not a question of our allowing him to do it as a favor to *him*. The obligation is all on the other side. It is we who are graciously permitted to hear.[32]

Dever advocated persons of either gender undertaking the work of public ministry, if qualified, in a common endeavor of men and women. Her argument was prophetic. Yet what most other Lutherans—men and women—wanted in the pulpit was a masculine intellectuality to communicate the Good News, a perception Lutherans shared with other conservative Christians. Lutherans were not alone in dealing with these matters. If fundamentalist conservatives were preoccupied with finding "real men" to fill their pulpits (in reaction to the growing feminization) New York and New England Lutherans in particular were looking for the "right men."[33] Here was a somewhat more nuanced response to changing gender relations in a church which apparently attracted a less than desirable type of male candidate for the Lutheran ministry.

Who were wanted? Male candidates "with modern and good education, yet with sound conviction, thinking freely and independently, are needed for the task." "There is too great a fear of modern thought, as though all of it were unsound, and could not exist with zeal. True conviction on a modern basis is possible and necessary." "It is one of the problems that our seminaries face—how to adjust their courses to modern thought, and yet conserve the truth. In the transition we must not loose our heads." Here was an important new idea among New York Lutherans—transition from a German-speaking religious subculture to a modern American culture with freedom to think yet an ability to maintain confessional convictions. It was neither confession-against-culture sectarianism like that found in the Missouri Synod and among the most conservative elements of the New York Ministerium; nor the culture-before-confession attitude of General Synod Lutherans in the New York Synod. It was a bold ideal which stimulated a farsighted proposal—campus ministry to Lutheran students at public and private universities. "The Church is not in touch with young men at the great universities." Not "all our ministers can be trained at the Church Institution." The idea was to promote spiritual growth at a time of intellectual maturing with the added prospect of recruitment for the ministry. Much work would be done by local campus congregations but where institutional size warranted, a student pastor would be called to serve in the institution itself.[34]

By 1913 a fact-finding effort by committee members Samuel G. Trexler, William M. Horn, and F. B. Clausen, had discovered that Presbyterians and Methodists had begun such efforts, together with the General Council, at the important midwestern Universities of Minnesota and Wisconsin. Inquiries were begun within the region at "the five great universities of Cornell, Syracuse, Columbia, Yale and Harvard." The majority of national leaders were college educated it was pointed out. "Three of our leading men of to-morrow out of every four are now at our higher institutions of learning." In excess of eight hundred Lutheran students (by conservative estimate) were presently enrolled at the five above-mentioned institutions of higher learning. "These men will be leaders in the next generation. What is our Church doing to get the value of their increased usefulness?"[35]

The synod bought the argument with enthusiasm, and student pastor Samuel G. Trexler was appointed in 1913. Work was begun immediately at the five schools as well as at the Massachusetts Institute of Technology and New York University. Introductions to university administrations met with greater interest and support than was expected, with the exception of Columbia. At Cornell the pastor was appointed a Sage Chapel preacher, "the first time that our church has been thus recognized." Student associations were started at Columbia, Cornell, and Harvard; on Good Friday the Sacrament was administered to students in the Presbyterian Chapel at Ithaca. And at least two students—one at Harvard, the other at Syracuse—were identified as potential candidates for the ministry.[36]

By 1914 the number of potential candidates had grown to six—one at Harvard, two at Cornell, three at Columbia. Members of the New York Synod had indicated a desire to join in support of the Student Pastor, having benefited because of students turned to ministry by Trexler. Campus ministry objectives matured with success and experience to extend beyond the simple recruitment of men for the ministry. The same year the work was extended to four women's colleges—Smith, Vassar, Wellesley, and Mt. Holyoke, where there were fifty-three Lutheran students registered. Associations and reading circles were created at the four institutions where it was found that the "young women . . . are even more of the diaspora than are our men." Recognition of the pastor himself increased, with four institutions inviting him to preach, while Harvard's Board of Preachers promised the appointment of a "Lutheran Pastor for the coming year."[37]

The work grew year by year. In 1915 the two English-speaking synods formed a Joint Committee to support and supervise the student pastor's work. With Trexler's resignation to accept a call to Buffalo, the joint committee and the synod president assumed some of his work. The need was great for pastoral care among students at institutions already contacted. With Lutheran interest shown, Princeton requested a

Lutheran preacher to preach on two successive Sundays each month with an intervening stay to serve "as the recognized adviser of the students." Visits were made to a number of colleges and universities to keep up contacts. In some places local pastors visited and supplied pastoral care. Townspeople and one hundred active Lutheran students at Cornell, meanwhile, were moving towards the formation of a University-based church with a called pastor. There the need was so urgent that the synod managed to arrange a special call to supply a student pastor, the Lutheran chaplain to the First New York Cavalry then stationed in Texas, E. F. Keever. Within a year, and in anticipation of the war's end, he was looking forward to seeing a "Luther Parish House," pastor's residence, and a chapel "crowning one of the heights of these hills, and testifying to the permanence and value of our holy doctrine."[38]

William Horn replaced Keever at Cornell the next year, and within a short time "secured a number of the students there for the Christian ministry" including a law student who switched professions. Another student was found at Tufts through the efforts of Pastor Arthur P. Grammas, student pastor at Harvard. At Cornell the Lutheran Association included Dutch Reformed students at the University as well as members from Ithaca itself. A large manse was purchased "as Lutheran headquarters in Ithaca" because it was strategically situated at the entrance to the campus, a town-gown arrangement with a chapel which supported a mixed worship community composed of students and city residents. Horn played a more aggressive role than Keever and began encountering a university in which religion was actually a taboo subject in the classroom, yet where professors self-confidently taught beyond their competency in the use and misuse of the Bible. His work exposed the superficial veneer of cordiality existing between church and university at Cornell (as elsewhere), and established a more honest if somewhat more negative dialogue with modern learning in a secular setting. Horn also helped establish a parish unique to the synod. By 1924 a Lutheran chapel had been built at Cornell, an imposing structure large enough to entertain the entire synod at its 1925 convention.[39]

COOPERATION WITH THE SYNOD OF NEW YORK

Aside from providing an important new source of clergy candidates, the campus ministry of the New York and New England Synod provided an opportunity for cooperation and joint support with the New York Synod. Joint ownership was tentatively begun in 1914, the same year in which a Joint Commission of the General Synod and General Council divided up national mission territories and responsibilities. New York was one of the territories where joint adjudication was to occur with the synod with first claim to a mission field having exclusive right to it by joint agreement. Whereas the German-speaking and English-speaking segments of the New York Ministerium could not adjudicate their own mission-field differences, the two English-speaking synods managed to work out arrangements in several disputed territories, among them (of course) Brooklyn. In another (Jamestown, New York) the agreement actually allowed the creation of an Augustana Synod congregation with an amicable understanding of its territory and work vis a vis the already established synod congregation.[40]

The following year (1915), the second in which plans went forward for joint support and supervision of a student pastor, the two synods also arranged a joint meeting of home mission committees "to devise plans and methods in establishing missions in New York City." This growing cooperation contrasted with a response to a merger proposal received from the New York Ministerium. (To them the continuing division seemed justified, promising better results than "organic unity," largely because language differences could not yet be overcome. When the "rapid introduction of the English language" then taking place had run its course, foundations would have been laid for a natural merger.) Meanwhile the dual tasks of student work and home missions kept both synods busy working out detailed ways of cooperation in what was becoming a joint mission to English Lutherans in New York and New England.[41]

CONCLUSION—ENGLISH-SPEAKING CONVERGENCE

The Synods of New York, and New York and New England were on the verge of greater cooperative efforts when the national merger of the General Council, General Synod, and United Synod South transformed the magnitude of the task. Now three synods, the two English-speaking synods, and a New York Ministerium then being rapidly anglicized, were expected to consummate a marriage in New York and New England which had been contracted for by its national bodies in New York City. Getting to the altar would be more difficult than the proposal of marriage. In this the Synod of New York and New England was to play the role of both marriage broker and bride, sharing as it did important characteristics of the New York Synod and the New York Ministerium. The matter was complicated by the fact that this was a remarriage of sorts, after a long and painful period of divorce. A momentous reconciliation of such magnitude deserves its own chapter however, one which will bring this story and volume to a close.

NOTES

1 John Nicum, *Geschichte des Evangelisch-Lutherischen Ministeriums von Staate New York und angrenzenden Staaten und Landern*. (Reading: 1888), 284.

2 Karl Kretzmann, *The Atlantic District of the Evangelical Lutheran Synod of Missouri, Ohio, and Other States and Its Antecedents* (Erie, Pa.: Erie Printing Company, 1931), 33; Nicum, *Geschichte*, 318.

3 Kretzmann, *Atlantic District*, 33, 138-141, 148, 155; Nicum, *Geschichte*, 610-613, 318-19.

4 Eugene L Fevold, "Coming of Age, 1875-1900," *The Lutherans in North America*, ed. E. Clifford Nelson (Philadelphia: Fortress Press, 1975), 315. See BC, 617, 624.

5 Fevold, "Coming of Age," 317-18. Nicum, *Geschichte*, 318-19.

6 See Arthur Karl Piepkorn, *Profiles in Belief*, II, 28 ff; also Tappert, 12-15." Concerning the Dogma of Predestination," *Lutheran Church Review* 3 (1884): 223-5, 228-229, 226-227, 233, 236.

7 New York Ministerium, *Abstract English Minutes* (1900), 19.

8 **Supporters** of the unaltered Galesburg Rule, *protest party members*, and *opponents* of strict construction by year of representation were: 1873—*Drees*; 1874—**Volz, Schmitthenner,** *Ruperti*, Thomsen; 1875—**Frey, Schmitthenner**, *Ruperti*, Thomsen, *Krug*; 1876—**Hoppee, Frey, Volz**, *Halfmann, Moldehnke*, Erhart, *Krug*; 1877—**Hoppee, Volz, Schmitthenner**, *Moldehnke, Halfmann*, Hill, Hoeneke, *Baden, Krug*; 1879—**J. C. J. Petersen, Schmitthenner**, Koenig, *Baden, Krug*; 1880—**Hoppee, Schmitthenner**, *Moldehnke*, Hoeneke, *Baden*; 1881—**Petersen, Schmitthenner**, *Moldehnke, Kuehne, Baden*; 1885—**Petersen, Schmitthenner**, *Moldehnke*, Richter, Kuever, *Krug, Baden*; 1886—**Gomph, Schmitthenner**, Struckert, *Krug*. See list of Clerical Delegates, General Council, *Documentary History of the General Council of the Evangelical Lutheran Church in North America*, ed. S. E. Ochensford. (Philadelphia: General Council Publication House, 1912), 536-551, 563. Delegates position on Galesburg Rule to be found in New York Ministerium, *Minutes* (1876), 55-56.

9 Nicum, *Geschichte*, 332-4. New York Ministerium, [German] *Minutes*, (1887), 50-51, 67; (1890), 58-61. New York Ministerium, *Abstract English Minutes* (1900), 20; (1901), 52. See Richard W. Solberg, *Lutheran Higher Education in North America* (Minneapolis: Augsburg Press, 1985), 297-98.

10 New York Ministerium, *Abstract English Minutes* (1895), 8, 9; (1896), 16, 10.

11 Ibid. (1898), 12, 20; (1895), 16.

12 Ibid. (1899), 11, 17; (1900), 12-13.

13 Ibid. (1900), 13-14.

14 Ibid. (1902), 20-22. New York and New England Synod, *Minutes* (September, 1901), 6-7.

15 Ministerium, *Abstract English Minutes* (1902), 21ff, 35, 21 ff, 35, 39, 42, 46.

16 Kretzmann, *Atlantic District*, 17-22, 128. W. H. Luecke, "A Half Century of Testimony of Staunch Lutheranism in New York City, or The First Fifty Years of History of Trinity Lutheran Church in New York City," *Concordia Historical Institute Quarterly* XXXII. 1 (1959): 1-14.

17 Kretzmann, *Atlantic District*, 22-34; Congregational database.
18 Ibid., 35-47, 96-107, 108-115.
19 Figures taken from author's congregational database. Ministerium, *Minutes* (1896), 30; (1897), 32.
20 Ministerium, *Abstract English Minutes* (1899), 12; (1901), 13.
21 For New York Synod see Chapter 11. New York Ministerium, *Abstract English Minutes* (1900), 29-31.
22 Ibid. (1895), 18-19; (1900), 29-31.
23 New York Synod, *Minutes* (1900), 34-5; New York Ministerium, *Abstract English Minutes* (1900), 29-32.
24 New York Ministerium, *Minutes* (1929), 78; New York and New England Synod, *Minutes* (1902), 30.
25 Ibid. (1909), 11-12; (1910), 43.
26 Ibid. (1913), 36-9.
27 Ibid. (1914), 61.
28 *Abstract English Minutes* (1898), 18.
29 New York and New England Synod, *Minutes* (1910), 10; (1911), 46-7.
30 Peter N. Stearns, *Be A Man ! Males in Modern Society*, 2nd ed. (New York: Holmes & Meier, 1990), 78-79, 118-119. Betty A. DeBerg, *Ungodly Women. Gender and the First Wave of American Fundamentalism* (Minneapolis: Augsburg Fortress Press, 1990), 13ff; 86ff.
31 *Lutheran Cyclopedia* (1954), 572. J. L. Neve, "Shall Women Preach in the Congregation? An Exegetical Treatise," *LQ* 33 (1903): 412-413. Margaret R. A. M. Seebach, "Should Women Preach," *LQ* 33 (1903): 579-583. Margaret R. Seebach (1875-1948) published a popular biography of Henry Melchior Muhlenberg, *An Eagle of the Wilderness: The Story of Henry Melchior Muhlenberg* (Philadelphia: United Lutheran Publish House, 1924); and authored the hymn "Your Kingdom Come"—see *Lutheran Book of Worship* (Minneapolis: Augsburg Publish House, 1978), # 376.
32 Mary Dever, "Woman in the Pulpit," *LQ* 34 (1904): 287.
33 See Betty A. DeBerg, "Manly Christianity," *Ungodly Women* (Minneapolis: Augsburg Fortress Press, 1990), 86 ff.
34 New York and New England Synod, *Minutes* (1911), 46-7, 37.
35 Ibid. (1912), 31.
36 Ibid. (1913), 26,49-51.
37 Ibid. (1914), 40-4.
38 Ibid. (1915), 45; (1916), 16-18, 56-8; (1917), 49-50.
39 Ibid. (1918), 40; (1918), 40-51; (1924), 47-50; (1925), 3.
40 Ibid. (1914), 37, 67-9.
41 Ibid. (1915), 55-56, 46-7; (1916), 54-56, 56-57.

12

MERGERS

Forming the United Lutheran Church, 1918 and the United Lutheran Synod, 1918-1929

A merger of the General Council, the General Synod, and the United Synod of the South was first proposed on April 18, 1917. Twelve days before on April 6—Good Friday—the United States had declared war on Germany. Far from slowing down merger, wartime considerations demanded a swift resolution of this timely proposal. By June of 1918 a constitution was drafted and by November all three national bodies had approved the document. Of the district synods making up these three bodies, all but the Augustana Synod approved of the merger. November 11, 1918—Armistice Day—each body held separate meetings in New York City, then adjourned to regroup three days later in a constituting convention which ran from November 14th to the 16th, concluding three days after World War I.[1]

The new national church body, which moved beyond the religious pluralism the General Synod considered normative in shaping American denominational life, laid down a significant challenge to the New York Lutheran Church. All three New York Synods approved a merger which had occurred in their own back yard and with their help. But the merger enthusiasm which propelled the three national bodies to unite, did not carry over into all of the local synodical bodies. Eleven years lapsed before the three New York synods united to form a United Lutheran Synod of New York which shared the supradenominational confessionalism of its parent body.

THE UNITED LUTHERAN CHURCH IN AMERICA—1918

Lutherans had been preparing for a national merger for some time. The Lutheran Society of New York and the Lutheran Social Union had been bringing lay people together on social occasions since the Luther Jubilee of 1883. At the same time Lutheran leaders, especially clergy, were cultivating an intersynodical fellowship through organizations like Concordia, Koinonia, and the Lutheran Ministers Association of Metropolitan New York, behind all of which stood the ever more influential George U. Wenner. They all shared an experience of common endeavor and purpose. The Luther League, Lutheran Brotherhood, and Laymen's Missionary Movement were pan-Lutheran or interdenominational fellowship and service organizations which crossed synodical and national church lines in developing youth programs and stewardship campaigns for the national church. Lutheran students, educators, and editors had also organized on a pan-Lutheran basis before the turn of the century.[2] The three national bodies had worked out cooperative agreements in home mission in the 1890s and had been receptive to the three free conferences (1898, 1902, 1904) which had been called to explore what American Lutherans shared in common.

CONFESSIONAL CONVERGENCE

Confessional differences remained the divisive issue among Lutherans. Prof. Henry Eyster Jacobs of Mt. Airy Lutheran Seminary, leading confessional theologian of the General Council, tried putting the matter in perspective with his opening address to the Second General Conference of Lutherans held in 1902. Formal subscription to the Augsburg Confession was not the primary concern of the General Council. It was rather that "if the faith that is held and taught be actually that of the Augsburg Confession," though "the Augsburg Confession have never been read nor subscribed, the church so holding and teaching is an Evangelical Lutheran Church." A church should not only subscribe to the Augsburg Confession, but the faith should also be truly understood and used ("held and taught").

> "It is not subscription to the confession of faith, but it is the receiving, teaching and defending the faith of the confession, that determines our position. Our loyalty to the ampler confession (and as years advance our admiration of these documents only increases) in no way interferes with our cordial recognition as Lutherans of all who hold unequivocally and simply to the doctrines of the Augsburg Confession, even though they be unwilling to prescribe any further ecclesiastical test."[3]

General Council Lutherans wondered aloud if General Synod Lutherans actually believe what they professed!

Jacobs continued the dialogue in 1908, this time as the Council's "Official Visitor" to the General Synod's Richmond, Indiana Convention. There he presented six General Council theses which expressed the Council's misgivings about the General Synod's confessional stance. The confessional position of each general body was spelled out in the first two theses—the General Council accepted the Unaltered Augsburg

Confession without mental reservation and asserted that the rest of the *Book of Concord* was "in perfect harmony of one and the same faith"; the General Synod adhered to the Word of God, as contained in canonical Scriptures "as the only infallible rule of faith and practice" and viewed the Augsburg Confession "as a correct exhibition of the fundamental doctrines of the divine Word, and of the faith of our Church." Jacobs favored the Council's "more specific and carefully framed declaration concerning the Augsburg Confession" and continued by observing that these differences "resolve themselves ultimately into one great difference: The basis of the General Synod . . . is a less completely developed form of the same confessional basis as that of the General Council." If the General Synod were to take advantage of this less developed form to embrace some point of the *Altered* Augsburg Confession, or to repudiate certain doctrines in the unaltered form, it would be "a manifestly unfair use" of its doctrinal basis Jacobs warned. The difference, therefore, "becomes one between an *adequate and explicit and an inadequate and what has been found in practice to be an ambiguous statement* [original italics]."[4]

General Synod leaders considered this undeveloped form (so-called) more than adequate. Following Jacobs to the podium, Leander S. Keyser, General Synod Visitor to the previous General Council convention at Buffalo, reported on that convention's discussion and ratification of the Jacobs theses. Keyser had defended the General Synod confessional stance before the Council in Buffalo. That stance, it may be remembered, went back to a 1864 Resolution passed at York, Pennsylvania in "Repudiation of Alleged Errors in the Augsburg Confession," and to an 1869 formula of confessional subscription developed shortly after the General Council was formed. Both statements were reprinted in the 1869 Constitution adopted at Washington, DC as amplification of its doctrinal position. Having rejected the doctrines of transubstantiation, consubstantiation, "auricular confession and priestly absolution," the "Repudiation" declared that the Augsburg Confession, "properly interpreted, is in perfect consistence with this our testimony, and with the Holy Scriptures as regards the errors specified." Keyser now argued for a reasoned defense of this position out of self-respect for its own traditions and a regard for the Council. Therefore he presented a series of General Synod resolutions which affirmed the Augsburg Confession to be "the original, generic confession of the Lutheran Church" and "an adequate and sufficient standard of Lutheran doctrine." Furthermore Keyser insisted with regard to the remainder of the *Book of Concord* that "she holds those Symbols in high esteem" and recommends "that they be diligently and faithfully studied by our ministers and laymen." The General Synod agreed with Keyser's defense, passing his proposals as the "Richmond Resolutions" of 1908.[5]

A series of exchanges followed. The "Richmond Resolutions" were reported to the General Council by the Synod's visitor G. M. Grau, and the Council's response reported back to the General Synod at its 1911 convention. The General Council had spent some time discussing the adequacy of the General Synod's subscription to the Augsburg Confession. Grau defended that subscription, insisting that it was as complete as "that of any body of Lutherans whatever in any land or time." He granted that "it was not always, but it is so now." Like other American Lutheran bodies, the General Synod "has constantly tended to a more definite and precise doctrinal and confessional statement and unqualified subscription." To this helpful interpretation Professor Jacobs had responded affirmatively, indicating in his opinion that "eight points and half of the ninth were thus satisfactorily met, and he hoped that this last half point would be met as we came in the spirit of Christ to our work as a Church."[6]

Each body had an opportunity to articulate its position and to defend it in public, thereby reaffirming their past confessional stances and their present integrity. But the General Synod also tacitly accepted the Council's critique of 1908-1909. Always more open to mergers on a less specific confessional basis, and in some ways positively eager without due regard to confessional details, the General Synod accommodated its own more limited confessional position to the more "adequate and explicit" stance of the General Council. Accordingly it reworked the confessional parts of its constitution, presenting them for adoption at its 1913 convention. Article II continued to read that the "Canonical Scriptures of the Old and New Testaments" were received "as the word of God and the only infallible rule of faith and practice," while the Unaltered Augsburg Confession was still accepted "as a correct exhibition of the faith and doctrine of our Church as founded upon the word." Added, however, was another Article (III) on the other symbolical books. While the General Synod regarded the Augsburg Confession as a sufficient doctrinal basis for cooperation between synods, it also recognized the Apology, Smalcald Articles, the Catechisms and the Formula of Concord "as expositions of Lutheran doctrine of great historical and interpretative value, and especially commends the Small Catechism as a book of instruction."[7] Like Jacobs, the General Synod had come (in his words) to accept the Book of Concord "as years advance our admiration" for this "ampler confession."

EVALUATION OF GENERAL COUNCIL AND GENERAL SYNOD

This moment of convergence had been long in arriving. It was due to the persistence of General Council theologians, most notable Charles Porterfield Krauth and Henry Eyster Jacobs who steadfastly insisted on the superior confessional position of the General Council. Krauth in his critique of denominationalism, like his incisive analysis of what constituted confessional integrity in religiously pluralistic America, shaped the Lutheran confessional position as did few other theologians. Holding up the Augsburg Confession as a catholic document with the best potential for reconciliation among Protestant denominations was both farsighted and prophetic, while his insistent rejection of denominationalism's definitiveness kept pluralism from shaping the confessional consciousness of American Lutherans. Jacobs, as staunch in defining and defending General Council confessional standards, had what Krauth lacked (or suppressed)—an ability to draw together different positions in such a way that both parties could find a common expression of their confessional outlook in language acceptable to the General Council.

What, then, can be said of the General Synod and its confessional position? Could liberal American Lutheranism on the defensive say anything to a conservative confessionalism which was then very much on the offensive? In modifying its own stance in response to General Council criticism, did it have anything left to contribute confessionally to a united Lutheran Church? The answer is "yes."

In the first place General Synod theologians, as late as the first decade of the twentieth century, quite properly pressed their criticism of an *ahistorical confessionalism* which saw no change or development of Lutheran dogma between 1530 and 1580 when the *Book of Concord* was published. A sharp scholarly exchange had occurred between Gettysburg Professor James W. Richards and Theodore E. Schmauck between 1909 and 1911. Pastor, General Council president, president of the Mt. Airy Seminary Board, and Seminary professor, Schmauck's ahistoricity made him an early critic of the historical/critical method of Biblical scholarship.[8] Over against Richards's historical perspective, Schmauck maintained that the development of pure doctrine which had occurred in this period between 1530 and 1580 existed, by extension, in the General Council itself where doctrine developed "apart from any of the modifying factors of language, race and nationality." Richards, to the contrary, in amplifying the General Synod belief that the Augsburg Confession was a correct exhibition of the fundamental doctrines of the Divine Word and faith of the Church, insisted that it provided a sufficient confessional basis for a Lutheran Church. The *Book of Concord*, to the contrary (he insisted), had not been an instrument of concord in the Lutheran Church in America. It represented further developments in doctrine rather than a closed system whose letter was more important than the spirit of its theology. While Richards's attack was onesided, its intent was quite properly to criticize General Council ahistoricity, which it did with telling effect. So sharp were the differences between Richards and Schmauck that the General Council and General Synod seemed miles apart a few short years before merger.[9]

Secondly, the General Synod pushed for theological openness. None of the General Synod's theological formulae would find expression in the constitution of the United Lutheran Church, its synods, or congregations. Yet it brought with it a certain spirit of openness that was absorbed into the new church, a spirit of generosity which is more difficult to define. At the time of the 1918 merger, the General Synod's leading theologians resisted the idea that the whole *Book of Concord* was basic to sound Lutheranism, though General Council theologians were pressing them to do so.[10] Gettysburg theologians Milton Valentine and James W. Richards rejected the idea that one could not be Lutheran without affirming the fine theological distinctions of the Formula of Concord. For them the Augsburg Confession was basic, something that could not always be said of other General Synod leaders. For them the Formula of Concord pushed disputed points into unwarranted prominence, formulating with too-great specificity an exaggerated Lutheranism that was divisive rather than unifying. The irenicism of Philip Melanchthon (author of the "Apology" to the Augsburg Confession) was as important to them as the more discriminating incisiveness of Luther. Perhaps something of this General Synod distinction between a few confessional essentials and less essential specifics led to the ULCA's constitutional distinction between the importance of the Augsburg Confession and the lesser significance of the rest of the *Book of Concord*, a distinction articulated for the first time in a national Lutheran body in the General Synod's 1913 revision of its constitution.

The General Synod thus provided much needed resistance to confessional stridency. It functioned like a loyal opposition. If Krauth and the General Council believed that confessional theology must be accepted and thought through in terms of original intent and without reservation, the General Synod "thought *with* reservations" even as it became more confessionally responsible. Its concern for "evangelical freedom" and "Christian Liberty" brought into the new church Reformation themes which Enlightenment theologians had thought important, and which were also important in their own right. Because of this orientation, General Synod pastors and congregations had a greater understanding of and appreciation for American institutions and values, including American Protestantism. For similar reasons the General Synod also displayed a regard for the particularity of liturgies, values, and histories in congregations and synods which contribute to legitimate diversity in any open institution.[11] Again, the General Synod showed a greater degree of Christian charity toward other Protestant bodies and a more ecumenical spirit that would help differentiate ULCA Lutheranism from more isolationist forms of Lutheran confessionalism. Finally, it was more open to a discussion of social issues and questions of public policy as part of the Church's public ministry.

Nowhere did this appreciation for particular differences in a spirit of evangelical freedom leave a more enduring legacy than in the General Council-General Synod debate over the Common Service. While its chief architects were busy exploring historic Lutheran liturgies in search of a normative Lutheran service, James Richards reminded Lutherans that this "normal" service, which was compiled from a variety of liturgies, reflected these different liturgies which were composed for distinctive areas within Germany and within different countries in Europe. Though varied in structure, what they had in common were liturgical principles enunciated by Luther, Richards argued. They were all moderately conservative, tended toward simplicity, emphasized preaching and teaching of the Word, and displayed the importance of "Christian liberty."[12] It was this spirit of *adiaphora* which the General Synod kept alive at a time when rigid confessionalism was on the rise within the General Council.

THE QUADRICENTENNIARY—OCCASION FOR MERGER

Once eastern Lutherans successfully incorporated this more flexible posture into General Council confessionalism, little remained to keep the three bodies apart, except for official inertia. In 1914 a joint committee formed to plan the quadricentennial of the Reformation three years hence. The General Council had proposed such a celebration and planning committee in 1909. Now with Lutherans making plans to celebrate a common heritage, the suggestion was made by committee member E. Clarence Miller that "the celebration should be marked by the union of the three bodies in the year 1917." The committee demurred, feeling that the motion "premature."[13] Shortly however, caution would give way to cooperation, and cooperation would make continued separation unthinkable. This was especially true in the northeast.

In the meantime the three official bodies of eastern Lutherans, north and south, were moving toward the idea of merger, though with similar caution. In 1914 the North Carolina Synod proposed to the United Synod of the South that it press for organic union with the General Synod and General Council. But the General Synod demurred "in view of the obvious fact that present historical developments do not justify any hope of a union of the general bodies." Instead it proposed a federation which would "take a comprehensive view of all the general work and thus unify the co-operation now existing." It was towards this limited end that the United Synod of the South recommended (in 1916) that "a commission on Federation" be authorized to arrange a series of conferences in 1917 to define their cooperative work. The General Synod had in the meantime (1915), vested its own Committee on Practical Co-operation and Fraternal Conference with power to negotiate a federation with other Lutheran bodies authorized to do so. The General Council appointed a Commission on Lutheran Unity in 1915 as well. Though organic unity was thought unattainable, the three Lutheran bodies were prepared by 1916 to officially become involved in merger talks that might develop out of plans for the Quadricentenniary.[14]

MOVE TO MERGER

At the last meeting of the Joint Quadricentennial Committee its lay representatives again pushed for merger talks. On the evening before its last session, eight laymen gathered to discuss merger. They "resolved that this gathering request the Joint Lutheran Committee to arrange a general meeting of Lutherans to formulate plans for the unification of the Lutheran Church in America." The resolution was signed by the group's leader, the Honorable J. L. Zimmerman, treasurer of the committee. Speaking from legal experience Zimmerman believed that unification could legally merge the three bodies and take over all property. Clarence Miller, meanwhile, presented six brief items in a plan for merger. H. E. Jacobs (a third committee member) responded with a resolution to form a United Lutheran Church in America, "Believing that the time has come for the more complete organization of the Lutheran Church in this country." Three years of planning and celebration made the proposal more appealing and now highly appropriate. As reported to the General Synod by its president, V. G. A. Tressler (another committee member), merger occurred because the "sentiment prevailed . . . that the noblest memorial of the four hundredth anniversary would be the merging of the three general bodies represented." The presidents of the General Council, and the United Synod South, who concurred with Tressler, but were asked to form a committee "for formulating a constitution with an adequate doctrinal basis."[15]

Early on the three presidents appointed a Joint Committee to prepare a Statement of Faith and to frame a Constitution. The three also made a comparative study of the new General Synod Constitution, the General Council's "Principles of Faith and Polity," and the Constitution of the United Synod, South, and agreed on the order of the articles in the new constitution. It was they who also decided to incorporate the "Principles of Faith" into the new document. Subsequently a Joint Committee on the Constitution was appointed which met in May of 1917 with General Council President Theodore E. Schmauk chairing. Each item was discussed at length, and the decision made to establish a Commission of Adjudication to sort out future difficulties arising from the merger. Such difficulties as might arise, however, should not prevent merger. As Schmauk informed the General Council in his 1917 report of merger proceedings: "This problem was not of our making. Unity is the spirit of the age." The recently negotiated confession of faith pointed with hope to a potential union which would be stronger confessionally than the Council's own Fundamental Principles.[16]

CONFESSIONAL BASIS OF THE ULCA

The new constitution highlighted "the inner unity which we have with one another . . . in the common confession, defence and maintenance of our faith, and in united efforts for the extension of the Kingdom of God at home and abroad." It also amplified the new body's doctrinal basis. The ULCA received and held "the canonical Scriptures . . . as the inspired Word of God, and as the only infallible rule and standard of faith and practice." It accepted "the three ecumenical creeds" as "important testimonies drawn from the Holy Scriptures"; received and held (as well) the Unaltered Augsburg Confession as a correct exhibition of the faith and doctrine of the Evangelical Lutheran Church, acknowledging all churches which confess the same "to be entitled to the name of Evangelical Lutheran"; and recognized the Apology, Smalcald Articles, Large and Small Catechisms, and the Formula of Concord "as in the harmony of one and the same pure Scriptural faith."[17]

President V. G. A. Tressler commended the new constitution to the General Synod, observing that "as far as I can see, there is nothing in its doctrinal basis or its provisions for carrying on the affairs of our Church, which is out of harmony with the present constitution of the General Synod." His General Council counterpart, T. E. Schmauk, made the even more interesting observation that the new confessional basis "is, if anything, stronger confessionally than that found in our own Fundamental Principles." He was correct. The General Council constitution expressed the conviction "that the other Confessions of the Evangelical Lutheran Church, inasmuch as they set forth none other than its system of doctrine and articles of faith, are of necessity pure and scriptural." To use Henry Eyster Jacobs's felicitous phrase, fifty years' experience in using the *Book of Concord* "advance[d] our admiration" for this "ampler confession." While such changes had been quietly taking place within the General Council, the General Synod continued to insist publicly on a critical historical honesty in sorting out the authority of Scripture and the Confessions. The surprising result was a confessional basis which incorporated the various Confessions more fully into a (now) United Lutheran confessional perspective, while continuing to protect the primacy of Scripture. It was a confessional basis that both traditions—General Council and General Synod—contributed to from their (initially) very different perspectives.[18] Ironically, the General Synod led the way with the 1913 reformulation of its doctrinal statement!

PLANNING FOR THE FIRST NATIONAL CONVENTION

All three national bodies approved the new constitutions by November of 1917. Only one body demurred. On November 12 the Augustana Synod, a national body of Swedish-American Lutherans organized as a district synod of the General Council, withdrew from that body to the dismay of President Schmauk. Never comfortable in the predominantly German General Council, it severed its relationship, deciding to remain independent of the new church, though the vote was close. When it became clear that a majority would reject "the whole idea of merger" Columbia Conference president C. R. Swanson proposed a resolution that the "Augustana Synod does not at this time see its way clear to enter the proposed merger . . . but declares itself in favor of a confederation of Lutheran church bodies in North America." True to its word, the Augustana Synod remained close to the ULCA, shortly joining with it in the formation of the National Lutheran Council.[19]

With preliminary approval secured, a Ways and Means Committee took up the practical details of merger. It began by framing bylaws to consolidate the agencies and boards of the three bodies, then arranged for incorporating the new church, and planned its first convention, not without some difficulties. The greatest obstacle was drafting bylaws detailed enough to centralize the work of the church, yet broad enough to eventually include the Augustana Synod or other Lutheran bodies invited in the constitution's preamble to join the union. Augustana's withdrawal removed some of the difficulties. Another problem was finding sufficient corporate power to create a more centralized national church. After examining the corporation laws of various states, it was decided to incorporate under the Religious Corporations Act of the State of New York, a document originally drafted by the late John Nicum, Rochester pastor and president of Wagner College.[20]

FIRST ULCA CONVENTION

On November 14, 1918, three days after the Armistice, more than five hundred Lutheran delegates assembled at the Lutheran Church of the Holy Trinity (fig. 12.1), Sixty-fifth St. and Central Park West, in New York City, for the first convention session of the new church. Founded to help bring greater attention to Lutheranism in the nation's first metropolis, this English-speaking General Council church symbolized the spirit of confessional moderation about to be reconfirmed in a United Lutheran Church. Called to order by the Ways and Means Chair, General Council President T. E. Schmauk, the roll of participating synods was called. Immediately sixteen "declarations on the religious and moral issues" of the day were adopted, a reminder that this important occasion was set amidst other, more momentous events, to which American Lutherans related in a special way. Their eagerness to deal with contemporary events may have betrayed a German-American defensiveness but it also revealed a new Lutheran willingness to explore the relationship between Christ and culture.

The delegates thus quickly declared their hearts to be "deeply moved with joy because our arms have succeeded in overthrowing autocracy, opening up the way for a larger liberty, and . . . standing ready to oppose all anarchy among the people of Europe." National aggrandizement was branded "unChristian," while freedom's pursuit by small nations and the unhampered opportunity to develop national life, were considered consonant with the Gospel. All true democratic movements were believed to be in accord "with the principles of the Gospel and the spiritual priesthood of believers," thereby squaring confessional theology with democratic political thought!

figure 12.1
Church of the Holy Trinity, New York City

Even as Lutherans cautiously affirmed the affinity of democracy for the spirit of the Gospel, they insisted upon their own freedoms in a democratic society: "the Church is a distinct divine institution and the living organism of believers, who should not be disturbed in the freedom of their faith." Sin was considered the source of all war, while anarchy was branded as contrary to the will of God." No final unity of mankind could occur "apart from the teachings of Jesus Christ," and religious and moral convictions and motives were considered necessary to healing social ills which no concentration of state power could achieve. Clearly Christ had an affinity for democratic culture in this new Lutheran view. It would remain to be seen in what other ways this United Lutheran Church in America would be American.

AMERICAN LUTHERANISM REDEFINED

That evening the Convention was addressed in its first religious service by Henry Eyster Jacobs on the topic "The Race Set Before Us." His text was Hebrews 12:1 and 2—"Wherefore, seeing we also are compassed about with so great a cloud of witnesses, let us lay aside every weight and the sin which doth so easily beset us, and let us run with patience the race set before us, looking unto Jesus . . . who is set down at the right hand of the throne of God." It was a night for celebrating American Lutheran history. Jacobs recalled the struggle for religious liberty against Dutch Calvinist resistance some two-hundred and fifty years before by "a group of humble Lutheran laymen" on Manhattan Island, a group who sought the right to rear children in the Lutheran faith. Next Jacobs invoked the Muhlenberg ideal "of but one Synod for the entire country," predicting it would henceforth be difficult "to keep apart" Lutherans having the same name, a common history, the same Catechism, Confessions, Liturgy, and hymns. The race set before us "is to mobilize and co-ordinate our forces, by publicly acknowledging and more firmly establishing the inner communion we already have with one another."[21]

The wartime crisis had forced Lutherans like Jacobs to reexamine their orientation to America and its culture. Jacob's thoughts on that evening had previously been expressed to the General Synod's Susquehanna Synod under four headings:

I The Thorough Lutheranizing of the Lutheran Church in America
II The Thorough Americanization of the Lutheran Church in America
III The Lutheranizing of America
IV The Lutheranizing of the World [22]

It was the ULCA's "special mission" to bring the seed of the Gospel, with all its latent energy, to all for whom the Author of the Gospel intended it." This is one Gospel, not many—not one for the Scandinavian, another for Slav; one for the German, another for the American; one for East, another for the West; one for the North, another for the South. There can be no sectionalism nor provincialism in the Gospel. Nor should it be hedged around "with minutely drawn qualifications." As the Apology to the Augsburg Confession reminds, if less serious mistakes of brethren are not overlooked, the church will fly apart into schisms. "Our life is a beginning and setting out, not a finishing; he is best who approaches nearest the mind of the Spirit."[23]

Jacobs proposed a theological agenda for this new church in a free land which contrasted sharply with Germany, its universities, and a discredited state church system. Among American Lutherans a voice could be heard expressing a "Theology, new in form, but identical in substance with that of the Reformation, in the English language (now the world language) and in the terms of modern thought." It would embody a "new Symbolics . . . where European distinctions" and Reformation antagonisms are greatly modified, "combining fidelity to its confession with kindly consideration of other churches." The new church also needed readjustment to "more cordially welcome the new era, with its increased opportunities." As the Formula of Concord notes, "The church of every time and place has, according to its circumstances, the right to change, to diminish or to increase its extended arrangements, as may be deemed at any time most profitable." This means foreign missions based on "a new estimate of the real worth of man" derived from the diffusion of democratic principles and from the hard lessons of warfare, starvation and death.[24]

While it was not a night for sticking too closely to the text, Jacobs made a valid point. Identifying theological themes peculiar to the General Synod and the General Council, Jacobs managed to weave them together in a common strand that drew together separate pasts for the sake of a common future. It was vitally important that the new church come to terms with both the past and the present, with Germany and with America, for the sake of a new future. The Lutheran Church in America was coming of age in declaring a changed relationship to Europe. The offer to reconstruct the German church on a sound confessional basis, just as President Wilson offered to reconstruct Germany on the basis of liberal democracy, was a far cry from the symbolism of the old New York Ministerium's coat of arms—the German Double Eagle in imperious flight from east to west.

NATIONAL SYNODICAL BUSINESS

The second day the delegates moved to the Engineering Societies' Building and Auditorium on West Thirty-ninth Street, to address organizational matters on their agenda. Pastor Frederick W. Knubel (1870-1945), pastor of Atonement Lutheran Church in Manhattan, and a member of the New York Synod was elected president of the new national church body. Many expected Schmauk, who was chairing the session, to receive the majority of votes as leader of the General Council, because of his constructive role in merger preparations. Knubel was less tied to conservative and classical theology, however, and had become well known recently for his leadership in Lutheran wartime cooperative efforts. By the fourth ballot it was clear that the delegates preferred someone younger, less tied to the past and more open to other churches and traditions. This was a fortunate choice, for Schmauk died before the new church assembled for its second convention.[25]

Electing officials, approving the constitution and bylaws, determining sites for individual boards and then providing them with members, these and a host of other details took up the remainder of the delegates' time. Much of this business was accomplished in approving a lengthy report prepared by the Ways and Means Committee. Creation of the National Lutheran Council was among the most important matters laid before the convention. The Soldiers and Sailors Commission which Frederick W. Knubel chaired, had been organized to look after the interests of Lutherans in uniform with the outbreak of hostilities against Germany. The Armistice brought other problems to the Commission's attention including the need to represent Lutheran Church interests in Washington, D. C., where accusations of being pro-German (and presumably anti-American) were brought before the Judicial Committee of the United States Senate. In response the three predecessor bodies of the ULCA had joined with the heads of twelve other Lutheran bodies to form the National Lutheran Council at Chicago on September 6, 1918.[26] It was the results of this meeting which the new ULCA was now asked to join as part of a new and important umbrella organization for Lutherans in the United States.

A NEW KIND OF NATIONAL STRUCTURE

Equally important was approval of a constitution creating a new degree of centralized authority in a national Lutheran body. Whereas the General Council and General Synod had assumed the initiative in preparing educational and liturgical materials, and in adjudicating matters of discipline and doctrine, these were undertaken within the framework of a largely advisory body, whose synods met together in consultation to conduct their mutual business. Both were nineteenth-century bodies. The ULCA included such responsibilities in the earliest sections of "ARTICLE VI: OBJECTS," but went on to incorporate other matters within its jurisdiction—missions, the regulation of worship, appointment of editorial committees, preparation of literature, liturgies, hymn books and catechisms, the creation, organization and development of boards and committees for the work of the departments, and to exercise a general supervision over church affairs.

Where internal matters common to all synods were concerned, the new church had new power to act, though the consent and cooperation of individual synods was necessary where a specific synod was involved. Intersynodical dealings and disputes were now placed in the hands of a board of adjudication instead of being left to the synods concerned. While synods retained rights and jurisdiction in internal affairs when not expressly delegated to the ULCA, the national body was given the right to "protect and enforce" its doctrinal basis, the purity of preaching, and the right administration of the sacraments. All matters of doctrine and conscience on binding matters were to be referred to the Commission of Adjudication. Synods were prohibited from changing geographical boundaries without national permission and their "established lines of work" were allowed to continue for satisfactory reasons where "such privilege" is granted by the national body. Synods once largely independent were now to become integrated entities in a far more highly rationalized national church body. Nineteenth-century national councils and synods had been replaced by a twentieth-century national church.

Formation of the ULCA coincided with the modernization of the American Protestant denomination, a process which had begun in the 1890s and was reaching completion by the end of WWI. National church leaders sought to construct a national, bureaucratic superstructure upon a nineteenth-century regional denominational structure of congregations and synods, importing the philosophy and methods of the emerging business corporation to create a "national denominational enterprise." The new order was characterized by a hierarchical, bureaucratic structure of authority broken down into agencies and departments, given to normative rules, committed to a systematic division and specialization of labor, and administered by professional leaders. Churches were not alone in this attempt to master growth and change. The progressive Era was noted for ordering and developing national institutions. With America's churches the task involved mastering numerical, financial, and programmatic expansion. As already noted, the American denomination was mission-driven. Its agencies of mission (foreign and domestic) and church extension, together with a growing commitment to education from parish to university and to social welfare concerns, shaped the agenda for building a national church.[27] This was a twentieth-century phenomenon with roots (as we have seen) in the nineteenth-century.

The extent of modernization varied from denomination to denomination, with the degree of bureaucratization depending upon the size and influence of its urban, professional middle class. Among Lutherans this kind of influence emerged from the lay brotherhood organized to provide a role for lay skills, expertise, and commitment in the development of the church and its mission. The brotherhoods were an outgrowth of the Laymen's Missionary Movement, a highly successful prewar interdenominational crusade to heighten lay awareness of missions and the need for their support by local congregations. In the General Synod Lutheran members of the interdenominational LMM served as an in-house fundraising organization cooperating with secretaries of those GS boards which would benefit from the organization's efficient efforts. The Lutheran Brotherhood meanwhile grew out of simultaneous efforts to develop a men's service organization within the General Synod which relied on "the inspiration of a great missionary objective such as the Missionary Movement" in developing it own programs. Its successor, the ULCA's Lutheran Brotherhood of America, continued the LMM influence in a united Lutheran organization which focused on fundraising and mission development.[28]

Members of LMM and the denominational brotherhoods, with their commitments to mission and "systematic finance" (especially the "every member" canvas and the two pocket envelope), carried their enthusiasm for organizational efficiency into their respective national church bodies. And so it is no surprise to find that members of the LMM and Lutheran Brotherhood not only took an important lead in promoting Lutheran merger, but helped shape the bureaucratic structures of the new United Lutheran order of board (agency) committees and executive secretaries of sub-agency departments. But it was in the area of finance that this influence was most prevalent. The ULCA adopted "The Financial Plan" in 1918 which included two basic LMM/LB fund raising techniques—the every member canvas and the duplex envelope. With ULCA Treasurer E. Clarence Miller sitting on the national LMM Executive Committee such a move was not surprising. Two of four lay members of a special Committee of Fifteen chosen by the ULCA convention to examine the details of "The Financial Plan" were also LMM Executive Board Members. (Two other members of that same Executive Board sat as lay members on the Home Missions Committee.) The LMM's report to the 1920 national convention provided convincing evidence of the gains in membership and support that such measures could produce.[29]

NATIONAL STRUCTURE AND NEW YORK DEVELOPMENTS

Improved national church structure and finance added new life to American Protestant denominations, including the ULCA, though at the cost of an increasing secularization in which efficiency and instrumental values could override traditional matters of faith and piety. Yet the traditional, nineteenth-century regional structure of synods and congregations with its pastoral system (which in the Lutheran Church was rooted in the Ministry of Word and Sacrament) was remarkably persistent. Differences between pastors and national executives, and between parish "parochialism" and national interests, introduced a new level of tension and conflict into national church structures however. The ULCA attempted to strike a balance between the benefits of national organization and the continued vitality of synod structures and congregational ministry. President Frederick H. Knubel noted as much in his 1920 "Report." While extolling the ULCA's "developing organization with the strengthening position of the Constituent Synods, the enlarging conceptions of the boards and agencies, and the vigor of general organizations for men and women and young people," an emphasis on "great organization" likewise constitutes the gravest spiritual problem which the church faces. The church must be evaluated and valued in the fundamentals of its spiritual life—"the Divine-human Christ," "the faith and its scriptural confession," and the congregation with its "Means of Grace."[30]

It was this new level of tension, given the relatively strong emphasis in the ULCA on local institutions, with the extensive involvement of synodical mission superintendents, mission committees, and clergy conferences, and of local congregations in the actual development of ULCA missions, which prevented the immediate reorganization of New York's three area synods after 1918. In the northeast striking the right balance between continued synodical integrity and a developing national organization which include reorganized synods would take time and would involve a close assessment of each synod's mission potential in its present form. In the end it would be the lay leaders of the LMM and Lutheran Brotherhood with an efficient program of mission which would finally tip the balance in favor of restructuring.

FORMATION OF THE UNITED LUTHERAN SYNOD OF NEW YORK—1929

The new national body which all three New York Synods joined in 1918 displayed a different organizational reality than the predecessor bodies of which they had been a part. No provisions had been made by the ULCA for redistricting the new church's synods where territories overlapped as in New York. Distinctive forms of present work—i.e., German missions—could be continued with ULCA sufferance; changing territorial borders likewise required national church involvement. Where former General Synod and General Council synods existed in the same geographic region, realignment was a distinct possibility, though longstanding traditions and differences could well reinforce the status quo, in which case adjustments between overlapping jurisdictions would come before the Committee of Adjudication.

OTHER SYNODICAL MERGERS

The first merger to take place in these new circumstances was between the Pittsburgh Synods of the General Council and the General Synod after a satisfactory opinion was obtained on the legality of doing so. The "historical continuity of the merging Synods has been absolutely preserved," it was noted at the time, suggesting that continuity as well as change were to be important in this time of transition. But continuation in the ULCA was not a forgone conclusion with such readjustment, so that it was necessary for reorganized synods to request admission to the national body in substitution for the old organizations.[31] Once begun, in the face of theological and geographic differences, synodical merger was no easy matter as the New York Synods were about to demonstrate.

The Pittsburgh merger was a question of geographical overlap, and a matter of overcoming historical antagonisms between the General Council and the General Synod in western Pennsylvania. In another case reorganization took place to strengthen a weak portion of the church. The Northern Indiana Synod (GS) and portions of the Chicago Synod (GC) united to form a separate body, the Michigan Synod, centered in Detroit, with the understanding that Indiana congregations would unite with the Indiana Synod when the Michigan churches were strong enough to form their own organization. A new Illinois Synod was formed out of former congregations of the Chicago (GC), Northern (GS), Central (GS), and Southern Illinois (GS) Synods, replacing these now defunct bodies as the constituent synod in the area. The Indiana Synod, meanwhile, was formed out of the Olive Branch Synod (GS) and that portion of the Chicago Synod (GC) which did not enter the new Illinois Synod. This included former GC and GS congregations in Indiana around Indianapolis, plus GS congregations in southern Indiana, and across the Ohio River in Kentucky and Tennessee. Taken together this regional reshuffling led to a reorganization along state lines but with centers in the three urban areas of Chicago, Detroit, and Indianapolis.[32]

Other synodical reorganizations occurred over the next several years. Not all were granted existence in perpetuity. A Slovak Lutheran synod was formed by request directed to the Executive Board from the Slav-Hungarian Mission Board located in Harrisburg, Pennsylvania. Given permission to organize, the Slovak Evangelical Lutheran "Zion" Synod was formed at Braddock, Pennsylvania with the stipulation that it "gather its congregations into a harmonious unity as a Synod" to prove it could function separately within the ULCA.[33] The Ohio Synod, meanwhile, was organized in late 1920 uniting four state synods formerly belonging to the General Council and the General Synod. A similar merger occurred in North Carolina in 1921, and in Virginia in 1922. In 1923 two former General Synod bodies, the Central Pennsylvania and Susquehanna Synods were merged to form the new Susquehanna Synod. In Canada language differences were overcome in two former General Council bodies, the Canada Synod and Synod of Central Canada, with the creation of a new Synod of Canada.[34] Clearly what the New York synods hoped to accomplish was part of a significant restructuring of Lutheran boundaries in North America.

MERGER IN NEW YORK

Of all the reasons for merger, most prevalent were the needs to overcome language differences and to consolidate synods with different origins but overlapping territorial jurisdictions. Lutheranism in the northeast was faced with both problems. Whether Lutherans from different backgrounds in the same towns, villages, and cities would work together or at cross-purposes in the merger process was an open question. In such circumstances, it is surprising that the process of merger in New York ever began in 1917. It did, however, because New York Lutheranism was at the center of national Lutheranism. Indeed, the

New York proposal for synodical merger may have been the first in the new national church. On April 30, 1917, twelve days after the proposal for the national merger of the three general bodies, the presidents of the New York Ministerium, the Synod of New York, and the Synod of New York and New England met together in New York City and agreed upon an identical recommendation to their respective synods. Apparently the Synod of New York and New England took the initiative, prodded by Pastor William M. Horn, a member of that Synod's Executive Committee.

Three reasons were given. Such a move should be made in "accordance with the spirit" of the national proposal. The "expediency of union" was not an exceptional reason, however. Merger was also necessary "under the economic pressure of the war." In Synods without adequate funding with which to meet the challenges of home missions and urbanization, the war and its economic pressures played a significant role.[35] Accordingly the three presidents proposed to their respective bodies

> That each Synod at its coming meeting appoint a Commission of Three, the President of Synod, one minister, and one layman, to meet with similar Commissions appointed from the other two bodies, and if the action of the General Bodies shall be favorable to merging, to prepare plans for the merger of the New York Ministerium, the Evangelical Lutheran Synod of New York, and the Evangelical Lutheran Synod of New York and New England, into one Organization, and to report their findings to these respective bodies in 1918 at their annual meetings.[36]

Both English-speaking synods immediately complied with the request. However the Ministerium failed to appoint the necessary commissioners. The recommendation was submitted to the 1918 Ministerium convention and action to proceed approved, but the matter was never carried out. The Ministerium's inaction was reported at the 1918 convention of the New York and New England Synod with the observation that the parent body did not intend joining a synodical merger until General Council intentions were clear. A puzzled Ministerium president thought preoccupation with Wagner College's recent move to Staten Island may have prevented action. Whatever the reason, a New York merger was to *follow* not *precede* national action. The matter was again taken up therefore in 1919 by the Ministerium and quickly passed.[37]

A first meeting of the joint commission was postponed in anticipation of this action, so that merger talks did not get underway until mid 1919. When the commissioners met on May 26 the Ministerium had not yet appointed members. Discussion proceeded with only its president representing the body. The three presidents had met previously on three occasions to prepare a survey of the territory and the work of their respective synods. After considering these reports, various plans for partial cooperation short of merger were suggested, but a consensus finally emerged "that the best results would be accomplished" by an actual merger of the three synods. A second meeting in July, in which Ministerium commissioners were finally present, agreed that a constitution for merged synods prepared by the ULCA Executive Committee would serve as the basis for union, though with a few changes. It was understood that the proposed constitution would have to be accepted by the three synods without amendment, and (further) that when two synods had ratified it, the merger would be effective for the two ratifying bodies. With these important preliminaries concluded, plans were made to meet at First Church, Albany, on June 10, 1920, to consummate the union.[38]

The commission met again in November 1919, after the plan of merger had been presented to the three bodies, to hear of its progress. It was agreed that the constitution as adopted by the commissioners should be submitted to the three synods. Preliminary reports from the three bodies indicated however that "the merging of the three bodies could not be accomplished at once." This resistance which was noted at the November meeting of the commission materialized in the 1920 sessions of the merging synods. The New York and New England Synod's two conferences recommended the new constitution to the 1920 convention for ratification. It also noted that the synod "is on record for a constructive policy and a union of the three Synods, based upon the sound principles set forth in the Constitution of the United Lutheran Church in America." After considerable debate in the New York Synod over several objectionable articles, action on the document was deferred for a year and the constitution was sent to its three conferences with the understanding that if all three approved, a special session would be called for purposes of ratification. In the Ministerium, meanwhile, none of the conferences looked favorably on the plan of merger. When the Ministerium itself met, the proposed constitution was given careful consideration, especially "in view of the fact that we as a Synod have our special mission." It was therefore resolved "not to agree to a Merger at the present time." After two years of confusion and apparent stalling, it was finally evident that the Ministerium wished to continue as a separate synod of the ULCA for the sake of its German-language mission in the northeast.[39]

Plainly the Ministerium was not yet seriously interested in merger. Despite the losses associated with the "Protestpartei" and again with the withdrawal of the Synod of New York and New England, the Ministerium felt it had a singular mission which was best served by remaining apart. It had experienced growth in the first decade of the century, but had then declined in membership between 1910 and 1920. But again after 1920 its special mission seemed a source of growth with increased German immigration after World War I. Graph 12.1, measuring active (communing) membership, suggests something of the relative fortunes of the three synods discussing merger and the volatile nature of Ministerium growth. By the end of World War I there seemed good reason for a speedy, three-way merger to offset the declining fortunes of northeastern Lutheranism. After 1920 there were reasons for a merger of the two dynamic English-speaking Lutheran bodies, but a three-way union was more problematic. While the English-language bodies were free to develop a joint mission, it was the oscillating size and fortunes of the Ministerium and its dynamic of German-language ministry that could conceivably be hindered by merger, thereby affecting the size of the Lutheran community in the northeast.

NEW MERGER PLANS

At this point the New York and New England Synod emerged as the linchpin of merger. It related well to the two other synods (the Ministerium and the New York Synod) which found it difficult to relate to each other. It had initiated the merger talks in early 1917 and was the first (and only) synod to ratify the proposed constitution. It continued relating to the Ministerium (its parent) in terms of possible remerger, and to the New York Synod through a potential merger of cooperative English-mission efforts. Where the Ministerium was conservative and German-speaking, and the New York Synod liberal and English-speaking, the New York and New England Synod was a progressive English-speaking synod with a background of German-language and culture. The term "progressive" was then current in American politics and was applied by a New York and New England Synod delegate to a certain spirit in the Ministerium. What was seen in the Ministerium in 1913—"a new spirit . . . of progressiveness, a wider and broader outlook and a determination to make itself a more influential factor in determining the destines of the Church"—was partially a projection of its own attitude.[40] The Synod of New York and New England confidently moved forward into an English-speaking culture as it moved out of a German-speaking milieu. Unwilling to jettison its heritage, it was yet eager to engage the modern, urban world. The Synod shared this viewpoint with key elements within the Ministerium, on the one hand, while sharing a more liberal outlook on the other with its English-speaking General Synod counterparts.

Thus this particular synod's potential for linking together the other two bodies was quite good. But so was the stress that could shear the linchpin. In 1922, for example, the Ministerium proposed "to bring about a merger between the New York and New England Synod and our New York Ministerium." It looked to its English offspring for help in developing Wagner College, something the New York and New England Synod wanted to pursue if its own needs "receive proper consideration and attention." Simultaneously, the synod was drawn in the other direction, however. The New York Synod proposed further cooperation on a second mission superintendent as an expression of it's "eager desire" that all three synods should soon be one." The New York and New England Synod decided under the circumstances to seek a dissolution of the present merger committees in the three synods and to have all three appoint new members.[41]

IMPACT OF THE LUTHERAN BROTHERHOOD

This the New York Synod declined to do after heatedly debating the matter at its 1923 convention in the presence of a New York and New England delegate. The bridge synod was thus forced to reexamine its own position. It concluded that the time had come for merger and that the previous principles of merger enunciated by the ULCA should be followed. Again they asked for the appointment of new merger committees. At this point a determined laity made a bold move reminiscent of the lay members on the Quadricentennial Committee who initiated the national merger in 1917. The Lutheran Brotherhood—a layman's service and fund raising organization—memorialized the three New York synods on the proposed merger.

Intersynodical experience within the Lutheran Brotherhood in New York and acquaintance with pastors in the three bodies gave the membership reason for involvement and a fair prospect of success. The Synod of New York and New England Brotherhood observed in a memorial presented by Chair Rodney T. Martinson that membership in the ULCA meant "there are no doctrinal differences" to prohibit merger. Secondly, they insisted that the "differences in practice and language are not regarded by us worthy of being made an obstacle" to merger. What is more, extensive cooperation already existed among members of the three bodies through inner and home mission work, and through the Brotherhood itself. Larger interests, especially missions and education, would be helped by merger they argued, where presently they are being hampered. Finally, as laymen interested in finances and expenses associated with running three separate synods, the costs are disproportionate to the result. It is simply "wasting the Lord's money and diverting it from channels where it is most sorely needed."[42]

The Lutheran Brotherhood's intervention accomplished its purpose. By 1924 the Ministerium reported that it was ready to appoint a committee on a three-way merger. Within a year it was ready for a thorough discussion of the matter both by pastors and in congregations. While the president would not influence the decision, he did plead "that the whole matter be conscientiously discussed, in perfect quietness and earnestness." Synodical committees separately drafted proposed constitutions, and the results were compared with the ULCA's model constitution. Meanwhile a bill was pushed through the New York State legislature naming the members of the joint commission as the incorporaters of "The United Lutheran Synod of New York."[43]

The Ministerium discussed the new constitution in a special convention held at Albany during November of 1925. Congregations thoroughly discussed the matter beforehand and presented their objections at the special session. Given the congregational confessionalism to be found in the Ministerium the discussion was to be extensive, involving numerous questions, objections and recommendations. It was immediately apparent that the Lutheran Brotherhood had been wrong in its first assumption, namely that there were no doctrinal differences separating the synods. Congregationalism—if doctrine it was—was certainly one. St. Johns Lutheran Church, Jersey City, spoke for many other congregations when it insisted that no confessional basis for merger was acceptable except that spelled out in the Ministerium constitution, being the "confessional standpoint of a truly Lutheran synod." The Ministerium constitution was recommended as the basis for merger by St. Johns because it "safeguards most acceptably the inalienable rights and privileges of its congregation." Other congregations insisted that the merging synod adopt the name of the "Venerable Evangelical Lutheran Ministerium of the State of New York, etc." St. Johns, Passaic (NJ), objected to acknowledging other churches on the basis of the Unaltered Augsburg Confession alone; it also asked if German conferences were forbidden. Among its many other questions, St. Johns objected to making congregations conform in public worship to the dictates of a synod.[44]

The objections were so numerous that it was moved at one point that merger be scuttled in favor of following "our traditional policy unhindered."[45] Instead, the entire synod agreed that its confessional basis for merger would be the confessional position "laid down in our old Constitution." For the first (and last) time in its long history the Ministerium agreed on the rectitude of its own doctrinal basis:

> This body accepts all the canonical books of the Old and New Testaments, as the revealed Word of God and the only Rule of Faith; also the Confessions of the Evangelical Lutheran Church as contained in the Book of Concord of 1580 as the correct presentation of the Christian faith.[46]

Following a listing of the three ecumenical creeds and the other confessional contents of the *Book of Concord*, it was agreed that "All questions concerning the Faith of the Church and Administration of the Sacraments shall be decided in accordance with this rule of Faith."[47] A lesser standard was unacceptable!

The Ministerium's confessional position had already been referred to Henry E. Jacobs of the Philadelphia Seminary for commentary. His reply was designed to defuse the feelings and opinions of what he considered the "zealous students of our symbolical books." Specifically he referred to the concern for concord in the *Book of Concord* which he believed was too easily disrupted by dissensions when people judge one another too harshly. Among other things he pointed to the sections in the ULCA Constitution which shaped the doctrinal relationship between synods. Most specifically, Article II, Section 3 stated that the ULCA "receives and holds the Unaltered Augsburg Confession as a correct exhibition of the faith and doctrine of the Evangelical Lutheran Church, founded upon the Word of God; and acknowledges all churches that sincerely hold and faithfully confess the doctrines of the Unaltered Augsburg Confession to be entitled to the name of Evangelical Lutheran." It was enough then that synods within the general body—including the three New York Synods—relate to each other in terms of doctrinal sufficiency, namely mutual acceptance of the Unaltered Augsburg Confession. Anything more was unnecessary.[48]

Frederick Bosch, president of the Synod, did not take this tack however, when presenting the results of the special convention to the 1926 annual meeting of the Ministerium. Instead he noted that the New York Synod was ready for merger, and willing to take up important additions and alterations in the proposed constitutions after merger. Bosch indicated that in his view the Ministerium should "first know the requirements of a New Synod" before consenting to merger. Aside from doctrinal problems, he noted other matters of great concern, especially "the educational question." The issue was colleges and seminaries. The Synod of New York and New England had become closely allied with Muhlenberg College; the New York Synod had long supported the Hartwick Seminary, recently (1926) expanded to include a new college at Oneonta, New York; while the Ministerium was heavily indebted in support of Wagner College, and closely affiliated with Mount Airy Seminary. "Our synod has resolved" he concluded, "that we wish a merger with the two other synods, if a satisfactory basis can be found." But a true unity of spirit was necessary "in principles and in the plans of work" before the Ministerium could consent to union.[49]

The 1926 Convention proved a turning point in intersynodical merger negotiations. The Merger Commission of the New York Ministerium reported more positive results from its three-way discussion with the other two synods. The New York Synod had similar concerns about educational institutions and thus it had been proposed in the commission to "accept in all fairness the entire educational situation with respect to the institutions in which the three Synods now have interests." The new synod, should it materialize, would find itself supporting three colleges and two seminaries, a fateful decision that would guarantee insufficient funding for too many institutions already weakened by inadequate support. Two other issues were solved with fewer consequences. The question of a name was settled by accepting a new name associated with none of the predecessor bodies—the United Lutheran Synod of New York and New England. Meanwhile the demand that merger proceed on the doctrinal basis of the Ministerium constitution was tabled, perhaps in light of Henry Eyster Jacobs's observations on what was constitutionally necessary for doctrinal merger. Instead the Commission recommended "in view of the common subscription of the merging Synods, forming the United Lutheran Church in America to the doctrinal basis set forth in the constitution thereof as amply sufficient," that the doctrinal basis of the new church be accepted. Moreover, the New York Synod and the Synod of New York and New England should deliver declarations to the Ministerium "that their interpretation of the doctrinal basis of the said constitution so adopted is in full agreement with the doctrinal basis of the present constitution of the New York Ministerium."[50]

By means of such assurances the Ministerium reluctantly let go of its understanding of the symbolical books of concord as "the correct presentation of the Christian faith," in favor of a new formula by which they became "a true exposition and defense of the Divine Word; by which Rule and Confessions all questions of faith and practice shall be decided." The difference between "the correct presentation" and "a true exposition" no longer warranted separation among Lutherans coming to trust one another more fully, though the differences hidden behind the two phrases were still significant enough to require one final and rather lengthy discussion of doctrine at the 1928 meeting of the Merger Commission. It, too, concerned the doctrinal basis of the proposed constitution, and "turned largely about an interpretation of terms." The final solution of this longstanding issue, reached by accepting the doctrinal clause in the Constitution of the New York and New England Synod on the symbols and their interpretation of Christian faith, was not without its ironies. The phrase had originated in the 1890s within the Ministerium itself after the upset caused by the "Protestpartei." In the end the Ministerium found a solution to its distrust of the New York Synod by borrowing its own earlier language, now in English, from an offspring it had come to trust as a bridge into the larger world it was now (at last) willing to cross.[51]

THE CONCLUSION OF THE MATTER

One looks in vain for a classic Hegelian synthesis of theological opposites in the new United Lutheran Synod of New York. The United Synod's confessional stance was not a synthesis of General Synod Biblicism and General Council Confessionalism. The merger was not a merger of theologies based on a least common denominator, nor an evenly distributed set of political compromises which kept everyone happy. The New York Ministerium lost the battle, but won the war. Though unable to merge on the basis of its own doctrinal standards, developed over long years of theological disputation, the Ministerium entered a United Synod more fully committed to the confessional theology of the Lutheran Church than it had been at its own inception. And while the other two synods might have been satisfied to base their new confessional identities on the Unaltered Augsburg Confession, both swore that their understanding of the whole *Book of Concord* corresponded to that of the New York Ministerium. The senior synod had simply divested itself of its own extremism in substituting the language of its more progressive offspring, and in so doing the spirit of concord in the *Book of Concord* was more fully realized in 1929 than before.

Looking back over their respective histories, each of the retiring synod presidents reflected on the history of their particular body as it was coming to an end. What they said *and* how they said it reflected on those histories. Herman Brezing, Ministerium president, opened his last Annual Report with a quotation from St. Paul: "Jesus Christ, the same yesterday, today and forever." With five years of merger plans being concluded he observed "The Evangelical Lutheran Ministerium of the State of New York and Adjacent States and Countries, as such, will cease to exist." Amidst these changes "we naturally turn in thought to the unchanging Head of the Church, Jesus Christ, the same yesterday, today and forever."

Having glorified Him in the past in a Ministerium which served as "the bulwark of Evangelical Lutheranism" in New York State, "we are now entering upon a larger union with our brethren in the faith" in conformity "with His will." Having "begun, continued and ended our work in Him, we turn our face resolutely to the future because the same Lord Jesus Christ, the Head of the Church, watches over our destiny, and Him alone would we serve and glorify." Relinquishing his office, and conscious of serving in a "line of men" with whom his name will be linked," Brezing experienced "a certain sense of human satisfaction." He also had regrets. For the "miscarriage of certain purposes" he could not altogether absolve himself. But he desired "as a final word" to witness to a "new revelation" given him "of Christ as the Head of His Church and to acknowledge humbly His over-ruling guidance and His wise and manifold intervention."[52]

Merger was most difficult for the Ministerium. It gave up much which had been dear to it, and in so doing its president carried a certain burden of guilt and failure. The Ministerium's grief was palpable. Its past, stretching back beyond its own origins to the earlier confessionalism of Henry Melchior Muhlenberg and the Pennsylvania Ministerium, as well as to the Lutheran orthodoxy of William Berkenmeyer and the New York Classis, now seemed in jeopardy. Its future in the larger United Synod was uncertain. With declining fortunes in a changing world, hope could only be renewed by a vision and the assurance that the Lord of Life was the head of the new church. So persuaded, they brought to an end a tradition stretching back into the eighteenth century.

A newer synod with greater prospects and inherited problems, the New York Synod had a sense of future, having successfully negotiated a difficult transition to a modern, urban, mission-minded Lutheran body. Charles Leitzell, president of the New York Synod for nearly eight years, was also conscious of his synod's history stretching back well into the last century, beginning with that moment when the Hartwick Synod (the oldest of the three constituting synods) had broken away from the Ministerium. But he was more conscious of the New York Synod's history from 1908 and especially interested in developments during the 1920s. The real history of the synod "cannot be recited or tabulated," he observed, suggesting that the importance of the Synod was not to be measured by results. Fourteen congregations, 11,000 baptized and 5,000 communing members had been added to the synod in the past decade. This "splendid progress" must be put in perspective, however. A list of explanations qualified Leitzell's description of the recent growth. The return to peacetime had been difficult; many congregations were new missions with financial burdens; appeals for European relief and larger church needs had drawn away mission support; the "great principles of Stewardship were new to many of our people" and much prejudice had to be overcome in bringing congregations to an understanding of "the meaning of stewardship"; finally, synodical loyalty was at an ebb when the Synod of New York was formed, while the question of merger constantly before the new body meant commitments and actions were postponed to the detriment of church work.

Yet progress had been made in the face of such difficulties. Forces at work in the synod had at last been unified, "bringing 150 more or less independent congregations into a real unity of action and purpose, developing a real sense of synodical loyalty, giving pastors and people a larger outlook and causing them to think in terms of the kingdom rather than simply of the local church." Faced with the prospect of laying down his task at last, Leitzell did so with the satisfaction of having sought always "to do His will" and having a "conscience void of offense." While the synod had some misgivings and apprehensions about the future, nevertheless "we are looking forward with great expectancy to new relationships, to enlarged opportunities for service, and with a determination to work together "in such a way that our Lutheran Church on this territory will be greatly advanced and the coming of the kingdom . . . speedily hastened."[53]

Briefest of all was Samuel Trexler, president of the New York and New England Synod. The past was very much present in the future of the new church. His hope was that the last twenty-seven years' experience might be brought "into this union." Three characteristics of the

New York and New England Synod were important to remember. First was a decided "home mission impulse" which "throughout her career . . . has been her normal function." From thirty-seven congregations, the young synod had grown to a "full hundred purely through the missionary impulse." This feature of the synod's life "has about it the quality of rich romance" and gives promise of what might be achieved "under the united power of the merged Synod." A second emphasis has been "the appeal of the thousands of young people at the non-church institutions on this territory," leading to pioneering work in student ministry not only by campus pastors, but through local congregations as well. The third feature "worked out in the laboratory of our Synod" was the "system of information and education" by which congregations were made aware of the larger church and its mission. Despite absorption in local matters, all congregations had partaken of the "forward movements which have given the life of our Synod such joy and interest."[54]

THE UNITED SYNOD—A LUTHERAN EMPIRE

The United Lutheran Synod of New York (ULSNY) represented a monumental merger of northeastern Lutherans—454 pastors, 402 congregations, a baptized membership approaching a quarter million (214,000 +) and a communing membership of 100,000. (See Graph 12.1.) The congregations and their members were drawn from five states—Maine, Connecticut, Massachusetts, New Jersey, and New York. The territory was sufficiently large to require subdivision into eight conferences—the Western, Central, Eastern, New York, New Jersey, New England, Long Island and German Conferences. Together they represented in membership one-eighth of the United Lutheran Church in America, a veritable "Lutheran Empire" centered in the Empire State among people experienced in building regional and national structures, including the United Lutheran Church and the Federal Council of Churches. (See Map 12.1.) This Lutheran empire emerged when, as an official of the Federal Council observed, size was important in the modern United States.[55]

Its origins went back to a single synod, the New York Ministerium (1786). But it was also the merger of two traditions (General Council and General Synod), three predecessor bodies (New York Ministerium, Synod of New York, New York and New England Synod), and of six more distant synods—the Hartwick (1830), Franckean (1837), New Jersey (1861), Steimle (1866), and New York Synods (1867), and the restructured Ministerium (1867)—all of which were subdivisions of the original parent. It took two intermediate mergers—the New York and New Jersey Synod (1872), and the Synod of New York (1908)—to bring General Synod Lutherans to the point of merger with General

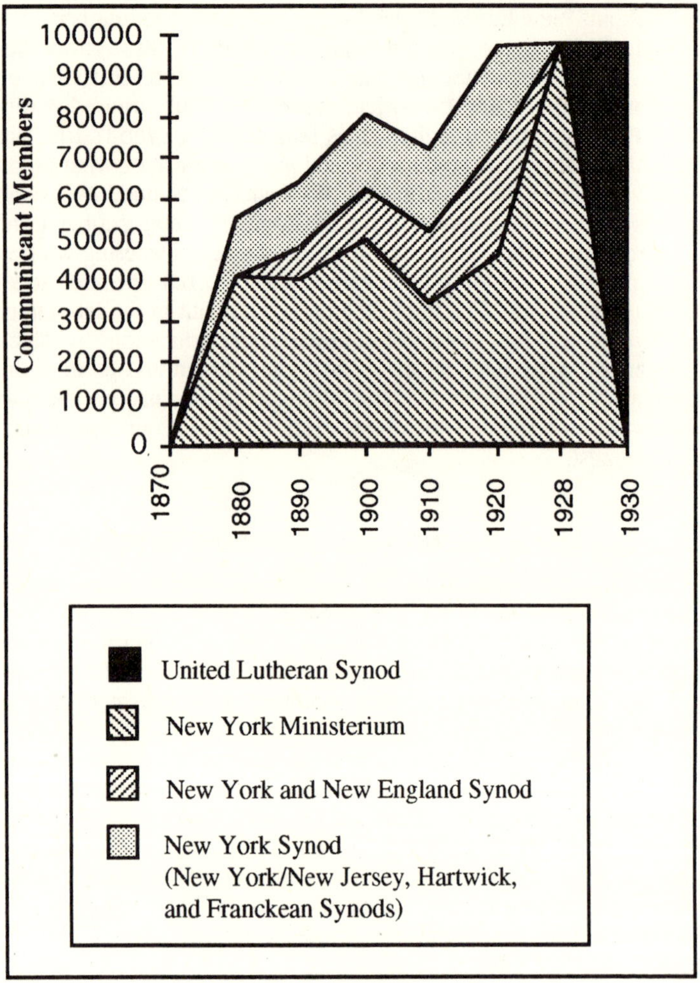

Graph 12.1
Formation of the United Lutheran Synod

Council Lutherans; meanwhile one further subdivision, the New York and New England Synod (1902), was necessary before General Council Lutherans were ready to unite with General Synod Lutherans. Moreover, this union represented a merger of three confessional traditions—liberal (New York Synod), progressive (Synod of New York and New England), and conservative (The New York Ministerium). But it also reflected a common confessional heritage traceable to the original New York Ministerium and the Muhlenberg confessional legacy.

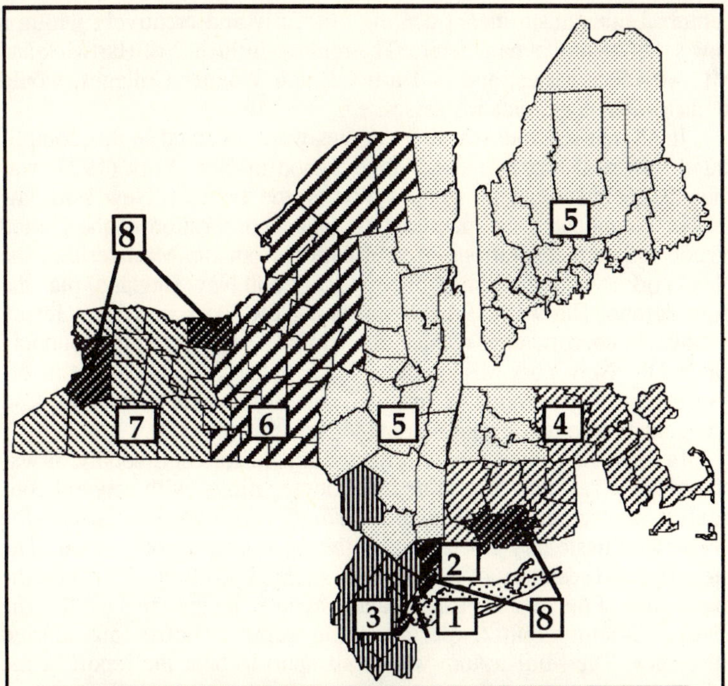

Conferences of the United Lutheran Synod of New York
(With Synod of Origin for Majority of Congregations)

1. Long Island - GC & GS (NY & NE Synod; Synod of New York)
2. New York - GC (NY Ministerium)
3. New Jersey - GS & GC (Synod of New York; NY Ministerium)
4. New England - GC (NY Ministerium)
5. Eastern - GS (Synod of New York; Hartwick; Franckean)
6. Central - GS & GC (NY Ministerium; Hartwick; Franckean)
7. Western - GC (NY MInisterium; NY & NE Synod)
8. German - GC (NY Ministerium)

Map 12.1
Conferences of the ULSNY 1930

Numerically, there was a 50/50 balance between German-speaking Conservative and English-speaking Liberal/progressive bodies. How these differing theological expressions of Lutheran confessionalism would affect politics within the new ULSNY was an open question. Thinking and acting within this complex matrix of early twentieth century Lutheranism meant dealing faithfully and creatively within a new set of historical parameters. The relative influence of Hartwick and Mt. Airy Seminaries, and of Hartwick and Wagner Colleges, would significantly shape such responses.

In all, ten separate synodical bodies were involved in this complicated historical process. The United Synod of New York (1929) was thus the tenth and, again, single synod on the territory. New York law further complicated this pedigree. Actual incorporation of the United Synod required resolutions of ratification from the Ministerium, the New York Synod, the Synod of New York and New England, plus the now defunct Hartwick, Franckean, and New York and New Jersey Synods. In consolidating its past, the United Synod voted the founding date of the New York Ministerium, 1786, as the official date of its organization, legitimizing a mildly scandalous genealogy but also recognizing a common confessional legacy.[56]

In form the United Synod reflected this historical diversity. It was organized as a synod of pastors and congregations, with a synod convention, conferences, and a ministerium, plus two auxiliaries—the Women's Missionary Society, and the Synodical Brotherhood. The president and secretary of Synod were salaried positions. Based on the experience of the two English-speaking synods, it was expected that the United Synod would experience the same benefits of salaried efficiency. The Ministerium was to sit apart to hear the report of the examining committee, to try cases of heresy and discipline, and to transact such other business as the synod might refer to it.

The greatest change involved the conferences. Larger in number and in size than in any of the predecessor bodies, the conferences were now charged, in addition to the usual function of carrying out regulations and resolutions of the synod, "to care for the interests and development of the Church upon its territory." They were in practice if not in fact, synodical organizations in their own right. Mission and benevolence development were particularly important parts of their activities. Also conference presidents were to serve as a committee advising the Synod president of conference needs and keeping conference records on the multitude of official events—pastoral installations, cornerstone layings, church dedications, memorials for deceased ministers—to be reported through the synod president to the synod convention.[57]

"WOMAN POWER"

The Women's Missionary Society represented a merger and reinvigoration of the Women's missionary societies inherited from the predecessor synods, together consisting of 691 women's groups, with a membership of 34,312. The oldest had originated with the formation of women's missionary societies in the General Synod, beginning with the Franckean Synod in 1879. The newest groups were the ten-year-old members of the Ministerium's Women's Missionary Society, organized at the formation of the ULCA so that Ministerium women might be represented in the Women's Missionary Society of the United Lutheran Church. The merger was welcomed, for United Synod women anticipated an increase in the "woman power" it felt would occur with a missionary society in every congregation. Overall, the new organization represented a continuation of the woman's role and public work first developed by the predecessor synods in the late 1870s and early 1880s. However by 1930 and the formation of the United Lutheran Church and Synod the women's missionary societies at the congregational level had also probably become one of the most important sources of theological education and spiritual formation for Lutheran women. A synodical field secretary kept in touch with the entire organization while its seven conference auxiliaries each had its own secretary. Together they kept in touch with congregations in the German Conference, the only group with no secretary. A request was made that pastors encourage the work of the society and help in the organization of congregational mission societies. Though the organization did not initially experience phenomenal growth, its size and influence were impressive—two hundred and four (204) congregational societies out of four hundred and two (402) congregations. So were its works. A missionary nurse was supported at the Chirala Hospital in India as was a teacher in Inner Mission work at the Konnarock Training School in Virginia. Partial support was provided for two schools in China. The woman's role in the home was extended into the congregation through the society, with the development of lay and professional leadership among the young becoming another major effort of the group. Young women's missionary groups, which had been organized in numerous congregations, focused on both mission concerns and leadership development among young women. Sixty-one Light Brigades were also organized for the missionary education of congregational children. Deaconess candidates were developed and supported. Young men for ministry were under the society's care as well as young women "preparing for Christian service."[58]

New to the Synod was a Synodical Brotherhood. Its immediate goal was the establishment of Brotherhoods in each congregation, or the reinvigoration of already established organizations, presumably those once a part of the eastern version of the Lutheran Brotherhood—in all at least 277 congregational units with a membership of 14,076. By comparison with men's groups in other denominations, or with Lutheran women's organizations, Lutheran men were noticeable by their relative absence from auxiliary church affairs in the first decades of the twentieth century. Perhaps this was because the men were lay men—competent in other areas of life, especially organization and finance—but secondary to clergymen in the church. Yet once organized in 1930 the Brotherhood focused on youth work—especially delinquent and problem boys—and addressed church issues with which they were concerned. At the beginning at least, these involved questions of finance and organization, including the financial costs of synod, topics which laymen had as good if not a better grasp of than pastors. Whatever the issue, with laymen delegates also part of a Synodical Brotherhood, organization of the ULSNY represented a significant increase in the role of lay men in the church. With meetings open to women, however, something of the rigid gender distinctions at the synodical level were softened for it was in the Brotherhood that men and women joined together for the first time in a meeting where synodical issues were addressed.[59]

Men, however, sat on local vestries and councils which traditionally had concerns in the area of church organization and finance. Such were the powers of these little oligarchies of trustees, at least in the late nineteenth century, that neither congregations, synods nor pastors had much control over them. And until women were accepted into positions of representative leadership, representation and voting rights were limited by law and/or custom to men. Women's voting status in the church in New York had actually declined since the relatively enlightened period following the Revolution. The old Ministerium, at least, had availed itself of that male legal privilege by disenfranchising women after being instructed by their conferences to do so. With congregations so organized, women delegates would not be elected to synodical gatherings, though no synodical constitution, including the new constitution of the ULSNY (or its parent body, the ULCA), defined delegates beyond the stipulation of communing membership in congregations. The lack of gender qualifications prompted the Texas Synod to memorialize the ULCA on the biblical propriety of electing women to church councils, synods, or national church boards. By 1936 the national body went on record affirming that election to such offices was "not contrary to Scripture" though a call to the ordained office of ministry indeed was.[60]

In addition to these auxiliaries, the United Synod was deeply involved in an elaborate Inner Mission effort. The working definition of inner missions put forward by William Alfred Passavant, American Lutherans' foremost inner missionary in the middle of the nineteenth century, indicates its potential extensiveness. Inner mission involved: 1) the scriptural revival of religion; 2) Christian education in Sunday schools, kindergartens, catechetics and Bible study, as well as in academies, colleges and seminaries; 3) the relief of temporal needs through funds, special societies, and institutions (including orphanages, hospitals and homes for the aged); and, 4) the enhancement of congregational worship through the development of the liturgy and congregational singing. This array of activity was all to be found within the new United Synod! Besides the congregational Sunday-, day-, and parochial-schools, or the local aid societies (both integral parts of inner mission within local parishes), all of which were too numerous to count, inner mission activity included: one seminary on the territory (Hartwick Seminary) and another receiving official support (Philadelphia Seminary); two colleges (Wagner and Hartwick); six orphan homes (Buffalo, Sulphur Springs, Syracuse, Wartburg, Bethlehem in Staten Island, and Children's Home in Brooklyn); at least two homes for the aged (Maria Louise Memorial and Wartburg, Mt. Vernon); two hospitals (Lutheran in Brooklyn and Lutheran of Manhattan); Emigrant House in Manhattan; the Immigrant Society of Manhattan; the Seamen's Mission also in the borough; an Association for the Relief of Indigent Germans; a German Home for Recreation of Women and Children; and the Inner Mission Society, and the Inner Mission and Rescue Work organizations of Manhattan.[61]

Confessional and ethnic differences led to the creation also of Missouri Synod and Scandinavian inner mission institutions. Thus in addition to United Synod entities one could count again as many inner mission institutions on the territory: two colleges (Concordia, Bronxville, and Upsala in New Jersey); a teacher's institute and seminary (also Bronxville); at least three homes for the aged (Wartburg in Brooklyn, Norwegian Old People's Home in Manhattan, and Swedish Augustana in Brooklyn); a Norwegian Deaconness Motherhouse in Brooklyn; Norwegian Lutheran Hospital in Brooklyn; the Lutheran Hospital Association consisting of twenty Missouri Synod congregations; and immigrant and seamen's missions (two Norwegian, one Swedish, one Danish, and one Finnish). While most of these institutions served specific groups outside of the United Synod, the interLutheran nature of inner mission work going back to Passavant made this group of institutions part of a larger Lutheran "Inner Mission" in the New York area. The existence of the Luther League of New York City with its *The Lutheran League Review*, of Koinonia (an intersynodical Lutheran pastor's group which met monthly for the discussion of papers presented by the members), of the American Lutheran Publicity Bureau in Manhattan, and of the Inner Mission Society with its *Inner Mission* periodical, meant that the United Synod was also involved in a diverse and complex interLutheran culture beyond its own boundaries dedicated to the enrichment of Lutheran religious life in the northeast. As George U. Wenner observed of the potential of this substantial religious body, the "simple faith and the catholic principles of our church should secure for us a wide field of useful and effective service."[62]

PROSPECT

The biggest organizational change, perhaps, came with the development of a new kind of superintending president of synod, a position unlike any previously employed by New York Lutherans. Who might fill that position was determined on the third ballot for president of the organizing convention. The new synod had come to life under the gavel of former Ministerium vice-president, Theodore Posselt, pastor of St. Johns Evangelical Lutheran Church of Albany (fig. 12.2), its meeting place.

figure 12.2
St. Johns Evangelical Lutheran Church, Albany, N. Y.

Posselt may have been a contender for the position, given the active role he played in organizing the new synod. Perhaps George U. Wenner, well known senior pastor of the New York Synod was in contention, or Charles Leitzell, its energetic president with a recent record of success in building a new synod out of disparate predecessor bodies. On the third ballot, however, the vote went to the president of the New

York and New England Synod, the Rev. Dr. Samuel Trexler. He, like Leitzell, had a successful record, and carried with him into the new synod a progressive sense of the church and its mission in a changing world. Having served as president of the bridge synod in the negotiations was no doubt also a large consideration with members of the New York Ministerium and the New York Synod. In any case these two larger synods cast their votes for the leader of the smallest organization, unusual in this kind of balloting. The two bodies shared the rest of the offices between them however. Pastor Paul Kirsch, of the Ministerium, was elected the new secretary. German secretary of the Ministerium, the Rev. Frederick Noeldeke, was elected to a similar position in the new synod. Mr. Fred Wefer, treasurer of the New York Synod, was chosen for that position in the United Synod.[63]

In his first report President Trexler gave an overview of the new body. The conferences were working and making the large organization effective. Where the ranks had been "rather thin" in the old synods, the mingling of congregations "previously separated" now enriched the life of the church. Paid officers had been effective in bringing "the new vision of the stronger Synod" to each congregation. It was also a diverse synod. Urban, suburban, and rural congregations were now at last brought into one organization. Included were churches "in the busiest thoroughfares of our largest cities as well as the church at the country crossroads." Beside congregations already 100 years old when Muhlenberg came to America in 1742, there are "new missions still in their swaddling clothes." "Color, [and] race" added to the diversity, giving to the new synod a "really comprehensive life." Unique, perhaps, was the distinction of having "so many of the forces which dominate this nation as well as the world." In all, the new synod was "standing but at the threshold of a new life for the Church on this territory."[64]

Trexler no doubt had in mind Transfiguration Lutheran Church, Harlem, the first permanent Lutheran congregation of African-Americans on the New York territory. It was formed in Harlem among Lutherans with roots in the Danish West Indies, the first place in the New World where Lutherans "pursued an organized and systematic program to bring black people into the church." In 1913 a prominent and influential West Indian, the secretary of the Pullman Porter's Union, called upon a local Danish Lutheran pastor, A. C. Kildegaard, to establish Lutheran services for West Indians in his congregation on Sunday evenings. This Danish West Indian Lutheran Congregation moved to Harlem in 1920 to better serve the West Indian community developing there. The Church was supplied during the early 1920s by the executive secretary of the ULCA Board of American Missions, Dr. Zenan M. Corbe, pastor of the Church of the Transfiguration in Philadelphia, and four of his parishioners who were students at Wagner College; in 1922 the church's staff was augmented by a deaconess,

Sister Emma Francis of the Virgin Islands, who had been trained in biblical studies at Freinwalde, Germany, and in nursing at Elizabeth Hospital in Berlin, and later returned to Fredricksted from Germany to co-found the Ebenezer Home for Girls. The congregation, by now renamed the Church of the Transfiguration in honor of Pastor Corbe, was also served by a Virgin Island student at Wagner, Paul Edward West, who after graduation from Wagner and Mt. Airy Seminary was called to Transfiguration where he served until his retirement in 1956. It was received into membership in the new United Lutheran Synod of New York and New England in 1929 and that is quite probably why it caught Trexler's attention. Like key congregations among German and Swedish immigrants in the New York area, Transfiguration became a mother church to other African-American congregations. The Church of the Holy Trinity would be organized in Jamaica, L. I. in 1934; in 1942 St. Pauls was organized out of Transfiguration members moving into north Harlem.[65]

Trexler finished his report on an unusual note—with a question. Exactly what did the life of the congregation in the new synod express? Having visited half the congregations, he and Secretary Kirsch had a good sense of what was happening at the new synod's grass roots. This was an important question to the new organization since together the congregations made up "The Church which is His body." Ideally, what they together represented was an incarnation of the living Lord, an expression of the Christ "in the richness and completeness of His personality." The reality "is oftentimes a distressing and blotted image, frequently so faint that no impression whatever is made." What diluted the image "is the entrance into the Church of a spirit of worldliness which leaves the congregation with a character not differing much from a score of secular organizations about it." Its cause was twofold, according to Trexler. Too many congregations had incurred financial obligations which were a burden and which had resulted in all "types of cheap devices for gathering money." To this "sorry picture" was added a church which uses worldliness "as a lure to bring young people into the Church." World lures and cheap fundraising devices in the United Synod were but part of what Trexler described as an "anaemic church life which meekly bows to every human whim" and which can never represent "the Christ whose mission was too great to be entangled with such a pathetic program."[66]

THE ANEMIC EMPIRE

We began this study with a brief description of a veritable Lutheran empire formed by Lutherans which in some ways reflected the material bigness and prosperity of the Empire State itself. What we could not then see was the impact which this material environment had on the spiritual life of its congregations and members. While Trexler was speaking only about Lutheran congregations forming the new United Synod, his concerns reflected the decay of discipline and piety, the loss of religiosity, and the rise of prosperity occurring throughout the Church in America after World War I—a change which historians have described as the decline of American Protestantism.[67] In the case of northeastern Lutheranism, a once rural and small-town collection of independent Lutheran synods had been transformed into a new and largely urbanized church—the United Synod—a veritable Lutheran empire in the northeast, arisen out of the cities and towns in the Hudson River hydrographic basin, and grown to large proportions with the growth of the Empire State and its environs. In this process of merger and urbanization, and with the rebuilding of a once rural infrastructure upon an urban base, cosmopolitan cultural forces transformed the church. Already by the 1880s the constituent synods of this new merger lamented the forces of secularity and materialism threatening rural and small town congregations. What Trexler saw about him was the further impact of these forces on an increasingly secularized Protestantism, which were badly distorting the piety and stewardship of a newly urbanized Lutheran church.

What Trexler lamented was the seeming ease with which a tradition-oriented, and confessionally conservative church had been drained of life ("anemic church life") so easily, so quickly, and so thoroughly in these circumstances. What he expressed was a traditional Lutheran piety which was uncomfortable with the larger world, with the profane, the secular, and the material world, and especially with the urbanized realities of the greater New York area. The Frenchman André Siegfried saw the same things when observing in his 1927 analysis of American religion that the traditional Lutheran distinction between the two kingdoms meant the saints "must live in the world as best they can and must carefully protect the purity of their spiritual lives." Lutherans differed from the predominant Calvinism of the American Protestant hegemony. Material concerns and wealth were rationalized as divine blessings and signs of God's favor by a Protestant ethic which more easily united religion and daily life. Siegfried noted that Lutherans, together with Roman Catholics and Anglicans (high church Episcopalians), resisted this general tendency towards worldly Protestantism. In the Lutheran case, as Siegfried noted, it was doctrine, ethnic origin, a terror of modernists, and an unsympathetic view of the "social church" (i.e., Social Gospel), which demarcated American Lutheranism's distinctive sphere.[68]

WHAT KIND OF DENOMINATION?

Other less than desirable forces may also have been at work within the Lutheran Empire having to do with its *raison d'être*. Just as New York Lutherans were putting the finishing touches on their own expression of united Lutheranism, the American theologian H. Richard Niebuhr developed a systematic criticism of confessional denominationalism in his *The Social Sources of Denominationalism*, published in October of 1929. Drawing heavily upon the disciplines of history and sociology—especially the insights of Ernst Troeltsch, Max Weber, and R. H. Tawney—Niebuhr argued that denominationalism "represents the moral failure of Christianity. . . . [B]efore the church can hope to overcome its fatal division it must learn to recognize and to acknowledge the secular character of its denominationalism." The church in America no longer had any viable denominational life in it; rather its denominational differences could be attributed to the pernicious influence of race, nationalism, sectionalism, social group, and economic class.[69]

Niebuhr doubted that official statements of faith contained the real "explanation of the sources and of the character of the prevailing differences" in a church. "Lutherans are distinguished, the interpreter of the creed tells us, by their belief in justification by faith alone, by their exaltation of the word of God as the primary means of grace, and by their profession of the priesthood of all believers." Not so. Divisions among Lutherans point to non-theological differences, that is secular distinctions. Divisions brought about by the Civil War, for example, were more deep-seated among Lutheran than among other Protestant bodies in America, lasting until 1918 according to Niebuhr, partly because northern churches (i.e., the General Synod) severely condemned all rebellion and insurrection, being "true to its inherited character as a child of the German state churches." Southern Lutheranism (he insisted) displayed a willingness to accommodate itself to American culture and life in ways which northern and western German Lutherans resisted. Immigrant Lutheran churches were (in his view) at risk of becoming "more a racial and cultural than a religious institution in the New World." Exaggerated confessional differences, meanwhile, could be attributed both to resistance to acculturation and to competitive denominational separateness. Finally, "race discrimination" had become "so respectable an attitude in America that it could be accepted by the church without subterfuge of any sort." Whereas prior to the Civil War "white and black Christians worshipped together," at the present time eighty-eight percent "of Negro Christians" were segregated by denomination or (within denominations) by conference.[70]

If Niebuhr was correct, a once-viable confessional theology had simply become the vehicle and protector of organizational differences, rather than a means of new life for an anemic church like that which Trexler described. Viewed from Niebuhr's perspective what could be said for the new United Lutheran Church and its United Lutheran Synod of New York? A bright spot according to Trexler was that color and race had given it something of a "really comprehensive life." Moreover, the ethnic, racial, language, cultural, and geographic divisions which Niebuhr so lamented in his criticism of denominations, had been challenged and in some cases overcome by the new unity of both the United Lutheran Church and the United Synod, something Henry Eyster Jacobs had noted with interest a decade before in his inaugural sermon before the assembled delegates of the ULCA in New York City. Yet Niebuhr's perspective was arresting for thoughtful Lutherans as for other Christians in America, and properly so. Writing in the 1931 edition of *Lutheran Church Quarterly* Charles M. Jacobs, son of Philadelphia Seminary's Henry Eyster Jacobs, and confidant of ULCA President Frederick W. Knubel, noted:

> Many of the author's facts are beyond dispute. There can be no doubt in the mind of any unprejudiced student that the manifold divisions among Lutherans in America are due, not so much to differences in "doctrine and practice" between the separate groups, as to differences in racial origin and in social and cultural inheritance. These differences, holding the Lutheran groups apart, have made anything like an even and harmonious doctrinal development impossible. They have also caused the doctrinal differences which do exist to be magnified far beyond their intrinsic importance. They have kept alive certain *theologoumena* which possess little reality outside of professors' studies and the classrooms of theological seminaries, and have made them slogans of ecclesiastical parties. As these slogans lose reality, new ones are found. Today it is not really differences in doctrine that hold the Lutherans of America apart, but differences of other kinds. They are partly racial; but chiefly they are environmental. . . . . The cause of them has to be sought in the history of the groups and not in textbooks of Dogmatics."[71]

Jacobs could have been reflecting on the unfolding history of New York Lutheranism with its intense environmental interactions of theology and geography. Lutherans like Jacobs were seeking to put their confessional past into historical and sociological perspective, and beginning to face a new present in which social divisions no longer represented faithful distinctions to be celebrated, but sinful divisions to be overcome.

A conserving attitude to a common confessional heritage, older than any of these American divisions, would be a cause of union in the future, not the division Jacobs predicted. Speaking prophetically he observed:

> Out of the chaos of American denominationalism we are witnessing the gradual emergence of a few types of churches, and these types have their prototypes in the Protestant Reformation. There is every reason to expect that this process will be accelerated in the next few decades and that we shall see church unions of large ex-

> tent and great significance. It is fairly safe to predict that by 1975 there will be not more than three, probably not more than two, great organizations of Lutherans in America; there may possibly be only one. The situation is by no means hopeless.[72]

By 1975 there were, in fact, just three large organizations, and they were on their way to further consolidation which would reduce the number to two in the next decade. And at least one of those organizations—the Lutheran Church in America—a successor body to the United Lutheran Synod, would originate in a "Commitment to Unity" which facilitated this reduction from three to two major national Lutheran bodies.[73]

Lutheran historian and Gettysburg Seminary professor Abdel Ross Wentz, in a review published the same year, observed somewhat more critically that *The Social Sources of Denominationalism*

> furnishes abundant scholarly proof that the denominational expression of Christianity is deeply ingrained in the very nature of things and cannot be laid aside at the behest of a group of professional reformers. . . . His book is a realistic investigation of the social forces which have led to the formation of the various denominations or churches and which are potent factors in perpetuating them in their separateness.[74]

But where Niebuhr saw only continuing separateness, Wentz saw the kinds of changes occurring which would eventually foster this commitment to unity. Wentz's 1931 "Presidential Address" to the American Society of Church History developed his argument at greater length. Rejecting the narrow sectarianism of an earlier period in American religious history, twentieth-century churches were (so far as Wentz was concerned) involved in developing a "new denominationalism" which displayed

> an inextinguishable longing for something like intellectual toleration and Christian cooperation. Herein lay the positive progress that may be credited to the period of sectionalism...So in religious life the supreme allegiance of the churches to Jesus Christ did not hinder them from being true to their separate histories and cultivating their denominational consciousness, while yet arranging among themselves such a division of labor as would leave no territory unoccupied to become the camping ground of such special privilege as the world, the flesh, and the devil. This was the spirit of the new denominationalism.[75]

The result has been a modified denominationalism marked by "(1) the persistence of the denominational type, and (2) the general recognition of the claims of generic Christianity." Thus to speak, as Niebuhr does, as though "denominations of our day" were merely competing rival camps "is an offense against the historical perspective. To insist that the present-day divisions among Christians are of necessity a scandal because they weaken the force of the Christian impact, and not to see that the divisions among Christians may be the integrated divisions of an advancing army, does violence not only to the lexicon but also to the historical sense." "The denominational lines of our day have deep social sources and far-reaching historical roots, so that they cannot be wished out of existence or commanded to disappear."[76]

FACING THE FUTURE WITH HISTORICAL AWARENESS

Eastern Lutherans like Jacobs and Wentz were not about to dismiss their past as a history of moral failure, to whatever extent they might recognize its shortcomings in light of Niebuhr's seminal study. The social sources of Lutheranism had their place—"deeply ingrained " is how Wentz put it—and were not to be denied, however limiting one might recognize them to be. Addressing the 1937 synod convention of the United Lutheran Synod of New York and New England, Pastor Augustus Steimle, describe the nature of the struggle with these deeply ingrained aspects of faith in the history of New York Lutheranism:

> Back of a living language stand customs, usages, a history, a literature, a culture. It is difficult, more difficult than superficial thought would assume, to separate religion from the culture in which it comes to us. We cannot escape our environment. The impress of our schooling goes with us through the years. Nor can we on the other hand eliminate the tingling of the blood in our veins that comes from our ancestors. So when we view this transition of Lutheranism in our country from its cradled forms in Europe to its utterly new and alien surroundings in America, let us look with sympathy and intelligence upon the pathetic struggles that meet us in the history of New York Lutheranism.[77]

While a church might move beyond these historic limitations in facing its "utterly new and alien surroundings," a sympathetic view of the past was necessary in Steimle's view if it was every to do so.

On the other hand pressing toward the mark required change. No matter how valid one's traditions and historical development, authentic historical existence (as the existentialist philosopher Martin Heidegger was to argue in the 1920s) requires that we see ourselves within the context of history since we cannot escape the inevitability of lives bound by present conditions and shaped by outlooks inherited from the past. Human beings are born willy nilly into a world not of their own making. They exist in a particular society that carries with it not only the weight of the past, but the tensions and conflicts of the present. Grasping that existential reality is necessary if the future is to be faced with courage and intelligence and faith.[78]

In the spirit of the times this growing ability to become more inclusive with an enlarged perspective and a more comprehensive set of shared interests was now being identified by the American philosopher, John Dewey, as at the heart of pragmatic thinking in a democratic society. As popularly misunderstood, "pragmatic" seems to sanction whatever idea works. Properly understood, however, "pragmatic" refers to working ideas adequate to the occasion. In the case of the merger of the three general bodies, the resulting confessional statement was more comprehensive and complex than those of the predecessor bodies. It was, to use the felicitous phrasing of Henry Eyster Jacobs, an "ampler confession," and one which conformed more completely to the function of the confessional canon as defined in the Formula of Concord, namely that "all doctrines" pertaining to Lutheran matters "should conform to the standards" of these confessional norms. The need in an age of religious pluralism to so act and think as to transcend particular and concrete (though limited and limiting) religious realities for the sake of something more adequately comprehensive Dewey would identify as at the very heart of life in a democratic society, a perspective that since has offered tantalizing possibilities for doing theology in a pluralistic context.[79] Dewey had little hope however for organized religion, a too pessimistic view if only because even as he wrote eastern Lutherans were managing such a process of change and growth.

For eastern Lutherans in the tradition of the ULCA this meant learning how to accommodate the conservative Reformation to the process of historical change. The tradition of the conservative Reformation must be honored and preserved yet not uncritically, for where traditionalism constrained vision, the past would have to be critiqued in the name of progress. How to honor the one without becoming hostage to the other? This was a tricky theological business requiring historical consciousness. Such an awareness would express itself in new and important ways in Lutheran church life by the 1930s. To it we can trace the beginnings of a sustained historical inquiry into the origins, development and merger of Lutheran synodical traditions in New York Lutheranism of which this volume is one development.

CONCLUSION—NEW SYNOD AND OLD MINISTERIUM

A further volume will be necessary to recount not only such growing historical awareness but the further forms which change would take. By 1929 a United Synod had merged two forms of eastern Lutheranism associated with the General Synod and the General Council. Further change would reflect those forces at work—geography and religious subcultures—which traditionally had shaped the development of the Minsterium tradition and legacy.

Geography would be one major source of further change. By mid-century the United Synod would begin breaking apart along subregional conference lines. New Jersey would withdraw to form its own Synod of New Jersey in 1950, eighty-nine years after the first experiment in New Jersey regionalism led to the formation of the original, English-speaking New Jersey Synod. Two years later the subregional nature of what remained was renamed the Synod of New York and New England.

With the merger of the ULCA and the Augustana Church, the American Evangelical Lutheran Church (Danish), and the Finnish Evangelical Lutheran Church (Suomi Synod) in 1962, and the subsequent formation or restructuring of synods in the northeast, New England congregations would become a separate synodical entity while New York itself would be divided into the Metropolitan New York and upper New York Synods. Smaller synods now dealt with the integration of former Scandinavian and German churches into new combinations of confessional and liturgical interests.

Finally, in 1988, with the formation of the Evangelical Lutheran Church in America (ELCA) from the LCA, the ALC (American Lutheran Church), and the AELC (Association of Evangelical Lutheran Churches), all of these geographically based synods would incorporate former German and Norwegian elements of the ALC and of the AELC (former Lutheran Church, Missouri Synod) into even more pluralistic confessional and liturgical entities. Neighboring congregations of great diversity, once organized along parallel lines, would now begin to converge, encountering each other in more complex communities of faith which would be confessed within the context of a growing and changing theological tradition.

Each of the present ELCA synods in the Northeast traces its official history and origins to the founding synod—the New York Ministerium. And yet each, along with its many congregations, contains a heritage which can only increase the complex nature of that Ministerium's ongoing legacy, leading (one can hope) to an "ampler confession." And each synod has doubtless had to ask, as did the new New York Synod and the reorganized New York Ministerium in 1867, what is new or old in this changing institution. In a present day marked by pluralistic diversity, a struggle for inclusiveness, converging (but also sometimes conflicting) confessional traditions but also a need for a unity which does no violence to heritage, the complicated history of the New York Ministerium, including its experience of dealing with such problems and possibilities, leaves a rich historical legacy which can inform us about faithful living in a changing world in which the faithful can still confess Jesus Christ to be Lord of the future.

NOTES

1 Fred W. Meuser, "Facing the Twentieth Century, 1900-1930," in *The Lutherans in North America*, Clifford E. Nelson, ed. (Philadelphia: Fortress Press, 1976), 375-6; Abdel Ross Wentz, *A Basic History of Lutheranism in America* (Philadelphia: Fortress Press, 1955), 282-3.

2 For documents relating to the Lutheran Society of New York see The Lutheran Society, Inc. Minutes, Publications, Correspondence, and Documents (Archives of Cooperative Lutheranism: RG 22: Lutheran Society of New York, Archives of the Evangelical Lutheran Church in America, Chicago, Illinois). Frederick H. Knubel, "Read at Memorial Service at Concordia, December 17, 1934," MNYS, SP 1, George U. Wenner. The Luther League of America was organized in New York, and the first state Luther League was the New York organization formed in 1893. For documents relating to the Luther League see Luther League of New York, Luther League of New York and successor bodies, 1893- , Minutes, programs, etc. (Metropolitan New York Synod Archives: RG 14, SP 5, Wagner College, Staten Island, New York). Lutheran Brotherhood of America (Archives of Cooperative Lutheranism: RG 30: Lutheran Church Men of America 1917-1966, Minutes and Printed Reports, Publications, Archives of the Evangelical Lutheran Church in America, Chicago, Illinois).

3 *The Second General Conference of Lutherans in America Held in Philadelphia, April 1-3, 1902* (Newberry, S. C.: Lutheran Publication Board, 1904), 30-31.

4 General Council, *Documentary History* (Philadelphia, 1912), 405-408.

5 General Synod, *Minutes* (1909), 54, 315, 60-61.

6 Ibid. (1911), 102.

7 Ibid. (1913), 126-7, 387ff.

8 John H. P. Reumann, "The Mt. Airy Biblical Tradition and Its Significance for the Future of the Seminary and the Church," *Philadelphia Vision—Mt. Airy Tradition: Essays for the 125th Anniversary of The Lutheran Theological Seminary at Philadelphia* (Philadelphia: Lutheran Theological Seminary at Philadelphia, 1991), 22.

9 Robert H. Fischer, "The Healing of the Schism Between the General Synod and the General Council: Sources for a Reevaluation," *Gettysburg Seminary Bulletin* 48.4 (Fall, 1968): 38. On Schmauk see Schmauk, T. E. and C. Theodore Benze, *The Confessional Principle and the Confessions of the Lutheran Church*, 1911. James W. Richards, *The Confessional History of the Lutheran Church* (Philadelphia: Lutheran Publication Society, 1909), 617, 228, 232.

10 Meuser, "Facing the Twentieth Century," 374.

11 On the nature of this "little tradition," as compared with the great tradition of confessional church bodies, see James P. Wind, *Places of Worship. Exploring Their History*, *The Nearby History Series*, David E. Kyvig, ed. (Nashville, Tennessee: American Association for State and Local History, 1990) 4: 18ff.

12 Michael B. Aune, "The Corporate and Confession Character of Worship: The Common Service Debate," *Word and World* VIII. Winter, No. 1

(1988): 32-41.

13 "Historical Report of the Merger," United Lutheran Church, *Minutes* (1918), 39.

14 See Richard C. Wolf, ed., *Documents of Lutheran Unity in America* (Philadelphia: Fortress Press, 1966), 267-271. For a detailed account of the celebration see Otto H. Pannkoke, *A Great Church Finds Itself* (Quitman, Ga. 1966), pp. 44-62.

15 "Historical Report of the Merger," United Lutheran Church, *Minutes* (1918), 37-42. General Synod, *Minutes* (1917), 81.

16 "Historical Report of the Merger," 40. Richard C. Wolf, ed., *Documents of Lutheran Unity in America* (Philadelphia: Fortress Press, 1966), 116-17.

17 United Lutheran Church, *Minutes* (1918), 63.

18 General Synod, *Minutes* (1917), 82. General Council, *Minutes* (1917), 24. General Council, *Documentary History*, 180. For a survey of the literature related to rapprochement see Fischer, "The Healing of the Schism," 32-41.

19 G. Everett Arden, *Augustana Heritage: A History of the Augustana Lutheran Church* (Rock Island, Ill.: Augustana Press, 1963), 279-80.

20 "Historical Report of the Merger," 41.

21 Henry Eyster Jacobs, "The Race Set Before Us," ULCA, *Minutes* (1918), 11-19.

22 Faith R. Burgess, "The Public Face of Mt. Airy," *Philadelphia Vision—Mt. Airy Tradition: Essays for the 125th Anniversary of the Lutheran Theological Seminary at Philadelphia* (Philadelphia: Lutheran Theological Seminary at Philadelphia, 1991), 44.

23 Jacobs, "The Race Set Before Us," 11-19.

24 Ibid.

25 *Minutes* (1918), 36; (1920), 27, 54-55, 101, 108. Fred W. Meuser, "Facing the Twentieth Century. 1900-1930," *The Lutherans in North America*, Clifford E. Nelson, ed. (Philadelphia: Fortress Press, 1976), 376.

26 ULCA, *Minutes* (1918), 44-54; (1918), 53-4. Frederick K. Wentz, *Lutherans in Concert. The Story of the National Lutheran Council 1918-1966* (Minneapolis: Augsburg Publishing House, 1968), 14-17.

27 See Ben Primer, *Protestants and American Business Methods, Studies in American History and Culture, No. 7* (UMI Research Press, 1979), esp. 1-3, 35, 38, 46. ULCA, *Minutes* (1920), 30-32.

28 Primer, *Protestants and American Business Methods*, 95-96. General Synod, *Proceedings* (1913), 81, 23 ff; (1915), 19, 156, 255; (1917), 88-89. On the Lutheran Brotherhood also see National Lutheran Council, *The Lutheran World Almanac and Annual Encyclopedia for 1921* (New York: The Lutheran Bureau, 1920), 457. Wentz, *Lutherans in Concert*, 86.

29 Ibid., 121, 153, 170, 173, 183, 191, 204, 218-19, 232, 248, 82-4, 50-1, 106-7. How developed was the national ULCA in these directions by such forces? Extensive departmentalization and substantial executive salaries were hallmarks of advanced bureaucratization in the national Protestant denomination. For example, The Domestic and Foreign Missionary Society (D & FMS) of the Protestant Episcopal Church (a highly bureaucratized structure) supported 300 missionaries with a staff of seventy-eight (78), organized into eleven departments by 1920. Episcopal executive salaries averaged $4,500 in 1910, when the average pastor in the United States earned $800. The combination of the ULCA's five (5) mission boards with

nine (9) departments, supported approximately 390 missionaries with a staff of twenty-three (23) including fifteen (15) executives. Lutheran executive salaries for the two largest boards averaged $3,000. Executive salaries for the smaller boards ran from $1,500 to $2,500. The new ULCA thus had a well developed bureaucratic structure but with fewer staff and slightly lower salaries than the D & FMS. ULCA, *Minutes* (1920), 68, 130.

30 Primer, *Protestants and American Business Methods*, 185-191.

31 ULCA, *Minutes* (1920), 66-68.

32 Ibid., 67-8. Wentz, *Basic History*, 288-89.

33 ULCA *Minutes* (1920), 68.

34 Wentz, *Basic History*, 289-90.

35 Ministerium, *Extract English Minutes* (1919), 19. Synod of New York and New England, *Minutes* (1917), 19-20.

36 Ibid.

37 New York and New England, *Minutes* (1918), 70. New York Ministerium, *Minutes* (1919), 18-19, 38.

38 New York Synod, *Minutes* (1919), 57. New York and New England Synod, *Minutes* (1919), 53-4.

39 New York Synod, *Minutes* (1920), 58-9; (1919), 58. Synod of New York and New England, *Minutes* (1920), 40-42. New York Ministerium, *Minutes* (1920), 33.

40 Synod of New York and New England, *Minutes* (1913), 48.

41 Ibid. (1922), 64.

42 Synod of New York and New England, *Minutes* (1923), 67, 80-81. Meuser, "Facing the Twentieth Century," 403, 432.

43 Synod of New York and New England, *Minutes* (1924), 46; (1925), 41, 70. New York Ministerium, *Minutes* (1925), 23-4.

44 Ibid. (1926), 3-7.

45 New York Ministerium, *Minutes* (1926), 8.

46 Ibid. (1926), 9.

47 Ibid.

48 United Lutheran Church in America, *Minutes* (1918), 10-12.

49 Richard W. Solberg, *Lutheran Higher Education in North America* (Minneapolis: Augsburg Press, 1985), 297. New York Ministerium, *Minutes* (1926), 38-9.

50 Ibid., 71, 70.

51 "Constitution of the United Lutheran Synod of New York," United Lutheran Synod of New York, *Minutes* (1929), 54. Synod of New York and New England, *Minutes* (1928), 43; New York Ministerium, *Minutes* (1902), 33.

52 New York Ministerium, *Extract English Minutes* (1929), 17-19.

53 Synod of New York, *Minutes* (1929), 19-32.

54 Trexler's autobiographical account of the Synod bears the romantic title *Crusaders of the Twentieth Century* (New York), 1927. Synod of New York and New England, *Minutes* (1929), 8.

55 See Martin E. Marty, *The Noise of Conflict, 1919-1941, Modern American Religion* (Chicago: The University of Chicago Press, 1991) 2: 25, 48, 36.

56 ULSNY, *Minutes* (1930), 80-89, 93.

57 Ibid., 54-77.

58 New York Ministerium, *Minutes* (1929), 78-9; ULSNY, *Minutes* (1929),

106; (1930), 120-122: (1931), 194-6. On the spirituality of women's mission societies see Betty A. DeBerg, *The Spirituality of Lutheran Women's Missionary Societies, 1880-1930, Lutheran Mission in North America*, Marvin Huggins, ed. (Chicago, Illinois: Lutheran Historical Conference, 1992) 15: 1994.

59 ULSNY, *Minutes* (1929), 106; (1930), 122; (1931), 196-97; (1932) 138; (1933), 72-3.

60 John Nicum, *Geschichte des Evangelisch-Lutherischen Ministeriums von Staate New York und angrenzenden Staaten und Landern* (Reading: 1888), 389. James Kenneth Echols, "Charles Michael Jacobs: Servant of the Church," *Philadelphia Vision —Mt. Airy Tradition: Essays for the 125th Anniversary of the Lutheran Theological Seminary at Philadelphia* (Philadelphia: Lutheran Theological Seminary at Philadelphia, 1991) 37.

61 Passavant quoted in August Sueflow and E. Clifford Nelson, "Following the Frontier," *The Lutherans in North America*, E. Clifford Nelson, ed. (Philadelphia: Fortress Press, 1975). The original is to be found in George H. Gerberding, *Life and Letters of W. A. Passavant, D. D.* (Greenville, PA: Young Lutheran Co., 1906), 281, 283-4. George U. Wenner, *The Lutherans of New York* (New York: The Petersfield Press, 1918), 150-53.

62 Ibid., 130. Materials related to The Lutheran Society of New York are to be found in Record Group 22 and Koinonia materials in Record Group 32 of the Archives of Cooperative Lutheranism deposited in the Archives of the Evangelical Lutheran in America, Chicago, Illinois. See Helen M. Knubel, ed., *An Introductory Guide to Lutheran Archives and Collections* (New York City: Archives of Cooperative Lutheranism. Lutheran Council in the USA, 1981), pp. 57-8, 77.

63 Ibid. (1929), 5, 94.

64 Ibid. (1930), 37.

65 Harry J. Kreider, "Negro Lutheran Work in New York," *LCQ* 20 (1947): 270-273. John A. Kaufmann, ed., *Biographical Record of the Lutheran Theological Seminary at Philadelphia 1864-1962* (Philadelphia: Lutheran Theological Seminary, 1964), 131. Jeff G. Johnson, *Black Christians. The Untold Lutheran Story* (St. Louis: Concordia Publishing House, 1991), 36-52.

66 ULSNY, *Minutes* (1930), 38-9.

67 See Winthrop S. Hudson, *The Great Tradition of the American Churches* (New York: Harper & Brothers, 1953), 195ff.

68 Andre Siegfried, *America Comes of Age. A French Analysis* (New York: Harcourt, Brace and Company, 1927), 33, 47. On the use of Siegfried for the writing of American religious history from a Lutheran perspective see Mark A. Noll, "The Public Church in the Years of Conflict," *Christian Century* 108.17 (1991): 552-559.

69 H. Richard Niebuhr, *The Social Sources of Denominationalism* (New York: The World Publishing Company, 1957), 25.

70 Ibid., 12, 196-97, 223, 236, 240, 259.

71 C. E. Jacobs, Review of H. Richard Niebuhr's *The Social Sources of Denominationalism*, *LCQ* 4 (1931): 100.

72 Ibid., 101.

73 For the origins and development of the Lutheran Church in America, see W. Kent Gilbert, *Commitment to Unity, A History of the Lutheran Church in*

America (Philadelphia: Fortress Press, 1988)

74 Abdel Ross Wentz, "Recent Discussions of Christian Unity," *LCQ* 4 (1931): 83.

75 Abdel Ross Wentz, "Permanent Deposits of Sectionalism in American Christianity," *LCQ* 9 (1936): 36.

76 Ibid., 37.

77 Augustus Steimle, "Our Story: Sesquicentennial Address, United Lutheran Synod of New York, Albany, June 9, 1936," *LCQ* 10 (1937):183.

78 Marvin Perry, et. al. , *Western Civilization. Ideas, Politics and Society*, 3d ed. (Dallas, Texas: Houghton Mifflin Company, 1989), 757.

79 See Jerome Paul Soneson, *Pragmatism and Pluralism. John Dewey's Significance for Theology, Harvard Dissertations in Religion,* Bernadette J. & Francis Schussler Fiorenza Brooten, ed. (Minneapolis: Fortress Press, 1993) 30: esp. 87-91, and Chapter 6.

SELECTED BIBLIOGRAPHY

The following bibliography, which contains all works cited and consulted, includes a selected list of archival materials for those readers wishing to explore the topic of Lutheranism in the northeast.

ARCHIVAL DEPOSITS

General

Knubel, Helen M., ed. *An Introductory Guide to Lutheran Archives and Collections*. New York: Archives of Cooperative Lutheranism. Lutheran Council in the USA, 1981.

ARCHIVES OF THE METROPOLITAN NEW YORK SYNOD (MNYS)

Hormann Library, Wagner College Staten Island, New York Record Groups

Franckean Synod. *Journal*. 1837-1908. MNYS, RG 4.

________. *Proceedings of a Convention of Ministers and Delegates from Evangelical Lutheran Churches, in the State of New-York*. Albany, 1837. MNYS, RG 4.

Hartwick Synod. *Minutes*. 1830-1908. MNYS, RG 3.

New Jersey Synod. *Minutes*. 1860-1872. MNYS, RG 5.

________. *Minutes of the Convention . . . which resulted in the formation of the Evangelical Lutheran Synod of N. Jersey*. Easton, Pa., 1861. MNYS, RG 5.

New York and New England Synod. *Minutes*. 1902-1929. MNYS, RG 9.

New York and New Jersey Synod. *Minutes*. 1872-1908. MNYS, RG 8.

New York Ministerium. *Entwurf der Constitution und Nebengesetze des Evangelisch=Lutherischen Ministeriums des Staates New York- und angrezender Staaten und La[nder]*. New York: Lutherischen Verlags=Vereins, 1878. MNYS, RG 2.

________. *Minutes*. Typescript transcription, Metropolitan New York Archives, 1786-1818. MNYS, RG 2.

________. *Minutes*. 1820-1929. MNYS, RG 2.

________. *Minutes of the Evangelical Lutheran Ministerium of the State of New York and Adjacent States and Countries for the Years 1807 to 1818*

Inclusive. MNYS, RG 2.

________. Transcript of manuscript protocol, 1786-1806 (German). 1786-1806. MNYS, RG 2.

New York Synod. *Historical Statement of the Evangelical Lutheran Synod of New York*. New York, 1867. MNYS, RG 7.

________. *Minutes*. MNYS, RG 7.

St. Matthew Lutheran Church. Transcript & Translation of manuscript "Protocol." 1868-1886. MNYS. Uncatalogued.

Steimle (German New York Synod). *Minutes*. 1866-1872. MNYS, RG 6.

Synod of New York. *Minutes*. 1908-1929. MNYS, RG 10.

United Lutheran Synod of New York and New England. *Minutes*. 1929-1936. MNYS, RG 12.

Van Alstine, Nicholas. *Historical Review of the Franckean Evangelical Lutheran Synod of New York*. Philadelphia: Lutheran Publication Society, 1893. MNYS, RG 4.

Special Collections (Record Group 14)

Barnett, J. N. *History of the Gilead Evangelical Lutheran Church, Centre Brunswick, Rensselaer Co., NY. and the Vicinity*. Fort Wayne, Ind.: Gazette Co., 1881. MNYS, SP 2

Belfour, Edmund. *Historical Sketch of St. Paul's Evangelical Lutheran Church, in Schoharie, New York*. Pittsburgh: Foster, Dick & Co., 1896. MNYS, SP 2

Bloomhardt, Paul F., and Frederick Henrich. *A Short Biography of Frederick August Kaehler, DD., LL.D. And a historical sketch of the English Evangelical Lutheran Church of the Holy Trinity*. Buffalo, N. Y.: Otto Ulbrich Co., 1937. MNYS, SP 2.

Bougher, Aubrey N. "A Diamond Year History of Christ Lutheran Church, Rosedale." *The Evangelical Lutheran Church of Christ 75th Anniversary Journal & History, 1913-1988*. Privately printed, 1988. MNYS, SP 2.

Brueckner, H. *Seventy-Fifth Anniversary of St. Matthew's Evangelical Lutheran Church, Eighth and Hudson Sts., Hoboken, NJ*. Privately printed, 1933. MNYS, SP 2.

Clarkson, David. *History of the Church of Zion and St. Timothy of New York 1797-1894*. New York: G. P. Putnam's Sons, 1894. MNYS, SP 2.

Documentary History Committee. "Obituary Entitled Wenner, George Unangst." *The Lutheran* (November 17 & 22, 1934). MNYS, SP 1, George U. Wenner.

Ekhardt, Florence, and Alfreda Kastner Tesman. *History of the Lutheran Church, Newburgh, New York, 1709-1987*. Privately printed, 1987. MN YS, SP 2.

Grottke, Theodore L., and Erna H. Grottke. *A History of Christ Evangelical Lutheran Church, Airmont, Suffern, New York*. Dexter, Mich.: Thomson-Shore, Inc., 1990. MNYS, SP 2.

Heins, Henry H. *Swan of Albany. A History of the Oldest Congregation of the Lutheran Church in America*. Rensselaer, N. Y.: Hamilton Printing Company, 1976. MNYS, SP 2.

Hoffmann, Hugo W. *The History of St. Paul's Evangelical Lutheran Church, Brooklyn, NY., from 1853-1903*. Mt. Vernon, N. Y.: Wartburg Printing House, 1903. MNYS, SP 2.

Kieffer, G. L. "The Fulfillment of the Faith the Fathers Had in George U. Wenner." A compilation of references to George U. Wenner in the synodical proceedings of the United Synod of New York and New England and predecessor bodies. George U. Wenner. MNYS, SP 1.

_______. "George Unangst Wenner." *The Lutheran* (November 10, 1934). George U. Wenner. MNYS, SP 1.

[Knubel, Frederick H.]. Memorial to Dr. George Unangst Wenner. "Read at memorial service at Concordia, December 17, 1934." George U. Wenner. MNYS, SP 1.

Kosbab, Charles W. *The Rochester Lutheran Conference of the United Lutheran Synod of New York and New England and the United Lutheran Church in Americas 1809-1962*. Rochester, NY: Typescript by Charles W. Kosbab, 1962. MNYS, SP 2.

Kraeling, E. C. J. *Unser Zion. Dis Geschichte der Zions-Gemeinde in Wort und Bild. Eine Jubilaums-Gabe der Geminde dargereicht*. Mt. Vernon: Wartburg-Waisenhauses, 1905. MNYS, SP 2.

Krotel, G. F. *A Discourse Delivered on the Tenth Anniversary of the Evangelical Lutheran Church of the Holy Trinity, of New York City*. Privately printed, 1878. MNYS, SP 1, G. F. Krotel.

Luther League of New York. *Luther League of New York and successor bodies, 1893- , Minutes, programs, etc*. Metropolitan New York Synod Archives: 1893-. MNYS, SP 5.

Memorial of the Rev. Henry N. Pohlman, DD. Albany: J. Munsell, 1875. MNYS, SP 1.

N. L. C. Bulletin. "Dr. G. U. Wenner Dead." reprinted in *The Lutheran* (November 10, 1934). MNYS, SP 1, George U. Wenner.

Olsen, Arthur C. *Upon This Rock. St. Peters Evangelical Lutheran Church of Greenport, Long Island, NY*. Greenport, N. Y.: 1959. MNYS, SP 2.

Runyon, I. Searles. *The Record of the First Twenty-five Years 1906-1931. The Inner Mission Society of the Evangelical Lutheran Church in New York City*. Privately printed, 1931. MNYS, SP 2.

Seventy-fifth Anniversary 1865-1940. The Church of Gustavus Adolphus, New York City, NY. New York: 1940. MNYS, SP 2.

Thomforde, Christopher. *St. Paul's Lutheran Church 1809-1984, Church and Clara Barton Streets, Dansville, NY*. Privately printed, 1984. MNYS, SP 2.

Uehling, Carl T. *St. John's Evangelical Lutheran Church, Newark, New Jersey, Founded October 10, 1833. The One Hundred and Twenty-fifth Anniversary*. Privately printed, 1958. MNYS, SP 2.

Wenner, George Unangst. *Sixty Years in One Pulpit*. New York: The Petersfield Press, 1928. Unpaginated. MNYS, SP 1, George U. Wenner.

_______. Undated letter, but ca. 1923. MNYS, SP 1, George U. Wenner.

Zum Goldenen Jubilaum der evang. luth. Dreieinigkeits-Gemeinde zu Middle Village, L.I. Brooklyn: Albertype Co., 1906. MNYS, SP 2.

ARCHIVES OF COOPERATIVE LUTHERANISM, CHICAGO (ARCL)

Record Groups

Koinonia, 1896-1973. Minutes and Constitutions, Correspondence, and Documents, ARCL, RG 32.

Lutheran Church Men of America 1917-1966, Minutes and Printed Reports, Publications, ARCL, RG 30.

The Lutheran Society, Inc. Minutes, Publications, Correspondence, and Documents. ARCL, RG 22.

PRIMARY SOURCES

BOOKS

Arndt, Johann. *True Christianity. The Classics of Western Spirituality*. ed. Peter Erb. New York: Paulist Press, 1979.

The Augsburg Confession with Explanatory Notes and Observations. Troy, NY: Hartwick Synod, 1837.

Buffalo Synod. *Synodical Letter*. 1848.

Dern, John P. Translated by Simon Hart and Sibrandina Geertruid Hart-Runeman. *The Albany Protocol. Wilhelm Christoph Berkenmeyer's Chronicle of Lutheran Affairs in New York Colony, 1731-1750*. Ann Arbor, Michigan, 1971.

Dillenberger, John, ed. *Martin Luther. Selections from his writings*. New York: Doubleday Anchor, 1961.

Erb, Peter C., ed. *Pietists. Selected Writings*. New York: Paulist Press, 1983.

The First General Conference of Lutherans in America Held in Philadelphia, December 27-29, 1898. Philadelphia, 1899.

General Council. *Documentary History of the Evangelical Lutheran Ministerium of Pennsylvania and Adjacent States*. Philadelphia: General Council Board of Publication, 1898.

General Council. *Documentary History of the General Council of the Evangelical Lutheran Church in North America*. ed. S. E. Ochensford. Philadelphia: General Council Publication House, 1912.

General Council. *Minutes*. (1867-1918).

General Synod. *Minutes*. (1830-1918).

Graubau, Johann A. *Lebenslauf des ehrwu(")rdigen J. A. Grabau*. Buffalo: Reinecke & Zecsch, 1879.

Hazelius, Ernest Lewis. *The Confession of Augsburgh. . . . To Which Are Added a Life of D. Martin Luther, And Some Extracts from His Works*. New York: James Oram, 1813.

Jacobs, H. E., ed. *First Free Lutheran Diet in America. Philadelphia, December 27-28, 1877*. Philadelphia: J. Frederick Smith, 1878.

________. *Second Free Lutheran Diet in America. Philadelphia, November 5-7, 1878*. Philadelphia: Lutheran Publication Society, 1879.

Kerr, Hugh T., ed. *Readings in Christian Thought*. Nashville: Abingdon, 1966.

Krauth, Charles Porterfield. *The Conservative Reformation and its Theology: As Represented in the Augsburg Confession, and in the History and Literature of the Evangelical Lutheran Church*. New York: J. B. Lippincott & Co., 1871.

Kreider, Harry Julius. *The Lutheran Church in New York. 1649-1772. Records in the Lutheran Church Archives at Amsterdam, Holland*. New York: The New York Public Library, 1946.

________. *Protocol of the Lutheran Church in New York City, 1702-1750*. New York, 1958.

The Lutheran Church in New York. 1649-1722. Records in the Lutheran Church Archives at Amsterdam, Holland. New York: The New York Public Library, 1946.

Lutheran Church in New York and New Jersey, 1722-1760. Lutheran Records in the Ministerial Archives of the Staatsarchiv, Hamburg, Germany. New York, 1962.

Meyer, Carl S., ed. *Moving Frontiers: Readings in the History of the Lutheran Church —Missouri Synod.* St. Louis: Concordia Publishing House, 1964.

Missouri Synod. *Reports*. St. Louis, 1890, 1900, 1910, 1920.

Nevin, John. *The Anxious Bench*. Chambersburg, 1843.

________. *Geschichte des Evangelisch-Lutherischen Ministeriums von Staate New York und angrenzenden Staaten und Landern*. Reading, 1888.

Pauck, Wilhelm, ed. *Martin, Luther: Lectures on Romans*. Philadelphia: Westminster Press, 1961.

________. *Melanchthon and Bucer*. Philadelphia: Westminster Press, 1969.

Pelikan, Jaroslav, and Helmut T. Lehman, ed. *Luther's Works. American Edition*. Philadelphia and St. Louis: Fortress Press and Concordia Publishing House, 1955-.

Schmauk, T. E. and C. Theodore Benze. *The Confessional Principle and the Confessions of the Lutheran Church*. Philadelphia: General Council Publication Board, 1911.

Schmucker, Samuel Simon. *Definite Platform, Doctrinal and Disciplinarian, for Evangelical Lutheran District Synods: Constructed in Accordance with the Principles of the General Synod*. Philadelphia: Miller & Burlock, 1855.

The Second General Conference of Lutherans in America Held in Philadelphia, April 1-3, 1902. Newberry, SC.: Lutheran Publication Board, 1904.

Spener, Philipp Jakob. *Pia Desideria*. ed. Theodore G. Tappert. Philadelphia: Fortress Press, 1964.

Strobel, P.A. *Memorial Volume to Commemorate the Semi-Centennial Anniversary of the Hartwick Lutheran Synod, of the State of New York*. Philadelphia: Lutheran Publication Society, 1881.

Tappert, Theodore G., ed. *The Book of Concord*. Philadelphia: Muhlenberg Press, 1959.

________. *Lutheran Confessional Theology in America. 1840-1880*. New York: Oxford University Press, 1972.

Tappert, Theodore G. and John W. Doberstein, eds. *The Journals of Henry Melchior Muhlenberg*. Philadelphia: Muhlenberg Press, 1942.

Tauler, Johannes. *Johannes Tauler. Sermons. The Classics of Western Spirituality*. New York: Paulist Press, 1985.

Valentine, Milton. *Christian Theology*. 2 vols. Philadelphia: Lutheran Publication Society, 1906.

Van Engen, John, ed. *Devotio Moderna. Basic Writings*. New York City: Paulist Press, 1988.

Wolf, Richard C., ed. *Documents of Lutheran Unity in America*. Philadelphia: Fortress Press, 1966.

ARTICLES

Kretzmann, Karl. "The Constitution of the First Lutheran Synod in America." *Concordia Historical Institute Quarterly* IX (1936): 17-34

[Philadelphia Seminary Faculty]. "Concerning the Dogma of Predestination." *Lutheran Church Review* 3 (1884): 223-236.

Schaff, Philip. "Address to Evangelischer Verein fur innere Mission." *Concordia Historical Institute Quarterly. Nietzsche and Schaff on American Lutheranism*. ed. August R. Suelflow. January 1951. 23: 149-57

Seebach, Margaret R. A. M. "Should Women Preach." *Lutheran Quarterly* 33 (1903): 579-583.

MICROFILM CORPUS OF AMERICAN LUTHERANISM (MCAL)

BOOKS

Berkenmeyer, Wilhelm Christoph. . . .*Getrouwe Herder-en Wachter Stem aan de hoog- en neder- duitsche Lutheranen in dese gewesten, eenstemmig te Zyn-vertoont met twee Brieven en andere Redenen Lutherscher Theologanten aangaande 't van Dierensche Beroep, en de Henkelsche Bevesstiging*. New York: J. Peter Zenger, 1728. MCAL 21:1.

Bjorck, Erik Tobias. *A little olive leaf put in the mouth of that (so called) Noah's dove, and sent home again to let her master know that the waters are abated from off the face of the ground, and that for the sake of Jesus Christ, whose servant to the end of my life I shall endeavor to be*. New York: William Bradford, 1704. MCAL 1:1:

Braun, Anton Theodor. *Dr. Martin Luther's Shorter Catechism, tr. from the German*. Troy: R. Schermerhorn, 1811. MCAL 4:8.

Ernest, J., ed. *Hymns of Praise*. Loonenburg (Athens), 1792. MCAL 1:6.

Falckner, Justus. *Grondlycke Onderricht van seke re voorname Hoofd-stucken, den waren, loutern, saligmakendon, Christlycken Leere. . . .* New York: William Bradford, 1702. MCAL 20:11:128.

Hazelius, Ernest Louis. *Exercises at the installation of the Rev. J. P. Goertner, in St. Paul's Church, Johnstown, January 3, 1827*. Johnstown: Montgomery Republican, 1827. MCAL 7:3.

________. *Materials for Catechization on passages of the scripture, containing the doctrines of Christian faith and morality. For the instruction of youth, especially in the Ev. Lutheran Church*. Cooperstown: H. & E. Phinney, 1823. MCAL 6:6.

Kunze, Johann Christoph. *Hymn and Prayer Book for such Lutheran churches as use the English language*. New York: Hurtin & Commardinger, 1795. MCAL 1:9.

________. *King Solomon's great sacrifice at the dedication of his temple. A sermon preached on the 19th Trinity Sunday, Oct. 11, 1801, at the dedication of the new erected English Lutheran Church called Zion, in the city of New York*. New York: Nichols, 1801. MCAL 1:13.

________. *The rudiments of the shorter catechism of Dr. Martin Luther*. Philadelphia: Steiner, 1785. MCAL 1:7.

Kurtz, Benjamin, and J. G. Morris, ed. *Lutheran Observer*. Baltimore: published independently, 1834-1851. MCAL 8-14.

Lintner, George Ames, ed. *The Lutheran Magazine, published by the Western Conference of Lutheran ministers in the state of New York*. Schoharie: L. Cuthbert, 1827-1831. MCAL 3:1:

Lintner, George Ames, and Ernest Hazelius. *Exercises at the installation of the*

Rev. J. P. Goertner. Johnstown, 1827. MCAL 7:3: 24.

Naskov, P. *The Articles of Faith. . . . in forty sermons. . . .* New York, 1754. MCAL 1:2.

New York Ministerium. *A collection of hymns and a liturgy for the use of the Ev. Lutheran Churches, to which are added prayers for families and individuals*. Germantown: Billmeyer, 1824. MCAL 6:7.

________. *A liturgy for the use of the Evangelical Lutheran Church*. Philadelphia: Billmeyer, 1814. MCAL 19: 2.

Quitman, Frederick Henry. *Evangelical Catechism, or a short exposition of the principal doctrines and precepts of the Christian religion. For the use of the churches belonging to the Ev. Lutheran Synod of New York. To which are added: I. A scriptural advice to the young. II. Sir M. Hale's Character of a true Christian. III. An address to those who wish to be confirmed. IV. A sketch of the history of religion. V. A collection of prayers for parents and children*. Hudson: Norman, 1814. MCAL 5:2: 192.

________. *Three Sermons: the first preached before the Ev. Lutheran Synod, convened in Christ's church, in . . . Claverack, on ... the 7th of September, 1817; and the 2nd and 3rd on the Reformation of Martin Luther*. Hudson: Norman, 1817. MCAL 5:6: 42.

________. *A treatise on magic, or on the intercourse between spirits and men; with annotations*. Albany: Balance Press, 1810. MCAL 4:7: 76.

Schaeffer, Frederick Christian. *An address pronounced at the laying of the corner stone of St. Matthew's church, New York, October 22, 1821; with the ceremonial on the occasion*. New York: E. Conrad, 1821. MCAL 6:3.

Smith, Charles A., ed. *Lutheran Pulpit and Monthly Religious Magazine*. Albany: J. Munsell, 1837-1838. MCAL 3:2.

Strebeck, George. "Dr. Martin Luther's catechism." *Hymn and Prayer Book*. New York: Hurtin & Commardinger, 1795. MCAL 1:9.

________. *A collection of (299) Evangelical hymns, from different authors and collections, for the English Lutheran Church in New York*. New York: Tiebout, 1797. MCAL 1:10.

________. *A sermon preached (by courtesy) in the German Reformed Church at New York*. New York: Tiebout & O'Brien, 1796. MCAL 1:12.

________. *The wrath to come, discussed in three sermons . . . the certainty and endless duration of future punishment, maintained against the doctrine of the Universalists*. New York: Nichols, 1803. MCAL 4:2.

Weygand, John Albert (tr.). *The whole system of the XXVIII Articles of the evangelical unvaried confession presented at Augsbourgh, to the Emperor Charles V by the Protestant princes and states . . . to be compared with the translations of the Moravians, printed at London in the year 1749, wherein most the half hath been left out*. New York: Parker & Weyman, 1755. MCAL 1:3.

Williston, Ralph, ed. *A choice selection of evangelical hymns from various authors, for the use of the English Evangelical Lutheran Church in New York*. New York: Totten, 1806. MCAL 4:5.

SECONDARY SOURCES
BOOKS

Abell, Aaron Ignatius. *The Urban Impact on American Protestantism, 1865-1900*. Cambridge: Harvard University Press, 1943.

Ahlstrom, Sydney E. *A Religious History of the American People*. 2 vols. Garden City: Image Books, 1975.

Aland, Kurt. *A History of Christianity. From the Reformation to the Present. A History of Christianity*, Vol. 2. Philadelphia: Fortress Press, 1986.

Althaus, Paul. *The Theology of Martin Luther*. Philadelphia: Fortress Press, 1966.

Anderson, Hugh George. *Lutheranism in the Southeastern States. 1860-1886. A Social History*. The Hague: Mouton, 1969.

Arden, G. Everett. *Augustana Heritage: A History of the Augustana Lutheran Church*. Rock Island, Ill.: Augustana Press, 1963.

Atlantic District, Lutheran Church-Missouri Synod. *Marching with Christ*. 1956.

________. *A Diamond Jubilee History 1906-1981. Atlantic District-Lutheran Church Missouri Synod*. New York City: 1981.

Bachmann, E. Theodore. *They Called Him Father*. Philadelphia: Muhlenberg Press, 1942.

Balmer, Randall. *A Perfect Babel of Confusion. Dutch Religion and English Culture in the Middle Colonies. Religion in American Series*. ed. Harry S. Stout. New York: Oxford University Press, 1989.

Bebout, John E. and Ronald J. Grele. *Where Cities Meet. The Urbanization of New Jersey. The New Jersey Historical Series*. ed. Richard M. and Wheaton J. Lane Huber. New York: D. Van Nostrand Company, Inc., 1964.

Beck, Walter H. *Lutheran Elementary Schools in the United States*. St. Louis: Concordia Publishing House, 1965.

Bittinger, Lucy Forney. *The Germans in Colonial Times*. New York: Russell & Russell, 1968.

Bonomi, Patricia U. *Under the Cope of Heaven. Religion, Society, and Politics in Colonial America*. New York: Oxford University Press, 1986.

Brown, Dale. *Understanding Pietism*. Grand Rapids: William E. Eerdmans Publishing Company, 1978.

Buck, Charles. *A Theological Dictionary, New American (corrected) Edition revised by the Rev. George Bush*. Philadelphia: Thomas Cowperthwait, 1838.

Buehring, Paul H. *The Spirit of the American Lutheran Church*. Columbus, Ohio: Lutheran Book Concern, 1940.

Burr, Nelson R. *A Critical Bibliography of Religion in America. Religion in American Life*. ed. James War and A. Leland Jamison Smith. Princeton: Princeton University Press, 1961.

Butler, Jon. *Awash in a Sea of Faith. Christianizing the American People*. Cambridge: Harvard University Press, 1990.

Cassedy, James H. *Demography in Early America. Beginnings of the Statistical Mind, 1600-1800*. Cambridge: Harvard University Press, 1969.

Christiano, Kevin J. *Religious Diversity and Social Change*. New York: Cambridge University Press, 1987.

Clark, Delberr W. *The World of Justus Falckner*. Philadelphia: Muhlenberg Press, 1946.

Clasen, Claus-Peter. *The Palatinate in European History, 1559-1660*. Oxford: Basil Blackwell, 1963.

Clatterbaugh, Kenneth. *Contemporary Perspectives on Masculinity. Men, Women and Politics in Modern Society*. San Francisco: Westview Press, 1990.

Cobb, Sanford H. *The Story of the Palatines: An Episode in Colonial History*. New York: B. Putnam's Sons, 1897.

Commager, Henry Steele. *The American Mind. An Interpretation of American Thought and Character Since the 1880's*. New Haven: Yale University Press, 1950.

Conlin, Joseph R. *The American Past. Part Two. A Survey of American History Since 1865*. New York: Harcourt Brace Jovanovich, 1987.

Conser, Walter H. Jr. *Church and Confession: Conservative Theologians in Germany, England, and America 1815-1866*. Macon, Ga.: Mercer University Press, 1984.

Countryman, L. William. *Dirt, Greed, and Sex. Sexual Ethics in the New Testament and Their Implication for Today*. Philadelphia: Fortress Press, 1988.

Cragg, Gerald R. *The Church and the Age of Reason 1648-1789*. Harmondsworth, England: Penguin Books, 1970.

Cremin, Lawrence A. *American Education. The Metropolitan Experience 1876-1980*. New York: Harper & Row, 1988.

Cronmiller, Carl R. *A History of the Lutheran Church in Canada*. Toronto: Synod of Canada, 1961.

Cross, Whitney R. *The* Burned-over District.The Social and *Intellectual History of Enthusiastic Religion in Western New York, 1800-1850*. New York: Harper & Row, 1965.

Current, Richard N., et. al., *American History. A Survey. Volume II: Since 1865*. New York: Alfred A. Knopf, 1987.

Currie, Robert, Alan Gilbert, and Lee Horsley. *Church and Churchgoers. Patterns of Church Growth in the British Isles Since 1700*. Oxford: Clarendon Press, 1977, 238.

Dawson, Christopher. *Religion and the Rise of Western Culture*. London: Sheed & Ward, 1950.

DeBerg, Betty A. *Ungodly Women. Gender and the First Wave of American Fundamentalism*. Minneapolis: Augsburg Fortress Press, 1990.

Douglas, Ann. *The Feminization of American Culture*. New York: Alfred A. Knopf, 1977.

Drach, George, and Calvin F. Kuder. *The Telugu Mission*. Philadelphia: General Council Publishing House, 1914.

Ebeling, Gerhard. *Luther. An Introduction to His Thought*. Philadelphia: Fortress Press, 1970.

Elert, Werner. *The Structure of Lutheranism*. 1962.

Ellis, David M., James A. Frost, Harold C. Syrett, and Harry J. Carman. *A History of New York State*. Ithaca, New York: Cornell University Press, 1967.

___________. *A Short History of New York State*. Ithaca, New York: Cornell University Press, 1957.

Epstein, Barbara Leslie. *The Politics of Domesticity. Women, Evangelism, and*

Temperance in Nineteenth-Century America. Middletown, Connecticut: Wesleyan University Press, 1981.

Epstein, Klaus. *The Genesis of German Conservatism*. Princeton: Princeton University Press, 1966.

Farley, Edward. *Theologia: The Fragmentation and Unity of Theological Education*. Philadelphia: Fortress Press, 1983.

Faust, Albert Bernhardt. *The German Element in the United States*. 2 vols. New York: Arno Press and the New York Times, 1969.

Ferm, Robert L. *Piety, Purity, Plenty. Images of Protestantism in America*. Minneapolis: Fortress Press, 1991.

Ferm, Vergilius. *The Crisis in American Lutheran Theology*. New York: Century Co., 1927.

Finke, Roger, and Rodney Stark, *The Churching of America, 1776-1990. Winners and Losers in Our Religious Economy*. New Brunswick: Rutgers University Press, 1992.

Fischer, David Hackett. *Albion's Seed. Four British Folkways in America. America: A Cultural History*. New York: Oxford University Press, 1989.

Forster, Walter O. *Zion on the Mississippi*. St. Louis: Concordia Publishing House, 1953.

Franklin, John Hope. *From Slavery to Freedom. A History of Negro Americans*. 5th ed. New York: Alfred A. Knopf, 1980.

Gaustad, Edwin Scott. *Historical Atlas of Religion in America*. Revised ed. New York: Harper & Row, 1976.

General Council. *Proceedings of the Convention held by representatives from various Evangelical Lutheran Synods in the United States and Canada accepting the Unaltered Augsburg Confession*. Pittsburgh, 1867.

Gerber, David A. *The Making of an American Pluralism. Buffalo, New York, 1825-60*. Chicago: University of Illinois Press, 1989.

Gerberding, George H. *Life and Letters of W. A. Passavant, D. D.* Greenville, PA: Young Lutheran Co., 1906.

Gilbert, W. Kent. *Commitment to Unity. A History of the Lutheran Church in America*. Philadelphia: Fortress Press, 1988.

Glatfelter, Charles H. *Pastors and People: German Lutheran and Reformed Churches in the Pennsylvania Field, 1717-1793*. Breinigsville, Pennsylvania: The Pennsylvania German Society, 1980.

Gobbel, A. Roger. *On the Glorious Hill. A Short History in word and picture of the Lutheran Theological Seminary at Gettysburg*. Lancaster, Pennsylvania: Pridemark Press, 1976.

Goldman, Mark. *High Hopes. The Rise and Decline of Buffalo, New York*. Albany: State University of New York Press, 1983.

Gottwald, Norman K. *The Tribes of Yahweh. A Sociology of the Religion of Liberated Israel, 1250-1050 B. C. E.* Maryknoll, N. Y.: Orbis Books, 1979.

Grane, Leif. *Peter Abelard. Philosophy and Christianity in the Middle Ages*. English ed. New York: Harcourt, Brace & World, Inc., 1970.

Gustafson, David A. *Lutherans in Crisis*. Minneapolis: Fortress Press, 1993.

Hallenback, Wilbur C. *Urban Organization of Protestantism*. New York: Harper and Brothers, 1934.

Handy, Robert T. *A Christian America. Protestant Hopes and Historical Realities*. 2nd ed. New York: Oxford University Press, 1984.

________. *A History of the Churches in the United States and Canada*. New York: Oxford University Press, 1977.

________. *Undermined Establishment. Studies in Church and State*. ed. John F. Wilson. Princeton: Princeton University Press, 1991.

Hansen, Marcus Lee. *The Problem of the Third Generation Immigrant.* Rock Island, Illinois: Augustana Historical Society Publications, 1938.

________. *The Atlantic Migration, 1607-1860. A History of the Continuing Settlement of the United States. Torchbook Edition*. ed. Oscar Handlin. New York: Harper & Brothers, 1961.

________. *The Immigrant in American History*. ed. Arthur M. Schlesinger. New York: Harper & Row, 1964.

Hatch, Nathan O. *The Democratization of American Christianity*. New Haven: Yale University Press, 1989.

Hazelius, Ernest L. *History of the American Lutheran Church, from Its Commencement in the year of Our Lord 1685 to the Year 1842*. Zanesville, Ohio: Edwin C. Church, 1846.

Heathcote, C. W. *The Lutheran Church and the Civil War*. Privately published, 1919.

Heilbronner, Robert L., and Lester C. Thurow. *Economics Explained.* Englewood Cliffs, NY: Prentice-Hall, 1982.

Herberg, Will. *Protestant-Catholic-Jew. An Essay in Religious Sociology*. New York: Doubleday & Company, Inc., 1960.

History of Suffolk County, New York. New York, 1882.

Hoffman, Bengt R. *Luther and the Mystics. A re-examination of Luther's spiritual experience and his relationship to the mystics*. Minneapolis: Augsburg Publishing House, 1976.

Holmes, Nigel. *Designer's Guide to Creating Charts and Diagrams*. New York: Watson-Guptill, 1984.

Hudson, Winthrop S. *The Great Tradition of the American Churches*. New York: Harper & Brothers, 1953.

Jacobs, Henry Eyster. *A History of the Evangelical Lutheran Church in the United States. American Church History*. Second ed. New York: Charles Scribner's Sons, 1899.

Jenny, Gerald. *The Young People's Movement in the American Lutheran Church*. Minneapolis: Augsburg Publishing House, 1928.

Johnson, Jeff G. *Black Christians. The Untold Lutheran Story*. St. Louis: Concordia Publishing House, 1991.

Jones, Madlwyn. *American Immigration*. Chicago: University of Chicago Press, 1960.

Jordan, Winthrop K. *White over Black. American Attitudes Toward the Negro, 1550-1812*. Chapel Hill: University of North Carolina Press, 1968.

Jungkuntz, Theodore R. *Formulators of the Formula of Concord. Four Architects of Lutheran Unity*. St. Louis: Concordia Publishing House, 1977.

Klein, Christa R., with Christian D. von Dehsen. *Politics and Policy. The Genesis and Theology of Social Statements in the Lutheran Church in America*. Minneapolis: Fortress Press, 1989.

Klein, Milton. *New York: The Centennial Years 1676-1976*. Port Washington, NY: Kennikat Press, 1976.

Kreider, Harry J. *The Beginnings of Lutheranism in New York*. New York:

United Lutheran Synod, 1949.

________. *History of the United Lutheran Synod of New York and New England. Volume I: 1786-1860*. Philadelphia: Muhlenberg Press, 1954.

________. *Lutheranism in Colonial New York*. New York: United Lutheran Synod, 1942.

Kretzmann, Karl. *The Atlantic District of the Evangelical Lutheran Synod of Missouri, Ohio, and Other States and Its Antecedents*. Erie, Pa.: Erie Printing Company, 1931.

________. *The Oldest Lutheran Church in America. A Brief Chronicle of Events in the History of the Evangelical Lutheran Church of Saint Matthew in the City of New York, 1664-1914*. New York City: privately published, 1914.

Kuenning, Paul P. *The Rise and Fall of American Lutheran Pietism. The Rejection of an Activist Heritage*. Macon, Georgia: Mercer University Press, 1989.

Lawyer, John D. *A Scripture Guide to the Mode of Baptism: Being a Discourse Delivered by Request of the Evangelic Lutheran Church at Argusville, NY., May 12, 1844*. Albany: E. H. Pease, 1844.

Leclercq, Jean. *The Love of Learning and the Desire for God. A Study of Monastic Culture*. New York: Fordham University Press, 1961.

Lindbeck, George. *The Nature of Doctrine*. New York: Westminster Press, 1984.

Mabee, Carleton. *Black Education in New York State: From Colonial to Modern Times*. Syracuse: Syracuse University Press, 1979.

Mann, William J. *Life and Times of Henry Melchior Muhlenberg*. Philadelphia: General Council Publication Board, 1911.

________. *Lutheranism in America: An Essay on the Present Condition of the Lutheran Church in the United States*. Philadelphia: 1857.

Marty, Martin. *Modern American Religion, Vol. 2: The Noise of Conflict, 1919-1941*. Chicago: University of Chicago Press, 1991.

________. *Modern American Religion, Vol. 1. The Irony of It All. 1893-1919*. Chicago: University of Chicago Press, 1986.

Maurer, Wilhelm. *Historical Commentary on the Augsburg Confession*. Philadelphia: Fortress Press, 1986.

McKivigan, John R. *The War against Proslavery Religion. Abolitionism and the Northern Churches, 1830-1865*. Ithaca: Cornell University Press, 1984.

McPherson, James M. *Battle Cry of Freedom. The Civil War Era. The Oxford History of the United States*. C. Vann Woodward, General Editor. New York: Oxford University Press, 1988.

Meinig, D. W. *Atlantic America, 1492-1800. Colonial American Geography as Matrix of Culture. The Shaping of America. A Geographical Perspective on 500 Years of History*. New Haven: Yale University Press, 1986.

Miller, Perry. *The New England Mind: The Seventeenth Century*. New York: Macmillan Co., 1939.

Moldenke, Edward F. *Geschichte der St. Petri Gemeinde*. New York: privately published, 1887.

Morris, John G. *Life Reminiscences of an Old Minister*. Philadelphia: privately published, 1896.

Nadel, Stanley. *Little Germany. Ethnicity, Religion, and Class in New York*

City, 1845-80. Urbana: University of Illinois Press, 1990.

National Lutheran Council. *The Lutheran World Almanac and Annual Encyclopedia for 1921*. New York: The Lutheran Bureau, 1920.

Neve, J. L. *A Brief History of the Lutheran Church in America*. 3d. ed. Burlington, Iowa: German Literary Board, 1934.

Nichols, James H. *Romanticism in American Theology*. Chicago: University of Chicago Press, 1961.

Nicum, John. *The Doctrinal Development of the Evangelical Lutheran Ministerium of the State of New York*. Syracuse: privately published, 1887.

Niebuhr, H. Richard. *The Social Sources of Denominationalism*. New York: The World Publishing Company, 1957.

Noll, Mark A. *A History of Christianity in the United States and Canada*. Grand Rapids, Michigan: William B. Eerdmans Publishing Company, 1992.

Oberman, Heiko A. *Luther. Man between God and the Devil*. New Haven: Yale University Press, 1989.

Olson, Oscar N. *The Augustana Lutheran Church in America: Pioneer Period, 1846 to 1860*. Rock Island, Ill.: Augustana Book Concern, 1950.

Osmer, Richard Robert. *A Teachable Spirit. Recovering the Teaching Office in the Church*. Louisville: Westminster/John Knox Press, 1990.

Ozment, Steven E. *Homo Spiritualis. A Comparative Study of the Anthropology of Johannes Tauler, Jean Gerson, and Martin Luther (1509-1516) in the Context of Their Theological Thought. Studies in Medieval and Reformation Thought*. ed. Heiko A. Oberman. Leiden: E. J. Brill, 1969.

Pannenburg, Wolfhart. *Systematic Theology*. Volume 1. Grand Rapids, Michigan: William B. Eerdmans Publishing Company, 1991.

Pannkoke, Otto H. *A Great Church Finds Itself*. Quitman, GA: privately printed, 1966.

Pelikan, Jaroslav. *The Christian Tradition IV: Reformation of Church and Dogma (1300-1700)*. Chicago: University of Chicago, 1984.

Perry, Marvin et. al. *Western Civilization. Ideas, Politics and Society*. 3d ed. Dallas, Texas: Houghton Mifflin Company, 1989.

Pfatteicher, Philip H. *Commentary on the Lutheran Book of Worship*. Minneapolis: Augsburg Fortress, 1990.

Pfatteicher, Philip H., and Carlos R. Messerli. *Manual on the Liturgy—Lutheran Book of Worship*. Minneapolis: Augsburg Publishing House, 1979.

Piepkorn, Carl Arthur. *Profiles in Belief. The Religious Bodies of the United States and Canada*. 4 vols. New York: Harper and Row, 1978.

Potash, P. Jeffrey. *Vermont's Burned-Over District: Patterns of Community Development and Religious Activity, 1761-1850. Chicago Studies in the History of American Religion*. ed. Jerald C. Brauer and Martin E. Marty. Brooklyn: Caarlson Publishing Inc., 1991.

Preuss, Robert. D. *The Theology of Post-Reformation Lutheranism. A Study of Theological Prolegomena*. St. Louis: Concordia Publishing House, 1970.

Primer, Ben. *Protestants and American Business Methods. Studies in American History and Culture, No. 7*. UMI Research Press, 1979.

Pugh, David G. *Sons of Liberty. The Masculine Mind in Nineteenth-Century America. Contributions in American Studies*. ed. Robert H. Walker. Westport, Connecticut: Greenwood Press, 1983.

Reed, Luther D. *The Lutheran Liturgy. A Study of the Common Liturgy of the*

Lutheran Church in America. Philadelphia: Fortress Press, 1947.

Rice, E. W. *The Sunday School Movement, 1780-1917, and the American Sunday School Union, 1817-1917*. Philadelphia: Union Press, 1917.

Richards, James W. *The Confessional History of the Lutheran Church*. Philadelphia: Lutheran Publication Society, 1909.

Riforgiato, Leonard R. *Missionary of Moderation. Henry Melchior Muhlenberg and the Lutheran Church in English America*. London: Bucknell University Press/Associated University Presses, 1980.

Rosenberg, Carroll Smith. *Religion and the Rise of the American City. The New York City Mission Movement, 1812-1870*. Ithaca, New York: Cornell University Press, 1971.

Rosenberry, Lois Kimball Mathews. *The Expansion of New England. The Spread of New England Settlement and Institutions to the Mississippi River 1620-1865*. New York: Russell & Russell Inc., 1962.

Rosenwaike, Ira. *Population History of New York City*. Syracuse: Syracuse University Press, 1972.

Ryan, Mary P. *Cradle of the middle class. The family in Oneida Country, New York, 1790-1865*. New York: Cambridge University Press, 1981.

Sachse, Julius Friedrich. *German Pietist of Provincial Pennsylvania*. New York: 1970.

________. *Justus Falckner, Mystic and Scholar*. Philadelphia: New Era Printing, 1903.

Sagarra, Eda. *A Social History of Germany. 1648-1914*. New York: Holmes & Meier Publishers, 1977.

Sattler, Gary R. *God's Glory, Neighbor's Good*. Chicago: Covenant Press, 1982.

Schaff, Philip. *America: A Sketch of the Political, Social, and Religious Character of the United States of North America*. New York: 1855.

Schenk, Hans Georg Artur Viktor. *The Mind of the European Romantics. An Essay in Cultural History*. London: Constable and Co. Ltd., 1966.

Schlesinger, Arthur M. *The Rise of the City, 1878-1898*. New York: Macmillan, 1933.

Schmid, Heinrich. *The Doctrinal Theology of the Evangelical Lutheran Church*. ed. Charles A. Hay and Henry E. Jacobs. Philadelphia: Lutheran Publication Society, 1889.

Schmucker, Samuel Simon. *The American Lutheran Church, Historically, Doctrinally, and Practically Delineated, in Several Occasional Discourses*. Springfield: D. Harbaugh, 1851.

Schorske, Carl E. *Fin-De-Siecle Vienna. Politics and Culture*. New York: Vintage Books, 1981.

Sellers, Charles. *The Market Revolution. Jacksonian America, 1815-1846*. New York: Oxford University Press, 1991.

Shriver, George. *Philip Schaff. Christian Scholar and Ecumenical Prophet*. Macon, Georgia: Mercer University Press, 1987.

Siegfried, Andre. *America Comes of Age. A French Analysis*. New York: Harcourt, Brace and Company, 1927.

Smith, Timothy L. *Revivalism and Social Reform. American Protestantism on the Eve of the Civil War*. New York: Harper & Row, 1965.

Solberg, Richard W. *Lutheran Higher Education in North America*.

Minneapolis: Augsburg Press, 1985.

Soneson, Jerome Paul. *Pragmatism and Pluralism. John Dewey's Significance for Theology. Harvard Dissertations in Religion*. ed. Bernadette J. & Francis Schussler Fiorenza Brooten. Minneapolis: Fortress Press, 1993.

Spaeth, Adolph. *Charles Porterfield Krauth*. Philadelphia: General Council Publishing House, 1909.

Sprague, William B. *Annals of the American Lutheran Pulpit. Or Commemorative Notices of Distinguished Clergymen of the Lutheran Denominations in the United States*. New York: Robert Carter & Brothers, 1869.

Stange, Douglas C. *Radicalism for Humanity: A Study of Lutheran Abolition*. St. Louis: Oliver Slave, 1970.

Stark, Rodney, and William Sims Bainbridge. *The Future of Religion. Secularization, Revival, and Cult Formation*. Berkeley, California: University of California Press, 1985.

Stearns, Peter N. *Be A Man! Males in Modern Society*. 2nd ed. New York: Holmes & Meier, 1990.

Stein, Alice. *The Church at the Campus Gate. A Half-Century of the University Ministry*. Ithaca, New York: Lutheran Association of Ithaca, 1990.

Stein, K. James. *Philipp Jakob Spener: Pietist Patriarch*. Chicago: Covenant Press, 1986.

Stoeffler, F. Ernest. *German Pietism During the Eighteenth Century. Studies in the History of Religions*. Leiden: E. J. Brill, 1973.

________. *The Rise of Evangelical Pietism. Studies in the History of Religions*. Leiden: E. J. Brill, 1971.

Sweet, William Warren. *Revivalism in America*. New York: Scribner's, 1944.

Tappert, Theodore G. *History of the Lutheran Theological Seminary at Philadelphia, 1864-1964*. Philadelphia: Lutheran Theological Seminary, 1964.

Thompson, Bard, ed. *Liturgies of the Western Church*. New York: World Publishing, 1961.

Trexler, Samuel. *Crusaders of the Twentieth Century. A Lutheran Story in the Empire State*. New York: The Macmillan Company, 1927.

Troeltsch, Ernst. *The Social Teaching of the Christian Church*. 2 vols. London: Allen & Unwin, 1931.

U.S. Bureau of the Census. *Historical Statistics of the United States*. Washington DC, 1960.

United Lutheran Church in America. *Common Service Book of the Lutheran Church with the Hymnal*. Philadelphia: The Board of Publication of the ULCA, 1917.

United States. *Eighth Census of the United States*. Washington DC, 1866.

________. *Fourteenth Census of the United States*. Washington DC, 1921.

________. *Ninth Census of the United States*. Washington DC, 1871.

________. *Progress of the Nation. Eleventh Census of the United States*. Washington DC, 1891.

________. *Seventh Census of the United States*. Washington DC, 1851.

________. *Tenth Census of the United States*. Washington DC, 1881.

________. *Thirteenth Census of the United States*. Washington DC, 1911.

________. *Twelfth Census of the United States*. Washington DC, 1901.

von Hahmann, Ernst H. *1868-1938. In Memory of the Seventieth Anniversary of Trinity Evangelical Lutheran Church, Guy Park Avenue, Amsterdam, NY.* Amsterdam, NY: Recorder Print, 1938.

[Wedekind, A. C.]. *Jubilee of the English Lutheran Church of St. James in New York City.* New York: Roberts & Sherwood, 1877.

Weiser, Frederick S. *Love's Response: A Story of Lutheran Deaconesses in America.* Philadelphia: United Lutheran Church Board of Publication, 1962.

Welch, Claude. *Protestant Theology in the Nineteenth Century.* 2 vols. New Haven: Yale University Press, 1972.

Wenner, George U. *The Lutherans of New York.* New York: The Petersfield Press, 1918.

Wentz, Abdel Ross. *A Basic History of Lutheranism in America.* Philadelphia: Muhlenberg Press, 1955.

________. *Gettysburg Lutheran Theological Seminary.* Gettysburg: Lutheran Theological Seminary, 1965.

________. *Pioneer in Christian Unity: Samuel Simon Schmucker.* Philadelphia: Fortress Press, 1967.

Wentz, Frederick K. *Lutherans in Concert. The Story of the National Lutheran Council 1918-1966.* Minneapolis: Augsburg Publishing House, 1968.

Wertenbaker, Thomas Jefferson. *The Founding of American Civilization. The Middle Colonies.* New York: 1938.

Wiederaenders, Robert C., and W. G. Tillmanns. *The Synods of American Lutheranism.* St. Louis: Concordia Print Shop, 1968.

Williams, Peter W. *Popular Religion in America. Symbolic Change and the Modernization Process in Historical Perspective.* Englewood Cliffs, New Jersey: Prentice Hall, 1980.

Wind, James P. *Places of Worship. Exploring Their History. The Nearby History Series.* ed. David E. Kyvig. Nashville, Tennessee: American Association for State and Local History, 1990.

Wittwer, Norman C. Jr. *The Faithful and the Bold. The Story of the First Service of the Zion Evangelical Lutheran Church Oldwick, New Jersey.* Redwood City, CA: Monocacy Book Company, 1984.

Wolf, Edmund Jacob. *The Lutherans in America. A Story of Struggle, Progress, Influence and Marvelous Growth. With an Introduction by Henry Eyster Jacobs.* New York: 1889.

Wood, Forrest G. *The Arrogance of Faith. Christianity and Race in America from the Colonial Era to the Twentieth Century.* New York: Alfred A. Knopf, 1990.

Wuthnow, Robert. *The Restructuring of American Religion. Society and Faith since World War II. Studies in Church and State.* ed. John F. Wilson. Princeton, New Jersey: Princeton University Press, 1988.

Young, John J. *This History of St. John's Evangelical Lutheran Church 79-83 Christopher St. New York City from 1855-1905.* New York: privately published, 1905.

BOOK SECTIONS

Adams, James Luther. "The Voluntary Principle in the Forming of American Religion." *The Religion of the Republic.* ed. Elwyn A. Smith, 217-246. Philadelphia: Fortress Press, 1971.

Ahlstrom, Sydney E. "Theology in America." *The Shaping of American Religion*. ed. James War Smith and A. Leland Jamison, 232-321. Princeton: Princeton University Press, 1961.

Anderson, H. George. "Early National Period." *The Lutherans in North America*. ed. E. Clifford Nelson, 81-146. Philadelphia: Fortress Press, 1975.

Brereton, Virginia Lieson, and Christa Ressmeyer Klein. "American Women in Ministry. A History of Protestant Beginning Points." *Women in American Religion*. ed. Janet Wilson James, 171-190. Philadelphia: University of Pennsylvania Press, 1980.

Burgess, Faith R. "The Public Face of Mt. Airy." *Philadelphia Vision—Mt. Airy Tradition: Essays for the 125th Anniversary of the Lutheran Theological Seminary at Philadelphia*, 40-51. Philadelphia: Lutheran Theological Seminary at Philadelphia, 1991.

Dorn, Jacob H. "Religion and the City." *The Urban Experience. Themes in American History*. ed. Raymond A. Mohl. and James F. Richardson. Belmont, California: Wadsworth Publishing Company, 1973.

Echols, James Kenneth. "Charles Michael Jacobs: Servant of the Church." *Philadelphia Vision —Mt. Airy Tradition: Essays for the 125th Anniversary of the Lutheran Seminary at Philadelphia*, 33-40. Philadelphia: Lutheran Theological Seminary at Philadelphia, 1991.

Fevold, Eugene L. "Coming of Age, 1875-1900." *The Lutherans in North America*. ed. E. Clifford Nelson, 255-358. Philadelphia: Fortress Press, 1975.

Fischer, Robert H. "The Confessionalism of American Lutheran Church Bodies of German Background." *The Church and the Confessions*. ed. Wilmos Vajta and Hans Weissgerber. Philadelphia: Fortress Press, 1963.

Frazier, E. Franklin. "The Negro Church: A Nation Within a Nation." *Denominationalism*. ed. Russell E Richy, 209-228. Nashville: Abingdon, 1977.

Jacobs, Henry Eyster. "The General Council." *The Distinctive Doctrines and Usages of the General Bodies of the Evangelical Lutheran Church in the United States*, 87-118. Philadelphia: Lutheran Publication Society, 1893.

Kloss, Heinz. "German-American Language Maintenance Efforts." *Language Loyalty in the United States*. ed. Joshua A. Fishman. New York: Humanities Press, 1968.

Mead, Sidney E. "Denominationalism: The Shape of Protestantism in America." *Denominationalism*. ed. Russell E. Richy, 70-105. Nashville: Abingdon, 1977.

________. "The Fact of Pluralism and the Persistence of Sectarianism." 247-266. ed. Elwyn A. Smith, Philadelphia: Fortress Press, 1971.

Meuser, Fred W. "Facing the Twentieth Century. 1900-1930." *The Lutherans in North America*. ed. Clifford E. Nelson, 359-452. Philadelphia: Fortress Press, 1976.

Oberman, Heiko A. "Simul Gemitus et Raptus: Luther and Mysticism." *The Reformation in Medieval Perspective*. ed. Steven E. Ozment, 219-253. Chicago: Quadrangle Books, 1971.

Reumann, John H. P. "The Mt. Airy Biblical Tradition and Its Significance for the Future of the Seminary and the Church." *Philadelphia Vision—Mt. Airy Tradition: Essays for the 125th Anniversary of the Lutheran Theological Seminary at Philadelphia*, 15-31. Philadelphia: Lutheran Theological

Seminary at Philadelphia, 1991.

Ryan, Mary P. "A Women's Awakening. Evangelical Religion and the Families of Utica, New York, 1800-1840." *Women in American Religion*. ed. Janet Wilson James, 89-110. Philadelphia: University of Pennsylvania Press, 1980.

Smith, Elwyn A. "The Voluntary Establishment of Religion." *The Religion of the Republic*. 154-182. ed. Elwyn A. Smith, Philadelphia: Fortress Press, 1971.

Smith, Timothy L. "Religious Denominations as Ethnic Communities: A Regional Case Study." *Denominationalism*. ed. Russell E Richy, 185-206. Nashville: Abingdon, 1977.

Tappert, Theodore. "The Church's Infancy. 1650-1790." *The Lutherans in North America*. ed. E. Clifford Nelson, 3-80. Philadelphia: Fortress Press, 1976.

Valentine, Milton. "The General Synod." *The Distinctive Doctrines and Usages of the General Bodies of the Evangelical Lutheran Church in the United States*, 34-61. 3d. ed. Philadelphia: Lutheran Publications Society, 1893.

Welter, Barbara. "The Feminization of American Religion: 1800-1860." *Clio's Consciousness Raised. New Perspectives on the History of Women*. ed. Mary S. Hartman, 137-157. New York: Octagon Books, 1976.

CONFERENCE PROCEEDINGS

Butler, Jon. *Power, Authority, and the Origins of American Denominational Order. The English Churches in the Delaware Valley 1680-1730. Transactions of the American Philosophical Society,* 68 (February, 1978), 3-85.

DeBerg, Betty A. "The Spirituality of Lutheran Women's Missionary Societies, 1880-1930. Lutheran Mission in North America " *Lutherans and Missions. Lutheran Historical Conference, Essays and Reports 1992,* 14 (1992), 142-160.

Scholz, Robert F. "Henry Melchior Muhlenberg's Relation to the Ongoing Pietist Tradition." *Lutheranism and Pietism. The Lutheran Historical Conference. Essays and Reports 1990*, 14 (1992), 40-66.

EDITED BOOKS AND MAGAZINES

Adams, Thomas, et. al., ed. *Population, Land Values, and Government. Studies of the Growth and Distribution of Population and Land Values; and of problems of Government. Regional Survey*. New York: Arno Press, 1974.

Bodensieck, Julius, ed. *The Encyclopedia of the Lutheran Church*. Minneapolis: Augsburg Publishing House, 1965.

Deitz, Charles E., ed. *New York Ministerium Legacy*. New York City: Metropolitan New York Synod, 1986.

Hoffman, Bengt, ed. *The Theologia Germanica of Martin Luther*. New York: Paulist Press, 1980.

Jackson, Samuel Macauley, ed. *The New Schaaf-Herzog Encyclopedia of Religious Knowledge*. Grand Rapids: Baker Book House, 1977.

James, Janet Wilson, ed. *Women in American Religion*. Philadelphia: University of Pennsylvania, 1980.

Kolb, Robert, ed. *Andreae and the Formula of Concord. Six Sermons on the Way to Lutheran Unity*. St. Louis: Concordia Publishing House., 1977.

Lueker, Edwin L., ed. *Lutheran Cyclopedia*. St. Louis: Concordia Publishing House, 1975.

Ochensford, S. E., ed. *Documentary History of the General Council of the Evangelical Lutheran Church in North America*. Philadelphia: General Council Publication House, 1912.

Ozment, Steven E., ed. *The Reformation in Medieval Perspective*. Chicago: Quadrangle Books, 1971.

Reumann, John A., ed. *Biographical Record of the Lutheran Theological Seminary at Philadelphia 1864-1962*. Philadelphia: Lutheran Theological Seminary, 1964.

Spitz, Lewis W., and Wenzel Lohff, ed. *Discord, Dialogue, and Concord*. Philadelphia: Fortress Press, 1977.

Stoeffler, F. Ernest, ed. *Continental Pietism and Early American Christianity*. Grand Rapids: Wm. B. Eerdmans Publishing Company, 1976.

ARTICLES

Aune, Michael B. "The Corporate and Confession Character of Worship: The Common Service Debate." *Word and World*, 8 (winter, 1988): 32-41.

Bainbridge, William Sims, and Rodney Stark. "Sectarian Tension." Reprinted from *Review of Religious Research* in *Religion: North American Style*. Second Edition. Patrick H. McNamara, ed. Belmont, Ca.: Wadsworth Publishing Company, 22 (December, 1980): 118-131.

Bauslin, David H. "The Genesis of the 'New Measure' Movement in the Lutheran Church in This Country," 40 (July, 1910), 360-91.

Bouman, J. A. "Retrospect and Prospect: Some Unscientific Reflections on the Four Hundredth Anniversary of the Formula of Concord," *The Sixteenth Century Journal*, 8, (1977), 85-104.

Dever, Mary. "Woman in the Pulpit," *Lutheran Quarterly*, 34 (1904), 284-287.

Durnbaugh, Donald F. "Work and Hope: The Spirituality of the Radical Pietist Communitarians," *Church History*, 39 (1970), 72-90.

Fink, R. A. "Women in the Church," *Lutheran Quarterly Review*, 4 (1874), 220-233.

Fischer, Robert H. "The Healing of the Schism Between the General Synod and the General Council: Sources for a Reevaluation," *Gettysburg Seminary Bulletin*, 48 (1968), 32-41.

Fortenbaugh, Robert. "American Lutheran Synods and Slavery, 1830-1860," *Journal of Religion*, 13 (1933), 72-92.

________. "The Representative Lutheran Periodical Press and Slavery, 1831-1860," *Lutheran Church Quarterly*, 8 (April, 1935), 151-172.

Froehlich, Karlfried. "Church History and the Bible," *Lutheran Quarterly (NS)* 5 (1991), 127-142.

Giese, E. F. "The Chasm between the German and English in the General Synod," *Lutheran Quarterly*, 7 (July, 1877), 409-400.

Grislis, Egil. "Ernest L. Hazelius: Ecumenical Theologian of the Southern Lutheran Church," *Gettysburg Lutheran Theological Seminary Bulletin*, 45 (August, 1965), 22-39.

Hiller, Alfred. "History of the First Ten Years of the Synod of New York,"

Lutheran Quarterly, 49 (April, 1919), 247-268.

________. "History of the Lutheran Church in New Jersey," *Lutheran Quarterly*, 28 (1898).

Horn, Henry E. "Steps Toward a Modern Piety." *Word & World*, 8 (1988), 18-24.

Horst, Mark. "The Problem with Theological Pluralism," *Christian Century*. 103 (Nov. 5, 1986), 971-974.

Hull, William. "The Lutheran Church in Columbia County, NY," *Lutheran Quarterly* 10 (1880), 33-55.

________. "The Lutheran Church in Dutchess County, NY," *Lutheran Quarterly* 11 (1881), 381-397.

________. "The Lutheran Church in Ulster County, NY," *Lutheran Quarterly* 12 (1882), 539-548.

Jacobs, C. E. "Review of H. Richard Niebuhr's The Social Sources of Denominationalism," *Lutheran Church Quarterly*, 4 (1931), 100-102.

Jacobs, H. E. "The Common Hymnal," *Lutheran Church Review* 29 (1910), 250-275.

Keiter, Charles R. "Immigration in the Nineteenth Century in Its Relation to the Lutheran Church in the United States," *Lutheran Church Review*, 31 (1912), 272-279.

Kline, M. J. "The Genesis of the General Synod," *Lutheran Church Quarterly* 49 (1919), 44-60.

Knoll, Mark A. "The Public Church in the Years of Conflict," *Christian Century*, 108 (1991), 552-559.

Krauth, Charles Philip. "Our General Synod," *Evangelical Review*, 5 (October, 1853), 239-80.

Kreider, Harry J. "The English Language Schism in the Lutheran Church in New York City, 1794-1810," *Lutheran Church Quarterly*, 21 (1948), 50-60.

________. "Laymen and the High Cost of Living in 1864," *Lutheran Church Quarterly*, 20 (1947), 81-84.

________. "Negro Lutheran Work in New York," *Lutheran Church Quarterly*, 20 (1947), 261-273.

________. "New York Synod Convention in Wisconsin, 1860," *Lutheran Church Quarterly*, 19 (1946), 408-411.

________. "New York Synod Recovers Its Ancient Records," *Lutheran Church Quarterly*, 19 (1946), 292-296.

________. "The Oldest Lutheran Church in America," *Lutheran Church Quarterly* 18 (1945), 57-9.

Kuenning, Paul P. "New York Lutheran Abolitionists: Seeking a Solution to a Historical Enigma," *Church History*, 58 (1989), 52-65.

Luecke, W. H. "A Half Century of Testimony of Staunch Lutheranism in New York City, or The First Fifty Years of History of Trinity Lutheran Church in New York City," *Concordia Historical Institute Quarterly*, 32 (1959), 1-14.

Maurer, Heinrich H. "Studies in the Sociology of Religion and American Sectionalism. The Pennsylvania German," *American Journal of Sociology* 30 (1925), 412-414.

Neve, J. L. "Shall Women Preach in the Congregation? An Exegetical Treatise," *Lutheran Quarterly*, 33 (1903), 409-413.

Nicum, John. "The Confessional History of the Evangelical Lutheran Church in the United States," *Church History*, 4 (1890), 101-109.

Richards, James W. "The Confessional History of the General Synod," *Lutheran Quarterly*, 25 (Oct., 1895), 458-90.

Schlesinger, Arthur Meier. "A Critical Period in American Religion, 1875-1900," *Proceedings of the Masssachusetts Historical Society,* 64 (1932), 523-547.

Schmucker, Beale M. "The Lutheran Church in the City of New York," *Lutheran Church Review,* 3 (1884), 203-222, 276-295.

Scholz, Robert F. "Clerical Consociation in Massachusetts Bay: Reassessing the New England Way and Its Origins," *William & Mary Quarterly* Third Series, 29 (July, 1972), 391-414.

________. "The Confessional Stance of Henry Melchior Muhlenberg and the Early Pennsylvania Ministerium," *Lutheran Quarterly*, 1 (1987), 439-456.

________. "Was Muhlenberg a Pietist?" *Concordia Historical Institute Quarterly*, 52 (summer, 1979), 50-65.

Seilhamer, Frank. "The New Measure Movement Among Lutherans," *Lutheran Quarterly*, 12 (May 1960),121-43.

Smith, R. Morris. "The Liturgical Development of the General Synod of the Evangelical Lutheran Church in the United States," *Lutheran Quarterly*, 47 (1917), 491-514.

________. "The Liturgical Development of the General Synod of the Evangelical Lutheran Church in the United States," *Lutheran Quarterly*, 47 (1917, 65-90.

________. et al. "Liturgical Development Within the Evangelical Lutheran Church in the United States," *Lutheran Church Review*, 36 (1917), 469-519.

________. ed. "Special Liturgical Section—Liturgical Developments within the Evangelical Lutheran Church in the United States," *Lutheran Church Review* 36 (1917), 455-519.

Smith, Timothy L. "Historic Waves of Religious Interest in America," *Annals of American Academy of Political and Social Science* (1960), 9-19.

________. "Religion and Ethnicity in America," *American Historical Review* 82 (1978), 1155-1185.

Stange, Douglas C. "The 125th Anniversary of Fraternal Appeal," *Concordia Historical Institute Quarterly* 40 (1967), 354-59.

Steimle, Augustus. "Our Story: Sesquicentennial Address, United Lutheran Synod of New York, Albany, June 9, 1936," *Lutheran Church Quarterly* 10 (1937), 171-184.

Stuckenberg, Mrs. J. H. W. "Thought on Woman's Education," *Lutheran Church Review* 17 (1887), 571-589.

Suelflow, Roy A. "The Relations of the Missouri Synod with the Buffalo Synod up to 1866," *Concordian Historical Institute Quarterly,* 27 (April, 1954).

Venable, Charles Leslie. "The Case for Full Membership in the Federal Council of Churches," *Lutheran Church Quarterly* 15 (1942), 225-239.

Weigelt, Horst. "Interpretations of Pietism in the Research of Contemporary German Church Historians," *Church History,* 39 (1970), 236-241.

Wenner, George U. "Woman's Ministry in the Church," *Lutheran Quarterly* 26 (1896), 471-476.

Wentz, Abdel Ross. "Permanent Deposits of Sectionalism in American Christianity," *Lutheran Church Quarterly,* 9 (1936), 27-38.

________. "Recent Discussions of Christian Unity," *Lutheran Church Quarterly* 4 (1931), 76-90.

Wolf, Edmund J. "History of the General Synod," *Lutheran Quarterly* 19 (July, 1889), 420-58.

NEWSPAPERS AND MAGAZINES

Horst, Mark. "The Problem with Theological Pluralism." *Christian Century.* 103 (Nov. 5, 1986), 971-974.

"22 Races Seek Hospital Care of Lutherans." *New York Herald Tribune.* May 22, 1927: Region 7 Archives at Philadelphia.

UNPUBLISHED MANUSCRIPTS

Butler, Jon. "A Spiritual Tower of Babel: Shifting Structure and Functions of Religious Diversity in Colonial Pennsylvania, 1680-1760." 1983.

Fischer, Robert H. "William Alfred Passavant and the Church's Ministry of Mercy." 125th Anniversary of the Wartburg Home, October 17, 1992. Wartburg Home, Mt. Vernon, NY: The Passavant Society of the Wartburg Home, 1992.

Van Alstine, Robert W. "Steadfast. A Biography of Rev. Nicholas Van Alstine, DD." (1814-1900). typescript: 1982.

DISSERTATIONS

PH. D

Bost, Raymond M. "The Reverend John Bachman and the Development of Southern Lutheranism." PH. D. dissertation, Yale University, 1963.

Bronner, Frederick L. "The Observance of the Sabbath in the US, 1800-1865. " PH. D. dissertation, Harvard, 1937.

Deitz, Reginald W. "Eastern Lutheranism in American Society and American Christianity. 1870-1914. Darwinism—Biblical Criticism—The Social Gospel. " PH. D. dissertation, University of Pennsylvania, 1958.

Flesner, Dorris A. "The Galesburg Rule: A Study of Lutheran Exclusivism." M. Div. thesis, Divinity School, University of Chicago, 1953.

Fortenbaugh, Robert. "The Development of the Synodical Polity of the Lutheran Church in America to 1829." PH. D. dissertation, University of Pennsylvania, 1926.

Glasco, Laurence Admiral. "Ethnicity and Social Structure: Irish, Germans, and Native-Born of Buffalo, NY, 1850-1860." PH. D. dissertation, State University of New York at Buffalo, 1973.

Haney, James Lawton. "The Religious Heritage and Education of Samuel Simon Schmucker: A Study in the Rise of 'American Lutheranism.' " PH. D. dissertation, Yale, 1968.

Haug, Hans R. "The Predestination Controversy in the Lutheran Church in North America." PH. D. dissertation, Temple University, 1968.

Huber, Donald L. "The Controversy over Pulpit and Altar Fellowship in the General Council of Evangelical Lutheran Church, 1866-1889." PH. D. dissertation, Duke University, 1971.

Huff, G. L. "A Historical Study of the Sabbatarian Issue in the Lutheran Church in America, 1830-1860." M. Div. thesis, Gettysburg Seminary, 1961.

Kuenning, Paul P. "American Lutheran Pietism—Activism and Abolitionist." PH. D. dissertation, Marquette University, 1985.

Lapham, James Sigurd. "The German-Americans of New York City 1860-1890." PH. D. dissertation, St. John's University, 1977.

Lehman, L. L. "Lutherans and the Movement for Temperance (1827-1859)." M. Div. thesis, Gettysburg Seminary, 1961.

Lentz, Kenneth R. "Life and Theology of Joachim Oporin. Professor and Teacher of Henry Melchior Muhlenberg." PH. D. dissertation, Heidelberg, 1970.

Nelson, Harvey LeRoy. "A Critical Study of Henry Melchior Muhlenberg's Means of Maintaining His Lutheranism." PH. D. dissertation, Drew University, 1980.

Peters, Clarence. "Development of the Youth Programs of the Lutheran Churches in America." M. Div. thesis, Concordia Seminary, St. Louis, 1951.

Scholz, Robert Francis. "'The Reverend Elders.' Faith, Fellowship, and Politics in the Ministerial Community of Massachusetts Bay, 1630-1710. " PH. D. dissertation, University of Minnesota, 1966.

Thurau, R. H. "A Study of the Lutheran Sunday School in America to 1865." PH. D. dissertation, University of Pittsburgh, 1946.

INDEX

ABOUT THE AUTHOR

ROBERT F. SCHOLZ (B.A. University of Minnesota, M.Div. Lutheran Theological Seminary at Philadelphia, Ph.D. University of Minnesota) is Senior Pastor of St. David's Lutheran Church, Massapequa Park, Long Island, New York, and Adjunct Professor of History at Hofstra University, Hempstead, Long Island. He is Historian of the Metropolitan New York Synod, Evangelical Lutheran Church in America, and is chair of its Archives Advisory Committee, which has oversight of the New York area Lutheran Archives and of its historical research projects. He has written articles and book reviews in the area of American religious history. He has served parishes in suburban Philadelphia and on Staten Island, and was chaplain of the College at Wagner College, where he directed the Core Program and also taught in the history and religion departments. He has also taught at the University of Washington and Long Island University. He is a member of the Lutheran Historical Conference and currently serves on its Board.